FORMULA 1
THE AUTOBIOGRAPHY

FORMULA 1
THE AUTOBIOGRAPHY

Edited by Gerald Donaldson

TED SMART

First published in the United Kingdom in 2002 by Weidenfeld & Nicolson

This edition produced for
The Book People Ltd
Hall Wood Avenue,
Haydock,
St Helens WA11 9UL

A CIP catalogue record for this book is available from the British Library

The text and picture acknowledgements on p360 constitute an extension to this copyright page

"Formula One", "Formula 1", "F1" and "FIA Formula One World Championship" (together with their non-English translations and permutations) are Trademarks or Registered Trademarks of the Formula One group of companies. All rights reserved

ISBN 0 297 84308 7

Text Contributors: Origins - Mark Hughes; The Fifties - Simon Taylor; The Sixties - Eoin Young; The Seventies - David Tremayne; The Eighties - Nigel Roebuck; The Nineties - Adam Cooper; The New Millennium - Adam Cooper

Consultant editor: Quentin Spurring

Photo research: David Winter

Editorial consultant: Philip Dodd
Designed for David Costa & Partners (Wherefore Art?) by Emil Dacanay, assisted by Elina Arapoglou and Sian Rance
Design director: David Rowley

Printed and bound in Italy by Printer Trento

Half-title page, from left: Jean Behra, Jose Froilan Gonzalez, Cesare Perdisa, Harry Schell and Mike Hawthorn at the drivers' briefing - British Grand Prix, 1956.
Title pages: The gloved hands of Mario Andretti, whose Formula 1 career spanned 14 seasons.

Introduction

by Gerald Donaldson

In this book the full spectrum of the Formula 1 experience is vividly brought to life by the voices of those who experienced it. Described in their own words - by the drivers, the women in their lives, the team personnel, race officials, media representatives and many other personalities - what follows amounts to the most penetrating and revealing study of the pinnacle of motorsport ever undertaken.

Covering more than 100 years of competition, and featuring over half a century of the Formula 1 World Championship - 680 Grands Prix held at 60 separate venues in 23 different countries - the book defines a sporting phenomenon, showing how it began, how it evolved and how it works.

Through the reality of the spoken word, accompanied by a profusion of compelling images from the sport's best photographers, the book takes us on a high-speed journey through time. These eyewitness accounts, colourful impressions, evocative descriptions, candid opinions and entertaining anecdotes show us what took place - there and then, here and now.

The book is organised chronologically into seven chapters, each one devoted to a particular era: *The Origins, The Fifties, The Sixties, The Seventies, The Eighties, The Nineties* and *The New Millennium.* Combined, they document and preserve for posterity a tumultuous world of contrasts: of humour and heartbreak, of glamour and grime, of celebration and sadness.

In the final section of the book an extensive biographical section provides further insights into the lives of many of the people whose voices can be heard in the book, while a bibliography lists reference books and sources of further reading.

Throughout the book the major technological developments of the cars are documented, but the emphasis is firmly on the people in the sport. For it is the men, not the machines, who most capture the imagination, as one of the greatest Formula 1 stars pointed out before he was killed.

AYRTON SENNA: "After all, the public are interested in the people. OK, they follow the racing and the fighting on the circuit, but the racing and the fighting are done by real people. They are the ones that by their personality, by their character, by their instinct, end up making the show boring or exciting. That is what gives the show some shine or some darkness. People who watch are interested about the driver that is in the car. The way he looks, not only physically, but the way he looks through his eyes, the way he speaks, by his voice being soft, sharp. The way he makes his answers, the contents of his answers, the enthusiasm he passes on, the instincts of fighting, all those things. And we are all different. Therefore what holds people, what gets people and holds them in admiring you, is what you are."

The Formula 1 circus has always attracted exceptional people and provided them with a wonderfully dramatic stage on which to perform. They are a disparate lot, strong personalities from many cultural and social backgrounds, united - and often divided - by a common cause: the quest for success in a high-pressure environment, where the clock never stops, excellence is taken for granted and the pursuit of perfection is the constant goal.

RON DENNIS: "We all have an intense desire to win, and those desires tend to put people into a sort of personality showcase, and therefore you get a complex situation. It brings out both weakness and strength of character."

Amongst the fascinating cast of characters there are examples of great cameraderie, though the fierce competition in such volatile circumstances inevitably leads to conflict and controversy. There is also plenty of laughter and always - despite this being such a mechanically-oriented endeavour - a great deal of very deeply felt human emotion.

The book is full of tears - of heartwarming joy and unbearable grief - and what it reveals is a sport that inspires passion like no other, both in those who participate in it and those who watch it. For many, the drivers are supermen, performing heroic deeds at the highest level of motorsport, filling us with wonder and thrilling us with their exceptional skill and daring.

Quite remarkable, especially in the old days when the sport was so deadly, is how phlegmatically the drivers faced their incredibly perilous profession.

In 1932 the legendary team entrant Enzo Ferrari handed Tazio Nuvolari, one of the sport's first superstars, a return ticket to Sicily, where he was to race an Alfa Romeo in the Targa Florio.

TAZIO NUVOLARI: "Ferrari, people say you're a good businessman, but I can see you're not. You should have given me a one-way ticket. When you set off for a race, you must be aware of the chance that you will be making the return journey in a wooden box."

Nuvolari won that Targa - over 44 miles to the lap on primitive mountain roads - with a sensational drive, deeply impressing a riding mechanic who had never raced with him before.

PARIDE MAMBELLI: "Nuvolari asked me if I was afraid. Then he told me that, whenever he took a bend too fast, he would yell, so that I could protect myself as best I could, by wedging myself between the seat and the dashboard. I spent the whole race, from start to finish, in a huddle. He started yelling at the first bend, and he didn't stop yelling until the last one."

Formula 1 people are fond of saying their sport is like going to war. In the past, when it was interrupted by real conflict among nations, certain racing heroes performed heroically under the guns of war. When peace returned and racing resumed the sport offered a way of forgetting, becoming even a unifying force, as former enemies combined their efforts to do battle in the World Championship series that was formally organised in 1950.

Below: Ferrari team mates before the start of the 1959 German Grand Prix at the Avus circuit, Berlin - from left to right, Phil Hill, Dan Gurney and Tony Brooks.

From that point on Formula 1 went from strength to strength, though from the time when horseless carriages were first raced the sport has always had its critics.

These days some naysayers see it as the most politically incorrect pursuit imaginable - a dangerous, environmentally unfriendly waste of vast amounts of money which is spewed out from the exhaust pipes of ridiculously and unnecessarily high-tech cars.

With its warts and all revelations this book lets everyone have a say, even Formula 1's severest critics, some of whom are featured players within it.

demanded, the sensation of speed is like a drug that makes us come alive so that we become intoxicated by the exuberance of our own velocity - as is the case with some of the featured players in the book.

These latter-day knights in shining armour lead us on crusades to exotic destinations in faraway countries. Their extraordinary vehicles are getaway cars that transport us into wondrous flights of fancy as we ride with them vicariously into the great unknown, to places like the mighty Spa-Francorchamps circuit in Belgium.

In 1963 the great Jim Clark conquered Spa in his Lotus and won the Belgian Grand Prix, though

Since most of us are too timid to achieve great adventures in speed on our own we look to Formula 1 drivers to do it for us.

TYLER ALEXANDER: "I think this thing is like an overbred cocker spaniel, and most of it is created by the media, because it isn't anything different than it's ever been. You come here, you fuck around with a car, it's got four wheels and a motor in it, you start it up, and you're on.

"The people here are supposed to be stars, but they all put on their pants one leg at a time, though some of them have their head so far up their arse they stagger around like lunatics.

"Some 'purists' say all the money these days has spoiled Formula 1 as a 'sport'. It's a phoney load of bullshit to call something a sport when it's really a business. Once upon a time it was a sport, yes, but that was an awful long time ago. It was a business to us when we started. I mean, that's what we were doing for a living. That's all we did then, and that's all we do now."

It is worth noting that the speaker of those words (race engineer Tyler Alexander) has been a fixture in Formula 1 for nearly 40 years, unable to leave its enduring allure and enjoying every minute of his love/hate relationship with the sport that is his life.

The book shows how Formula 1 is, in many ways, the perfect sport for the new millennium - a high-speed, technologically driven form of escapism from the cares of everyday life. In today's fast-paced world, where our feelings have become dulled, yet instant gratification is

his 280-mile journey, comprising 32 laps around the treacherous 8.7 mile track, was not without misadventure.

JIM CLARK: "The gearbox started dropping out of top and, at Spa, that's not funny. You wind up the car to 9500rpm on the straight, when suddenly all hell is let loose and you make a grab for the lever and pull it back into gear before the revs go off the clock. Once this happens, you're waiting for it to happen again. Here I was with Graham Hill on my tail and pressing, and I was approaching the Masta kink at 150mph, holding the gear lever in place with my right hand, and moving my left hand to the bottom of the steering wheel.

"The car often needs a correction in the kink and, by keeping my hand low on the wheel, I could twirl it round with one hand and hold the slide. But doing this lap after lap was not in the least pleasant. Fortunately, Graham's BRM retired and I could ease off - which was just as well because then there was a sudden thunderstorm."

Unlike most of the modern circuits, which have been sanitised (some would say emasculated) in the interest of safety, Spa remains a raw, risky challenge. In many ways it is the star of the show, with the hair-raising Eau Rouge section a featured attraction. When trying to describe the sensation of negotiating Eau Rouge the drivers tend to bring portions of their anatomy into play.

MARTIN BRUNDLE: "It is terrifying. You're heading downhill, flat out in sixth gear and it's like, 'I'm not gonna lift this time.' Your heart says you're not going to lift and your brain says you are. Your brain seems to have this little muscle attached to your foot."

RUBENS BARRICHELLO: "It is just fantastic! You feel that if you do not hold on to your heart it will come out your mouth."

MARK BLUNDELL: "It is like nothing on this earth. It is incredibly daunting and you have to drag up a hell a lot of commitment as you come out of La Source and head down the hill. On the way into Eau Rouge you are really studying the size of your balls."

Yet some drivers feel that Spa, which in 1960 was the scene of the worst weekend in Formula 1 history, is a too dangerous throwback to the past.

RALF SCHUMACHER: "Many drivers love Spa. I can understand this because the circuit is very fast and there is no question it is a real test of bravery. It also has a lot of history and tradition. But in my opinion the

on earth. That absolutely fantastic feeling when you put the ultimate qualifying lap together. Getting the lap right, getting the corner right, knowing that nobody else could have done better than you in the car. Sometimes I shout in the cockpit. When I've done a good job and come past the finish line, I shout. I'm so happy!"

Derek Warwick never had the pleasure of winning a Grand Prix, but Nelson Piquet did - 23 times. While some drivers weep when they win, Piquet's overflowing depth of feeling found another outlet.

NELSON PIQUET: "There is nothing, not one thing, as good as beating somebody you respect and winning a Grand Prix. I sometimes piss my pants on the slowing down lap! It is a feeling you cannot imagine."

Far from leaving nothing to the imagination, the realities found in the pages of this book fuel our imaginative fires even higher, especially for those

In many ways we are a dream for people, not a reality. That counts in your mind. It shows how much you can touch people. AYRTON SENNA

time for Spa as it now stands has run out. Yes, corners like Eau Rouge are a big thrill, but the danger factor is too high."

For modern drivers this book will be an eye-opener, with the past experiences of their peers serving as a sobering reminder of the terribly harsh realities that were so often a sad feature of the sport.

JODY SCHECKTER: "Even after my big Silverstone accident, I felt I was 'unhurtable', and I went on feeling that way until I witnessed the result of François Cevert's fatal accident at Watkins Glen in '73. I was the first person on the scene. It gave me a big jolt - I mean, it really brought the whole thing home to me. It was the biggest fright I've ever had. From then on all I was trying to do in Formula 1 was save my life."

Yet for the drivers the pleasures to be found in the cockpit have always outweighed the pain.

DEREK WARWICK: "There's unbelievable elation. There's pleasure in a Formula 1 car like nothing else

who must follow the sport from a distance. Only comparatively few fans are able to attend Grands Prix in person, where the sights, sounds and smells, the all-pervasive aura of drama and the sheer magnitude of the spectacle amount to a sensory experience that can be almost tasted and touched.

This book plunges us into the midst of a maelstrom of racing adventures, exposing us to a myriad of spine-tingling sensations. It provides fantastic views of cars hurtling through landscapes in a blur, bombards the eardrums with the primal scream of engines revving to the point of bursting, fills our nostrils with the lingering odours of burnt fuel, tortured rubber, white hot metal. The mind reels at the enormity of this assault on the senses, boggles at the preposterousness and improbability of the speed - even on the slowest circuit of all, in the streets of Monte Carlo. With this book we can put Formula 1 into its proper perspective, comprehend its complexities, savour its nuances and, especially, appreciate its heroes even more.

At a time in history when real heroes are in short supply, this book shows how Formula 1 provides a forum for the best drivers to personify the ancient definition of a hero: a man of superhuman strength, courage and ability, an illustrious warrior of extraordinary bravery, fortitude and greatness of soul.

In the past, before the sport's current huge audience existed, Formula 1 drivers performed in relative anonymity and were mourned by comparatively few when they fell. The book pays tribute to the exploits of these unsung heroes, and respectfully documents the tragedies that too often befell them.

Better known in these days of celebrity sports personalities are the more recent examples of lost heroes such as Gilles Villeneuve and Ayrton Senna. So widespread was the tremendous outpouring of grief after Senna's death in 1994 that even those who knew little about Formula 1 began to realise the depth of passion to be found in the sport, among the drivers who live their lives at the limit, and among the fans who follow them with almost religious devotion.

AYRTON SENNA: "In many ways we are a dream for people, not a reality. That counts in your mind. It shows how much you can touch people. And as much as you can try to give those people something, it is nothing compared to what they live in their own mind, in their dreams, for you. And that is something really special. Something, really, really special for me."

This book takes us into the heart and soul, the brilliant mind of the special man that was Senna. While many dreams died with him, and with those of his peers who preceded him, Formula 1 always carried on, providing yet more heroes - and villains, more adventures - and misadventures, more material for this book.

Some oldtimers feel that Formula 1 has suffered because of the huge amounts of sponsorship funding that have transformed it into the world's most expensive sport. Certainly that was the opinion expressed by one of the sport's originals, who in 1982 decried the coming of money.

ENZO FERRARI: "The introduction of so-called sponsors, which have nothing whatsoever to do with the progress and development of the automobile, has harmed the relationship between teams and drivers in the vast majority of cases. Sponsors have a decisive influence on the constructors by suggesting or even dictating the choice of the driver who will give them the best publicity."

Yet surely Enzo Ferrari, one of the real racers of all time, would not be displeased to see the famous team he founded spending over $300 million a year, including paying its superstar Michael Schumacher over $30 million, to make Ferrari's 21st-century presence the most powerful in its long history.

The presence of big money in Formula 1 has brought with it a marketing-minded, PR-conscious mentality that makes extensive use of spin-doctoring to put the brightest possible shine on the sport's public face. Some think this has created a Formula 1 devoid of strong personalities, stifling the voices of its more colourful characters. Not so, according to one of the current stars, who is also the outspoken son of one of the sport's legendary drivers.

JACQUES VILLENEUVE: "I will leave Formula 1 if I can't say what I think. There are already too many robots here. Only the power of money wants this type. Fans want drivers with character."

One aspect revealed by the events that unfold in the following pages is that, despite undergoing constant change over the years, Formula 1 history often repeats itself. Examined individually, certain periods of that history might seem more drama-packed than others, but there has never been a dull decade, as the man who has been most responsible for creating the modern version of the sport observes.

BERNIE ECCLESTONE: "Everybody says the old days are the best, don't they? That's because as you get older you like to think the old days were the good old days. But I don't think that way. I think each era has got its own special thing."

Below: Heidi Wischlinski (left, then David Coulthard's girlfriend) and Erja Hakkinen share the stress of watching their men in the cut and thrust of battle during the 1998 season.

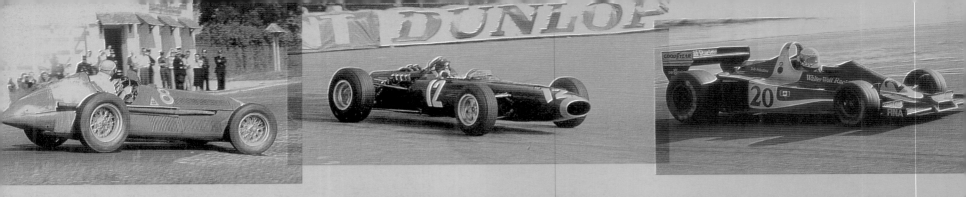

ALAN JONES • JACQUES LAFFITE • CARLOS REUTEMANN • GILLES VILLENEUVE • JOHN WATSON
NIKI LAUDA • DIDIER PIRONI • PATRICK TAMBAY • MICHELE ALBORETO • EDDIE CHEEVER • DEREK
WARWICK • AYRTON SENNA • NIGEL MANSELL • GERHARD BERGER • JEAN ALESI • FRANK
WILLIAMS • PATRICK HEAD • RON DENNIS The Nineties (P246) ALAIN PROST
NELSON PIQUET • GIOVANNA AMATI • JAMES HUNT • AYRTON SENNA • GERHARD BERGER • JOHN
WATSON • PATRICK TAMBAY • NIGEL MANSELL • THIERRY BOUTSEN • RICCARDO PATRESE
JEAN ALESI • FRANK WILLIAMS • PATRICK HEAD • FLAVIO BRIATORE • BERNIE ECCLESTONE
MAX MOSLEY • PROFESSOR SID WATKINS • MICHAEL SCHUMACHER • MARTIN BRUNDLE
MIKA HAKKINEN • ERJA HAKKINEN • MICHELE ALBORETO • MICHAEL ANDRETTI
LUCA DI MONTEZEMOLO • EDDIE IRVINE • JOHNNY HERBERT • MIKA SALO • DAMON HILL
DAVID COULTHARD • RUBENS BARRICHELLO • JACQUES VILLENEUVE • HEINZ-HARALD FRENTZEN
RALF SCHUMACHER • GIANCARLO MINARDI • EDDIE JORDAN • JACKIE STEWART • ALAIN PROST
RON DENNIS • CRAIG POLLOCK • ROSS BRAWN The New Millennium (P310)
MICHAEL SCHUMACHER • MIKA HAKKINEN • DAVID COULTHARD • JUAN PABLO MONTOYA • RALF
SCHUMACHER • JENSON BUTTON • KIMI RAIKKONEN • JACQUES VILLENEUVE • EDDIE IRVINE
FRANK WILLIAMS • JACKIE STEWART • NIKI LAUDA • RON DENNIS • ROSS BRAWN • RUBENS
BARRICHELLO • JEAN ALESI • JOHNNY HERBERT • HEINZ-HARALD FRENTZEN • PROFESSOR SID
WATKINS • ALAIN PROST • JARNO TRULLI • FLAVIO BRIATORE • MAX MOSLEY • BERNIE ECCLESTONE

The Origins

Sir Henry Segrave, the 1920s racing driver and World Speed record holder, wrote: "The attainment of speed is an instinct inherent in the normal human being and in the vast majority of animals, and one which has played a most important part in the process of evolution." This instinct came into play as soon as the first automobile was driven. It has been the life force of motor racing ever since, though the first competitions for horseless carriages were conceived not as sporting contests, but as exercises in technology and propaganda. This was a romantic era, with daredevil drivers wrestling monstrous machines to high adventure on the open road. The danger that lurked around every bend often led to disaster, yet the brave pioneers raced on.

CHARLES JARROTT (the first successful British racing driver): "Obviously the competitive element existed between the various manufacturers of [the] cars taking part. They entered for the race in the hope that they could successfully beat their rivals. But the general idea underlying the whole event was the desire to prove to the world that motor-cars would go, and that they were capable of travelling long distances in a reliable and speedy manner. The events were looked upon as educational both to the public and to the manufacturer, in the evolution of vehicles, which were something more than mere pieces of machinery made for sale and barter. And lessons were learned, experience and knowledge gained, and that side of the sport which was influenced by the financial aspect of the event was satisfied in these rewards, and the extermination of all opposition to each individual interest was not thought of."

Commerce may have been behind the first automotive competitions of the mid-1890s but, once the very first start flag dropped, that innate human desire for speed also became a factor. It was at that moment that motor racing became a sport.

Opinions still differ as to when this took place. In April 1887, *Le Vélocipède* organised a 'race' round the streets of Paris in an attempt to publicise the virtues of the new breed. Given that only one entrant made it to the startline - Albert, Comte de Dion on his steam-powered quadricycle - it can more fairly be described as a demonstration.

In 1894, *Le Petit Journal* organised a 'trial' from Paris to Rouen (80 miles), with a panel of judges to decide the winner, based on criteria such as ease of handling, practicality and running costs. As such, it was not a race either, but there was much interest in who would complete the course first. It was de Dion in his steam 'tractor', at 11.6mph. He was not, however, awarded the prize: the tractor's boiler required a stoker, and this did not meet the objectives of the competition. Georges Lemaître's petrol-driven Peugeot was instead declared the 'winner'.

Doubtless aggrieved, de Dion was an instigator, with several other motoring notables, of the French Touring Club, which soon became the Automobile Club de France (ACF). These included Emile Levassor, Armand Peugeot and de Dion's fellow steam car producer, Léon Serpollet. Their purpose was the organisation of a true race.

A British journal outlined the event in June 1895:

THE ENGINEER: "Now that the difficulties in the way of mechanical road traction have been in great part overcome, a vast amount of interest was taken in the trials, [but] several makers were not satisfied with the way in which these trials were carried out... Upon the initiative of Count de Dion, of De Dion Bouton et Cie, the makers of a steam carriage that last year beat all the other vehicles in the race to Rouen, it was decided to organise a much more severe test, which should consist of a race from Paris to Bordeaux and back, a distance of about 744 miles."

A prize fund of almost 70,000 francs was on offer, with 31,500 francs for the winner. Only the conductors of the car, of whom there had to be at least two, could effect repairs, using only tools carried with them. The demands of roadgoing practicality were still implicit in the rules. But the big difference this time was that the winner would be the car which completed the course in the least time. A race!

The 1895 Paris-Bordeaux-Paris motor race was widely publicised by magazines such as *La France Automobile,* and thousands of spectators turned up at the Arc de Triomphe in Paris on the dawn of 11 June - the dawn of motorsport itself. Here 27 vehicles convened before making their way to the starting point in Versailles. The first car - a Peugeot driven by its designer Louis Rigoulot - started at midday, the rest following at two-minute intervals.

THE ENGINEER: "As the contest was one of speed, it was not to be expected that the competitors would take any special precautions to ensure safety, and not long after the carriages had left Versailles, it was reported that one of the two Serpollet vehicles had come to grief and had fallen over a bridge."

Comte de Dion's steamer led at first but broke down before reaching Tours. This put Levassor's Daimler petrol-engined Panhard-Levassor into a lead it never lost. At 3.30am, on reaching Ruffec, about 120 miles short of Bordeaux, Levassor found his intended relief driver asleep, and decided to press on. By the time his nearest rivals reached Bordeaux, he was over three hours into his return journey. The relief driver never did get to drive; he simply kept Levassor company and helped with repairs.

News spread of Levassor's epic solo drive as he made his way back to Paris. A smashed gas lamp meant he had to cover the final night stretch at much reduced pace, but he made it to Porte Maillot at lunchtime, two days after the start, still over five hours ahead of the next man, at an average of 14.9mph. He received an appropriately wild reception.

On account of seating only two, Levassor's car was not eligible for the winning prize money, which went instead to the Peugeot of Koechlin, third-placed of the nine finishers. Regardless of the money, however, Levassor had won the motor race. At Porte Maillot, there stands an evocative stone carving of him. France was the dominant car-producing nation for many years to come and remained at the centre of the motor racing movement. But the sport was not lost to other countries.

In the month before that 1895 event in France, there had in fact been a short race in Italy, from Turin to Asti. Only five entered and, of the three finishers, one was Simone Federmann's winning Daimler omnibus, the others motorcycles.

In Belgium, Baron Pierre de Crawhez was a motivating force in establishing a national motor club in December 1895 to organise races.

That same year in America - where a race for steam tractors had been staged on a horse racing track as early as 1867 - the *Chicago Times-Herald* backed a 92-mile race from Chicago to Waukegan and back, but only two turned up from an original entry of almost 100. It was restaged a few weeks later and this time six competitors made it to the start, although only Frank Duryea's winning Duryea and Oscar Mueller's Mueller-Benz finished - partly on account of a snow storm.

In Britain, the law prohibited competition on public highways. Every vehicle not pulled by a horse was required to be preceded by a man carrying a red flag. It was not until 1896 that the red flag law was repealed, under pressure from a small but increasing band of motorists who argued that the car did not require the draconian precautions framed for giant, steam-powered traction engines.

For 1896, the ACF organised a second epic event, from Paris to Marseilles, a distance of 1062 miles, run in stages of no more than 170km (106 miles) in order to avoid night driving. Petrol-powered cars dominated the results. De Dion's steamer led, helped by improved Michelin pneumatic tyres, but still the science was imperfect and he retired after suffering numerous punctures. Levassor lost a dominant lead when his Panhard overturned after hitting a dog. Although he rejoined and finished fourth, the internal injuries he had incurred would take his life the following year. Thus the first motor racing hero was tragically also the sport's first driver fatality.

THE AUTOCAR: "Trees and other obstacles scattered over the roads by a storm brought several of the autocars to an untimely end. And then the competitors were much impeded by the stray dogs and other animals that insisted on taking too close an interest in the vehicles. The dogs especially have to be educated up to an understanding of the autocar. Apparently the sight of the vehicle rushing along at the rate of 25mph conveys to these quadrupeds the impression that it is running away, and they are seized by an insane desire to get under the wheels and stop it. Thus the race has been fatal to the dogs. At least 15 are known to have lost their lives in this way. The friend of man has been anything but a friend of the autocar."

Mayade's Panhard won the ACF event, but he was killed in a non-racing accident soon afterwards in very similar circumstances to that of Levassor. Panhard's response was one of the first illustrations of how the new sport directly improved the cars of the early motorists.

CHARLES JARROTT: "[Levassor's] most lamentable accident happened entirely due to the [tiller] mode of controlling the steering. [It] would not have occurred had his car been fitted with wheel steering. [Mayade] was driving a touring car and was proceeding along a French road when he met with an obstacle. The steering was wrenched out of his hands and he himself was precipitated onto a kilometre stone, and sustained injuries from which he afterwards died. Very much as a result of these accidents, wheel steering was adopted by the Panhard and other firms who were engaged in building cars capable of travelling at any great speed, ie 20mph."

By the time of the next big event - the Paris-Nice of 1898 - technology was advancing notably. As well as the new steering wheel from Panhard and Bollée, Michelin had largely perfected the pneumatic tyre, and more power was being extracted from the engines - as much as 8hp - by the expedient of cooling them better and making them bigger. Then, in mating together two Daimler twin-cylinder Phénix engines, Panhard was able to endow its racers with 2.4-litres. By 1900, 5.3-litre, 20hp Panhards would be fighting with monster 7.3-litre Mors of 28hp.

With power came a price: the first driver fatality during a motor race happened during a minor event at Périgueux in 1898. The Marquis de Montaignac's Landrey-et-Beyroux came up to pass the smaller Benz of de Montariol, who moved aside. As the Marquis raised his hand in thanks, he briefly lost control and forced the Benz down a ditch, severely injuring the riding mechanic. De Montaignac looked back to see what had become of his rival, and again lost control. His car rolled into the same field, with fatal consequences for both de Montaignac and his mechanic.

Above: Some of the first horseless carriages had steam engines. Albert, Comte de Dion, transported a nattily attired pit crew in his De Dion-Bouton steam-powered machine in the 1894 Paris-Rouen 'trial'.

Suddenly in the distance a little speck appeared and a sound like the droning of a bee could be heard. This sound became more and more distinct as the speck approached, leaving behind a fan-like tail of dust. It was George Heath on his 70hp Panhard, just returning from a final run round the course, and we crouched into the hedge as the bounding, swaying monster came on to us. And I shall never forget my sensation as, with an appalling crash, he shot by, leaving us enveloped in a huge dust cloud.

CHARLES JARROTT

As competition between the marques intensified, manufacturers began employing paid professional drivers, rather than relying on employees or favoured customers. Many were former cycle racers, such as Panhard's Fernand Charron, who became the acknowledged ace of the new sport.

CHARLES JARROTT: "Dare-devil, dashing and full of the winning spirit, his wins were hard-fought and hard-won. Without being what is ordinarily called nervous, he nevertheless was a mass of nerves, and he received little assistance from his physique to carry him through the strain and stress of driving a racing car at full speed throughout the long day. An old-time French champion cyclist, he is slightly built, small, dapper and as quick as lightning when the occasion calls for quickness. He is charmingly courteous. As a really brilliant driver, Charron at his best had no equal."

Charron won both major events of 1898, the second of which, the Paris-Amsterdam, was a race that crossed national borders for the first time. International competition soon followed. Gordon Bennett, an American newspaper millionaire who was in Paris to set up the *Paris Herald*, had partly funded the first city-to-city events and competed in some of them. For 1900, he proposed the Gordon Bennett Cup - an idea sparked by a war of words between Charron and Alexander Winton, an American car manufacturer and racer, as to the relative merits of French and American cars.

The objective was to stimulate foreign competition to the still-dominant French. Those countries with national motor clubs - France, Belgium, Britain, Germany, Italy and the USA - could enter up to three cars each in an annual race. The first would be held from Paris to Lyons and thereafter the winning nation would act as the host the following year. The national teams were distinguished by the colour schemes of the cars: blue for France, yellow for Belgium, red for the USA.

The ACF selected Charron, Léonce Giradot and René de Knyff, all Panhard drivers. This incensed the rival Mors team, whose cars had been presenting an ever stronger challenge to the Panhards in recent races. In protest, Mors decided to have its man 'Levegh' run the race unofficially. Winton represented America in a car of his own design. Belgium entered Camille Jenatzy in a Snoek-Bolide of 10.6 litres, but the Benz chosen to represent Germany was not readied in time.

In the race, Winton's claim for the USA quickly faded, as he was left far behind by the French cars. Levegh led much of the early going in his 'outlaw' Mors before a breakdown lost him time and paved

the way for another Charron victory. The Panhard driver suffered an accident ten miles short of the finish after hitting a dog, but got going again, with riding mechanic Henri Fournier holding in a damaged water pump drive. Levegh was unofficially second ahead of Giradot. Of the 'foreign' entries, Winton was an early retirement, while Jenatzy got hopelessly lost and retired in a fit of pique. As a demonstration of French superiority, the Gordon Bennett was resounding.

If France was still the racing capital, Germany leapt into the lead in the technology stakes in 1901. Car design took a quantum step with the introduction of Daimler's 'Mercedes' model, designed by Maybach. Even as a 'touring' customer car, it rendered everything else obsolete, racers included. In all of automotive history, the 1901 Mercedes still stands as arguably the biggest advance made in one sweep over existing technology. Its engine features were immediately copied by Panhard and Mors.

Not only were such machines incomparably faster than their primitive counterparts of a few years earlier, but they were also reliable. In those very early days, race driving had been as much an exercise in mechanical problem-solving as driving ability. No longer was this so.

The 1901 Gordon Bennett race had introduced a maximum weight - creating the first racing formula - in an attempt to curb speeds by indirectly limiting engine swept volume, but manufacturers managed to retain their massive engines by making chassis construction more efficient or flimsier, depending upon their expertise. Still the speeds rose.

CHARLES JARROTT: "In the rapid march of progress, new cars were built for each event. Months saw extraordinary progress and, working as the makers were in order to get their machines out for the event, they invariably failed to do so until the very last minute. In each event a long line of practically untried new motor cars formed up, their capabilities to be tested and their merits discovered over hundreds of miles of unknown road. And much of the charm of the sport lay in its glorious uncertainty. In addition to the excitement of driving a new and practically untried machine, you also had the fact that you were driving a much faster machine than you'd ever driven before, because the power of the motors was increased for each event and, with all these glorious elements of uncertainty, a feeling that you were perhaps driving faster than anyone had ever driven before. To secure real and exciting sport, obviously the spice of danger was an added interest because, since we were not then accustomed to the speeds, this sense of danger always existed."

Unfortunately the danger extended to the spectators. In 1901 came the accident that had been waiting to happen for the previous six years. Although the Paris-Berlin race was manned extensively along the route by soldiers, they could not be everywhere along its 687 miles. At Monchenot, a boy walked onto the road to watch a car leave his sight. He was hit at full speed by the next competitor and killed instantly. Fournier won his second major victory of the year, but even such continued success by France in international competition (it also won the second Gordon Bennett Cup thanks to Giradot's Panhard) was not enough to dissuade the French government from slapping an immediate ban on motor racing.

The power of the emergent industry - France would produce over 8,000 cars in 1902 - was demonstrated when it pressured the government into overturning the ban in time for the 1902 Paris-Vienna race. This was won in style by Marcel Renault in one of his brother's 'small' 5.4-litre machines and, because no major incidents blighted the race, motor racing seemed to be off the hook once more. The Gordon Bennett was incorporated into this event, but only as far as Innsbruck. Selwyn-

Francis Edge's British Napier was the only finisher in this class and gave the British car industry a conundrum: Britain was eligible to stage the 1903 race, but public road racing had always been banned there.

In the light of the policing problems of city-to-city events, Belgium's pioneering Circuit des Ardennes race of 1902 was well-timed. It was the first major race to consist of laps round a circuit - even if that lap was 53.5 miles long.

The race was staged over six laps of a circuit of closed public roads, which allowed it to run non-stop, with no 'neutral' sections through towns. It would also be much easier to police the crowd - a timely consideration given the spectator fatality in the 1901 Paris-Berlin.

Charles Jarrott, who won the race, drove his 13.6-litre, 70hp Panhard from the Paris factory to the starting town of Bastogne.

CHARLES JARROTT: "Half past four and we had our car out and took up our position. While sitting on my car, an English newspaper correspondent asked me the inevitable question of how I felt. I had to confess that instead of, as usual at the start of a race, feeling very

Above: Thousands of spectators watched transfixed as Belgian daredevil Camille Jenatzy hung onto his thundering Mercedes for 355 miles to win the 1903 Gordon Bennett race on the Athy circuit in Ireland.

keen, my feeling was one of boredom more than anything else, as for some reason this race did not appeal to me. I could imagine the 60-odd cars traversing that small 53-mile circuit, and the prospect of sitting in dust for over 300 miles was not exhilarating.

"We set off at 5.32am. I had been unable to find time to take the opportunity of going over the route, and I therefore started off ignorant of what was in front of me, not knowing where the turns were, how far they were off, or what the road was like. One of the first things I came upon, almost immediately after the start, was Jenatzy's car, smashed into ten thousand pieces. It appeared almost impossible that anyone could have escaped from such a wreck alive.

"The clearest impression I have of this race was the anxiety of keeping the car at full speed through the blinding dust cloud which enveloped the whole course... Among the pine forests, it hung as thick as a stifling pall, worse than a London fog, and at times it was only possible to judge the direction of the road by watching the tops of the trees."

Opposite: Early cars, like this turn-of-the-century Mercedes, had massive 10-litre engines that cranked out power equivalent to that of nearly 100 horses. Too often, those horses ran amok, causing grievous harm to passengers and bystanders alike.

For almost six hours, Jarrott overcame the hazards to win the race for Panhard when Fernand Gabriel's Mors rolled to a halt, only 7km out from the finish.

With hindsight, the Circuit des Ardennes was a critical development of the sport on its way to becoming 'Grand Prix' racing. Another was the inevitable major tragedy in a city-to-city event - ironically the next major race after the Ardennes.

Monster machines, terrible dust clouds, a pre-dawn start, 314 entrants, three million spectators, drawn like moths to a flame by the stories of fantastic speed, power and heroism. All the ingredients for tragedy were present for the 1903 Paris-Madrid.

THE AUTOCAR: "The engines of the first half dozen cars were now running, and while the din of the buzzing monsters was almost deafening, the blue haze of burnt lubricating oil rose up in huge volumes, poisoning the morning air. One of the officials scribbled something on a car and, lifting the lid of the tea caddy-shaped metal box affixed to the side of the De Dietrich, asked Jarrott to get ready. The cool hand settled himself, his

mechanician took the seat and the first speed was slipped in. The voice of the official timekeeper could just be heard through the exhausts of the many engines; but the crowd had ceased to shout and whistle and sing. There was a tenseness in the air, and high above a lark's song, as he mounted heavenward, came down clear to the earth. 'Dix,' cried the timekeeper - 'cinq, quatre, trois, deux - partez!' In went the clutch, and with a wave of his hand Jarrott sped away on his De Dietrich, opening the Paris-Madrid race, which Fate had already decreed should have no end."

CHARLES JARROTT: "What do I remember of that race? Long avenues of trees, top-heavy with foliage, and gaunt in their very nakedness of trunk; a long never-ending white ribbon, stretching away to the horizon; the holding of a bullet directed to that spot on the skyline where earth and heaven meet; fleeting glimpses of towns and dense masses of people - mad people, insane and reckless, holding themselves in front of the bullet to be ploughed and cut and maimed to extinction, evading the inevitable at the last moment in frantic haste; overpowering relief, as each mass was passed and each chance of catastrophe escaped; and beyond all a

horrible feeling of being hunted. Hundreds of cars behind, all of them at my heels, travelling over the same road perhaps faster than I, and all striving to overtake me, pour dust over me and leave me behind."

Early leader Louis Renault averaged 70mph on the stage into Chartres, and his top speed of 90mph was faster than the official Land Speed Record of the time. But Louis's brother Marcel, the hero of the Paris-Vienna the year before, tried to pass Léon Thery in the dust when he left the road, hit a tree and was fatally injured. Then Lorraine Barrow swerved to miss a dog at 80mph on a tree-lined stretch: his mechanic was killed instantly, and Barrow died some days later. Riding mechanic Nixon was killed after his driver Leslie Porter swerved into a wall when confronted with a closed level crossing: the Wolseley overturned, trapping the mechanic beneath it, then caught fire. Philip Stead received fatal injuries when his De Dietrich overturned. Jarrott was a friend and team mate of both Barrow and Stead and had dined with them the evening before their accidents.

Above: The romance of racing on open roads became a nightmare in the 1903 Paris-Madrid. Mercedes-mounted Marious Barbarou and his mechanic survived, but several lives were lost, including that of Marcel Renault, brother of car company co-founder Louis Renault, who was second in this last inter-city race.

CHARLES JARROTT: "As I approached, Barrow was raising a glass to his lips and, seeing me walking towards him, he set it down and expressed his delight that I had got to the start safely and then, seeing me still lugubrious and unhappy, he slapped me on the back and again raising his glass exclaimed: 'Whatever is the matter with you! Are we not all here? Let us eat, drink and be merry, for tomorrow we die!' - words spoken in jest but fulfilled to the bitter end."

Terrible though the list was, these were competitors. But an accident at Châtellerault finally signed the death-warrant of the event. A child walked into the road and a soldier immediately ran to pull him clear. Tourand's Brouhot hit and killed both of them, then speared into the crowd, killing another soldier and injuring many spectators.

At the overnight halt in Bordeaux, the French government halted the race, impounded the cars and chartered special trains to take them back to Paris. They were towed to the trains by horses.

Louis Renault had been the first into Bordeaux but, on corrected time, the victor was Gabriel's Mors at 65mph, with Renault second. Gabriel had started 168th and so had a terrible time of the dust clouds.

CHARLES JARROTT: "An extraordinary piece of driving, it stands unequalled and will always stand alone."

No longer would races run from city to city. The Ardennes format was recognised as the way forward. The British government - which had granted a special act of parliament (before the Paris-Madrid debacle) for the 1903 Gordon Bennett Cup to be staged in pre-republic Ireland - could at least console itself that its event conformed to this pattern. It was a race in which Mercedes, which had entered the sport in the ill-fated race to Madrid, converted its technological leadership to racing prominence, as Jenatzy beat the previously dominant Panhards and Mors.

However, Thery's Richard-Brasier won the 1904 Gordon Bennett, defeating Mercedes on its home ground. France was obliged to host the 1905 competition. On a circuit near Clermont-Ferrand, Thery again won, beating Felice Nazzaro's Fiat. This home victory allowed the French to bring the Gordon Bennett series to an end by declining to stage the following year's event. The ACF had a better plan - and a characteristically chauvinistic one, perhaps induced by the growing threat from Mercedes and Fiat.

SAMMY DAVIS: "Three cars [the limit on a single national entry] could not by any possibility involve more than three firms. The French therefore suggested that the countries should be represented by a team numerically in

proportion to the size of a national industry and, the defects of that being obvious, went on to suggest a new type of race where manufacturer competed against manufacturer, instead of nation against nation, and all who wanted might enter."

The name of this new competition? The Grand Prix.

LAURENCE POMEROY (author of *The Grand Prix Car*): "The ACF were activated largely by the desire to have a French win and, by opening the race to an unlimited number of cars from each country, they did much to ensure one, as France was the dominant producer of automobiles."

A 65-mile course of largely straight public roads round the Le Mans countryside was devised, with temporary tracks of wooden planks through fields by-passing any major villages. The event would be held over two days, 26-27 June, with two races of six laps. Thirteen teams, ten of them French, entered a total of 34 cars at £200 each.

The Gordon Bennett maximum weight limit of 1000kg was maintained and the cars were generally similar to those seen in 1905. But a new stipulation was made whereby only the driver and riding mechanic could work on the car. Three companies - Renault, Fiat and Itala - immediately grasped that the outcome of the race would depend on the speed of tyre changes. They gladly accepted the Michelin innovation of detachable wheel rims.

SAMMY DAVIS: "The Le Mans circuit was crammed to capacity. As the early morning mist rose patchily, it became apparent that it was going to be one of the hottest days in creation, and that caused no little peevishness, since many of the drivers decided then and there to take off some clothing.

"The whole of France in the role of spectator was prostrate wherever shade was available, to escape the burning heat, here and there sufficient energy being developed to watch the intense labours of a mechanic and driver changing tyres, a process that took five minutes and was like handling red hot metal made worse by the penetrating smell of hot rubber."

The race soon surrendered to the Renault of Ferenc Szisz. It was not the outright fastest car - that was Paul Baras's Richard-Brasier - but it lost the minimum of time in stoppages. He was followed home by Nazzaro's Fiat with 21-year-old Albert Clement, in the Clement-Bayard manufactured by his father, close behind in third position - a heroic achievement given that his car did not have detachable rims. The race and its format were a success, and history was set on a new course. For

some years, the French reserved the right to the term 'Grand Prix'. Other races of similar concept were held elsewhere, and the Kaiserpreis of 1907 was in all but name a German Grand Prix, while the Targa Florio was an early incarnation of the Italian Grand Prix. But the biggest, most prestigious event for the next few years would remain the Grand Prix de l'ACF.

It was decided to have a common formula for 1908, based on cylinder bore size. The Fiats were again the quickest cars, but this year their reliability deserted them in both the Targa Florio, won by Itala, and the Grand Prix, in which Christian Lautenschlager's Mercedes was victorious. The Fiats were left to win the Florio Cup and the new Savannah Grand Prize, an American Grand Prix in all but name, held on a purpose-built, 25-mile track in Georgia.

Thus the French marques did not win a major event in two years, and were twice defeated on home ground. And 1908 was the first year in which the motor industry produced more cars than it could sell. For the first time, the expense of motor racing looked like something the French could do without. They instigated the 'Self-Denying Ordnance' with which a cartel of manufacturers brought Grand Prix racing to a halt.

But the manufacturers' withdrawal simply proved that the sport had a life of its own. There were other companies - progressive ones like Peugeot, Hispano-Suiza and Delage - which saw no reason to cease their activities in 'voiturette' (small car) racing. They still raced, and people still massed to see them. New heroes were made, new engineers came to the fore. Regardless of official labels, voiturette racing became the new 'Grand Prix', and racing simply left the abstainers behind. This much was suggested in 1912 when the ACF organised an official 'Grand Prix' once more, with no limit on engine swept volume (although there was a class for voiturette cars).

Top right: Ferenc (François) Szisz prepares to fire up his 13-litre, Michelin-shod Renault for the 1906 Grand Prix de l'ACF, at Le Mans in France. Szisz, a Hungarian, went on to glory - winning this first ever automobile Grand Prix.

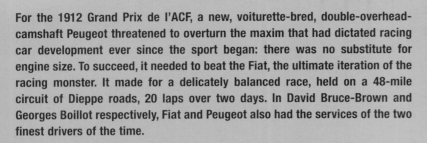

For the 1912 Grand Prix de l'ACF, a new, voiturette-bred, double-overhead-camshaft Peugeot threatened to overturn the maxim that had dictated racing car development ever since the sport began: there was no substitute for engine size. To succeed, it needed to beat the Fiat, the ultimate iteration of the racing monster. It made for a delicately balanced race, held on a 48-mile circuit of Dieppe roads, 20 laps over two days. In David Bruce-Brown and Georges Boillot respectively, Fiat and Peugeot also had the services of the two finest drivers of the time.

PETER HELCK (contemporary American journalist): "David Bruce-Brown was big in stature, strong in heart and hands. With the requisite competitive spirit and a passion for thundering speed, he was the ideal racing man. For many close followers of the sport he was supreme."

DAVID SCOTT-MONCRIEFF (contemporary British journalist): "Boillot at the wheel of a Peugeot had acquired almost legendary fame. An overpowering, swollen-headed man who played to the gallery, he might in his general attitude have stepped right out from the pages of a Dumas novel. He was a virtuoso of the road and he knew it. His long string of triumphs had brought sporting France to his feet."

From the start, the race condensed into a Fiat versus Peugeot struggle of epic proportions - Old Guard versus New Order.

SAMMY DAVIS: "It was magnificent; the huge Fiat ran all-square, rock-steady, belching smoke and flame on acceleration. The Peugeots owned a fiercer snarl, and their cornering was superb, [Jules] Goux alertly quiet, Boillot handling his car with just that apparent exaggeration of gesture which inevitably fitted with his d'Artagnan character and yet was a mere disguise to sheer skill."

By the fourth lap, Bruce-Brown was edging out his lead from Boillot, who had the second Fiat of Wagner snapping at his heels. Goux could lend no support to his team mate after his Peugeot ran out of fuel, forcing the mechanic to refill at the roadside, which merely earned a disqualification. At the end of the first day's racing, after six-and-a-half hours of intense struggle, Bruce-Brown led Boillot by two minutes.

SAMMY DAVIS: "For the survivors the sight of the morrow's dawn produced intense depression, fine drizzle such as all drivers fear making the outlook miserable as the teams struggled into ponchos and waterproofs. The serried ranks of umbrellas gathered to witness the fight, and one by one the cars left.

"A rumour seemed to run before the wind, grew, became certain - Boillot's Peugeot was leading. Incredible as it seems, the Fiat had run out of fuel and, since there was nothing else to do, had to be replenished by the roadside in spite of the regulations."

But now Wagner began to press Boillot. The Peugeot was suffering a clutch malfunction and Wagner took a brief lead. But the outcome was decided, as in 1906, by tyre changes. Fiat clung to old-fashioned wooden-spoked 'military' wheels, with detachable rims. Peugeot had taken advantage of regulations that no longer specified wheels to be an intrinsic part of the car that could not be changed, and had fitted fully detachable Rudge Whitworth wire-spoked wheels - as used for years on its voiturette cars. Aided by much quicker tyre changes, Boillot held on at the front for a historic victory. The monster cars that had ruled racing since the turn of the century had put up a hell of a fight, but had been vanquished by science. Reinforcing the message, the final result had Victor Rigal's 3-litre voiturette Sunbeam in third place, ahead of the similar machines of Dario Resta and Medinger, with an array of full-size Grand Prix cars behind them.

There was no stopping the Peugeots after that. They romped to victory in the remaining race of the season, the Grand Prix de France (a rival to the French Grand Prix set up by a different organising body), then plundered America too by taking apart the 1913 Indianapolis 500. The maximum swept volume was reduced to 5.5-litres for a new fuel consumption formula at that year's Grand Prix, but it made no difference to Peugeot's form, Boillot and Goux scoring a 1-2 in defeating the rival Grands Prix Delages.

The new, scientific era tempted back into the arena the most technology-led manufacturer, Daimler, which had learned new lessons working on airplane engines. In the 1914 Grand Prix, Daimler fielded a new Mercedes with separately forged pistons and four valves per cylinder, and it was too much for the Peugeots. Boillot drove a heroic race, but his early chase of Max Sailer's Mercedes, which had deliberately been sacrificed as the team hare to break the Peugeot, proved fatal to his engine, which expired on the last lap. Mercedes scored a crushing 1-2-3 victory.

When the Mercedes Grand Prix engine would next be seen, it was in a fighter plane. There were to be no more Grands Prix until after the First World War.

SAMMY DAVIS: "There was something more than motor racing in the air as the crowds made their way dustily from the course. Never before had there been that curious but indefinable feeling and everybody was extraordinarily quiet. Had the gift of foresight been ours what, I wonder, would one have thought; as it were there was quite distinctly the feeling that a menacing though invisible force had been manifest."

Main picture: In the 1914 Grand Prix de l'ACF at Lyons, Georges Boillot's number 5 Peugeot failed to stop a Mercedes juggernaut led by Christian Lautenschlager. It was the last major European race before the outbreak of war.
Inset: When the Great War ended the survivors raced again, among them André Lagache and René Léonard, at Le Mans in 1919.

There had come faintly on the wind the echoing thud of guns. The brooding shadow was death, the end had come to a generation. SAMMY DAVIS

THE EMERGENCE OF FERRARI

In the wake of the wartime annihilation of Europe's infrastructure, racing took time to get restarted. A brave attempt to return to normality was made by Vincenzo Florio with his 1919 Targa Florio, but it was not until 1921 that a full-blown Grand Prix was held.

Nothing forces the pace of technology like war, and research into piston-driven aero engines had led to startling development of the internal combustion motor. The straight-eight, short-stroke engine of the Fiat 801-402, designed by Guido Fornaca for the new 3-litre Grand Prix formula of 1921, has been described as 'the first high-speed engine'. It produced its maximum power at 4250rpm, compared with 2800rpm for the 1914 Mercedes and 2200rpm for the 1912 Peugeot. The Fiat's 115bhp represented 38bhp/litre, compared with 25 for the Mercedes and 17 for the Peugeot. This engine formed the basic blueprint for racing motors of the next four decades.

The new Fiats were not ready in time for the first post-war French Grand Prix, held at Le Mans around a much shorter circuit (of eleven miles) than had ever been used for a major European race. The American Duesenberg company, which had itself played a key role in the wartime development of the eight-cylinder aero engine, set the pace with its own straight-eight car, developed from the machines it had raced at Indy for the previous two years, and equipped with a hydraulic braking system. Jimmy Murphy took it to victory, beating fellow American Ralph de Palma in a French Ballot.

The Fiats appeared five weeks later for their home race - named the Italian Grand Prix, so establishing a precedent that other countries would follow. On a circuit in Brescia, the Fiats were by far the fastest, but tyre failures handed the win to Jules Goux's Ballot.

A 2-litre formula was introduced for 1922 and Fiat dominated over Sunbeam. The British company, in employing former Peugeot and Ballot designer Ernest Henry, proved conclusively that Fiat's engine philosophy had overtaken that of Henry's, which was still rooted in the pre-war period. It was a season of two significant milestones.

In France, the cars started *en masse* from a starting grid for the first time, rather than at timed intervals, so that spectators could be sure that the car in front on the track was leading the race. The grid was determined by lots drawn from a hat.

In Italy, the Grand Prix was held at a new circuit: Monza. Tracks built specifically for racing were common in the USA, notably Indianapolis, and in Britain there was Brooklands, but Monza was the first Grand Prix circuit that did not comprise public roads. It enabled the organisers to charge spectators for the first time, and France soon followed with Montlhéry, Spain with Sitges.

With the inauguration of Monza, the significance of the Targa Florio waned, but in 1922 it was the scene of the debut of a forced induction race engine. In the first international race Mercedes was allowed to enter under post-war settlement terms, the company entered two supercharged cars. The technique would lead to huge increases in power outputs and was immediately adapted by Fiat for its 1923 Grand Prix car, which was soon producing 65bhp/litre.

Fiat's pacesetter status meant that its race engineers became much in demand by rival teams. Sunbeam sacked Henry and in his place recruited Fiat designers Vincent Bertarione and Walter Becchia. Enzo Ferrari, now driving for the emergent Alfa Romeo team, played a key role in the further depletion of the Fiat ranks, immediately after Fiat had dominated the 1923 Italian Grand Prix.

Main picture: Dario Resta's Sunbeam pursues Louis Wagner's Alfa Romeo during the 1924 French Grand Prix at Lyons, where patrons in the restaurants willingly ate the dust raised by their racing heroes. Wagner's team mate Giuseppe Campari won and was the toast of the town.
Inset: Laura and Enzo Ferrari (on the right) enjoy a picnic at the 1924 Parma-Poggio Hillclimb, scene of Enzo's debut as a driver five years earlier.

The wind howling round one's ears and air pressure trying to force our heads back amply demonstrated the real thrill of racing, the full exhilaration of speed.

ENZO FERRARI: "I began to wonder whether I might not be able to tempt some young technicians away from Fiat. One such man had already left Turin for Milan on my instigation; this was [Luigi] Bazzi, who was already a close friend of mine in 1923. Employed in Fiat's racing division, after the Tours Grand Prix in France he had a difference of opinion with Ing. Fornaca and decided to come to Alfa.

"Bazzi at once got to work on the P1 [Alfa Romeo Grand Prix car] and its 2-litre, six-cylinder engine. Between one test and another, he suggested we might try to snatch Vittorio Jano, a young and very promising technician of Fiat's. Thus, in September 1923, I was back in Turin - not looking for a job this time, but offering one. We had a talk, I told him the advantages of joining Alfa and, the following day, he signed up.

"I had never met Jano before. Bazzi had described him as a man with a formidable will, but no description would do credit to this extraordinary man and his fertile brain. With Jano, there came over to Alfa also other technical staff of less renown. Once in Milan, Jano took command of the situation, introduced a military-like discipline and in a few months succeeded in turning out the P2, the machine that made such a sensational debut in 1924."

That debut came in a minor race, at Cremona a couple of months before the 1924 European (French) Grand Prix at Lyons. Antonio Ascari won with the P2, against little front-line opposition, but its speed suggested it would be on a par with the Fiat. This was unsurprising, given that the P2 was a detail refinement of the 1923 Fiat with which Jano had been intimately involved, with a similar engine providing a similar 135bhp.

The 1923 Fiat was matched against the P2 in France; the battle had extra spice not only because of the grudges between the two teams, but also because, in Ascari, Alfa had the one driver likely to be able to challenge Fiat's acknowledged maestro of the era, Pietro Bordino.

ENZO FERRARI: "I first met Ascari in Milan in 1920. He was not very tall, but of athletic build, fair, elegant and with a flair for business. He was, in fact, already selling cars. It was not long before we were calling Ascari 'the maestro'. He was a man of strong character, exceptionally active and endowed with real courage. He was largely self-educated and when I met him had already acquired a wide engineering knowledge. As a driver, he was extremely daring and something of an improviser. He was a *garabaldino*, in fact, as the slang expression goes for drivers who put courage and verve before the cool calculation of those who succeed in judging corners perfectly every time, endeavouring lap by lap to approach closer and closer to the very limits of tyre adherence."

The Fiat/Alfa contest might have been relegated to secondary interest had things gone according to plan at Sunbeam, which had devised a superior supercharging development. At first, Henry Segrave led comfortably, but an engine misfire condemned the Sunbeam effort, and soon there was a gripping battle between Bordino and Ascari. Sammy Davis of *The Autocar* had a unique journalistic vantage point for this race: he was the riding mechanic for Count Louis Zborowski, a privateer with a 1923 Indy Miller. The following year, the requirement of carrying a riding mechanic would be dropped from the regulations.

SAMMY DAVIS: "The evening before the race, being restless, we both went for a walk in the dark along a pleasant country road, both very silent and preoccupied for a time, neither of us being able to avoid the inward conviction that rather serious things might happen on the morrow. We walked a long way. Conversation gradually came back. Gradually the state of our feelings was found to be mutual. When we returned we understood each other very thoroughly indeed.

Stones flung from other cars'
rear wheels flicked past one's ears
as dangerously as the bullets
they strongly resembled.
SAMMY DAVIS

"Next day, not daring to have much breakfast as the race was extremely long, we felt pretty awful until we arrived at the pit, amid all the excitement and bustle of bands and crowds, but there still remained a funny feeling. Lining up for the start that feeling became more definite, while the machines, in pairs, were being arranged along the road.

"Ahead of us Segrave who, as last year's winner, headed the line with Divo, the Delage crack, nibbling his little finger, and even Nazzaro was fidgety, symptoms of great comfort to me, who had imagined that my own internal depression was due to inexperience.

"Suddenly the order to start engines, a deafening high-pitched drone, an official gesticulated through the smoke, a motor cyclist moved off, and after him went all the cars in pairs. The motor cyclist shot to one side, a big flag fell, and away we went in an inferno of noise and enormous clouds of smoke. All my funny feelings disappeared, and as I watched the cars behind with an occasional glance at the gauges in front, the joy of the thing came back in full measure - I might have been a different person.

"Our run up the sinuous base of the triangular course was a real joy, but the long straight up and down the 'Montagnes Russes' at 117mph, with the Miller's engine going really well, was the more so because every field, every house and every point of vantage was black with spectators innumerable.

"In between miles each gauge had to be watched, the oil gauge needle particularly on corners where the surge of the oil gave evidence of a low level, air pressure had to be maintained in the fuel tank, an occasional glance given outside to see that nothing worked loose, and that the tyre treads were standing up.

"Two rounds later, we had to stop to replace a loose distributor wire. Suddenly, Zborowski leapt like a gazelle over the front wheel.

"There was a terrific roar, a sense of something a millimetre from the back of one's overalls, a whirlwind, then a shower of stones. Bill Guinness had passed at full speed in the Sunbeam. I had to keep my head under the scuttle and Zborowski was forced to use the fan-shaped wire stone guard, looking through which was no fun at all, even after I had given him a pair of new, clean goggles and scraped the dirt and flies from the old pair. It was undoubtedly those shattering bumps which caused our downfall.

"It began when Zborowski said: 'Steering's gone.' Looking over the side I then noticed that the forward shock absorbers were dangling loose. Overshooting the pit once more earned us a most lengthy rebuke from the pit *commissaire*. When I got to the front of the car I nearly fell over with astonishment; the whole of the front axle had parted from its underslung spring on one side and was resting on the lower flange of the frame, while on the other side two badly bent bolts, out of four, were all that retained the thing in position! We had driven nearly a complete lap like that and the axle might have come adrift at any moment! Dejectedly, we gave up and retired, blacker than the proverbial tinker."

Above: Enzo Ferrari, with mechanic Guilio Ramponi, at the wheel of a 1923 Alfa Romeo. Ferrari, who also wanted to be an opera singer or a sportswriter, won 13 of his 47 races.

Alfa Romeo's debut was victorious, and it was the final straw for Fiat. Bordino had been narrowly leading after his exciting battle with Ascari, but the pace the Alfa forced upon him made his brakes give out. After Ascari encountered an engine problem, Guiseppe Campari's sister P2 won narrowly from Divo's Delage.

ENZO FERRARI: "Not only was Guiseppe Campari an exceptionally skilful driver, but an indomitable fighter, too, a man who - for the sake of winning - would disregard danger in the same way as he disregarded little inconveniences that smacked of the ridiculous.

"During practice for the Mille Miglia on one occasion, I was going over the Raticosa Pass with him. Our seats were simple banquets, as they were then called, that is to say, fixed to a simple cross-piece itself secured to the chassis by means of four bolts and wire. At a certain moment liquid began to spray into our faces from the wooden floor. Above the roar of the motor, I shouted to Campari, 'I hope a pipe hasn't gone. Better stop and see!'

"There was no reply. I gazed at him in astonishment. What sort of man was this who would disregard a risk of this kind? I regarded him from head to foot and noted that, from the legs of his overalls - always too short - there protruded long cotton underpants tied by a tape. And it was from here there came that liquid which the airstream blew about the cockpit.

"Astonished, I turned to my companion, addressing him in the Milanese dialect as I knew he would answer this: 'Peppin,' I shouted, 'What's up?'

"'Hey, you don't expect me to stop on a trial run, do you?' replied Campari. 'While you're practising, you've just got piss your pants, that's all!'"

Following its defeat in France Fiat did not appear for its home Grand Prix at Monza a few weeks later. Ascari won effortlessly, leading an Alfa 1-2-3-4 despite the presence of a new team of supercharged Mercedes. In one of them Zborowski, awarded a works drive after such promising showings as a privateer, was killed.

ENZO FERRARI: "Fiat had drivers of the mettle of Nazzaro, Bordino, Pastore and Marchisio, but they were badly beaten all the same. This gave Fiat food for thought and caused them to consider the effort which racing cost them and balance it against any benefits from their successes. From that time on, Fiat - who had raced ever since they first came into being - restricted their motor sport activities to sporadic appearances in certain events."

After Fiat's withdrawal, Alfa Romeo's P2 dominated in 1925, winning the inaugural World Championship for manufacturers, but the company was having one of its periodic financial crises. Ascari's death in the French Grand Prix gave it a justification to withdraw from racing at the end of the year. Sunbeam was in a similarly perilous state financially, and that left only the French Delage and Bugatti teams as reliable entrants for 1926, when a new 1.5-litre formula was introduced in an effort to contain the escalating speeds.

The withdrawals came close to stopping Grand Prix racing in its tracks. In the 1926 French Grand Prix, for example, only three cars took the start, all Bugattis, and for the last 50 miles only one of them was running! A British Grand Prix was held for the first time, round an improvised circuit within the Brooklands speed bowl. With an entry of nine cars, it was one of the more successful events of the season. Such a dire level of support detracted from the achievement of Delage and Robert Benoist in winning all four major Grands Prix of 1927. After that, even Delage withdrew, financially exhausted.

As with the Self-Denying Ordnance of the pre-war years, however, the sport ultimately transcended the circumstances of the manufacturers which had withdrawn as a result of the world financial recession. Instead, a new breed of independent entrant emerged, existing on start and prize money (feasible now with the advent of enclosed circuits) as well as contributions from wealthy pay-drivers and component suppliers. Several star drivers became independents, buying their own cars and making their living from them rather than relying on the programme of a manufacturer.

Bugatti became a kind of customer race car producer and provided most of the racing hardware for such entrants - a role the Type 35 filled to perfection. Maserati fulfilled a similar role on a smaller scale, although both had works teams. Scuderia Ferrari was formed with Alfa Romeo's equipment and emerged as the most hard-hitting of all the new-style racing outfits.

It was a time of technical stagnation, but also of a competitive intensity that established a brilliant new generation of drivers, with Tazio Nuvolari and Achille Varzi at its vanguard. The emergence of the modern-style Grand Prix calendar became clear, as more races meant more income for those teams relying on the sport for their existence.

Above: The day before the 1933 Italian Grand Prix Giuseppe Campari announced he was going to retire and become a professional opera singer. In the race his Alfa overturned and Campari was killed, one of three drivers to die on a dreadful day at Monza.

René Dreyfus was one of the competitors when the most famous Grand Prix of them all was staged for the first time, in 1929.

RENE DREYFUS: "Antony Noghes, the president of the *Commission Sportive* of the Automobile Club de Monaco was trying to get a new race onto the international calendar. There were Grands Prix all over Europe, several in France alone, and he saw no reason why his country should not have one too. That there really was not an awful lot of room in the tiny principality did not concern Antony in the slightest. After all, the city did have streets and the race could be run on them. Antony went to the [FIA] in Paris who thought he was crazy - but he convinced them. And thus was born the Grand Prix de Monaco of 1929.

"I had to be there. In addition to the *classement général,* the race was also to include a separate classification for 1500cc cars - which just happened to be the displacement of my [Bugatti] Type 37A.

"Thirteen drivers would be gridded: an unlucky number, but three cars entered failed to make it to the starting line. One of them was a 1750 Alfa which was to have been driven by the Alfa Romeo dealer from Modena, but Enzo Ferrari had some problem with his car and didn't make the start.

"Absent from the race too - and most ironically - was Louis Chiron. Prior to the decision for the Grand Prix, Freddy Hoffmann had arranged for Louis to race a Delage at the Indianapolis 500 and so the only native Monegasque who could possibly have participated in the first Grand Prix de Monaco couldn't because he was in America instead.

"I remember meeting Rudolf Caracciola for the first time. He was there with his white SSK Mercedes; nobody thought he could possibly perform well with that big car on that serpentine circuit, but he would do a fantastic job. His drive in Monaco, during which he led for several laps before shredding tyres dropped him to third, was stunning.

"The Bugatti of the Frenchman who had entered as 'Philippe' was painted blue. He was Philippe de Rothschild, a quite good driver, but either his distinguished family objected to his participation in motor sport, or possibly he did not wish them to know of it. Pseudonyms were commonplace in racing at this time.

"Another Bugatti was painted British racing green, to be driven by a man who spoke French like a Frenchman, who had entered the race as 'Williams' and whom we all called Willie. Some said he was a wealthy sportsman, others thought that he was one of the livery men who operated from the Place de l'Opéra in Paris and hired out his car and chauffeur services to wealthy clients who wished to travel elegantly from Paris to Berlin, for example. No one knew for sure. What we did know was that he was a charming but very reserved gentleman."

'Williams' went on to win the race, with Dreyfus winning his class. The mysterious Englishman was actually William Grover-Williams, who had been a professional chauffeur for a famous portrait artist, Sir William Orpen. When Orpen ended his affair with one of his models, Eve Aupicq, there was a settlement that made her a wealthy woman. It included the artist's Rolls-Royce as well as the services of Grover-Williams. They became lovers and later married, and Grover-Williams was able to buy his way into top-flight motor racing. Once there, his prowess led him later to become a works Bugatti driver.

RENE DREYFUS: "That first Monaco Grand Prix had been a great success. There were no accidents, the race had been an interesting one, and very well attended. Everybody was certain there would be a Monaco Grand Prix in 1930."

**There was, and Dreyfus won it - using the very Bugatti that the enigmatic 'Williams' had driven to victory in 1929.
René Dreyfus not only raced for Ettore Bugatti, whose cars supported Grand Prix racing almost single-handedly during this era, but also for the Maserati brothers and, later, Enzo Ferrari.**

RENE DREYFUS: "I guess you could say Bugatti's cars were avant-garde, in that they made everything else look old-fashioned by comparison. But perhaps more accurately, Ettore Bugatti was very much of the moment - and everybody else was late. It was not so much a matter of technical specifications which made Bugatti so modern as it was the look of a Bugatti - there was a delicacy to the design; it was a little jewel of a race car, not the rough diamond that was the usual competition car. Yet the car's delicacy was deceiving, for what the Bugatti really was, was an aggressively sophisticated racing car...

"At that time the Bugatti was less powerful than the Maserati, but it was much more tractable, had much more finesse. The difference between the two cars was one of sophistication. It was in abundance at [Bugatti factory] Molsheim. It was not in [Maserati base] Bologna. At that time, getting out of a Maserati and into a Bugatti was rather like leaving a hardware store and going into Tiffany's.

"Because it was small and because, too, it was run by brothers - solid, down-to-earth, friendly people with no sense of the pompous in them, no flamboyance -

the Maserati organisation was a true democracy. Brothers, drivers, mechanics - we were a fraternity. And no one pulled rank - ever. 'Come,' Alfieri would say, 'let's look at some improvements we've made to the cars.' We would look then return to his office and examine the drawings. 'What do you think of this,' the brothers would ask, 'what do you think of that? Let's learn about this, let's discuss that.'

"The difference between being a member of the Bugatti team and the Scuderia Ferrari was virtual night and day. I lived with [Bugatti's] Costantini, I visited with Ferrari. With Ferrari, I learned the business of racing, for there was no doubt he was a businessman. Enzo Ferrari was a pleasant person and friendly, but not openly affectionate. There was, for example, none of the sense of belonging to a family that I had with the Maserati brothers, not the sense of spirited fun and intimacy that I had [at Bugatti].

"Enzo Ferrari loved racing, of that there was no question. Still, it was more than an enthusiast's love, but one tempered by the practical realisation that this was a good way to build a nice, profitable empire. I knew he was going to be a big man one day. Ettore Bugatti was Le Patron, Enzo Ferrari was The Boss. Bugatti was imperious, Ferrari was impenetrable."

ENZO FERRARI: "As my trade mark, I continued to use the rampant horse, the story of which is a simple and fascinating one. The emblem was emblazoned on the fighter plane of Francesco Baracca, the ace of World War I, who was shot down at Montello.

"In 1923, when competing in the first Circuito del Savio, at Ravenna, I made the acquaintance of Count Enrico Baracca, the hero's father; as a result of that meeting, I was subsequently introduced to the ace's mother, the Countess Paolina Baracca, who one day said to me,

'Ferrari, why don't you put my son's rampant horse on your car? It will bring you luck.'

"I still have Baracca's photograph, with his parents' dedication in which they entrust the horse to me. The horse was, and has remained, black; whilst I myself added the gold field, this being the colour of Modena."

Opposite: The inaugural Monaco Grand Prix was held in the streets of Monte Carlo on 14 April 1929. Rudolf Caracciola averaged nearly 50mph to finish third in a 7.1-litre Mercedes SSK. The race became a permanent fixture and, with only minor track modifications but massive increases in speed, it remains the most glamorous, and the most dangerous, destination on the Formula 1 tour.

Overleaf: The first Monaco winner was the mysterious 'Williams' - here powering his Bugatti Type 35 past a Delage. Williams enhanced his aura of mystery by becoming a British secret agent during the Second World War.

The circuit, laid out entirely within the Principality, works out to be just over three kilometres. It goes without saying that the track is made up entirely of bends, steep uphill climbs and fast downhill runs. Any respectable traffic system would have covered the track with DANGER signposts, left, right and centre. *NICE-MATIN*

IF YOU SUGGESTED RUNNING A RACE HERE FOR THE FIRST TIME, YOU WOULD BE

CONSIDERED TO BE MAD AND OUT OF TOUCH WITH REALITY. PHIL HILL IN 1966

1930s

In 1930, Alfa Romeo bought back the P2s owned by Achille Varzi and Gastone Brilli-Peri and, encouraged by Enzo Ferrari, returned to Grand Prix racing, with these two as its lead drivers.

Varzi had come to the fore in 1929, using his privately-owned P2. He had begun the year continuing in partnership with fellow motorcycle ace Tazio Nuvolari, the pair having previously decided to pool their resources and drawing power, using a pair of Bugattis. Two such giants of competitive intensity made uneasy partners. Varzi flew the coop and sourced one of Alfa's mothballed P2s. With this he won a string of victories, often at the expense of Nuvolari's tired Bugatti. For the Montenero Grand Prix at Leghorn in July, Nuvolari arranged himself an Alfa, although merely a 1750 sports model. He finished second to Varzi's P2 and set the fastest lap. That was impressive in itself, but the fact that he was in a plaster body corset, having broken his ribs in a motorcycle race the week before, made it something more than that. The legend of Tazio Nuvolari had just reached critical momentum.

When Brilli-Peri was killed during the 1930 season-opening Tripoli Grand Prix (there were suggestions of suicide brought on by a romantic disappointment), it created a vacancy at Alfa Romeo, and Nuvolari was chosen to fill it. This made Varzi and Nuvolari team mates once more, a situation that lasted two races before Varzi again moved on and bought himself a Maserati. It underlined the uneasy professional relationship of the pair. Their rivalry and opposing personalities would ignite front-line motor racing for years to come, just as it had motorcycle racing in the mid-1920s. They were to fight many epic duels over the next few seasons - notably in the 1930 Mille Miglia, the 1931 Targa Florio, the 1933 Monaco Grand Prix and the 1934 Mille Miglia.

GEORGE MONKHOUSE (journalist and photographer): "The very sight of Nuvolari has for some reason which I cannot explain always sent tingles down my spine. Perhaps it was just his dynamic personality, but I know that I was not alone in this feeling. He is a wiry, dapper little man with a most purposeful chin. His racing get-up was always colourful, a bright scarf, a red or blue [linen] helmet, giving relief to the sombre brown sleeveless leather jerkin in which he usually drove if the day was cold or wet. In fine weather he donned a bright yellow pullover and white helmet, but wet or fine, round his neck he always wore his lucky charm, ironically enough a golden tortoise. To see Nuvolari in his heyday, chin out, sitting well back in the driving seat, his outstretched hairy brown arms flashing in the sun as he made his blood-red Alfa perform seemingly impossible antics, not once, but corner after corner, lap after lap, the tyres screaming and the crowd yelling themselves hoarse, was quite fantastic. There was something soul-stirring about Tazio Nuvolari, for wherever he drove, thousands of spectators, whatever their nationality, 'squeezed' for him, hoping against hope that he would achieve the impossible, nor did he often disappoint them."

RENE DREYFUS: "Varzi was an aloof sort. An elegant, meticulous man and fastidious, the pleat on his coveralls had to be just so. His driving suit was made to order for him at an expensive shop in Milan; later most of us flattered Achille by comparison and went to the same shop to be outfitted."

ENZO FERRARI: "Varzi the driver was no different from Varzi the man: intelligent, calculating, grim when necessary, ferocious in exploiting the first weakness, mistake or mishap of his adversaries. He could be well described as pitiless."

RUDOLF CARACCIOLA: "The elegant Milanese, [Varzi was] seemingly soft and certainly a little too soft with regard to women and the horde of his admiring camp followers. But that was certainly never allowed to be manifest in the car. The same man, whose kindness was often misinterpreted and put down to weakness, was hard as steel the moment he got behind the steering wheel of his car."

PIERO TARUFFI (a team mate to both men): "Nuvolari delighted the crowd with his wizardry, while Varzi, cornering like a white line, used to leave many spectators almost indifferent. Varzi [had] a calculating temperament which, even in races with huge prize money at stake, prevented his exerting more than the minimum effort necessary to win."

ENZO FERRARI: "I have often been asked what there was special about Nuvolari's driving - in what way it was distinctive. All manner of things have been written and said about that famous style of his. It is always the same, in all forms of achievement: a man becomes a legend and, if he is a boxer, it is claimed that he can slay a bull with a blow of his fist; and, if he is a racing driver, he always takes all corners on two wheels."

'After racing against him several times, I began to wonder what there was special in the style of that grim little man, whose performance was invariably the more brilliant the greater the number of bends, which he referred to as 'resources'. So one day in 1931, during practice for the Circuito delle Tre Province, I asked him to take me along with him for a while on the 1750 Alfa that my Scuderia had allotted to him.

"At the first corner, I was certain that Tazio had taken it badly and that we were going to end up in the ditch; I braced myself for the shock. Instead, we found ourselves at the beginning of the straight with the car pointing down it. I looked at Nuvolari: his rugged face betrayed not the slightest emotion, not the slightest sign of relief at having avoided a 180 degree skid. At the second bend, and again at the third, the same thing happened. At the fourth or fifth, I began to understand how he managed it, for from the corner of my eye I noticed that he never took his foot off the accelerator, but kept it pressed flat on the floorboards. Bend by bend, I discovered his secret.

"Nuvolari went into the bend rather sooner than would have been suggested to me by my own . . .

suddenly pointing the nose of the car at the inner verge just where the bend started. With the throttle wide-open - and having, of course, changed down into the right gear before that frightful charge - he put the car into a controlled four-wheel skid, utilising the centrifugal force and keeping the machine on the road by the driving force of its rear wheels. Right round the whole of the bend, the car's nose shaved the inner verge and, when the bend came to an end, the machine was pointing down the straight without any need to correct its trajectory. Seeing him do it so much as a matter of course, I soon grew accustomed to this extraordinary performance although I had the impression every time that I was hurtling down the switchback slope of a figure-of-eight, with the same feeling of numbness that we have all experienced at the end of the dive."

Opposite: Nuvolari led his team mates Varzi and Campari to a 1-2-3 victory for Alfa Romeo in the 1930 Mille Miglia. Early on the morning of the second day Varzi was in front. Nuvolari playfully switched off his lights, crept up on his rival and swept by to win.
Above:"Grim and ferocious" Varzi (left in top photo and left, inset) became a drug addict. The lucky charm of the dapper and daring Nuvolari (right in top photo and right, inset) was a

ENZO FERRARI, HERE FLOGGING AN ALFA ROMEO WHILE MECHANIC ONGARO HANGS ON: "It must be remembered that there are two sorts of drivers: those who race because they are enthusiasts and those who do so merely because they are ambitious.

"The former end up in one of two ways: they either kill themselves or they go on racing till they are white-haired. The latter give up at their first failure or after their first success. It will be realised, consequently, what a maelstrom of conflicting feelings, ambitions, stubborn wills and complexes is let loose on the track."

The 1932 season was dominated by Jano's new Alfa Romeo P3. A genuine single-seater, it was the lightest Grand Prix car (770kg) and, with 190bhp from its 2.6-litre twin supercharged straight-eight, also the most powerful. Yet the company withdrew on the eve of the 1933 season, a victim once more of a financial crisis. It handed its old Monza models to Enzo Ferrari, and later in the season released its P3s to him as well. So this was another season fought out by independents, the results split between Bugatti, Maserati and Scuderia Ferrari. But it was the final one: the factories were coming back, encouraged by a new formula and a sinister new political backdrop.

In October 1932, the AIACR had announced a new Grand Prix formula, to take effect from 1934. It stipulated only a 750kg maximum weight. The aim was to provide a more tightly defined formula, while pegging speeds to the level reached by racing cars such as the P3. The AIACR assumed that any bigger and more powerful cars would weigh more than 750kg. The formula unwittingly attracted two German manufacturers - but Mercedes and Auto Union were interested because they could drive a horse and cart through the intent of the formula.

Benito Mussolini and his officials were already a feature of Italian racing when Adolf Hitler was made chancellor of Germany in 1933. A car enthusiast, he could also see the propaganda value that racing offered the nation. The sport came to be an integral part of the Nazi party's 'Strength Through Joy' programme. The two German manufacturers were given all the budget they needed to implement their assaults on the soft target of 750kg Grand Prix racing.

NAZI PROPAGANDA PAMPHLET: "The Führer has spoken. The 1934 Grand Prix formula shall and must be a measuring stick for German knowledge and German ability. So one thing leads to another: first the Führer's overpowering energy, then the formula, a great international problem to which Europe's best devote themselves, and finally action in the design and construction of new racing cars."

RENE DREYFUS: "We realised that Germany's new chancellor was an automobile enthusiast and wanted his country's car to be supreme, the most powerful, the fastest, the most everything. That he envisioned supremacy in a contest other than on a race track was the furthest thing from our minds."

Hitler's subsidy has been described as 'not so much an offer, as an order' for Mercedes to go racing. Naturally it obeyed. Auto Union was a more surprising contender. Both companies had in common a measured empirical methodology that bulldozed aside beliefs founded on the intuitive fine-honing of the Italian and French constructors.

ENZO FERRARI: "The new [750kg] formula, without any limit on engine size, obviously offered enormous possibilities for the metallurgical industry and led to the adoption of new materials, of the new magnesium alloys and the wide use of so-called white steels. By this means Mercedes and Auto Union were able to fit engines of 6 litres or more in cars having a weight of only 750kg, while we had not been able to do better than 2.6 litres."

PIERO TARUFFI: "I do not believe that the manufacturers in those days understood much about a car's behaviour on corners. They did not know about slip angles and the cornering power of tyres and so were ignorant of the effects of oversteer and understeer on a car's behaviour, and of how these could be diminished or increased to produce the desired characteristic. This was largely because design was usually entrusted to excellent draughtsmen, brought up on practice rather than theoretical engineering. This began to appear very clearly under the formula setting a limit to maximum weight. The successful firms were those rich in technical resources, like Mercedes-Benz and Auto Union who left everyone else behind."

Cars such as the Alfa Romeo P3 and Maserati 8CM - the fastest machines of 1933 - had reached the point where their power (around 200bhp) was no longer the limiting factor. Their relatively primitive chassis technology made them so unstable that they could not really use any more horsepower.

GIANBATTISTA GUIDOTTI (Alfa Romeo test driver/race manager): "The hardest job was not to get them round corners, but to keep them on the road where straights allowed the cars to approach their maximum speeds."

The chassis of both the German contenders of 1934 were the first capable of handling ferocious horsepower. In a sport in which it had taken almost 40 years to reach 200bhp, Mercedes was getting 430bhp from 4 litres by the end of its first season. It made for the most visually exciting and dramatic era the sport had ever seen. And it coincided with the careers of four of the all-time greatest drivers: Nuvolari, Varzi, Caracciola and, later, Bernd Rosemeyer.

The big, naturally aspirated V16 engine of Prof. Ferdinand Porsche's Auto Union was mounted behind the driver but ahead of the rear wheels - a layout that had actually first been introduced to Grand Prix racing by the futuristic but abandoned Benz *Tropfenwagen* back in 1923. There was a direct connection between the two cars, as explained by Ferdinand Porsche's son.

DR FERRY PORSCHE: "Our business manager was Adolf Rosenberger, who had been a successful [amateur] racing driver in the 20s. He had driven the mid-engined *Tropfenwagen* and told my father that it was an extraordinary car - he had been very impressed with it. After listening to Rosenberger's experiences we came to the conclusion that, as our new engine was going to produce a great many horsepower, we must have most of the weight over the rear axle, which is why the Auto Union was mid-engined."

The Mercedes W25 was more classical in concept, with a front-mounted, supercharged straight-eight,

Above: Team boss Enzo Ferrari demonstrates how Achille Varzi should put his foot down in an Alfa Romeo.

but highly progressive in detail. Like the Auto Union (and the Benz *Tropfenwagen* before it), the W25 featured independent suspension for all four wheels and hydraulically operated brakes. The gearbox was sited at the rear for better weight distribution and the twin-cam engine had four valves per cylinder. The Auto Unions were finished in a dramatic-looking silver but, initially, the Mercedes were traditional German racing white. They too came to be silver following the weigh-in for their first race, when they were found to be 1kg over the 750kg maximum.

HERMANN LANG (then a Mercedes team mechanic): "We were all standing around discussing what was to be done about the extra kilo. Anyway, the decision was taken to remove the paint and so we set to work. The cars had been painted white very carefully in order to get an excellent finish, but the bodies were of hand- beaten aluminium and so were very uneven. This meant that there was quite a lot of filler applied before the paint was sprayed on and it was probably this filler, rather than the paint, which pushed the cars over the limit. So were born the 'Silver Arrows'."

Auto Union's Hans Stuck gained the first of the new-generation German victories in a full Grand Prix, with a dominant drive, appropriately in the German Grand Prix on the daunting Nürburgring. He followed it up with another in Switzerland. Then came the Italian Grand Prix, and a remarkable comeback by Rudolf Caracciola. In practice for the 1933 Monaco Grand Prix, the German ace had crashed his Alfa Romeo badly, severely injuring his right leg. He had not raced since, and Mercedes prepared its Grand Prix programme without him. Almost a year after his accident, Louis Chiron invited him to drive a lap of honour in Monaco.

RUDOLF CARACCIOLA: "Returning to the race course had shaken me more than I had thought. That was my world, that was where I belonged. A man is a racing driver as another is a hunter. From instinct, from an urge that originates deeper than conscious thought. I had always had contempt for the others, for the boys who sat at the steering wheel only to hunt down retirement pay. You are a racing driver because it is your fate, or you will never be one.

"The evening before the [Monza] race, we sat in a bar in Milan. [Team manager Alfred] Neubauer was discussing our chances. He always did that with loving thoroughness but I could not bear to listen any longer and got up and went outside. I had enough trouble with my own worries. What good were his tactical tricks if my leg didn't come through?

"The year before, on the eve of the Monza race, there had been more contestants. Chiron told how cheerful they

I had to drive again. It was the only way to endure life. RUDOLF CARACCIOLA

had all been, how they had made Campari sing, how they had laughed about him and the way he forced his bulk down into his Alfa *monoposto*. Before the race he admired a chronometer, donated by Pirelli, and said that after the race, which he intended to win, he would like to have at least two of those. Also, he had told the mechanics to put aside a whole roast chicken for him because he would come back with a wolf's hunger. But he never came back from that first lap. Nor did Borzacchini.

"Chiron told me that Lehoux had tried to make a deal with Czaikowsky not to open up to full speed until the last few laps. It hardly seemed right to challenge Fate once more on the ill-omened day. But Czaikowsky refused to go along with the notion. So he too failed to return. He was thrown off the course at the same spot as Campari and Borzacchini.

"All three drivers were brought to lie in state. Green fir-tree branches decked the walls and you could not see the coffins for flowers and wreaths. Their friends passed by in silence, and the public crowded in awe before the dead heroes of the racing sport.

"But we drivers kept our colleagues fresh in our memories - their words, their actions, their personalities were always kept alive in our talks. The deaths of our comrades was not gruesome to us - to us it seemed as if they would reappear in the door at any moment to join the conversation. What if I were thrown

out at the curve tomorrow? 'Another Victim of Monza', the newspapers would say, and I couldn't help thinking how many had been left on the road. But it must be a good death, I thought - it must be a quick one. At least it would be better to go this way than to die in some lingering fashion."

Caracciola's performance was nothing less than heroic in the 1934 Italian Grand Prix. Despite fearful pain from his leg injury, he had fought and already won a battle with Hans Stuck's Auto Union when, quite unable to continue, he handed his car to team mate Luigi Fagioli, and shared the victory. Subsequently the 1935 season surrendered to him, with victories in five of the nine major Grands Prix.

One he did not win though, was the German Grand Prix, in which Nuvolari made inspired use of the pact that many believed he had with the devil. By this time, the German machines were developed yet further from the frighteningly fast visions of 1934: Mercedes boasted 462bhp, Auto Union having to cope with 'only' 375. Scuderia Ferrari was still relying on Jano's old Alfa P3, now bored out to 3.8-litres and mustering 330bhp.

Nuvolari's victory should not have been possible: there were nine Auto Unions and Mercedes present at the Nürburgring that day in July.

THE AUTOCAR: "Mist cloaks the pine-clad mountains amid which the course lies. Patches of light fall upon the distant hilltops but the track is wet and glistening. The cars are pushed up to the start as files of Nazi troopers parade, and impressive anthems blare from the loudspeakers. As soon as 11am approaches, all other sounds are drowned by the roar of exhausts. In a few seconds even these give place to the shrill sound of the Mercedes superchargers, then an electric signal releases the champing cars. It is a tremendous sight as white, red and green cars fight for the lead before the sweeping hairpin after the stands."

As the mid-race pitstops approached, with his fuel load now low, Nuvolari revealed his searing pace for the first time, picking off von Brauchitsch and moving up to second place when Fagioli made his stop.

THE AUTOCAR: "The excitement in the grandstands is indescribable. Here they are! Nuvolari leads! Rosemeyer is second. Rosemeyer - he has passed Caracciola. 'Caratch' is on his tail, and von Brauchitsch wheel-to-wheel behind. There they go down the valley. Now von Brauchitsch is past

Caracciola, and Rosemeyer worries Nuvolari's rear wheels.

"When the eleventh lap arrives all four of the leaders are in at the same time. It is a sight for the gods as mechanics leap to the wheels, and others insert the gigantic funnels for the refills. Nuvolari leaps from his car and walks up and down sucking a lemon. The Germans are busy with their cars, like ants. Jacks go under, wheels are spun off, churns of fuel emptied in. German pit work wins! Off goes the first Mercedes - von Brauchitsch's car. Then Rosemeyer with the Auto Union, and almost at the same time the other Mercedes - Caracciola's - gets away with supercharger screaming. Nuvolari's car is still in the pit! Fuel is still being emptied in as the jack is let down. The Mercedes mechanics laugh and give the Italian a good-natured cheer as he flashes past their pits."

Alfa Romeo's fuel pumping device had broken, losing Nuvolari over a minute to the German machines. His stop took 2m14s, compared to 47s for von Brauchitsch. He rejoined sixth. If what he had been doing immediately before the stops was wondrous, what he now produced was verging on the mystical. Rosemeyer

fell out of the picture with another visit to the pits, bu in two laps Nuvolari passed Fagioli and made up ove a minute on Caracciola in a car that was in no way comparable. Now only von Brauchitsch was ahead. The German was a quick driver but his spectacular style was hard on his tyres, and soon his right-front was dangerously worn. What to do? Another stop would be a certain surrender, and so agonisingly he pressed on.

THE AUTOCAR: "With two laps to go, Nuvolari's scarlet Alfa is only 32s behind the leading Mercedes. Into the last lap and von Brauchitsch seems to have stabilised the gap Then, the Karussel announcer is on the air: 'Von Brauchitsch is followed closely by Nuvolari! Von Brauchitsch has burst a tyre! Nuvolari has passed him! Now the little Italian appears and a shout goes up as never before was heard. Von Brauchitsch brings his car over the line on the rim! Von Brauchitsch climbs from his car. He is crying like a child."

Up on the podium, there was no recording of the Italian national anthem. That's how confident the Germans

had been! No matter, Nuvolari had the record somewhere, and conjured it like a rabbit from a hat. It was not the only magic he had woven that day - just the perfect flourish to what stands as arguably the greatest Grand Prix victory of all time.

Mercedes and Auto Union continued to dominate. A European Drivers Championship was inaugurated in 1935, with scores taken from five of the principal Grands Prix. Rudolf Caracciola won in 1935 and 1937, Bernd Rosemeyer in 1936. By the end of the formula, the 5.7-litre Mercedes was producing 646bhp, the 6-litre Auto Union 520bhp, and streamlined versions were approaching 250mph on the long straights of the Avus track in Berlin.

The Auto Union's power, combined with a layout that put the driver way up front, a long way from the tail slide, made it perhaps the most demanding Grand Prix car of all time. It was in such a machine that Rosemeyer made his Grand Prix debut in 1935. He had no car racing experience of any kind prior to this, having graduated directly from motorcycles. Yet he won his first Grand Prix after just half a season, and became the European Champion in his first full season.

RUDOLF CARACCIOLA: "Smiling, as if it were sheer play, he had won his victories. And yet he too had to pay for them and fate had demanded the highest payment of all from him. Rosemeyer [who was killed while attempting to set a speed record on an *autobahn*] was honoured with a state funeral in Berlin. All of we colleagues and racing drivers in our racing overalls had escorted him to his final resting place. The music, the muffled drums accompanied our slow steps. The monotonous rhythm penetrated our hearts

and translated itself into words: 'You today and I tomorrow, you today and I tomorrow...'"

Such foreboding did not stop Caracciola taking his winning habit into the new 3-litre formula of 1938. The new formula did little to contain power - the supercharged engines of both German teams produced over 420bhp - and even less to curb lap speeds, which continued to rise. The double blows of Rosemeyer's death and the descent into drug addiction by Varzi, his erstwhile team mate, finally paved the way for Nuvolari to race a competitive car once more, his gigantic ability having been squandered on unworthy machinery for four years. Nuvolari signed for Auto Union in mid-season 1938, by which time Caracciola was well into his championship stride. Nonetheless, Nuvolari won on his third appearance for the team, at Monza. Then came Donington and a stunning victory.

RODNEY WALKERLY (*The Motor*): "He came through the bends with his elbows flashing up and down like pistons, the steering wheel jerking quickly from side to side - and yet all the time the car ran as if on rails. There's little doubt that Tazio was driving on top of his form. He is 46 years of age. He was driving a car he said last year was unmanageable. And yet he was driving as he drove 15 years ago, doing things no one else can do, and slowly catching up after his two pitstops to his rivals' one."

Fagioli's former Mercedes mechanic Hermann Lang, who had been taken on as a full works driver in 1937, had won for the first time at Tripoli that year, a result

he repeated in 1938. At the same time as Lang's promotion, the team had to get Hitler's express permission to employ rising British star Richard Seaman - who embarrassingly won the German Grand Prix in 1938. Seaman had mixed feelings about his big career break, particularly as the political situation worsened, as later recalled by his wife.

ERICA SEAMAN: "In February [1939] we went to Berlin for the motor show, where all the Mercedes drivers had to appear in racing overalls to shake the hand of Der Führer. I remember the night before, Dick saying, 'Here I am about to shake hands with Hitler! What I should do now is phone the Home Office and say - 'If I kill him, will you give a million pounds to my widow?'"

RENE DREYFUS: "What was happening in Europe now was incredible. Things were changing cataclysmically, but it seemed as if we were trying to pretend they were not. In racing circles we had been aware of, but somewhat apart from, the political situation. Certainly we saw the swastikas, we heard the Fascist songs, we were neither blind nor deaf. And during the year past, because we were often on the road to Germany, we could see the movement of troops and we could sense the military build-up. But as drivers, we were simply French, Germans, Italians and British, and we were all friends."

Tragically, Seaman would lose his life after crashing out of the lead of the 1939 Belgian Grand Prix at Spa. Knocked unconscious in an impact with a tree, he was trapped inside the burning car, with rescuers unable immediately to understand the mechanism of the removable steering wheel. It was a season on which Lang stamped his authority, even over Caracciola in what was still very much 'his' team. But it was Nuvolari who won in Yugoslavia - on the very day England declared war on Germany.

HERMANN LANG: "We all went home very depressed. We were told not to travel through Hungary, as our safety could not be guaranteed, so we had to go through Yugoslavia to Austria, and some of the roads were just country lanes in the fields. We eventually arrived home with the war four or five days old. We all had company cars - mine was a lovely 3.4-litre drophead - we had hardly driven through the factory gates when they were confiscated, as were our trucks.

> "The military had taken over Mercedes and motor racing was over for a long time to come."

Above: In 1948 Giuseppe Farina, winner of the first post-war Monaco Grand Prix, received his trophy from Prince Rainier.

37

The Fifties

With the sport formally organised into an annual series of Grand Prix races contested by cars conforming to specific technical rules, the Formula 1 World Championship proved to be a formula for success. By the end of the decade Formula 1 had become the pinnacle of motorsport. The dramatic exploits of drivers like Farina, Ascari, Fangio, Gonzalez, Hawthorn, Collins and Moss made them household names. Exotic cars from the likes of Ferrari, Alfa Romeo, Maserati, Mercedes, Cooper and Vanwall were sources of wonder. Amidst the fiercely competitive racing, examples of great camaraderie and sportsmanship further captured the public's imagination. Sadly, there was also too often the need for mourning, as many of the heroes lost their lives.

In 1945, in a Europe still ravaged by the Second World War, motor racing of sorts got under way with surprising rapidity in France and Italy. The newly formed Fédération Internationale de l'Automobile, a Paris-based association of national bodies, took over the administration of international motor sport, in place of the pre-war AIACR. The FIA soon convened to rationalise the muddled multitude of racing classes from country to country. It laid down specifications for three types of single-seater racing cars and, for ease of reference, called them Formulae A, B and C.

Formula C was to provide inexpensive racing, using readily available 500cc motorcycle engines. Formula B, with a 2-litre upper limit on engine swept volume, was based on the pre-war 'voiturette' class. Formula A was intended to recreate the great days of pre-war Grand Prix racing.

In 1938, the Grand Prix formula had catered for 3000cc supercharged and 4500cc unsupercharged engines, while the voiturettes were equipped with 1500cc supercharged power units. Hoping to attract the pre-war machines that were available, the FIA set the new Formula A at 1500cc supercharged, 4500cc unsupercharged.

Before long, A-B-C metamorphosed into 1-2-3, and the term Formula 1 became current.

The title 'Grand Prix' was used for a plethora of races around Europe, and some of these were merely Formula 2 events. There had been a championship of sorts for manufacturers in the 1920s and, in the 1930s, a Champion of Europe had been voted by committee,

based on performances at selected races. In 1949, the International Motorcycle Federation came up with a World Championship, based on points scored in nominated major races, and the FIA seized on the idea. The first Formula 1 World Championship was announced for 1950.

Given that the races were all in western Europe (until Argentina in 1953), this was a somewhat grandiose title. In an attempt to make it more global, the Indianapolis 500 was included, and would remain on the list for 11 seasons. But this was never more than a gesture: Indy was run to very different rules, and for different cars and drivers. The only serious attempt by a Formula 1 contender to earn points at Indy was an unsuccessful visit by Alberto Ascari in 1952.

In that first 1950 season, with only six Formula 1 rounds – in Britain, Monaco, Switzerland, Belgium, France and Italy – many of the other non-championship Grands Prix around Europe, at tracks like Barcelona, Zandvoort, San Remo, Pau, Pescara and Albi, continued to carry considerable prestige and attract strong entries. Gradually, as the number of championship rounds grew, these non-championship events lost status – although, well into the 1960s, there were still four or more Formula 1 races a season in Britain. Eventually the term 'Grand Prix' was allowed by the FIA to describe only a national qualifying round of the World Championship, and works Formula 1 cars no longer raced in any other events.

This gradual process carried with it a significant shift in the Formula 1 driver's ambitions and rewards. The arrival of the World Championship in 1950 created surprisingly little interest at the time, among either the competitors or the spectators. What mattered was winning a race, not scoring points. In Formula 1 today, for drivers, teams and TV audiences alike, everything has become subordinated to the fight for the World Championships for Drivers and Constructors. Winning a race has become merely a means to the overriding end of winning a title.

When the World Championship began, even crash helmets were optional. Until they were made compulsory, in 1952, most drivers wore a linen or leather head-covering, and the crash helmets that did appear were usually adapted from polo or riding hats. Some drivers even raced in jacket, shirt and tie. But the cockpit of a Grand Prix car was a hot and oily place, and most of the professionals opted for short-sleeved T-shirts, cotton trousers with elasticated ankles and light driving slippers.

In due course, the tyre companies offered the drivers lightweight overalls. It was the first glimpse of personal sponsorship, with the name of the tyre manufacturer in small, neat, sober letters on the breast pocket. The difference, of course, was that the driver was quite content to display this name in return for a free set of overalls.

The cockpits of 1950s Grand Prix cars were big, high and open by today's standards, with the driver in a substantial seat above the propshaft, sawing away at a big steering wheel with his elbows out in the slipstream and his legs either side of the gearbox. On occasion, a disintegrating clutch would burst through the bellhousing and inflict leg injuries. Stomach muscles and kidneys would take a tremendous pounding on the bumpy tracks of the day, and Stirling Moss and others used to wear broad waist belts to support their abdomen during a long race. And the races were long: the 1954 German Grand Prix at the Nürburgring, which Fangio won for Mercedes, lasted over three and three-quarter hours. (At the start of the 21st century, the German Grand Prix at Hockenheim occupied just 78 minutes.)

Most drivers preferred the idea of being thrown out to staying with the accident, and seat harnesses, while they featured in American racing in the 1950s, did not appear in Formula 1 until the late 1960s. By then, cornering speeds were enormously higher but, with the tubular frame chassis being replaced by the monocoque, the cars were becoming stronger for their weight. Provided fire was not involved, it now became preferable in most accidents for the driver to remain inside the car.

Above: Fangio's Alfa Romeo failed to finish the 1950 British Grand Prix, the first race for the Formula 1 World Championship.
Opposite: Geoffrey Crossley's illustrious competition included the Swiss Baron Emmanuel de Graffenried, the Argentinian ace Juan Manuel Fangio and the Siamese Prince Birabongse Bhanudej Bhanubandth.

In this country, if you were a racing driver, people thought there was something slightly rough about you. The press and the public had no interest: folk had not cottoned on to motor racing then. GEOFFREY CROSSLEY

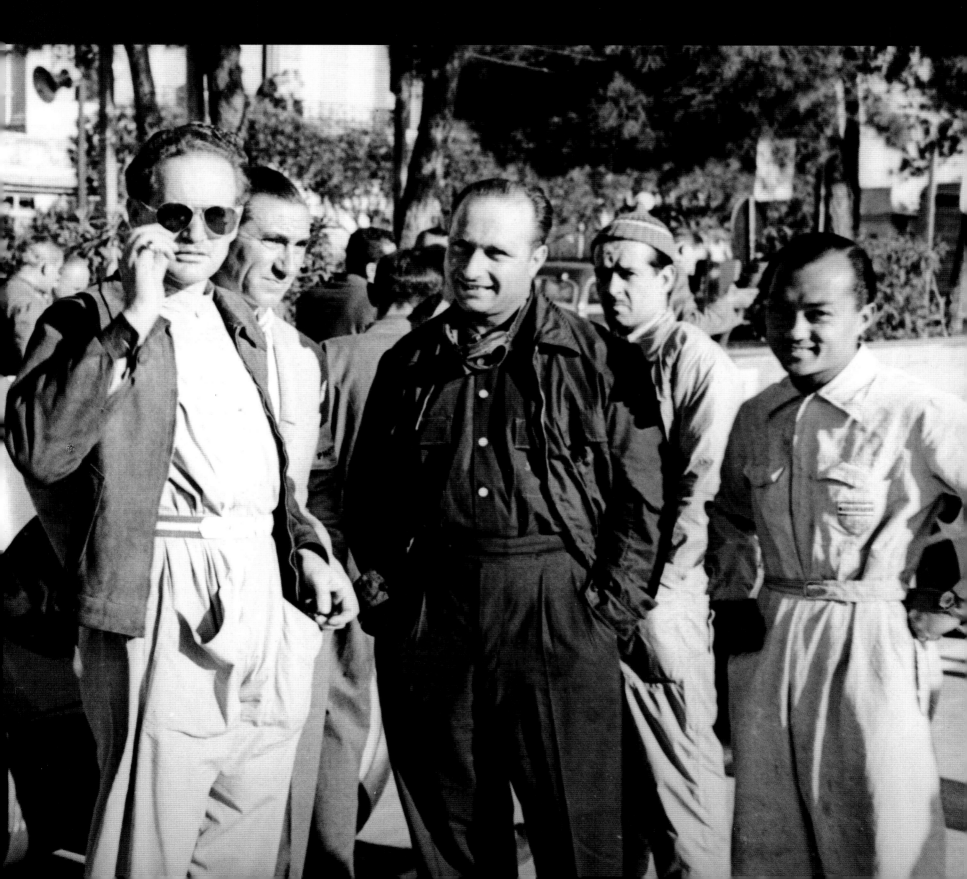

13 MAY 1950 - BRITISH GP (SILVERSTONE) It fell to the bumpy wartime concrete runways of the former RAF bomber base at Silverstone to host the first-ever round of the Formula 1 World Championship - although, interestingly, none of the contemporary coverage mentions the new championship at all! On 13 May 1950, a 21-car grid lined up in 4-3-4 formation for a 202-mile race in front of a 150,000-strong crowd.

Those 21 cars included four of the magnificent Tipo 158 Alfa Romeos which, apart from a year off in 1949, had been dominating Formula 1 since the war. The lead driver was the arrogant, stylish Italian, Giuseppe Farina, who had been winning Grands Prix for Alfa since 1936. Then there was the quiet, bandy-legged Argentine, Juan Manuel Fangio, who had astonished everyone with his first European season in 1949 in a Maserati effectively paid for by the Perón government. His string of wins had rapidly earned him, aged 38, a seat in the world's top racing team.

The so-called 'Alfetta' had originally been developed for the voiturette class before the war, using a twin-supercharged, straight-eight, 1500cc engine. Although a ten-year-old design, it was ideal for the new Formula 1. Alfa's closest rival was Ferrari, whose Type 125 used a supercharged 1500cc V12. But Enzo Ferrari was clearly not much impressed by the new World Championship series: he did not bother to send any cars to Silverstone, although, the following weekend, his full team was at Monte Carlo for the second round.

The only other works cars came from France: the Lago Talbots were big, heavy 4.5-litre machines, also a pre-war design, reliable but relatively slow. Britain's Grand Prix hope, the much-vaunted V16 BRM, was far from ready, although it did a couple of demonstration laps. Apart from half a dozen Maseratis of varying ages, the rest of the field was made up with British no-hopers: four ancient ERAs and a couple of Altas. An Alfa Romeo walkover was a foregone conclusion.

But, for the war-weary enthusiasts of the time, the whole event was magical, and the British press covered it with breathless enthusiasm.

BILL BODDY (*Motor Sport*): "The arrival of the cars before a big race never fails to thrill. That evening in the bars in Buckingham and adjacent towns there was only one topic of conversation — the Grand Prix. Even before 150,000 people flocked to the course we felt that motor racing had 'arrived' in England."

RODNEY WALKERLEY (*The Motor*): "Motor Racing in the grand manner came to Britain on Saturday. The long line of pits, the beflagged stands, the blue and gold of the royal box where the Royal Standard floated in the wind, was a spectacle of colour and movement which I found strangely stirring and heartwarming."

A less romanticised picture of what Grand Prix racing was really like in the 1950s came from the amateur driver who started 17th on that first grid with his privately owned Alta.

GEOFFREY CROSSLEY: "I towed my car behind a wartime Chevy truck I'd bought at an army disposal sale. You negotiated start money with the organisers, and you'd get a bit of prize money if you finished - £75 perhaps, or £100 if you'd done well.

"The fact that Silverstone was the first round of the new World Championship didn't really affect us. In fact, I don't think we even knew about it. The Alfas were in a race of their own — they were at least eight seconds a lap faster than the British cars, so they came past us every 15 laps or so."

Above: Guiseppe Farina (centre), Luigi Fagioli (second from right) and Reg Parnell (third from left) - 1-2-3 for Alfa Romeo in the first championship Grand Prix. Farina (opposite) went on to become the first World Champion.

The howling red Alfas ran in predictable 1-2-3-4 formation, with Farina leading Fangio, Fagioli and Parnell, until a rare mistake from Fangio: he clipped a straw bale, broke an oil pipe and retired.

GEOFFREY CROSSLEY: "My race was a bit of a disaster. There was a mix-up with my crew about pit signals, and after my refuelling stop I rejoined in something of a frenzy and was a bit too forceful with the gear lever, so I had to retire with bent gear selectors. After the continental races, there would always be a big gala dinner for the drivers and teams. I don't remember anything like that after Silverstone. I think we all just went to the beer tent."

21 MAY 1950 - MONACO GP (MONTE CARLO) Fangio's first World Championship victory came the week after Silverstone, when he lapped the rest of the field in a dramatic Monaco Grand Prix. High winds blew sea water onto the track at the Tabac corner, where the track surface in those days was stone paving slabs. On the first lap Farina, chasing Fangio for the lead, spun on the wet surface. Luigi Villoresi's Ferrari squeezed through, but fourth man Froilan Gonzalez crashed his Maserati, splitting open its full tank to add fuel to the soaking surface. More than half the field were eliminated in the ensuing pile-up. Gonzalez carried on in his battered and leaking car, only for it to burst into flames at the next corner. In all, 10 of the 19 starters were eliminated. Fangio had seen none of this, but as he approached the blind corner, he realised that it looked subtly different.

JUAN MANUEL FANGIO: "Instead of the white blobs of faces looking at me, I saw necks craned. I was in the lead, but people were looking to their right, which meant something more interesting must be happening round the corner. A photo I'd seen in an old album, of a pile-up in the 1936 Monte Carlo race, came back to me in a flash, and I started to slow. Round the corner there was a mass of crashed cars and fuel spilling all over the track. I managed to pull up inches from the wreckage, and work my way towards the gap that remained."

3 SEPTEMBER 1950 - ITALIAN GP (MONZA) Throughout the season, Ferrari's little supercharged V12 proved unable to stay with the Alfa Romeos, but Enzo Ferrari was now pursuing a different course. The 1500cc supercharged cars were fast, but thirsty: the Alfa engines, producing almost 250bhp per litre, used their methanol at a rate of around 3mpg, requiring both a prodigious fuel load and mid-race refuelling stops. Ferrari's new designer, Aurelio Lampredi, decided to opt for the unsupercharged, 4.5-litre alternative, and produced a simple, torquey, more fuel-efficient Ferrari V12.

Ignoring Indianapolis, Alfa Romeo won all six rounds of the first year's series, with three victories each for Farina and Fangio. In fact Fangio had the better season, for he also won non-championship Grands Prix at San Remo, Geneva and Pescara. But in the races that counted for points, Farina's fourth place and fastest lap in Belgium was enough to write his name indelibly into the history books as the first World Champion.

Over the winter of 1950-51, Alfa Romeo sought to meet the new Ferrari challenge. The Tipo 158 became the 159, the supercharged straight-eight of which was reworked to produce an impressive 430bhp. But the fuel consumption was even worse, and additional side tanks had to be fitted for some races. Aside from Ferrari, there were once again no serious challengers: the nimble little Gordinis with their production-based pushrod engines joined the Lago Talbots from France, the Maseratis were all run by private teams, and the BRM was still not a serious contender.

27 MAY 1951 - SWISS GP (BREMGARTEN) The opening round was on the tree-lined Bremgarten circuit near Berne, which had the reputation of being particularly treacherous when it rained. In the wet here, in 1948, the great Achille Varzi had died in the wreckage of his Alfa Romeo 158. Sure enough, on race day, the rain was torrential, but Fangio's drive was flawless. Piero Taruffi's Ferrari beat Farina's Alfa into second place, but finished almost a minute behind the Argentine.

Fangio was now just a month off his 40th birthday, honing the genius that was to give him a still unequalled five World Championships in six seasons. Years later, he named that Swiss victory as an important milestone, and for an unusual reason: it removed from his make-up a weakness that has dogged many a great driver.

JUAN MANUEL FANGIO: "The night before the race, before going to bed, I invited two friends to take a couple of laps of the circuit in my own car. I wanted to memorise it again, down to the last detail. Suddenly a cat darted across the road, and I ran it over. 'You've killed a black cat!' they shouted in unison, and began to make jokes about how unlucky it was to kill a black cat, especially the night before a race. Ascari, for one, had a terrible fear about black cats: if one crossed the road in front of him he would stop, turn round, and find another route.

"That night I couldn't sleep, thinking about killing that cat. Well, as it turned out, next day I led the race pretty much from start to finish, in the pouring rain. For me, that day marked the end of all superstition. In the beginning

everyone has his superstition. If fate is unkind to you on the day you happen to run over a black cat, you remain a slave to that superstition for the rest of your life."

1 JULY 1951 - FRENCH GP (REIMS) Alfa Romeo won in Belgium (Farina, after Fangio had a 15-minute delay with a refuelling stop that went horribly wrong) and in France (Fangio, after taking over Fagioli's car mid-race when his own developed a misfire). But a Ferrari was second on both occasions.

14 JULY 1951 - BRITISH GP (SILVERSTONE) Fangio's 27-year-old compatriot, Froilan Gonzalez, had joined Scuderia Ferrari at the French Grand Prix, standing in for Taruffi who was unwell, and had run strongly in second place before handing over his car to Ascari. This was enough to earn the chubby Argentine a permanent place in the team, and his performance in the British race was a sensation. He outqualified team leader Ascari as well as the Alfas of Fangio and Farina to take pole position, becoming the first man to lap Silverstone at over 100mph.

The BRMs finally turned up at Silverstone - for what was to be the only World Championship appearance by the V16 - although they embarrassingly missed practice altogether and had to start from the back of the grid. In the race Reg Parnell and Peter Walker brought both recalcitrant cars home in fifth and seventh places, but were way off the leaders' pace.

The race developed into a thunderous fight between the stylishly smooth Fangio and the wildly abandoned Gonzalez, and many of the straw bales lining Silverstone's featureless layout were shredded by the Ferrari's cheese-cutter grille.

BILL BODDY: "Gonzalez, a fat, dark little man, bare arms at full length, fought his sliding Ferrari, ran wide at Becketts, found a gap in the straw bales and went on."

SAMMY DAVIS (*The Autocar*): "On one lap he almost met his Waterloo when the Ferrari slid and hit a tub. The front of the car rose in the air, and Gonzalez just succeeded in holding it as it came down. Yet he did not seem to slow, rejoining the course and losing only about 60 yards to Fangio."

Predictably, the Alfas stopped for fuel first, but soon the Ferraris had to come in also. Ascari had already retired with a broken gearbox so, when Gonzalez came into the pits, he leaped out and offered his car to his team leader. He was pushed back into the cockpit, two churns of fuel were sloshed in, the worn tyres left untouched and he was sent out again, still in the lead. Fangio's Alfa was unable to catch him, for the rotund Argentine continued to drive like a man possessed.

After 162 minutes of racing, the battered Ferrari crossed the line almost a minute ahead of the Alfa Romeo. It was not merely the first time the Alfas had been beaten in a straight fight since the war. It was a historic first World Championship Grand Prix victory for Scuderia Ferrari - the start of a legendary roll of victories which would be lengthening still, five decades later.

ENZO FERRARI: "I had left Alfa Romeo so that I might show the people there what I was made of - an ambitious idea that might have ruined me! When for the first time in the history of our direct rivalry Gonzalez in a Ferrari showed his heels to the whole Alfa team, I wept with joy. But my tears of happiness were blended, too, with tears of sadness, for I thought that day: 'I have killed my mother!'"

At the next round, Ferrari vanquished Alfa Romeo again, Ascari beating Fangio by half a minute in the first post-war Formula 1 race at the Nürburgring. On its home soil at Monza, Alfa Romeo therefore made a giant effort, with three updated 159Ms among its four-car entry. The race crews practised their refuelling stops too, but their rehearsals almost ended in tragedy when Consalvo Sanesi's car caught fire and he was badly burned.

In the race, Fangio threw a tyre tread and then broke a piston. Farina stopped with a misfire, taking over Felice Bonetto's car to finish third. But the Ferraris of Ascari and Gonzalez finished a crushing 1-2.

At Alfa Romeo, there was fury and suspicion after this disappointment. Amid claims of sabotage within the factory, one or two of the workforce were dismissed. Ascari was within two points of Fangio in the World Championship; one round remained.

28 OCTOBER 1951 - SPANISH GP (PEDRALBES) At the Pedralbes circuit north of Barcelona, Alfa Romeo was determined nothing should go wrong this time. Ferrari was hoping to go through without a refuelling stop, but it also opted for smaller-diameter, wider wheels. In the heat and with heavy fuel loads, first Taruffi, then Villoresi, then Ascari and finally Gonzalez all needed to stop for tyres. Fangio meanwhile drove a faultless race, to score Alfa Romeo's last-ever Grand Prix victory, and to be crowned World Champion. Gonzalez was again the Ferrari star, coming back brilliantly to finish second and push Farina down into third place, both in the race and in the championship points table.

To vanquish Ferrari in 1952, Alfa Romeo realised that a completely new car was needed. It had insufficient funds to develop it, so approached the Italian government for a subsidy. When this failed to materialise, the company announced its withdrawal from Formula 1.

Opposite: 'Maestro' Juan Manuel Fangio won the first of his five driving titles in 1951.
Above: Reg Parnell salvaged fifth place from a recalcitrant BRM V16 in front of the British team's home crowd at Silverstone.

GONZALEZ'S SHORT, HEAVY BODY ALMOST OVERFLOWING THE COCKPIT:

NO STYLIST, THIS NEW STAR, BUT VERY FAST INDEED. SAMMY DAVIS

Alfa Romeo's withdrawal left no serious challenge to Ferrari, so the FIA realised that, unless something was done, every Grand Prix was likely to be a walkover. It had announced a new Formula 1, for 2.5-litre unsupercharged cars, but this would not come into force until 1954. Hoping to encourage opposition from Britain, France and Germany, the governing body decided that the 1952-53 World Championships would be for relatively plentiful Formula 2 cars. In fact, it ushered in two years of almost uninterrupted Ferrari domination.

While a few non-championship Formula 1 races continued to be run with sparse fields, the Formula 2 Grands Prix did succeed in attracting more works teams: two from Italy, one from France and, at varying times, up to four from Britain. But for two monotonous seasons, until the final Grand Prix of 1953, every single race was won by Ferrari. Of the 15 events during those two years, Ascari won eleven, nine consecutively.

Having experimented with a 2-litre V12, Ferrari opted for a simple, four-cylinder engine which was torquey, reliable and fast. Its only real opposition came from Maserati, whose six-cylinder A6GCM was not ready until mid-year. In its debut race, the non-championship Autodromo Grand Prix at Monza, Fangio - exhausted by driving overnight across Europe after a race with BRM the previous day in Ireland - crashed heavily. His injuries would keep him out of racing for the rest of the season, and would also hobble Maserati's efforts.

18 MAY 1952 - SWISS GP (BREMGARTEN) Subsequent events would suggest that Taruffi owed the only World Championship victory of his career to the absence of his team leader, Ascari, who was in the USA preparing for the Indy 500.

22 JUNE 1952 - BELGIAN GP (SPA) Having failed to take his Ferrari 375 to the finish at Indianapolis, Ascari returned to Europe to begin his outstanding sequence of Grand Prix victories at Spa-Francorchamps.

7 SEPTEMBER 1952 - ITALIAN GP (MONZA) Maserati had a works A6GCM for Gonzalez in the last 1952 round at Monza, and gave Ascari and Ferrari a fright. Gonzalez started with a light fuel load, and led magnificently until stopping to refuel just before half-distance. He still finished second, ahead of the Ferraris of Villoresi and Farina.

While Ferrari was untouchable all season, there were interesting signs of the emergence of several new teams and drivers. It was a thinly financed French team which came closest to challenging the Scuderia. Gordini scored third places with Jean Behra at Berne and Robert Manzon at Spa - and, in the non-championship Grand Prix at Reims, Behra sensationally beat the Ferraris of Farina, Ascari and Villoresi fair and square. A less publicised achievement of Behra was to get to Berne at all: his car was finished so late at Gordini's little factory in the suburbs of Paris that there was no time for the transporter to get it to Switzerland. So Behra jumped into the cockpit and drove it on the public roads across France, and over the Swiss border. Incredibly, the police of both countries and the customs officials at the border turned a blind eye.

HWM, which had fielded a full three-car Formula 2 team in European races since 1950, ran up to four Alta powered cars in each round, using promising young drivers like Peter Collins, Lance Macklin and Paul Frère. Frère finished fifth in his home race at Spa, and Connaught and Frazer Nash drivers also scored points occasionally.

The find of the year, however, was a tall young man named Mike Hawthorn, who always raced wearing a bow tie under his green windcheater. He burst onto the scene at the Easter Monday Goodwood international with a new Formula 2 Cooper-Bristol, winning two races and finishing second to Gonzalez's 4.5-litre Ferrari in the main race. Then he contested three Grands Prix, finishing fourth at Spa, third at Silverstone behind the Ferraris of Ascari and Taruffi, and fourth in the new Dutch Grand Prix at Zandvoort - so that, at season's end, he was fourth equal in the World Championship, and the best-placed non-Ferrari driver.

The pre-war ERA marque was revived with the new, Bristol powered G-type, but the car never lived up to the promise of its advanced specification. It was particularly galling to young Stirling Moss that, while he struggled with the complex ERA, Hawthorn was getting all the plaudits as Britain's rising new star with the simple, effective Cooper.

STIRLING MOSS: "It was just over-clever, and simply didn't work. ERA's Leslie Johnson told me David Hodkin, its designer, was a genius. But it was a project that made an awful lot of fuss about doing very little, and I became very disillusioned by the Clever Professor approach to racing car design."

Both Hawthorn and Moss had been noticed by the Ferrari team as impressive young talents. Moss was offered a works drive for 1952 by Enzo Ferrari, who summoned him to the non-championship race at Bari in September 1951. But, when Moss got there, he found the car he had been promised had been given to Taruffi instead, and thereafter he did not really trust the Commendatore. A year later, Hawthorn got the call to come to Modena, and signed for the 1953 season alongside Ascari, Farina and Villoresi to become Britain's first Ferrari works driver.

Alberto Ascari, in #2 Ferrari, won the Dutch Grand Prix (the start, above) and dominated the 1952 season.

Ascari, the driver, had a sure and precise style, but Ascari the man had an impelling need to get into the lead at the very beginning. ENZO FERRARI

It was like a Roman Holiday: we were the gladiators, and obviously none of the crowd lining the track were in the least bit worried that their antics might kill us, or themselves.

MIKE HAWTHORN

Opposite: Ascari, the eventual winner, leads Fangio at the start of an Argentine race that descended into madness.
Right: The Ferrari team fuels up for the Dutch Grand Prix of 1953. Farina (helmet) finished second, while Villoresi (right) failed to finish. Ascari (next to Villoresi) won this race and the 1953 championship.

18 JANUARY 1953 - ARGENTINE GP (BUENOS AIRES) The 1953 season began in January, in Argentina, for the first World Championship Grand Prix to be held outside Europe. The event inaugurated a new, Perón-financed autodrome on the edge of Buenos Aires, and 350,000 people thronged into the new stadium, many cutting through the fences to gain access without tickets. Then one enterprising individual threw a hook over one of the wire fences, hitched it to the back of a truck and dragged it down altogether. Crowd control broke down completely, and people clustered five or six deep on the very edge of the track, or actually on the road surface itself. Horrified by the potential danger, the drivers at first refused to start: but as the afternoon dragged on, and the crowd became more impatient in the baking heat, the organisers realised there would be a riot if the race did not take place. Reluctantly, the drivers took up their grid positions, with people lining the track on both sides.

MIKE HAWTHORN (his first race for Ferrari): "The crowd was edging further and further into the roadway, completely obscuring our view of the corners. Time after time I waved at them to get out of the way, but this only made them worse. They began standing in the roadway holding shirts and pullovers, which they snatched away at the last moment like a toreador playing a bull."

Surprisingly, it was not until lap 32 that the inevitable accident happened. A small boy dashed into the road in front of Farina's third-placed Ferrari. Farina swerved to avoid him, lost control and slid sideways into the densely packed crowd beside the track. Officially, ten people were killed, and more than 30 seriously injured, but the true numbers were probably much greater. For a while, there was mayhem: hysterical spectators were running around unchecked, and Englishman Alan Brown struck another child with his Cooper-Bristol, killing him instantly.

VICENTE ALVAREZ (*Autosport*): "Not satisfied with just getting near the track, the crowd clustered thickly at danger points, standing on the very kerbs and thus limiting the visibility of the drivers, creating a permanent risk of tragedy should a car spin out.

"And this is what happened as Farina came hurtling down the second straight. Trying to dodge an imprudent spectator, the Italian swerved to the outside and hit the crowd which was packed solid along the kerb at that point. Ten were killed and more than 30 injured. Farina emerged with an injured foot and the car was extensively damaged. This sad mishap caused mass confusion and, for some moments following, danger was still greater as spectators were running in all directions. One was struck by Alan Brown and seriously wounded."

Some of the more lurid contemporary accounts speak of ambulances crashing into each other, and of a policeman, trying to restore order, being kicked to death by a hysterical mob. Incredibly, the race went on. Ascari's Ferrari won by a lap from team mate Villoresi, with Gonzalez third for Maserati. Fangio, in his first race since his near-fatal Monza accident more than seven months before - and now displaying the distinctive stiff-necked stoop that would remain with him for the rest of his life - retired from second place with broken transmission. Hawthorn was fourth. Ascari averaged 78.129mph - in just over three hours of driving - which was far too fast in the dangerous conditions.

21 JUNE 1953 - BELGIAN GP (SPA) Back in Europe, and greatly helped by the talents of Fangio and Gonzalez, the latest Maserati gradually began to match the speed of the Ferrari, if not its reliability.

Marshals and police were unable to check the unruly mob, which swept beyond the enclosures and invaded the track. VICENTE ALVAREZ

We would go screaming down the straight side-by-side, absolutely flat out, grinning at each other, with me crouching down in the cockpit, trying to save every ounce of wind resistance. MIKE HAWTHORN

5 JULY 1953 - FRENCH GP (REIMS) On the long straights of the very fast, flat Reims road circuit, the cars would bunch up together in high-speed groups, running wheel-to-wheel at 160mph and slipstreaming past one another, and for nearly three hours a magnificent battle raged between the very evenly matched Ferraris and Maseratis. Gonzalez had opted once more to start on half-full tanks, and he took the lead from a weaving, darting, seven-car gaggle in pursuit. Ferrari's new boy had to adapt rapidly to the art of slipstreaming.

MIKE HAWTHORN: "We were hurtling along at 160mph, sometimes three abreast, down an ordinary French road. It was a bit frightening to see the nose of one of the other cars come alongside, then drop back again as the driver decided he could not make it before the next corner. The cars were evenly matched, and we could only get past each other by slipstreaming. The trick was to tuck in close behind the other man, get a tow from his slipstream, ease back the throttle as far as possible

without losing position, and then suddenly tramp on the pedal and use the surge of urge to nip out and pass him. Whereupon he would try to get into position to return the compliment. The slightest misjudgement could have meant disaster for everybody, but even so we usually managed a quick grin at each other when we passed - all except Farina, who sat scowling with concentration."

By the time Gonzalez made his inevitable pitstop, Fangio and Hawthorn had worked their way to the front of the group, and the two of them, Argentine maestro and English youngster, began a titanic struggle, with the lead changing between them on virtually every lap. The Maserati had a tiny edge over the Ferrari on straight-line speed, but the Ferrari's brakes and low-speed torque were superior, so that Hawthorn was able repeatedly to outbrake Fangio into the tight Thillois hairpin and pull away from the Maserati on low-speed acceleration. Then, as the speed built down the long undulating straight, Fangio would move alongside to challenge again.

MIKE HAWTHORN: "We were only inches apart, and I could clearly see the rev-counter in Fangio's cockpit. Once, as we came into Thillois, he braked harder than I had expected and I shunted him lightly, putting a dent in the Maserati's tail. That shook me for a moment, for I thought it would take some living-down. 'New Boy Shunts Fangio,' they would say. But he showed no resentment at all. He just kept on fighting every inch of the way, according to the rules, in the way that has earned him the admiration and respect of everyone in motor racing.

"I [had been] scared that the master was going to get very angry with such a newcomer, particularly in a World Championship event. Yet gradually I saw that he, too, was thoroughly enjoying himself. As we went down the straight from Garenne, practically wheel-to-wheel, I would catch his infectious grin, which did more than anything else to give me the confidence to keep it up. Some drivers in the top grade would have tried everything to put me off - but not Juan Manuel. Naturally he did his best to beat me fair and square, but it was one of those days for me, and that wonderful little F2 Ferrari did the rest.

"I had a totally unexpected bit of luck. As we swung into the last lap, it suddenly dawned on me that Fangio had not changed down into first gear for the Thillois turn. Perhaps he was having trouble with the gearbox? [It emerged later that such was the case.]

"Wheel-to-wheel we flashed round for the last time, and I knew that everything was going to depend on perfect timing of that last change into first gear on the last corner. We were only inches apart as we braked, changed down, and down again. Then I slipped into first, cut round the apex as close in as possible, straightened up the wheels and simultaneously slammed the throttle wide open. I gained the precious yards I needed and was leading by one second as the flag came down."

After the race, Hawthorn was mobbed by the excited crowd and was himself overcome with emotion.

RODNEY WALKERLEY: "The young British driver stood for his National Anthem with tears running down his cheeks. The crowd gasped with amazement when he took off his helmet and they saw his obvious youth, after a drive in which he matched every champion on the circuit with courage, speed and racecraft."

13 SEPTEMBER 1953 - ITALIAN GP (MONZA) Ferrari's clean sweep continued until an enthralling final round at Monza, the last World Championship race run to the Formula 2 regulations. The grid lined up Ferrari-Maserati-Ferrari-Maserati-Ferrari-Ferrari-Maserati, and a classic slipstreaming battle ensued.

After almost three hours of racing, a four-car group of two Ferraris and two Maseratis were wheel-to-wheel coming into the final Parabolica corner for the last time. Ascari and Farina in Ferraris were trying to shut out Fangio's Maserati: Marimon in the other Maserati was four laps down after a long pitstop. Halfway round the corner, Ascari, leading, suddenly found he had to

lap Jack Fairman's Connaught. Darting off-line, Ascari started to spin; Farina took to the grass to avoid him; Marimon hit Ascari; and Fangio stormed over the line - having averaged a speed of 110.64mph - to score a World Championship victory for Maserati at last. But the driving title went to Ascari, for the second year in a row.

ENZO FERRARI: "Alberto Ascari was unusual, both as a man and as a driver. Strong willed, he knew what he wanted and set about obtaining it punctiliously. He was one of the very few, for instance, who went into athletic training for the races.

"When leading, he could not easily be overtaken - indeed, I will go as far as to say that it was virtually impossible to overtake him. When he was second, however, or even farther back, he had not the combative spirit I should have liked to have seen on certain occasions."

Above: After almost three hours of racing at Monza, a four-car group of two Ferraris and two Maseratis were wheel-to-wheel. Ascari, leading, spun, avoiding a backmarker, and was hit by Marimon. Farina went on the grass to avoid them and Fangio stormed across the line to win for Maserati.

The new 2500cc Formula 1 was destined to remain in force for seven years, and this period of stability saw a fascinating swing of technical superiority from Italy to Germany to Britain, accompanied by the transition from hefty, front-engined, ladder-framed cars to dainty, lightweight, mid-engined spaceframes. But at the start of the new formula, little seemed to have changed. Ferrari and Maserati were still the only protagonists seriously challenging for victory, while Gordini, struggling on with marginal finance, was the only other works participant.

However, there had been rumours for some time that Mercedes-Benz was planning to return to Grand Prix racing; indeed it had briefly considered doing so in 1951, using a car based on its pre-war 1500cc supercharged Tripoli machine, but the adoption of Formula 2 for 1952 had ended the project. Instead, during the winter of 1952, the Daimler-Benz board secretly authorised the development of an advanced new Formula 1 car, capable of winning under the 2.5-litre regulations in 1954.

The ambitious programme called for a straight-eight engine with desmodromic valve gear and fuel injection, lying on its side in a spaceframe, with offset transmission and inboard brakes. There would be all-enveloping bodywork for fast circuits and open-wheelers for the twistier tracks. To lead the team, the funds were available to hire the best driver in the world. Accordingly, a successful approach had been made to Juan Manuel Fangio.

Lancia also decided to join the fray. Its new car was to use a V8 engine and, in a quest for consistent weight distribution throughout a long race, pannier fuel tanks were hung between the wheels on each side. Lancia lured the world's other top driver, Alberto Ascari, who had long complained to Enzo Ferrari about the Scuderia's poor rates of pay. But this was to prove a bad move for Ascari's career. The new Lancia was not ready until the end of the season, leaving him with nothing more than occasional guest drives with Ferrari and Maserati.

The new Mercedes-Benz cars would not be raced until they could be assured of victory, so their debut was set as the French Grand Prix in July. For the two rounds before that, in Argentina and Belgium, Fangio was released to return to Maserati, and he comfortably won both races in the new 250F.

4 JULY 1954 - FRENCH GP (REIMS) Then came Reims. Historians noted that, to the day, it was the 40th anniversary of the domination of the French Grand Prix at Lyons by the new, 4.5-litre, shaft-drive Mercedes Grand Prix car, on 4 July 1914.

And history repeated itself. The brand new W196 'streamliners' of Fangio and Karl Kling led virtually from start to finish, crossing the line almost side-by-side in a demonstration of crushing superiority. Gonzalez, now driving for Ferrari in one of its new, side-tanked Squalo ('whale') Tipo 553 cars, led the pursuit until his engine blew but, by the finish, the

silver streamliners were a lap ahead of everyone else. The Mercedes team was again led by the legendary Alfred Neubauer.

17 JULY 1954 - BRITISH GP (SILVERSTONE) For the British Grand Prix, more Mercedes superiority was expected - but the streamliners proved difficult to handle on the artificial Silverstone circuit. Fangio, clouting marker barrels and grappling with a recalcitrant gearbox, could do no better than fourth, a lap down, with Kling a lowly seventh. Gonzalez scored a fine win for Ferrari ahead of team mate Hawthorn, with Marimon's Maserati third. It was to be Ferrari's last victory for a while.

1 AUGUST 1954 - GERMAN GP (NÜRBURGRING) At the Nürburgring, Argentina's Onofre Marimon was killed during practice when his Maserati went off the track, plunged through a hedge and somersaulted. His compatriots, Fangio and Gonzalez, were stricken with grief at the death of their friend. Fangio, poker-faced, went out and won the race, while Gonzalez, having led initially, was overcome with emotion and was replaced by Hawthorn at his refuelling stop. Hawthorn's own Ferrari had broken its transmission, but he drove superbly to finish second.

5 SEPTEMBER 1954 - ITALIAN GP (MONZA) Having used the open-wheel Mercedes W196 to win in Germany and Switzerland, Fangio switched to the streamliner to win in Italy. But the hero of Monza was Stirling Moss.

With inspired performances in sports cars, Formula 3, touring cars and rallies, Moss had so far failed to make his mark in Grand Prix racing. He had spent the Formula 2 era grappling with underpowered and unreliable British cars - HWM, ERA, Connaught, Cooper-Alta - and started 1954 with his privately owned Maserati 250F. He was third at Spa, and was lying a brilliant second at Silverstone when a driveshaft broke with ten laps to go. He had shown Maserati that he merited a works drive and, from the German Grand Prix, his car was painted red.

At Monza, where Ascari had returned to Ferrari for the occasion, he and Fangio disputed the lead for the first half of the race, with Moss in their wake, taking on the two best drivers in the world.

STIRLING MOSS: "Slipstreaming Fangio and Ascari into the Curva Grande, I saw my chance, and slingshot past them both to take the lead. Ascari came back at me, but his engine broke almost immediately, so next time round I found myself holding an increasing lead. This was absolutely wonderful while it lasted - leading the Italian

Grand Prix as effective Number One for a major Italian works team - but 12 laps from the end my car began to trail a haze of smoke. I stopped at the pits for three gallons of oil to be added under pressure. But as I accelerated away those three gallons lay on the pit apron where the car had been standing. By the Curva Grande the pressure gauge had zeroed and I knew my race was over. I tried to limp on, but at the Curva del Porfido my engine seized.

"I coasted as far as I could, then hopped out and pushed the last half-mile. I sat on the tail waiting for Fangio to win, and then pushed it across the line to be classified tenth. Apparently an oil pipe had been clamped too rigidly against the chassis, and had cracked through vibration. Afterwards Fangio - like the great sportsman he is - greeted me as the moral victor."

29 OCTOBER 1954 - SPANISH GP (PEDRALBES) For its final round, the 1954 World Championship returned to the Pedralbes circuit at Barcelona. At last the new Lancia was ready: and clearly it was a serious contender. Ascari put it on the pole, a full second clear of Fangio's Mercedes, and led the early stages until his clutch failed. His team mate Villoresi was an early retirement with brake failure. Hawthorn's Ferrari won from the Maserati of an impressive youngster, Luigi Musso, who was

> What really impressed me was that, as I clambered out of the car, rummaging in my pockets for a rag to wipe my face, a mechanic appeared bearing hot water, soap, a flannel and a towel. Out there in the middle of the desolate Hockenheimring, this was forethought I could hardly credit. I thought then that to be associated with such an organisation could not be bad. STIRLING MOSS

running in only his third World Championship race. Fangio had an unhappy afternoon with an overheating Mercedes, finishing a distant third drenched in hot oil.

But in the World Championship, with six wins out of eight rounds, Fangio had long since put the title well out of reach. Ferrari drivers Gonzalez and Hawthorn finished second and third, half a point apart. It had been an impressive comeback season for Mercedes.

Two weeks after Barcelona, the Mercedes-Benz racing manager, Alfred Neubauer, sent a telegram to Moss, offering him a seat alongside Fangio for the

1955 season. The frenetically active Moss was not at home: he had flown to New York to do the American Mountain Rally for Sunbeam-Talbot. But, on his return, he flew to Germany to try the W196 at Hockenheim and, on a damp track, he equalled the lap record.

He duly signed for a substantial sum to drive for Mercedes-Benz in Grands Prix and sports car races.

Opposite and above: Fellow Argentinians Gonzalez and Fangio led the German Grand Prix, but were grief-stricken at the death of their countryman Onofre Marimon. Gonzalez, overcome by emotion after the fatality, was replaced by Mike Hawthorn, who finished second to Fangio.

ENZO FERRARI: "Political motives were behind the efforts of Hitlerite Germany, when the Mercedes and Auto Union cars swept the board everywhere. It was abundantly clear that this gigantic mechanical offensive was meant to enhance German prestige and the Nazi regime. The second Mercedes offensive, after the war, was for reasons of industrial prestige and economic policy.

The one great figure behind both these attacks was, of course, Alfred Neubauer, who was for years my personal adversary and became a good friend of mine.

"I first saw Neubauer when he was driving a Mercedes in the Targa Florio race in 1923 or 1924. He was lanky, with very pale eyes, a high-pitched voice, a prominent aquiline nose and brusque manners. 'He's not a very likeable sort of fellow, this German,' I thought to myself.

"Then, in 1934, we ran into one another again. It was the debut of the weight formula, and Mercedes and Auto Union - or, rather, Germany - had come to the conclusion that the time was ripe for their offensive. And Alfred Neubauer was the new general. He had grown so stout that I hardly recognised him. And, in the years that were to come, seemingly in pace with the increasing strength of Mercedes and Germany, Neubauer grew steadily fatter and fatter and became increasingly more authoritarian and dictatorial.

He was to be seen by the pits, casting scornful glances at his rivals and barking out commands in his Wehrmacht officer's voice, whilst his staff jumped to his orders as though on a parade ground.

"Very soon, he was a well-known personage in our little world, generally disliked - although this did not worry him in the slightest - yet he was highly esteemed and feared for his efficiency. I thought quite often of Neubauer during the war: indeed, I could not help thinking of him every time a German mechanised column passed in front of my workshops and some officer or other alighted and started shouting orders.

"In 1954, Alfred Neubauer turned up once more at the head of a team of sleek, silver cars. And he was fatter and more dictatorial than ever. Year by year, I watched him grow stouter and stouter with increasing concern: he and Mercedes and Germany seemed to grow as though they were one, pound by pound, success by success, mark by mark.

"This unhalting progress could not help making me think: 'If Neubauer doesn't stop putting on weight, it looks as though Germany is getting ready for another war.'"

The 1955 season promised much, with Mercedes-Benz, Ferrari, Maserati and Lancia all bidding for victory, Connaught and Vanwall providing an interesting second-string, and Gordini producing an ambitious straight-eight, semi-streamlined car. In fact it was to be a year of tragedy, and of almost total Mercedes domination.

16 JANUARY 1955 - ARGENTINE GP (BUENOS AIRES) The opening round in Argentina had an unreal quality, because of unprecedented heat. It was 36°C in the shade when the race began, and track temperatures of over 51°C were recorded. The race lasted more than three hours, and several drivers collapsed with heat exhaustion. As they stopped at the pits, they were relieved by team mates who had stopped earlier and had had a chance to recover, so that almost every car that finished was handled by two, if not three drivers. In all, there were 16 driver changes. The heroic winner was the indomitable 43-year-old Fangio, who drove without relief.

JUAN MANUEL FANGIO: "To be frank, I was at the end of my tether. I won that race simply by staying in the car. My leg was burning where it touched a tube in the cockpit. [He would carry the scars of this for the rest of his life.] To stop myself passing out, I tried to imagine that I was lost in the snow, and that I had to keep going or I would die of cold. There was a time when I thought I couldn't do it, but then my morale came back, and the will to win. When it was all over they had to lift me out of the car. They laid me on the floor of the pits and gave me an injection."

In his first drive for Mercedes, Moss was lying second until the heat vaporised his fuel. When his car ground to a halt out on the circuit, he got out and lay down.

STIRLING MOSS: "I was groggy from the heat, but not as much as the ambulance men and marshals who immediately surrounded me seemed to think. Despite my protests, I was bundled into an ambulance, and only set free when we found an interpreter."

Having escaped, Moss trudged back to the pits, where Neubauer sluiced him down with cold water and put him in the third Mercedes, which had already been driven by both Hans Herrmann and Kling. Moss brought it home in fourth place, behind the two shared Ferraris: Gonzalez/Trintignant/Farina second, Farina/Maglioli/Trintignant third.

3 MAY 1955 - MONACO GP (MONTE CARLO) The Monaco Grand Prix, as usual a race of attrition around the tight, hilly street circuit, was won by Maurice Trintignant's Ferrari from Eugenio Castellotti's Lancia. Fangio and Moss, who was fresh from his famous Mille Miglia win in a Mercedes 300SLR sports-racing car, circulated at the head of the field until first Fangio's car had transmission failure, and then Moss's broke its valve gear. This promoted Ascari into the lead in the new Lancia - but on the same lap he lost it at the chicane on the waterfront after the tunnel.

GREGOR GRANT (*Autosport*): "Ascari's Lancia came though the tunnel faster than ever, and suddenly swerved sideways into the hay-bales, bounced off a stone bollard and toppled into the water, narrowly missing an anchored yacht. The car disappeared in a cloud of spray and steam, and with it went Ascari. Then, to our immense relief, a blue helmet popped up out of the water and the Italian was tearing it off and striking out with a strong overarm stroke. Frogmen rushed to his rescue, and he was pulled aboard a boat. After first-aid, he was taken to hospital suffering from shock, bruises and a broken nose - fortunate to be alive at all."

ENZO FERRARI: "Ascari loved his family, but in his own way. I once asked him why he was so severe with his two beloved children. He replied: 'Every time I come back from a race, I always bring them something that will make them happy, and I usually try to give them everything they need - even if it is to satisfy a whim. All the same, though, I think it as well that I should be severe with them: I don't want them to get too fond of me, in fact. One of these days, I may not come back and they will suffer less if I have kept them a bit at arm's length.'

"On Thursday, after falling into the sea at Monte Carlo, Ascari turned up at Monza, where Castellotti was practising on the 3-litre sports model they were due to drive that weekend. Alberto remarked that, after an accident, one must as soon as possible get back behind the wheel again in order not to lose one's nerve; and, during the mid-day break, he asked if he could take the car round the track a couple of times. He set off wearing Castellotti's crash helmet and with his tie fluttering over his shoulder. The second time round, he was killed on the big, sweeping bend that is hardly a bend at all."

JUAN MANUEL FANGIO: "I have lost my greatest opponent."

The death of Ascari was a body blow from which Lancia, already in financial difficulties, never recovered.

5 JUNE 1955 - BELGIAN GP (SPA) Castellotti ran a Lancia in the Belgian Grand Prix as a private entrant, and outqualified Fangio's Mercedes to take pole position, only to retire with a gearbox failure. The following month, Gianni Lancia would hand over the entire racing shop - cars, spares and tools - to Ferrari.

By then, there had been an even bigger tragedy, which had shaken the entire motor racing world. During the Le Mans 24 Hours sports car race, one of the Mercedes 300SLRs, driven by Frenchman 'Pierre Levegh' (a pseudonym for Pierre Bouillon), had crashed into a crowded spectator enclosure. More than 80 people

In Argentina many drivers - including Farina (#10 Ferrari) and Kling (#8 Mercedes) - collapsed with heat exhaustion and had to be relieved by team mates. Driving without relief, the heroic 43-year-old Fangio won, although he had to be lifted out of his Mercedes at the finish.

had been killed, and across Europe there was an immediate shocked reaction. The French, German and Swiss Grands Prix were cancelled - indeed all circuit racing was banned in Switzerland, and remains so to this day.

In the three remaining rounds of the World Championship, Mercedes swept home in dominant 1-2 finishes, as it had already done in Belgium. Moss loyally shadowed Fangio in all of these save one.

16 JULY 1955 - BRITISH GP (AINTREE) Moss qualified on pole, a fifth of a second faster than his team leader.

STIRLING MOSS: "Without any formal discussion or team orders, I followed Fangio for some time, and then moved ahead. I felt he could have reversed the order if he'd really wanted to, but I felt I would at least make him work hard for it because here I was at last - leading my home Grand Prix.

"At 50 laps, I was some 12 seconds ahead, but Neubauer was signalling 'Pl' to me, which meant 'piano', so I had to slow down. Fangio was now very close, and one lap later he was on my tail. I just led to the chequered flag by 0.2sec, with his car's nose about level with my steering wheel. I had just won my first Grande Epreuve, and become the first Briton to win the British Grand Prix."

11 SEPTEMBER 1955 - ITALIAN GP (MONZA) Over a season and a half, the Mercedes-Benz W196s had started 15 Grands Prix and won 12 - seven times finishing 1-2. In sports car racing, the 300SLRs had won every time out - except at Le Mans, where the team had withdrawn, while leading, as a mark of respect after the accident. Now, having made its point, Mercedes quit motor racing. The cars went into the factory museum, and Fangio and Moss had to look elsewhere for 1956.

The nearest opposition to the mighty Mercedes team had come from Ferrari, with Maserati picking up a few points thanks to the efforts of Mieres, Musso and tigerish Frenchman Jean Behra. The underfinanced British Connaught team ran solely in non-championship events, apart from an abortive three-car entry in the British Grand Prix, but they scored a much-lauded victory in the Syracuse Grand Prix. A shy young dental student, Tony Brooks, who had never before driven a Formula 1 car, beat the works Maseratis of Musso, Schell, Taruffi and Mières. Brooks fought off Musso in a battle that lasted almost two and a half hours, and set a new lap record.

Meanwhile there was another, better-financed British team in the wings: Vanwall. Bluff, tough industrialist Tony Vandervell was an early BRM supporter who, frustrated by its lack of progress, fielded an old 4.5-litre Ferrari called the Thin Wall Special (after the bearings that had made his fortune), and then his own car, the Vanwall. He signed Mike Hawthorn as his lead driver, but it was a short relationship.

For the new season, Ferrari developed the D50 Lancias, and continued also with the Super Squalo design using the Lancia V8 engine. Fangio took over as team leader, but kept his options open by signing for only one season in a team that included the young British driver Peter Collins, as well as Castellotti, Musso, Spanish aristocrat Alfonso de Portago, and Belgians Olivier Gendebien and Paul Frère. Moss returned to Maserati, joining Behra, Gonzalez, Villoresi and Taruffi.

With the help of Colin Chapman, whose Lotus cars were dominating the small sports car racing classes of the day, Vanwall had completely redesigned its car, with cigar-like aerodynamic bodywork, and the Franco-American Harry Schell as its lead driver. Somehow Connaught was persevering, although its straitened finances meant that it would appear in only two championship rounds. And BRM was back, its overly complex V16 design succeeded by a simple, lusty four-cylinder car, the P25, which was light, powerful and very fast. After an unhappy season at Vanwall Mike Hawthorn decided to give patriotism another try; Ron Flockhart and Syracuse winner Tony Brooks, abandoning his dentistry, completed the team.

3 JUNE 1956 - BELGIAN GP (SPA) Fangio predictably won the opener in Argentina. In Monte Carlo, Moss scored a magnificent victory, leading from start to finish. Then Collins won both the Belgian and French rounds for Scuderia Ferrari - but, in both these races, the Vanwall began to show some real form.

1 JULY 1956 - FRENCH GP (REIMS) Schell found the slippery Vanwall to be tremendously quick on the long straights of Reims, where he qualified fourth, ahead of the Maseratis of Moss and Behra, and ran in the leading quartet until his engine failed. Team mate

Hawthorn (on loan from BRM) was called in and Schell took over his car, rejoining in eighth place. His ensuing drive was the stuff of legend: the three Ferraris were at the front in the order Fangio, Castellotti, Collins, but the Vanwall wound them in.

DENIS JENKINSON (*Motor Sport*): "The Ferrari pit thought Schell was a lap behind, having not noticed that he'd taken over Hawthorn's car. So they did not give their drivers any warning of the approaching Vanwall.

"The terrific progress of the green car had the crowd on its feet. Setting a new lap record, Schell was now only 12 seconds behind the Ferraris. Each lap he got closer and the crowd cheered louder, and in a panic the Ferrari pit realised their mistake and gave their trio the press-on signal. But they could not shake the Vanwall off, for Schell had really got the bit between his teeth and he was determined to break up the red cars. The mixed Ferrari team of Argentine, Italian and British drivers had to work together, and they deliberately drove along the straights side-by-side to keep the green car from going by, for without any doubt it was quicker on maximum speed."

Nevertheless Schell managed to fumble past both Collins and Castellotti at the hairpin, and tucked in behind Fangio. It was too good to last: soon he was in the pits to mend a broken fuel-injection linkage, and he finished a distant 10th. Fangio stopped with a fuel leak, so Collins won from Castellotti. But it had been a historic sight, a green car winding in the red Ferraris and disputing the lead - something that had never happened in seven years of the World Championship.

5 AUGUST 1956 - GERMAN GP (NÜRBURGRING) The Nürburgring is called the mother and father of all road racing circuits. Fangio, however, found it more like their beautiful daughter...

JUAN MANUEL FANGIO: "The Nürburgring was always my favourite track, from the first day I ever drove on it, in an Alfetta in 1951. What happened to me was like what happens when a friend speaks to you about a woman you don't know, and when you meet her she turns out to be much more attractive than you imagined.

"The relationship wasn't easy of course. Getting to know the Nürburgring was like getting to know a woman. You can't memorise 176 curves in over 14 miles, just as you can't memorise 176 feminine wiles after a short acquaintance. But I fell totally in love with the Nürburgring and believe I finally managed to master it. It was as is if I had screwed all its secrets out of it, and got to know it once and for all.

"There was always fear at the Nürburgring. Fear is not a stupid thing. Winning is not a question of courage, but of faith in oneself and in the car. A car is like a creature that lives, with its own emotions and its own heart. You have to understand it and love it accordingly. I knew many drivers more courageous than me. They are dead now."

2 SEPTEMBER 1956 - ITALIAN GP (MONZA) They went to the final round on the full banked circuit at Monza with Fangio leading on points, Moss unable to catch him, but Collins still with an outside chance.

The Italian championship decider was magnificent, as Monza races so often are, but the use once more of the punishingly bumpy, high-speed, banked circuit underlined the primitive state of tyre technology at the time. From the start, Ferrari team mates Castellotti and Musso, bent on glory, rushed away to fight over the lead, slipstreaming each other down the straights and thundering wheel-to-wheel around the bankings. Collins drew alongside Fangio, pointing to their rapidly disappearing team mates, but the Old Man shook his head and wagged an admonishing finger. He knew better than anyone that this was one race that would not be won in the opening laps.

DENIS JENKINSON: "This was a real end-of-season battle and there were no holds barred. Castellotti and Musso threw caution to the winds and forgot all possibilities of tyre troubles. It was clear they were out to win or blow each other up, and halfway round the fifth lap the trouble started, for both cars threw their left-hand rear tyre tread, and both drivers slithered to a stop in the pits and screamed for new tyres. On the very next lap, de Portago had his left rear tyre tread come off. After a hair-raising 160mph slide down the banking, he motored slowly back to the pits, but could not continue as the suspension had been damaged."

Moss, having started an untypical sixth on the grid, had now worked his way to the front, and took the lead from Fangio. Schell's Vanwall was once again showing its straight-line speed and also briefly held the lead.

DENIS JENKINSON: "Musso and Castellotti were making up time rapidly, going as hard as they knew how. Castellotti was screaming round the very edge of the south banking and about to join the finishing straight when once more his left rear tyre threw its tread and the car spun helplessly off the banking onto the infield. It struck a barrier and ricocheted back onto the track, still spinning wildly, crossed the inner track and came to rest on the grass. A rather furious and somewhat shaken Castellotti got out completely unhurt.

"The race was now becoming fantasy and on lap 11 Collins had the left rear tyre burst and stopped at the pits. All these troubles were caused by the terrific centrifugal loadings due to the high speeds round the bankings, together with the roughness of the concrete."

Then Fangio stopped at the pits with a broken steering arm. In a long stop, it was replaced, but Ferrari sent out Castellotti in the car; clearly it was planning to put Fangio into Musso's car, for Musso, driving the race of his life, had got back up to second place behind Moss. When he came in for fresh tyres, Fangio stood by, ready to get in, but Musso stared straight ahead, stony-faced, and stormed back into the race.

When Collins came in for more tyres, however, he willingly handed his car over to his team leader - even though it was he who was battling for the title with Fangio. It was an astonishingly sporting gesture.

PETER COLLINS: "It's too early for me to become World Champion - I'm too young [he was 25]. I want to go on enjoying life and racing, but if I become Champion now I would have all the obligations that come with it."

While all this high drama was being played out, Moss had built up a comfortable lead - until there were only five laps to go.

STIRLING MOSS: "I felt the Maserati falter and die beneath me. No fuel! I spotted [Luigi] Piotti, the Italian Maserati privateer, coming up behind and gestured frantically for him to give me a push towards the pits. He understood, offered up the nose of his car to the tail of mine, and punted me gently round to the pits."

A few precious gallons were sloshed in and Moss rejoined, but Musso's Ferrari had gone past to lead his home Grand Prix with four laps to go. But there was more left in the script for this incredible race. On the next lap, as Musso came onto the home straight, his steering broke. He slewed sideways across the track and skidded to a halt inches from the pit wall, to be helped from the cockpit, sobbing with disappointment.

So Moss cantered home to score his third World Championship victory, and Fangio and Collins shared the second-place points. Schell had long since retired, so Flockhart's Connaught was third, a lap down. With Fairman finishing fifth, a further two laps in arrears, this was Connaught's best-ever result in a World Championship event.

Fangio was the World Champion for the fourth time. Moss, who had actually led many more laps during the season, was once again the runner-up, three points behind.

Monza 1956 had been a race that epitomised a golden era in Formula 1: a brave, flat-out battle between ambitious team mates; a young driver giving up the World Championship title for his team leader; and nobody protesting when the winner, in trouble, took advantage of a push from another car. Back then, Formula 1 really was a sport.

Opposite: In France, Collins (#14) overtook his Ferrari team mate Castellotti (#12) to win. In Italy (above), with the championship at stake, Collins handed over his Ferrari (#26) to his other team mate Fangio, who finished second to Moss (lower right), the winner for Maserati. But Fangio, thanks to an unselfish Collins, won his fourth driving title.

The 1957 season was even better than 1956. Now there were three marques genuinely capable of victory, for Vanwall had further improved its car and team leader Tony Vandervell had recruited Stirling Moss.

STIRLING MOSS: "I had many reservations, but this was clearly the first green Grand Prix car I had ever driven which showed such winning potential."

Fangio moved back to Maserati, joining Behra and Schell, while Hawthorn returned to Ferrari alongside his close friend Collins, and Musso and Castellotti. Gordini had disappeared, having never had the funds properly to develop its eight-cylinder car. BRM would only contest three rounds, failing to score a single point. Connaught would have a final swansong at Monaco, where young Stuart Lewis-Evans finished a creditable fourth, and then put up the shutters.

13 JANUARY 1957 - ARGENTINE GP (BUENOS AIRES) Fangio scored his habitual victory in the opening round in Argentina. The 250Fs of Behra, Menditeguy and Schell followed the defending champion home. The Ferraris were outpaced, and though de Portago finished fifth, four cars retired with mechanical failures, including that of Castellotti. Sadly, this was the last Grand Prix for both these Ferrari drivers.

ENZO FERRARI: "Eugenio Castellotti was a country gentleman from the agricultural town of Lodi. He had got into motor racing at his own expense, paying for his first sports cars out of his own pocket. It cannot be said that he was a driver of outstanding class or impeccable style; but none can deny that he was a big-hearted and extraordinarily generous young man, with great determination and pluck. Castellotti was killed in a banal accident during a test run (in the latest Ferrari 801) on the Modena track. He was going through a confused and

conflicting time emotionally , and it is probable that his end was brought about by a momentary slowness in his reactions. (Castellotti, aged 27, had asked his fiancée Delia, an actress, to give up her career, which she didn't want to do). He was bitter and absent in his manner. At the second lap, he crashed into one of the concrete barriers."

Alfonso de Portago was killed in a horrendous accident in the 1957 Mille Miglia. Running fourth at the time, and within 75 miles of the finish line, de Portago had a tyre burst while his Ferrari sports car was travelling at 170mph. The car flew off the road, snapped off a telephone pole, careened through a group of spectators, flipped over a bank and somersaulted back onto the road. The death toll - nine spectators (five of them children), de Portago and his co-driver - caused public outrage, and the historic Mille Miglia was never run again as a race.

ENZO FERRARI: "A gentleman driver of professional calibre was the late Marquis de Portago. The Spanish nobleman was a man possessed of a high degree of physical courage; he was to be found on bobsled tracks, steeplechases, motor races or anywhere else where you can risk your neck. On the whole, he was an unusual type, followed wherever he went by his fame as a Don Juan, looked upon everywhere as a sort of 'magnificent brute' on account of his air of personal neglect with his stubbly chin, his hair in need of a cut, his shabby leather jacket and his loose-jointed gait. It cannot be denied that he made quite an effect on the women, for he was tall and good looking."

19 MAY 1957 - MONACO GP (MONTE CARLO) Moss's first Grand Prix in a Vanwall was at Monaco, and he led from the start from Collins, Hawthorn and Fangio.

STIRLING MOSS: "Approaching the chicane on lap four, I hit the brake pedal as normal, and I swear there was a system failure. The team said they could find no problem later, but

I am adamant the front brakes had gone when I hit that pedal. The now over-braked rears instantly locked, and my only course was to go straight on, smashing through a pole-and-sandbag barrier, crushing the Vanwall's nose and breaking my own against its steering wheel. Collins and Hawthorn crashed their Ferraris in the general confusion, and Fangio - of course - dodged through completely unscathed and went on to win."

It was Monaco 1950 all over again. Brooks brought his Vanwall home second, and everyone else was at least two laps behind.

Almost unnoticed was the true sensation of this race: Jack Brabham's Cooper. Cooper had already made the new 1500cc Formula 2 its own with a sized-up version of its highly successful rear-engined Formula 3 car, using a proprietary four-cylinder Coventry Climax engine. For Monaco, Rob Walker funded an enlarged (1960cc) engine, and the fiercely determined Australian Brabham drove the little car brilliantly, profiting from others' problems to rise to third place - until the fuel pump drive sheared on lap 99. The Cooper coasted down the hill to the entrance to the tunnel and ground to a halt. But it took more than that to stop its driver.

JACK BRABHAM: "In those days, I didn't like to be beaten. So I got out of the car and pushed. I pushed the thing through the tunnel, down to the chicane, up to the Tabac corner and along the harbour side to finish sixth - and last. The worst thing wasn't so much the exhaustion as losing third place. And the really scary part was pushing it through the tunnel with all those cars screaming past in the near darkness."

7 JULY 1957 - FRENCH GP (ROUEN) Fangio dominated, finishing almost a minute clear of the Ferraris of Musso, Collins and Hawthorn, and holding the 250F in magnificent, oversteering drifts as he thundered

through the sweeping downhill bends after the start. Neither Moss nor Brooks took part, the former suffering from a severe sinus infection, while the latter had been injured crashing his Aston Martin at Le Mans a couple of weeks earlier. The Vanwalls were handled by Lewis-Evans and Roy Salvadori: neither finished, but Lewis-Evans drove so well that he was promptly hired as the permanent number three driver.

20 JULY 1957 - BRITISH GP (AINTREE) In the British Grand Prix, back at the Liverpool venue, Aintree, Vanwall finally won a clear victory in a World Championship Grand Prix. Moss was discharged from the London Clinic in time for first practice, while Brooks was still not fit enough to do a full Grand Prix

distance, and so would hand over his car to Moss mid-race if necessary. And it was necessary: Moss, starting from pole, was building a strong lead when, 20 laps into the 90-lap race, his engine went off-song. After a quick pitstop failed to cure the problem, Moss stopped again, Brooks was signalled to come in, and Moss rejoined in Brooks's car in ninth place.

MOTOR SPORT: "It was bound to come sooner or later, and it was very fitting that the climax of all Mr Vandervell's efforts should be achieved in the British Grand Prix. Everyone paid tribute to him for getting together the team of drivers, mechanics and technicians that made it possible for a thoroughbred British Grand Prix car to win the British Grand Prix."

Opposite: Fangio (#32 Maserati) won in the streets of Monte Carlo (above), a week after Ferrari's dashing playboy driver, the Marquis Alfonso de Portago (opposite, top right, with cigarette) was killed.

Drove like hell and was 1st around 70th lap. Car super and OK at end. STIRLING MOSS (DIARY ENTRY FOR 1957 BRITISH GP)

This is one of the classic drives of all time, by perhaps the greatest driver of all time. I was witness to it, and in fact I finished fifth in that German Grand Prix. I know the word 'incredible' is much devalued these days but what Fangio did on the 4th of August in 1957 was, and remains, absolutely that. STIRLING MOSS

4 AUGUST 1957 - GERMAN GP (NÜRBURGRING) The Vanwalls may have triumphed on the smooth tarmac of Aintree, but they were nowhere two weeks later on the tortuous Nürburgring. Their hard suspension made them almost undriveable around the 14-mile Eifel circuit, where they were airborne several times a lap, leaping sideways over the bumps. Moss finished a distant fifth, Brooks was ninth having been sick in the cockpit and Lewis-Evans crashed.

But this was to be one of the great Grands Prix of all time - one that would live on not only as Fangio's final victory, but also as his finest.

JUAN MANUEL FANGIO: "From the start the two Ferraris of Hawthorn and Collins took the lead. I let them do so, and in fact I was surprised at the way they kept passing each other instead of working together as a team. Instead of thinking about how to get out in front together, they were playing around for the lead. I kept behind for the first two laps, and that allowed me to study their style of racing. On the third lap, I took advantage of the fact that they had stopped dicing with each other, and challenged and overtook both.

"When I came into the pits I had a 28-second lead. I stopped the car and got out. While I was having a drink, Bertocchi and Ugolini were putting me in the picture about the state of the race. My mechanics were working away, but they weren't doing a good job. I don't know whether they were nervous or what, but the fact is that I lost all the advantage I had gained, plus another 48 seconds. While they were working, I heard the two Ferraris pass, one very close to the other. When the mechanics finally lowered the jack, they had taken much longer than they had first allowed for. There were ten laps left of the 22-lap race. When I set out again I felt quite disappointed, as I was losing a race that could win me the championship.

"I had to get the tyres bedded in, so on the next lap I was 51 seconds behind. After that, the car really began to perform to my liking. The Nürburgring is one of those tracks where you lose touch with things; you think you're going fast and you're not going fast at all. I began to use higher gears. I had learnt from

experience that if you left the car in a higher gear for some of the faster curves, and as long as you went in at the correct angle, you came out with the engine revving at a faster rate on the following straight, which made a difference in terms of time. It wasn't very comfortable, feeling the lack of grip as the car went round, but after all, I had to win. I began to take nearly all the bends in a higher gear than I would have normally used.

"That's how I was driving when I came to the dip below the bridge, where I had passed Gonzalez in 1954 in order to gain the lead in the first lap. This time, I didn't lift my foot off the accelerator. Normally, we took that curve in fifth, trying to skim rather than jump, so as not to jolt the car and allow a margin for error when it landed. This time I took it without slackening at all, with my foot down. I tried to stick well to the inside of the dip, where the car took off, and I touched the ground on the opposite side of the track, uncomfortably close to the fence. There were no guard rails in those days. In my mirror I saw the cloud of dust I'd raised at the edge of the track. It was a risk worth taking. The curve linked two straights, and I had treated it as if it were just one straight. I knew I'd make up some seconds there.

"They told me afterwards that there had been quite a stir in the Ferrari pits. As I seemed at first to be losing rather than gaining after my pit stop, they had told their drivers to reduce their pace. But they looked at their stopwatches after the first lap in which I'd used the higher gears, they couldn't believe their eyes. I had made up ten seconds!"

On the 20th lap, with two laps to go, race leader Hawthorn was two seconds ahead of his Ferrari team mate Collins and three seconds ahead of Fangio's flying Maserati.

JUAN MANUEL FANGIO: "On that lap, I saw a red blur disappearing round a bend, among the trees, and I said to myself: 'I'll certainly catch that Ferrari.' The pits had signalled to me that there were not two cars in front of me, but only one. I had no idea that the other was only a few metres in front of the one I had seen. On the Adenau descent, I saw the two red cars, one behind the other. I knew I was going to catch them.

That day I made such demands that I could not sleep for two days afterwards.

JUAN MANUEL FANGIO

"By the time we passed the pits, I was tailing them. We came into the second to last lap, passed the semi-circle, onto the straight behind the pits, and on the way into the left-hand North curve, I got on the inside of Collins. I had pressed the Maserati a bit too hard, and it was too far over coming out of the curve. Collins gained some yards on me and overtook me again, and placed himself strategically for the next curve.

"I didn't want him to think he had got the better of me, so I stuck to his tail through a series of bends until we reached a short straight that led upwards to a bridge. I got alongside him. At the speed we were going, it seemed that there wouldn't be room for two cars. I had overtaken him before, and Collins gave way, I got in front of him at the little bridge and went down the toboggan run that followed it. And there was Hawthorn's Ferrari, right in front of me, going down into a right-hand bend.

"I accelerated through the various bends that followed. I started tailing him, and was beginning to work out how many chances I had left to overtake him, when the opportunity suddenly presented itself. After that series of curves came a short straight, which ended in a 90-degree turn to the left, followed by an equally sharp turn to the right. On the straight stretch, Hawthorn pulled to the right to get his angle. I saw my chance, and cut in on his inside. Hawthorn must have suddenly seen a red blur to his left, because he quickly pulled over as if startled."

MIKE HAWTHORN: "It was now a straight fight between Fangio and me and I was driving right on the limit as we rushed through the endless tree-lined curves to Hocheichen and on to the Quiddelbacher Hohe, but just as I was going into a slow right-hander Fangio cut sharply inside me and forced me onto the grass and almost into the ditch. If I hadn't moved over I'm sure the old devil would have driven right over me!"

JUAN MANUEL FANGIO: "The Englishman collected his wits again, but not enough to press me hard. I made a point of getting away from him before reaching the straight, because there he might have taken advantage of my slipstream and passed me. My lead was sufficient for him not to be able to stick close to me. I kept it up for the whole of the last lap, and won the race."

MIKE HAWTHORN: "As we started the last lap he had the vital yards in hand which prevented me from getting to grips on the corners and he crossed the finishing line 3.6 seconds ahead of me. This race had been every bit as exciting for the drivers as the spectators, and even though Peter and I had been beaten, we enjoyed every moment of it."

JUAN MANUEL FANGIO: "What a celebration there was! I was carried here, there and everywhere on people's shoulders. [Hawthorn and Collins] were both very good lads. Both appreciated me, and their congratulations were sincere."

When I managed to get to the podium Hawthorn and Collins were ecstatic, as if they had been the winners. They never stopped congratulating me and shaking me by the hand. JUAN MANUEL FANGIO

This Homeric victory clinched Fangio's fifth World Championship. His average speed for the entire three and a half hours, pitstop included, had been faster than the lap record he had set the previous year. As they carried him shoulder-high from his car, the full story of that immense effort was etched into his oily, sweaty face.

JUAN MANUEL FANGIO: "That day I had everything turned on and firing on all cylinders. I was ready to do anything. Whichever way you look at it, it was an extraordinary race. When it was all over, I was

convinced that I would never be able to drive like that again - never. I had reached the limit of my concentration and will to win. Those were the two things that allowed me to take the risks I did that day. I knew I could win, but I knew equally I could lose.

"I was stretching myself to the limit. I was trying out new things, pushing myself further at many blind spots where I had never before had the courage to go to the limit. I was never a daredevil, never a spectacular driver. I would try to win as slowly as possible. Until that race I had never demanded more

of myself or the cars. Whenever I shut my eyes it was as if I were in the race again, making those leaps in the dark on those curves where I had never before had the courage to push things so far. For two days I experienced delayed-action apprehension at what I had done, a feeling that had never come over me after any other race, a feeling that still returns to me this day when I think about that time. I had never driven as I drove then, but I also knew I'd never be able to go so fast again - ever."

And he didn't. It was to be his last victory.

18 AUGUST 1957 - PESCARA GP (PESCARA) Next the World Championship paid its only visit to the magnificent Pescara road circuit in Italy - at almost 16 miles, the longest track ever used for a World Championship round. It covered a fast, narrow triangle of public roads over a section of the Mille Miglia course, running along the Adriatic coast and winding steeply through country villages into the Abruzzi mountains. The British journalist who knew the course from his famous, victorious ride with Moss in the 1955 Mille Miglia could not conceal his enthusiasm.

DENIS JENKINSON: "The entire circuit is composed of normal everyday Italian roads. It runs slap through villages, and contains every known hazard of normal motoring such as kerbstones, bridges, hairpins, rough surfaces and every type of bend and corner imaginable. Out in the country section, the road is bordered by fields, trees, high banks, hedges, sheer drops and concrete walls; in fact the whole thing is pure unadulterated road racing."

And this was exactly the challenge that allowed Moss's genius to excel. By the second lap, he was leading, from Musso, Fangio and Behra, and there he stayed for almost three hours in intense heat on this unbelievably demanding circuit. The atmosphere of 1950s Italian racing was admirably captured by the editor of *Autosport.*

GREGOR GRANT: "The stands were packed to capacity, and several fights broke out among the crowd after noisy arguments over seats. Safety arrangements were not impressive, mainly comprising straw bales behind which stood those unable to find seats. Later an even bigger and better fight broke out in the stands, with a strapping young Italian matron stopping a stiff uppercut, and following it up with a slashing attack on her assailant with the back of a seat. In next to no time fists were flying: then peace reigned again as the *polizia* interfered. Meanwhile, Horace Gould's Maserati had collected the straw bales at the chicane and finished up in a vineyard with its radiator hanging from a tree."

The battle is not between driver and driver, nor even between car and car, but between the combination of car and driver against natural surroundings. DENIS JENKINSON

Musso split his oil tank and burst his engine. Fangio, by now a long way behind Moss, slid on the spilled oil and clouted a wall, coming into the pits to change a buckled wheel. By two-thirds distance, Moss, worried by fluctuating oil pressure under braking, was able to make a precautionary stop for more oil, but he still led Fangio home by more than three minutes in one of the most gruelling Grands Prix of all time.

GREGOR GRANT: "Fangio came in looking extremely tired, but he was out of his car in no time to congratulate his rival. Being a real World Champion, he also went into the Vanwall pit to shake hands with Tony Vandervell, David Yorke, Vandervell's 10-year-old son Colin, and all the Acton mechanics."

8 SEPTEMBER 1957 - ITALIAN GP (MONZA) For the final round at Monza - this time, to everyone's relief, not using the banked section – the three Vanwalls headed qualifying in the order Lewis-Evans, Moss and Brooks, with Fangio relegated to the outside of the four-car front row. It was a dramatic confirmation of Vanwall's achievement. Even 12 months earlier, the sight of three green cars heading all the red ones on the Monza starting grid would have been inconceivable.

The race developed at once into a typical Monza slipstreaming battle, with Moss, Behra, Fangio, Brooks and Lewis-Evans all taking turns at leading. But Lewis-Evans retired with a split header tank, Brooks was delayed with a faulty throttle linkage and Behra's V12 Maserati overheated. Moss pulled away to another comfortable victory over Fangio, with Wolfgang von Trips's Ferrari third.

It had been a fascinating year. Every race had been won by Fangio or Moss, and Moss was the runner-up for the third year in succession. For the first time since 1950, Ferrari had failed to score a victory. Waiting in the wings was the biggest technological change since the start of the championship: the mid-engined revolution.

Opposite: Fangio was second best to Moss on the magnificent Pescara circuit in one of the most gruelling Grands Prix of all time.
Below: Moss and Fangio won all the races in 1957, but for the third year in succession Moss was runner-up to Fangio in the championship.

In its ninth season, the World Championship came of age. There were ten rounds on three continents, and an enthralling battle for the title between two great British drivers which went all the way to the final round in North Africa. In the end, this battle was resolved by a single point. It was also the first year of the International Cup for Constructors: six different marques scored points, the title going to Vanwall.

But it was also a year of tragedy. Motor racing in the 1950s was accepted as dangerous, and fatalities at all levels, from international to club racing, were not infrequent. Strangely, however, the only Formula 1 driver who had died thus far during a World Championship event was Onofre Marimon, during practice for the 1954 German Grand Prix. But, in 1958, three of the small band of works Grand Prix drivers - almost a quarter of the hard-core regulars - died. And, in a cruel irony, the new World Champion was killed in a road accident three months after clinching his title.

There was also a highly significant change in the Formula 1 regulations.

DOUG NYE (author, *Cooper Cars*): "The International Sporting Commission decided to extend the 2.5-litre formula for a further three years, but with some far-reaching changes. Methanol fuels were banned, replaced by 100/130 octane aviation spirit; and [the] race distance was slashed from a minimum 500km, or three hours' duration, to only 300km, or two hours. Fuel consumption on AvGas was far more modest than on methanol, so tankage could have been reduced even without the cut in race distance. Under the new formula, cars could be smaller and lighter: they could be built like Coopers and Lotuses."

The strong Vanwall team of Moss, Brooks and Lewis-Evans continued as before. Ferrari's driver strength was also little changed, but its new car, smaller and lighter, was an expanded version of the V6-engined Formula 2 Dino. BRM continued with the four-cylinder P25, using Behra and Harry Schell as its main drivers. Cash-strapped Maserati effectively disappeared as a works team, although the evergreen 250F continued to be campaigned by several private owners. The little mid-engined Coopers were run both by the works team and by privateer Rob Walker. Lotus made its first appearance, with its slender, front-engined Formula 2 chassis fitted with a larger Coventry-Climax motor for Cliff Allison and Graham Hill.

19 JANUARY 1958 - ARGENTINE GP (BUENOS AIRES) For the first round in Argentina, only Ferrari sent works cars, so a Maranello walkover was expected, even though Fangio and Behra were present in privately entered Maseratis. But shortly before the race, while Rob Walker was on a skiing holiday in Switzerland with his family, he had a telephone call from Moss's manager, Ken Gregory.

ROB WALKER: "He asked if I would allow Stirling to drive my Cooper in Argentina. My first reaction was to wonder how on earth we could get the car there in time, as I couldn't possibly have afforded the cost of air freight. However Ken said the Argentines were so keen to have Stirling in the race that they had offered to pay for the car and two passengers to fly to Buenos Aires, and so I agreed to go ahead. I decided not to go myself, as my son Robbie's first half at Eton started just before the race and I naturally wanted to be with him then. Anyway, it was important to have two mechanics available to prepare the car properly, so Alf Francis and Tim Wall used the two free tickets.

"When they rolled the car out of the aeroplane at Buenos Aires, the Argentines were absolutely furious to discover that they had paid so much money to fly such an insignificant-looking beetle halfway across the world, even if Stirling Moss was going to drive it, and the Ferrari team dismissed it out of hand. However, when Stirling was third fastest in first practice they began to sit up and take notice."

STIRLING MOSS: "I was horsing around with [wife] Katie when she accidentally stuck her finger in my eye and scraped 4mm off my cornea. It hurt like hell. A doctor gave me some drops and pain-killers, but I had to drive for the rest of practice with an eye-patch, which was possibly unique! On the Saturday, I only did three laps because my vision was still blurred. On race morning, the doctor did what he could, but said it would be five days before my eye healed.

"Fuel economy was good and we quietly planned to run non-stop, but we were told our tyres would not last more than 30 to 40 laps, while the race was over 80 laps. The Cooper wheels were retained by four studs instead of centre-lock knock-offs, so any tyre change would have been a fatal handicap.

"I started quite well (from seventh on the grid) and was fourth behind the Maseratis of Fangio and Behra and Hawthorn's Ferrari, and then took third. But on lap four, I struck trouble. The gearbox was rigged with a clutch-interlock mechanism to stop it jumping out of gear. Far from jumping out, I now had the thing jammed in second! I did almost a complete lap like that. I tried to change gear all the way round, running the engine up to 6000rpm, putting out the clutch and trying to move the lever, but still it was jammed solid.

"I was just about to pull into the pits when suddenly it freed. By sheer providence, a stone had flown up and jammed under the interlock mechanism and opened it for me. It was incredibly lucky."

While all this was going on, Moss dropped to fifth, but now, changing gear without using the clutch, he worked back up to second behind Fangio but ahead of Hawthorn, Behra and Musso, all the time trying to drive cleanly and undramatically to preserve his tyres. When Fangio made his mid-race stop, Moss was in the lead.

STIRLING MOSS: "To lull the opposition, Alf made a great display of preparing fresh tyres for me in the pits. But of course to stop would have killed any chance we had of winning. Ever since half-distance, I'd been watching my front tyres closely, and also studying my rears in the mirrors, and occasionally craning round for a proper look when I had the chance. I knew what I was looking for, and with about 14 laps to go I saw it.

"A little white spot began flicking round the left-hand tyre, where the tread had worn through and the white breaker strip between tread and carcass had been exposed. The other tyres were soon going, too. These spots became longer and longer, they became a continuous line and then began to broaden into an undulating band which had now darkened as the casing proper was exposed. Then the bands became indistinct, looking fuzzy as the tortured carcass began the first stage of shredding by growing tiny hairs.

"Alf and Tim signalled to me that Musso was closing fast. I slowed and slowed, balancing my lead against my tyres, in an increasingly desperate state, and tensed for a burst all the time. Now I was actively seeking out the oily, slippery bits of road, and keeping off anything abrasive where adhesion, and wear, might be high. But Musso had begun his charge just too late, and I won, by 2.7 seconds.

"I could scarcely believe it. We had beaten the powerful Ferraris with a little 2-litre special with its clutch inoperative. It was Cooper's first-ever Formula 1 victory, and only the fourth-ever in World Championship Grands Prix by a British car. Vanwall had won three the season before, and each time I'd been the lucky chap behind the wheel."

It was also the first World Championship Grand Prix victory by a mid-engined car. Then as now, things changed quickly in Formula 1: within barely a couple of seasons, the front-engined car would disappear completely.

18 MAY 1958 - MONACO GP (MONTE CARLO) The second round of the season brought another surprise victory for Rob Walker's little Cooper, this time with Maurice Trintignant at the wheel. It was the moustachioed Frenchman's second Monaco win, and the greatest drive of his career, and that night he was the hero.

Left: When Moss finished in front in Argentina with his Cooper's engine in the back, it heralded the end of front-engined cars.

ROB WALKER: "Maurice spoke no English at all, and if he understood any he certainly wasn't letting on. He used to rely upon Harry Schell to teach him phrases suitable for various social occasions, one of which was important enough for Harry to write it down in Maurice's diary so there could be no mistake about it. So when Maurice was introduced to an English-speaking lady, Maurice would thumb through his diary and then, with a dazzling smile, he would recite, 'Ow do you do - weel you slip wiz me tonight?' I believe that this direct approach had almost as many successes as failures."

During the race, Behra was the surprise early leader in the BRM until its brakes failed, and then Moss and Hawthorn began their Vanwall versus Ferrari battle that was to last the entire season. Both led, but both retired, and the little Cooper led home the Ferraris of Musso and Collins. The first two rounds had been won by a private entrant using a modified Formula 2 car, and Cooper now led the new constructors' championship - while Musso, with two second places, led the Drivers' points table.

26 MAY 1958 - DUTCH GP (ZANDVOORT) Moss led from start to finish in the Vanwall while, after Brooks and Lewis-Evans had retired, Schell and Behra produced BRM's best performance to date by finishing second and third.

15 JUNE 1958 - BELGIAN GP (SPA) It was Vanwall versus Ferrari again a week later at Spa, but this time it was Brooks versus Collins, because Moss, leading away from the start, missed the gearshift into fifth and blew his engine. Collins's engine expired, so Brooks cantered home from Hawthorn and Lewis-Evans. Apart from the shared Aintree drive with Moss the previous season, it was Brooks's first World Championship win, and his average speed of 129.9mph around the daunting Spa circuit made it the fastest road race ever run in Europe. Further back, Cliff Allison scored the first World Championship points for Lotus in a distant fourth place.

Now Ferrari had not won a World Championship race for almost two years. Indeed, every event since Fangio's great win in Germany the previous year had been won by a British car.

6 JULY 1958 - FRENCH GP (REIMS) Ferrari was back on top in France – in tragic circumstances. On the circuit that had kick-started his Formula 1 career five years before, Mike Hawthorn put his Ferrari on pole, and led from start to finish.

Fangio, now 47 years old, had not appeared since the Argentina race, but Maserati came up with a new, much lightened *'piccolo'* version of the 250F which the great man entered under his own name. It was not quick enough, and he only qualified on the third row. And his mind was full of retirement.

JUAN MANUEL FANGIO: "Things were changing. For me, the atmosphere was not like before, when it was a sport for enthusiasts. During my first season in Europe, I often had to repair my car with my own hands. Now everything was done by proxy. Since 1956 I had been discussing contracts, advertising, and all that sort of thing - I was surrounded by it. Me, who had never raced thinking about the money I would win. I had known the feeling of not being able to wait for the day of the race, for the contest to begin. Now I was 47, and I had rivals aged 25. They had the road in front of them, and I had run it already. Racing no longer gave me satisfaction: it had become an obligation. And when racing begins to feel like work, well..."

Nevertheless, being Fangio, he drove a brilliant race, charging through from eighth on the grid to wage a furious battle with Moss for second place, and getting ahead of the Vanwall on the 12th lap. A dozen laps later, however, he pulled angrily into the pits, waving a piece of broken metal.

JUAN MANUEL FANGIO: "I stopped at the Maserati pit and threw the clutch pedal at the feet of Guerrino Bertocchi. It had broken in two. They had drilled holes in it to lighten it! I did without the clutch for the rest of the race, changing gear by ear. I finished fourth. I stopped the car in the pits and, by the time I had got out of it, my decision was made."

Fangio never raced again. In his last race, he had had a wheel-to-wheel battle with Moss, his greatest admirer and his successor as the acknowledged best driver of his era. Out of respect, Mike Hawthorn had refused to lap him late in the race after his stop. Behind Hawthorn, Moss was second and Wolfgang von Trips, in another Ferrari, third. Collins ran out of petrol on the final lap but was classified fifth, though there were no post-race celebrations.

ENZO FERRARI: "When eagerness for victory grips a determined driver he is liable to take incalculable risks, especially when his direct rival is animated by the same stubborn will to win. At Reims there were two men - team mates Musso and Hawthorn - at the wheels of two equally powerful cars and each equally anxious to win. I do not think there was any personal animosity between them. They admired one another and were good friends, even though they were of widely differing temperaments.

"Musso had won at Reims the previous year. The circuit was one that suited his style and he was therefore full of confidence. Like Hawthorn, Musso was after the World Championship and he, too, had a good chance of winning it. But on that bend, they probably engaged in a brief, ruthless battle, Hawthorn in front and Musso about twenty yards behind him. I am convinced that, in the excitement of the chase, Musso kept his foot down."

Musso was chasing Hawthorn into the long, very fast right-hand Gueux sweep after the pits when they came up to lap the slower Maseratis of Gerino Gerini and Troy Ruttmann. Both gave Hawthorn room, but then moved across to take their line through the corner. Musso, trying to stay with Hawthorn, tried to go around the outside and his car got away from him, sliding broadside into a field beside the track. It cartwheeled, throwing him out, and he died shortly afterwards.

At this, the halfway point in the season, Moss and Hawthorn were level with 23 points each. Hawthorn had earned the extra point for fastest lap at Monaco and Reims, and Moss had taken it at Zandvoort. It was clear that a Briton was going to end the year as World Champion and, for the first time, the general media in Britain began to give Grand Prix racing widespread coverage. In the constructors' championship, Ferrari was leading Vanwall by 28 points to 22.

Ferrari's winning form continued. Collins came through from sixth on the grid to lead the British Grand Prix from start to finish, in a superbly polished drive. Moss should have been his closest challenger, but his diary for that day records his disappointment.

19 JULY 1958 STIRLING MOSS (diary entry): "Collins's Ferrari was so fast he passed me at full bore. I stayed second, leaving Mike and catching Peter a little, then a rod broke at 25 laps. I've had it for the championship. The Vanwall is just too slow."

Moss's retirement left Hawthorn to take seven points for second place and fastest lap. Roy Salvadori's works Cooper was an impressive fourth - the four-cylinder Climax engine had now been stretched to 2.2-litres - ahead of Lewis-Evans's Vanwall and Schell's BRM.

3 AUGUST 1958 - GERMAN GP (NÜRBURGRING) In Germany, Moss, at his brilliant best, led from the start, building a big lead and setting a new lap record, only to be stopped on the fourth lap with a faulty magneto. This put Collins and Hawthorn in front, but Brooks was driving magnificently. From 30 seconds back, his Vanwall relentlessly wound in the two Ferraris. On lap 10, he got past Hawthorn and began to pressure Collins, and on lap 11 the Vanwall got ahead and Brooks went on to win. But behind him a tragedy unfolded.

The Peter Collins accident happened directly in front of Mike Hawthorn, and it was a dreadful blow to him, for the team mates enjoyed a friendship of a closeness unusual in Formula 1 before or since. In his book about the 1958 season, *Champion Year*, Hawthorn remembered how he had woken Collins in the Nürburgring Sporthotel that morning.

MIKE HAWTHORN: "I went along to their room fairly early. Louise [Collins's American film actress wife] was already awake, but Pete was still asleep, snoring his head off. I looked down at him sleeping there and for some reason I felt happy looking at him. He is one that won't die, I thought. Then he woke and saw me looking at him and swore at me for waking him.

"In the race, after Brooks passed us, Pete was driving as well as he had ever driven. We went into the little dip which is the Pflanzgarten. Pete went into the dip all right, but as he accelerated out of it he seemed to me to be going too fast. He was trying hard to catch Tony and in the heat of the moment he didn't turn into the corner early enough. When he did turn, it was obvious he was too wide: only a yard, maybe two yards, out of line, but it was enough.

"His back wheel hit the bank and the car lifted. God, I thought, the silly fool, we're both going to be involved in this. I was just thinking up some choice words to say to him when we climbed out of two bent Ferraris when, without the slightest warning, fantastically quickly, his car just whipped straight over. It came as a completely paralysing shock. There was a blur of blue as Peter was thrown out, and I put the brakes on hard and almost stopped as I looked round. I saw the car bounce upside down in a great cloud of dust before it came to rest."

Hawthorn raced on but, before completing another lap, his transmission failed and he stopped out on the circuit. He asked a marshal to telephone the pits for a report on Collins's condition, and was told, "A bit bruised, but all right." After the race had finished, while the crowd cheered for Brooks's victory, Hawthorn got a lift back to the pits, and stopped at the scene of the accident. He found Collins's damaged crash helmet, a shoe and a glove. Louise had already been taken by Ferrari

Above: For Fangio, here being overtaken by Moss's Vanwall, the French Grand Prix was his last. Peter Collins (inset) won in Britain, then was killed in Germany.
Opposite: Hawthorn's championship year was blighted by the deaths of his Ferrari team mates Musso and Collins, who was Hawthorn's best friend.

I decided not to lap the Old Man, but instead to watch him. He had all his old skill, and his placing of the car for a corner was, as it always had been, an immaculate line.

MIKE HAWTHORN

team manager Tavoni by road to the hospital in Bonn, where Collins had been received with severe head injuries. Mike drove there, too, with Harry Schell and, when he got there, they told him his friend was dead.

ENZO FERRARI: "I had a very high opinion of Peter Collins, both as driver and as man. My last memory of him is when I shook his hand before he left for the Nürburgring; looking at him, I was suddenly seized by a strange feeling of infinite sadness. As I went back into my office, I could not help wondering whether it was some sort of presentiment."

Back in England, a shattered Hawthorn considered giving up motor racing straight away. But the show had to go on. With three races to go, he led Moss by 30 points to 24, and in three weeks the circus was due in Portugal for the eighth round, on the street circuit of Oporto.

25 AUGUST 1958 - PORTUGUESE GP (OPORTO) Everything seemed to go according to plan for Moss. He qualified on pole position and led virtually from start to finish, apart from a few laps in the early stages when Hawthorn's Ferrari got in front of him. He also set a new lap record on the way - a vital part of his afternoon's work, because it would earn the critical extra point. Hawthorn, whose Ferrari's brakes were fading badly, gradually fell back from the Vanwall and, at two-thirds distance, he came into the pits to have them adjusted, rejoining in third place. He then drove absolutely on the limit, at least until his brakes wilted again, and retook second place - and in so doing he lowered Moss's new lap record by a further 0.21sec. Urgently, Vanwall team manager David Yorke hung out a signal informing Moss of the lap record: 'HAW-REC'. But Moss misread the signal - he thought it said 'HAW-REG', meaning Hawthorn was maintaining a regular pace in second place and was no threat. He could almost certainly have set a faster lap but, with a huge lead, and anxious to conserve the Vanwall's reliability, he did not.

STIRLING MOSS: "This misunderstanding ultimately cost me the World Championship. It really irritated me: I'm sure I could have taken the record back if only I'd realised."

There was more drama to come. When Moss took the chequered flag, with Lewis-Evans's Vanwall behind him a lapped third, Hawthorn was just ahead of him, with his last lap still to do. The Ferrari was now almost brakeless again - and Hawthorn spun and stalled. As the only man left on the same lap as the leader, his second place was secure - but only if he could restart and get to the flag.

STIRLING MOSS: "On my slowing-down lap, I came across his stalled car and saw him struggling to push-start it in the direction of the race, uphill. I slowed beside him

and bawled, 'Push it downhill – you'll never start the bloody thing that way!' Which he did, ensuring his second place."

But a marshal reported to the organisers that he had seen Hawthorn driving his car against the direction of the race. If this were proven, he would be disqualified. That evening, after the prizegiving, Mike was asked to attend an official inquiry.

MIKE HAWTHORN: "I was ushered into a room in which the officials were seated round a large table. I felt like a schoolboy up before the headmaster after being found smoking behind the fives courts, or caught out of bounds with the maths master's daughter, which is even more serious, but far more fun."

Hawthorn was told to wait outside, and the officials then called in Moss.

STIRLING MOSS: "I spoke up for Mike because it looked as though they might disqualify him, and I didn't want to win the championship by default. I'd seen him stall the car and I'd told him to go down the hill and restart. I explained that he wasn't on the circuit: he was on the escape road, so there was no question of him going against the traffic.

"It cost me the championship, but so what? It depends on which way you want to win it. I liked Mike, so I volunteered the information."

CHRIS NIXON (Hawthorn's biographer): "With this one remarkable act of sportsmanship Moss kissed the World Championship goodbye. One can only wonder if Mike would have done such a gentlemanly thing for the driver that he thought of as the abominable arch-professional, had the situation been reversed."

7 SEPTEMBER 1958 - ITALIAN GP (MONZA) The championship was still open. Once again Moss qualified on pole, and there was a great Monza slipstreaming battle for the lead involving Moss, Hawthorn and his American team mate Phil Hill, who was having his first proper Formula 1 works drive. But, after only 17 laps, the Vanwall's gearbox tightened up and then destroyed itself. Now, if Hawthorn could win the race, he would be crowned champion. Brooks's Vanwall had already been into the pits to investigate an oil leak, dropping to ninth place. Yet, in a typically brilliant drive, Brooks almost unobtrusively worked back up to the leading group and, as Hawthorn's clutch started to slip in the closing stages, he went through to win. Hill was told to slow and keep station behind Hawthorn. So the title fight lived on to the final round, to be held a whole six weeks away on the high-speed road circuit outside Morocco for the first (and only) World Championship round in North Africa.

19 OCTOBER 1958 - MOROCCAN GP (CASABLANCA) Hawthorn was now on 40 points, Moss 32. A win and a fastest lap for the Vanwall driver would bring his

total to 41: but the rule which only allowed each driver to count his best six scores meant that Hawthorn could only improve his total by finishing second or higher. In Casablanca tension was running high again.

JEAN HOWARTH (Hawthorn's future fiancée, who later married Innes Ireland): "Mike was still very nervous about the race, but once we got there he calmed down a lot, as the waiting was almost over. He blew his top when he first got a look at the Ferraris, though. We went to the garage and found them covered with dust sheets and, when he pulled the sheet off his, it had the number 2 on it. That's when he really hit the roof, for both Peter and Musso had been killed racing that number. Mike just wouldn't go near the car again until it had been changed. Olivier Gendebien agreed to swap, so Mike took his number 6. He felt a bit better after that and set fastest time in practice, but the battle for the championship had really got to him."

Vanwall's strategy was for Brooks and Lewis-Evans to gang up on Hawthorn, keeping him out of second place while Moss went for victory and that crucial fastest lap. Ferrari, meanwhile, opted to sacrifice Hill as a 'hare' to put pressure on Moss. In the race, in fact, the young American held second place, but could not stay with the Vanwall. Brooks demoted Hawthorn from third. But then it started to go wrong for the Vanwall team: Brooks's engine seized on a fast part of the course and he spun wildly on his own oil, fortunately coming to rest without further damage.

Then, late in the race, a similar fate befell another Vanwall. As Lewis-Evans went through a high-speed sweep on the far side of the circuit the engine blew and the rear wheels locked. The stricken car went into a series of slides before hitting a tree and bursting into flames. The injured Lewis-Evans managed to get himself out of the wreck, enveloped in flames, and was helicoptered to a nearby hospital.

Moss now had a huge lead and, with Hawthorn in a distant third place, the Ferrari pit signalled to Hill to slow down and let Hawthorn by. Thus Moss cantered home 84 seconds ahead of Hawthorn to score a full nine points for victory and fastest lap - but Hawthorn had won the World Championship by one point.

Moss was the first to congratulate him.

STIRLING MOSS: "My congratulations were genuine, but I could not hide my deep depression because of poor Stuart's crash as well as my own disappointment. It really did hurt. But within days the knot in my stomach relaxed, and I realised it didn't really matter - not that much. I became far more philosophical and, perhaps, more mature."

Moss had won five of the 10 rounds, and led three of the others. Hawthorn had only won one race, but his five second places and the Ferrari's reliability had told in the end. Significantly, in the next New Year's Honours, Moss was awarded the OBE, but there was no recognition of Hawthorn - nor of Tony Vandervell, whose magnificent determination had put together the best Formula 1 team of its era. With six wins from nine starts, Vanwall had dominated the first-ever Constructors championship.

When the Formula 1 circus flew back to London from Morocco, lying in the back of the chartered Viscount, dreadfully burned, was 28-year-old Stuart Lewis-Evans. As the aircraft landed at London Airport, an ambulance was waiting to take him to the famous Burns Unit at East Grinstead Hospital - but he died the following Saturday. It was the first time in almost a decade of his involvement in motor racing that any of Tony Vandervell's drivers had been more than slightly hurt. It took its toll on Vandervell. In January 1959, the owner of the first champion Formula 1 team announced his retirement.

Five weeks before, Hawthorn had announced his retirement. Enzo Ferrari had told him to name his price for the 1959 season, but Hawthorn was not interested - he said he could not explain all the reasons, even to himself (though the death of Peter Collins was doubtless a factor), but wanted to go out at the top.

When Stirling Moss won in Morocco (opposite) he was on course to win the championship. Instead, his remarkable sportsmanship enabled Mike Hawthorn (above, with Moss) to take the driving title.

Mike Hawthorn, a fair lad with a rather absent manner, was disconcerting on account of his ability and his unpredictableness. Capable of facing up to any situation and getting out of a tight corner with a cold and calculated courage and an exceptional speed of reflexes, he was nevertheless liable suddenly to go to pieces. All in all, though, he was a driver who on his good days had no reason to fear any rival. ENZO FERRARI

Having decided not to defend his title in the 1959 season, Mike Hawthorn began to lay plans for expanding his business interests, and a fortnight later announced his engagement to Jean Howarth. But in January Hawthorn lost his life when his Jaguar road car was involved in a notorious car accident on the Guildford bypass in Surrey. He was 29 years old.

The new season got off to a late start. Four of the previous year's Formula 1 'name' drivers were dead. Vanwall was gone. The Belgian Grand Prix was cancelled due to the organisers' financial problems, and the Argentine and Moroccan Grands Prix had disappeared from the calendar. However, there was a new event in the USA, to be run at the end of the season on an unsuitably bleak and bumpy track on the Sebring airfield in Florida.

Tony Brooks had moved to Ferrari, joining Phil Hill, Jean Behra, Cliff Allison and Dan Gurney. BRM continued with Schell, Jo Bonnier and Ron Flockhart. Aston Martin finally appeared with the long-awaited single-seater version of its successful DBR1 sports-racer, a big, heavy front-engined car which was outdated before it turned a wheel, and co-opted Roy Salvadori and Carroll Shelby from its sportscar team.

But Cooper looked in excellent shape. There was now a full 2.5-litre version of the four-cylinder Coventry-Climax engine, producing a torquey 240bhp alongside the 280bhp of the heavier, bulkier Ferraris and BRMs. There was to be a three-car team for Jack Brabham, Masten Gregory and young Bruce McLaren, while Stirling Moss decided to throw in his lot with private entrant Rob Walker for the full season. Because of worries about how the works Cooper's Citroën-based gearbox would deal with the extra power, Walker's privately entered car was equipped with a Colotti gearbox - which turned out to be a big mistake.

10 MAY 1959 - MONACO GP (MONTE CARLO) After disposing of Behra's rapid Ferrari, Moss had the Monaco Grand Prix in his pocket, holding a lead of almost a minute after 81 laps, when the Walker Cooper's gearbox failed. This left the win to Brabham's works Cooper. Brooks, lying second 20 seconds down, was in no state to challenge: overcome by fumes, he had vomited in the Ferrari's cockpit. Everyone else was lapped at least twice.

At various times during his career, Moss had to endure criticism from uninformed observers to the effect that he was a car-breaker - that he often failed to finish because his driving style was more punishing on the car's mechanical components.

GREGOR GRANT (*Autosport*): "In truth, on a circuit such as Monaco, Moss is now in a class by himself. At no

time did he appear to be caning his motor car, and his passage around the circuit was as smooth and delightful to watch as anything ever witnessed. It was an exhibition of virtuosity in Grand Prix racing such as few drivers can ever display."

31 MAY 1959 - DUTCH GP (ZANDVOORT) Moss, trying to conserve his suspect transmission, made a cautious start, but worked his way to the front with 15 laps to go. Two laps later, the gearbox broke again.

This misfortune cleared the way for a truly historic victory: BRM, in its tenth season, finally won a Grand Prix. Jo Bonnier was on fighting form all weekend, taking pole position from Brabham and Moss, and disputing the lead with Brabham before drawing away. Once Moss had retired, the bearded Swede romped home to win by 14 seconds from Brabham, with Gregory's Cooper third.

Notwithstanding the fact that Cooper now had a clear lead in the Constructors championship, the maiden victory by BRM caused much joyful comment.

GREGOR GRANT: "Last Sunday's great victory was just about the best tonic that motor racing could have had. For ten long years, the men of Bourne have tried vainly to win a *grande épreuve*, only to have their hopes dashed time and time again. The venture has had more criticism than anything else in motor racing, but all connected with BRM cannot help but feel that the empty years have come to an end, and that their cars will contribute to the prestige of British automobile engineering, every bit as much as have Vanwall and Cooper-Climax."

This rejoicing was premature. It would be three long years before BRM would score its second Grand Prix win - once again at Zandvoort.

5 JULY 1959 - FRENCH GP (REIMS) At Reims, the weather was tremendously hot, and melting tar meant that the circuit was breaking up. Brooks was masterly all weekend, earning pole position, leading from start to finish and giving Ferrari its first win for almost a year. Gregory's Cooper stormed through from seventh on the grid to second place by the third lap but, within five more laps, he was completely exhausted by the heat and came in to retire, his face cut and bleeding from the flying stones. Trintignant in the Walker Cooper got up to second place, spun at the hairpin on melted tar and loose gravel, push-started his car on his own and then came into the pits completely exhausted, to be doused with cold water. Others were retiring with radiators punctured by stones, and the noses of the cars and the drivers' helmets were scarred and dented.

DENIS JENKINSON: "Of all the drivers, Brooks was looking the most comfortable, avoiding the flying stones by awaiting his opportunity to lap slower cars, whereas the others, who were still racing against each other, were all getting badly cut about the face. Flockhart had his goggles broken and took them off, only to collect another stone in the eye, and he raced on in a bloody state, while McLaren was also badly cut. On the straights, Brooks tried to get fresh air by leaning his head over the side of the cockpit. Phil Hill was virtually standing up in the cockpit, and Brabham had his elbows over the cockpit sides trying to deflect air on himself. The air temperature outside was so hot that these antics made little difference, the only advantage being that it was different hot air from that in the cockpit.

"With 14 laps to go, Moss began to speed up, so that, as Hill and Brabham got played-out, Moss closed on them. [Here, and in the British Grand Prix, Moss was

Opposite and top right (in the 1958 Moroccan Grand Prix): Mike Hawthorn's bittersweet championship year was his last. Five weeks after announcing his retirement he was killed.

77

driving a British Racing Partnership BRM while the Rob Walker Cooper had its gearbox problems sorted out.) The American Hill was in a terrible state, his judgement for braking having gone completely, and he overshot, spun and went sideways on the hairpins nearly every lap, driving in a wild daze. Brabham was beyond going any faster, so that when Moss took third place from him he put up no fight at all. On lap 40 Moss set a new lap record and was gaining rapidly on Hill, who was in no state to receive such a challenge.

"Then at the end of lap 43 Moss failed to appear. Since before half-distance the clutch had stopped working on his BRM, the drive being solid, and now he had overdone things on Thillois hairpin and was going sideways at about 60mph in the middle of the road. Without the clutch working, he could do nothing to stop the engine stalling as he revolved, and he came to rest in a horrid silence. He made several struggling attempts in the heat to push-start the car in gear, but it was quite impossible. So, rather than sit by the roadside in the heat, he suffered disqualification by enlisting outside help, and drove quietly back to the pits, very hot and very clapped-out, the car quite undamaged.

"Just before this happened, the straw bales on the corner had ignited themselves and, while the Moss episode was in progress, pale blue smoke could be seen rising, causing the more imaginative newspaper journalists to rush to telephones and pour out the gory details of how Stirling Moss had escaped death. The bottom of Fleet Street was revealed by the man from the *Daily Mirror*, who described the Moss spin as a 'miracle escape' and went on to give details of a mythical crash into a barrier at more than 100mph."

So all Moss had to show for his efforts, as was the case in Holland, was the single point for fastest lap. Brooks and Hill made it 1-2 for Ferrari, and Brabham increased his World Championship points lead with third place.

JACK BRABHAM: "I was nearly collapsing at the wheel, so I broke the windscreen away to try to get some air. Every car I got near showered me with bricks and stones. I was coasting into the corners rather than braking, because my feet were so badly burned I could hardly put any pressure on the pedals. At the end I had to be lifted out of the car."

Meanwhile, 21-year-old Bruce McLaren, in only his second Grand Prix in a Formula 1 car, fought through to fifth at the finish.

BRUCE McLAREN: "At the finish I took off my helmet and cried my eyes out. I don't know why, but I wept uncontrollably for several minutes."

This extraordinary Grand Prix, which had lasted over two hours in that baking heat, was almost immediately followed by an hour-long Formula 2 race. Having paused only to clean up their bleeding faces and soak themselves with cold water, half the Formula 1 drivers took part, including Brabham and McLaren. The irrepressible Moss won it in Rob Walker's Cooper-Borgward, and set the fastest lap at an average of over 121mph.

18 JULY 1959 - BRITISH GP (AINTREE) There would be no points for Ferrari: strikes in Italy prevented the red cars from making the trip. It was here that Brabham really started looking like this year's World Champion. He put his works Cooper on pole and led from start to finish, showing echoes of his Australian speedway roots as he powered through Aintree's tighter corners in oversteering slides.

His only pressure came from Moss, in the pale green BRM once again. Thanks to a slipping clutch, Stirling had only qualified on the third row, but he stalked the Cooper until needing a stop soon after half-distance for fresh rear tyres.

Then, with nine laps to go, Moss started to suffer a fuel starvation, so he brought the BRM in for a quick top-up. McLaren went through to second place, and the closing laps were enlivened by a wheel-to-wheel battle between the maestro and the talented novice as Moss fought to get his second place back.

Above: Brooks (#24 Ferrari) won at Reims with a masterly drive in boiling heat.
Opposite, top: Burgess (#18 Cooper) stopped for a drink. Moss (#2 BRM, opposite, below) pushed his stalled car and collapsed.

I took a frightful battering from flying stones. The mixture of sweat and blood in my goggles was like pink champagne.

BRUCE MCLAREN

DENIS JENKINSON: "It took Moss just one lap to get on the tail of McLaren, and the next lap he was by. But getting away from the young New Zealander was another story. On lap 71, McLaren drew level with Moss as they went past the pits, but there was insufficient length of straight for him to get in front, and on the next lap they were only a foot apart and lapped Trintignant on the right-hand side."

BRUCE McLAREN: "I wondered if Stirling was getting annoyed. I glanced across: to my surprise Stirling was thoroughly enjoying himself and gave me an encouraging thumbs-up sign!"

Jenkinson's downbeat description of the scene at the finishing line underlines how relaxed the rules were then about track access.

DENIS JENKINSON: "It seemed impossible that McLaren could stay with Moss as they weaved past slower cars, but stay he did and they took the last corner still with only a foot or two between them. As they accelerated towards the line, which was now crowded with photographers and officials, leaving space for only one car, Moss drove straight at the people on the right of the road, making them jump out of the way, to leave McLaren room to try to take him on the left. This was indeed a very sporting manoeuvre and, though the New Zealand driver tried to draw up alongside, second place went to Moss and the BRM."

It was the first Grand Prix that Moss had finished that season, and he again drove the fastest lap - but this time he had to share his new lap record, and the extra point, with the impressive McLaren.

2 AUGUST 1959 - GERMAN GP (AVUS) This year, the German Grand Prix forsook the Nürburgring to visit the unsuitable and dangerous, banked Avus track in East Germany, on the edge of Berlin. This was as different from the tortuous 'Ring as it was possible to imagine.

The Avus offered a flat-out run down one carriageway of a dead-straight *autobahn*, a hairpin at the end, a flat-out run back on the other carriageway, and then an immense steep banked turn, paved with bricks, sweeping round to connect with the *autobahn* once more. The average lap speed was over 150mph, albeit with the g-forces on the banking making the cars bottom on their suspensions. Tyre life was an obvious concern, so the organisers decided to split the race into two one-hour 'heats'.

At Reims, Jean Behra had been fired from the Ferrari team following an angry scuffle in the pits with team manager Romolo Tavoni, after his engine had blown. On the Saturday afternoon at the Avus, Behra entered his own Porsche in a supporting sports car race. Rain had made the banking treacherously slippery, and he lost control of the car, which spun over the lip of the banking and hit a concrete block-house. The impact almost cut the Porsche in two. Behra was flung out against a flag mast and killed instantly.

Consequently, the German Grand Prix was run in an atmosphere of gloom and foreboding. As expected on this high-speed track, the Ferraris dominated. Brooks won both heats and, on aggregate results, Gurney was second and Hill third. Moss was back in Rob Walker's Cooper after much development work on its Colotti gearbox, but it lasted precisely two laps before breaking again. The works Coopers of Brabham, Gregory and McLaren failed too, although not before Gregory had bravely run wheel-to-wheel with the Ferraris on the banking.

The BRP BRM, being driven by Hans Herrmann, came to the end of its career when its brakes failed at the hairpin. The car cartwheeled end-over-end in an immense and much photographed accident. Herrmann was thrown out but, miraculously, he suffered only abrasions from being catapulted down the track.

23 AUGUST 1959 - PORTUGUESE GP (MONSANTO) Finally, Moss's luck turned. In the next two Grands Prix, in Portugal and Italy, his transmission held together, and the Walker Cooper scored handsome victories. The Portuguese round, on the Monsanto Park circuit just outside Lisbon, was a perfect demonstration of Moss's superiority: he headed every practice session and ended up on pole more than two seconds faster than everyone else. He led from start to finish and lapped the entire field.

STIRLING MOSS: "I pulled away without over-straining my car, and when I saw that Jack had crashed while chasing me I slowed right down by the pits to shout to John Cooper that he had gone off but seemed OK. I eased down and down, treating my car - and especially its gearbox - like Dresden china, and it held together. This was my first Grand Prix win of the season, and I was so pumped-up with delight I couldn't sleep a wink that night."

Brabham's accident was potentially very serious. He came up to lap local driver Mario de Cabral entering a 130mph right-hander when the Portuguese moved across on him. Brabham was forced off the track and his car took off over the straw bales, felled a telegraph pole and rolled back onto the track, throwing Brabham out into the middle of the tarmac. Brabham sat up and found himself looking straight into the radiator of Masten Gregory's car, which just missed him and went on to take second place from Gurney's Ferrari. Brabham was taken to hospital with cuts and bruises.

13 SEPTEMBER 1959 - ITALIAN GP (MONZA) Moss had pole again but, rather than rushing away into the lead on this punishing circuit, he drove a very canny race, letting the Ferraris set the pace. Brooks burned out his clutch at the start, but Hill took an early lead, with Moss keeping in touch just ahead of Gurney, and Brabham fourth. Just before half-distance, the Ferraris came in for fresh tyres: the Walker Cooper had been fitted with knock-off rear wheels to allow rapid rear tyre changes, and Ferrari assumed Moss would also stop for rubber. And, just as in Buenos Aires the previous year, Alf Francis stood in the pit-lane holding up a wheel as Moss went past. Francis could not believe that Ferrari would fall for the same trick again - but they did.

DENIS JENKINSON: "Finally it became obvious that Moss had no intention of stopping for tyres and had led the Ferrari team into a trap. It was a perfect case of Moss suiting his strategy and his decisions to the pattern of the race. He led the field home at a new record speed, still with ample tread on his tyres — whereas Brabham in third place had worn his tyres dangerously thin."

Ferrari, with five cars in its home race, had to be content with Hill's second place and Gurney, Allison and Gendebien following Brabham home, fourth, fifth and sixth.

With only one round to go, three drivers had a chance of taking the title. Brabham, Brooks and Moss had each won two races, and each had one second place to his name: once again Moss had to

Main picture: Lap speeds averaged over 150mph on the treacherous track at Avus. Jean Behra (inset) got into a fist fight in practice, then was killed when his car flew over the banking. Opposite: Stirling Moss practises his art at the 1959 Portuguese Grand Prix.

win and set fastest lap at Sebring to be sure of the title. But the US Grand Prix was not scheduled to take place for another three months! They all had to possess themselves in patience until a couple of weeks before Christmas.

12 DECEMBER 1959 - US GP (SEBRING) Almost inevitably, Moss took pole position in Florida, three full seconds quicker than his main rival for the title, Brabham. And he set off in quest of his goal, pulling away in the lead - until, after only six laps, the Colotti gearbox gremlins reappeared, and he coasted to a stop. Meanwhile, Brooks was rammed on the first lap by team mate von Trips and decided to stop to have the damage checked. The Coopers of Brabham and McLaren circulated at the head of the field, and the result of the championship looked a foregone conclusion. But, on the last lap, Brabham's car spluttered and died - out of fuel!

McLaren went on to win - at 22 years, 3 months and 12 days, the youngest-ever Grand Prix winner - with Trintignant's Walker Cooper second and nearly caught on the line by Brooks's Ferrari. Brabham pushed his car the last quarter-mile to cross the line fourth, and collapsed.

JACK BRABHAM: "They helped me into an official's caravan. I flopped out for a quarter of an hour or so to get my breath back. Then it suddenly dawned on me. I'd won the World Championship. I just couldn't believe it."

The first decade of the Formula 1 World Championship ended with an Australian winning the title with a British car. Thanks to the efforts of both the works and Walker teams, Cooper conclusively beat Ferrari to the constructors' championship.

It was a very different picture from that first race at Silverstone in 1950. Then the Italian Alfa Romeos had been in a class of their own, and the British had had to do their best with uncompetitive pre-war equipment. But now, British cars and teams would go on to dominate most of the next 40 seasons.

It is the ability to go fast and conserve his tyres, and to plan the strategy of his actions while he is racing, that makes Moss the great artist that he is. DENIS JENKINSON

The Sixties

In each season, there was a driver so dominant that his rivals openly acknowledged him as the best. When the decade started, it was Stirling Moss, until a mysterious crash ended his career. Jim Clark assumed the mantle, until his fatal accident in 1968, when Jackie Stewart took over. Money was a reliable yardstick: first Moss, then Clark, then Stewart were the best paid. The others had to accept that earnings would always be linked with success on the track. A sharp improvement in the earning power of the Grand Prix driver was one of many fundamental changes - the front-engined racing car disappeared; television coverage arrived, and with it sponsorship. But the decade was also deadly, and its tragedies sparked Stewart's crusade for improved safety measures.

Jack Brabham and Cooper won the 1960 titles, as they had the previous year. Brabham was the perfect driver for the father-and-son team of John and Charles Cooper. A rugged Australian who brought seat-of-the-pants engineering to Formula 1, Brabham was backed up by his like-minded team mate, Bruce McLaren. McLaren won the first Grand Prix of the 1960s - and one of his McLaren cars would win the final Grand Prix of the decade.

7 FEBRUARY 1960 - ARGENTINE GP (BUENOS AIRES) Nothing was easy in those days. For the first race of the season, the Cooper and Lotus drivers were forced to sit out practice because the Blue Star Line's *Scottish Star* had been delayed by engine trouble, and was being towed into Buenos Aires harbour. The Argentine Post Office was on strike and all cables and letters of information on the race had gone astray. The national airline was also on strike.

BRUCE McLAREN: "I flew for two days from New Zealand in a Super Constellation, [and] arrived in New York to find my Comet flight south cancelled - and I had just missed a Pan-American Boeing. It took me nearly half a day to persuade the airline to hand over my ticket, which they were holding for me, and I finished up pounding down to Buenos Aires in a DC3. This took a further 36 hours and I arrived in the Argentine capital two days late and a physical wreck."

Throughout the season, Andrew Ferguson, the team coordinator, kept a detailed diary of Cooper's adventures...

ANDREW FERGUSON: "In Buenos Aires, our drivers sat around for the first three practice sessions. Stirling was fastest but he was kind enough to allow Jack a practice run in his Rob Walker Cooper on the understanding, of course, that there would not be any fireworks. Bruce contented himself with a two-hour walk round the circuit, only to find later that he had been walking round the motorcycle circuit. Our drivers were given half an hour's practice prior to darkness, their only worry being the density of the crowds on the edge of the road, thereby being a second or so slower per lap for fear of annihilating some of the paying customers. Just before the cars lined up on the grid, pre-race tension was relieved by a tremendous fight between a dozen or so spectators in the grandstand and Jack [Brabham] was able to make a fine cine-film of the fracas. At the finish of the race, Bruce was rather unnerved by the hospitality of the crowds, and was under the impression that they intended to kill him..."

BRUCE McLAREN: "As I rolled the car into the pits I thought I had found a riot. There were spectators fighting, police struggling with them, officials pushing, cameras shoved in my face, people screaming. I was dragged into the grandstand. I tried to walk but my feet weren't touching the ground - I was being propelled by three burly, sweating policemen on each arm. Down in South America, they don't just show enthusiasm - they go mad!"

13 MAY 1960 A crash during practice for the non-championship Silverstone International Trophy took the life of the popular Harry Schell. The experienced, Paris-born American, who had been racing in Formula 1 since 1950, lost his Yeoman Credit team Cooper on a wet track at Abbey Curve, hit a retaining wall and was hurled out of the cockpit.

Above: Sweeping through the Ardennes forest, Belgium's majestic Spa circuit proved to be as lethal as it was picturesque. Jack Brabham's Cooper won on this disastrous weekend.
Opposite: The Team Lotus drivers of Colin Chapman (left) included (to the right) Innes Ireland, Jim Clark and Alan Stacey. Stacey crashed fatally at Spa when hit in the face by a bird.

ROY SALVADORI: "Harry was a number one character in motor racing. He spoke many languages, he was tall and good-looking, he had tremendous wit and charm. His driving was inconsistent but on occasion he would hit tremendous form, such as at Reims in 1956. His death was a tragic loss for everyone."

29 MAY 1960 - MONACO GP (MONTE CARLO) STIRLING MOSS (the first Grand Prix winner in a Lotus): "Racing simply became more scientific. Lotus made the racing car an artistic piece of work, but using science. John Cooper was more of a fundamentalist, a terribly talented blacksmith who had done as much as Lotus, maybe more, in a different way."

6 JUNE 1960 - DUTCH GP (ZANDVOORT) JACK BRABHAM: "I made the best start. Moss was following me closely at first, and round the esses just prior to the finishing straight, I touched one of the kerbstones at the side of the track and hooked it out, right into Moss's path. It flattened his front tyre for him and might easily have knocked his wheel off - he seemed to think I'd done it on purpose."

Dan Gurney crashed after a brake hose burst going into the Tarzan corner and his flying BRM killed a spectator. Gurney was fortunate to escape with only a broken arm...

DAN GURNEY: "It was terribly unfortunate that the boy was killed. But it was as though I had nothing to do with it. I didn't have a choice in my own mind. He was on the other side of a good-size hill, in a lane for spectators that had barbed wire on both sides of it, so he was in the right place. But that was maybe 100 yards from the track. I arrived there in the air, having been pretty doggone high, and there was no way to see it. I went through an advertising sign, everything. It was sobering to think that, hey, this is part of the business, also."

19 JUNE 1960 - BELGIAN GP (SPA) A black weekend began with a huge accident to Stirling Moss, who broke his nose, three vertebrae, several ribs and both legs.

BRUCE McLAREN: "Moss had been recording very fast times on the second day of practice at Spa and when I saw him leaving the pits as I swooped down from La Source hairpin, I jumped at the opportunity to follow him and learn more about the circuit. I sat in behind as he accelerated up the hill, up through the woods to the long left-hander before the plunge down to Burnenville corner. He left me going down the hill and opened a gap of a hundred yards or so. We swung into the long right-hand curve made blind by farmhouses immediately beside the road. I had a strange feeling something was wrong and backed off a fraction."

STIRLING MOSS: "I was holding the car in a sweeping right-hand bend at 140mph when the left rear wheel snapped off. I did the only thing possible under the circumstances. With the wheel gone the rear of the car slid out left, I threw the steering hard left to correct, and stood on the brakes. I reckon I took 50mph off the top. Yes, I must have done at least that. I remember looking back and seeing that the wheel wasn't there anymore. The car spun I think twice and hit the embankment backwards. I think my neck snapped back and [that] knocked me out."

BRUCE McLAREN: "I was shattered to see Moss's Lotus spinning wildly on the road in front of me. It hit the left side of the road, rocketed across to the right and bounced

wildly in the air. There was so much dust that I lost sight of the car. I had the brakes on hard and slid to a stop as the Lotus came to rest. At first I thought Stirling was still in the cockpit and, well aware of the ghastly risk of fire, raced back to the wrecked car. To my amazement it was empty!"

STIRLING MOSS: "I don't remember getting thrown out of the car or flying through the air. The next thing I remember is being on my hands and knees in the dirt. I think I landed that way, but am not sure. I wasn't scared in the car because I was too busy. But I was scared now on my hands and knees. I thought I was going to die. I couldn't breathe, you see. I couldn't see either, and that worried me, but mostly I couldn't breathe."

BRUCE McLAREN: "Stirling was asking for artificial respiration, but with the thought of possible internal injuries, I persuaded him to lie still and keep his mouth open until his breath came back. I felt sure he was only winded. The only thing I had forgotten was that he had false teeth and might have swallowed them. Fortunately he hadn't."

ANDREW FERGUSON: "It took a long time for the ambulance to arrive for Stirling and, by this time, a queue of cars some 200 yards long had stopped at the scene. In an effort to hurry the arrival of the ambulance, Mike Taylor was dispatched to the pits in his Lotus, and unbeknown to everyone, he disappeared at La Carrière corner."

INNES IRELAND: "Mike Taylor was in the prototype Lotus I had raced in Argentina and the early-season races and he had gone off the road on a fast, 130mph corner. Instead of taking the right-hand curve as he meant to do, he just went sailing straight on. How he was not killed, I can't imagine. The car went across a damned great ditch, shot into the air, hit a tree which was completely uprooted, and finished up smack into another tree. Somehow or other he came out of it with only a few broken bones, although he had a neck injury which gave him trouble for some months after.

"When I visited him in hospital he said, 'The steering broke. I turned the wheel and nothing happened.' The steering column had sheared off and I must say it gave me a few uncomfortable moments when I realised how long I had been driving that car."

Taylor successfully sued Lotus for damages and retired from the sport. Chris Bristow, though, was not lucky enough to have that option.

JACK BRABHAM: "I led the race from start to finish but young Chris Bristow lost control of his Yeoman Credit Cooper and hit the side of a house plus a couple of concrete posts and a fence. The accident looked terrible when I passed, and it was."

JIM CLARK: "I was almost put off racing completely, for I was the first to arrive on the scene at Burnenville when Chris Bristow was killed. Chris was a very keen young driver who was one of Stirling's protégés, and he tried very hard indeed in every race in which he competed. In this race he was in the midst of a tremendous battle with Willy Mairesse, who was having his first Grand Prix drive in a Ferrari. Mairesse had a similar temperament to Bristow in that he went into racing hell for leather. Coming down the hill, I heard Bristow got himself over on the outside of the bend and in the wrong line. He tried to get the car across to the other side but lost control completely. The car rolled over and over, killing him instantly before throwing his body out on the circuit. Mairesse just missed being involved in this ghastly crash.

"I came bustling down behind them and no one had any flags out to warn me of what was round the corner. I saw a marshal suddenly dash out on to the road, waving his arms and trying to stop me, and the next thing I saw was another marshal run from the far side of the road. I remember thinking, 'Where is he going?' And then he bent down and grabbed this thing by the side of the road. It looked just like a rag doll. It was horrible and I'll never forget the sight of this mangled

body being dragged to the side. I was almost sick on the spot. I remember at the end of the race finding that my car was spattered with blood."

Team Lotus driver Alan Stacey also lost his life.

JACK BRABHAM: "Towards the end of this disastrous race, Alan Stacey, who was driving a works Lotus, was apparently hit in the face by a bird, [and] lost control of the car which hit a bank and caught fire. Alan was thrown out and killed instantly and the car careered across a field on fire."

JIM CLARK: "Thankfully I didn't see Alan's accident or the car and I was only told about it at the end of the race. Had I seen my team mate's accident right after Bristow's I am convinced that I would have stopped there and then, and retired from motor racing for good. Yes, it was a terrible race."

INNES IRELAND: "I saw Alan lying in the ambulance. He looked as if he was asleep, the way I'd seen him a hundred times in countless hotel rooms. I just couldn't believe my eyes. I was completely devastated. I don't think I had ever seen anyone dead before. I simply turned round in absolute horror and ran away."

JIM CLARK: "I had only known Alan for a year. He was a terrific personality and very good company. He thought a lot about the techniques of racing and could explain things. He had tremendous guts, for very few people knew that Alan had only one leg. His right leg had been amputated below the knee in a childhood motorbike accident, and he had an artificial leg. He always used to have a machine with a motorcycle twist-grip throttle on the gearlever because he couldn't heel-and-toe. He had developed a technique of blipping the throttle with his twist-grip and changing gear while using his feet on the clutch and brake.

"Despite his disability, Alan was determined that nothing and nobody should stop him racing. Not only did he develop his racing technique, but also one for hoodwinking the doctors at the compulsory check-ups which were insisted on before races by the organisers. We all liked him and were prepared to assist in this ploy. When it came round to the knee reflex test, he would cross his left leg over his artificial one. The doctor would tap it and find it satisfactory. At this point one of us - usually Innes Ireland - would ask some pointless question to distract the doctor's attention. Alan would then perform a clever little shuffle which still left his good leg uppermost. This was always good for a chuckle as we filed out of the examination room."

INNES IRELAND: "Alan got a great deal of fun out of that leg. Many a chambermaid had run from his room at the sight of an apparently dismembered leg hanging over a chair, complete with shoe and sock."

Above: When Chris Bristow's Cooper somersaulted off the circuit at Spa, Jim Clark was first on the scene and was nearly sick at the sight.
Opposite: Stirling Moss made an amazing comeback from his serious injuries at Spa. Back on track in the streets of Oporto he went on to finish third in the championship won by Jack Brabham.

BILL GAVIN (journalist and Jim Clark's biographer): "I was staying with the Cooper team at the Hotel Val d'Amblève at Stavelot and Team Lotus were there also. Jack Brabham had won the race for Cooper and, to distract his wife's attention from the sad events of the day rather than celebrate his victory, he gave a little dinner party. So we were all on one side of the restaurant pretending to celebrate Jack's victory, while on the other side Team Lotus were silently mourning the loss of Alan Stacey. Naturally they were all terribly dejected and once I noticed that Colin Chapman was crying.

"I was astonished when Jack Brabham got up from our table with a bottle of champagne in his hand, walked across the room and offered it to the Team Lotus lads for a drink. He filled their glasses and they all smiled at Jack and congratulated him on his win. Thereafter they were more at ease, and what might have seemed like a tactless gesture on Brabham's part was probably the best thing that could have happened."

JIM CLARK: "When drivers die like this, you vow that you will never race again. You honestly lose all interest in racing, and just want to get as far away as possible. Then your mind begins to function again and slowly everyday things start to crowd their way back. I don't think I am callous but I have somewhat been blessed with a bad memory for such things. A day later you feel a little bit better, three days later and you are packing your bags for another race. You keep telling yourself that you must overcome emotion, but at their height your emotions can wield great power over your body and your mind. You can make rash decisions and you have to live with them until you regain your self-control. You assume the burden in your own mind even though it was not your fault. It is a kind of guilt by association and you don't initially realize what everyone in such a predicament should realize - no matter how you feel, you still come back to reality and the living world."

14 AUGUST 1960 - PORTUGUESE GP (OPORTO) At Oporto, Stirling Moss made an amazing comeback from his accident at Spa. Ignoring the searing pain from his broken bones, he forced himself through a vigorous exercise regimen. Five weeks after his crash, he broke the lap record testing at Silverstone. Two weeks on, he won a non-championship race in Sweden and, two weeks after that, he raced in Portugal.

ANDREW FERGUSON: "Oporto - a road circuit in the fullest sense - was to be the scene of the clinching of the drivers' championship for Jack, the manufacturers' championship having already been won by our works Coopers. The majority of the team went to Portugal by Webbair but, to celebrate his solo pilot's licence, Jack decided to fly down in his Cessna. Very fierce storms were encountered and the occupants of the Webbair flight were rather concerned for Jack's safety. On running into dense cloud, Jack had come lower and lower until, in the end, he was reduced to following the coastline - which needless to say added miles to his journey. But he arrived safely and the team was most relieved."

4 SEPTEMBER 1960 - ITALIAN GP (MONZA) ANDREW FERGUSON: "Everyone applauded Phil Hill's most deserved victory at Monza, especially after a season when he had tried so hard and certainly caused us to think hard on a number of occasions."

Jack Brabham completed the year as World Champion in the Cooper.

JACK BRABHAM: "In 1960, I really enjoyed being World Champion. I felt that five victories in a row was not a bad record and I finished the year with 43 points. Bruce was second on 34. I think it was Bruce's best year and it was certainly Cooper's."

The British teams were not ready for the first season of the 1500cc Formula 1. Since the new formula had been announced late in 1958, they had mistakenly believed that the governing body could be persuaded to retain the 2.5-litre limit. BRM had no engines at all, so Graham Hill took matters into his own hands.

GRAHAM HILL: "Even before the end of 1960, I started dashing around to buy 1.5-litre four-cylinder Formula 2 Coventry Climax engines wherever I could - they had suddenly got a bit scarce. I spent a lot of my own money, but at least I was sure of having an engine and, of course, BRM ultimately repaid me."

BRM and Coventry Climax hastily designed 1.5-litre V8 engines. In contrast, Ferrari had the luxury of two engine types - its Formula 2 65deg V6, and the later development of a 120deg V6. Its 190bhp was to prove sufficient to maintain Ferrari's superiority on circuits where Stirling Moss's skill could not compensate for the 150bhp achieved by the four-cylinder Climax engine in his Lotus.

Porsche had contested only six Grands Prix over the previous three seasons but, with established expertise in small competition engines, the company now became a contender with its four-cylinder, air-cooled, 'boxer' motors.

14 MAY 1961 - MONACO GP (MONTE CARLO) INNES IRELAND: "For Monaco, we were trying a new five-speed ZF gearbox and, in practice, I was pressing on, and changing gear just as I was entering the tunnel. I intended to snick the gear lever very, very quickly into fourth gear, but the habit of years with the old, conventional gate was my downfall. Instead of fourth gear, I selected second. The odd thing was that, just as I was letting the clutch in, and in the fraction of a second before it bit, I thought to myself: 'Christ, I'm in the wrong bloody gear!'

"But even as the thought flashed through my mind, the back wheels were locking up solid. Since the Lotus was still set up to take the curve, it just flew off the road. For me, it was the most extraordinary experience because, being in almost pitch darkness, I had no idea which way the car was pointing. In no time at all, I had hit the tunnel wall. And the noise!

"I can remember the colossal crashing and banging that echoed in the enclosed space. I think the car was going backwards when it hit the wall and I was thrown out of it. I was thrown, I suppose, some 50 to 80 yards and probably owe something to my Army parachute training for not hurting myself worse than I did. I scraped my elbow down to the bone and stripped lumps off my back in landing, but it could have been worse. The other injuries - a fractured knee-cap and an inch or so off the front of my shinbone - happened, I think, as I was leaving the car."

For Monaco, Stirling Moss put Rob Walker's Lotus on pole. Half an hour before the start, Alf Francis, perhaps the most famous mechanic in Formula 1 history, had to perform heroic makeshift repairs.

ROB WALKER: "One of the mechanics noticed that a chassis tube was cracked right next to the aluminium fuel tank. Alf didn't hesitate for a moment. He moved the car away from the pit area, got the oxy-acetylene welding gear from the lorry and, having wrapped the petrol tank in wet cloths as far as it was possible to do so, he calmly began to weld the crack. It was a very brave thing to do, and typical of Alf. I watched him for a bit but after a while discretion overcame valour, and I retired to a safe distance. I don't suppose Alf fancied being blown up any more than I did, but he never hesitated to do what had to be done and I don't think his hand trembled once throughout the whole operation."

Francis wheeled Moss's car onto the grid with the bodywork side panels removed.

ROB WALKER: "For this race Stirling decided he wanted the side panels removed to help keep him cool. Apparently he had tried this during a very hot race on the Tasman Series and it had worked very well. I was rather worried that it would infringe some regulation or other."

STIRLING MOSS: "In 1961 at Monte Carlo, I was absolutely flat out at my own rating. That is very unusual. Other people, even other drivers, may say, 'Well, old Moss was flat-out coming through such-and-such a bend,' and perhaps I was, and perhaps what they took to be ten-tenths I reckoned was only eight-tenths. But in this race I was on the limit."

RICHIE GINTHER (second for Ferrari): "Monaco was 100 laps then, and lasted going on three hours. I was right on the limit all the way, and I think Stirling was too. He and I were first and second in qualifying and, in the race, we got three seconds under our qualifying times! Unbelievable, really, when you think back on it. Hey, any time you've done well against Stirling, you know you've really done something."

STIRLING MOSS: "A racing car is an animate object, not an inanimate one. It has character. There are things it will do and things it won't do. Your job is to find out what it will do and then push it as far as possible. But you mustn't push it too far or it will turn on you, as a person would.

"I have no desire to build a car myself, only to take something someone else has built and extract the maximum from it. I guess you would say that I am a conductor rather than a composer. I would be no good as a jazz musician. I don't want to improvise, merely to play the music exactly as it is written. If I were a painter, I wouldn't like to mix my own paints, merely to take paints already mixed and make the best possible picture out of them. I suppose that would make me a bad painter."

18 JUNE 1961 - BELGIAN GP (SPA) Phil Hill was on pole position at Spa, and it seemed logical that he would be allowed the win if all went according to the team plan. The problem was that there was no Ferrari team plan...

PHIL HILL: "There had always been tension with Ferrari. Ever since I joined the team back in 1956, I'd been involved in many flare-ups and witnessed even more. You could never really relax with Ferrari, because there was always someone who wanted to see you screw up, who was ready to take your place if you didn't keep your wits about you.

"The drivers argued with the engineers, and the team manager argued with the drivers, and the mechanics argued with everybody - and it was even more upsetting in '61 when the World Championship would be in the balance. My team mate, [Wolfgang von] Trips, wanted it very much, and so did I. And despite the fact that we were members of the same team, we each knew that we'd have to fight with everything we had to win the battle. Therefore the tension continued to build."

2 JULY 1961 - FRENCH GP (REIMS) History was made on the Reims road course. Ferrari brought a fourth car for the promising young Italian, Giancarlo Baghetti, who had won non-title races at Naples and Syracuse. On the long straights, the powerful Ferraris were in their element, but this time there were team orders, and Phil Hill was not happy. Despite his championship lead, he was to let Trips win. He deliberately stormed away in the opening laps, then backed off to let Trips overtake. It all came to nought when Trips had a stone through his radiator, and cooked his engine. Hill led again until he spun on the melting tarmac, and stalled when his foot was knocked off the throttle as his gyrating car was clipped by Moss. Ginther led, but also retired with overheating. Baghetti, in his first World Championship race, inherited victory. But he would never win again.

I love to feel a racing car around me, to feel the way it holds me.
I love to make it do all that it was built to do, and then a little bit more. STIRLING MOSS

I'll never retire.
I love racing too much. STIRLING MOSS

8 AUGUST 1961 - GERMAN GP (NÜRBURGRING) The ever-fickle Eifel weather played an important part in the German Grand Prix, with intermittent rain falling throughout the day. Before the start, everyone fitted Dunlop's rain tyres. Then the rain stopped, and Dunlop wanted all the teams to change to harder-wearing dry-weather tyres. The works and Walker Lotus teams decided to risk it on 'wets'.

JACK BRABHAM: "I found out that Moss had rain tyres on, so I had to rush around to get some, but we only had time to change two tyres. I went out with two rain tyres on the front and two ordinary tyres on the back. I led from the start until we came upon a wet patch. The front wheels went round but the back ones didn't, so I lost the back and, by the time I'd got it straight, I'd gone through a hedge and was driving down behind it. I stayed there and watched the race from behind the bushes."

Moss took over the lead in his Walker Lotus with Phil Hill trying to hang on in the Ferrari, while his team mate and championship rival von Trips was flying in third. In the last laps, the two Ferraris fought ferociously, trading lap records. Trips took the flag in second place, with Hill on his exhausts after a hectic last lap.

ROB WALKER: "Stirling provided me with one of my proudest moments when he stood on the winner's rostrum in the pouring rain, with an enormous laurel wreath around his shoulders, while 200,000 Germans listened to our national anthem. When Stirling won at Monaco, I thought that neither he nor anyone else could possibly drive a finer race. At the Nürburgring, I thought he had. Looking back on them today, I really don't know which of these two drives was the better. What I do know is that both of them were absolutely magnificent."

STIRLING MOSS: "It is a fine thing to win, to hear your country's anthem played just for you, but I believe I like the competition better than the victory, the fighting better than the winning. I like to feel the odds against me. That is one of the reasons why I do not drive for a factory. I want to beat the factory in a car that has no right to do so. If I had any sense I would have been driving for Ferrari all these years. But I want to fight against odds, and in a British car.

"Of course, racing is dangerous, particularly at places like the Nürburgring. I like it that way. Without danger there wouldn't be any point to it. It would be just a game that anyone could play. It would be like climbing a mountain with a net ready to catch you if you fell. What's the point to that? You might just as well walk up a ladder. Racing is a kind of Russian roulette. You never know when the chamber will come up loaded. Racing's a gamble. I like to gamble, to bet I can do something no one else can do."

Top: In his home race Wolfgang von Trips was second to Moss. For Moss (opposite) it was the final victory before his career-ending crash. For Von Trips, it was the last race of his life.

10 SEPTEMBER 1961 - ITALIAN GP (MONZA) The combined, 10km Monza *autodromo* was used for the Italian Grand Prix, with the road course and the full banked sections. For this ultra-fast track, Hill was given a new, faster-revving Ferrari engine and was told it had more power, but instead he found himself struggling, and was only fourth fastest of the six Ferraris entered. What particularly irked him was being bettered by a newcomer, Ricardo Rodriguez, the young Mexican who was having his first Ferrari Formula 1 drive. Enzo Ferrari was at the track for practice and Hill demanded a new engine for the race.

There was no impending sense that this race would decide the World Championship but, with von Trips on pole and Rodriguez alongside him, Hill was wound up tight.

PHIL HILL: "Life is a struggle whatever work you do, but at least in any other business you don't have to risk your life. For me, race day is always the same. I'm asleep in a warm bed, the sun is shining in the window, and I start to wake up and I'm lying there all warm and secure. And then I start to think: this is not just any day. This is a very special day. This is race day. Then in an instant all the warmth and security is gone, the bed is cold, and I sit up wide awake."

Hill's Ferrari team mate - nicknamed 'von Krash' earlier in his career, and later 'Taffy' - was equally wary of the dangers of his profession.

WOLFGANG VON TRIPS: "The line between maximum speed and crashing is so thin - so thin."

In the race he crossed that line for a final time.

ENIS JENKINSON: "Coming off the South Banking to end the opening lap, there were seven cars closer together than seemed reasonable and, though they crossed the timing line in the order Phil Hill, Ginther, Rodriguez, Clark, Brabham, von Trips and Baghetti, it meant nothing, for by the time they were out of sight the order had changed completely."

JIM CLARK: "I was on Taffy's tail, slipstreaming round the Vialone to keep up as we came down at full speed to the braking point for the North Curve. I was preparing to overtake him and my front wheel was almost level with his back wheel as he started to brake. Suddenly he began to pull over towards me and he ran right into the side of me. I honestly don't think 'Taffy' realised I was there. I am sure that, when he passed me earlier, he had decided his was the faster car and I would be left behind. Everything happened at lightning speed. We touched wheels and I had a split-second to think about the accident before it actually happened. I thought: 'God, he can't do this.' I remember mentally trying to shout at him to look in his mirror and see me."

DENIS JENKINSON: "What happened next was one of those strokes of ill-fortune that strike every so often, for the German's Ferrari spun, and shot up the grass bank on the outside of the straight and flung von Trips out. It cannoned off the wire mesh protecting fence and bounced back on the track, after rolling over a number of times, and stopped a crumpled wreck nearly in the middle of the track. Clark's Lotus also spun as a result of the impact, stayed on the track most of the time and came to rest on the grass verge, the driver badly shaken but unhurt. The unfortunate von Trips landed heavily and, though being taken to hospital, he died before anything could be done, the only saving grace being that he died not knowing that his Ferrari in running berserk killed 11 spectators leaning on the fence and injured many more, three of these dying later.

"With the whole field being so close behind, it was remarkable that no other cars were involved in the crash, and for those in the grandstands and pits, and around the rest of the circuit, the race went on, details of the accident being unknown and unannounced by the organisers."

PHIL HILL: "I had been ahead of the accident and, as we came round on the next lap, I saw the two cars by the edge of the road. The accident looked bad, but no worse than many others. I turned my thoughts to the job in hand: winning the Italian Grand Prix."

JACK BRABHAM: "I think it was just one of those unfortunate things than can happen at any time on a slipstreaming circuit. I am staggered that we never had more of this type of accident, particularly at Monza, because when you get a pack of cars switching and swapping places in the first few laps, you've got a potentially dangerous situation. I've always tried not to get mixed up in those early battles and tend to sit back and watch rather than get involved because it's all so pointless. I don't think either Jimmy Clark or Taffy von Trips were carving each other up as was suggested at the time. Jimmy was always a driver you could drive really hard against and be quite confident that he wasn't going to do something stupid. I'm not even sure that theirs were the only two cars involved - it could have been a third one which touched one of the other two and caused the Lotus to veer enough to touch the Ferrari."

PHIL HILL: "Ricardo Rodriguez? He's damn brave, that's all I can say. I know he's a skilled driver, you understand, but to do the things he's doing, you've got to be way out, and if he lives, I'll be surprised. By the way, there was another party involved in the Trips accident. Trips didn't just arbitrarily move over on Clark, you know. He moved because he had to, to avoid someone on the other side."

One by one, the other Ferraris trickled down the pit-lane with broken engines and, at the finish, Hill led Dan Gurney's Porsche by half a minute. But Hill's victory, even his World title, paled into insignificance when he was finally given the dreadful news of the fatalities.

PHIL HILL: "I was stunned, deeply shocked. The papers reported that I broke down and sobbed, but that was not true. There were no tears. When you've lived as close to death and danger as long as I have, then your emotional defences are equal to almost anything. Von Trips died doing something he loved and he was willing to accept the risks. Just as I am willing. When I love motor racing less, my own life will become worth more to me, and perhaps I will be less willing to risk it."

8 OCTOBER 1961 - US GP (WATKINS GLEN) When Enzo Ferrari withdrew from the final race of the season, as a mark of respect for his fallen driver von Trips, it meant that Phil Hill was denied an opportunity to race in front of his home crowd as the new World Champion.

PHIL HILL: "I tried to persuade Ferrari to send one car for me, but he wouldn't budge because he had his championships in the bag. He played the role of the martyr to the hilt, to tell the truth, meeting the press with several days' growth of beard and looking distraught and grief-stricken. They were all crocodile tears to me - he was putting on a show, as he'd done many times before. I went to Watkins Glen, of course, but I was just driven round on a lap of honour on the back of a convertible. I was really sick about that, for that day should have been the crowning glory of my career, the biggest day of my life."

Instead, that day belonged to Innes Ireland, who achieved his only Grand Prix victory. Ireland took the lead after both Jack Brabham and Stirling Moss had retired but, near the end of the race, his Lotus was keenly challenged by Dan Gurney's Porsche...

INNES IRELAND: "Those final five laps were absolute misery. I became convinced that, on the brink of success, I was bound to run out of fuel. Each lap seemed interminable and the suspense was agonising. All I could do was pay attention to keeping on the road and to go on muttering prayers. Every time I came past the pits, I could see from the signals that Gurney was closing. Four laps, three, two, one, still with the Lotus going, though Heaven knows where the fuel was coming from. And then - victory."

"I really did feel marvellous at winning that race. I had been a bit lucky, certainly, but I reckoned Team Lotus were overdue for a bit of luck. And now we had won our first championship Grand Prix. Everyone in Lotus was beside himself with delight. How little I realised that the future held not a greater glory - but a rather nasty kick in the teeth. Sixteen days after winning that race for Team Lotus, I was thrown out on my ear!"

Stirling Moss had won several times in Rob Walker's privately entered Lotus and Colin Chapman could see the value of the kind of dedication and professionalism that Moss demonstrated. Feeling that Ireland was a carry-over from a previous generation of roistering racing drivers, in it for the thrills and the parties, Chapman had decided to sign Jim Clark as his 1962 team leader with Trevor Taylor, who had dominated Formula Junior for Lotus, as his number two.

INNES IRELAND: "I suppose winning the Grand Prix at Watkins Glen should give me the memory of a great race, but somehow it doesn't. The memory was spoiled forever, for it was the last race I drove for Team Lotus. I am, of course, proud of the fact that I became the first Scot ever to win a World Championship event, but somehow this seemed disconnected from the race itself."

Hill's championship by default meant that the credit he got for his driving never equalled the effort he put into it.

ENZO FERRARI: "Phil Hill was not a top-flight driver, but he was safe and useful on fast circuits. He loved long straights and flat-out bends, but he was not so keen on the twisty bits and more-difficult circuits which demanded continuous accuracy. He could show precision all right on courses where high speed was the determining factor."

PHIL HILL: "Racing brings out the worst in me. I don't know what I would have become if I hadn't become a racing driver, as a person, I mean. I'm not sure I like the person I am now. Racing makes me selfish, irritable, defensive.

"There are 30 other guys trying to get where I am. I have to be on my guard all the time. I even have to hang around the cars when I could be doing something useful, in order to make sure the mechanics are doing what I have asked them to do. We're not allowed to touch the cars. I don't hang around the cars all the time because I like to, but to protect my interests. If I could get out of this sport with any ego left, I would."

Opposite: The infamous banking was used for the last time, though it was not the scene of the disaster at Monza.
Above: Count Wolfgang von Trips.
Below: The Von Trips Ferrari ran berserk, killing its driver and 11 spectators. His team mate's death made a deeply shocked Phil Hill the 1961 champion.

The 1962 season brought dramatic changes in the driver and team hierarchy. Cooper's double World Champion, Jack Brabham, left to start his own team, Lotus recruited Jim Clark, and Stirling Moss's career came to a premature halt. BRM team owner Sir Alfred Owen had decreed that, if it failed to win a Grand Prix during the season, the team would be disbanded. Happily, BRM won four of the nine Grands Prix, and both the titles. It was the defending champion, Ferrari, which failed to win all year.

23 APRIL 1962 A crash at a non-championship race at Goodwood on Easter Monday ended the career - and almost the life - of Stirling Moss, the acknowledged leader of the international pack, who had agreed a deal with Ferrari for the upcoming season. Enzo Ferrari had agreed to provide updates of the 1961 title-winning cars to Rob Walker's privately owned team. At Goodwood, however, Moss was driving Walker's Lotus and, to this day, he has absolutely no recollection of the crash.

Michael Cooper, a professional photographer, agonised over a nightmare he had the night before the race, but was too embarrassed to broach the subject with Moss. This dream lured Cooper to walk across the centre of the circuit to St Mary's corner, on the far side from the pits, and his were the only photographs of the accident, as it happened.

MICHAEL COOPER: "In my dream, Moss left the track at St Mary's, crossed a wide area of grass and slammed into the bank with a muffled, thundering CRUMP which threw the driver out of the cockpit and he just seemed to keep on going up. I could only presume that this meant he had died. But it was hardly the sort of story that I could go and tell Stirling..."

Moss led initially, then ran into gearbox problems, and Graham Hill took the lead in the new 1.5-litre BRM V8. Moss lost three laps in the pits and stormed back into the race. Out in front, Graham could see Stirling coming up behind, but he knew that Moss was several laps behind and was not a threat to his first Formula 1 victory. When Moss came up behind Hill, a marshal waved a blue flag to inform the leader that a faster car wanted to overtake. Some think that Hill waved acknowledgement to the flag marshal, and that Moss mistook the wave as a signal to overtake. He shaped up the Lotus to pass the BRM, but Hill turned in towards his line through the curve. The next moment, the Lotus was on the grass verge, headed for disaster.

GRAHAM HILL: "I never acknowledge the blue flag. I never have and I certainly didn't do it then. Stirling came up alongside with all four wheels on the grass and I gave up racing and just watched. The Lotus went over a bump, there was a flash of flame from the exhausts and it went straight into the bank."

Hill's theory was that the brakes must have failed on the Lotus, while Bruce McLaren speculated that the car's steering might have broken, or the throttle might have stuck open. In any case, Moss was critically injured, and taken to hospital in a coma. He did not wake properly for 38 days.

ROBERT EDWARDS (Moss biographer): "An X-ray revealed that the impact of the crash, through deceleration (120mph to nought in perhaps three seconds), had physically detached the right side of his brain from his skull, which accounted for his deep coma. The other injuries - the double fracture of the left leg, the broken left arm, the crushed left eye socket and cheekbone - were, in medical terms, relatively trivial by comparison."

Stirling Moss never raced a Formula 1 car again, although he did compete in Historic races.

20 MAY 1962 - DUTCH GP (ZANDVOORT) There was a fundamentally important technical innovation in the paddock at Zandvoort for the first Grand Prix of the 1962 season. Colin Chapman's monocoque Lotus 25 established design principles that have survived to the present day, and immediately impressed rival teams.

GRAHAM HILL: "The Lotus monocoque chassis did away with all the tubes. It was rather like an eggshell or an aircraft fuselage, and I must say it was the most beautiful-looking car and extremely functional. The car looked right, which is always a sure sign."

JIM CLARK: "The Lotus 25 was virtually shaped around me, and I had two long aluminium boxes on either side of me in which the rubber fuel tanks were carried. The boxes were secured at each end by a light steel frame. Another box behind my back, in the shape of a wedge, carried more petrol.

"It was a great benefit for the designers from an aerodynamic point of view, but at first it held some difficulties for the driver. For example, the worm's eye view of the track which this position gave meant re-orientating oneself with the features of the track to which one had become accustomed."

STIRLING MOSS: "On the Lotus 25, you have to shift gears by bending your wrist back and forth. There's no room for bending your arm. Bloody ridiculous!"

But the revolutionary Lotus was not an immediate winner. Hill's BRM V8 won in the Netherlands.

GRAHAM HILL: "I won my first World Championship event after four years of Grand Prix racing. The car went beautifully - I had absolutely no problem with it at all. It was a repeat of the first Grand Prix win that BRM ever achieved, with Jo Bonnier in the 1959 Dutch Grand Prix. That was the only Grand Prix that BRM had won to date and here they were, three years later, winning in Holland again. Everyone was tickled pink and the future certainly looked good for us at that stage."

3 JUNE 1962 - MONACO GP (MONTE CARLO) The Monaco grid produced a healthy mix of cars, with Jim Clark on pole in the Lotus 25, Graham Hill second in the BRM and Bruce McLaren on the outside of the front row with his Cooper. Ahead of them lay nearly 195 miles through the treacherous streets of Monte Carlo.

ROBERT DALEY (American journalist): "This is what road racing is all about: the race cars are speeding down hills, rounding acute, reverse camber corners at speeds normal men would not dare on a wide, straight highway. The skill and control which goes into this is incredible, thrilling, and it fills the spectator with wonder. Wonder is one of the chief emotions motor racing gives. The drivers maintain a control of their machines which seems absolute. And yet at the last moment spectators cower, unable to believe that such speed, such dust and noise can really be controlled at all."

At the start of the race, there was a typical Monaco *carambolage.* Willy Mairesse forced his Ferrari between Clark and Hill going for the first corner, but then missed his braking point and slithered wide, which let McLaren and Hill through, while Clark was baulked. Richie Ginther's throttle stuck wide open as his Ferrari left the fifth row of the grid. As they braked for the hairpin, it hit Trintignant's Lotus, which spun into Ireland's Lotus, Taylor's Lotus and Gurney's Porsche. A flying wheel killed a marshal.

McLaren found himself leading, but Hill overtook him. Clark made up for his delay at the start and also passed McLaren, but dropped out with clutch failure. With only 13 miles left, Hill's BRM ran out of oil and he stopped, leaving McLaren with the lead over Phil Hill's Ferrari.

BRUCE McLAREN: "With three laps left, the team began feverishly hanging signals on the pit board. They were timing the gap back to Phil Hill and hurriedly putting it on the board for me to read as I went past on the other side. They were working fast, with only seconds to get the figures from the stopwatch to the board, and on one lap they dropped all the numbers. As I accelerated past, John was frantically trying to pick them up and hold them on the board. I had time to chuckle.

"Phil was still five seconds behind. I didn't think he could pick that up in two laps and, by holding my pace, was sure he would be a couple of seconds away at the finish. Even if he were on my tail, there was nowhere to pass on that last half-lap. Especially if I didn't want to let him! As I braked into the chicane for the last time, I couldn't see the Ferrari in my mirror, but on entering the left-hander at Tabac there was a red dot about 200 yards behind. I had won."

PATTY McLAREN: "I remember going to the palace after Bruce had won. The winners were always invited to this amazing cocktail party. A crowd of us went together including Bette and Graham [Hill], Bruce and myself. We were running slightly late and we arrived at the wonderful palace and there was a corridor that you couldn't see the end of. It looked like it was half a mile long with this polished, polished floor, and I'm walking very sedately trying to hurry them along. I think we'd probably had a few drinks at the hotel after the win and the boys started skating on the polished floor. I arrived at the door at the end and suddenly the door swings open and it's Princess Grace! Talk about embarrassment! The boys all nearly fell in a heap behind me but she took it all well."

At this point, the two Hills were sharing the lead in the World Championship. But the defending World Champion was beginning to question the wisdom of continuing in his profession, especially given the particular pressures facing a Ferrari driver.

PHIL HILL: "They think I should go out there in an inferior car and sacrifice myself to the honour and glory of Ferrari. There have been too many sacrifices already. I won't be another. I won't be one of their sacrifices.

"I would so love to get out of this business unbent. I have a horror of cripples. Even when I was a little boy I couldn't bear to look at anyone who was deformed, could not bear to see them suffering. I guess I've always worried about ending up that way myself. I want to get out of this in one piece. Do you know, I've never been hurt in an accident.

"I now wonder about the intrinsic value of what I do. Does it have any intrinsic value? I have become a cynic. I no longer believe that driving race cars is so important."

Lola team mates Roy Salvadori and John Surtees (opposite left), and 19 of their peers, were beaten by Bruce McLaren's Cooper at Monaco.

17 JUNE 1962 - BELGIAN GP (SPA) Jim Clark won for the first time in the Lotus 25, but the long, high-speed road course at Spa-Francorchamps proved as dangerous as ever.

DENNIS MAY (*Car & Driver*): "During practice at Spa, at a point near the end of the lap when Graham Hill was doing about 145mph, a local woman carrying a bucket of water started to cross the road in front of him. She makes a habit of doing this when cars are passing her cottage door at 145mph, he was to learn afterward, having an idea that it establishes her civic rights or something. This time, she hesitated halfway across. If she hadn't, it would have been *finis* for Hill, woman, BRM, bucket and all."

Graham Hill and Bruce McLaren disputed the opening lap, but battle was joined when Trevor Taylor and Willy Mairesse came along to join in, and Clark had gathered up the leading group from his modest start. The battle between Taylor and 'Wild Willy' Mairesse, slipstreaming back and forth, swapping the lead, was towing Hill and McLaren with it, and Clark was holding station in fifth.

BRUCE McLAREN: "Trevor and Willy were dicing wheel-to-wheel and at 140mph-plus swooped up the hill after the pits side by side. Going into the first left-hander, I was sure one would back off and let the other through. I braked, because it looked as though they were going to take the corner abreast - and they did! If there was going to be an accident, I had no intention of being in it, so I sat back a safe 20 feet."

DENIS JENKINSON: "This was a pretty cut-throat battle between these two, inexperience in one cockpit and exuberance in the other, and all at an average that was still over 130mph. There was nothing to choose between them, Taylor brought up in the tough school of Formula Junior, Mairesse in rallies, both a little out of their depth and fighting hard. On lap 26 it happened. Taylor was in the lead as they left the very fast left-hand bend at Blanchimont and the two cars touched at over 100mph. The Lotus cut down a telegraph pole and crashed into a ditch, and the

Ferrari caught fire and landed upside down. Fortunately both drivers were flung out, Taylor escaping with only a shaking and Mairesse needing first-aid for slight burns and numerous cuts and gashes."

TREVOR TAYLOR: "Willy got too close. Our Lotus used a ZF gearbox with its selector rod sticking out the back, and he got close enough to nudge me out of gear with the nose of his Ferrari! I immediately snapped sideways, but I've got to thank Mairesse, because his car then pushed me straight again before I hit the telegraph pole broadside, which wouldn't have done me any good at all..."

8 JULY 1962 - FRENCH GP (ROUEN) The French Grand Prix was this year moved from Reims, and held at Rouen for the first time since 1957. The works Porsches had been absent from Belgium because of factory troubles, and this time it was Ferrari's turn to miss a race because of industrial disputes in Italy. After Graham Hill's leading BRM was halted by an engine failure, Dan Gurney claimed his and Porsche's first Grand Prix victory.

ENZO FERRARI: "The points that struck me most about Gurney were his great physical fitness and the exuberance with which he told me about his early racing, his ambitions and his wide family circle. He was courageous, gave everything he had without reserve. I remember him as strong, simple and dedicated."

5 AUGUST 1962 - GERMAN GP (NÜRBURGRING) The British Grand Prix had been a runaway for Jim Clark, but the next race brought excitement from the start of practice when the Dutch privateer, Count Carel Godin de Beaufort, set off with a TV camera mounted on the back of his Porsche.

DENIS JENKINSON: "Going down the deep descent into Fuchsrohre, the camera mounting broke loose and the TV camera fell off de Beaufort's Porsche, he not realising it immediately. Soon after, Graham Hill came charging down the hill at 140mph, through the gentle ess-bend, to find this large object lying in the road.

"There was no possible hope of avoiding it and, as the BRM ran over it, the oil radiator and pipes were ripped off and the oil poured out onto the road and the car's rear tyres, and Hill found himself spinning through the bushes and trees. By a miracle the car stayed upright, even though the right-hand rear wheels and suspension was ripped off, and with a crashing of undergrowth the car came to rest, with Graham shaken and bruised. McLaren was following and slowed, realising something was amiss, but his team-mate, Tony Maggs, arrived with no prior warning and replicated Hill's pirouettes.

"For the sake of getting a few feet of bad film, two drivers' lives had been risked and two cars demolished, but the all-powerful television racket seems to be able to get away with such things. When everyone got back to the pits and the various stories were pieced together, there was a right old shindig and practice ended in a bit of a shambles one way and another."

Come race day, heavy rain delayed the start for an hour. Dan Gurney was on pole in his Porsche, with Graham Hill (BRM), Jim Clark (Lotus) and John Surtees (Lola) across the front row. When the flag fell, Clark was caught stalled. In trying to demist his goggles, he had forgotten to turn on the fuel pumps after starting the engine. But he made up for that by passing 17 cars on the opening lap! Gurney and Hill were disputing the

lead on the steaming wet track, with Surtees in their spray, but the two front-runners encountered different cockpit problems. Hill's fire extinguisher came loose and was bouncing about beyond his reach, while Gurney's battery dislodged itself and he went wide trying to fix it, letting Surtees through. The leading trio stayed incredibly close together in the appalling conditions, with Clark closing at a rate which became beyond even his considerable abilities.

DENIS JENKINSON: "Clark's driving was almost unbearable to watch. Time and again he was in almost uncontrollable slides on the wet and slippery surface, but always he was the master of the situation, until on his 11th lap when he got into two really big slides in fifth gear, and he was lucky to get away with them. Until this point he had been driving in one of those inspired trances that are brought on by being niggly with oneself, but after nearly losing the car completely at very high speed, he came to a more reasonable sense of proportion and decided to ease off and settle for a very firm and well-won fourth place.

"After two and half hours on a rain-drenched track that demands intense concentration in the dry, Hill, Surtees and Gurney crossed the line with only 4.4sec covering first to third."

12 SEPTEMBER 1962 - ITALIAN GP (MONZA) Graham Hill won comfortably, and the second place finish by his BRM team mate Richie Ginther was especially satisfying, given that it was Ferrari's home race.

BROCK YATES (Enzo Ferrari biographer): "Ferrari invited Ginther back for 1962. He handed him a contract that was more or less the same as the one he had offered the year before. Ginther scanned it, then refused to sign it. 'Sign it or you'll never drive in Formula 1 again,' said Ferrari darkly. Ginther wadded up the paper and tossed it in Ferrari's lap. Ferrari said nothing, then buzzed for one of his assistants. 'Take the key to Signor Ginther's car and check in the trunk to make sure the jack is still there,' Ferrari said imperiously."

29 OCTOBER 1962 - SOUTH AFRICAN GP (EAST LONDON) GRAHAM HILL: "The championship was wide open until the final round in South Africa. I was going to have to dock some of my points because only the best five races of the total of nine could be counted. If Jimmy won in South Africa, he would take the championship."

The two title contenders were on the front row of the grid, with Clark's Lotus on pole. Clark simply motored into the distance, taking Hill's

championship chances with him. By half-distance, the Lotus was nearly half a minute in front. But falling oil pressure forced it out of the race - and the titles went to Hill and BRM.

GRAHAM HILL: "It was not until I saw Jimmy stopped at the pits for two consecutive laps that I realised I was going to win the race. In fact I didn't even have to win it. With Jimmy out, it wouldn't matter whether I finished or not. I'm not going to knock my good fortune. I was delighted to have won and what made it all the more pleasurable was the fact that I had won in the BRM, a car which at one time had been the laughing-stock of motor racing."

1 NOVEMBER 1962 For a non-championship Formula 1 race in Mexico City, Ferrari had not entered, so Rob Walker agreed to enter a Lotus for the young Mexican Ricardo Rodriguez.

ROB WALKER: "Ricardo had been motorcycle champion of Mexico when he was 13, he'd started racing cars when he was 15, and he'd become a works Ferrari Formula 1 driver by the time he was 19. I think the locals in Mexico really expected him to win, which was a lot of pressure for such a young man to handle.

"He was fastest in practice until a few minutes before the end of the first session, [when] John Surtees went slightly quicker. Ricardo got back into the car and as the mechanics were settling him in, he crossed himself and kissed his father's hand, and then he went out to beat Surtees's time. On his first flying lap, he lost it at about 120mph on the bumpy part of the banking and he was thrown out onto the Armco barrier and killed."

Walker's mechanic, Alf Francis, was able to confirm that nothing had broken on the car and that the accident had been caused by driver error. This was a minor consolation for Walker, who had never suffered the trauma of having a driver killed in one of his cars.

Tragically, shortly after Rodriguez had been killed, it happened again. Walker agreed to give a trial to Gary Hocking, a young Rhodesian motorcycle racer who had won the 350 and 500 World Championships in 1961, in a three-race December season in South Africa. Hocking was killed in the Walker Lotus during practice for the Natal Grand Prix at Durban.

Top left: Graham Hill won in Holland, Germany, Italy and South Africa, en route to the 1962 driving title.
Opposite: The low-slung Lotus 25 was virtually shaped around Jim Clark, who sped through a barnyard to win brilliantly in Belgium.

The lying-down driving position, though not completely new to me, required some time to become accustomed to. But once I had mastered the new position, I wondered how I had ever driven a racing car any other way.

JIM CLARK

Porsche having withdrawn at the end of 1962, Dan
Gurney moved to Jack Brabham's team for the 1963
season, while Phil Hill had grown tired of the politics
at Ferrari and now joined a defection of several
personnel, to form the new ATS team. Young Chris
Amon signed to race Reg Parnell's Lola in place of
John Surtees, who replaced Hill at Ferrari.

BROCK YATES: "Surtees was a giant in the sport. He had
already won the World Motorcycle Championship for MV
Agusta and was much loved in Italy, a favour he returned
in kind. He was brave to a fault and a skilled car and
chassis tuner. His effortless transfer to four-wheeled
racing - an entirely foreign discipline - had been
accomplished by only a few men, including Nuvolari,
Rosemeyer and Varzi, and was a major accomplishment
in itself. That Surtees was instantaneously a contender
against the best in the business, bordered on the
miraculous. They called him 'Big John' in deference not
to his physique, but to his heart."

JOHN SURTEES: "I was originally asked out to
Maranello at the end of 1960. I wasn't very happy with
the political scene there and I wasn't very happy with
all the drivers they seemed to have on their books.
And frankly, I realised I didn't really know enough about
car racing. By this stage I'd only done four GPs, a
couple of Formula 2 races and three Formula Junior
events. So I thought, judging by past experience, it
wasn't right to go somewhere new like this as such a
novice. I decided then not to go into a hornet's nest like
that at the time without some sort of knowledge, so
I didn't accept the offer until 1963."

9 JUNE 1963 - BELGIAN GP (SPA) DENIS JENKINSON
"When the art of high-speed driving is being
demonstrated to its fullest, and if the driver happens to
be one of the top names in Grand Prix racing - such as
Jimmy Clark - then one's cup of pleasure as a spectator
is full to overflowing.

"In these days of apparent safety and security all
around us, with 'civilisation' blinding us into a state of
almost lethargic torpor, where we have no need to
indulge in anything the slightest bit risky, it is
a wonderful sight to see a man, by his own choosing
do something that is really stretching the safety
factor to the limit; deliberately flirting with danger for
no real gain other than his own personal satisfaction.
To see this happening a few feet away from me at
anything up to 150mph is a wonderful sight and I am
never ashamed to admit to a distinct 'prickly' feeling
behind the eyes."

Left: 'Fearless' John Surtees conquered the fearsome Nürburgring,
despite having his Ferrari's mirrors filled by Clark's Lotus.
Opposite: Always awesome, Spa was terrifying in the wet.
Clark tamed the treacherous track to win by a full five minutes.

4 AUGUST 1963 - GERMAN GP (NÜRBURGRING) At a circuit where they had both won magnificently in the past, Juan Manuel Fangio and Stirling Moss were interested spectators. They saw a succession of accidents and a fine maiden victory for John Surtees.

Willy Mairesse was making his first appearance for Ferrari after a serious accident at Le Mans. The brave but foolhardy Belgian was soon back in hospital, crashing at the Flugplatz and smashing his arm so badly that he never drove a Formula 1 car again. A flying wheel from his Ferrari killed a track marshal. Chris Amon crashed the Parnell Lola when the steering broke, and fellow Kiwi Bruce McLaren crashed heavily in his Cooper in an unexplained accident.

BRUCE McLAREN: "I had been a little sceptical when Stirling Moss woke from his Goodwood accident and said, 'If you told me I'd been hit by a bus, old man, I'd have believed you.' I thought he must have had some recollection of at least the initial stages of getting involved in his accident. Now I know how blank that space can be. I woke up in Adenau hospital, not far from the Nürburgring, and only logic told me I must have gone off the track somewhere. How, when or where I had not the slightest idea, and apart from what people have told me since, I still do not recollect anything leading up to, or surrounding the accident. I must have banged my head somewhere, as I was out cold for about an hour. It seems that the mind conveniently whitewashes anything it would be better not to remember."

As the race continued, poleman Jim Clark's engine lost its edge and Surtees stormed into the lead in his Ferrari, setting records as he went on to win his first Grand Prix on four wheels and Ferrari's first victory since 1961. His winning average speed was faster than the previous lap record.

ENZO FERRARI: "John Surtees embodied all the great virtues. What I liked about John, known to British fans as 'Big John' and to Italians as 'Son of the Wind,' were the mechanical knowledge, selfless enthusiasm and dedication that he lavished on the sport. He neglected no detail, carefully weighing up his opponents, the cars and the circuits. He gathered every little crumb of knowledge that might come in useful. He was the same with his cars - he was never satisfied because he knew that with racing cars there is always 'something else' to be added, by dint of hard thinking or precise calculation."

8 SEPTEMBER 1963 - ITALIAN GP (MONZA) The Monza event was scheduled to run over the combined circuit incorporating the unloved bankings but after three cars had suffered suspension failures on the first day of practice, aid came from an unexpected quarter. The police demanded that the bankings were not to be used, fearing a repeat of the accident in 1961 that had killed Wolfgang von Trips and 13 spectators. Already Chris Amon was in hospital, having suffered another high-speed accident in the Parnell Lola.

CHRIS AMON: "It was the second day of practice and it was the first time I'd had competitive power that season. I did about three laps and then just lost it in the second Lesmo. I had no seatbelts in those days and I went sideways off the track. The front end hit a tree, the back end hit a tree, and I carried on over the side. The gearbox finished up 50 yards away.

"I wasn't very well afterwards. I'd broken several ribs and became the focus of other patients' attention in hospital when they realised I was a racing driver. I'd just turned 20. I had one night in there and they put me on the plane back to England with the rest of the crew on the Sunday night. Everybody feels sorry for you when you've hurt yourself and they tend to try and cheer you up and make you laugh - and with broken ribs, laughing is no laughing matter."

Having won at the Nürburgring, John Surtees was already the new hero of Italy when he started at Monza from pole position in the new 'Aero' Ferrari. Surtees led the opening laps but a valve dropped in his V6 engine. Jim Clark's victory for Team Lotus clinched the World Championship, but the thrill of his achievement was tempered when the police ushered him away to be questioned over his involvement in the 1961 accident. In contrast, BRM's Richie Ginther was so delighted with his second place that he drove his Fiat Topolino up the steps of the hotel that evening.

6 OCTOBER 1963 - US GP (WATKINS GLEN) Richie Ginther was popular with the American crowd at Watkins Glen because he was still in the running for second place in the championship, which he eventually shared with his BRM team mate Graham Hill. Appropriately, they finished 1-2 in the US race - and BRM won some money.

TONY RUDD (BRM manager): "When I collected the starting money - $100,000 for first and $75,000 for second, all in $100 bills - Cameron Argetsinger, the race organiser, and his staff were very concerned that I planned to drive back to the Glen Motor Inn by myself. I had not given it any thought, so I was relieved to get back, pay the hotel bills and share the money out. After this, there was not enough left to worry about!"

28 DECEMBER 1963 - SOUTH AFRICAN GP (EAST LONDON) Jim Clark started his Lotus 25 on pole in South Africa, and won going away to collect a record seventh Grand Prix victory for the season.

COLIN CHAPMAN: "Jim drove the same monocoque Type 25 chassis all season to win the seven Grands Prix. There was no difference between his car and the others on the team - except that his was more worn out, and we also tried alternative gearboxes on the other cars. As a matter of interest, when Jim has gone out in one of the other cars he has always gone as quick, or even quicker, than he had done in his own car."

The 1964 season went down to the wire, but John Surtees had resuscitated Scuderia Ferrari to the point where he could challenge Jim Clark's Lotus and Graham Hill's BRM all the way to the last round in Mexico. The first Japanese entry in Formula 1 was a bold new car from Honda, which appeared for the German Grand Prix driven by the relatively unknown American, Ronnie Bucknum.

10 MAY 1964 - MONACO GP (MONTE CARLO) In the season-opener, Graham Hill and Richie Ginther scored a 1-2 for BRM for the second year in succession. Besides being a reliable number two to Hill from the driving point of view, Ginther's mechanically oriented mindset gave him an insight into the direction Formula 1 technology might take in the future.

RICHIE GINTHER: "I think there's so far to go that no one has envisaged an end yet. People who think they've reached an end just aren't far-thinking enough. Racing cars have been getting smaller every year. Each season we say they'll never get any smaller - but they always do. They have to. It's getting to the point now where designers are trying not only to make an engine as powerful, reliable and light as possible, but also as physically small as it can be. Because the smaller the engine is, the smaller the car is going to be. When they get the engine down to the width of the driver, it will be the size of the driver that governs the width of the car. We haven't quite reached that stage yet, but when it does arrive, it will suit a small guy like me just fine..."

14 JUNE 1964 - BELGIAN GP (SPA) On the final lap of an extraordinary race at Spa, Bruce McLaren's Cooper appeared in the lead - but it was coasting with a dead engine downhill towards the finish line at 10mph, while Jim Clark's Lotus closed at 100mph and took the lead yards from the chequered flag. Clark was unaware he had won, and ran out of fuel on the slowing-down lap. He came back into the pits riding on the back of the car of his new team mate, Formula Junior champion Peter Arundell.

BRUCE McLAREN: "The last lap in Belgium was completely chaotic. Given another half-gallon of petrol, Dan Gurney would have won; given another quart of petrol, it would have been Graham Hill's race; and given just another teaspoonful, I would have won. At least that's how it appeared on the surface after the finish of that fantastic race in which four different people led briefly on the last lap."

28 JUNE 1964 - FRENCH GP (ROUEN) DENIS JENKINSON: "The French race was held at Rouen again. The circuit of *Les Essarts* is the one that will always conjure up memories of the great Fangio when he was at the top of his career in 1957. Possibly the finest action photographs ever taken were made at Rouen in that year when Fangio threw his 250F Maserati into opposite-lock power-slides down the 130mph swerves after the pits, mainly just for the fun of it, to let everyone appreciate that he really was the master of his machine. Since those old-fashioned days, science and design have improved Grand Prix cars out of all recognition and if a car needs opposite steering lock through a fast bend, there is something amiss and adjustments must be made. Today, 1957 seems like an heroic age, but I have no doubt that, in 10 years, the 1964 French Grand Prix will seem like an heroic age."

Dan Gurney's victory was the first for the Brabham team, and Jack Brabham set a new lap record chasing Graham Hill's BRM to the flag, missing a 1-2 by eight-tenths of a second.

2 AUGUST 1964 - GERMAN GP (NÜRBURGRING) Honda appeared for the first time at the Nürburgring, a daunting circuit indeed for the Californian debutant, Ronnie Bucknum.

JOHN TOMERLIN (*Road & Track*): "In March, Bucknum was approached by a representative of Honda and flew to Tokyo to climb behind the wheel of the first Formula 1 car he'd sat in in his life. 'It was the most frightening experience I've ever had,' he said, 'and personally I thought I was pretty bad.'

"Honda did not think so. It signed him to a contract guaranteeing him four races in 1964, or the equivalent in payment, a contract which, Bucknam said, 'I think makes me one of the best-paid drivers in the sport.'"

British-born Rhodesian works Honda motorcycle rider Jim Redman was also at the Nürburgring, where he declined the opportunity to make his four-wheel racing debut.

JIM REDMAN: "Sochiro Honda was a genuine and modest person. To see him working, in his overalls, in the midst of his engineers, you'd never imagine he was the 'big boss'. He was the personal inventor and owner of an incredible number of patents and was never happier than when he had solved a problem with his team of engineers, or when he found a way to beat his rivals in the races. He knew how to instil in all his employees his love of a job well done and his sense of loyalty. He and his team took enormous pride in everything they did and his employees would have worked an eight-day week and a 25-hour day if he asked them."

John Surtees started from pole and won comfortably to give Ferrari its first Grand Prix victory of the season. Sadly, however, the dangerous Nürburgring claimed another victim. After crashing his privately entered Porsche in practice, Dutch amateur Count Carel Godin de Beaufort - an overweight and jolly man who painted his cars a patriotic orange - died from his injuries the day after the race.

23 AUGUST 1964 - AUSTRIAN GP (ZELTWEG) The first World Championship race in Austria was held on the bumpy runways and perimeter roads of the Zeltweg military airfield, and there were many suspension failures during practice. In his home Grand Prix, young Jochen Rindt made his Formula 1 debut in Rob Walker's Brabham-BRM.

HEINZ PRULLER: "Photographers were at the airport as the top drivers arrived and tried to arrange the classic handshaking photographs - Rindt and Clark, then Rindt with Hill - but Jochen was determined to avoid being obtrusive. He didn't yet feel like master in his own home, but more like a guest in his country.

"The drivers' briefing was held in English and Jochen missed a point. When he asked, one of the English drivers turned round and suggested: 'Don't worry, just follow us.' For Rindt there seemed hope of a World Championship point but brake trouble forced him into the pits and later the steering failed."

ROB WALKER: "I remember Jochen had taken the trouble to find out when I was arriving and met me at the airport. He was such a charming young man, so full of youthful enthusiasm and so grateful for the drive. He never forgot that I gave him his first Formula 1 drive and, when the Osterreichring was inaugurated some years later, he said to me: 'I want you to be the first person I ever drive round this circuit,' and he took me round in a Mercedes 500SEL. It was very touching."

In the race, the rough track surface caused mechanical mayhem, and 11 drivers failed to finish. Among them was Phil Hill, now driving for Cooper in what would be his final season. The ill-handling car hit track-side haybales and caught fire. Although Hill tried to quell the blaze, it was burned to a crisp.

Lorenzo Bandini gave Ferrari its second win in successive races, his only Formula 1 victory in a career that would end in the most horrible way in 1967.

MIKE HAILWOOD: "At a post-race party in Austria, Jim Clark and Innes Ireland arrived wearing kilts but, Innes being Innes, had elected to wear nothing underneath. As the evening progressed, Innes became more and more enthusiastic and eventually decided to dance on the table. All the girls became very excited, but it was just too much for Graham Hill, who dashed outside and returned with a nice prickly cactus. Poor old Innes and his girlfriend spent the next week occupied with a pair of tweezers and a magnifying glass, pulling out the spines!"

6 SEPTEMBER 1964 - ITALIAN GP (MONZA) To the delight of the 'tifosi', John Surtees put his Ferrari on pole at Monza, but Ronnie Bucknum was just as happy to qualify the Honda on the fourth row.

RONNIE BUCKNUM: "We were really making progress. I was delighted when Jim Clark came up to me and said: 'My goodness, you've never raced here before and you're halfway up the grid!' I knew we had a lot of power, maybe as much, if not more, than the others but the brake pads were only so-so and it was difficult to stop. The brakes were only good for a few laps."

In the race, Bucknum's brakes lasted 13 laps before they forced him into retirement. Surtees had no such trouble, and gave the Scuderia its third consecutive victory.

4 OCTOBER 1964 - US GP (WATKINS GLEN) The result at the Glen, Graham Hill winning from John Surtees, left both of them in contention with Jim Clark for the World Championship as the teams headed off to Mexico for a gripping finale.

25 OCTOBER 1964 - MEXICAN GP (MEXICO CITY) Dan Gurney put his Brabham on pole and went on to win the race, but the title went to John Surtees after Lorenzo Bandini responded to frantic Ferrari pit-signals in the final laps to allow his team leader to finish second. Bandini was the pivotal man in the title chase: earlier, he had accidentally (he maintained) punted Graham Hill's BRM, flattening its exhausts so that Hill had to stop for repairs.

BROCK YATES: "At first the British press grumped that Bandini had been assigned to bump Hill into the weeds so that his team mate could win the Championship. But no less an authority than Hill denied this. Pulling himself up to his considerable height, the regal mustachioed Englishman, whose blue helmet carried the stripes of the London Rowing Club, snorted: 'Of course he didn't mean to do it. It was just bloody bad driving!'"

After seven Grand Prix seasons, 1961 World Champion Phil Hill retired from Formula 1.

MARY HEGLAR (author of *The Grand Prix Champions*): "After reaching the top in 1961, the inner drives that had compelled him to race continued to lose their grip and, following a frustrating 1964 season, Phil left not only the Cooper team, but Grand Prix racing as well. This was a half-step back from the precipice, a compromise between his need to compete and his ever-stronger belief that to do so was folly."

PHIL HILL: "It's strange, you know. You almost have to be out of this business, and sufficiently detached, to be capable of being objective enough to see where you've been. In the minds of some people who are still involved, they might make another judgement of you as an individual, such as 'He's not the type and maybe shouldn't have been one of us', or something like that. I know how I feel about automobile racing today, I feel I understand my reasons for participating a helluva lot better than I did while I was doing it. With these insights I can only have even greater respect and admiration for those who participate over the long term in face of such obviously conflicting motivations, even though much of the conflict is sub-surface."

Success can only be achieved with a kind of pioneer spirit and the repeated use of three tools: failure, introspection and courage. SOCHIRO HONDA

Opposite: For Honda's debut at the daunting Nürburgring, a pensive Ronnie Bucknum was entrusted with handling the screaming V12 engine that developed 220bhp at 12,000rpm.
Above, inset: Count Carel Godin de Beaufort was fatally injured in his Porsche 718.
Overleaf: Jim Clark's Lotus crew informs him that he is 25s ahead of second-placed Jackie Stewart and the rest are miles behind at rain-sodden Spa. Mechanic Dick Scammell (right) later became head of Cosworth Engineering.

I don't think Jim Clark ever liked Spa, but I think that was incentive to dig down.

There's no doubt about it - like a great artist, they've got something extra. ALLAN McCALL

Jim Clark of Team Lotus won the opening round of the 1965 season in South Africa on New Year's Day, and five more - the Belgian, French, British, Dutch and German Grands Prix in succession. Besides the World Championship, Clark won the British and French Formula 2 championships, and the Tasman Series in New Zealand and Australia - and he also became the first non-American to win the Indianapolis 500 race since 1916.

This year was also notable for the debut of another Scot who would make an indelible mark on the sport. Jackie Stewart was recruited from great success in Formula 3 racing to become Graham Hill's team mate at BRM. Before the season was over, he had secured the first of what was to become a record number of Grand Prix wins.

30 MAY 1965 - MONACO GP (MONTE CARLO) Graham Hill started his BRM from the pole and won in Monaco for the third time in a row - although it was not without misadventure.

GRAHAM HILL: "The race had been on for about 25 laps and I was in the lead when I came over the brow of a hill towards the chicane at about 120mph and [was] just getting on the brakes when I saw Bob Anderson in his Brabham creeping along and blocking my line into the chicane. I locked up the brakes and ran down the escape road, leaving some rare old skidmarks, and came to a griding halt. I had to get out of the car, push it backwards onto the track, climb in and start the engine. All this took time and I'd dropped back to fifth. I was pretty narked about this, as you can imagine, though I made it back into the lead and scored the hat-trick of wins.

"Later that night, we went to the Tip-Top, a little bar which is a popular meeting place for all the British contingent. I look in every year, and every year the owner treats me to a drink - this time it was champagne."

13 JUNE 1965 - BELGIAN GP (SPA) ALLAN McCALL (Team Lotus mechanic): "Jimmy was so unpunishing with the car. Brake pads - we only used to have to replace them on his car after four or five races. The biggest thing for him was that the car repeated itself. It had to be consistent. Once it was consistent, he'd work on it from there. It didn't have to be a consistently good car, it just had to be consistent. I never knew any other driver with the ability to carry that extra bit of speed around the corners that came to Jimmy so easily without molesting the machinery."

1 AUGUST 1965 - GERMAN GP (NÜRBURGRING) Jim Clark's first win on the notorious Nürburgring clinched the World title with three races still to go.

12 SEPTEMBER 1965 - ITALIAN GP (MONZA)
Newcomer Jackie Stewart's first Grand Prix victory was accomplished by slipping inside his veteran BRM team leader Graham Hill on the South Turn, the last corner of the last lap.

JACKIE STEWART: "It was difficult for me in this particular situation because my car was definitely quicker through the South Turn than Graham's. I didn't know what to do. I really didn't. I'd finally resolved that we should try for a dead heat. Now that sounds corny, but put yourself in my position: I would obviously have loved to win my first Grand Prix, but at the same time I had Graham to respect and also the will of BRM. We hadn't been given any signals on a finish formation, so I was in a difficult situation.

"What happened? Going into the corner I was on the inside, which is the accepted line, and Graham went wide, only to strike the loose stuff that gets pushed to the outside of a corner during a race. When you get onto that there's nothing much you can do about it. You can't brake or steer in the normal way, you've got to try and pussyfoot the car round in the best way you can. That's what happened."

24 OCTOBER 1965 - MEXICAN GP (MEXICO CITY)
Richie Ginther started the last Grand Prix of the 1.5-litre formula from the second row of the grid, but he led the field into the first corner. The race then became a battle between the Californian friends, Dan Gurney in the Brabham and Ginther in the Honda, with Gurney setting fastest laps as he shaved Ginther's lead.

RICHIE GINTHER: "When Dan was closing on me, I knew exactly what I was doing. There's a hairpin on the circuit and I was allowing him to come back at me because I was saving my car. I knew how much I could let him have. I didn't do anything stupid. I couldn't let myself go too much in case I lost concentration, but I was letting him come. I had a fuel mixture control on the dashboard and I had it at 'lower rich' to protect the engine, but I could alter the control to anywhere from 'full rich' to 'full lean' and the difference was 300 revs on the straightaway. My car was that much better than his."

Ginther's first Formula 1 victory was also the first for Honda, and for its tyre supplier, Goodyear.

YOSHIO NAKAMURA (Honda team boss): "After the race I sent a telegram to Honda headquarters in Tokyo echoing the words of Julius Caesar: 'I came, I saw, I won!'"
BRIAN HART (former racer and engine builder): "One of my greatest memories is Nakamura and his men actually making the Honda work. Most of the time it was

very difficult to get the engine to run on 12 cylinders. It had these massive long exhaust pipes which looked like tentacles, as if an octopus was being sucked from the engine, and it was tuned like 12 motorbikes. Nobody had ever revved engines so high. The other engines were running about 10,500rpm. When Ginther won in Mexico he was running 12,500. And the noise the thing made was unbelievable!"

The outcome of the World Championship was the achievement of an outstanding partnership between the entrant and his team leader, based on deep mutual respect.

COLIN CHAPMAN: "Jim will always have a go and give his very best. In all the time I have known him, I have seen him have remarkably few 'off' days. This is a tremendous morale-booster for the team as a whole. The mechanics will work really hard preparing the cars when they know the man in the cockpit is going to make the most of what they give him. It means that all the hard work is converted into race-winning potential. He gets on better with mechanics than most drivers. He has a good personal relationship with them and even when things go badly wrong, he's far more likely to let me have it, rather than to moan to the mechanics."
JIM CLARK: "Colin is a hard taskmaster and yet he still retains that knack of getting people to work near-miracles for him. Many a time I've seen him talk mechanics into doing what they genuinely think is impossible. But somehow he fires them with some of his own tremendous enthusiasm, and the job gets done. The thing is, if it's really necessary, he'll always be prepared to roll up his own sleeves and lend a hand, and I think people respect him for that."

Graham Hill (above and left) won Monaco for the third time in a row, a sideways Stewart and a stalking Bandini finishing third and second, respectively. Inset, right: 1965 World Champion Jim Clark.

The maximum swept volume of the Formula 1 engine was increased for the 1966 season from 1500cc to 3000cc, and the reaction to this big change by some of the teams was to adopt complex, multi-cylinder engines, in search of supposedly huge horsepower advantages.

BRM designed a complex, 16-cylinder device. Cooper dusted off the ageing Maserati V12. Ferrari (deploying a 3-litre version of its sportscar race engine) and Honda also came along with twelve-cylinder motors. As an interim measure, Lotus was compelled to persevere with a four-cylinder Climax engine, and this effectively rendered Jim Clark incapable of defending his title. Against most expectations, he lost it to a man accustomed to taking the simplest approach to any engineering problem. Jack Brabham commissioned Repco (Replacement Parts Company) in Australia to build a V8, based on the block of an obsolete Oldsmobile V8 saloon car engine. Even with modest useable power, it would win the World Championship two years in succession.

Most significantly for the brave men in the cockpits who were racing sometimes fragile race cars on often ridiculously dangerous tracks, 1966 was the year when Jackie Stewart began a then controversial safety crusade that would save many lives over the years.

22 MAY 1966 - MONACO GP (MONTE CARLO) While awaiting the H16 BRM engine, which would not be ready until late in the season, Jackie Stewart won the opening round at Monaco with a 2-litre V8, as used in that winter's Tasman Series. John Surtees had to drive the heavy new V12 Ferrari while team mate Lorenzo Bandini had the lighter, 2.4-litre V6. Surtees led the race until the differential broke. He was not a happy man...

JOHN SURTEES: "This was where one of the big differences came with [Ferrari team manager Eugenio] Dragoni. I considered that our purpose in going to Monaco was to win the race - not just to put on a demonstration of how the new 3-litre car would perform. It was taking too big a chance to expect the new car to finish. I considered that the 2.4-litre car was the one to win at Monaco, purely on the grounds of reliability - in other words, horses for courses.

"My troubles with Dragoni started with the first race I drove for Ferrari back at the beginning of the 1963 season. But for the sake of the team we - or at least I - held a 'truce' because it was only when we were away from the factory that these situations seemed to occur.

"When I started with Ferrari, the team was at a low ebb, but this suited me fine because there was such tremendous potential. I think a lot of chances were just thrown away in the past few years and this was usually because Mr Ferrari had to rely virtually entirely on what he heard back from others, and most of the people around him were sometimes ill-advised themselves, or at least weren't quite aware of what was going on.

"I had looked upon the 1966 season as being the pay-off year in the investment that I'd put in, in the way of time and effort, during the 1.5-litre formula, and this was one of the things that kept me with Ferrari despite my differences with the team management. But unfortunately these other people realised what the 3-litre formula meant to me and the possible success I could gain, and they took it as an opportunity to create impossible situations."

12 JUNE 1966 - BELGIAN GP (SPA) The notoriously fickle weather in the mountainous Ardennes Forest region of south-eastern Belgium played havoc with the national Grand Prix. While it was dry on the starting grid, a downpour began at the far end of the 8.749-mile track, which was treacherous even in fine conditions.

JACK BRABHAM: "Unfortunately not everybody on the grid knew that it was already raining out on the other side of the circuit. One or two people had been given the news, which was their good luck, and apparently the spectators were being told it was raining at Malmedy, but no one thought of letting us in on the news.

"As we went into Burnenville - which is probably the fastest and most difficult corner on the whole course - I realised that the road surface had just had a shower of rain. It is difficult enough to get round Burnenville in the dry, but in the wet, and when you're not expecting it to be wet, it is diabolical! It wasn't actually raining there, but the surface was very slippery, and so far as I was concerned it was completely unexpected. We were doing about 135mph when we found ourselves sliding."

DENIS HULME: "There were cars going in all directions when we hit the rain. I thumped up the back of [Jo] Siffert's car and the front wheels on my Brabham splayed out. I stopped it up against a kerb and got out to bash the wheels until the tie-rods were more or less straight again. When I heard the others coming round on their second lap, I left the car and shinned up the bank - there was no way I was going to stay down on the road with that lot hammering through! Then I got down and started to drive slowly round to the pits. Each time I heard the field bearing down on me again, I'd park the Brabham and race up the nearest bank."

JACK BRABHAM: "Halfway down the straight, the shower had started to form puddles on the road and the rear tyres were aquaplaning. On the approach to the kink in the straight, I just couldn't see how Jochen Rindt was going to get through the tweaks without getting into trouble. I was already trying to slow down when Rindt's Cooper began to go round like a top. I've never seen a car go round and round so many times so quickly and violently. He was right in front of me and gave me a grandstand seat.

"The amazing thing is that, while he was spinning, he kept going round the corners. It was a miracle that he stayed on the road and the embarrassing thing was that I was catching him up, because he was slowing down quicker through spinning than I could slow down using the brakes in a straight line. As he finished spinning for the last time, I was nearly on to him, but luckily he finished on the right side of the road, and left me enough room to squeeze past on the left.

"Rindt really impressed me. After a spin like that, to drive as he did for the rest of the race and finish second was little short of fantastic. I think if I'd had a spin like Rindt's I would have given up motor racing for life!"

While Brabham also survived, and finished fourth in the race, several cars spun off and crashed heavily at the 150mph Masta Kink. Among them were the BRM team mates Jackie Stewart and Graham Hill, whose car finished up a steaming wreck alongside Stewart's.

GRAHAM HILL: "Jackie was still in the car and obviously in some sort of pain. He looked terribly helpless. I leapt out of my car and rushed to see what I could do for him. The side of his car had been pushed in and had trapped Jackie. The fuel tank had split and he was soaked in petrol. The first thing I did was to turn off the switches to stop the fuel pump pumping petrol everywhere, and also to make sure there were no sparks flying around. The raw fuel was burning Jackie. It is very strong stuff and it can take all your skin off just by chemical action.

"I tried to lift Jackie out. He was pretty dazed and complained of pain in his shoulder and I then realised that I would have to take the steering wheel off before I could get him out, as it was jammed up hard against his leg. I ran off to ask a marshal to find a toolbox - he brought one back and we undid Jackie's steering wheel, took it off and got him out. Our immediate fear of the BRM going up like a torch was now over and we took him to a small farm building nearby. In there I took all his clothes off because they were soaked in fuel.

"No assistance had arrived, so I ran to a marshals' post again and telephoned from there for an ambulance; when I got back it was just arriving. The first thing the nurses did when they saw Jackie was to cover him up again with his petrol-soaked overalls, so I had a big battle with them. They seemed more concerned about their embarrassment than about Jackie's pain."

JACKIE STEWART: "I thought the nurses were nuns. To this day, I can't make up my mind whether they were there, or whether they were just part of my semi-delirium. I had broken my collarbone and dislocated a shoulder, and I had some ribs cracked. I had a sore back and concussion. But my main concern was the petrol. As it was I had substantial petrol burns and eventually all my skin would come off.

"The building I was in, the so-called medical centre, was just a shack. I lay there on the concrete floor littered with cigarette butts and dirt. They stuffed me into an old ambulance and provided a police escort to go to the hospital in Liège, which was quite a few miles away.

I was in a rather desperate state, heading straight for a house on the left. I thought I was going in right through the front door, and remember thinking to myself, 'This is it.' JACK BRABHAM

Opposite: Stewart, Hill and Gurney compare notes in the calm before the storm that created complete chaos at Spa. Half the field crashed in the first-lap cloudburst, among them Hill, who rescued Stewart from his wrecked car.

As a driver, Jackie Stewart left Formula 1 a better place than he found it. Everyone racing today has reason to be grateful for Jackie's pioneering courage and persistence. MURRAY WALKER

Jackie spoke for all of us.
He was the only one with the balls to do it. CHRIS AMON

They said I had no guts. Christ Almighty! When did *they* ever crash at 150mph?

JACKIE STEWART

The Nürburgring was even more dangerous than Spa. Anyone who says he loved that track is either a liar or he wasn't going fast enough...

JACKIE STEWART

"On the way, the ambulance driver lost the police escort and didn't know how to get to the hospital. In spite of all those problems, I was in London at St Thomas's Hospital six hours after my accident, which was a terrific effort, thanks to Louis Stanley, who was instrumental in forming the Grand Prix Medical Unit after my accident.

"From then on while I was with BRM, I had a set of spanners that fitted my steering wheel, taped inside the cockpit. These were painted in day-glo colours with a description of how to remove the steering wheel in the language of whatever country I happened to be racing in. This was a small but important point if you got trapped as I had."

This accident in Belgium triggered Jackie Stewart's determination to improve safety standards in Formula 1. He pioneered the use of seat harnesses and fireproof overalls for the drivers, and guard-railing and run-off areas for the circuits. But at first Stewart's personal crusade was not without its critics among the drivers.

The prevailing attitude at the time was outlined by Stirling Moss who, despite his nearly fatal accident at Goodwood in 1962, did not share all of Stewart's safety concerns. Writing in his 1963 autobiography, *All But My Life*, Moss had this to say...

STIRLING MOSS: "I am president of the Grand Prix Drivers Association and we try to induce the promoters to improve the circuits, make them safer, mainly for the spectator. We do not advocate taking out trees, for instance, eliminating things that make for interest. We don't want 'spin-off' zones and that sort of thing. We like the natural hazards. We'd like to race around Hyde Park or Central Park without any changes at all in the topography. We accept the hazards, as at Monaco, of hitting a building or going over a drop; after all, it's no fun gambling for matchsticks.

"I think most of us in the GPDA are against seatbelts in Grand Prix cars. I like seatbelts in closed cars, but in a racing car I want to be thrown out, or have the choice, mainly because of the danger of fire. I will not use a belt in a race. At a race in Riverside, USA, I was told that seatbelts were mandatory. It was going to cost me thousands of dollars, but I told the mechanics to load the car and pack up. The promoters came around and we compromised. I said they could put a seatbelt in the car, if they liked, as long as the ends were buckled together under the seat so they couldn't fly around, and so that no one would think, looking into the car, that I was going to use it. The thing was put right out of sight. But it was in the car and I suppose that satisfied the insurance brokers or whatever. I thought it was a piece of flaming hypocrisy."

Chris Amon, although he would later fully support Stewart's efforts, was at first fearful that improved circuit safety standards would lead to more dangerous driving by some of his peers.

Opposite: Crash-prone Willy Mairesse miraculously survived this fiery accident in his Ferrari at Spa in 1962, though he later committed suicide.
Above: Jackie Stewart - here flying his BRM in 1966 - was terrified at the notoriously dangerous Nürburgring, yet won there a record four times.

I was the first driver ever to win a Grand Prix in a car bearing his own name - as all the journalists wrote over and over again. JACK BRABHAM

CHRIS AMON: "Stewart I take my hat off to, because his attitude was never ambivalent. He worked hard for circuit changes, and he drove hard. But absolutely fairly.

"However, there are people in this business who worry me. At GPDA safety meetings, they'd shout about cutting trees down, flattening banks and erecting guardrail all over the place. I'm surprised some of them didn't ask for guardrail in their hotel rooms. After all, most people die in bed! Okay, fine, then you'd get into a race with some of these crusaders, and find they'd happily put you over their precious guardrails without giving it a thought! This was something I never could understand.

"I wasn't anti-safety - no one wants to get killed or maimed - but I thought it was a double-edged sword, because more safety also meant more indiscipline.

"When I started, going off the road meant hitting a telegraph pole or a house or something. And it meant that for the other guy too. So respect for each other - common sense, really - was essential, and it stayed with me. But some of these people screaming for run-off areas and catchfencing and stuff gave the impression they intended to use it before the weekend was through."

JACKIE STEWART: "My attitude was that, as a driver, I was being paid for my skill. I wasn't being paid to risk my life. But it was a very tough job to get any support for what I wanted to do. There was criticism from some of the drivers and the media and people said that if Jackie Stewart couldn't stand the heat, he should get out of the kitchen. I was accused of trying to wrap the drivers in cotton wool. It was said I removed the romance from the sport, that the safety measures took away the swashbuckling spectacular that had been. In that 1966 Belgian Grand Prix, I ended upside down in a ditch with fuel leaking all around me and with no marshals, no safety crew to help me. So Graham Hill and Bob Bondurant, who had also crashed, had to get me out of the wreckage.

"As it turned out, I only had a broken collar bone, but when you see all these things happening you say this is just ridiculous. Here was a sport that had serious injury and death so closely associated with it, yet there was no infrastructure to support it, and very few safety measures to prevent it. So I felt I had to do something."

3 JULY 1966 - FRENCH GP (REIMS) John Surtees had won in Belgium for Ferrari, but the first man to win

World Championships on two wheels and four had tired of the internal politics at the Scuderia, and caused a sensation by quitting the team the following week. He appeared at Reims in a Cooper.

7 AUGUST 1966 - GERMAN GP (NÜRBURGRING)
JACK BRABHAM: "The German Grand Prix was extremely wet. It was a shocking race and a very dangerous one. I guarantee we drove every lap under a different set of circumstances, because of rain showers on different parts of the circuit. One lap you would come round and the track was dry and the next lap it would be all wet. And then you would hit rivers running across the road. I got a lot of satisfaction out of winning that race, because it was the first Grand Prix I had won at the 'Ring. I look back on that as more satisfying for me personally than perhaps any other race."

Driving in only his fourth Grand Prix, Englishman John Taylor, perhaps unsighted by the first-lap spray at the Flugplatz corner, hit the back of Jacky Ickx's Formula 2 Matra with his privately entered Brabham-BRM, which crashed and caught fire. The former RAF officer succumbed to his burn injuries a month later in hospital at Koblenz.

JACK BRABHAM: "We finished the season as champion constructors and I'd taken my third world championship for drivers. Obviously I was more pleased with these two things coming together than I had been in the Cooper days - or maybe more satisfied would be a better way of putting it. When you are older you definitely appreciate things more, and I felt that our designer Ron Tauranac, Repco, Esso, Goodyear, the accessory firms and all my mechanics were as much involved and as much to be praised as the driver.

"People used to think that we were financed entirely by Repco but this was not so. There was no direct financial backing from Repco at all, but their help came in a different way. Repco lent us the engines for three years. If we sold any, the money went to Repco, and any that were unused or obsolete went back to them.

"Phil Irving designed the engine, based on two main factors. One was that the engine should be capable of installation in existing Brabham chassis. The other was a desire to keep down frontal area to existing limits with the Climax engine, so we could keep the excellent penetration of the 1965 cars.

"We also aimed at making the Repco engine a mechanic's dream from the point of view of accessibility, with easy maintenance and replacement of parts. When we received the engine it was all we hoped it would be. It was giving over 300 horsepower to start with, it was very flexible and it had very good torque. It was an ideal engine to drive."

Opposite: Jochen Rindt starred for Cooper at scenic Watkins Glen, but the year belonged to Jack Brabham (above at Spa).

I thought Jochen was the sort of person who drove at ten-tenths most of the time. He was always driving that near the edge that something was liable to happen to him through no fault of his own. JACK BRABHAM

The New Zealander Denny Hulme won only twice in 1967 (although on the most difficult circuits, Monaco and the Nürburgring) but, even though Jim Clark won four times, the title was secured by Hulme at the final round. His happiness with this achievement was spoiled by two more fatal accidents during the season, which occurred while Jackie Stewart continued to pursue what was still mostly a single-handed safety crusade.

JACKIE STEWART: "The first helmet I had was a British Herbert Johnson model, because Stirling Moss used to have a Johnson. It was white and it was beautiful, but then I realised that it didn't give very good protection, so Paddy Hopkirk brought me over an American Bell helmet. The next thing was the heavy-duty overalls that Jo Bonnier was wearing. They were really heavy things and very uncomfortable. Then there was the 'Nomex' underwear, the balacalava, the seat harness and a series of things that kept developing."

Also in 1967, Ford Motor Company paid Cosworth Engineering £100,000 to develop a new 3-litre race engine. The deal proved to be probably the biggest bargain in Formula 1 history.

2 JANUARY 1967 - SOUTH AFRICAN GP (KYALAMI)
ROY SALVADORI (former driver and now Cooper Maserati team manager): "When Jochen Rindt and Pedro Rodriguez joined us early in 1967, they didn't get on at all well. For the first race of the season in South Africa, we couldn't get Rindt's car right. His engine blew and, though Pedro lost a couple of gears, he still won the race.

"Coming back on the aircraft to London, we were all together and Pedro wanted to learn gin rummy by playing with Jochen's manager, Bernie Ecclestone, and me. He insisted that we play for money - feeling lucky after he'd just won his first Grand Prix - and we stripped him. Jochen was desperate to play Pedro too, just to get into a fight with him. So he played Pedro, and Pedro won every game. Jochen was so angry that he packed up his briefcase and his hand luggage, and moved away from our seats, and when the plane stopped to refuel at Nairobi, he got off the plane and stayed there!"

7 MAY 1967 - MONACO GP (MONTE CARLO) In a race with only six finishers, Denny Hulme won the Monaco Grand Prix by a whole lap.

DENNY HULME: "I suppose I was lucky at Monaco, because Jackie [Stewart] broke down and I went on to win. This was the win I needed to set me up and I think it came partly because of oil on the circuit in the early part of the race. The car was handling superbly and, on the slippery circuit, it didn't seem to lose anything in lap times compared with my rivals. I don't know why this was so. It was just that the characteristics of the car were terrific that day. You could have talked to it and it would have gone round the corners. Monaco gave me a morale boost for the rest of the season because I knew that I was competitive and it was just a matter of staying there."

The Monaco Grand Prix was marred by Lorenzo Bandini's appalling accident, in which the handsome Italian was trapped for some time in his fiercely burning Ferrari. It was a day of infamy for the sport, made all the more terrible by the fact that the disaster was captured live on television and shown around the world.

ALAN HENRY: "On lap 82, as Bandini took the chicane on to the harbour front, his 312 clipped the inside wall with its right-hand wheels. It ran wide to the left, climbing up the straw bales, a wheel came off, the car turned over on to the track - and erupted into a horrifying pillar of flame. By the time Bandini was extricated from the Ferrari's smouldering remains, he was dreadfully burnt and, despite fighting for his life for three more excruciating days, eventually succumbed to his injuries.

"One can only begin to imagine what a trauma it was for Chris Amon, passing the scene of his team mate's accident again and again for the remainder of the race. His Ferrari was briefly delayed with a pitstop to change a deflated Firestone tyre, punctured on some of the accident debris, but Chris did well to come home third behind Hulme and Graham Hill's BRM."

CHRIS AMON: "I had gotten to know Lorenzo well and he was particularly supportive of having me in the team. I think his crash was a result of sheer fatigue. It was a long race, the thick end of three hours, and it was very hot that day. I know that by about the 75th lap I was actually starting to get cold in the car, which meant that I was totally dehydrated. I'm sure Lorenzo went through the same thing, and it was purely a lapse of concentration that caused him to run wide and hit the bales."

JOHN SURTEES: "Bandini had virtually cried and pleaded with me not to leave Ferrari the previous year. I said to people on the team: 'Look, you will kill the lad because of the sort of responsibility he'll face - an Italian in a Ferrari car isn't on.'"

ENZO FERRARI: "Bandini had an honest background as a mechanic, a precise and unhurried style, and an *amour propre*. He did very well in every type of car, a fact which made me liken him to Ginther, although I really thought of him as a potential Collins. His determination, loyalty and attachment to the team made me especially fond of him."

4 JUNE 1967 - DUTCH GP (ZANDVOORT) As Colin Chapman had used the Dutch Grand Prix for the debut of his monocoque Lotus 25 in 1962, so he used it five years later to launch his Lotus 49, a car tailored to the compact new Ford-Cosworth DFV. The engine was an immediate success. Graham Hill, now driving for Team Lotus, was on pole, and Jim Clark won the race.

KEN TYRRELL: "I went to Zandvoort when the Ford engine had its first outing and I was obviously very impressed with what it had done in practice and qualifying. I had lunch with Cosworth's Keith Duckworth and he was walking around like a cat on hot bricks, nervous as hell, and I said, 'You don't expect it to finish its first race. Don't worry about it. If it doesn't finish, it's already shown how good it is.' And of course it won. When I got back from that race, I ordered three of those engines."

DENNY HULME: "I knew the Lotuses were fast but I felt we had the edge on reliability. If he finished, Jim looked like the winner almost every time, but frankly I didn't feel that the Lotus 49 was the best car in the world. The greatest thing about it to my way of thinking was the engine. So far as handling was concerned, I thought that our cars were better.'

18 JUNE 1967 - BELGIAN GP (SPA) A week after he had won the Le Mans 24 Hours for Ford, co-driving A.J. Foyt, and pioneered the art of spraying champagne on the rostrum, Dan Gurney won again at Spa-Francorchamps - this time in his own Formula 1 car.

NIGEL ROEBUCK: "On the podium, the perennially luckless Gurney looked a little dazed. Two wins in seven days! Clark, who always considered Dan his only true rival, was delighted for him."

14 AUGUST 1967 Formula 1 lost one of its last privateers when Englishman Bob Anderson crashed while testing his four-year-old Brabham-Climax on the club circuit at Silverstone, prior to shipping it to Canada. The former motorcycle racer lost control on the rain-soaked straight and his car struck a marshals' post. Anderson was not wearing a seat harness and suffered severe chest and throat injuries, but no doctor was present, and half an hour passed before medical help arrived. He succumbed in hospital a few hours later.

10 SEPTEMBER 1967 - ITALIAN GP (MONZA) A year after quitting Ferrari, John Surtees rubbed it in for Italian fans by winning sensationally at Monza

for his new team, Honda. In the most thrilling finish for years, Jim Clark led going into the final lap, but had Surtees and Jack Brabham hard on his tail. Suddenly the Lotus slowed, starved of fuel, and Surtees took the lead. Then the Brabham-Repco outbraked the Honda V12 in the final corner, only to slide broadside across its bows, and Surtees held off his rival in a frantic dash to the chequered flag, to win by less than a car's length.

Although he coasted into third place, the result eliminated Clark from the title chase. Now he would not take the championship even if he won the final two Grands Prix - but it didn't stop him from doing just that. After winning in Mexico, Jim Clark invited third-placed Denny Hulme into his huge wreath of laurels as a celebration of Denny's title.

The new World Champion was nicknamed 'The Bear' and it described him perfectly, both for the people who liked him and those who didn't. He came across vividly as the claw-swiping grizzly to a legion of journalists who clashed with him. The International Press Association awarded him its 'lemon' prize two years in a row for being the least communicative Grand Prix driver. His reputation as a growler fed upon itself and grew to the point where Denny almost felt obliged to be gruff. He was a modern PR man's worst nightmare. And it all came about because all he really wanted to do was go racing and go home.

DENIS HULME: "I know it's very much a necessity for the sport to get worldwide publicity, but I still think it would survive without the so-called freeloading people. I had a pretty hard row to hoe to get to be World Champion and maybe I'm bitter about it. It was hard work, you know, it really was. I got where I did through very hard work. The press never gave me a fair crack of the whip until I was World Champion, so after that I clamped down on them.

"If they print the truth, OK. If they don't print the truth, that's where I mainly get bitter. A journalist is only going to make a slip once and I never forgive that. He's not a good journalist from there on in.

"I do vent my feeling a lot of times, by shouting at people at the wrong time, you know. But I say what I think, whether it's the right or the wrong time, but that doesn't particularly worry me. As long as I've said what I think, that's the main thing."

Opposite: Chris Amon emerges from the terrible pillar of smoke and flame where his trapped Ferrari team mate Lorenzo Bandini (inset) lies dying.
Top right: Denny 'The Bear' Hulme edged out his boss 'Black Jack' Brabham to win the 1967 driving title. Together they collected the Constructors' Championship for Brabham.

Jack could give the impression that he was a bit vague sometimes. He was quite good at that - particularly with anyone who wanted to talk about money. But he knew exactly what he was doing, and where he wanted to go.

DENNY HULME

You accept the fact that Formula 1 is totally futile and stupid and still you carry on, because what

is out there on the track is so exhilaraiting for the selfish man behind the wheel. JACKIE STEWART

Jimmy ranked with, perhaps even out-ranked, Nuvolari, Fangio and Moss, and I think we all felt he was in a way invincible. To be killed in an accident with a Formula 2 car is almost unacceptable.

BRUCE McLAREN

The face of Formula 1 changed forever in January 1968 when the Team Lotus cars were re-liveried from the traditional British colour scheme of green with a central yellow stripe, to the red and gold of a Player's Gold Leaf cigarette packet. Traditionalists were appalled, but the age of commercialism had arrived, and typically Colin Chapman was first to seize the opportunity. This season Ken Tyrrell put a package together to compete in Formula 1 as a private entrant, with a chassis from Matra, the new Ford-Cosworth engine, Dunlop tyres - and Jackie Stewart as his trump card. The Tyrrell/Stewart partnership would soon become one of the most successful in Formula 1 history.

Early in the year, Formula 1 was changed forever in the most tragic way, when one of the greatest racing drivers of all time lost his life.

1 JANUARY 1968 - SOUTH AFRICAN GP (KYALAMI) Jim Clark won for the 25th time. It was his 72nd and last Grand Prix.

7 APRIL 1968 - HOCKENHEIM The great Jim Clark only ever made small mistakes, and had very few accidents. The biggest crash of his career killed him when a rear tyre deflated and came off the rim of his works Lotus during a Formula 2 race at Hockenheim in Germany.

GRAHAM HILL: "At Hockenheim I remember soldiering on in about eighth place and, every time I came into the infield, I could see Jimmy in front of me on one of the twisty bits of track - then he disappeared. I thought perhaps he had gained a bit on me, or lost a bit, and was just in a different part of the circuit. About the same time I also noticed on the back straight, on one of the fastest bits of the circuit, that there were some skid marks going off the track and into the trees. I realised straight away that whoever had gone off there was in serious trouble, but it never occurred to me that it could have been poor Jimmy. For me, it was very touching to find in Jimmy somebody who wasn't hard and cynical but was basically a warm, honest person."

COLIN CHAPMAN: "Jim raced because he loved it. Naturally, he made a lot of money out of it, but to him it was a sport, not a business. If he had his way, at the end of a race he would creep away into obscurity until it was time for the next race. He was not interested in the glamour or the thrills."

JACKIE STEWART: "Nobody knew what was going on inside Jim. He was an incredibly private person. He isolated himself. But you could see his anxiety, and it got worse as he got older. He had a stiffness in his

shoulders. He was the coolest, calmest, most calculating racing driver in the world, yet he continually chewed his fingernails with nervousness. In a way he was a terribly highly tensed man and yet the moment he slipped into a racing car he changed."

Innes Ireland, having retired from driving in 1966, was now the Sports Editor of *Autocar* magazine. He wrote an acclaimed obituary for his fellow Scot...

INNES IRELAND: "I have known Jim Clark for perhaps longer than any of his contemporaries, for my father was a veterinarian surgeon in the area of the Clark farms in Scotland - in fact I bought one of my first racing cars from his brother-in-law, another farmer nearby. We spent two good years together in Team Lotus in 1960 and 1961. But to my great regret, I did not know him as well as I might, for our early friendship was later clouded over by the circumstances of my leaving Lotus.

"His past performances need no recollection here - they are indelibly printed in the record books for posterity. He had a great love for his heritage, which was the basically simple, rustic life of farming and animal husbandry: but his dedication to motor racing was even greater, for he forced himself to leave all this behind to concentrate on his chosen profession. And it is in this light that we must remember him, for he died as he lived, giving his all in a racing car.

"I am sure that he would express no regrets at the violence of his passing and surely this is answer enough for us who are left. I can only say to look at it as he would have done - otherwise his life has been in vain. And to those who still question the wisdom of people who wish to risk their lives in racing cars, I would say that motor racing, as a sport, is the most exacting, demanding, exhilarating and, above all, satisfying sport in which a man with red blood in his veins could indulge."

CHRIS AMON: "I don't think Jimmy's death slowed anybody down but I think it probably cast some doubts in people's minds because, if it could happen to him, it could happen to anyone. A lot of us had a sort of 'bullet-proof' attitude at the time and it certainly put a dent in that."

COLIN CHAPMAN: "For me, Jimmy will always be the best driver the world has ever known."

7 MAY 1968 A month to the day after Jim Clark had died, his former Lotus team mate Mike Spence was killed during practice for the Indianapolis 500.

His fellow Scot Innes Ireland (top left), Lotus boss Colin Chapman (centre, inset) and the entire racing world found it hard to believe that the great Jim Clark was dead.

12 MAY 1968 - SPANISH GP (JARAMA) GRAHAM HILL: "I was delighted to win in Spain for the team after the sadness we all felt. It was my first Grand Prix win since the American race in 1965, so it was a long time since I had seen the chequered flag."

8 JUNE 1968 Italian all-rounder Lodovico Scarfiotti, the proud winner of the 1966 Italian Grand Prix at Monza for Ferrari, was a works Cooper driver in 1968. He was killed on the day before the Belgian Grand Prix, practising for a round of the European Hillclimb Championship at Rossfeld, when his Porsche sports-racing car flew off the road into a clump of trees.

9 JUNE 1968 - BELGIAN GP (SPA) The Belgian Grand Prix that summer produced another freak result. Several cars had the lead during the race and, at the chequered flag, the winner was convinced he had finished second...

BRUCE McLAREN: "I crossed the finishing line at Spa, gave a bit of a wave at the chequered flag, braked hard, pulled in behind the pits and tried to drive the car back up to our transporter. Second place in the Belgian Grand Prix wasn't too bad. I'd got boxed in quite badly at the start and had to get through most of the field, but I was feeling quite pleased. Our crew seemed pleased too, and they had been jumping up and down as I crossed the line. There were so many people milling about at the back of the pits that I had to stop the car and climb out.

"One of the BRM mechanics, Cyril Atkins, ran up talking excitedly about Jackie Stewart's last-minute pitstop and shouted something like 'What a finish! You crossed the line number one,' he said. My number was five - I wasn't quite sure what he was on about. Then he shouted 'You've won! Didn't you know?' I didn't know, and it's about the nicest thing I've ever been told. I had won a Grand Prix in a car with my name on the nose!"

23 JUNE 1968 - DUTCH GP (ZANDVOORT) In Holland, the Stewart/Tyrrell partnership paid its first dividend, although it was accomplished with a comparatively small budget. Ken Tyrrell, who had been successful as a Formula 2 entrant with Matra, got the Formula 1 chassis free from the French aerospace company. His biggest bill for the season was for engines, five Cosworth DFVs at £7500 each. The driver, who never signed a contract but confirmed their deal with a handshake with Ken Tyrrell, was not that expensive either, although the canny 'Wee Scot' would go on to become the first millionaire racing driver.

JACKIE STEWART: "When I drove for Ken in Formula 2 in 1964 I had maybe £150 in the bank. If someone had said to me in those days that I was going to earn £5000 a year, I would have thought it was fantastic. But then, when I started out with Ken in Formula 1, I saw that I could make £8000 or £9000 a year and

That year of 1968 was horrific, with a driver being killed on or about the seventh of each month. On the seventh day of each month you weren't that keen to go out in the car. CHRIS AMON

suddenly that was awful big money. There weren't a lot of people making that sort of money then who weren't executives or something of the kind."

7 JULY 1968 - FRENCH GP (ROUEN) The victory by new Ferrari recruit Jacky Ickx on the Rouen road course was the first achieved by a car fitted with a rear aerofoil. Sadly, it is also remembered for a more sombre reason. Driving a Formula 1 car for the first time at the age of 40, Jo Schlesser crashed his Honda and was burned to death in the cockpit. His team mate, John Surtees, had urged Honda not to race the unproven new car in which Schlesser lost his life.

20 JULY 1968 - BRITISH GP (BRANDS HATCH) Rob Walker bought a Lotus 49 for Jo Siffert, but the Swiss destroyed it in a huge accident in initial testing at Brands Hatch.

ROB WALKER: "That was bad enough, but when the wreckage was taken back to our workshops in Pippbrook, a spark from one of the mechanic's drills ignited fuel vapour, and the whole lot went up. I lost what remained of the Lotus, of course, but also my ex-Seaman Delage, as well as scrapbooks and souvenirs collected from 30 years of racing. It was heartbreaking.

"We carried on. A new Lotus 49 was completed by our mechanics just before the British Grand Prix at Brands Hatch. And we won! It was Seppi's first World Championship Grand Prix victory and for me, after all the drama of our last visit to Brands Hatch, it was like a fairytale."

Opposite: Jo Schlesser died when his Honda crashed on the second lap of his first Grand Prix.
Below: Jackie Oliver (pictured with a Lotus mechanic) was the miraculous survivor of a violent accident in the same race.

4 AUGUST 1968 - GERMAN GP (NÜRBURGRING)

JACKIE STEWART: "Even in perfect conditions it really was a ridiculous place - over 14 miles to the lap, more than 170 corners - the most dangerous circuit in the world, where over 100 people had been killed over the years. In the car you would be leaping six feet in the air from one bump to another, trees and cliffs and rocks and ditches on every side. I thanked God whenever I finished a lap there.

"In all, I won four times there. Nothing gave me more satisfaction than to win at the Nürburgring, and yet I was always afraid. When I left home to race in the German Grand Prix, I always used to pause at the end of the driveway and take a long look back at my house. I was never sure I would come home again.

"In that 1968 race, I found myself going into the first corner lying third behind Graham Hill and Chris Amon. The spray was absolutely unbelievable - I couldn't see anything at all! I couldn't see my braking distance marks; I couldn't see the car in front. I tried to get out of the spray and go up the inside, and by doing this,

I managed to see a little more clearly. I hate to think what was going on behind me! This situation continued for the majority of the lap, but I passed Chris on the hill towards Adenau.

"The track is narrow, the undulations so pronounced, the bends so numerous, that you can hardly remember where you are on the circuit even on a clear day, but in fog and ceaseless spray you just have no idea at all. In addition, you are continually worried by the fact that you are aquaplaning and almost always losing control, and you feel sure that the man in front is doing the same thing so that at any moment he is going to appear just in front of you pointing in the wrong direction.

"After passing Chris, it was then a case of finding the right spot on the circuit to overtake Graham. This I dearly wanted to do before the start of the straight, so I managed to come out of the small Karussel at the end of the swallow-tail corner pretty well and I got an advantage on Graham at this point, overtaking him just entering the last corner before the straight. This meant

that I had the complete home straight to myself without any hindrance from spray. I knew what Graham was going through because at the speed reached on the straight, which was getting on for 170mph, the spray was staying at road level for a tremendously long time due to the hedges keeping it back - and of course with no wind, and the mixture of fog and mist, you can imagine how impossible visibility was from behind.

"After this, it was only a matter of driving as fast as I possibly could because you simply can see nothing in your mirrors with so much spray around unless the next car is very close behind you. After two laps I had an advantage of 34 seconds or so and I managed to build up steadily on this, trying as hard as I could to stay on the road since there were so many times when one was almost sliding off, or hitting some new puddle that wasn't there on the previous lap.

"With only three laps to go, it really started to pour down with rain all round the circuit, and the track became really treacherous. At a point about half a mile from the Karussel I entered an S-bend in third gear and

Nürburgring, 1968 - thick fog and rain. You could hardly see the road. There were probably close to 400,000 spectators, though they mustn't have seen much of it. It was just a great wall of spray. I cannot remember having been more frightened in a racing car.

JACKIE STEWART

suddenly lost control in a deep river of water which was running across the road. The car immediately started sliding, the engine stalled, and I was hurtling across the road towards a marshal who was standing beside his post completely unprotected. He dived one way; then decided to jump the other way; then suddenly he just froze, and I knew I was going to hit him. But just then the wheels got a little bit of grip and I managed to regain control. Graham, in fact, who was some way behind, arrived at the same corner and spun off, but by this time the marshal had moved his position to somewhere a bit safer!

"At last, I took the chequered flag just over four minutes ahead of Graham. It was a tremendously satisfying race to win, but I was very pleased to get it over with. I can remember thinking as I went down to the South Turn after taking the chequered flag that this was perhaps my greatest ambition as far as winning on any circuit is concerned.

"But that 1968 race should never have been held, and having won it by such a big margin gave me more credibility when I demanded changes in the interest of safety. Even after I had won there four times I was criticised, and if I had wanted to win a popularity contest, I wouldn't have done what I did."

6 OCTOBER 1968 - US GP (WATKINS GLEN) Jackie Stewart won the US race but it was Mario Andretti, driving a third Lotus 49, who made Formula 1 history by qualifying on pole position in his first

Grand Prix. The Italian-born American star led the race initially before retiring with a clutch failure, but it whetted his appetite for more.

MARIO ANDRETTI: "I was lucky because the Lotus 49 was the car of the moment - it would be like a rookie getting into a Ferrari or McLaren today. It suited my style because I felt immediately in control, and very much at home. It was light and forgiving with a beautiful little gearbox. You could drift it. It was like a dream. Right away I was at the limit. That's when I truly fell in love with a Formula 1 car. I felt: 'This is where I belong.'"

3 NOVEMBER 1968 - MEXICAN GP (MEXICO CITY) Graham Hill clinched the championships for himself and Team Lotus with a victory in Mexico. It emerged later that he had been fortunate...

GRAHAM HILL: "For this race, we'd devised a scheme whereby we could flatten the rear wing. I had an extra pedal over the top of the clutch and, after I'd finished changing gear, I'd press this pedal and put the wing flat for extra speed down the straights. When I took my foot off it, the wing snapped back into the right position for the corners. Shortly after the start of the race, this pedal went light, and I saw in my mirror that one of the two rubber straps that operated the whole system had broken. So the World Championship rested on a single rubber band..."

Opposite: Stewart's stunning margin of victory in appalling conditions at the notorious Nürburgring was the result of outstanding skill and exceptional courage.
Above: Hill (foreground) was second to Stewart in Germany, but went on to beat him by eight points to win the 1968 championship.
Overleaf: Jochen Rindt's ill-fated Lotus led from the start at Montjuich Park

We all get scared, but I get scared that something will happen with the car.

It's the cars that break, not the drivers. JOCHEN RINDT

The last season of the decade began with the cars sprouting ungainly wings on various parts of the chassis. Rear-mounted aerofoils had first appeared on the Ferraris and Brabhams the previous season, in Belgium, but their function was not fully understood by the rival teams. But now everybody had realised that the wings helped the cars stick to the road, and the designers experimented furiously with them. The pioneer in the field had reservations...

RON TAURANAC: "I really think that racing would be better without wings, even though we used them first. I reckon they have served their purpose and helped development, but it's got to the stage now where you could design a really good car, and it wouldn't work without a wing. If a wing falls off a car now, it just isn't competitive. If wings aren't banned, they should at least be strictly regulated with some form of maximum span. There are no regulations at all governing wings because the regs were written before the wings appeared."

4 MAY 1969 - SPANISH GP (MONTJUICH PARK) For the Spanish Grand Prix in Barcelona, wings were extended to their ultimate, Colin Chapman having found that the higher the rear wings were raised on the Lotus 49s, the better the lap-times of Graham Hill and his new team mate, Jochen Rindt. At the start of the race, Rindt stormed away into the lead with Chris Amon's Ferrari and the Lotuses of Jo Siffert and Hill behind. Hill passed Siffert but almost immediately careened off the track into the guardrail. The rear wing supporting struts had collapsed. Hill escaped unharmed but, as he checked the damage, Rindt's wing failed at the same point on the circuit.

HEINZ PRULLER (Rindt biographer): "On the 20th lap, and at a speed of about 140mph, Jochen's wing gave way. The aerofoil bent back, and this resulted in the lifting effect which Jochen had always feared. The rear of his car rose up and appeared to climb the guardrails, which had fortunately been raised on Jochen's insistence a few weeks earlier; the car was thrown to the right, collided with the remains of Hill's Lotus, turned over and slid along the track upside down.

"Graham's 'golden hands' which had rescued the trapped Stewart at Spa in 1966, now came to Jochen's immediate assistance. Petrol was running everywhere in enormous quantities; the smallest spark could have started an inferno. Jochen's face was bleeding badly but he was conscious and muttered: 'Shit!' The next day, lying dazed in hospital with concussion, a broken jaw and a broken nose, Rindt mumbled to his wife Nina: 'I always wondered what Jimmy felt at Hockenheim. Now I think I know: nothing.'

"Jochen told me that he thought his bad luck was destroying him that summer. His bad luck affected him as much as the atmosphere in the team and he argued constantly with Chapman. The moment Jochen started to talk to Chapman, the conversation disintegrated into nothing. He therefore took to phoning Bernie Ecclestone (his manager), and Bernie thereupon telephoned Chapman at Lotus.

"When they arrived at the Nürburgring for the Formula 2 race that Jochen would win, both Chapman and Rindt realised that things just couldn't go on. For three hours they squatted in the transporter; they even missed half the Friday morning practice. Chapman showed Jochen a huge photo of him in an English newspaper, captioned 'Is this man the perfect race driver?' Chapman said: 'Don't believe it, Jochen. You're far from it. You're fine in the car but you're a bastard outside.'"

Five days after his crash in Spain, Rindt wrote a letter to Chapman from his home in Geneva. The letter was judged so controversial that the English publishers of Rindt's biography, written after his death (following a mechanical failure in a Lotus) by his Austrian journalist friend, Heinz Pruller, chose not to print it. The letter, in English, was reproduced in the appendix of the German language edition.

JOCHEN RINDT: "Dear Colin,

I just got back to Geneva and I am going to have a second opinion on the state of my head tomorrow. Personally I feel very weak and ill. I still have to lay down most of the day. After seeing the new Doktor [sic] and hearing his opinion we can make a final decision on Monaco and Indy.

"I got hold of this incredibly [sic] picture which pretty much explains the accident. I didn't know it would fly that high.

"Now to our whole situation, Colin. I have been racing F1 for 5 years and I have made one mistake (I rammed Chris Amon at Clermont-Ferrand) and I had one accident at Zandvoort due to gearselektion [sic] failure - otherwise I managed to stay out of trouble. This situation changed rapidly since I joined your team. Levin, Eifelrace F2 wishbones and now Barcelona [all accidents caused by mechanical failure].

"Honestly your cars are so quick that we would still be competitive with a few extra pounds used to make the weakest parts stronger. On top of that I think you ought to spend some time checking what your different employees are doing. Please give my suggestions some thought. I can only drive a car in which I have some confidence and I feel the point of no confidence is quite near."

Top left: Hill stands by the remains of his Lotus moments before his team mate Rindt crashed into it.
Opposite: Before the race Rindt was worried about the fragility of the rear wing. Its failure left him lucky to suffer only a concussion, a broken jaw and a broken nose.

18 MAY 1969 - MONACO GP (MONTE CARLO) The outrageous high-mounted wings were abruptly banned on safety grounds, after the first day of practice at Monaco.

7 SEPTEMBER 1969 Jackie Stewart ran over a hare at the start at Monza, then won his fifth race in a row.

JACKIE STEWART: "It sprinted right into my path. My right front tyre hit it. There was no question of me deviating even a fraction to avoid it. I would have had an accident and taken half the starters in the Italian Grand Prix off the road with me. I went through agonies for the next few laps, thinking a bone had lodged in the tyre and it might suddenly deflate."

5 OCTOBER 1969 - US GP (WATKINS GLEN) Graham Hill's Lotus was fitted with experimental Firestone tyres which were badly worn late in the race, and Hill spun, stalling the engine. He had to get out and push-start his car, then headed back to the pits for a tyre change. He had had a bad accident and had been unable to do up his seat harness.

GRAHAM HILL: "I'll never know whether this was a good thing or a bad thing. The right rear tyre collapsed and the car went out of control. It veered off the track, hit a bank, shot me out and rolled over. I carried on rolling along the ground. The car ended up upside down. I had broken my right knee just on the joint, dislocated the left one and torn all the ligaments.
  "I can remember very little of the accident, except going backwards at high speed. I must have been a bit dozy in hospital because I can remember some of the lads coming to see me directly after the race and I told them to tell Bette that I wouldn't be dancing for a while."

Hill's young team mate, Jochen Rindt went on to win his first Grand Prix.

JOCHEN RINDT: "There was no overpowering feeling of happiness, perhaps because I should have won so often in the past.

Jackie Stewart fully understood that his Drivers title and Tyrrell's Constructors championship resulted from a team effort.

JACKIE STEWART: "Ken is so practical. That's his talent in my mind. He's such a practical man. This can be taken the wrong way but it's not meant to be - he has such a simple mind, it's not a complicated mind, it's not full of little devious, intricate plans. Everything has to be slotted in the right way and that's where the success came from. He chooses his mechanics and crew well. They're as solid as the Rock of Gibraltar. They are no-nonsense, practical people. Few smoke or drink, simple things like that. I don't mean that to be a criterion, but it's a funny thing that they all very conservative - and very good.

Until the last moment I didn't believe the car would last. Not until the final lap, and not quite even then.

JOCHEN RINDT

Right: Jochen Rindt recovered from his accident at Montjuich to win for the first time at Watkins Glen - where his team mate Hill crashed heavily and badly injured both legs.

The Seventies

Competition became more and more fierce, but with it came a series of appalling accidents that shook Formula 1 to its very foundations. There were some miraculous escapes, but far too many drivers perished in 'the cruel sport'. This mounting toll created a sense of doom, so the racers - and their families and friends - were forced to prepare themselves for the worst. After burying several of his peers, Jackie Stewart abruptly retired, although his safety crusade eventually began to pay dividends. Humour occasionally leavened the heartbreak, as with the arrival of the colourful Hesketh team, whose driver James Hunt featured in the dramatic 1976 championship showdown with Niki Lauda, whose heroic comeback from near death astonished the world.

Above, from left: Robin Herd, Alan Rees, Graham Coaker and Max Mosley (later, president of the FIA) used an acronym of their names for their new team. But the initial success of March was resented.

You could feel the annoyance, hatred almost, of some of the Grand Prix establishment because we'd pulled it off. For our part, we were pretty arrogant, as one tends to be when one's young. I suppose it was hubris. MAX MOSLEY

Seven different drivers and five different teams won races in the rollercoaster season of 1970, despite the arrival of a car which established design principles that endure to this day. Colin Chapman's innovative Lotus 72, with its chisel nose, wedge-shaped aerodynamics and side-mounted radiators, would become the class of the field. Sadly, though, this was also a deadly year...

7 MARCH 1970 - SOUTH AFRICAN GP (KYALAMI) Jack Brabham was 43 years old going into the new season, and he knew it would be his last at the wheel of a Grand Prix car. And yet, after Jackie Stewart and Chris Amon had set the pace in practice in South Africa with their Marches, the 'Old Man' romped home a dominant winner.
March was an acronym for the names of the company's founders: Max Mosley, Alan Rees, Graham Coaker, Robin Herd. But March's ambitions seemed so outrageous - the company had only begun producing Formula 3 cars in 1969 and now planned a complete range of proprietary racers from Formula Ford right through to Formula 1 - that the motor racing press had taken to calling it 'Much Advertised Racing Car Hoax'.

MAX MOSLEY: "Robin and I walked from our pit, which was at the bottom end of the lane, up to the front of the grid, savouring the whole thing. Everything we'd set out to do, we'd done - there were two of our cars sitting at the front with equal times. It was one of the most extraordinary moments of my life. For our part, we were pretty arrogant, as one tends to be when one's young. I've often talked over those times with Robin and we agree that the biggest mistake we made was being too pleased with ourselves."

19 APRIL 1970 - SPANISH GP (JARAMA) Jackie Stewart won in Spain, but it was to be the only time that his March achieved the feat and, near the end of the season, his entrant, Ken Tyrrell, fielded his own car. The year had started safely, but an indication of the tragedies that lay in wait came in Spain when Jackie Oliver's BRM broke a stub axle and crashed into Jacky Ickx's Ferrari. Both drivers escaped, but both their cars were consumed by fire.

JACKIE OLIVER: "It was the first lap of the race. I was coming downhill when the inside hub broke. It snapped off. The wheel came off. I lost the brakes. I swerved to avoid Bruce McLaren going into the downhill hairpin - nearly 180 degrees of hairpin. I tried to go across the grass to cut out the hairpin, but I was going too quickly - about 100mph. The car swivelled and hit Jacky Ickx

as he was accelerating his Ferrari out of the hairpin. It was the worst thing that can happen. The Ferrari was carrying 48 gallons of fuel."
JACKIE STEWART: "It was my moment of horror. As I came round on my second lap I saw the smoke from the two burning cars before I got round the corner. But I was travelling too fast to do much about it. I was faced with a wall of fire. In an instant I decided to go on, and I actually drove through the flames and smoke. By then I had decided to give the car full throttle. It was all over in a second or two. But when I think about it I realise that it was miraculous nobody was hurt."
JACKIE OLIVER: "I wasn't trapped, although the bulkhead was crumpled and I had to lever it away. In the flames it was like being in a dark room. You can't see anything. I got out of the car. Everything sizzled. The Perspex visor of my helmet bubbled and blistered. A Spanish marshal thought the helmet was on fire. He grabbed me and tried to pull it off. I was kicking him on the shins. I rolled around on the ground to put out the flames."

Bruce McLaren finished second in Spain with a car of his own design.

BRUCE MCLAREN: "People have just lately begun to compare me with Colin Chapman. I think Colin is a lot cleverer than I am. In fact, I know he is. He is a very sharp, quick thinker. Chapman will innovate for the sake of innovating.
"I am not interested in building the fastest car. I think you have to be capable of getting on the front row of the grid to be sure of winning a race, but I'm all for reliability, too. We haven't yet built our ideal Formula 1 car, but we're working on it!
"As to my driving, I don't feel I've really won a race unless I've beaten the best guys in motor racing. Unfortunately, a basic caution has stayed with me from my early days, when to shunt the car would have meant the end of my career. I know I am considered to be the perfect Number 2 in a team, the eternal runner-up. That aggravates me. I'd much rather win, of course, but the ability isn't always there. Sometimes it is, sometimes I can do it. I wish I could do it all the time, but I have no illusions. I know I can't. Stewart, Rindt and Andretti all seem to be able to go faster than I can. So does Denny. He used not to be able to, but he certainly can now. He's just plain better. Jack Brabham is amazing - he has this tremendous ability to put one great lap together.
"But in 1959, when I began my first season in a works Formula 1 team, for Cooper, I was under instructions not to bend the car. I was 22, and I drove carefully and sensibly, and I didn't bend the car, but maybe that caution stayed with me too long."

The fuel bags ignited. The fuel sprayed out. The air was full of petrol vapour and droplets. It went up like a napalm bomb. JACKIE OLIVER

10 MAY 1970 - MONACO GP (MONTE CARLO)
Monaco provided the most dramatic finish of the year, when Jochen Rindt suddenly came alive and pressured Jack Brabham into a costly mistake in the last corner. The new Lotus 72 was still proving troublesome so Rindt was in the now ageing 49C, and sulking along in fourth place, when he suddenly scented a chance of victory and began pushing the well-used Lotus for all it was worth - and then some.

ANDREW MARRIOTT (*Motoring News*): "The race could well go down in the annals of motor racing history as one of the great epics, for the Austrian snatched the lead on the last corner as Jack Brabham barrelled straight on at the Gasometer Hairpin. It was a race of changing fortunes and one should not lose sight of the fact that Jackie Stewart took the lead at the start and pulled into a strong lead before a transistor box let him down. Spare a thought, too, for both STP March drivers, Amon and Siffert, who easily could have been at Brabham's heels on those last vital laps, save for last-minute retirements. But Rindt takes the glory for his fantastic performance in the second part of the race and his super-human last lap of 1m 23.3s, which is a new record for the fascinating circuit.

"What a fantastic last lap it was, with Rindt driving faster than he ever has done before or is likely to again. Round the Station hairpin, they were nose to tail and, by the time they dived into the darkness of the tunnel, there was still only feet in it. Rindt had three chances, the chicane, the Tabac and the Gasometer hairpin. There is no way past at the chicane and, for that matter, there was no room at the Tabac either. It had to be Brabham's race.

"That dash down to the hairpin is one of motor racing's all-time great moments. In front of Brabham and Rindt were two backmarkers. Which side should Brabham go, for one of the chaps was in the middle of the road?

"The veteran Australian chose the inside, a quick glance in his mirror to see where Rindt was, and all of a sudden it was all happening right into the eyes of the world's watching millions. Brabham smashed on to the brakes but he simply could not stop in time. He scrubbed off most of the speed, but unbelievably failed to make the turn and nudged quite slowly into the Armco. For Rindt, it was like a fairy tale and he accelerated back up towards the Automobile Club to take the chequered flag for a staggering win."

Above: Bruce McLaren and Mario Andretti race past the still flaming wreckage from the Ickx/Oliver collision at Jarama.

THE DEATH OF BRUCE McLAREN

2 JUNE 1970 The McLaren team missed Monaco, after team founder Bruce McLaren had been killed in a testing accident at the Goodwood circuit in rural Sussex.

DAVID PHIPPS (*Autocourse*): "Tuesday, June 2nd, 1970, was one of those perfect English summer days to which only a Shakespeare or a Wordsworth could do justice. We were planning to go down to Goodwood to watch Bruce testing his 1970 CanAm car. He had promised to drive me round the track in it, once it was sorted out to his satisfaction, and this was to be the day.

"We were a bit late getting away, but it was such a glorious morning there didn't seem to be any great urgency. The sun shone from a cloudless blue sky, the chestnut trees were in full flower, and the countryside could never look more beautiful. We sang almost all the way there.

"When we reached the circuit, instead of the expected and well-known sounds of a McLaren test day, there was an ominous silence hanging over the whole area, as still as the warm summer air. We drove right up to the pits, saw the pit counter strewn with tools, and the transporter open but empty. Then we heard that dreadful, urgent, two-note ambulance siren...

There was nothing that we, or anyone else could do. Bruce was dead, they said. And I couldn't understand how the sun could keep on shining, the birds go on singing. Everything was the same; and yet nothing could ever be the same again.

"Bruce was a very competitive person, though with an easy-going charm and infinite good nature. Certainly, anyone who knew him learned a lot from just knowing him. I would clearly like to think that a little of his rare quality has rubbed off on all of us."

When he died Bruce McLaren's cars had won four races. Three decades later McLaren had become one of the most successful teams in motor racing history.

To do something well is so worthwhile that to die trying to do it better cannot be foolhardy. Life is measured in achievement, not years alone. BRUCE MCLAREN

Pedro loved Spa for the same reason I loved it. Spa was Grand Prix racing as we always thought it should be. CHRIS AMON

7 JUNE 1970 - BELGIAN GP (SPA-FRANCORCHAMPS)
BRM's hopes for its P153 were finally justified on the fastest track of them all, Spa-Francorchamps, where Pedro Rodriguez beat Chris Amon's March after a scintillating performance by the bold and underrated Mexican. The challenges of this daunting circuit in the Belgian forest aroused strong passions among the drivers.

JACKIE STEWART: "Along with the Nürburgring, Spa is one of the two most dangerous circuits in the world. Very fast, with lap speeds in excess of 150mph, through the Ardennes forest, so that if you go off you're almost certain to hit a house or land in the trees. Frequently, without warning, it rains, and the course is so long, almost nine miles around, that it can be wet on one side and perfectly dry on the other; you can find yourself driving into a downpour on dry tyres at speeds as high as 190mph.

"This year, after practice ended, we had a GPDA meeting which turned into a hassle when Ickx and Rodriguez stood up to insist they're going to run even if it rains. Ickx and Rodriguez say they're duty-bound to run even if it's pissing with rain, because people have come to see them. To listen to them, you'd think they had a mission.

"I understand their sentiments, but their lack of prudence completely baffles me. If it's raining, there's going to be a problem not only of spray but speed, of extreme aquaplaning. If you lose control, it's not like at other tracks where you just spin down the road and stop before hitting something solid. Here you're going to obliterate yourself. It's not difficult to imagine three or four of us being wiped out in an afternoon, not to mention the possibility of our taking a couple of hundred spectators with us.

"Jacky Ickx has an image that is the direct opposite to mine. He has short hair, I've got long hair; he wears three-piece suits, I go Mod; he talks about risks, while I talk about safety. I like Jacky and I say this not as a concession, but his temperament is uneven. You see it in his driving.

"And now he wants to drive Spa in the wet. Doubtless, the man is among the top three or four drivers in the world, but he still can't come to grips with the fact that Spa, his very own Belgian Spa, is lethal. In the meeting Ickx finished up by saying that we're all test pilots and must accept the possibility we might crash and die.

"Pedro? Certainly not one of your more stable individuals. His thinking rarely goes to depth, and now I'm almost certain he's incapable of anything short of an emotional response. His wet-weather reputation has been won mainly in sports cars where not everyone goes fast, and I wouldn't classify him as one

Rodriguez is everything the neophyte thinks about racing drivers. Hot-blooded, Latin, and totally irrational. JACKIE STEWART

of the more prominent drivers. He's too excitable. He might be coming out of the pits with no hope of winning and you'd be coming up on him, and still he wouldn't let you by, not gracefully. Instead of thinking, 'Well, this guy's about to lap me, I ought to let him through, I can tuck in behind him,' Pedro will try to race with you. He's all heads down. In practice he gets terribly excited, and when he's in one of these states it's best to stay away from him."

JOHN BLUNSDEN (*Motor Racing Year*): "It rarely happens that Grand Prix teams openly applaud the victory of rivals, but there was almost universal cheering the moment that Pedro Rodriguez swept across the finishing line at Spa to record the first BRM victory for four seasons. It was not just the fact that BRM had at last broken their 'duck' with a 3-litre car, but also the manner of the victory, for Rodriguez had won his race the hard way, not by default.

"He had made an excellent start from the third row of the grid, and was fourth at the end of the first lap, behind Amon's March, Stewart's March and Rindt's Lotus 49C. On lap three he moved ahead of the Lotus into third place, by which time Amon had temporarily lost his lead to Stewart, and then won it back again. Lap four, and

Rodriguez also passed Stewart to run second to Amon, and on lap five the Mexican put the BRM into the lead.

JACKIE STEWART: "It was a good win for Pedro. He drove well, and as Jochen and I were watching from the pits, it was pretty clear he was holding off Chris, showing a discipline he seems to be able to muster only on high-speed circuits. Perhaps Pedro gets bored when the danger isn't obvious.

"But I want Spa stopped. I say this categorically. I don't think the place is safe or right for modern racing. It's the fastest road course we visit, true, but the fables that have been built up around the place are absurd, absolute crap. The notion that it's a maker of men is ridiculous.

"Those people who say they like Spa? Bullshit. Nobody likes Spa. I defy any man to say he likes the place, to tell me he doesn't think twice before leaving home, and continue to think about it on his way there and then think about it the night before he's going to drive. A cloud of depression hangs over everybody. Anybody who claims he likes the place, says that he drives it at ten-tenths, is simply not telling the truth. He's conning himself, either that or he's never done the place at speed and doesn't know what he's talking about."

Opposite: Eau Rouge, Spa's breathtaking rollercoaster-ride-of-a-corner, separated the men from the boys. Stewart braved it best to take pole, averaging 151.638mph.
Top right: Pedro Rodriguez (left in picture) and Chris Amon finished first and second at Spa. Rodriguez averaged 149.942mph, while Amon got fastest lap, at 152.077mph.

137

21 JUNE 1970 - DUTCH GP (ZANDVOORT) Tragedy again stalked the Formula 1 circus when it arrived in Zandvoort for the Dutch Grand Prix. Revisions to the Lotus 72 had turned it into a winner, but there were no celebrations for Jochen Rindt after the death of his close friend, Piers Courage, who crashed his De Tomaso and succumbed in the flaming wreckage.

At Monaco, Courage's entrant Frank Williams had found himself quietly watching Piers and Sally having a drink together - the dashing blade and his pretty wife savouring their seemingly carefree existence.

FRANK WILLIAMS: "I don't know why, but for some reason I just thought to myself, 'It's all too good.' Just over a month later, Piers was gone."

JACKIE STEWART (diary entry): "June 21, 1970: Most of what follows is in retrospect. I couldn't keep the diary after the race, not with Piers dead, nor could I do it for days afterwards. Even now, it's difficult.

"Both Helen and I have now seen more of life and death than most people see in two lifetimes. Four weeks after Jimmy died in '68, it was Mike Spence at Indianapolis; four weeks later, another friend, Lodovico Scarflotti; four weeks more, to the day, it was Jo Schlesser in Rouen; and two weeks ago, Bruce McLaren at Goodwood. Now it's Piers. It just keeps on...

"Helen had come to Zandvoort, the boys were home with their nanny, and we thought it would be a good time. Helen comes only to the races where there's a nice ambience, and what with the sea and all, we thought it would be fun at Zandvoort. She was watching from the pit roofs with all the other girls, with Norah Tyrrell, Nina Rindt and Sally Courage. Short of Nina and Jochen, she's been closer to Sally and Piers than to almost any of our friends, and up on the roof there she and Sally were doing lap charts together, sitting side by side on folding chairs.

"We'd gone 23 laps when smoke started billowing from behind a far corner of the circuit. It was a fast, top-gear corner taken around 140mph, and it was obvious that a car had crashed heavily, but even at a speed reduced to extreme caution I could not be sure who it was.

"In the pits, Ken realised what had happened and shouted up to Helen, 'See to Sally. Piers has crashed.' Sally, meanwhile, caught sight of the smoke and just blew her top. Helen took her out of the pit area to a car parked at the back and told her she had heard an announcement over the loudspeakers that Piers was all right, a report that had come in from a course marshal who thought he had seen him walk away from the wreck. Sally calmed down a bit, Helen left her and went to collect their charts and stop watches.

"Ken had heard the announcement too, and when I came by the pits he showed me a pit board sign, 'Piers O.K.' I couldn't imagine anyone being all right in that mass of smoke and flame, but I didn't get another signal, so

I worshipped the guy. He was totally adorable. Everybody in motor racing turned out for his funeral. And there were plenty of red eyes from the hard guys.

FRANK WILLIAMS

For the past two weeks Sally had been wonderful, spending time with Pat McLaren to make things easier after Bruce's death. Her nerves were on end and she was all wrung out with tension. JACKIE STEWART

I kept on driving. I finally finished second to Jochen and drove back to the pits. As I was stepping out of the car, Ken motioned me to remove my helmet so I could hear what he had to say, and it was then, I think, that I knew Piers was dead.

"Someone had given me a Coke and I remember smashing the bottle against the ground as I went off to the transporter. Yet, despite it all, my mind was cold. Absolutely cold. In neutral. All my concentration had been exhausted and I felt empty as I always do at the end of a race. Piers's death had come as a shock, but there was no way left for me to show it. I was drained. There was nothing left inside me.

"Helen had been asked to give Sally the tragic news, and Ken told me they'd gone back to the hotel. I was thinking more about them than about Piers - about Helen's strength, Sally's reaction - and as I changed my clothes in the transporter, I got someone to find a friend of mine who is a doctor. I didn't know if there was a doctor with Sally and I thought she might need one. The main thing was to get her back to her family in London, where she could be cared for and away from the press. As it was, the photographers had already started to gather in the hotel lobby by the time I arrived. Sally was quiet from a sedative Helen had given her on the way over, and Helen herself had been crying. But she managed to stay strong - how, I don't know. Frank Williams, Piers's entrant, was there too. He had been Piers's best friend for years, and was taking it hard. He needed to be with somebody now and he stayed with me all the while.

"There were people to be called and arrangements had to be made to get Sally back to England. Frank called Piers's mother, but he was in no condition to do anything else. I was tired. I never eat when I race, so I was hungry, and finally we got together for supper with Louis Stanley, who was also helping, and we sorted out what still had to be done. Sally, after a while, was flown back to London by Jochen and Nina, while I spent most of the night making telephone calls and finally got to bed about 1:30 in the morning. Helen, fortunately, was already out, as she had taken a pill."

"June 22, 1970: In the morning Helen returned to Geneva, I stayed on. There had to be an accident report and the police wanted me to help them. Frank Williams, Louis Stanley and I drove out to the circuit to reconstruct the accident. The crash had set off a complete bank of grass and it was still smouldering in places. There was a horrible, tragic smell in the area and it was absolutely quiet, only the wind coming off the sea, rustling the dune grass, and the three of us there on that empty road.

"Later the police wanted to know what we planned to do with the wreck. I thought about a scrapyard but then realised people might take bits of it for souvenirs and that sort of thing, so I knew this was out of the question. Frank just said, 'Get rid of it...I don't ever want to see it again... Get it away,' and I had it hauled to Amsterdam or Rotterdam, maybe - I can't remember - where it was melted in an incinerator and the remaining bits chopped up after they cooled."

Left: Sally Courage had helped comfort Bruce McLaren's widow, Pat, after McLaren died at Goodwood. At Zandvoort, Sally was time-keeping for her husband, Piers.
Above: After Zandvoort, Helen Stewart (left in picture) and Nina Rindt had to comfort their widowed friend Sally.

Oh God, not another one.

COLIN CHAPMAN

7 JULY 1970 - FRENCH GP (CLERMONT-FERRAND) In France, Jackie Stewart and American veteran Dan Gurney talked about the dangers of their profession.

DAN GURNEY: "This is a cruel sport. Not long ago I lay awake in bed and I counted all the people I've known who died in racing. And after a while, maybe an hour, I counted up to the number 57."

JACKIE STEWART: "This is in many ways a strange sport. For a driver it offers a unique assortment of experiences and sensations, so extreme at some times that you wonder if they can all come from the same world. When the racing bug bites it is often impossible to shake it off. It seems to affect your entire body and somehow gets into your bloodstream. It can be the world's most exhilarating sport, but it can also be the most cruel."

18 JULY 1970 - BRITISH GP (BRANDS HATCH) Dan Gurney retired from Formula 1 racing after the British Grand Prix, but Jackie Stewart stayed on.

JACKIE STEWART: "It was hideously dangerous then. The statistics were that, if you raced for five years, there was a two out of three chance you were going to die. I saw far too many of my friends killed and it is the most horrible thing you can imagine. First you see the destruction of the car and the man's body. Then you see the hopeless tearing of the heart in his family and friends and the way they are invaded by despondency about their future. You see how the fans and your own family view what is happening and how bad it is for them and yet you go out and do it again."

16 AUGUST 1970 - AUSTRIAN GP (OSTERREICHRING) In Austria, Jacky Ickx raced the Ferrari 312B to its first victory but, even though Jochen Rindt failed to finish his home Grand Prix, his points total to date put him on course to become his nation's first World Champion.

6 SEPTEMBER 1970 - ITALIAN GP (MONZA) On 5 September, Jochen Rindt was killed during practice for the Italian Grand Prix at Monza. His Lotus 72 crashed when one of its inboard front brake shafts snapped as he was approaching the Parabolica corner at nearly 200mph. Initially in practice, Rindt was hampered by a fuel feed malfunction, and then Colin Chapman decided that the 72 should run without its wings to boost its straightline speed - thought to be 10mph down on the Ferrari's.

JOCHEN RINDT: "It is absolutely incredible. The car is almost 800rpm faster on the straight without wings. I can reach the rev limit almost anywhere around the track. Without wings I shall easily beat 1 minute 26 seconds, and I will be able to do this without a tow."

DENIS JENKINSON (*Motor Sport*): "Then things changed with an air of quiet descending and a complete lack of activity, and news arrived that Rindt had crashed badly on braking for the Parabolica while in close company with Hulme. As always happens on these occasions, the rumour-mongers were soon spreading stories, but it was ominous that Team Lotus packed up and disappeared into the paddock, to be followed by the Rob Walker team with their new Lotus 72, and eventually confirmation came through that Rindt had been killed in the accident. Hulme reported that he had seen the Lotus swerve about under heavy braking from 190mph and then turn sharp left into the guard rail amidst a cloud of dust, a wheel broken off by the impact coming out of the dust cloud and bounding across the road in front of him."

MIKE DOODSON: "From all accounts, the car went unstable under heavy braking before turning sharp left on to the sand and hitting the barrier, twice, very hard. The front end disintegrated and wheels, a fuel tank and other debris flew back across the track, Hulme taking violent evasive action but hitting a smaller piece."

HEINZ PRULLER: "Bernie Ecclestone (Rindt's friend and manager) started running. He ran so quickly that he reached the Parabolica before the much younger mechanic, Eddie Dennis. He wanted to go to Jochen's assistance and he believed that this was the time to take a look at the car.

"In the meantime they had got Jochen out of the car. Bernie picked up the white helmet, one shoe and - on the right-hand side of the road - a wheel with parts of the suspension, which he passed on to Eddie to put by the car. The Lotus was stuck in the sand, five yards from the crash barrier and five yards from the track."

JACKIE STEWART: "As I put on my helmet, the tears started rolling. I went back into the pit in order to regain control over myself; then I climbed into the car. While the mechanics strapped me in, I started crying again. I tasted salt. I sat there and people tried not to look at me and I knew there was nothing I could do to stop the crying, so I went out. And as soon as I got going, the crying stopped. I was all right. When I got to the Parabolica, I went around slowly, searching for the marks where Jochen went off. I ran four laps and my last lap was the fastest I had ever done Monza, and the fastest I was to do that weekend. It will be said I was trying to hurt myself, that it was suicidal, but it wasn't. It felt the same as any other lap.

"I finished second in the race and felt completely empty, drained and exhausted as all the pressures of the past two days collapsed. I felt capable of nothing and absolutely lost."

DAVID PHIPPS: "Until the 1970 season, those who believed in the ability and promise of Jochen Rindt were for ever at war with those who wrote him off as being a driver of 'sound and fury signifying nothing'. He was still a controversial character up till the day he died.

HERBIE BLASH (Lotus mechanic): "Chapman shot off immediately. Just went. Nina was at home in Switzerland, so we had to get Jochen's belongings back up to her at Begnins. When I arrived at Geneva there were banner headlines in German, 'Jochen Rindt Killed'. As I drove up to the house, Nina was at the bedroom window and waved like mad. I can imagine now that it was as if it was Jochen coming home, although of course it couldn't have been.

"There was nobody else in the room, just Sally Courage and Nina. There I was, sitting on the settee between these two women. What can you say in a situation like that?

"All of a sudden, Natasha, who was six and upstairs, cried out, 'Papa, Papa.' Both girls burst into tears, and

where Emerson Fittipaldi, a veteran of only three Grands Prix, scored a fortuitous and very emotional victory for Lotus. It made Jochen Rindt the sport's only posthumous champion.

EMERSON FITTIPALDI: "At last I came into the pit straight, and down towards the finish line, and I saw Colin jumping in the air and throwing his hat. When I was young, I looked at books and magazines in Brazil and I remember lots of photos of Colin throwing his hat for Jim Clark. And it was hard for me to believe that he was doing it now for me! Me, winning the American Grand Prix! I was just so happy I couldn't take it all in.

"Jacky Ickx composed a much discussed *Adieu To Jochen Rindt* with his father (a former sports writer) and closed with the following words: 'When, after four years of courage and disappointment, success in Grand Prix racing finally came to him, he became a different person. At the moment when he climbed into his car for the last time he was particularly happy. He had the looks and manners of a contented man. There can be little doubt that he remained happy until the very moment of his accident, for we drivers are always happy behind the wheel. The two seconds of the final drama cannot have changed things, for there is something passionate about fighting a car that has gone mad. Rindt would not have had even one second

Jochen was a mercurial person, one of Nature's rebels; a boy born to upset the establishment, to speak his mind without fear or favour - and to pack as much living as possible into his 28 years. DAVID PHIPPS

there I am, 21 years old and not knowing what life's about, with one arm round Sally Courage and the other round Nina Rindt."

4 OCTOBER 1970 - UNITED STATES GRAND PRIX (WATKINS GLEN) Now, victories for Jacky Ickx in the final three races could make him champion of the world - a title he no longer wanted in the tragic circumstances. The Belgian won in Canada, but a broken fuel breather lost him his chance in America,

25 OCTOBER 1970 - MEXICAN GP (MEXICO CITY)
HEINZ PRULLER: "Jacky Ickx won the Mexican Grand Prix and with 40 points he became runner-up to Jochen in the World Championship, ahead of Clay Regazzoni (33), Denis Hulme (27), Jack Brabham and Jackie Stewart (25 each) and Pedro Rodriguez and Chris Amon (23 each). Seeing the ever-increasing points score behind the drivers' names always reminded me of those war films in which the fighter pilots chalked up their victories. In the World Championship of 1970, crosses disfigured the final listings.

of fear (the excitement only comes later) and he would not have suffered. The duration of a life should not be measured in days or hours, but by that which we achieve during the time given to us. There isn't a single one of us who hasn't left his hotel room in the morning well aware that he may not return, but this does not prevent us from achieving complete happiness. On the contrary, perhaps it enables us to be all the more so. The knowledge that everything could finish before the end of the day enables us to enjoy the wonders of life and all that surrounds it all the more.'"

Opposite: Jochen Rindt - here relaxing with Jackie Stewart - became the only posthumous World Champion.
Above: Rindt won four races in a row, including the British Grand Prix, where he barged his Lotus 72C past Jack Brabham's Brabham BT33.

The 1971 season had two colour schemes: Tyrrell blue and Stewart tartan. Ultimately that colour combination would yield 25 Grand Prix victories and three driving titles, but the '71 season was perhaps the best of them all. Stewart won six of the 11 races, and his team mate François Cevert one other.

BRM won two races, but it also lost its best drivers when both Pedro Rodriguez and Jo Siffert were killed. As team mates in the Gulf Porsche sportscar team in 1970 and 1971, they had the equipment and management attention to fulfil a potential largely wasted by Formula 1 teams. Both were courageous, determined fighters with big hearts and massive wills to win.

Louis Stanley paired them together at BRM in 1971, and their sheer fighting spirit lifted the team. Without them, BRM was never quite the same again.

6 MARCH 1971 - SOUTH AFRICAN GP (KYALAMI) Mario Andretti won the opening race in South Africa for Ferrari. It was his first Grand Prix victory.

MARIO ANDRETTI: "This was one of those events that you longed for, the ones where you thought, 'I've got to put this one under my belt'; those are the ones you remember. Then that feeling of driving into Victory Lane or crossing the finish line, it's indescribable. When you finally do put it under your belt, what a beautiful, beautiful relief. But it's more a sense of accomplishment because you know the importance and you did it. It's a tremendous payoff. It really is."

Andretti's promotion to the rank of race winner was offset by yet another addition to the ever-growing number of drivers killed on the job.

11 JULY 1971 TIM PARNELL (BRM team manager): "We'd gone to Silverstone, we were all ready for the British GP, we'd tested, the cars were looking good and fit, and then some stupid idiot rang up from the blinking Norisring and they kept pestering Pedro, pestering him to drive this bloody car there. It was an old clapped-out car that'd been doing some film work. I said to him, 'You're crazy to go there,' but the money they offered was too much, and in the end he just went. The ironic thing is that he got into the lead with the thing; he should never have been in the lead with this clapped-out car, but there it was. Tragic. Your life's thrown away in a clapped-out car in a clapped-out bloody race."

JO RAMIREZ: "If anybody offered Pedro a wheelbarrow to race, he would go and race it. He was just a racer all the way. Pedro didn't agree with all the safety campaigns that people like Jackie Stewart did - he believed that when it's your turn to go, you gotta go, regardless."

After Pedro Rodriguez had been killed, Jo Siffert rose magnificently to the occasion to win for BRM in Austria. It was only his second Formula 1 victory.

JO SIFFERT: "With the first win for Rob [Walker, in Britain three years before], I was surprised, but terribly happy. This year was at a different stage in my life. And it was BRM's first victory since Spa last year. Many times BRMs have been in good positions and maybe never finished. So this was also happy for the team."

ROB WALKER: "In the fullness of time 'Seppi' and I developed what I suppose you could almost call a father and son relationship. When he was not in Switzerland or a German- or French-speaking country he was very dependent on us, and he was the first driver for whom I was able to act as a true mentor. When Stirling drove for me I was learning from him, but with 'Seppi' the roles were reversed. He was a superb driver who was just so brave he scared me witless. I admired him enormously."

Left: The death of his brother Ricardo in 1962 had failed to slow Pedro Rodriguez down. Sadly, Pedro's number came up in the summer of '71.
Opposite: Jo 'Seppi' Siffert (left in picture) with BRM team manager, Tim Parnell.

God is the only one that can tell you this is the end of the line. You can be racing, in the street, in church, you can be anywhere. Nuvolari, he raced thirty years, every week, and he died in bed of illness. PEDRO RODRIGUEZ

Seppi was just like Pedro, a wonderful man. When he'd come into the pits you'd just see the aggression drain away and he'd become again the gent he always was.

I put my hand up in the air as we crossed the line, on the basis that, even if I hadn't won, the judges would think I had because my hand was up. PETER GETHIN

5 SEPTEMBER 1971 - ITALIAN GP (MONZA) The Italian Grand Prix fell to jockey's son Peter Gethin, who won in a 'photo finish' as he narrowly led four other cars across the Monza line to win the fastest Formula 1 race ever run. Gethin's winning average speed of 150.75mph is a record likely to stand forever.

A margin of 0.61s covered the first five cars after 196 miles of flat-out racing. It was the closest ever multi-car finish, and Gethin's advantage over the second-placed car was measured at a hundredth of a second - the narrowest ever winning margin.

For the first 37 laps, the race was a high-speed, slipstreaming dogfight, with Peterson, Jackie Stewart, François Cevert, Clay Regazzoni, Mike Hailwood, Jo Siffert and Chris Amon taking numerous turns at leading. From lap 37 to 46, Amon seemed to exert a measure of control, only to have his advantage wiped out in the blink of an eye. The hapless Kiwi would finish sixth, half a minute behind the leading group.

CHRIS AMON: "I had enough breathing space to think about my preparation for the end of the race. I had a stack of tear-off visors, like we all used back then, but when I went to tear off the top one so that I had a clear view for the remaining laps, all of them came off at the same time."

On the last lap, the front-runners frantically jockeyed for position. With only 500 yards to go, Peterson, Cevert, Gethin, Hailwood and Howden Ganley lunged *en masse* for the finish line.

PETER GETHIN: "I was working my strategy backwards from the finishing line. The BRM was very good through the gears at Parabolica so I knew that if I was into the top three going into or halfway round the corner, the car

The fastest race in history was also the closest ever multi-car finish, with Gethin (opposite), Peterson, Cevert, Hailwood and Ganley separated by less than a second.

was capable of winning. When Ronnie and François were running side by side I went flying down the inside of them, a bit on the grass I seem to remember. But I couldn't stop anyway. If either of them had come across I would have hit them. I remember thinking I was in the right place, the lead, so whatever I did, even if it meant going off, I was going to keep my foot down in every gear. I went through the first part of the corner sideways, using maximum revs. I think Ronnie had an engine problem, maybe a broken exhaust, but in any case he came out of my slipstream after we had crossed the line.

The results stood, with Peterson fractionally mistiming his swoop out from Gethin's slipstream and crossing the line 0.01s the wrong side of glory. Cevert was 0.08s behind the March, Hailwood 0.09s behind the Tyrrell. Ganley, fifth after the best race of his career, was another 0.43s down in another BRM.

TIM PARNELL: "After we got the car from *parc fermé* we pushed it back into the paddock, and of course the usual track invasion had happened. The *tifosi* were all over the place. But do you know what? I'll never forget the fabulous applause they gave us. It was amazing! A tribute not only to a fantastic race, but to BRM - the British Ferrari, perhaps."

Later that night, there was a party for the BRM mechanics at the Serenissima Hotel in Monza. Louis

Stanley and his wife, Jean, sister of BRM owner Sir Alfred Owen, swept up in their Cadillac from the opulent Villa d'Este hotel on Lake Como.

TIM PARNELL: "It was a terrific party, as you can imagine, after our second consecutive victory. Then when Big Lou came to leave, they discovered that his Cadillac had a puncture."

PETER GETHIN: "Yes, there I was, changing the left rear wheel. I'd just won the Italian Grand Prix, my one and only F1 victory, and there I was sweating away, with all the other drivers laughing at me."

Stewart's young team mate, François Cevert, took the finale when he achieved his maiden win in America. With this season, Jackie Stewart and Ken Tyrrell solidified a relationship that became one of the greatest in the history of the sport - every bit as good as that between Jim Clark and Colin Chapman.

JACKIE STEWART: "Ken Tyrrell is a very special man. When I was racing with Ken I couldn't have asked for a better, more professional, more precise team manager, and I don't think there was another one that good when I was driving. Mercedes-Benz's fabled manager Alfred Neubauer was out of my era. Everyone gave him credit for being a great team manager but I didn't see necessarily an enormous likeness between him and Ken. He was much more austere, and Ken has never

been that. His decision-making was always immediate and positive. He'd say: 'Let's do this.' And just do it. Everything was imminent, there wasn't any soft time."

MIKE DOODSON: "For Tyrrell, finding a budget for 1971 had been a question of parlaying the talent of his driver, Jackie Stewart, into sufficient cash to pay rent, wages, suppliers and the invoices from Cosworth engines. The wage bill may have seemed high at the time, but only eight men had been involved in the construction of the first Tyrrell. Today, McLaren employs exactly that same number in its paint department alone."

After a few safe races, yet another fatality plunged the sport into gloom again. When Jo Siffert became the only driver ever to die in a BRM, after a freak accident in the non-championship race at Brands Hatch intended to celebrate Jackie Stewart's championship, the heart was ripped from BRM. Siffert had collided on the grid with Ronnie Peterson's car, and something broke as he plunged down the fast straight towards Hawthorn's Bend at the back of the circuit.

TIM PARNELL: "We think that crash broke the bracket that held the radius arm. I had a lot of letters from fans afterwards, and one was from a spiritualist who said something broke behind Seppi's left shoulder. And that's exactly what did happen. It was spooky. He hit a bank, the car rolled over in flames and he died through lack of oxygen. His only injury was a broken ankle."

In 1971 I got mononucleosis. And then in 1972 I got a duodenal ulcer that haemorrhaged. Both of those things took an immense amount out of me. JACKIE STEWART

The 1972 season featured a new colour scheme at the front, as Emerson Fittipaldi became the sport's youngest-ever World Champion in his striking, black-and-gold John Player Special Lotus 72. After a year in the doldrums, Lotus was awake again. The 25-year-old Brazilian won five races to Jackie Stewart's four as they dominated an otherwise unremarkable season.

23 JANUARY 1972 - ARGENTINE GP (BUENOS AIRES) Everyone sat up and took notice when Carlos Reutemann, driving for Brabham (now owned by an up-and-coming entrepreneur named Bernie Ecclestone), put his BT34 on pole position for his first Grand Prix, in his homeland.

ALAN HENRY: "Reutemann was destined to start the revitalised Brabham team off on a heady note. Using Goodyear's soft G52 compound, he whistled round the 2.121-mile Buenos Aires autodrome to grasp pole position in a magnificent 1m 12.46s, edging out Jackie Stewart's Tyrrell 003, which shared the front row on 1m 12.68s.

"The race was run in predictably sweltering conditions, but the Brabham team nonetheless opted to run the same Goodyear compounds as that on which Carlos had qualified. It was a mistake. Stewart eased immediately into the lead at the start. Reutemann hung on brilliantly in second place for the first eight laps, and he drifted back to fourth place before stopping for fresh rubber on lap 45. The BT34's left-hand tyres were replaced with a pair of G31 covers and Reutemann romped back to an eventual seventh place at the finish - an impressive drive even if it did have a disappointing outcome."

14 MAY 1972 - MONACO GP (MONTE CARLO) Jean-Pierre Beltoise, a former motorcycle racer, drove with a crippled left arm, a legacy of a horrendous accident early in his career. In the treacherous streets of Monaco, he hustled his under-powered BRM P160B to fourth place on the grid, behind champion-elect Emerson Fittipaldi's Lotus and the Ferraris of Jacky Ickx and Clay Regazzoni. But nobody really rated his chances of winning the race, even when race day dawned cold and very wet. Ickx, after all, was the recognised rainmaster...

LOUIS STANLEY: "The omens were hardly favourable. Instead of Riviera sunshine, Monte Carlo was soaked by sheets of torrential rain that went on hour after hour, leaving the most diabolical road conditions imaginable. Twenty-five cars went to the grid, the largest number seen at Monaco. Jean-Pierre, on the

Beltoise is a tough little blighter with a lot of courage. JAMES HUNT

inside of the second row, had an inspired start: he surged through a narrow gap, overtook Jacky Ickx's front-row Ferrari as they braked for Ste Devote, and disappeared up the hill in a cloud of spray. He led from then on throughout the 80 laps, never looked challenged, handled the BRM superbly, set the fastest lap and had the measure of the situation.

"It was a fantastic victory, BRM's fifth win in the Principality. Jean-Pierre was inspired. *Le Monde* made him a national hero with front-page headlines. Afterwards he expressed delight with the BRM. It was smaller and lighter to drive with better torque. At the celebration dinner afterwards he savoured to the full what was to be his only World Championship victory. But what a way to do it!"

4 JUNE 1972 - BELGIAN GP (NIVELLES) Fittipaldi's championship cause was aided by the absence of Stewart, who invalided himself out of the race due to the effects of a duodenal ulcer. The hyperactive Scot had simply been doing too much.

JACKIE STEWART: "At Monte Carlo, for instance, I was involved in all kinds of sponsor's functions, entertaining guests, speaking at breakfasts and dinners, and so on. At that time I was doing something literally every day. And I was doing six or eight countries a week, sometimes five or six countries a day. And

I was testing much more than is ever done today. We would go to Kyalami and do two Grand Prix distances a day for something like 18 days. And the same at Paul Ricard. In those days there really was a tyre war on, and no restriction on testing. And it wasn't just F1.

"I was doing CanAm racing at the same time, for instance. Europe one week, America the next. And the Americans knew much more than the Europeans how to make appearances dynamic. I would fly in and that same night I would do cocktails and a dinner and the next night I'd be flying by private plane and we'd do a whole lot of different cities and different states. Then you'd be getting on a plane on Sunday night, you'd be flying back, and you'd be testing on the Tuesday or Wednesday and Grand Prix racing on the Friday, Saturday and Sunday. And then you'd be going back to test the CanAm car or do another set of appearances.

"I'm not trying to belittle what the current guys do, but they really don't understand how heavy the load was in those days. It was a new discipline. Then there were the deaths you had to deal with. On 11 June 1972 - my birthday - Jo Bonnier was killed at Le Mans. Jo was mostly responsible for us moving to Switzerland. His two sons went to school with Paul and Mark, and I took space in Jo's office complex. He also worked hard with me on improving safety, and now he had been killed."

Top right: Jean-Pierre Beltoise raced with a crippled arm. His wife, Jacqueline, was the sister of François Cevert.

Despite his enormous talent, he's never won a Formula 1 race. It's something else, something to do with his character, with will. JACKIE STEWART

2 JULY 1972 FRENCH GP (CLERMONT-FERRAND) Time and again, Chris Amon threatened to win Grand Prix races, only for his car to break down. Many believed that he was as quick as Jim Clark on his day, which meant that Amon should have been the equal of Jackie Stewart or Emerson Fittipaldi in 1972.

At the French Grand Prix, on the daunting mini-Nürburgring called Clermont-Ferrand, he came closer to victory than ever before, and this time in a blue Matra. The New Zealander took a comfortable pole position, almost a second faster than Denny Hulme in a McLaren.

AUTOCOURSE RACE REPORT: "At the start Amon took the initiative, with Hulme. Stewart overtook Hulme, who was not happy with the handling of his McLaren. But there was nothing the Scot could do about the leading Matra. Or was there? At the end of the 20th lap, just over half-distance, Stewart swept by in the lead while poor Amon headed for the pits. A punctured front tyre was changed and Amon resumed, now eighth and his hopes of victory evaporated.

"With a few laps remaining Cevert was fourth, but who was this in fifth place? It was Amon, going faster than ever! The Matra had set a succession of record laps and Amon was slicing through the field back into the points. He overtook Cevert and finished third. The French Grand Prix proved that Stewart is usually the lucky one and Amon is always the unlucky guy."

JOHN BLUNSDEN: "Another lap and Amon might have been second. It was one of those out-of-this-world efforts which rightly had the spectators on fire, and it was hardly surprising that Amon was called on to accompany Stewart on his lap of honour."

JACKIE STEWART: "I was the only one who avoided the stones that day, that's why I didn't get a puncture."

CHRIS AMON: "Balls! The bloody road was littered with stones. That race was a little hard to cope with. With the pit stop I lost 90 seconds and threw caution to the wind. I was all over the place. Anywhere there was available track, I was on it, and I didn't get another puncture. I don't altogether follow Jackie's logic on that one."

JACKIE STEWART: "Chris is a very open and relaxed guy who's great fun to be with, although sometimes he gets terribly tied up, particularly during practice. Anger can boil up inside him which you never suspected was there, and by now his mechanics have a fairly thorough description of it. They call it Chris's 'wobblies'. There are three kinds, each corresponding to the intensity of his mood: the white, the rainbow, and the purple wobblies. The white variety is when he gets out of his car, his face ashen, throws his gloves down, and shouts: 'Fucking car!' and storms off. The rainbow type is when he explodes at everything in sight. The purple wobblies, the peak of his outbursts, are the same, but more so.

30 JULY 1972 - GERMAN GP (NÜRBURGRING)
If Lotus had a strong year, it was again miserable for Ferrari, whose revised B2 was still not a consistent match for the Lotus 72 or the Tyrrell 003 and its successor, the 005. Nevertheless, Ferrari had its occasional moments in the spotlight, in particular at the old Nürburgring, where Jacky Ickx scored a dominant victory, the best of his five for the Scuderia.

ENZO FERRARI: "Ickx was a combination of daring and calculation. For four years we pursued a title. His occasional behaviour, which gained him the nickname 'enfant terrible', hasn't stopped me remembering an adult young man and the impression of his fine driving and fearlessness in the rain."

ALAN HENRY: "Determined to avenge his defeat in the 1971 German Grand Prix, Jacky outqualified Stewart's Tyrrell by 1.7s at the Nürburgring. He led the 14-lap event from start to finish in faultless style and team mate Regazzoni backed him up with a splendid second place. The Swiss also turfed Stewart into the barrier as the Tyrrell driver attempted to pass him in the Hatzenbach forest on the last lap. Jackie was livid, but Clay simply shrugged his shoulders. 'He was off line,' he grinned sheepishly.

EMERSON FITTIPALDI: "Ickx was getting well ahead but Clay was driving very hard, in fact it was quite frightening to see."

ENZO FERRARI: "The inimitable Clay never lets up. *Bon viveur*, dancer, playboy, footballer, tennis player and, in his spare time, driver. He's the ideal guest at the most unusual fashion shows, the great resource of women's magazines."

Emerson Fittipaldi secured the drivers' championship with a win in the Italian Grand Prix.

10 SEPTEMBER 1972 - ITALIAN GP (MONZA) EMERSON FITTIPALDI: "1972 was a fantastic year. The car was competitive everywhere we raced and I usually qualified in the first two rows. The car was very reliable as well and we won the championship because of our finishing record just as much as being able to drive fast. It's like any time you win a championship, it was a real team effort.

"And, you know, it was a great pleasure to win the championship by winning the race at Monza. I remember the feeling on the victory lap that day. It was just fantastic!"

Opposite: Chris Amon was arguably the best driver never to win. His failure to do so provoked many arguments.
Right: Emerson Fittipaldi, though beaten by Jackie Stewart in France (below), out-drove everyone to win the 1972 championship.

The 1973 season brought an era to an end, and saw the first seeds of the new order that would replace it. There was a gripping battle for the championship as Tyrrell and Lotus dominated the races, with intervention from McLaren, but once again the year was marred by tragedy. Genuine heroism is rare in sport but in 1973 two examples earned George Medals for bravery for Mike Hailwood and David Purley.

Almost from the start, Jackie Stewart knew that it would be his last season as a racing driver. But only three other people were privy to the secret of his intended retirement.

JACKIE STEWART: "I only told Ken Tyrrell, and Walter Hayes and John Waddell at Ford. We had lunch in London, but I didn't want anyone else to know. Even François didn't know that I was going. He was nearly going to leave Ken - an offer from Ferrari was tickling him. I told him he needed one more year with me. I think he would have won the championship in 1974 for Ken."

Tyrrell went into the season with revised 006/2 versions of its 005 model, updated to incorporate new deformable chassis structures demanded by

Above: Jackie and Helen Stewart outside their house in Switzerland. "I made the decision to retire in April that year," said Stewart. "I only told three people. Helen never knew. I didn't want her thinking of ten green bottles."

the regulations. Ferrari was back in the doldrums as the first version of the 312B3 flopped, but Lotus still had the trusty 72s, with superfast Swede Ronnie Peterson joining reigning champion Emerson Fittipaldi. McLaren had a sleek new wedge-shape car called the M23 for Denny Hulme and Peter Revson. BRM partnered Ferrari refugee Clay Regazzoni and Jean-Pierre Beltoise with the young, unrated Austrian Niki Lauda, and the sinister-looking black UOP Shadow team was a welcome newcomer.

3 MARCH 1973 - SOUTH AFRICAN GP (KYALAMI) Clay Regazzoni's season with BRM had started with a bang in Argentina, where he led until his tyres went off. But the Swiss with the bandit moustache nearly came to grief at Kyalami when he crashed early in the race. In seconds the BRM was aflame, with 'Regga' unconscious in the cockpit. Only the intervention of Mike Hailwood, who had crashed in the same incident, saved his life. The multiple motorcycling champion dived into the flames to rescue him.

MIKE HAILWOOD: "It started on the second lap. Carlos Reutemann was in front of me. Dave Charlton was in front of Reutemann. At the first corner, Charlton started to lose it. He got the car sideways. Reutemann managed to squeeze through the gap.

"Charlton's car began to come back, as a spinning car does. I went over its nose which bent the left suspension. Then Charlton was out of the way beside a guardrail. I was creeping along. The next thing I knew was a great thud and crash."

Regazzoni's car had crashed into Hailwood's Surtees on the bend. Then the Ferrari of Jacky Ickx crashed into them both. Ickx managed to jump clear, but he was slightly injured.

MIKE HAILWOOD: "I was enveloped in flames. The cars were burning merrily away. They were interlocked. I undid the straps of my harness and extricated myself. I could see that 'Regga' was slumped unconscious in the BRM. I leaped across and undid his seat belts. I was trying to pull him out by one arm which was all I could get at. To pull a man out of a car like that is a difficult thing at the best of times. The BRM's left side was stoved in. It was burning. I just couldn't pull him out by one arm.

"There was petrol everywhere. I burst into flames. Frantically, I ran across to the other side of the track where there was grass and sand. I flung myself down and rolled around to put out the flames.

"Regga's blaze was extinguished by marshals and officials who were trying to get him out. Then the car

burst into flames again. I went back, grabbed him under the armpits, and with a couple of marshals, got him free. He was still unconscious, though not seriously hurt as it turned out."

CLAY REGAZZONI: "It was so brave of Mike, and there is no doubt I owe him my life."

PAULINE HAILWOOD: "I can recall vividly that Mike came walking up the pit lane and he looked terrible, worse than I'd ever seen him look all the time I had known him. He was tight-lipped, drawn and ashen-faced. And he was more than a bit anxious to get away from the place. In fact, he was very agitated about leaving and couldn't wait, so we got on the bike we'd come on and rode off. And in total silence, too. I thought he must have had one really big hairy moment and didn't want to talk about it. I thought he must have scared himself so much he just wanted to forget.

"The next morning the papers arrived and I was staggered to see what he had done. I read about it, and I still couldn't believe what my eyes were seeing in black and white in front of me. But there it was. Mike had seen Clay's predicament. A marshal was standing there doing nothing, apparently having given up any hope for Clay's chances. But not my Mike. In he went and he only came out when his clothes caught fire. He doused them out and went in again. This time he managed to haul big old Clay to safety."

For his bravery, Hailwood was later awarded the _Prix Rouge et Blanc Jo Siffert_ - an award named for the Swiss driver who had died in a flaming crash in 1971. Hailwood was also given the Ladbroke award for Courage in Sport and the Golden Goblet award for courage by the Swiss Automobile Club. In 1974, Hailwood was subsequently presented with the George Medal, Britain's highest civilian award for bravery.

JACKIE STEWART: "I didn't see much other than smoke and flame because I was busy trying to win the race. But it did not surprise me at all when I was told what Mike had done in saving Clay's life and putting his own very much at risk. It just seemed to me that if anybody was capable of such action, it was good old Hailwood. He wouldn't even consider the danger if he knew he was in a position to do something to help."

1 JULY 1973 - FRENCH GP (PAUL RICARD) By mid-season, Ronnie Peterson had established himself as the quicker Lotus driver. His first victory finally came in France after upstart Jody Scheckter, in a third McLaren, had led until colliding with Emerson Fittipaldi.

Despite 'SuperSwede' Peterson's superior speed, Colin Chapman's refusal to impose team orders (in stark contrast to Tyrrell, where Cevert was required to

ride shotgun to Stewart where possible) had a detrimental effect on the title aspirations of both Peterson and Fittipaldi.

14 JULY 1973 - BRITISH GP (SILVERSTONE) The American driver Peter Revson eventually won his first Grand Prix in a race that had got off to a shaky start when Jody Scheckter sent all and sundry spinning at Silverstone. Sheckter started a chain reaction exiting Woodcote Corner on the second lap and nearly wiped out half the field.

All three Surtees were damaged, along with Beltoise's BRM, Andrea de Adamich's Brabham, Jackie Olivier's Shadow and Roger Williamson's works March. Mercifully, de Adamich was the only driver to be injured, suffering a broken leg.

JOHN SURTEES: "That man has just wiped out my entire Formula 1 team."

JODY SCHECKTER: "I just pushed a mite too hard and suddenly the thing came around on me."

PETER REVSON: "After I won a friend called the next day and told me an interesting story. He said he was watching the race and he got a view of the accident involving Jody Scheckter. 'You know,' he said, 'I saw your team-mate after he crashed. It was just like he had the plague. Nobody would talk to him. He was just allowed to sit and sulk on his own.'

"My friend said he realised how cruel the sport is. He said over and over again that the winner is the winner but he is only one man. The losers are everybody else and nobody wants to know them. He

found it remarkable that there sat Jody Scheckter, who had been touted as the next great ace, and he had his first-lap shunt at Silverstone and suddenly he was disregarded."

The other man to star at Silverstone was James Hunt, who drove Lord Alexander Hesketh's March to fourth place in only his third Grand Prix. A Formula 3 driver who had gained a reputation for erratic driving and spectacular accidents, 'Hunt the Shunt' had a lucky escape in the Scheckter incident, when debris removed his car's tall airbox.

JAMES HUNT: "I crouched down, put my head under the dashboard and closed my eyes. I had a very lucky escape. I'd suffered badly from nerves all morning. I'd really been in a terrible state. So I was very surprised to find that, while we were waiting for the race to be restarted, I wasn't at all nervous. I suppose in a sense the event as such had started, so I was no longer jumpy.

"But I have to confess I don't remember a lot about the race. After being passed by a hell of a lot of people at the start, I made up a lot of places. Perhaps I shut my eyes again and just kept my foot in it."

Race winner Revson, a member of the wealthy family that owned the Revlon cosmetics empire, collected more than just the winner's trophy, having backed himself to the tune of £50 at odds of 14 to 1.

> When I said to him, 'Jesus, I don't believe it. You did all that and never even mentioned it to me,' he just replied, 'Firemen do it every day.'
>
> PAULINE HAILWOOD

PETER REVSON: "On the grid, no matter what anyone thinks or supposes, there are butterflies. It is the pressure I put on myself to win. There is a lot at stake and you must realize it. There is reputation, there is pride, there is money. If you are not prepared to understand that, to sacrifice for it, you are not prepared to be a winner. If I just went out there to run a race, there wouldn't be that kind of pressure, and I don't think I'd feel the butterflies.

"You must also be prepared to be apprehensive about being hurt or killed. That feeling exists. The thought of being killed does occur to you if you're a racing driver. But if it occurred a lot, you couldn't drive. Although it's ever present, it can be made to serve a purpose. What we do is fairly dangerous and that's why I feel we should make as much money as we can."

Top right: For his heroism in rescuing Clay Regazzoni from the flames after his crash at Kyalami (top left) Mike Hailwood earned Britain's highest civilian award for bravery.

I was trying to get people to help me, and if I could have turned the car over he would have been all right.

DAVID PURLEY

29 JULY 1973 - DUTCH GP (ZANDVOORT) In the long and sometimes sad history of motor racing, few incidents have left such an indelible stain on its character as the accident in which 25-year-old Roger Williamson was the needless victim of fire at Zandvoort during the Dutch Grand Prix of 1973.

Williamson had worked his works March up to 13th position by the eighth lap of the race, running just ahead of fellow-Briton David Purley, who was driving a similar car under his private LEC Racing banner. A star in F3 and F2, Williamson was gaining experience prior to graduating full-time to F1 in 1974 with a McLaren M23 entered by his mentor, Tom Wheatcroft, the British builder who later restored the pre-war Donington Park circuit and assembled its collection of historic racing cars.

Then, going into the first of two very quick fifth-gear right-hand curves out on the back of the Zandvoort circuit, Williamson's left front tyre exploded.

Purley saw the red March veer left, strike the kerb and then hit the Armco barrier. It rode along the top of the rail, which had been incorrectly installed in sand, not concrete. The barrier leaned backwards, and became a launching ramp. Williamson's March flew, then landed upside down on the opposite side of the track. Fuel leaked out. There was a momentary eruption of flame but, as the car came to rest, just on the apex of the second fast right-hander, the fire temporarily died down. Purley, a former paratrooper, stopped his car and ran to Williamson's aid. He found him alive and conscious, but trapped in the cockpit of the upturned car.

Around him, marshals stood transfixed, unable to impel themselves to go near the smoking car. None of them was wearing the correct fireproof clothing. Their fire extinguishers failed when Purley tried to use them.

MAX MOSLEY (then March team owner): "You would have thought that with double-waved yellows, you would have made the fire truck go back to the scene. The whole thing was a fuck-up that wouldn't happen today, because we

have sensible people running the races, and sensible people in the medical and emergency cars. It wouldn't have happened. In the end it always comes down to the same thing: it's not the cause of an accident that matters, it's the consequence."

Aghast at the inaction all around him, Purley attempted by himself to push the car over onto its wheels, all the while hearing Williamson pleading for help to escape. Purley strained so hard that he

ruptured blood vessels in both arms. He implored other marshals to move forward and help. None did. The fire gained hold again. The marshals let it burn.

DAVID PURLEY: "I just couldn't turn it over. I could see Roger was alive and I could hear him shouting, but I couldn't get the car over."

MAX MOSLEY: "Had the car not been upside down, Roger would have got out of it. The marshals were very cowardly. If that had happened opposite the pits, everybody would have turned it up the right way whether they were dressed properly or not. It was possible to do it."

The Dutch organisers put about a story that Williamson had died in the impact. The official report later confirmed what Purley already knew: Williamson had been alive and uninjured, but had died of asphyxiation.

MAX MOSLEY: "All the organisers did for Roger was to get the car back to the garage, then come to ask if a couple of us would go down and get the cadaver out. That was their only real concern. It was all so unnecessary. It could and should have been avoided. Roger was a good driver, sensational. He would have been a big star."

BRM team boss Louis Stanley, an ardent campaigner for safety, summarised the horror of the tragedy, and its bitter poignancy, in a piece of powerful and forthright prose...

LOUIS STANLEY: "Williamson's entrant and patron, Tom Wheatcroft, was distraught with grief. He asked if I would go with him to the mortuary for the identification as he was too upset to face the ordeal alone.

Above: Alone, anguished and distraught, David Purley tried in vain to get poor Roger Williamson (inset) out of the burning car.
Opposite: François Cevert was destined to be the cruel sport's next victim.

"The road out of the circuit was jammed with spectators making their way home. Sand dunes that minutes before had been natural grandstands for human ant heaps had reverted to gentle undulations with flickering waves of marram grass. Soon the crowds were left behind and we drove along quiet side lanes on a lovely summer's evening that neither of us saw.

"The mortuary was a simple building with a church-like atmosphere except that instead of an altar there was a coffin. The attendant gave me a key to unscrew one end and the lid was raised. If ever there was a condemnation of motor racing it was there. Roger Williamson, in stained flame-resistant suit, had both hands raised before his face as if to fend off the approach of death. The instinctive urge was to take those outstretched hands and help him out. The formalities completed, the lid was screwed back. Roger Williamson was now only a name on the roll of racing victims."

19 AUGUST 1973 - AUSTRIAN GP (OSTERREICHRING) Stewart's victories in Holland and Germany brought him within reach of the crown for the third time. But a win by Ronnie Peterson in Austria delayed his celebrations. The Swede had deferred to Fittipaldi in the race, trying to help his team mate keep his title chances alive. In the event, his chivalry went unrewarded as Fittipaldi failed to finish.

9 SEPTEMBER 1973 - ITALIAN GP (MONZA) When Peterson found himself leading Fittipaldi in the next race, at Monza, he stayed in front. Stewart, delayed by a puncture, fought back brilliantly to finish fourth, enough to win the title whatever Fittipaldi did.

RONNIE PETERSON: "I would gladly have let Emerson through if Jackie had finished fifth, but I was going to leave it as long as possible. I was being shown the boards and when Jackie moved to fourth place, I reckoned that was it, so I stayed in front of Emerson."

23 SEPTEMBER 1973 - CANADIAN GP (MOSPORT) The penultimate Grand Prix, in Canada, ended in farce, when nobody was sure if it had been Fittipaldi, Revson, Jackie Oliver in a Shadow, or even Howden Ganley in an Iso Marlboro who had won. The confusion was caused when, for the first time in Formula 1 history, the field ran behind a pace car. (Following Roger Williamson's fatal accident at Zandvoort, a new rule required a pace car to come onto the track and hold the field in check in the event of a serious accident.) As a result, the exact running order was the subject of considerable conjecture and the identity of the race winner remained in doubt for some time. Finally the timekeepers awarded the race to Revson.

7 OCTOBER 1973 - UNITED STATES GP (WATKINS GLEN) The final race of the season at the picturesque Watkins Glen circuit, should have been Jackie Stewart's final race. But late on Saturday morning his team mate François Cevert went out to post a fast time, and never came back. His Tyrrell crashed heavily in the ultra-fast Esses and the popular Frenchman with the flashing eyes was killed. Stewart, to whom he was like a younger brother, never raced again.

JACKIE STEWART: "Helen and I went to Niagara Falls with François just before the race that should have been my 100th and last Grand Prix. But I withdrew after François was killed. He was quick - at some races towards the end quicker than me though he wasn't always able to do it on a repeating basis. It was a terrible accident and I knew that he was dead at the scene, and one of my regrets to this day is that I didn't stay with him. But I just felt such disgust at the loss, the waste, that I drove slowly back to the pits."

JO RAMIREZ: "During one of his stops just a few minutes before his accident François said to me: 'Watch my times. I'll fix them. Do you notice that I am driving Tyrrell No. 6, chassis No. 006, engine No. 66 and this is the 6th of October. It's my day.'"

In a biography published shortly after his death François Cevert revealed a fatalistic outlook on the dangerous life he led...

FRANÇOIS CEVERT: "At Monza in 1970 when we were told that Rindt was dead it gave me a shock. The day before I had gone off after a spin at 300kph. He had killed himself at only 200kph. That night I had to take sleeping pills.

"The next day I finished sixth in the race and we celebrated with champagne; it was the first time I had scored a point in the World Championship. This lightheartedness might seem out of place. It is not, for we all know, everyone of us, that there is death in our contract. The more I drive the more I realise it could happen to me; but in fact it would take more courage for me to give up racing than it does to go on.

JACKIE STEWART: "François, more than anything else, apart from the talent, had enormous charm. And that was a human, natural charm. That wasn't just for the ladies, although he attracted a great deal of attention in that department. He mixed comfortably with the mechanics and everyone else.

"We still have a beautiful photograph of François in our home. He was a great pianist. His great piece was Beethoven's Pathétique piano sonata. Every time I hear it there is only one man in my mind, and that applies to Helen and the whole family. I don't know if those who read this believe in life after death, but François Cevert's spirit is still absolutely buzzing around."

For Ken Tyrrell, the Cevert accident was without question his lowest point, for the charming Parisian was universally loved within the tight family atmosphere of Tyrrell, and his death was a shattering blow.

François had become part of our little family. His enthusiasm and character were such that he sort of lightened our lives. He was always outgoing and there was a sparkle about him. The loss of François must have been close to losing a son. KEN TYRRELL

I am very attached to life, I am very happy to be alive. But I don't think I can give up racing, because it is that that I love above everything else.

FRANÇOIS CEVERT

For the first time in nine years, a Formula 1 season began without Jackie Stewart, the three-time champion whose record of 27 Grand Prix victories would endure for many seasons to come. Although Stewart would have several tempting offers to return, he stayed retired and never regretted it.

JACKIE STEWART: "My motor racing has been a wonderful experience. If I had the chance to live my life again, I would not change a thing. The personal pleasure which I have been allowed to enjoy has been so intense that it has often frightened me. Motor racing has projected my life into a kaleidoscope of colour, movement and sensation, which I honestly feel has magnified my appreciation of living far beyond what would have been possible had I done almost anything else. To have lived so vibrantly and experienced so much by the age of 34 has been a great privilege. I wish for my fellow participants in the sport that they also have the capacity and the time, as I had, to appreciate the full flavour of perhaps the world's most exciting sport.

"Like most things in life, however, the finest do not come cheaply. In my racing career I have lost many friends. If there were a magic wand, for me its only task would be to bring these friends back. That isn't possible, of course, but it is possible to remember that they were able to do the one thing which gave them more enjoyment than anything else. There are two sides to the fast spinning coin of motor racing and I consider myself fortunate that mine came down the right way up. I am content with my decision to stop."

As the 1974 season unfolded, nobody emerged as the new Jackie Stewart. But Niki Lauda looked an increasingly good bet. The Austrian had joined Scuderia Ferrari, which had taken major steps to effect a revival for its famed Prancing Horse team.

Fiat was now the major investor in Ferrari, and its chief executive, Gianni Agnelli, had persuaded Enzo Ferrari to give a young Roman lawyer a chance to coordinate the operation. When Luca di Montezemolo stepped up to the plate, technical guru Mauro Forghieri was freed of his management duties and was able to focus wholly on massaging the B3 into a competitive package for 1974. The ever-popular Clay Regazzoni was back, after being dropped at the end of 1972 and enduring a troubled year with BRM. Initially Ferrari tried to lure back Chris Amon, then went after Peter Revson, before settling on Lauda, who had impressed Il Commendatore.

When he first visited the Maranello factory and Fiorano, the team's private test track, Lauda was equally impressed.

That first year chez Hesketh was Alexander's ragtime fling. KEITH BOTSFORD

NIKI LAUDA: "The first time I see all this, I recognise the tremendous potential of the place. I found myself wondering why didn't this team walk away with every race? But it was not all a bed of roses.

"Compared to the '73 BRM, the Ferrari handling was much worse but the engine was much better. I realised immediately that the understeer problem needed to be fixed. I remember that first test at Fiorano I got out and said, 'This car is total shit, it understeers like hell!'

"But nobody ever says this to old man Ferrari. I say it to Forghieri first, then to Ferrari, too. Then Piero, Ferrari's son, got really worried because you can't say this to Ferrari. His car is always the best. I said: 'No, I told you, the car is total shit, it understeers and doesn't work.' So then old man Ferrari says, 'What happens if I fix the car? How much can you go quicker?' I said: 'Half a second.' Then he said to me, 'Fine. I'm gonna tell Forghieri now to do whatever you say to do, but if you don't go five-tenths quicker, you are out.' It was the first thing he told me.

"So I made Forghieri my best friend and said, 'Fuck it, do something! Change the roll centre at the front.' He did that and it was the real problem. Ten days later we tested again with a different front suspension, and I was six-tenths quicker. From that moment on I had the full confidence of the old man, how to develop the car. And Forghieri liked it too, after he'd been chucked out before. He was back, to prove to everybody that he was in charge again. The combination made it all go better."

At the opposite end of the spectrum from Ferrari, the oldest and most famous team in the sport, was Hesketh Racing, an audacious new venture funded by an eccentric young British aristocrat and featuring a colourful cast of characters led by a driver with a reputation for crashing: James Hunt.

KEITH BOTSFORD (British journalist): "Alexander, Lord Hesketh, the scion of a grocery fortune and a member by his mother of the McEwen clan of writers and painters, is one of the outsize figures that give motor racing a certain piquancy. He was then in his mid-twenties, the owner of a great house at Towcester (near Silverstone), a fat, ebullient, sporty sixties character, far from unshrewd and a splasher. It had entered his head - as it later entered the heads of Walter Wolf, an oil-exploration magnate, and David Thieme, whose authorised biography claims a start as an art designer in love with violet and a finish as a millionaire petroleum broker - that motor racing was a fun scene. Consequently he was putting together a Formula 1 team from scratch: with nought but money and some pretty savvy associates.

"His manager, 'Bubbles' Horsley, was a man of patchy but occasionally brilliant talent. His number one driver was James Hunt, 'Master James' as he was christened, because of his genteel upbringing and sometimes deliberate rudeness. Master James was the man who had escaped his minor public school in a big, rebellious way: bare feet, filthy T-shirts, exquisite girls and all; but as a driver, he was both very quick, very aggressive and, as drivers at the time said, bloody dangerous. No one had a more spectacular record of accidents than Master James; hence his sobriquet of 'Hunt the Shunt'.

"Champagne and pheasants in hired marquees with Lady Hesketh, Alexander's mother, complete with black eye-patch, presiding in a state of distraction; helicopters that flew ice and birds and more champers in and out of circuits; Master James cavorting among the Beautiful People with the exquisite Suzy, his model of a wife who eventually left him for the actor Richard Burton. It was a year of parties and night life, some good race results in an ever- improving car designed by Dr Harvey Postlethwaite, PhD."

13 JANUARY 1974 - ARGENTINE GP (BUENOS AIRES) The year started well for Ferrari, with Lauda and Regazzoni finishing second and third in Argentina.

NIKI LAUDA: "This I remember well, with Denny Hulme winning! I will never forget this, I was lying second and I could have won that race. But I got so worried that the brakes or something goes wrong so I took it easy and said to myself that second place was good enough. But if I would have pushed I could have won that one."

27 JANUARY 1974 - BRAZILIAN GP (INTERLAGOS) Regazzoni finished second in Brazil and moved to the head of the championship points table.

22 MARCH 1974 In private testing at Kyalami, in South Africa, Peter Revson was killed after his Shadow suffered suspension breakage. The rich American, who could have been a playboy but was instead a serious racing driver, had mentally prepared himself to survive a serious accident.

PETER REVSON: "If I were to be in a serious accident, I've decided I could live with the consequences and some are very unpleasant. I've heard people say they'd rather be dead than disfigured. I don't agree. If I were in a really bad wreck I'd spend some money on a plastic surgeon. I've seen racing drivers who have had very bad accidents and who are back driving race cars. They don't look like Valentinos, but people don't turn away from them in horror, either. I'd be thankful my faculties were still intact."

ROGER SILMAN (Revson's mechanic on the Shadow DN3): "I wondered what we were going to get with Peter, but I was enormously impressed. We had found somebody who very much wanted to help build the team. I had the impression that he didn't expect the team to be a world beater immediately, but he was quite prepared to help build it.

I would be lying if I said accidents don't worry me. I don't like pain, but I have a high threshold for it.

PETER REVSON

"I was astonished at just how professional he was. He was very, very capable, and had this ability to turn on a really quick lap. I think he was extremely capable; I'm not sure I'd describe him as being one of these really outstanding natural talents, a sort of Ronnie Peterson or someone like that, but in terms of being able to apply himself and to produce that quick lap when it was all-important - you sometimes work with drivers who are just unable to put it together and find anything else when it counts - he'd definitely got that. The accident was terrible. It was my first experience of being so close to somebody like that. A lovely bloke..."

TONY SOUTHGATE (Shadow designer): "Unfortunately, what happened was that the car was of low build and it hit the Armco at a shallow angle. It struck it at 45 degrees and wedged itself under the barrier, then tried to wrap itself round it and broke its back. The steering column was crushed on to his chest. The barrier didn't do its job of bouncing the car off. The ironic thing is that three days later they changed all that and made it three double fences."

Opposite: from the left - Alexander 'The Good Lord' Hesketh, James 'Hunt The Shunt' Hunt, Anthony 'Bubbles' Horsley and Harvey 'Doc' Postlethwaite, PhD.
Right: Peter Revson, a member of the Revlon cosmetics family, could have been a playboy. Instead, he devoted his life to the sport that, sadly, took it away.

It was noted that the principals of Hesketh Racing traditionally spent their Sunday night post-race debriefings in Trader Vic's bar at the bottom of the London Hilton hotel, where they drank Mai Tais until daylight. GERALD DONALDSON

7 APRIL 1974 At Silverstone, the Daily Express International Trophy race was won convincingly by James Hunt. Although it was a non-championship event, there was a strong Formula 1 contingent, including Lotus star Ronnie Peterson, whom Hunt relieved of the lead by overtaking him at 160mph in the notorious Woodcote corner.

IAN PHILLIPS (*Autosport*): "James Hunt's average speed of 133.58mph made this the fastest post-war race held in Britain. To see James bring the car up from a poor start and catch and overtake Ronnie Peterson in a historical moment at Woodcote was overwhelming. It gave a breath of fresh air to Formula 1 and a shot in the arm for British patriotism."

GERALD DONALDSON: "Led by the motoring press, the Hesketh Racing effort captured the imagination of more and more racing fans. James was hailed as the new British racing hero, the man most likely to succeed Jackie Stewart as the next British World Champion. His difficult rise from obscurity, his former 'Hunt the Shunt' reputation, his anti-establishment characteristics and his underdog status served to increase his stature in the eyes of the fans.

"But his fame spread beyond racing enthusiasts as the popular press took note of this new 'Golden Boy' of British sports. James's popstar good looks made young girls swoon and his girl-chasing reputation impressed red-blooded young males. His defiance of convention and party-loving ways were good copy, as were the colourful antics of Hesketh Racing, which sometimes seemed reminiscent of a bizarre Monty Python sketch.

"The raffish young ex-public schoolboys were engagingly eccentric and reports of their hijinks spread from the sports pages of the newspapers into the gossip columns."

8 APRIL 1974 - SPANISH GP (JARAMA) By Jarama, for the Spanish Grand Prix, there was no stopping Niki Lauda as he claimed his first Formula 1 victory. All season, the 312B3 remained the car to beat in his hands, as a fascinating battle developed between the young man's *brio* in an excellent car, and the more experienced Emerson Fittipaldi's cunning stealth in a McLaren M23 that was a match for the Ferrari on certain tracks.

7 JULY 1974 - FRENCH GP (DIJON-PRENOIS) In qualifying, Formula 1 suddenly realised it had a new star: a quiet, unassuming young Welshman named Tom Pryce, who was called up from Formula 3 racing to fill the Revson vacancy at Shadow. Pryce burst onto the scene with a stunning blend of speed and car control that would later be associated with Ayrton Senna and Michael Schumacher.

TREVOR FOSTER (former Shadow mechanic, now joint managing director at Jordan): "Suddenly Tom went out on the normal Goodyears we were getting at Shadow in those days and he was *very* quick. He qualified third, right behind Lauda and Peterson and ahead of Regazzoni, and people just couldn't believe it.

"At the garage at Dijon he just came in and sat quietly in the corner. He had this plain white racing suit, the one he'd always had, with just 'Tom Pryce' written on it and his blood group, and that was it. He just couldn't understand what all the fuss was about, that's the thing. It didn't overawe him at all. Everyone wanted to interview him, wanting this and wanting that, and he said, 'All I'm doing is driving a Formula 1 car.'"

6 OCTOBER 1974 - UNITED STATES GP (WATKINS GLEN) Victory in Canada late in the year pushed Fittipaldi back into contention as they went for the showdown at Watkins Glen in upper New York state. Lauda had won pole positions in Austria and Italy, but both races had ended with engine failures, and his chance of the championship finally slipped away when he crashed again in Canada after leading. Regazzoni's second place there, behind Fittipaldi, gave both men 52 points

as they prepared for the final battle, while Scheckter was an outsider for Tyrrell.

Ferrari's American outing was a flop, both drivers hampered by malfunctioning suspension dampers. Fittipaldi stroked home to fourth place - behind Reutemann, Hunt in the Hesketh and Reutemann's team mate, Carlos Pace - and won the title. Fittipaldi's greater experience and calmer temperament had won the day. Lauda, who finished fourth after an instructive year, filed that bit of data away in his mental computer...

For the second successive year, Watkins Glen's treacherous steel barriers claimed the life of a Formula 1 driver, in an accident frighteningly similar to that which had killed François Cevert. Helmuth Koinigg, a wealthy young Austrian competing in only his second Grand Prix, is believed to have suffered a punctured tyre, causing his Surtees to veer off the road at very high speed. The car tore through three layers of catchfencing and slid between two guard rails, and the driver was decapitated.

Opposite: The Good Lord issues a refuelling commandment. Hijinks aside, Hesketh's hunt for success was serious.
Above: Clay Regazzoni jumped to victory at the Nürburgring, while Tom Pryce (inset, right) leapt into prominence on his debut, though Fittipaldi topped the standings in 1974.

If ever any year of the Seventies had a driver's name on it, it was 1975. The name was Andreas Nikolaus Lauda. As Jackie Stewart had enjoyed with Tyrrell in 1971, the frail-looking, buck-toothed Austrian went racing in the comfortable knowledge that his Ferrari was the best car. Niki won five Grands Prix to achieve his first World Championship. He also fell in love.

NIKI LAUDA: "Summer 1975, that incomparable late summer, Lauda the computer, Lauda the technician, Lauda the calculator, Lauda the cool customer, is almost World Champion. But the computer is in love. 'Action Ibiza', we manage it several times in those weeks, secret journeys for which we need a discreet and silent pilot, Marlene and I. They are the most beautiful days of my life."

27 APRIL 1975 - SPANISH GP (MONTJUICH) The Spanish Grand Prix was one of the great scandals in Formula 1 history. The teams were literally held hostage and forced to race on a track whose safety levels were completely unsuitable. Only the fact that the paddock was located within a derelict sports stadium, so that the organisers could realistically threaten to lock in the teams until they co-operated, prevented a boycott.

DENNY HULME: "All the drivers could still remember the accidents with Armco that had killed Roger Williamson, François Cevert, Peter Revson and Helmuth Koinigg. They knew we should have taken more of a stand at Watkins Glen in 1973, where Cevert was killed. Some felt that the GPDA's apathy was a factor in Koinigg's death there a year later."

JACKIE STEWART: "It's hard to believe how many Armco barriers weren't assembled correctly. I actually went round Barcelona myself, checking for loose bolts."

Emerson Fittipaldi, the reigning World Champion, was so incensed, and felt so strongly about the matter of principle, that he did only three slow practice laps, with one hand in the air, and refused to race.

EMERSON FITTIPALDI: "I have no doubts that what I did was correct in the circumstances. I believed then, and I still believe, that the organisers of the race were completely irresponsible. It was a very difficult weekend for me, very difficult. Particularly when none of the other drivers supported me."

In the end, team chiefs organised parties of their mechanics to tighten the loose bolts on the barriers. In this spirit of camaraderie, practice was completed, and the race went ahead. It was initially marred by several accidents. Then came a tragedy on the 26th lap when the single rear-wing post broke on Rolf Stommelen's race-leading Embassy Hill. The car slid along the top of a guardrail, plunging into a marshal's post. A Spanish fireman and an American photographer were killed. Stommelen sustained broken legs.

NIGEL ROEBUCK: "After the accident the Guardia Civil was just lashing out at anyone and everyone. There was complete bedlam. It was just unforgettable, seeing Rolf still slumped in the wreckage of the car at the top of the hill, conscious and staring straight ahead, and clearly in huge pain from broken legs. Under the monocoque there was a body and the place was strewn with wreckage. There was a total absence of control. It really was the scene from Hell."

22 JUNE 1975 - DUTCH GP (ZANDVOORT) He was the Golden Boy whose movie idol looks cloaked a hair-trigger temper, whose nickname reflected the number of cars he had trashed in a career that was going nowhere until fluke circumstance pushed him into Formula 1. Yet, in Holland, James Hunt rose above his reputation and came of age. He resisted everything that Niki Lauda and Ferrari could throw at him to score an historic maiden Grand Prix victory in the white, blue and red car owned by Lord Alexander Hesketh.

Zandvoort's flowing, high-speed nature suited the Ferraris perfectly. Lauda and Clay Regazzoni wrapped up the front row with ease, but Hunt was third fastest, only half a second shy of the Austrian. And then the harsh northerly wind on raceday brought with it the rain. Lauda jumped into an early lead on the very wet track, pursued from the second row by Scheckter. Regazzoni was third, ahead of Hunt. That order remained for the first seven laps, but at the end of his seventh Hunt dived for the pits to change from rain tyres to slicks. It was a bold gamble.

JAMES HUNT: "The track was beginning to dry quite quickly, but to begin with there were only two dry strips with slippery wet stuff either side which made it tricky if you had to go off it to pass anyone. But I knew that switching tyres then was the right thing to do."

Hunt was on trial, chased by Lauda - the computer, the metronome - who had learned the previous year that mistakes could cost him titles. Now Lauda was driving utterly within himself, the master of his emotions and his actions, waiting for race leader Hunt to make the kind of mistake for which he was infamous.

'BUBBLES' HORSLEY: "I've always considered that his weak point might be to lead a race all the way to the flag under pressure. Zandvoort has proven me happily wrong. I am now even more convinced that James Hunt is fully capable of becoming a British World Champion."

Above: Niki Lauda (left) and Emerson Fittipaldi (right) chased the championship in 1975.
Opposite: In a dramatic duel in the Dutch dunes James Hunt defeated Lauda at Zandvoort to win for the first time.

I settled myself down, and focused on avoiding mistakes. I could not have had greater pressure than I did in that race. I lacked experience leading races, which is why I cocked up a couple of times earlier that year. But now my education was complete. For once I didn't make any mistakes, and after that it became easier. JAMES HUNT

PETE LYONS (*Autosport*): "The point about the Nürburgring which is dismissed by many of its critics is that for some people it represents ever romantic justification for the endeavour they call motor racing.

"Yes, it's too long to be easily managed; sure, much of the safety apparatus is sub-standard; granted, its kind of challenge is increasingly outside the mainstream of modern short circuit racing.

"The fact remains that hundreds of thousands of people go there every year and further hundreds of thousands wish they could. They sleep on rain-sodden ground and endure grey rainy mornings and they line the 14 miles of fencing on both sides and face the track and pay attention. The 'Ring is a special place. It is a place that holds our imagination and which, rightly or wrongly, we believe offers the greatest test of those we hold to be heroes. The 'Ring is a place where we can watch and truly understand that we could not do this thing ourselves."

I revise my market value, naturally. Every public creature has its market value. Mine goes up 30%. Otherwise nothing has changed in my life as a result of being World Champion - absolutely nothing.

NIKI LAUDA

17 AUGUST 1975 - AUSTRIAN GP (OSTERREICHRING) During a warm-up session on the morning of the Austrian race, American star Mark Donohue crashed when his Penske March 751 suffered a catastrophic puncture. The car went through several layers of catchfencing and he received a blow on the head. The former CanAm sportscar champion was brought round by an injection from an attending doctor and spoke lucidly to Emerson Fittipaldi before he was taken to hospital. There, he seemed to be fine.

Unfortunately, the flight to the hospital had increased the pressure on a brain haemorrhage, and Donohue began complaining of an increasingly unbearable headache. He subsequently lapsed into unconsciousness, and an emergency operation to open his skull and relieve the pressure came too late. By the following Tuesday, he was dead.

While uncertainty remained that a catchfence pole had inflicted the ultimately fatal blow to Donohue's head, his death prompted a re-evaluation of the safety device. Catchfencing - chainlink fencing anchored by wooden posts - had been introduced by circuit designer John Hugenholtz at Zandvoort in 1962, where John Surtees was one of the first men inadvertently to test it when his Lola crashed.

3 AUGUST 1975 - GERMAN GP (NÜRBURGRING) Niki Lauda finished third at the Nürburgring, having started from pole after an extraordinary qualifying lap.

NIKI LAUDA: "It was the ultimate madness: a first-ever Nürburgring lap under seven minutes. This came during Saturday qualifying and was possible only because I was in a special sort of mood that day and ready to go for broke to an extent I have never permitted myself since.

"As I flashed past the pits I glanced in my rear-view mirror and saw the mechanics waving their hands in the air. I knew then that I had cracked the seven-minute barrier. To be exact, my new Formula 1 lap record was 6:58.6. And that's how it stands to this day - no one has ever driven the 'Ring faster.

"The problems posed by the Nürburgring were obvious at a glance. Its layout made it the most difficult circuit imaginable. It was well-nigh impossible to render safe 14.2 miles of mountainous, tree-lined track. In the long term, a circuit like the 'Ring couldn't survive.

"It was increasingly plain that, as lap times got faster and faster, we were endangering not only our lives but the sport of motor racing itself, by failing to do something about track safety, especially at the Nürburgring. Responsible drivers, responsible journalists and responsible race officials started working to improve matters, with Jackie Stewart as standard-bearer.

"I steeled myself to drive that fast lap in 1975 although my brain kept telling me it was sheer stupidity. The antithesis between the modern-day racing car and the Stone Age circuit was such that I knew every driver was taking his life in his hands to the most ludicrous degree."

JOHN SURTEES: "I was a big advocate of catchfencing. What happened was that the Lola broke a steering arm as I was coming over the rise and into the corner leading on to the main straight. There were two things I recall: one is that the fencing slowed me down, the other is that I ended up in the bicycle park. I landed there, but the fencing undoubtedly slowed me down. Without the fencing, it would have been an enormous accident because I had no steering."

JACKIE STEWART: "Catchfencing was one of the best safety devices I had the misfortune to experience. In practice at Kyalami in 1973 I had a brake failure. Had chainlink fencing not been there, I would have died. There is no question about that. I was doing 176 miles an hour, and even the spinning did nothing to wipe off speed. I just tried to forget about it, until I opened my eyes and there was a white wall in front of me, which was the concrete. The fencing had slowed me down, otherwise that really would have been a big shunt."

In Austria, 37-year-old Vittorio Brambilla won his first and only Grand Prix victory. In torrential rain, the exuberant and stocky Italian - nicknamed 'The Monza Gorilla' - controlled his March wonderfully well, only to crash moments after he crossed the finish line.

AUTOCOURSE: "Brambilla told his mechanics later that the throttle stuck so he switched off the ignition, but the car somehow got away from him. Tyres splashing water on all sides, it rapidly went past the point of no return, and the man who had just won the race began watching his cool-off lap from over the left side of his cockpit.

"As if on ice, the car slid and slid and slid, losing hardly any speed, diagonally across to the right side of the hill beyond the pits. The speed was still high when at long last the big rounded nose went crunch into the guardrail. The car whipped round and rebounded and carried on up the hill toward the crest."

7 SEPTEMBER 1975 - ITALIAN GP (MONZA) Clay Regazzoni won in Italy, where Niki Lauda opted

for a 'standard' engine to be sure of finishing. **Third place was sufficient to clinch him Ferrari's first World Championship since John Surtees's in 1964, and Italy went mad. But Lauda kept his feet on the ground.**

NIKI LAUDA: "Monza, and the World Champion title. The consequence: my professional goal has been reached, and next year I shall earn more money. No festivities, except little ones, just the two of us, Marlene and I. A few quarrels with friends about it, but honours bore me, it's not for them that I have become World Champion. The official prize from the sport authorities, a dinner service for twelve, soon finds another good home. What could I do with these giant dishes? I felt like a head waiter with them: 'More fish, my lord?'"

Opposite: The partnership between Lauda and team leader Luca di Montezemolo brought success for Ferrari.
Above: Lift-off for a Lotus at the Nürburgring, where Niki Lauda's lap of "ultimate madness" resulted in an unbeatable record.

75 THE DEATH OF GRAHAM HILL

29 NOVEMBER 1975 During the evening, television programmes in Britain were interrupted by newsflashes. A light aircraft, piloted by Graham Hill, who was returning from a test at Paul Ricard in the south of France with members of his racing team, had crashed on Arkley Golf Course in north London. There were no survivors.

The weather that fateful winter night was foul. A dripping fog wreathed the environs of Elstree airfield, where the countryside of Hertfordshire crept gently towards the suburbia of North London. Not far away stood the private school where 15-year-old Damon Graham Devereux Hill was being educated, and the beautiful detached house which stood in its own grounds at Shenley, where the Hill family lived and Bette, Graham's wife, was entertaining guests. At the small airstrip nearby, several cars stood in the damp air, awaiting owners who would never return.

Hill's decision not to divert to Luton cost him more than his own life. It killed rising star Tony Brise, designer Andy Smallman, team manager Ray Brimble and mechanics Tony Alcock and Terry Richards. Hill, twice a World Champion, had competed in 176 Grands Prix before retiring from the cockpit earlier the same year to run his Embassy Hill team.

COLIN CHAPMAN: "I think that as a character, Graham was an example of what is best in a professional racing driver, he really worked at it."

You know the risks, you accept them. If man can't look at danger and still go on, that man has stopped living. If the worst ever happens, then it means simply that I've been asked to pay the bill for the happiness of my life, without a moment's regret.

GRAHAM HILL

Graham Hill with his children. Son Damon (centre) would later continue the family tradition and become a champion.

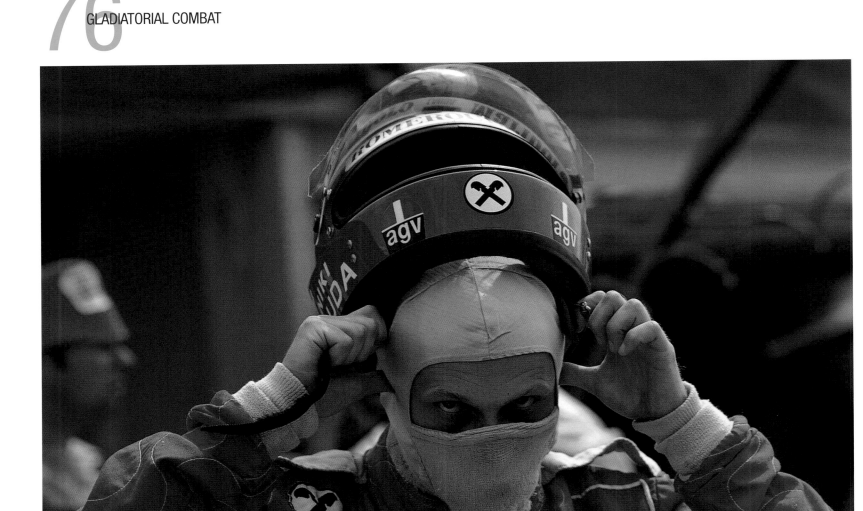

1976 was the most gripping season of the decade. The reality was more dramatic than a Hollywood scriptwriter's most preposterously fanciful screenplay: two close friends fighting tooth and nail for the World Championship - a charismatic English sex symbol versus an Austrian computer; two top teams locked in battle; political infighting that marred at least three races; a fiery, life-threatening crash that befell one of the leading contenders; a magnificent balls-to-the-wall fightback from adversity by the other; and an astonishing final scene set at the foot of a volcanic mountain in Japan.

Following Lord Hesketh's announcement that he simply could not continue spending so much of his inheritance on trying to make James Hunt the World Champion, Hunt found himself without a drive for 1976. But there was an unexpected vacancy when McLaren's Emerson Fittipaldi made a last-minute decision to join his brother, Wilson, in a new team funded by Copersucar, Brazil's national sugar industry. It was almost in desperation that McLaren hired Hunt.

EMERSON FITTIPALDI: "When I look back on it, I realise that leaving McLaren was one of the biggest mistakes I ever made in my life."

Hunt and McLaren were immediately fast but took a while to hit their rhythm. The season began strongly for Niki Lauda, who won the opening two races in his highly competitive Ferrari. His team mate, Clay Regazzoni won the third race, a new event in California.

2 MAY 1976 - SPANISH GP (JARAMA) In Spain, Hunt edged out Lauda, who was nursing bruised ribs after overturning a tractor at his home in Austria the previous week.

But Hunt's triumph was shortlived. Half an hour after the finish, the scrutineers found Hunt's McLaren M23 to be 1.8cm too wide, and disqualified the car. McLaren immediately lodged an appeal.

TEDDY MAYER (McLaren team manager): "It's like being hanged for a parking offence!"

13 JUNE 1976 - SWEDISH GP (ANDERSTORP) Tyrrell had stunned the Formula 1 circus with a bizarre, six-wheeled car for Jody Scheckter and Patrick Depailler. In Sweden, Scheckter scored the only victory for this maverick device.

4 JULY 1976 - FRENCH GP (LE CASTELLET) Just before Hunt won in France, he learned that his Spanish victory had been reinstated on appeal. Effectively he earned the points for two race wins in one weekend.

18 JULY 1976 - BRITISH GP (BRANDS HATCH) Hunt became embroiled in further controversy after winning the British Grand Prix at Brands Hatch, and then having it taken away. Lauda and Hunt qualified on the front row. However, at the start, Regazzoni beat Hunt into the first corner, but tangled with Lauda, triggering a multiple shunt. The race was red-flagged so that the accident debris could be cleaned up.

Hunt's damaged car was brought back to the pits, where the McLaren mechanics rebuilt its front suspension and wheeled it out for the restart. This seemed to contravene a rule that stated that no driver

Above: Niki Lauda and James Hunt, contrasting characters yet fast friends, fought hammer and tongs for the 1976 title.

might restart a race unless his car had completed the red flag lap. The stewards decreed that the local hero would not be allowed to restart his home race.

AUTOCOURSE: "Well, sir. You should've heard the crowd when that was announced! Do you think of the Brits as quiet, well-mannered, stiff-upper-lip sorts of people? The roar of their disapproval, rising from 77,000 throats, turned the Kentish skies an even deeper blue."

Fearing a riot, the authorities allowed Hunt to restart the race, and he went on to catch and pass Lauda to win. But later (24 September) it was ruled that Hunt was ineligible to run, and Lauda was declared the victor. It was rough justice, especially since Regazzoni had started the accident and Ferrari was the ultimate beneficiary.

1 AUGUST 1976 - GERMAN GP (NÜRBURGRING) In Germany, *Autosport* reporter Pete Lyons recorded a memorable vignette from the mighty Nürburgring, where - after what was to come on race day - Formula 1 cars would never race again.

PETE LYONS: "At mid-morning on Saturday the rain had stopped but down in the Foxhole the road was still streaming wet. Shallow sheets of rainwater were rippling down diagonally from kerb to kerb across the kinks of the track. It was many long minutes into the session before an engine could be heard nearing the Fuchsrohre section. It came through thinly at first and intermittently, isolated bursts of power modulated by passage over hill crests and across valleys and filtered through the shaggy limbs of millions of trees, but each time it was nearer and clearer, until with abruptness it was here, just up over the top of the ridge on the entrance to Schwedenkreutz. The sudden straining of the engine was cut off, there were cracklings and blippings.

"Then from a new direction, around the shoulder of the hill, the car came powersliding out of the Aremberg hairpin. It was little and slithered on its tyres, and spray was rising up behind. The driver's helmet bobbed as the car lunged over humps and waggled between the kerbs. It hurled itself forward under the road bridge - throwing ahead of it a brief reflection of noise from the concrete surfaces - and dropped down the hill. But the smoothness of the descent was interrupted as once, twice, three times and more the

driver slacked off his foot on the way down to the bottom. The black shape of the car dissolved in the boiling grey water thrown up by the tyres. Then even that vanished, and there was nothing left but the hard horn of the engine: moments of strong driving power, then tentative slackenings and cracklings.

"Minutes passed. The twin paths left by the rain tyres gradually filled in, and the road glistened again. The silence of the forest crept back slowly, like the confidence of a frightened wild animal.

"But a new noise was crashing through the wood. Another car, the second, and this one was running harder. Down the valley a wet metallic blur, the turmoil of vapour streaking along behind. From kerb to kerb, running nearly straight as the road weaved, down to the distant bottom of the dip, and not for an instant did the driver's foot ease. The strident engine howled unchecked as the car became a comet of water spray up the other side, arcing quickly out of sight under the trees. Hard - long, confident bursts of power through the swerves. Hard - sharp deceleration at the next crest. Hard - quick, sure acceleration away. The noise hung in the air angrily, abandoned by the speeding machine."

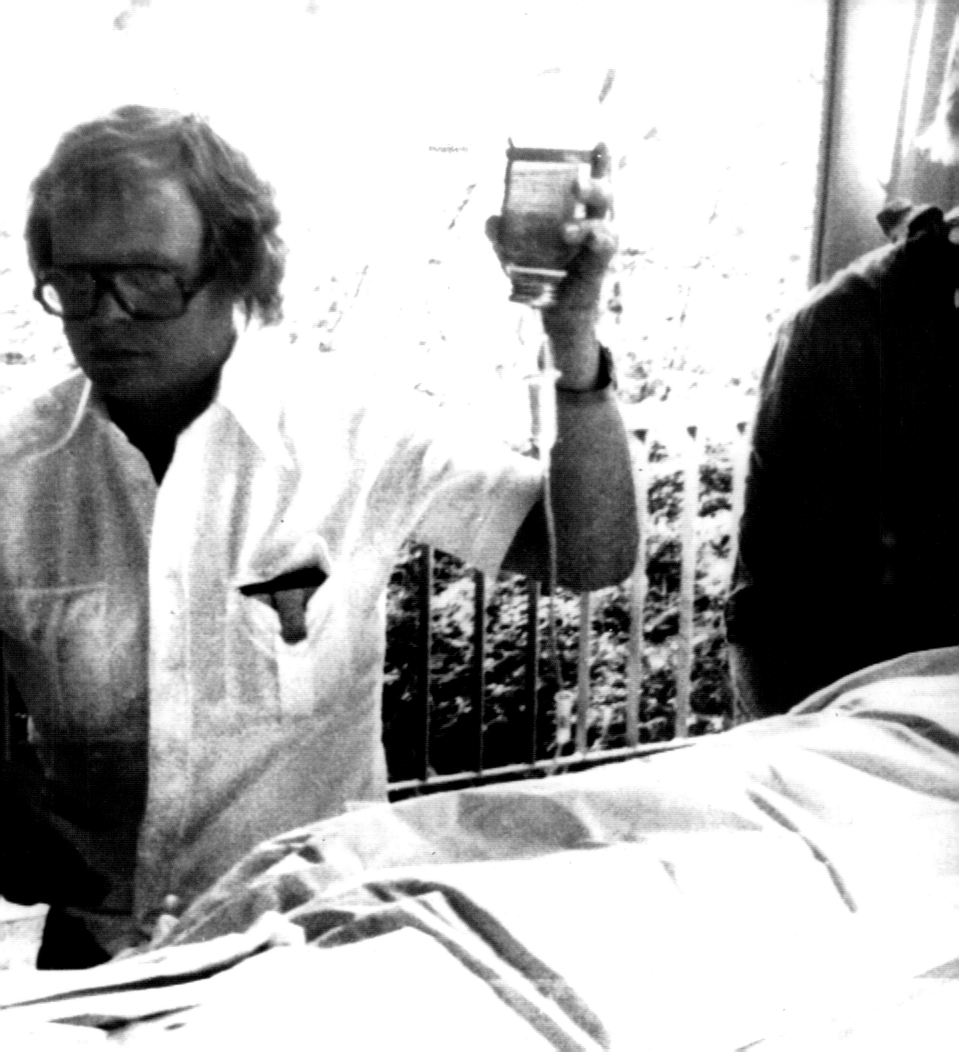

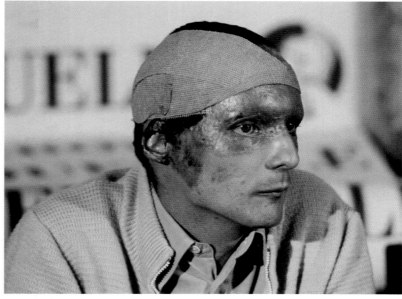

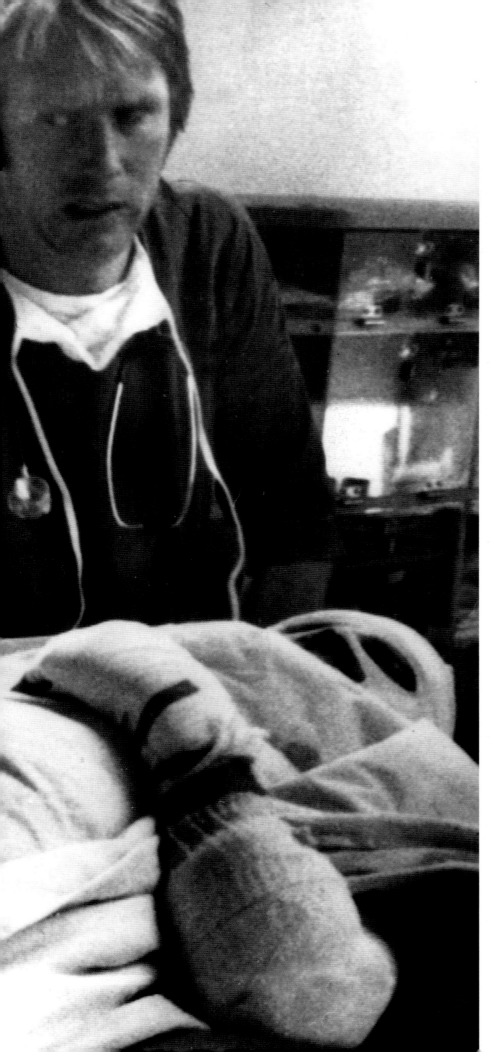

The race began under overcast skies, with James Hunt on pole, and Niki Lauda beside him. The damp track was drying, so Lauda stopped at the end of the first lap to switch from rain tyres to slicks. He was working his way back through the field when, just after Adenau and in the fast left-hander before the right-hand Bergwerk corner, his Ferrari went out of control.

NIKI LAUDA "I have of course seen films and TV video pictures of the accident dozens of times. I am driving down the Bergwerk, take the left turn at kilometre 10.6, and touch the apex at the concrete kerb. The car breaks away at the back and I put on opposite lock and drift - quite normally, nothing too dramatic. Speed: a bit more than 200kph an hour. Suddenly the car moves to the right, a much more violent movement than would be caused by a steering wheel movement and crashes through the fencing, bounces against the embankment and is hurled back so that the fuel tank breaks away. At the same time a pole knocked my helmet off. My Ferrari stands right across the track, Brett Lunger's car crashes into it and sends it 100 metres further. Merzario, Lunger, Edwards and Ertl save my life, by pulling me out of the burning wreck. Most marvellous of all was what Arturo Merzario did: he rushed straight into the flames and managed to get my safety belt undone. His action changed nothing in his attitude to me. He couldn't stand me before, and had often attacked me in the Italian press, and afterwards he did the same. He was a completely selfless saviour. He pulled out a fellow he really disliked."

JAMES HUNT: "I was well ahead of Niki on the road, maybe a mile ahead of him, so I knew nothing about the accident and drove 13 miles around the full lap until about two miles from where it happened before I saw the 'race stopped' flag signals were out.

"Apparently Niki's car had been on fire, but he got out of it and had talked to one or two of the drivers. He was burned a little bit around his face and wrists but it didn't look serious, and everything was fine. Niki was off to hospital, and obviously wouldn't be racing again that day but he'd have his burns patched up and we'd see him in Austria. That was the story we had then. It was still all we knew after I had won the race.

"But the next morning we realised that Niki was in a very bad way indeed. We were very concerned but there was little or nothing one could do. I couldn't visit him, so I went home and sent him a telegram. I can't remember what I said but it was something provocative to annoy him and then I told him to fight, because I knew if he was annoyed and fighting, he would pull through. If he relaxed and gave in, he would probably die. You've got to stay conscious and physically fight it yourself, and I knew Niki would be aware of that."

Given up for dead, Lauda survived by sheer force of will, though his disfigurement provoked some disgusting behaviour.

I lie in bed and think it will soon be all over. I am tired, and want to go sleep and know nothing more. All over me there are tubes going in and out. I hear voices, see a movement, feel giddy, then I think I mustn't go, mustn't go, and I cling to the voice as if to a rope, because as long as I can hear voices I am still alive, and I fight and fight and won't give in. I hear Marlene's voice. I can't see her, I can't speak but I can hear her, which cranks me up to think once more. I understand my situation: accident, fire, hospital, burnt, lungs turned to shit.

I AM BANDAGED, BLIND AND DUMB. A MAN APPEARS: I UNDERSTAND IT'S THE PRIEST. HE SPEAKS IN LATIN, IT SOUNDS LIKE A JUDGEMENT, THE LAST RITES. YOU CAN DIE FROM AN EXTREME UNCTION LIKE THAT JUST AS YOU CAN DIE FROM SHOCK. THE PRIEST SAYS NOTHING KIND, NEVER MENTIONS THE POSSIBILITY THAT I MIGHT RECOVER. IT MAKES ME SO CROSS. I WANT TO SHOUT,

'Hey, stop! This is the worst fuck-up you make in your life. I am not going to die!' NIKI LAUDA

It was suddenly very important to me that Niki should live, in a way that I hadn't realised, and I felt awful because there was nothing I could do about it. There I was sitting at home enjoying life even when I didn't particularly want to, when I wanted to go and help or do something and I couldn't. It was a strange time for me. When I heard he was beginning to recover I was immensely relieved.

JAMES HUNT

THE REACTION OF THE FANS WAS HELPFUL, ENCOURAGING, OFTEN TOUCHING. PEOPLE WROTE AND TELEPHONED OFFERING THEIR SKIN, OR THEIR EARS, TOLD ME THEIR EXPERIENCES OF BURNS AND SKIN TRANSPLANTS. A LITTLE BOY SENT ME HIS TOY FERRARI BECAUSE HE HAD HEARD MINE WAS BURNT. NIKI LAUDA

NIKI LAUDA: "As for the journalists, there were wide differences between them. The hyenas among them behaved in a way that went beyond everything. They tried all ways to get a photograph of my unrecognisable swollen head. The hospital was besieged, the idiotic photographers had to creep in unnoticed, they tried to bribe the nurses.

"Sensational newspapers went on for weeks with special Lauda accident reports. Headlines were: 'Niki Lauda's fight with death!', 'My God, where is my face?' And in the text: 'Niki Lauda, the fastest racing driver in the world, hasn't got a face now - it is nothing but raw flesh, the eyes are popping out.' This was illustrated with two nice photographs of my face covered in bandages, naturally on the front page. Two days later readers were given good news with the headlines, 'Niki Lauda will pull through.... but how can a man live without a face?"

"In the text it went on: 'How can he go on living with no face? However frightful it may sound, even when his body has recovered, he won't be able to see anyone for six months. Only by 1979 will his new face be ready. Nose, eyelids, lips will be made, but this face will not resemble his former face. Only by his voice will his friends be able to recognise the racing driver.'

"My first press conference was horrible. 'What did your wife say when she saw your face?' asked one of them. You could get up and go or else give stupid answers. Had Marlene asked for a divorce, had I got complexes about my appearance, what was going to happen about my ear? - even the most primitive tact or good manners were apparently forgotten when talking of Lauda.

"I find it obvious that one should treat a cripple in a normal manner and not keep referring to his imperfection. People are sometimes surprised that I am so 'cold' or 'hard', but you have to be damned hard to deal with these sort of situations. I answered the question 'How I was going to get used to my face?' by saying I didn't need a face, only a right foot. There is really no point having a complex about losing half an ear. It makes it easier to talk on the telephone. What other answer could one give to such an idiot? And nobody seems to realise that the answer follows from the question, they all think I am a hard devil."

15 AUGUST 1976 - AUSTRIAN GP (OSTERREICHRING) In Austria, Ulsterman John Watson scored his first Formula 1 triumph in style, and the only Grand Prix victory for American entrant Roger Penske, whose driver Mark Donohue had died at the Osterreichring the previous year.

29 AUGUST 1976 - DUTCH GP (ZANDVOORT) Having finished fourth in Austria, Hunt took further advantage of Lauda's absence with a victory in Holland.

12 SEPTEMBER 1976 - ITALIAN GP (MONZA) At Monza, Lauda sensationally returned to the cockpit, little more than a month after he had been given the last rites. His head was still swathed with blood-soaked bandages protecting his terribly scarred face, and the gruff Austrian was rightly hailed as a hero.

JACKIE STEWART: "Niki had no right to be driving there because he was nowhere near healed. It was the most courageous thing I have ever witnessed in sport."

NIKI LAUDA: "At Monza I hid the truth. I was rigid with fear. Terrified. Diarrhoea. Heart pounding. Throwing up.

"The first time the Ferrari skidded in practice I was scared. Being scared was intolerable. I said to myself, 'You can't drive a car like that.' Then I waited quite consciously for the skid and began with the precision work of handling the drift. After that it was not so hard, the worst was behind me. I had crossed the threshold and was once more at my normal rate. Next day I was fourth in the race, which some people thought was quite good."

10 OCTOBER 1976 - USA EAST GP (WATKINS GLEN) Without Lauda to do the testing, Ferrari had lost its edge. Hunt garnered another 18 points with brilliant victories in Canada and America. Early on the morning of the US race, Hunt was still sleeping in his hotel room. Suddenly the door burst open and into the room goose-stepped his championship rival, fully dressed in racing regalia including his helmet.

NIKI LAUDA: "Vake up! Today I vill vin zee championship!"

But Lauda only managed third in the race and, going into the final showdown in Japan, the points total was Lauda 68, Hunt 65.

24 OCTOBER 1976 - JAPANESE GP (MOUNT FUJI) That finale went down in history. Not because of the terrible weather at the spooky venue in the shadow of Mount Fuji, nor for pole-winner Mario Andretti's resurgent victory for Team Lotus. First there was an argument over whether the race should even be started, given the torrential rain that had inundated the track.

Then came Lauda's bold decision to pull out of the race after only a lap.

NIKI LAUDA: "I drive slowly, keep away from the other cars so that none of them shall run into me. I think how stupid this race is. You can't see. In this water on the track you are as helpless as a paper boat. Even going slowly you could be washed away. After the second lap I go into the pits. I am not going to drive, because it is madness. For me it was the limit. For me there is something more important than the World Championship."

Hunt still needed points to get the title, and he set about getting them in the most spectacular way. In appalling conditions, he led for 61 of the 73 laps, until deciding to play it safe, and dropping behind Andretti and Depailler into the third place that was all he needed. But then, in a final Hollywood twist, he picked up a puncture and had to make a pitstop that dragged on and on because the car's jack malfunctioned.

EOIN YOUNG: "Back on track again, Hunt was a different man. The calculating tactician had been replaced by a racer with a red mist of anger descending. How could he have blown the title like that? He cursed the tyres and cursed his luck.

"In a mounting fury, Hunt slammed round those closing laps, caution cast to the winds, and it was this final desperate lunge at the whole blasted season that carried Hunt back into the World Championship. Almost without realising it, he passed Regazzoni's Ferrari and Jones's Surtees, to claim third place."

Hunt's podium finish was just enough to clinch the title but, when he exited the cockpit of his McLaren, he exploded in a towering rage at team manager Teddy Mayer, blaming him for screwing up the tyre change and costing him the championship.

JAMES HUNT: "I was absolutely determined not to think I was World Champion and then get disappointed, because there were 300 good reasons why something should have gone wrong. It was only really when I checked the laps and when the organisers said I was third - and there were no protests in the wind - that I allowed myself to start believing it.

"Let's hope that no fool blames [Niki] for packing it in. He's come through a terrible accident and his comeback has been heroic. But I think he made the right decision and I feel awfully sorry for him. I feel sorry for anyone who's got to race in such ridiculous circumstances."

NIKI LAUDA: "Praise for the World Champion, James Hunt. He is of all the drivers the one I like best. I value him, I am fond of him, he is the only one I know fairly well in private life. He is relaxed, easy and unworried. He does

Poor Niki. In a perfect world we would have shared the World Championship but that is impossible.

JAMES HUNT

what amuses him, and I like that. All the quarrels between McLaren and Ferrari in 1976 never made any difference to James and me personally. We had divergent interests and each had to fight for his own side, of course, but that had nothing to do with us two men. He is a marvellous driver and brilliantly talented. When he is rested, he is the hardest man to beat."

Refusing to believe that Niki Lauda would ever recover his full powers, Enzo Ferrari hired Carlos Reutemann - who had been recruited to drive at Monza, where Ferrari never expected Lauda to appear - and gave the Argentine the job of developing the cars for 1977. On learning this, Lauda was livid...

NIKI LAUDA: "I telephoned old man Ferrari and had the most decisive talk that I had in all my four years with his team. 'What did this mean?' I asked. Well, he said, since I (Lauda) had made a wrong decision, all decisions henceforward were to come from him, he would take it in hand himself. 'Wrong decision, what did he mean?' Monza, he said - I shouldn't have raced at Monza. If I had missed

the race because of my accident we should have lost the World Championship in a way that would have looked better. I was utterly furious and shouted at him that perhaps for an Italian it would be all right to lie in bed and lose in a way that looked well, but when I fight, I fight and I don't lie in bed. If I lose the World Championship on the road, well I accept it. Thanks, goodbye, I slammed the receiver down.

"I was all in, depressed and furious. Why had I been through hell, got myself out of hospital, worked every minute on my body to recover, given everything I had to it, just to be treated in this way at the end of it all. Naturally when the old man said Monza he meant Fuji. If at Fuji I had driven like an angel through the water, everything would have been grand.

"I tried to put myself in his shoes. Okay, he pays for Ferrari to race and Ferrari to win. He pays for the World Championship, and then all of a sudden the fool Lauda won't drive because it's too dangerous for him. But when I go on thinking as Ferrari must be thinking, I can't help coming to the human situation, for after all he's got a man under contract, not an ape. He can give the ape a kick up

the arse and order him to drive, but a man must be expected to think. And if he didn't consider me an idiot before, then he must accept the result of my thoughts.

"When I think over the whole picture, including the Nürburgring, and when I add the quite special pressures on Niki Lauda in that autumn of 1976 and look back on at all, I can't see one iota of a possibility of it being fair to punish me for Fuji. In those days my fury against Ferrari was so deep that from then on I never again felt happy in the team."

Left: Hunt, Lauda and Peterson considered it ridiculous to race in the torrential rain at Mount Fuji.
Opposite: Reigning champion Lauda walked away from his number 1 and handed the title to Hunt (inset, sleeping on the plane flight home).

Now that Niki Lauda was out of favour at Ferrari, he knew that he needed to do something special if he was going to be champion in 1977. The fast-developing prowess of his team mate Carlos Reutemann further eroded Lauda's status at Ferrari. Lauda, now matured as the analytical strategist par excellence, focused on the long haul.

The opposition was strong, especially Team Lotus. Colin Chapman had been working on the concept of the Lotus 78 for two years in great secrecy. Four hundred hours of wind tunnel testing - unheard of at that time - went into it. The 78 had phenomenal cornering ability and was the dominant car of the season. Mario Andretti won four races for Lotus, and should have won others, but his championship campaign suffered through poor engine reliability and his own penchant for first-lap accidents.

The 1977 season was notable technically not only for the advent of the ground-effect Lotus, but also for the appearance of the first turbocharged engines.

9 JANUARY 1977 - ARGENTINE GP Walter Wolf's new team won the first race, on its first try, with Jody Scheckter driving. It was a fabulous result for Scheckter, and for new team owner Wolf, an Austro-Canadian oil magnate, but no doubt hard to swallow for Frank Williams, who had sold out to Wolf and was back home in England when the team he started in 1973 finally won a race.

FRANK WILLIAMS: "I recognised that Frank Williams Racing Cars was in a deep hole, and it required extraordinary entrepreneurial skills which I believe I didn't have at the time. It was better to make an accommodation. As for that win in South Africa it was just the team owned and run by the guy who bought my dud business, that's all."

5 MARCH 1977 - SOUTH AFRICAN GP (KYALAMI) NIKI LAUDA: "The first victory since my accident. A telegram from the Old Man: 'You are still yourself - as before, but more than ever!' Such rubbish! He sent the telegram not for me but only because his car had come in first.

"In the race, a crazy accident - because of a marshal, who ran across the track. The misery over the deaths and the joy over my victory mingled to something indescribable."

The death of young Welshman Tom Pryce during the South African Grand Prix was the personification of the needless racing tragedy. Pryce had made a slow start but was fighting his way back through the field when his Shadow team mate, Renzo Zorzi, rolled to a halt opposite the pits on the 21st lap, his car beginning

James Hunt, the defending World Champion, found himself struggling in the 1977 season until the new McLaren M26 came fully on song, after which he won three times. But with the title came responsibilties that Hunt found tiresome.

JAMES HUNT: "I can tell you, the business of being champion is nearly as tough as trying to stay champion on the track. It's almost a relief to get back to the simple life on the circuit, but I realise that isn't the way I should be looking at it. But the last few months have been absolute bloody hell. There was hardly a single day when I did not attend at least three public functions. I just worked 14 to 20 hours a day. Wearing work. I appeared here, I appeared there. Here I picked up a cup, there an award. And what do I do with them? I don't want a lot of useless bowls cluttering up my life.

"Why the hell can't I be more like Niki, who ignores all the bullshit that goes with the championship, though I must say he is sometimes harsh with the fans."

Hunt described one incident in which a young fan came up to Lauda in a race paddock and presented him with a gift...

JAMES HUNT: "It was a scrapbook which he had collected together. Niki simply took the book and said: 'Yes, now go.' Even if the book was awful, which it certainly was, I think Niki should have taken it, given the kid a smile and some chat. I would have. The fans make us what we are.

"Still, there's a temptation, when the 74th person grabs you and gives you an earful of bullshit, to tell him: 'Fuck off. Leave me alone.'

"But that person's probably travelled three hundred miles and especially wanted to talk to you. You need their support and it's nice to have and it's not their fault they've caught you at a bad moment. They didn't mean any harm, you have to remember that. But sometimes it's very wearying, very tiring.

"Short of locking myself up in a room, I can't get away from it and the problem is that the nice people don't often come up and talk. It's the pushy ones who barge through and make you perform. You feel like some sort of mechanical toy. When they confront you it's like throwing the switch and you're supposed to do or say something clever."

But some thought Hunt's irreverent attitude, especially his habit of dressing down for all occasions, was bringing the sport into disrepute.

JACKIE STEWART: "He might have been a modern young person who was anti-establishment but his habit of dressing too casually, wearing inappropriate clothes even when meeting royalty, I thought was bad form. Whereas the Jim Clarks, Graham Hills, the Jackie Stewarts if you like, were always fairly well presented, James seemed to want to go over the top the other way. I certainly didn't approve of that because I was by then deeply involved with multinational corporations associated with the sport, and I was worried that James was projecting the wrong image."

Above: Hunt horrified the establishment and struggled with the responsibilities that came with the championship.
Right: Poor Tom Pryce was already dead as his Shadow flew out of control down the straight at Kyalami.

to smoke. **Seeing the wisps of smoke, Jansen van Vuuren, a 19-year-old ticket clerk at Jan Smuts Airport who was acting as a pit-lane marshal that weekend, began a fateful charge across the road, lugging a fire extinguisher. Hidden in the dip before the brow were four cars travelling at maximum speed.**

ALAN REES (Shadow team manager): "As Tom was coming through the field there was only one more in that pack that he had to overtake, and that was Hans Stuck. Stuck was the one who avoided the guy who ran across the road, and he did it so quickly that Tom was left out there. He wouldn't even have known about it. He wouldn't have known anything about it, I'm sure of that. Stuck obviously saw the guy at the last moment and just swerved, and Tom was right in his slipstream and couldn't avoid the marshal."

ALAN HENRY: "I was down at Crowthorne corner and saw it all, although it didn't register with me what was happening at the time. I just saw a car out of control and slamming into the barriers. I walked up the left-hand side of the track after it was over in a fairly zonked frame of mind because there was no doubt about poor Tom. And John Surtees popped out of one of those little caravans the teams had, took me in, sat me down and gave me a whisky, which I always thought was a nice gesture. I appreciated that a lot. Tom was certainly quick enough to go all the way in the sport. It would just have been a matter of calming himself down and getting the right equipment."

FRANK KEATING (writing in *The Guardian*): "Tom Pryce had asked me not to forget to give him a full report of the England versus Wales rugby international when he arrived back home today from the South African Grand Prix. But now he's not coming back. He is just another tear-stained wail in the tragic litany of lives and loves lost in the name of his sport."

JAMES HUNT: "The system let Tom down, and it is time that something was done to prevent the possibility of a recurrence. I strongly believe that creating a squad of professional marshals, who travel to each and every Grand Prix, is the only sensible way to go for the future."

It makes me extremely angry when we lose drivers of the calibre of Tom. People do not listen enough to the drivers, yet we are the ones who take the greatest risk. JAMES HUNT

Our engine became famous
for blowing up its pistons,
and our British friends
called it 'The Big Yellow
Smoking Teapot'.

FRANÇOIS CASTAING

3 APRIL 1977 - USA WEST GP (LONG BEACH) Mario Andretti's win at Long Beach with the Lotus 78 was the first for a ground-effect car. Ground-effect became the watchword from 1977 onwards, and today's cars still generate much of their aerodynamic downforce in this way.

Colin Chapman is generally credited with harnessing ground-effect for Formula 1, but his design team, Peter Wright, Tony Rudd and Ralph Bellamy, all played a part. They established that the airflow beneath the car was even more significant in generating downforce than the flow over its bodywork. By installing venturi beneath the Lotus 78 in the form of profiled underwings, like an aircraft's but inverted, they could create a low-pressure area.

Effectively, this 'sucked' the car towards the ground, and caused much less aerodynamic drag than was generated by external wings. The key to success lay in creating a proper seal between the wide sidepods of the race car and the ground, via flexible 'skirts'.

COLIN CHAPMAN: "I think there are ten solutions to every problem and you should never be satisfied with the first one. You work them all out, then find one that has particular merit in terms of simplicity, elegance, cost, refinement. When you've wrung it to death, and can say, 'That's the essence' - then you build it."

16 JULY 1977 - BRITISH GP (SILVERSTONE) When a bulbous, yellow-and-black racing car turned up for the British Grand Prix in 1977, and qualified 21st in the 26-car field, few onlookers felt inclined to take it seriously. Some observers even sniggered.

Every other manufacturer had opted for the 3-litre naturally aspirated engine laid out in the regulations. In contrast, Renault, fresh from successes in sportscar racing which had advanced its turbocharging technology, took the huge gamble to build a car complying with the alternative rules, those that allowed 1.5-litre engines with forced induction. Thus was born the first 'turbo' in Formula 1.

PETER WINDSOR (*Autocar*): "A start, is how the Renault turbo's Formula 1 debut is best described. After the first day of practice, the car had yet to qualify. A turbocharger had already broken [larger turbochargers were used for the Renault's first appearance] and the Michelin tyres did not seem soft enough for the afternoon chill. But on Friday, a warmer day, the car was quicker. It was still very slow in acceleration and it was not good under

braking. But Silverstone, of all circuits, is kind to both those traits. Jean-Pierre Jabouille qualified with two rows of the grid to spare and, for the first time, there were two French radio stations to be heard in the pits on the night before the race.

"By the time of its first pitstop, lap 12, the Renault was lying 18th, ahead of such runners as Emerson Fittipaldi (Copersucar), Brett Lunger (McLaren), Patrick Neve (March) and Vern Schuppan (Surtees). Further, Jean-Pierre Jabouille was on the tail of Riccardo Patrese's Shadow - a fair achievement for a team so completely new. A split inlet manifold was what first stopped the Renault, another broken turbocharger was what finally halted it. But it was a start."

FRANÇOIS CASTAING (Renault Sport technical director): "From then we started discovering how tough it is to race at the level of F1. Even in those days. We were new, car all new, Michelin tyres new. I figured right away they were the way to go. But we went on to discover all the miseries of turbocharging with pump fuel. We were quick in qualifying but rarely finished. Half of the retirements were the engine not being reliable enough, the other half the inexperience of the team.

"After I left racing I was reading books about World War II and I found out everything that happened to us as far as understanding combustion and turbocharging, I could have learned enormously from all the work done by the British companies between 1940 and 1943 when they were supercharging the aircraft engines.

"The reason why the Spitfire went from 1500 horsepower to almost 3000 over three years is simply because they understood better how to control compressions, to design pistons and other parts that could support higher boost pressures. I've discovered all kinds of documentation since that I wish I'd read in '77."

Although nobody realised it at the time, the Renault was the future. It took another two years for Renault to win a race but, by 1984, all the major teams would have 650bhp turbocharged engines for the races, and most had special qualifying engines that developed up to 1500bhp. The turbo would rule until it was finally outlawed when Formula 1 catered only for 3.5-litre naturally aspirated cars from 1989.

Left: Renault's revolutionary new turbocharged V6 provoked sniggers at first, but then proved to be the only type of powerplant to have.
Opposite: The skirts on the Lotus - here on Mario Andretti's car at the 1977 French GP - raised eyebrows, but quickly became fashionable as their aerodynamic secrets were revealed.

You can only get design information from experience. It's suck-it-and-see engineering.

COLIN CHAPMAN

Gilles Villeneuve was an unknown quantity when he arrived at the British Grand Prix in 1977. After he had roundly beaten James Hunt and several other Formula 1 drivers in a Formula Atlantic race in Canada, Hunt recommended that McLaren give Villeneuve a trial run.

PETER WINDSOR (*Autocar*): "The Canadian Formula Atlantic star headed the list of pre-qualifiers after the Wednesday session, during which time he spun many times. In qualifying he indulged in a further bout of spins and finally outqualified his McLaren team mate, Jochen Mass. Villeneuve looked untidy, but then you would expect him to be. What you did not expect was the composure and resignation with which he accepted his speed. After practice, he could be seen walking round the paddock, tiny inside a new Marlboro McLaren jacket, almost unnoticed as he and his wife Joann mused over the biggest day in his career so far. Or was it that it did not seem such a big day? In the Marlboro motorhome, Villeneuve slipped into the McLaren briefing almost embarrassed, almost as an intruder.

"Next day, Villeneuve earned himself honours by running an early seventh, losing time to have a faulty water temperature gauge inspected and finishing a hard and clean 11th. His fastest race lap was bettered only by race-winner Hunt, Watson, Nilsson and Scheckter. It was enough to move Jackie Stewart to remark: 'He's got it.' Indeed he had, in spades. Formula 1 met a new hero that British summer day.

28 AUGUST 1977 - DUTCH GP (ZANDVOORT) Even before the end of the season, Niki Lauda had decided he would leave Ferrari and join Bernie Ecclestone's Brabham team in 1978. With his victory in Holland, Lauda was close to clinching his second title.

NIKI LAUDA: "The date of the win at Zandvoort suited my plan for giving notice splendidly. I wanted straight away, after the victory, to make it clear that I wouldn't make another contract with Ferrari, because once again it wouldn't suit their scheme of things. A win, practically World Champion, more on top than ever - and even so the fellow wants to leave?

"Four years of pressure are enough, four years of blowing hot and cold are the maximum. One couldn't blame the Old Man for all this. But the domination of the Old Man along with the unpredictability of the Ferrari underground and the spikiness of Mauro Forghieri - all that was too much for a fifth year.

"Forghieri (the technical director) was one of the chief reasons why I left Ferrari, but I must admit there is a lot to be said for him. He is a good chap, even more, he's a technical genius. Unfortunately he is also crazy. He makes snap decisions, ignores realities, insists he is right, and then you can't argue with him. He has got the psychological finesse of a sand viper. One important thing he has never understood in his life: that you must persuade a man, and having persuaded him you must not endlessly change your mind. When the Ferrari went well and all was perfect, he considered me a very good driver, perhaps the best. When things went wrong, I was an idiot.

"Ferrari, the racing team, is unique in the world, and it has unique problems too. They begin with the myth of Old Man Ferrari, who is such a sacred figure for the Italians that they go flat on their faces before him. When I say 'Ciao, Enzo', bystanders are always shocked, because hardly anyone calls him anything but President, or *Commendatore*, or even *Ingegnere*. His people are so much in awe of this monumental patriarch that it is a source of misunderstandings and mistaken decisions. They would rather please the Old Man by telling him something nice (untrue) instead of something less nice (true)."

On 29 August, Lauda met with Enzo Ferrari in his office at Modena.

NIKI LAUDA: "I am not much of a hand at 'historical merit' and the cult of legends. For me, Enzo Ferrari was just the chief of my racing team, and I always treated him with respect, but straightforwardly. When I wanted to talk with him I knocked on his door and went in, whereas even for his closest colleagues the ritual is to ask for an interview.

"In his office the show is a bit terrifying I must admit: the empty room painted dark blue, the great portrait of his dead son Dino, usually with candles burning in front of it, and at the writing table the aged President. If you feel a bit upset by all this, you feel more upset still on the way out, impressed by so much quiet grandeur. If you talk to him properly, all goes normally."

ENZO FERRARI: "I asked Lauda what he wanted to tell me. He became embarrassed. 'I remember,' he began, 'having made a promise, and it was not to leave the Ferrari team while you were still there. But today I find I can't keep it, because I no longer have the motivation to stay.' 'What motivation?,' I asked him. He answered by saying he couldn't find the right words in Italian, and began to speak in English.

Above: Gilles Villeneuve rapidly went from a nobody to one of the biggest names in the sport.

"I stopped him and exclaimed: 'If you want to say unpleasant things, then use the Italian language which you understand perfectly well.' I shouted: 'You, when you made your promise did you take my age into consideration, my eighty years and my illness?' Lauda went on in a fragmentary way and wasn't able to do more than just allude to this 'motivation.' I assure you that no new deals were ever offered him or new financial agreements discussed.

"Lauda was one of the greatest, and I still consider him to be so. A judgement? I never make judgements, I limit myself, when pressed, simply to giving my opinion, which, in the case of Lauda the man, I'd rather keep to myself."

11 SEPTEMBER 1977 - ITALIAN GP (MONZA) For 1977, the BRM team created a new car, an oversized, underpowered monster known as the P207. The year began badly when it failed to fit the packing crate intended to take it to Argentina.

Throughout the season, things got worse and, at Monza, the sole BRM for Belgian driver Teddy Pilette failed to qualify. After that, the team with 197 Grand Prix starts, 11 pole positions, 17 victories, 15 fastest laps and the 1962 World Championship closed its doors.

Between his race wins, Niki Lauda finished second six times, third once and fourth once. His progress throughout the season was simply irresistible. In the end he had 72 points. Scheckter trailed on 55, Andretti and Reutemann 47 and 42 and Hunt on 40.

There was always furore at Ferrari. The Old Man was a dictator. Forghieri was a genius, but also a madman.

NIKI LAUDA

Mario Andretti's World Championship in 1978 was a long time coming. The Formula 1 career of the charismatic, Italian-born American had been sporadic due to his commitments in American racing, where he was a full-fledged superstar. Yet he took pole position in his first Grand Prix, at Watkins Glen with Lotus in 1968, and in 1971 he won the South African Grand Prix with Ferrari.

Rejoining Team Lotus in 1976, Andretti worked with Colin Chapman to rebuild the team. By 1978, when the Lotus 79 ground-effect car was fully developed, Andretti, backed up by Ronnie Peterson, was well equipped to pursue the driving title in earnest. Ferrari, meanwhile, had hired the unproven Gilles Villeneuve to partner the experienced Carlos Reutemann in a new car, the T3, designed specifically around the products of its new tyre supplier, Michelin. In the final analysis, ground-effect won Lotus half of the 16 races, while superior engine power and radial tyres won Ferrari five of the other eight.

17 JUNE 1978 - SWEDISH GP (ANDERSTORP) When Niki Lauda blipped the throttle of his unusual-looking Brabham Alfa Romeo in the pits during a quiet test at Brands Hatch, onlookers wondered why the car seemed to drop momentarily on its suspension. Shortly afterwards, as the reigning World Champion sped to Lotus-crushing victory in Sweden, they found out.

NIKI LAUDA: "I tell you, it was the easiest win I have ever scored. You could do anything with that car!"

Earlier attempts at regulating against the use of fans to create suction beneath the cars had reckoned without the ingenuity of Gordon Murray, then Brabham's chief designer. To cool the car's Alfa Romeo flat-12, Murray mounted a large air/water heat exchanger above the engine, fed by cool air from a large fan - which just happened to draw its air supply from the Brabham's underbody area. As a result, the fan also sucked the car down towards the road surface. It stuck like glue...

ALAN HENRY: "A total of five teams protested the Brabham's eligibility at one time or other over the Swedish Grand Prix weekend, their feeling being that the primary reason for the fan was to provide download. Gordon Murray and team owner Bernie Ecclestone stuck to their guns, insisting that its primary function was cooling.

"The race won, the rulemakers promptly bowed to pressure and banned 'fan cars'. The Brabham never ran in that configuration again."

The race at Anderstorp was also notable for the performance of a rambunctious Italian youngster, Riccardo Patrese, driving for Arrows. Patrese came in for much criticism for the robust manner in which he rebuffed local hero Ronnie Peterson's attempts to deprive him of second place. His peers believed that he had crossed the line between what was and was not acceptable behaviour on the track.

2 JULY 1978 - FRENCH GP (PAUL RICARD) James Hunt finished third in France, his best result of a season in which his motivation waned considerably.

TEDDY MAYER (McLaren boss): "I can get James to talk about women, backgammon, tennis, golf, business, taxes, living in Spain, food, childhood, but I can't get him to talk to me about racing cars."

ALISTAIR CALDWELL (McLaren team manager): "James needed to be competitive and if he wasn't quick he was disappointed. I think his interest in motor racing was never that great anyway. He didn't want to work at it. He wanted it to be easy. So when it became hard work he lost interest. He wanted to just turn up and be the star and when that didn't happen he was not happy.

"He tried to be professional. But he was always lazy. We should have hired a more competent test driver and got the car quicker. Then, on race day, we could have dragged James in on his leash, strapped him into the car and let him loose like a mad dog."

JAMES HUNT: "It's difficult, when you're used to a good car and you go to a bad one, to maintain interest and competitive edge. In testing, I find it a great struggle to slog around endlessly in a car that is so fundamentally bad that whatever you do to it doesn't

change anything. And afterwards, to sit around and talk about this depressing fact for two hours is something I strenuously try to avoid.

"As far as racing goes, it's true I've got no peace of mind at the moment. I only get that from winning. I must win if I am going to stay in motor racing. I don't really like the sport and will only continue as long as I think I can win. I don't see myself racing on into the 1980s. It is too dangerous. I am not going to carry on risking my life indefinitely. There are too many other things I want to do."

13 AUGUST 1978 - AUSTRIAN GP (OSTERREICHRING) In Austria, Ferrari's new recruit, Gilles Villeneuve, made it to the podium for the first time, finishing third behind Ronnie Peterson and Patrick Depailler. It sometimes seemed that Villeneuve was in over his head in his early Grands Prix. In 1977, after his impressive debut with McLaren, Enzo Ferrari entered Villeneuve for the last two races, in Canada and Japan. In the latter event, Villeneuve rammed Peterson's Tyrrell from behind, flew over it and crashed into a group of spectators who had strayed into a restricted area, two of whom were killed.

Early in 1978, Villeneuve was being called unflattering names, some of which alluded to his propensity for airborne accidents, such as 'Air Canada' and 'The Pilot'. There were jokes that he would quickly become a friend of Lauda (an avid aviator and later to become the proprietor of his own airline) because they were both keen on flying.

But the fans loved his spectacular style and, as he added an element of circumspection to his repertoire, Villeneuve increasingly became a front-runner who stayed for the course.

Opposite: Lotus boss Colin Chapman threw his cap in the air whenever one of his cars won.
Above right: McLaren boss Teddy Mayer tore his hair in despair over Hunt's wandering mind.

10 SEPTEMBER 1978 - ITALIAN GP (MONZA) Monza appeared to crown what should have been the most memorable season of Mario Andretti's illustrious career. It was here at the Italian shrine of speed that he had first become inspired by the sport.

MARIO ANDRETTI: "Monza takes me back to the days when dreams were still dreams. In 1954 Aldo (his brother) and I went there to watch the Grand Prix. We were just kids. Of course we had to get there ourselves and we never told our father where we'd been. He didn't approve of racing at all, thought there was something... dishonourable about it. But I remember seeing my hero Ascari and just thinking what I'd give to be there, sitting in a race car, part of a Formula 1 team."

In the 1978 Italian Grand Prix, Andretti's Lotus crossed the line first, just ahead of the constant shadow of the Ferrari driven by Gilles Villeneuve. But then both were adjudged to have jumped a chaotic start, and Niki Lauda inherited the win. Andretti's jump-start penalty dropped him to sixth. He had still won the title, but the race was marred by a serious accident in which his team mate, Ronnie Peterson, had sustained badly broken legs.

JAMES HUNT: "It was a black day in the history of motor racing and one that I would like to be able to forget. At the start Riccardo Patrese [behind him in an Arrows] made what can only be described as an Italian home start and was right up alongside me on the outside of the track.

"I was slap in the middle of the pack, with Ronnie on my left. As we approached the funnel where the tracks divide, Patrese, with nowhere to go, without warning, barged over me, pushing me into Ronnie. In the ensuing sandwich my car flew up in the air and slid sideways down the middle of the track. Behind me all hell broke loose."

ALAN HENRY: "Suddenly, about 300 yards away from the start, cars began to tangle with each other and Ronnie's 78 came into violent collision with another car. The Lotus crashed nearly head-on into the angled guardrail which blanks off the entrance to the disused banked circuit. The front end was ripped off and the car exploded in flame as fuel lines were severed.

"Then the blazing machine cannoned back across the circuit and suddenly cars were going everywhere. Hunt's McLaren, Reutemann's Ferrari, Daly's Ensign, Lunger's McLaren, the Shadows of Stuck and Regazzoni, the Tyrrells of Depailler and Pironi and Brambilla's Surtees were all involved and crashed to a chaotic halt."

JAMES HUNT: "I tried to pull Ronnie clear but found one of his legs trapped between the steering wheel and what remained of the chassis. Flames and smoke enveloped the whole car again but the marshal flattened them and, with additional assistance now on hand [from Shadow driver Clay Regazzoni], we managed to wrench the steering wheel clear. I picked Ronnie up by the epaulettes of his uniform and dragged him clear of the car. I knew then that Ronnie's injuries must be pretty severe as there was virtually nothing left to the front end of the car."

ALAN HENRY: "After an unnecessary delay, an ambulance arrived and he was whisked away by helicopter to the Niguarda Clinic. Vittorio Brambilla, unconscious following a blow on his head from a flying wheel, was also removed to hospital, while Hans Stuck suffered from delayed shock a short while afterwards and was unable to take part in the restart."

MARIO ANDRETTI: "At this stage we thought Ronnie would be OK and I was able to think about the win that evening. Monza was where my dream really began. To win it where I saw my first Grand Prix, where I really first became passionate about Formula 1 and about racing, was a wonderful blessing."

The following day, Ronnie Peterson suffered a fatal pulmonary embolism. Andretti was shattered, the more so since it seemed that the popular Swede's life had not been in danger.

MARIO ANDRETTI: "I got a call from Emerson Fittipaldi early in the morning, saying that there was a problem with Ronnie, that things didn't look so good. My wife Dee Ann and I went down to the Niguarda Hospital, and a friend of Ronnie's met us there, suggesting that we didn't even get out of the car. He told us Ronnie had just died. There were

Above: At first, Ronnie Peterson's injuries seemed not to be life-threatening, but a few hours later he died.
Opposite: The deaths of his Swedish friends Peterson and Gunnar Nilsson made Mario Andretti's championship year a sad one.

a lot of press people and photographers there, trying to interview me. I didn't want to talk at all, but I just said something like 'Unhappily, motor racing is also this.'"

Mario Andretti and Phil Hill (in 1961) have been the only American World Champions. Each clinched his title in the Italian Grand Prix on Sunday 10 September, at Monza. Each entered the race with only his own team mate in contention for the championship. In each case - Wolfgang von Trips and Ronnie Peterson - the team mate suffered fatal injuries during the race, and the American became the World Champion.

At Monza, James Hunt pointed the finger firmly at Riccardo Patrese as the cause of Ronnie Peterson's accident. In fact, filmed evidence suggested that it was Hunt who had triggered the carnage, but Hunt was a former champion and had dragged Peterson from the burning wreckage. As pressure grew, Patrese's fellow drivers forced the organisers of the US Grand Prix East to decline his entry.

Patrese missed the race before returning to the Arrows cockpit for the finale, in Canada. Eventually he was cleared by an Italian court and, in later years, some of those who had judged him regretted their actions. Not Hunt. As a television commentator, he steadfastly criticised Patrese whenever the Italian appeared on his monitor. Nor did Patrese, who went on to compete in a record 256 Grands Prix, ever forget.

RICCARDO PATRESE: "The others, I can understand why they did what they did. But Hunt? He made my life miserable, and for something he had done rather than me."

8 OCTOBER 1978 - CANADIAN GP (MONTREAL): In the final race of the season, Jean-Pierre Jarier (replacing Ronnie Peterson at Lotus) was leading when he coasted to a halt with an engine failure. This paved the way for the local hero to win his first Grand Prix.

GILLES VILLENEUVE: "I was out in front with a big lead and I didn't know what to do. I kept saying to myself: 'Ferrari is the best car, it doesn't break, it never breaks.' And it didn't. To win a Grand Prix is something, but to win your first Grand Prix at home is completely unthinkable. This is the happiest day of my life!"

Meanwhile, the new World Champion reflected on the loss of so many fellow drivers.

MARIO ANDRETTI: "I've had just four really close friends - among the drivers - in all the years I've been racing. Billy Foster, who I knew well for just a couple of years, was killed in a NASCAR accident at Riverside in '67. Then Lucien Bianchi and I were very close. I always used to stay with him when I came to Europe, and we drove together at Le Mans one year. He was killed there in '69 in a testing accident. And the other two were Ronnie Peterson and Gunnar Nilsson, who was my team mate at Lotus in '76 and '77 and died of cancer a couple of weeks after the end of the '78 season.

"Gunnar's illness... you just find it hard to accept that something like that can happen so quickly to a man so young. Gunnar was such a loose, extrovert kind of a guy you couldn't help but get along with him.

"Ronnie was different, quiet and reserved. He took more getting to know. I mean, we'd known each other for years, but only when we became team mates did we become really close friends. For all his reserve, he had a really great, dry sense of humour. There's such a hole in motor racing now, and it'll never be filled, no question about it."

You know, team mates aren't necessarily friends. It happens or it doesn't. MARIO ANDRETTI

Why is one driver quicker than another? He's got more confidence. Sometimes he

gets it by over-riding certain fears and getting away with it. That lures you on.
MARIO ANDRETTI

It did not take rival teams long to figure out why the Lotus 79 had been so fabulously successful in 1978, even if some may not have fully understood more than the principles of ground-effect aerodynamics. Ligier stunned everyone in the opening two races, as Jacques Laffite romped home to easy and unexpected victories. The French team then slumped for a while, only to recover with a victory for Patrick Depailler in Spain.

3 MARCH 1979 - SOUTH AFRICAN GP (KYALAMI) It soon emerged that Ferrari had the best car. The boat-like 312T3 could win no beauty contest, but cramming the wide Italian flat-12 engine into a ground-effect chassis proved effective. Gilles Villeneuve underlined its potential and his own brilliance by winning the third race in South Africa. Another ace in Ferrari's pack was Michelin's radial tyre, which continued to be a bonus against Goodyear's crossply. Villeneuve won again in America, but his team mate Jody Scheckter took the crucial victory, at Monaco.

Ferrari team orders decreed that whichever driver was ahead in the standings at the seasonal mid-point would subsequently get the help of his team mate, even if they were both in contention for the title.

27 MAY 1979 - MONACO GP (MONTE CARLO) By Monaco it was clear that Lotus fortunes had faded and Mario Andretti would be unable to defend his crown. Neither Andretti nor his new team mate, Carlos Reutemann, came close to winning a race. The new Lotus 80 was too adventurous, and the 79 was outdated, and the Andretti/Chapman partnership suffered.

MARIO ANDRETTI: "Working with Colin was no trip to Paris, you know? He and I had some monumental arguments. We were struggling. Colin was getting bored and was looking for something totally new which never really materialised. Colin used to detest it whenever a driver volunteered some engineering suggestions. He was: 'Just drive the bloody thing!' and I'm: 'Yeah, I'll drive the bloody thing but I can't drive it because you don't know what you're doing!' We used to really go at it.

"We didn't make any progress in '79. If anything we went backwards. And then the frustration sets in and you start doubting yourself. You can't always blame the equipment. You drop into a no-man's-land. It is really the worst feeling in the world. It's like going to war with no bullets. You know you are going to get shot at, and you know you can't defend yourself."

Another former World Champion was seeking a rejuvenation: James Hunt had moved from McLaren to Walter Wolf Racing.

Opposite: Hunt's beloved dog, Oscar, was always there, while wife Suzi (who left him for Richard Burton) was only one of the women in his life.

JAMES HUNT: "I decided that on the professional level I had grown stale with the McLaren team. Our relationship had gone as far as it possibly could but this new team are a tremendous stimulus. I think they're going to provide me with a challenge that I so desperately want.

"I've still got it in me to be a winner. I know it's still there even after a year like 1978. I am convinced that once I get back into the right car the good results will come. My aim is to be World Champion in 1979 so that I can go out of this business on a high. That's the way I want to retire."

Many thought Hunt's chances of winning the title again were unrealistic.

JACKIE STEWART: "I think James has lost a great deal of the spirit he once had. I think he still desires success, the financial rewards. But desire is different from spirit and that, I think, has gone. James has never been shy about saying he drives for the money and possibly that's why he decided on one more season rather than retiring last year.

"Another thing is that James has become very acutely aware of the dangers of motor racing, which is one of the main reasons I retired when I did."

In Monaco, James Hunt's Wolf retired with transmission failure, and its driver walked away from the sport. Sometimes during his career, Hunt would be physically sick before a race, when the nervous tension got to him. But when he had a competitive car beneath him, his caution would evaporate. Winning was everything. But he had not had a winning car since 1977, and the Wolf was no answer. Long before Monaco, the fear had taken Hunt. The battle was no longer worth the risk.

On 8 June 1979, he announced his retirement, after a relatively short career that brought him 10 wins and one World Championship in 92 Grands Prix.

JAMES HUNT: "I wanted to have a really good final year, but it became clear to me that our car would never get there. If you haven't got an absolutely competitive car these days, you can forget it. And quite frankly, it's not worth the risk to life and limb to continue under those circumstances. I didn't want to end up in a box or permanently injured. The main thing was self-preservation."

JACKIE STEWART: "You would have likened James's rise to that of someone in the pop music industry rather than in sport. It was a very sudden rise to adulation and big money. It's hopelessly intoxicating and very confusing. Your entire world is fantasy and candy floss. But there's a side to this business which I think has gotten to James: driving a racing car endlessly, testing chassis, developing tyres, sitting in searing heat for an unacceptable number of hours, presentations, cocktail parties and dinners with people you don't want to be with. He wants to do things his way, but unfortunately you can't. If you're going to stay in the sport, you have to compromise - or you can retire and stay retired. I think he's making the right decision."

> I reckon I've had a fair crack at the whip. I've done six seasons in Formula 1 and I thought that was enough for anybody. JAMES HUNT

1 JULY 1979 - FRENCH GP (DIJON-PRENOIS) French veteran Jean-Pierre Jabouille finally achieved a first Grand Prix victory for Renault's turbocharged car - and in France, mother country of the very first Grand Prix (in 1906). Yet an extraordinary battle for second place stole the show. The verdict went to Ferrari's Gilles Villeneuve over Jabouille's team mate, René Arnoux. If any race encapsulated everything that Villeneuve stood for - his car control, his fighting spirit, his sheer bravado - this was it.

Time and again at Dijon, Arnoux would force ahead of Villeneuve, who wore out his tyres trying to keep his underpowered Ferrari up with the Renault. And time and again, Villeneuve would somehow scramble back ahead. Several times in the final laps their cars touched, interlocked wheels and ran off the road. At the finish, Villeneuve and Arnoux were elated and congratulated each other.

standout team in the latter part of the season. Having reformed his team after selling out to Walter Wolf, Frank Williams entrusted the design of his cars to Patrick Head, and their partnership in 1979 produced the highly competitive FW07, the first ground-effect Williams. The first victory fell to veteran Clay Regazzoni, at the team's home race in Britain, but it was his Australian team mate, Alan Jones, who quickly became a formidable force in Formula 1.

29 JULY 1979 - GERMAN GP (HOCKENHEIM) ALAN JONES: "When I came to Frank he was still one of the game's all-time least successful constructors. Everyone told me I was crazy, taking a big step backwards in my career. I knew Williams were a good, tight little team. It should have won races in 1978, but wasn't reliable enough. It began halfway through 1979 and things got even better after that. Not bad for a so-called loser and a beginner."

"We soon found out we had a charger. Whenever he had the chance in 1978, AJ passed car after car and would have won races if his car hadn't broken down. On one occasion that year, I remember turning to Patrick and saying, 'I don't mind if we don't finish. I've had my money's worth, because he's not just a good driver, he's an exciting driver.' And I hadn't been excited by a driver's performance in many years. I found out then what he has since confirmed time and time again: that AJ is the sort of driver who puts in the fast laps you need. He responds best when he's really got to hang it out.

"AJ was pretty much our age, a bit of a swashbuckler, took his work very seriously but played hard away from it. A man's man."

26 AUGUST 1979 - DUTCH GP (ZANDVOORT) In the Dutch Grand Prix, Gilles Villeneuve endeared himself forever to those who love never-say-die spirit by trying

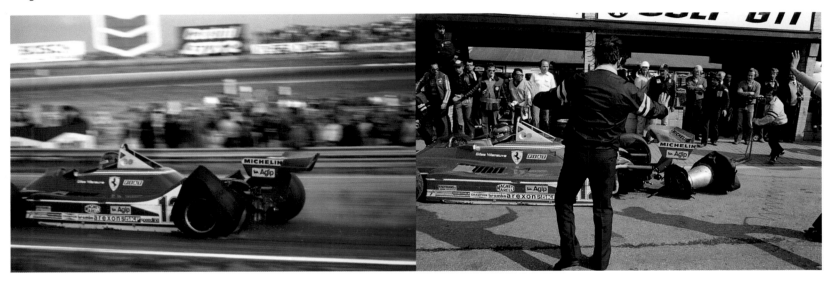

RENE ARNOUX: "No, I am not sad to be third. All you needed was for one or the other of us to become frightened and there might have been a terrible accident. But Gilles drove a fantastic race. I enjoyed it very much!"

GILLES VILLENEUVE: "I tell you that was really fun! I thought for sure we were going to get on our heads, you know, because when you start interlocking wheels it's very easy for one car to climb over another. But we didn't crash and it's okay. I enjoyed myself amazingly!"

Although some of their elder rivals were outraged, labelling their breathtaking duel dangerous and foolhardy, at least one of them approved.

MARIO ANDRETTI: "Aw, it's just a coupla young lions clawin' themselves."

Renault failed to win again in 1979. But Williams started a winning streak that would make it the

FRANK WILLIAMS: "The first thing I had on my mind when I formed the present team was to find a good professional driver. We weren't over-ambitious - we couldn't afford to be. We didn't go after Niki Lauda or Jody Scheckter: they were beyond our reach, both financially and in terms of their status in what we conceived as a small, highly professional team. We wanted work rather than glamour. We wanted the sort of pro who, if the car finished races, would bring us results.

"AJ was the man, but it was no piece of exceptional judgement or foresight or intuition on my part. AJ knows perfectly well I didn't rate him that highly when he joined us. I acknowledge that we were lucky he became available at just the right moment. But I had no idea he would be as good as he is. His brief from me was simple: 'Don't crash our cars, for we can't afford that many spares; finish in the points and work hard to help us develop our new car.'

to continue after an accident caused by a rear puncture. He had just taken the lead, passing Alan Jones in a seemingly impossible manoeuvre - round the outside of the difficult Tarzan corner. Villeneuve kept going, with the deflated tyre flailing itself to bits, destroying the rear suspension, and trailing behind like a crazed anchor. He staggered the wreckage into the pits, demanded that it be repaired, and was enraged when this proved impossible.

9 SEPTEMBER 1979 - ITALIAN GP (MONZA) By the time of the Italian Grand Prix, Villeneuve's only hope of prolonging his title aspirations was to disobey Ferrari team orders and pass Scheckter, who led initially. But the Canadian was an honourable man. While racing right on the South African's gearbox, Villeneuve was never tempted to pass and dutifully finished second to Scheckter, whose first-place points clinched the 1979 title.

Above: Villeneuve's fighting spirit - at Zandvoort he tried racing on three wheels - stole the show, though his Ferrari team mate Scheckter took the title (opposite).

JODY SCHECKTER: "I must say that during those last few laps - as much as I trusted Gilles - I was looking in my mirrors more than usual. I would have been very surprised if he tried anything, but I always look for surprises.

"At Monza I lived the best moments of my life when I switched off the engine and got out of the car. I saw the crowd going wild, climbing the fences, waving Ferrari flags. I had a lump in my throat as I walked through the paddock with all the police around me.

30 SEPTEMBER 1979 - CANADIAN GP (MONTREAL) In Montreal, Villeneuve never gave Jones a moment's peace, fighting tooth and nail for a victory that finally went to Jones, who raised his rival's arm in tribute as they stood on the podium.

PATRICK HEAD: "Alan was behind Gilles for 15 laps or so, waiting for an opportunity, and eventually he got him set up for the hairpin and came down the inside. They went round together, just about tapping. Gilles just didn't give up, and the moment Alan took a bit of a breather and dropped half a second, wham! Gilles just closed right up again."

ALAN JONES: "I just couldn't believe it. That guy just would not accept that he was beaten. I sweated like hell pulling out a couple of seconds on him, relaxed in a couple of corners, and there he was in my mirrors again. That bloody red shit bucket was all over me!"

FRANK WILLIAMS: "Although I don't particularly agree with his daredevil style, Villeneuve has done more for Grand Prix racing this year than all the other drivers combined."

Two days before the Jones-Villeneuve duel, Niki Lauda abruptly decided he no longer wanted to fight the Formula 1 wars. In practice on Friday, the battle-scarred veteran pulled his Brabham into the garage and parked it permanently.

NIKI LAUDA: "Suddenly I felt a sense of emptiness, a total lack of interest in what I was doing. I braked, steered towards the pits, and it was over. There's another world. It was a decision I made alone, and then discussed with Ecclestone and my sponsors. They understood. I often said that to be a good Formula 1 driver a man has to have a special kind of heart and mind. I don't know which of these two changed in me, the heart or the mind.

"I only know that ten years of racing, the same people, the same work, the same rhythm, the same problems, have not been enough to make me want to start another Grand Prix. Initially, I got pleasure from all these things I've mentioned, but I suddenly didn't feel this way any more. 'Where am I?' I asked myself. 'What am I doing in this car, now that I know all there is to know about tyres, engines, wings, suspension? Let's start something new,' I told myself, 'learn new things.'

"They have mostly been ten happy years for me. Perfect. I did something I enjoyed, and which made me rich: what more could I want? I say that it enriched me, but above all, it enriched my soul, not my wallet. Suddenly I'd had enough, thus my need for other things, my interest in planes. Maybe in ten years, perhaps sooner, I will look for something else, other objectives. Routine doesn't suit someone like me."

So Niki flew from Montreal to Los Angeles to finalise the purchase of a cargo aircraft he intended to add to the three business aircraft he already owned in a venture that was to become Lauda Air.

7 OCTOBER 1979 - US EAST GP (WATKINS GLEN) Before winning at Watkins Glen, Villeneuve added another chapter to his rapidly growing legend. The patented spectacular display of heroics took place in practice on Friday when the track was soaked and few people even ventured out of the pits. In fact, most drivers thought the flooded tarmac was simply undriveable. Gilles did not share their opinion and what followed was witnessed by several prominent journalists.

DENIS JENKINSON: "When we saw him going out in the rain, we said, 'This we've got to see!' Some members of the press, who think they know it all, don't bother to go out when it rains. But I was out on a corner in the rain watching him and all the hardball members of the press were with me. We had to see this. It was something special. Oh, he was fantastic! He was unbelievable!"

NIGEL ROEBUCK: "Gilles was the one bloke who made you go and look for a good corner in a practice session because you knew that, where everybody else would go through as if on rails, Gilles would be worth watching. That day in the rain at Watkins Glen was almost beyond belief! It truly was. You would think he had 300 horsepower more than anybody else. It just didn't seem possible. The speed he was travelling didn't bear any relation to anybody else. He was 11 seconds faster! Jody was next fastest and couldn't believe it, saying that he scared himself shitless! I remember Laffite in the pits just giggling when Gilles went past and saying, 'Why do we bother? He's different from the rest of us. On a separate level.'"

JEFF HUTCHINSON: "The spectacle of him pushing that Ferrari to the limit, with great rooster tails of water cascading off its rear wheels, just for the sheer fun and thrill of it, made the wet feet and miserable wait worthwhile. He lapped at an average speed of just over 100mph!"

GILLES VILLENEUVE: "That was fun! I was flat in fifth on the straight, about 160mph. It should have been faster but the engine had a misfire and was down about 600 revs. But for that I could have gone quite a bit faster, but then maybe I would have crashed."

BEING A RACING DRIVER'S WIFE IS A HORRIBLE, LOUSY JOB. YOU'RE THE STAR RACING DRIVER'S WIFE, BUT REALLY YOU'RE THE STAR OF NOTHING. JODY SCHECKTER

I know it sounds spoilt, but I hate living in hotels, having everything done for me. I feel like a five-star prisoner. PAM SCHECKTER

The Eighties

This most turbulent decade was ridden with strife on several fronts. The dispute between the sport's governing body and those handling its commercial interests - and the teams affiliated with each faction - was nothing less than a fight for control over Formula 1. The divisiveness threatened to tear the sport apart. Teams and drivers were united in their condemnation of absurd rules, inappropriate venues and a frightening lack of safety measures that put lives at risk more than ever. A drivers' strike was a rare show of solidarity in a decade otherwise noted for fierce feuds between drivers, especially team mates. Amidst the turmoil there was some great racing, with the likes of Piquet, Prost, Mansell and Senna making indelible marks on the sport.

Throughout the 1980 Grand Prix season mere motor racing was jostled aside by the column inches devoted to a civil war between FISA (Fédération Internationale du Sport Automobile) and FOCA (Formula One Constructors Association). Row followed row, over qualifying tyres, missed driver briefings, race boycotts, technical changes, the coming ban on skirts, financial controls. Towards the end of the year FOCA agreed to give way, conditionally, to FISA on the question of skirts. By then, however, Shylock had yet greater delusions of grandeur, and a pound of flesh was insufficient. FISA wanted the whole carcass.

KEITH BOTSFORD: "For the past several years, the sport has been afflicted by a long, boring war between two factions seeking to control Formula 1 for their own ends. One is the 'official' motor-racing establishment, headed by one Jean-Marie Balestre, a fiery, hot-headed Frenchman determined to exercise the power given him by the rules. Rules which, needless to say, have been codified by M. Balestre and his predecessors. The other, representing the majority of the constructors, is FOCA, headed by the tiny,

meticulous and shrewd figure of Bernard Ecclestone. The division between the two is basic. The Paris bureaucracy is top-heavy and not exclusively concerned with Formula 1. Balestre's power derives from the Third World and their votes. Ecclestone's interests are exclusively within Formula 1, and it is he who truly professionalised the sport. Both sides recognise the need for an impartial administrative body, but Balestre has wielded his power with what seems to FOCA to be partiality. To Balestre, FOCA is simply greedy."

1 MARCH 1980 - SOUTH AFRICAN GP (KAYALAMI) FISA announced that the next season the rules would be changed to ban skirts, an essential item of the ground effect principle.

JEAN-MARIE BALESTRE: "The ban on skirts for 1981 is just our first move towards re-establishing the FISA as the head of motor sport. All the cars will be inspected for conformity to the new regulations, and any cars which do not conform will be excluded from the World Championship. Any driver, team, constructor or car

which goes into 'pirate' racing will be banned for life. I hope everything will be done in cooperation with the FOCA. It is not my intention to drive Bernie Ecclestone out of racing, but for all the usefulness he has displayed, he has also made many mistakes out of impetuosity.

"When I was elected as President of the FISA I found a total mess, and I had to re-establish all the structures within it. Now I can tell you that the bulldozer is *en marche*! I have the drivers queueing up on my side, and all the people who matter are lining up to get FISA armbands. There have been widespread defections from the Ecclestone camp."

MAURO FORGHIERI: "In the first place, this rule is not a new one, because the skirts - as they are at the moment - are illegal, anyway! They are rigid. At first everyone was using fixed, flexible skirts, and that was OK, because the rules say you cannot fill the gap between the car and the ground with something elastic. Then Chapman brought in rigid, sliding skirts, and won the World Championship. OK, fine, but now I think is the time to take them off. We can go racing tomorrow without skirts, no problem."

Above: Jean-Marie Balestre (FISA) and Bernie Ecclestone (FOCA) were embroiled in a power struggle for control of the sport.
Opposite, top: Clay Regazzoni was permanently paralysed in a dreadful accident at the Long Beach circuit (opposite, below).

PATRICK HEAD: "If the skirts ban does go ahead, it will certainly succeed in its stated aim of slowing the cars down. We'd lose at least 90% of the downforce produced between the car and the road, and we'd need to get that back as soon as possible.

"However, I do agree that cornering speeds should be reduced. We've reached a point where an unchangeable factor comes into play. The drivers are all very fit and strong, yet they cannot cope with the loads imposed on them in certain types of corner. We're getting to a point where we're going beyond human capabilities. If it were my decision, I'd prefer to keep skirts - with a limitation on their overall length - and do away with wings."

30 MARCH 1980 - USA WEST GP (LONG BEACH) Nelson Piquet easily took his first Grand Prix win, but the day was marred by an accident to Clay Regazzoni, whose Ensign was running fourth in the late stages of the race. Regazzoni soon knew he had to face the unimaginable: his spinal cord had been severely damaged, and he was paralysed. Some similarly injured had recovered fully, notably the Swiss skier Roland Collombin, but others had not. Over the next couple of years Regazzoni underwent operations without number, his hopes of walking again constantly raised, then finally dashed.

CLAY REGAZZONI: "At Long Beach we had, for the first time, titanium pedals in the Ensign, and when I pressed the brake pedal there was not the slightest resistance from it. Nothing. I tried to pump it. Still nothing. I had to lose speed, and changed down from fifth to third, but Zunino's Brabham was parked in the escape road. I hit it, then bounced into the barrier. For about ten minutes I lost consciousness. Then I remember terrible pain in my back, and realised I couldn't move my legs.

"I was in hospital for a long time, and felt very sorry for myself, but when something like this happens, you move into a different world - a world you never thought about. And you feel ashamed. I remember Gunnar Nilsson talking about the children in his cancer hospital, how he had had years of good life which they would never have.

"As for me, I can drive my Ferrari Daytona. I have my driving school for handicapped people. I can still got to races, be part of them. I don't want to be pitied. I have accepted that the miracle will not happen, but life can still be worth something."

FRANK WILLIAMS: "I was enormously saddened by Clay's accident. He was very different from most racing drivers, in that he was - and is - an absolute gentleman, who loved motor racing for its own sake. A totally adorable character."

ALAN JONES: "Clay Regazzoni had a very good, natural, easy balance. He was a dispassionate driver in his last years. All of us become that way as we look on the racing world with a colder eye and recover from our early enthusiasms. Clay was once invited by Louis Stanley to look over BRM. Lou was there in his three-acre office and took Clay through his works and said: 'My boy, you have seen my car and my organisation - with my team and my factory we will make you World Champion.' Clay said: 'Fucka the Championship, how mucha you pay?'"

1 JUNE 1980 - SPANISH GP (JARAMA) The Spanish Grand Prix of 1980 did not take place, according to the official records for the sport. But there was a race - appropriately at Jarama, one of the bloodiest battles of the Spanish Civil War - which saw the serious beginnings of the FISA-FOCA War. The FOCA teams rebelled against the proposed banning of skirts, declaring that the ruling would favour the 'grandees', with their turbocharged engines. After much squabbling in practice, FISA declared the race 'illegal'. The FISA teams, (Renault, Ferrari, Alfa Romeo) withdrew from the race. Formula 1 was in deep crisis.

ALAN JONES: "Whatever fucking Balestre or anyone else says about it, that was a Grand Prix as far as I'm concerned, and I won it."

JEAN SAGE (Renault Sport): "We don't want to make any trouble - if the race is in the World Championship, we take part, but if it's just a show, we don't. It's a very easy decision for us. As soon as the race lost its FISA sanction we could not race. It was as simple as that. We are on the side of FISA - as a governing body, no matter who is running it."

FRANK WILLIAMS: "I refuse to be administered by an incompetent - this is my livelihood. All Balestre has is an armband - he doesn't run any cars, he doesn't pay my bills, he doesn't have one penny invested in my business, or any of the other teams here.

"What does the future hold? If the split happens, Balestre's lot will have eight or ten cars. They won't have any Grands Prix because all the circuit owners care about is making a profit - and the only profits come from Grands Prix. I would say that most Grands Prix will be run next year, with or without FISA. I don't say it will be an easy route, but we're not going to go out of business."

PATRICK DEPAILLER: "I am concerned about the conflict between Ecclestone and Balestre because I think it could kill Formula 1, as serious as that. If no one had raced in Spain, that would have made a big problem with the spectators. Someone had to race - at least half the field - just to please them.

EMERSON FITTIPALDI: "Grand Prix racing will be much better, and more popular, when it is organised by professionals. I hope FOCA breaks away, and runs the World Championship for itself. Ferrari, Renault and Alfa Romeo can join us if they wish."

MARIO ANDRETTI: "The great shame is that the public - our customers - suffer the most from this sort of dispute. They don't know anything what's happened. They come to see a race - and they see only half of one. The problem is that we have two sides who won't compromise, but every business has to be run on compromise."

29 JUNE 1980 - FRENCH GP (PAUL RICARD) ALAN JONES: "Knowing that Renault had backed Balestre over Spain and that the French had combined with the Italians to put the season, and my title, into jeopardy, I went to France in a fighting mood. I not only wanted badly to win that race, I wanted my win to be a personal gesture of defiance. I think it was my best race of the year, and certainly the most satisfying - it doesn't get better than beating the Frogs at home. The Ligiers were definitely quicker, and I won the race by keeping the pressure on

them. I love doing that, wearing someone down, inching up on them - it's really satisfying to know that what you're doing, lap after lap, is working. After the race we flew the Union Jack above our motorhome to really rub it in."

13 JULY 1980 - BRITISH GP (BRANDS HATCH) At Brands Hatch the reigning World Champion announced that this would be his last season, and another driver spoke about the danger factor - in what proved to be the last race of his life.

JODY SCHECKTER: "My decision to retire has nothing to do with the fact that I'm having a bad season. Serious drivers don't do that - if they did, we'd only have five cars on the grid. My reason for stopping is that racing used to be an all-consuming passion for me, but to be successful you need to give it 110%, and I don't have that commitment any more.

Above: Alan Jones, here leading Pironi's Ligier in France, won the championship with Williams.
Opposite, top: Patrick Depailler, though worried about the lack of safety, was driving as hard as ever on the day he died.

I am courageous, but I am not mad. PATRICK DEPAILLER

"When I started, my aim was to win the World Championship. I've done that now, and frankly the big passion is gone. I had a very good offer from Ferrari to stay on, and if I'd been a tennis player I'd have taken it, and done one more season just for the money. But that's not the way it is in racing, with all the dangers involved. I'd be very upset if I got killed doing something just for the money."

PATRICK DEPAILLER: "From a safety point of view, this place - Brands Hatch - is the worst. It is one of the quickest tracks, and the run-off areas are a joke - yet, as a track to enjoy, it is almost the best.

"I think I am courageous, you know, but I am not mad. If you don't have safety changes at the circuits, then you must keep cornering speeds down to what they were. The safety must be relative to the speed.

"Cornering speeds have become ridiculous, and something has to be done. We need a set of rule changes that are a good compromise for everyone involved. That is why we need a strong governing body, working with the designers.

"I think the way the cars are built now is just a joke. OK, they are good in a side impact because of the sidepods, but there is not enough protection for the driver's legs. Sitting right at the front does not worry me in itself, but we must have a strong structure around the legs."

1 AUGUST 1980 Patrick Depailler was killed instantly when his Alfa Romeo crashed at Hockenheim's flat-out Ostkurve during private testing. Marks on the road left no room for doubt: something on the car had broken as Depailler turned into the corner. In the best of circumstances, this was not a place to have an accident, but Depailler's chances of survival were wiped away by the absence of catch fencing, which, scandalously, was neatly rolled up behind the guardrail that day. The loss of Patrick, one of the nicest men ever to grace Formula 1, was hard to bear.

14 SEPTEMBER 1980 - ITALIAN GP (IMOLA) For once run at Imola, rather than Monza, the Italian Grand Prix resulted in an easy win for Piquet, followed by the Williams pair, Jones and Reutemann. Now, with two races to go, Piquet and Jones were but one point apart in the World Championship. For Villeneuve, though, Imola was the scene only of a miraculous escape.

GILLES VILLENEUVE: "When the right rear tyre went, on the approach to Tosa, that was it - I was just hanging on. I hit the bank very hard, and one of the front wheels hit my helmet, and at that instant I lost my sight. The car bounced back into the middle of the track, and I could hear all the other cars around me, but I couldn't see them.

"I can't describe the fear I felt - I thought I'd been blinded. I was just sitting there, waiting to be T-boned. Fortunately, everything began to clear up as they helped me out of the car. I had a check-up at the track hospital, and everything was OK, but I had a terrible headache, and wasn't allowed to fly the helicopter for 24 hours.

"Afterwards I thought a lot about that shunt. I'd hit barriers and walls and banks before, and once I'd broken my leg in a Formula Atlantic race at Mosport. After that I was never frightened of it - I thought, you know, you maybe get some fractures, go to the hospital, and they mend you. I'd only ever thought of accidents in terms of broken bones. But being blind maybe... Jesus, that was something I'd never considered."

28 SEPTEMBER 1980 - CANADIAN GP (MONTREAL)
ALAN JONES: "I've won the World Championship, and I'm so happy it was in a Williams. The great thing about driving for Frank is that you know that the money coming in is going towards making the team more competitive. Which isn't always the case, believe me.

"I would say we had the quickest car in Argentina, but that's about it. What's interesting is that we never qualified lower than sixth. At some places the Ligiers were in a class of their own - and qualified 20th at others. We were never dominant, but we were always there, and that's what makes a World Championship team. For that, we have to thank Patrick Head.

"I get pissed off when people say I'm only winning because these cars are easy to drive, and I've got a good one. Admittedly, a good driver won't win a race in a bad car, but that's always been the case. Who complained when Fangio and Moss cleaned up for Mercedes in 1955? Sure, they were the best drivers, but they had the best cars, too. A jockey won't win the Derby on a donkey."

JEAN-PIERRE JABOUILLE: "In my accident at Montreal, all I remember is that suddenly the car wouldn't turn. Before that, everything was normal. I don't know what happened, whether a wishbone broke, but I hit the guardrail very hard, head on, and suddenly there was a lot of pain.

"I was conscious the whole time. The car was so badly damaged that it took a long time to get me out, and I really felt the race should have been stopped - not for me as much as the rescue people. They were in a very dangerous place, completely unprotected, for a long time.

"The following year I moved from Renault to Ligier; people asked me if my right leg was OK now, and I kept saying it was no problem - I had to say that. In fact, the pain was very bad, I must say. I don't like to think of it even now."

5 OCTOBER 1980 - US EAST GP (WATKINS GLEN) A one-two by Jones and Reutemann gave Jones the driving title and put Williams on top of the world for the first time.

JACQUES LAFFITE: "Williams have won the constructors' championship, and I'm so happy for Frank. When I drove for him, in the early 70s, it was very hard, because he had no money. People always used to say he was no good at running a team, but that was stupid. He had no money, so how could he be good? Now he has the money, and the success is coming. I never doubted it would happen. He has a very good team - in fact, it is *too* good!"

ALAN JONES: "I liked Frank even before I worked for him. He was jovial and polite, and I put a high value on politeness. Civility is very important. Being civil doesn't detract from your inner combativeness or your interior strength. You don't have to be arrogant or rude to be a good fighter. The popular notion of the driver as arrogant, rude, macho and boorish, derives from Jochen Rindt and Niki Lauda, both Teutonic and both naturally aggressively offensive. They set a style: if you weren't rude and arrogant like some Hollywood stereotype of the SS officer, then you hadn't the balls to be a top racing driver."

I don't think that situation will happen again - but if it does, I think I will take the same decision I took in Brazil. When Jones says he doesn't trust me, he's absolutely right. He shouldn't. CARLOS REUTEMANN

An uneasy truce prevailed in the war between FISA and FOCA as the teams assembled at Long Beach in March 1981. It was a good race, too, free of politics, but in Argentina the hydraulic suspension on Nelson Piquet's Brabham heralded the ridiculous cars which stayed with us throughout the year.

At the end of 1980, FISA banned skirts, and decreed there should be a six-centimetre gap between car and ground, which would be rigorously monitored. Brabham's designer Gordon Murray came up with a clever system that circumnavigated the rule, allowing the car to pass muster at rest, but run very close to the ground at speed. To be competitive, everyone had to follow suit, but most systems were rather cruder, a switch in the cockpit allowing the driver to raise and lower his car, *à la* Citroën.

Thus, for the bulk of the season, every car was illegal - and everyone knew it, including those wearing FISA armbands carrying out checks in the pit lane. Farcical. On that point, at least, all racing people were agreed: the cars competing at the sport's pinnacle were absurd. To the designers they were a technical backwater, to the drivers an exhausting and lethal bore, to the spectators a joke. To the gentlemen of FISA they were, like most things, a mystery. For all that, however, the year saw a gripping struggle for the World Championship, and more competitive teams than ever before.

29 MARCH 1981 - BRAZILIAN GP (RIO DE JANEIRO) The Williams drivers dominated at Rio, but not in the order expected. In torrential conditions, Reutemann led reigning champion Jones from the start, Alan assuming that Carlos would eventually abide by his contract as the Number Two driver, and let him through for the win. It did not happen that way...

ALAN JONES: "I know exactly where I stand now - and, believe me, this situation won't occur again. No way will I sit back, waiting for Carlos to move over. I know the contracts we both signed, and I'd like to think that when you shake a bloke's hand he doesn't pretend a couple of months later that it didn't happen."

CARLOS REUTEMANN: "Alan had a reason to be upset - I can't disagree with that. It has affected our relationship since then. I had led all the way, and he was never right behind me, but always a few seconds back. Yes, I knew the terms of the contract, but still I was in a dilemma, because all through my career I'd started each race with the intention of winning it. When I saw the pit signal, telling me to give way, I said to myself, 'Right, if I give way now, I stop here on lap 57, or whatever it was, right in the middle of the track, and I leave immediately for my farm in Argentina. Finish.' That was my reaction. I was in a terrible situation. But... if I lift my foot now, I go home. Not a racing driver any more."

FRANK WILLIAMS: "It's true that Carlos did ignore the terms of his contract, and for that we exercised a certain financial penalty. But after that the matter was forgotten, as far as Patrick and I were concerned. Frankly, I just found the whole thing very boring! I don't care who gets the points. Why should I care which one of them wins? They're only employees, after all."

12 APRIL 1981 - ARGENTINE GP (BUENOS AIRES) FRANK WILLIAMS: "I think I will always begrudge Brabham their win in Argentina. Their cars were using skirts, and, so far as we were concerned, skirts had been banned.

"There was a lot of confusion about my protest. People got the impression I was protesting Gordon Murray's hydraulic system, which wasn't the case. That was a very clever idea. What I was protesting about was the skirts. If the Brabham was

considered legal, then we would all have to copy it. And FISA, for whatever reason, ratified the whole package. The day they did that was a very black day for racing, and started the farce which lasted for the rest of the season.

"I was the only bloke who protested the Brabham - no one else backed me up, and that's something I won't forget. Another big lesson learned. This is a big company now, you know, with 90-odd employees, and big money behind us. And I don't like to see it being messed around by what I consider to be incompetence on the part of others, people who have nothing whatever to do with it."

GORDON MURRAY: "I don't often get upset with people, but I feel absolutely disgusted with Frank Williams for the way he went about protesting our car. I've always got on well with him, but of late Frank has become the self-appointed Mr Motor Racing 1981, with his interviews and TV appearances, and so on. I've got enormous respect for what he and his team have done - but they've never done very much *original*. What annoys me so much is the way they seem to be protesting anything which might threaten them. The way they've carried on makes you wonder if they think they rule the world."

JEAN-PIERRE JABOUILLE: "The current rules are completely crazy. I did not believe it when Balestre and FISA accepted hydraulic suspension, solid skirts, and all that. Their decision was incredible! *Incredible!*

"How can you take Formula 1 seriously when it matters only to be legal in the pit lane? You can be illegal in the race

- if you were not, you would not go quickly enough even to qualify for it - but if you are illegal in the pit lane at the end, you lose the race! It is not only stupid, but also ridiculously dangerous. Bah!"

17 MAY 1981 - BELGIAN GP (ZOLDER) The shameful weekend at Zolder, almost every aspect of it disagreeable and acrimonious, made it clear that the winter 'agreement' between FISA and FOCA was nought but a truce, and an uncomfortable one at that. The new rule stipulating a six-centimetre gap between ground and car had been observed for precisely one race, at Long Beach. Now there was the farce of hydraulic suspension systems, of officials checking cars' ride heights in the pit lane, while knowing them to be illegally low out on the circuit.

And in Belgium there was also tragedy: a mechanic was killed in the pit lane during practice, another hurt at the start of the race - a start made chaotic by a drivers' and mechanics' 'demo' on the grid, and by resulting pigheaded obstinacy by certain constructors and officials. The whole thing was hateful.

Opposite: Carlos Reutemann's refusal to play second fiddle to his team mate Alan Jones led to discord at Williams.
Below and inset: Gilles Villeneuve hung onto his bucking bronco of a Prancing Horse to win in the streets of Monaco.

MARIO ANDRETTI: "I didn't agree with the timing, but since the mechanics had their minds made up to make a show of protest, we had to support them. I think they had a right to show a little respect towards the boy who was killed, and there are also certain points that we drivers are trying to make, which are totally ignored.

"A lot of mistakes were made at Zolder, and by a lot of people, not just us. To single us out is highly unfair. There were some very prominent constructors who caused the whole thing, by encouraging cars to be started when there were no drivers in other cars, and so on. If they had been patient, the whole thing would have been handled in an orderly fashion. There would have been a few minutes' delay to the start, and that would have been it.

"And to try to show us responsible for everything with a fine, I think, is pretty goddam shitty. The drivers are totally ignored in this sport, and it's time it changed. Quite honestly, I think Balestre is more on our side than Ecclestone. What are the constructors afraid of? It's those guys who want to keep the drivers disrupted, not FISA. Deep down, I really believe that they have something else in mind - as long as the drivers are not united, somewhere along the line they could set a price on us, manipulate us, like we're a bunch of idiots.

"It was criminal the way some of the constructors behaved on the grid at Zolder. Criminal. It showed a total disregard for human life. Just before the start - the *start* - I was told to shut the engine down. I looked around and saw that not everyone else was shutting down. I kept mine going, luckily, and all of a sudden the red goes on, and then the green, and another mechanic gets hurt. Beautiful, I says, lovely. Of course, that was the pressure of the goddam TV cameras."

31 MAY 1981 - MONACO GP (MONTE CARLO) GILLES VILLENEUVE: "Right now, I'm sore everywhere. Monaco is tiring, anyway, but this ridiculous go-kart ride we all have now is worse than ever. Bang, bang, bang! All the way through my helmet was smashing into the roll-over bar. What worries me more, though, is what's happening to the cars. The suspension is taking a hell of a beating, and think of what's going through the tyre sidewalls.

"Still, it's great to win in a place where you live, and I guess we'll have to stay in Monaco now. By the time I stop racing, my son Jacques will be 17, and he'll know so many girls here there's no way we'll be allowed to leave!"

ALAN JONES: "If I couldn't win it, I'm glad Gilles did, because I like him, and he's the rival I most respect. Second place wasn't the end of the world - and I got a lot of fun out of pressuring Piquet. He and I had a touch at Zolder, and afterwards he screamed to the press he was going to put me in the barriers at the first opportunity. He didn't have the guts to come and talk to me about it, face to face, but I couldn't really care less.

"I haven't got time to mess about with people like him. At Monaco he was making mistakes all over the place, and finally he parked it in the wall at Tabac. I don't often piss myself laughing in a racing car, but I got a good chuckle out of that!"

21 JUNE 1981 - SPANISH GP (JARAMA) This one was against the run of play. In theory, Jarama favours deftness rather than horsepower, handling over straightline speed. At Monaco, you looked to Williams or Brabham or Ligier to win. As at Monaco, you looked on incredulously as Gilles Villeneuve took it for Ferrari.

Above: Villeneuve's victory in Spain was a triumph for a determined man over a deficient machine.
Right: Prost's momentous first win, at home in France for Renault, was a milestone en route to a record-setting career.

GILLES VILLENEUVE: "We have a fantastic engine, the best facilities, Fiorano test track, and all the rest of it - and the chassis is *terrible*! You put on new tyres, and it's OK for four laps. After that, forget it. It's just like a fast, red, Cadillac, wallowing all over the place. The amazing thing is, it's so forgiving. I can get so sideways I'm almost looking over the roll-over bar - and still it comes back! But I'd sooner have it vicious, with some grip."

GORDON MURRAY: "I walked the circuit during the race, and I tell you, that is the greatest drive I have ever seen by anyone. You can't believe how evil that Ferrari was, yet, with all the pressure on him, Gilles never made a single mistake."

JOHN WATSON (third in the race): "That bloody Ferrari was getting in everyone's way - for the last 15 laps it was holding everyone up. Ridiculous!"

GILLES VILLENEUVE: "Watson's absolutely right - in fact, I couldn't understand why he and the others didn't pass me. Ask them what they were doing for the first 65 laps, while I was running flat out. After all, three of them were ahead of me on the grid."

5 JULY 1981 - FRENCH GP (DIJON-PRENOIS) A momentous day: the first of Alain Prost's 51 Grand Prix victories, and appropriately at home. Prost's Renault trailed Piquet's Brabham until rain red-flagged the race in its late stages. On its resumption, Prost gambled on Michelin's qualifying tyres for the 22-lap sprint to the flag. On a damp track, Piquet didn't have a prayer against him.

ALAIN PROST: "I was lucky with the rain, and I know it, but still this was such an important victory for me. It's the old thing everyone says: you win your first Grand Prix, and your mentality changes. Before, you thought you could do it; now you *know* you can."

> You are a winner, and you go into the record books, and you have the impression - totally warranted, by the way - that the world now sees you in a different light.
>
> ALAIN PROST

18 JULY 1981 - BRITISH GP (SILVERSTONE) Watson's win for McLaren was the first under the management of the team's new leader Ron Dennis. The McLaren MP4 featured a carbon fibre chassis that would soon become the norm. By finishing second Reutemann took the lead in the championship.

CARLOS REUTEMANN: "As for the World Championship, I don't really want to talk about it. I am leading on points now, and if it happens, it happens. Yes or no, life will be the same. The sun will be in the same place. At the moment everything is going well for me - too well, in fact, and that worries me. To be honest with you, I feel a little bit alone."

DIDIER PIRONI: "These stupid cars have to change. I can tell you, I feel stupid myself when I'm in the car, raising the suspension for the test in the pits, in front of all those spectators. How ridiculous it looks! It has to change because it is too stupid to stay. As for driving, there is no feel in the cars now they have no suspension movement. They are brutal to drive."

ALAN JONES: "If they don't change the bloody rules, I doubt that I'll stay in Formula 1. I'm not enjoying racing these things at all!"

EMERSON FITTIPALDI: "I remember the day I showed Ayrton, a mere boy in the European Formula Ford Championship, around the Zeltweg pits in 1981. One by one, I introduced him to all the team managers - that's right, I was the one who introduced Senna to Ron Dennis - and I had not done this before with any Brazilian driver.

"The difference was that I was convinced this was someone exceptional. My introduction went: 'This is Ayrton Senna. He has everything it takes to be World Champion.' These gentlemen of F1 were familiar with my reserved style, and they were very surprised. Senna simply gave an embarrassed smile.

30 AUGUST 1981 - DUTCH GP (ZANDVOORT) Alain Prost's second win, over Piquet and Jones, gave the Frenchman an opportunity to size up the rugged Australian.

ALAIN PROST: "The most fiery, the most powerful - I would even go so far as to say, the most violent - driver that year was unquestionably Alan Jones. It was no coincidence that he was the reigning world champion."

13 SEPTEMBER 1981 - ITALIAN GP (MONZA) Over the Monza weekend, the race - dominated by Prost - was somewhat overshadowed by news of World Champions, past and present. Alan Jones, the rumours went, was going to retire, and Niki Lauda, after two seasons away, would next year be making a comeback, with McLaren. There was even talk of a return by Jackie Stewart, who had quit eight years earlier.

JACKIE STEWART: "It's true I've received an incredible offer to come back, and although I feel I made the right decision when I retired at the top, it's very tempting.

I don't really need the money, but it's a hell of a hard job, turning down millions. I'm well off, but I'm not Niarchos."

NIKI LAUDA: "Yes, I asked McLaren for a lot of money, but everyone tries to get as much as possible in their jobs. It isn't the money that's bringing me back - racing is far too dangerous to do it for that reason alone."

FRANK WILLIAMS: "Niki is obviously taking a hell of a risk by coming back. He's been out of it for two years, and he's never been that strong physically. He's very determined, and I think he'll do a good job, but I have my doubts that he'll be quite what he was."

NIKI LAUDA: "How can I say how things will go? Maybe they'll be good, maybe bad. Maybe I'll finish up in the hospital. Who knows? People say comebacks never work out. Well, there's one good reason why I want to do it - to prove them wrong."

ALAN JONES: "Frank wasn't too thrilled when I told him I was probably retiring at the end of the season. The main reason for my retiring is simply that I want to go back and live in Australia. I started thinking a bloke had to be off his head running around the world, hanging about in airports, living in hotels. Perhaps, if we hadn't got into this stupid situation with cars like go-karts, I wouldn't have got so disillusioned with it all. I've always enjoyed my motor racing - and I haven't enjoyed it this year at all."

FRANK WILLIAMS: "Perhaps it's not as important to AJ as it was. After all, he's won the World Championship. I reckon he weighed everything up, was well satisfied by what he'd achieved, had made a pile of money, and decided to call it a day.

"But his decision so late in the season, besides being grossly inconsiderate to us, was a big setback for our plans. There was nobody of his calibre - like Villeneuve or Pironi or Prost or Piquet - available by September. They'd all done deals elsewhere.

"I don't think his late decision was deliberate - it's just that he's a very inconsiderate person. Every year I take a slightly tougher attitude towards drivers. You have to be realistic about them, to accept that most of them are in it to make as much money as they can. As soon as they're satisfied... gone! Right? And I'm probably particularly jaundiced about them at the moment. All I care about is Williams Engineering, and the points we earn. I don't care who scores them."

17 OCTOBER 1981 - LAS VEGAS GP (CAESAR'S PALACE) For the season finale - and the World Championship decider - the Formula 1 circus went for the first time to Las Vegas, where a Grand Prix belonged like Nureyev in the Rugby League Cup Final. Still, Bernie Ecclestone had done another deal, and so everyone did his bidding as usual. Reutemann versus Piquet versus Laffite is how it was in the standings, although Jacques's chances were strictly mathematical. The battle was truly between the South American pair separated by a single point, with Carlos a heavy favourite, for this track put a premium on stamina, which was always suspect in Piquet. Reutemann got a head start with a brilliant qualifying lap to get pole. But in the race Reutemann faded back to finish out of the points, handing the title to the fifth-place finisher, Piquet. Most thought Reutemann had simply given up, including the new World Champion.

NELSON PIQUET: "He braked early to let me pass when I came up behind him. He made it so easy for me I couldn't believe it."

PETER WINDSOR: "Carlos took pole with the Williams car FW07/12, but was worried that he had been designated FW07/17 for the race. On race morning he had to bed in brake pads, which would normally have been done on Friday or Saturday, instead of choosing a well-matched set of tyres.

"Unsure of a car he had barely driven, Carlos was shocked from lap one to feel a massive vibration through FW07/17. Clearly, the tyres were grossly mismatched. With no suspension travel the car became undriveable over the bumps, which deteriorated as the track surface crumbled. The car bucked and weaved through the fast left-handers.

"Carlos could still have emerged a hero if he had driven Piquet off the road, as Senna and Schumacher would do in the future, and thus won the 1981 championship. But that was not in style. As it was, he drove his heart out in Las Vegas and finished eighth."

FRANK WILLIAMS: "I've never had a problem with Carlos myself. The problems were always between him and Alan, and, to a lesser extent, between him and Patrick. It's true that Patrick never got particularly close to him, and that was part of the problem. I think Carlos thought, quite wrongly, that there were two distinct teams, with the top brass working for Alan. But that wasn't the case at all.

"As for the drivers themselves... well, all I can say is that they were extremely different types. They never had very much in common as individuals, although they did collaborate quite well on occasions. Their relationship really soured after all that stupid Rio business.

"After Silverstone, when Reutemann had a 17-point lead in the World Championship, the emphasis swung very discreetly to him. He had everything going for him. He got the best of everything - except that he needs psychological support more than most drivers, and perhaps we let him down a little there. He needs to be aware that everyone in the team is wearing a Reutemann lapel badge and an Argentine scarf, that sort of thing."

Meanwhile in Las Vegas, Alan Jones ran away with what he had announced as the final race of his career. The forthright Australian's absence would leave a void in the quotable character department so savoured by the media, a branch of the sport about which Jones had strong feelings.

ALAN JONES: "You have to handle the press and the media, because that's why the money's in the sport. I don't have much respect for them. Every writer has a favourite in the sport - that is, when they're not actually paid to support a particular driver or team or sponsor. The press are like the fans. They're for someone and against someone else. There are Ferrari freaks and Lotus freaks and then a huge number of ordinary hangers-on. We get to know them and there are a few of them we take seriously.

"Sometimes we're accused of being thick. I know a lot of people who thought that Ronnie Peterson was as thick as two planks, but of course nothing could be further from the truth: he was in fact highly intelligent, but just didn't care to have people think of him that way.

"A lot of drivers are thought of as just grown-up spoiled brats who would rather play tennis and swim or look at the birds than be made to sit down and think. A big part is played by the press: the I'm-too-stupid-to-think syndrome is an escape from the endless low-level questions they have to face from the idiots who write about them.

"But one cannot drive well without brains. No team-manager hires rock-apes: a fool in a Formula 1 car is a threat to himself and to others. And I don't just mean a fool intellectually or a fool in the racing car. I mean a man who can't think, can't reason, can't grasp what is required of him and can't control his emotions. Constructors look for potential World Champions, and recognise that to become a World Champion, a very special kind of intelligence is required."

KEKE ROSBERG: "The '81 season had been the worst of my life. I was 33, I'd been around for a long time, and Fittipaldi was so far off the pace that it gave you no chance to show people how you could race. I couldn't see where I would get a good drive. I had talked to Frank, but he said his team was settled for '82.

"Then, after Las Vegas, I heard that Reutemann had retired, and I thought, 'I bet that wasn't in Frank's plans', and got in touch with him again. Later he called me to go testing at Ricard, and I got a fantastic reception from the team - no suggestion that the big stars had gone and now they were stuck with me.

"The test went well, and finally Frank called me. He was just off to Saudi Arabia, in a rush. 'You can have the drive,' he said. I said, 'Frank, we haven't even talked about money or anything yet - but I'll take it!'"

While British fans (opposite) celebrated John Watson's win for a revitalised McLaren, a retiring Alan Jones (above) took potshots at the press and went home to Australia.

After a year of fooling around with 'six-centimetre gaps', of pretending that skirts were banned, FISA ran up the white flag for 1982. Skirts - fixed, not sliding - were now officially permitted once more, which meant in turn that suspensions had to be solid. All that mattered was crude downforce, and the cars, nasty to drive the previous year, now became hellish, with tyre side-walls acting as shock absorbers. Cornering speeds continued to climb, and for the driver there was no warning of the limit.

23 JANUARY 1982 - SOUTH AFRICAN GP (KYALAMI) The opening race was at Kyalami, but come the first day of practice, not a car ventured from the pit lane. The drivers were on strike.

During the winter they had each received a 'Superlicence' application form, and most had signed without troubling to read the small print. But Lauda, now back in Formula 1 with McLaren, noted a clause for which he didn't care, and drew it to the attention of Pironi, then president of the Grand Prix Drivers Association. What troubled Niki was the proposal that future superlicences be issued to a *driver and team.* The constructors claimed that this was simply to stop drivers from breaking contracts, but Lauda saw it as a means of subjugating them, putting them in the 'ownership' of their teams.

Therefore, when they arrived on the first morning, the drivers found a coach at the paddock entrance ; Niki invited them to board it. Once loaded up, the coach trudged off to Johannesburg, to the Sunnyside Park Hotel, while Pironi remained at the circuit, negotiating with Balestre and Ecclestone, these two for once in accord.

KEKE ROSBERG: "I very nearly didn't get on that bus, because I thought the whole thing was bloody stupid, and I could smell something wasn't right, but once you were on, you were on. Lauda and Pironi had planned it that way. That whole weekend Pironi behaved like it was the big weekend of his life."

Bernie Ecclestone, predictably, had snapped into combat mode from the outset, insisting that if his Brabham drivers Piquet and Patrese were not on hand for the first session, they would be sacked for breach of contract.

BERNIE ECCLESTONE: "It is people like Borg and McEnroe who bring in the crowds. If these drivers think they can do the same, I suggest that what they do is dress in all their gear, rent the New York Shea Stadium, which holds 56,000 people, and see how many turn up to see them. Then we would find out what the public really wants.

"We have been watching Ferraris for 50 years. Ferrari has had God knows how many drivers. They come and they go but still all that people want is to see a Ferrari.

"They cannot see the bleeding driver anyway! And they never make themselves available to the press. Really, I ask you, what asset are they?"

But as 10 o'clock came and went, Ecclestone's drivers, like their colleagues, were lounging in the sun. Later the FIA stewards announced that the race was to be postponed, that an application would be made for the suspension of the drivers' licences.

At the hotel the drivers pondered their next move. Clearly they would now have to spend the night there, and Lauda reasoned that if they took single rooms, unity would be lost. Therefore he organised a banqueting suite, in which mattresses were installed. And there the drivers stayed, awaiting news from the front. It wasn't until the morning that Pironi called with the news that the battle had been won.

KEKE ROSBERG: "That night Elio de Angelis played the piano - Mozart, I think - and Gilles played Scott Joplin. The best thing about it was that, for once, all the drivers

Strikes are no way for intelligent people to achieve their aims. KEKE ROSBERG

got along well together! Apart from Teo Fabi, that is, who ran like a chicken - said he was going for a pee, and never came back. He lost our respect for ever, not because he decided to leave, but because he betrayed us. He went straight to Ecclestone and Balestre, and told them everything we'd discussed.

"In the end, the drivers 'won', if you like, because we heard no more about the licence clause, but I hated the way it was done. That was my first race with Williams, and Frank was very tough with me - understandably, too, because here was this new driver, getting the big chance, and immediately letting him down."

After a night of indifferent sleep, and not entirely sure what had actually been agreed, the drivers returned to the track at Kyalami. A brief practice session, then an hour of qualifying, and that was it as far as race preparation was concerned.

Remarkably, in the circumstances, the race drew from Prost one of his greatest drives. After leading from the start, his Renault punctured a tyre after 41 laps, crawled back to the pits, rejoined eighth, and took the lead again on lap 68, with nine to the flag.

The team owners may have been livid about the drivers' behaviour; who were they to get high-minded? Within a few weeks *they* would strike, too. And they didn't relent.

DECISION OF THE STEWARDS OF THE MEETING
OF THE SOUTH AFRICAN GRAND PRIX

The Stewards of the Meeting of the South African Grand Prix have ascertained that the prequalification practice foreseen by the regulations has not been able to take place because of the refusal of the drivers to participate.

For the same reasons the first official qualifying session foreseen from 13h 20 to 14h 20 has not taken place because of the absence of drivers.

Furthermore, the Stewards of the Meeting have been informed by the FISA of the following official declaration made by the two drivers'representatives on the Formula One Commission : "If the FISA refuses to amend the text of the Super-Licence application the twenty-nine drivers who have signed the present note declare that they will not participate in the Grand Prix practices."

The Stewards ascertain that the drivers have carried out their threat and that the South African Grand Prix practices cannot be organized in application of the regulations, and as a result the race cannot take place without presenting very big safety risks.

In application of Article 141 of the Sporting Code, the Stewards of the Meeting consider themselves obliged to postpone the race because of a case of force majeure imposed by the attitude of the drivers and to postpone the Grand Prix for eight days.

Furthermore, for violation of Articles 68 and 69 of the Sporting Code and Article 8 of the F1 World Championship Sporting Regulations establishing the Super-Licences and for non respect of their signature and of their entry for all the World Championship races, the Stewards of the Meeting have decided the suspension of their international licence with immediate application for the following drivers : N. Piquet : R. Patrese : M. Alboreto : S. Borgudd : C. Reutemann : K. Rosberg : J. Watson : N. Lauda : N. Winkelhock : B. Salazar : E. de Angelis : N. Mansell : R. Guerrero : A. Prost : R. Arnoux : J. Mass : R. Boesel : C. Serra : A. de Cesaris : B. Giacomelli : E. Cheever : J. Laffite : G. Villeneuve : L. Pirro : P. Tambay : M. Baldi : J.P. Jarier : R. Paletti : D. Daly : D. Warwick : T. Fabi.

Notification of the present decision has been given to the drivers, or in absence their team manager.

21 MARCH 1982 - BRAZILIAN GP (RIO DE JANEIRO) An eventful day in Rio. Villeneuve led, until his tyres went off, and he crashed, after which Piquet and Rosberg fought it out. A combination of heat, high g-forces and solid suspension exacted terrible dues from the drivers, many of whom were at the end of their physical tether afterwards. On the top step of the podium, Piquet collapsed.

Afterwards Renault protested Brabham and Williams on the grounds that they had raced underweight, and FISA ultimately disqualified the two British cars, awarding the victory to Prost.

If there were no argument that the cars had been underweight, it was easy to sympathise with the teams responsible. While Renault and Ferrari, with all their cumbersome and weighty turbocharged cars, could just about get down to the weight limit, teams such as Williams, Brabham, McLaren and Lotus had no difficulty in undercutting it. Therefore, in the fight against the turbos, they took it upon themselves to restore some semblance of equality, by matching lower weight to their lower-powered engines.

The FISA regulation was that the minimum weight limit was 580kg - minus the driver, but including normal lubricants and coolants - which could be topped up after the race, prior to the checking of the car's weight. That being so, for ingenious minds it was the work of a moment to spot a loophole, and what they came up with was 'water-cooled brakes'. The car, equipped with a large water tank, would go to the grid with the thing full, spray its contents away in the early laps, run the bulk of the race 30kg under the limit, then have the tank refilled afterwards so as to be over 580kg for the post-race check.

COLIN CHAPMAN: "Now I admit that wasn't in the guy's mind when he wrote the rule - but exactly the same is true of turbos. When the equivalence formula was conceived, in the mid-60s, it was simply in case anyone wanted to supercharge engines left over from the 1.5-litre F1. When that rule was written, there was no such thing as a turbocharged petrol engine. Therefore, Renault, Ferrari and others are interpreting a rule in a manner in which it was never *meant* to be interpreted. And it's the same with our water-cooled brakes."

GILLES VILLENEUVE: "I think I probably enjoy driving - for its own sake - more than a lot of drivers, but I hate these cars. No one outside of Formula 1 can know how bad they are to drive.

"There is a moment, going over a bump and turning into a corner at the same time, when you lose vision. Everything goes blurred. Now we have skirts back again, the g-forces are unbelievable, and the steering is ridiculous heavy - like being in a big truck, with the power steering not working. Sometimes you feel you don't have the strength to pull it round a corner.

"And, of course, we have no suspension. You go over a bump, and you feel like someone is kicking you in the back. Your legs are flung around in the cockpit, and your head constantly hits the back of the cockpit or the roll-over bar. After a while, your sides ache, your head aches, and you become aware of not enjoying driving a race car.

"If you make love to a woman, and at the same time someone sticks a knife in your back, eventually you won't like making love so much, right? In the same way, if you like driving, but feel your head's being punched every time you come into a corner, eventually you won't like that so much. But... take away the knife, and I still like making love!

"The problem is that nothing is being done. And when we go to places like Long Beach and Monaco, where the g-forces will be less, it'll be forgotten. But Brands Hatch and Austria will be awful, and Zolder, I guess, will be quite a good killer.

"So many of the dangers we face are unnecessary, and could easily be removed. Look at qualifying. We have two sets of qualifying tyres for each driver in each timed session. You do one quick lap, and they start to go off, so you have just two opportunities to set your quick time.

"If I have only two chances to get a good grid position, I must wait until the track is clear. If there's someone in my way, I must just hope he's looking in his mirrors - I mean, I can't lift, because this is my last chance of a quick lap."

4 APRIL 1982 - USA WEST GP (LONG BEACH) Long Beach was memorable for a dominant victory by Lauda, in only the third race of his comeback.

25 APRIL 1982 - SAN MARINO GP (IMOLA) Imola '82 was a weekend of acrimony, which spawned eventual tragedy. The FOCA teams were on strike, sulky that

their 'water-cooled brakes' had been banned. So they stayed home, hurting the spectators, of course, but also themselves: Ferrari finished 1-2, and needed those points to win the constructors' title.

For Ferrari though, the price was way too high. As they cruised their last lap, Pironi suddenly spurted by the unsuspecting Villeneuve, ignoring team orders, stealing the win. After going briefly to the podium, Gilles stormed off.

A couple of days later the journalist Nigel Roebuck called Gilles. He spoke quickly and softly, as usual, cooler now, but soberly livid and disillusioned.

NIGEL ROEBUCK: "We were all staggered when Pironi appeared in the lead on the last lap."

GILLES VILLENEUVE: "Yeah, me also!"

NR: "Right after the race it was obvious you didn't want to talk to anyone. You went up to the podium, with Pironi, briefly, but then walked off before the ceremony was complete."

GV: "Well, I left because otherwise I would have said some bad things."

NR: "Have you talked it through with Pironi since?"

GV: "No. I haven't said a word to him, and I'm not going to again - ever."

NR: "Are you serious?"

GV: "Absolutely. I have declared war. I'll do my own thing in future. It's war. Absolutely war."

NR: "Well, tell me, where did it all begin to go wrong at Imola?"

GV: "OK, I'll tell you the facts, and leave you to decide. First of all - before the race even started - we knew we were extremely marginal on fuel. Forghieri told us to save fuel as much as we could. In fact, the cars were topped up on the grid. When René blew up I took the lead, and we got a 'slow' sign from the pits. You get a 'slow' sign, and that means 'hold position'. That has been the case ever since I have been at Ferrari.

"Do you remember Monza in '79? I sat behind Jody the whole way, knowing this was my last chance to beat him for the World Championship. OK, I hoped like hell he would break! But I never thought of breaking my word. I know all about team orders at Ferrari.

"Before this, our relationship [Villeneuve and Peroni's] had always been good, and I trusted him, but I won't make that fucking mistake again. I guess people will say I'm overreacting, but I don't see it that way. I trust people until they give me reason not to, but if they let me down, that's it."

ALAIN PROST: "The week before he died, Gilles called me several times - I was trying to help his brother in Formula 3 - and all the time he was talking about Didier. He was so angry, I couldn't believe it. Even now, I shiver when I think about it. And when the accident happened, I was absolutely sure why."

The bitter strife among feuding teams was overshadowed by Ferrari's internal conflict at Imola. Pironi's controversial victory over Villeneuve preceded tragedy.

He was there, looking like the hero who won the race, and I looked like the spoiled bastard who sulked. I knew it would look like that, but still I thought it was better to get away. GILLES VILLENEUVE

8 MAY 1982 After Imola the mood was low. When the teams - all of them - met up at Zolder a couple of weeks later, recriminations were rife, and much of pit-lane was a study in sullenness.

Grand Prix racing was split down the middle. And it was that same weekend, under a morose sky, that Villeneuve was killed in qualifying, thus reducing to trivia anything else which might have been wrong. He hit the slower moving March of Jochen Mass and had an enormous accident.

For many, racing's addictive quality was never more severely put to the test. Whatever had assailed this *soi-disant* sport in recent years, there had remained the spectacle of his genius to balance the scale. Now there seemed to be very little left.

A 21-year-old woman wrote to Villeneuve at Ferrari:

> "Hello Gilles: I still cannot believe that you are no more... I did not know Nuvolari but I will talk to my daughter with pride about you. I will be able to tell her that I delighted in you and cried for you. I have within me the sense of an infinite emptiness that I feel nothing will be able to fill except my tears. I hope that up there you have found a circuit and when the starting light is green, go Gilles."

Villeneuve achieved great fame with Ferrari through his magnanimity and daring. He taught us to appreciate the forces that mechanical parts have to withstand when a driver finds himself facing the unforeseen. Some people called him crazy. There was a chorus of criticism when I engaged him because he was an unknown entity. Well, Niki Lauda was also unknown when I took him on. **You have to admit I have a pretty good nose. In my eyes Villeneuve was one of my family. I loved him.** ENZO FERRARI

Gilles Villeneuve was universally mourned, his spectacular style created a legend. His son Jacques (inset, with his father) later made a name of his own in the sport.

EDDIE CHEEVER: "Think of the circumstances that day. Gilles was a fraction off Pironi at the time - and this was right after their falling out at Imola. Last qualifying run, a mixed set of used tyres... good lap, probably, a hundred revs more in the straight, through the chicane and up the hill Mass is in the way: is he going to go left or right? Gilles commits himself to the right, Mass also goes right to try and give him room You know how long that takes? It's a snap of your fingers."

PROFESSOR SID WATKINS (FIA Medical Officer): "I was very fond of Villeneuve - a good, honest bloke, as well as a genius of a driver. A lovely lad. When I first met him, I remember he said, 'I hope I'll never need you.' I was really very upset at Zolder when I got to his accident and it was obvious immediately there was nothing I could do for him. The final diagnosis was a fatal fracture of the neck just where the spine meets the base of the skull."

9 MAY 1982 - BELGIAN GP (ZOLDER) KEKE ROSBERG (second in the race): "That weekend was very difficult, very poignant. I had to work hard to put it out of my mind, I can tell you. But it didn't really hit me until the Monday, when I had to go up to the track to do a photo session. All that was left was garbage and Gilles's helicopter."

JODY SCHECKTER: "For Gilles, racing was a romantic thing. My preoccupation was keeping myself alive, but for him the thing was to be fastest, every race, every lap. And he was, I believe, the fastest racing driver the world has ever seen. If he could come back tomorrow, and live his life over again, I'm sure he would do it all the same way, and with the same love. That was the right word, in his case. More than anyone I've known, Gilles was in love with motor racing."

The crowds loved him because he, of all the men out there, was so clearly working without a net.

23 MAY 1982 - MONACO GP (MONTE CARLO) CLAY REGAZZONI (writing in the programme for the Monaco GP): "So long, Gilles. You were young, loyal, daring, simple and you loved to express yourself in our sport like no one has done in recent years. You had just attained the heights of glory and like a lightning bolt destiny cruelly stole your life. You leave an immense void. Your talents were fantastic exhibitions which the many fans you loved and for whom you always gave your best, will miss. They never will forget what you did and you will leave unperishable memories for automotive sport aficionados. Joann, Melanie and Jacques, like us, will always be proud of you. Adieu, Gilles."

13 JUNE 1982 - CANADIAN GP (MONTREAL) In Montreal - on the track now named Le Circuit Gilles Villeneuve - there was further tragedy, and again Didier Pironi was involved.

On pole position, he stalled the Ferrari at the start. Such occurrences have always been commonplace, especially in the turbo era, and usually those behind somehow find a path through. Young Riccardo Paletti, though, was starting a Grand Prix for the first time, and from the back of the grid. He hit Pironi's car at perhaps 120mph.

My father would ask me why I did things the hard way. The answer is: difficulty sharpens desire. ELIO DE ANGELIS

The rescue procedure, which was necessarily long and harrowing, was dealt with calmly and courageously, quietly impressing all who were there, but there was no saving Paletti.

Pironi, poker-faced in the midst of further turmoil, later came out and raced again. It seemed there were demons to be pushed from his mind, for, after several stops, he drove with complete abandon. More irony: at this, the track named for Gilles, he raced exactly as Gilles would have done.

3 JULY 1982 - DUTCH GP (ZANDVOORT) HARVEY POSTLETHWAITE: "Something very odd came over Didier at around that time. He went very...strange. He had big personal problems - with his wife, and sundry girl friends - but they didn't seem to concern him too much. It was more that he became incredibly arrogant and over-confident about everything - including the fact that he was going to be World Champion."

25 JULY 1982 - FRENCH GP (PAUL RICARD) Controversy again: Ricard was all Renault, but Arnoux spoiled the home team's afternoon by beating Prost, thereby ignoring his promise to help Alain's quest for the World Championship.

ALAIN PROST: "I thought the idea was unrealistic, but Arnoux suggested it. He gave his word, and he broke it. That was why I was angry. Afterwards he went on to the French press about how he had fought all this time, that he was always unlucky, the underdog. A martyr, you see - and the French love martyrs.

"That night I was driving home, and stopped for fuel. And the guy serving me says, 'You did the right thing, Monsieur Arnoux. Prost is a little shit, thinking everything should be handed to him on a plate.' He didn't even know what we looked like, but his prejudices were there. I was so embarrassed I gave him cash - I didn't want to offer a credit card with my name on it.

"I couldn't believe the bad publicity I got that week, and I told Renault I would leave if Arnoux stayed for '83, because you must trust your team mate. I remembered what happened with Villeneuve and Pironi at Imola. I learned a lesson from that."

8 AUGUST 1982 - GERMAN GP (HOCKENHEIM) At Hockenheim there was yet another appalling accident, and this time the victim was Pironi. In wet Saturday morning practice the Frenchman's Ferrari hit the back of Prost's slowing Renault and had a monumental crash. His legs were terribly injured and he had raced a car for the last time.

ALAIN PROST: "I was coming into the pits on that lap. Pironi couldn't see me because of spray, and hit the back of my car - he actually overtook me in the air. His car landed, tail first, in front of me, then bounced away, somersaulting down the road. Awful.

"From that day on, I admit it, I never felt the same about racing when the visibility was so bad. In fact, I thought it was fucking stupid."

DIDIER PIRONI: "Immediately after the accident, I felt no pain at all - it seemed like other accidents I'd had, when I hadn't been hurt. In fact, while they were working to get me out of the car, I was furious that now I would have to race the T-car, which wasn't set up so well. Then, in the helicopter, my legs began to hurt very seriously, and I looked at them for the first time, and thought maybe I wouldn't be driving in the race, after all."

HARVEY POSTLETHWAITE: "Everyone was pretty depressed, as you can imagine, and Enzo Ferrari asked me to join him the following day, to watch the race on TV. Tambay won it, of course, and the Old Man just sat there and cried. Fantastic, really, an incredible thing to witness. He went round and embraced everybody. The people here are *very* emotionally involved with racing."

29 AUGUST 1982 - SWISS GP (DIJON-PRENOIS) KEKE ROSBERG: "I learned a very good lesson at Dijon, because I lost my temper, and I was ashamed of myself - I could have caused an accident. I went berserk, which is a very dangerous thing to do in a race car, but de Cesaris was going to make me lose that race! I was chasing Prost for the lead, came up to lap de Cesaris, and lost ten seconds in three laps. He had more power, and it reached a point where I was banging my front wheel against the sidepod of his car - at 170mph at the end of the straight!"

25 SEPTEMBER 1982 - CAESAR'S PALACE GP (LAS VEGAS) From Caruso to Liberace. A fortnight after Monza, F1 found itself in Las Vegas again, and once more for a championship decider, this time between Rosberg and Watson. The odds were with Keke, who needed only a fifth place to be confirmed in the title, and finished precisely there. John took a fine second, but the dominant man - once the Renaults were gone from the picture - was Alboreto, who scored his first Grand Prix win, and got to meet Diana Ross afterwards.

DEREK ONGARO (FISA Circuit Inspector): "To be honest, I've hated every second of this season. There's something very wrong when the chequered flag comes down, and all you feel is relief that another race weekend is out of the way without someone getting killed."

In the tail of 1982, there remained one last sting. Shortly before Christmas, after returning from a meeting in Paris, Colin Chapman suffered a massive heart attack at his home in Norfolk. Set against all the other turmoil of the year, it was somehow less of a shock than it should have been.

BERNIE ECCLESTONE: "'Chunky' was my man. I really liked him. He was good company, one of the boys. He was a good businessman, he was probably the best designer there's ever been, and he was as quick as half the guys who ever drove for him. He was different from all the others, just a special guy."

The new world champion, Keijo 'Keke' Rosberg, was very much his own man, cheekily irreverent and possessing a well-developed streak of anti-establishmentarianism. After receiving the equivalent of a knighthood in his native land, the Flying Finn then had to deal with championship ceremonies conducted in a foreign tongue.

KEKE ROSBERG: "The only reason I went to the FISA prize-giving after winning the championship is the $10,000 fine I'd get if I didn't. So I arrive at the ceremony - the prize they're giving was my prize, remember! - and the whole business is in French. That really got up my nose. English is the language of motor racing. It's the only language everyone in the sport understands. I decided that if they were going to speak in their own language, why shouldn't I?

"I was very moderate. Too moderate. I only spoke a few minutes in Finnish, just to make my point. That's what I wanted to do: just to see what they would do about it, just to watch the expression on their faces. Unfortunately, I couldn't keep a straight face long enough. I started in four languages, went on in Finnish and then thanked everyone in four languages again."

Opposite: Splitting seconds - the Austrian Grand Prix was one of the closest finishes ever. De Angelis (right) beat Rosberg by 0.050s.
Above: As a champion smoker, Keke Rosberg was ideally suited as a high-speed billboard for his tobacco sponsor.

The season of 1983 began on an optimistic note: FISA had at last seen the folly of the ground effect era, had banned skirts, made flat-bottomed cars mandatory. It was a fine time to watch the drivers at their work, for the killjoy engineers, with all their computers and wind tunnels, had yet to find much in the way of new downforce to replace the old. For a short while, therefore, Grand Prix cars actually slid around again, and briefly F1 fans revelled in it.

Inevitably, though, there was a new madness. Fuel stops, revived by Brabham in mid-1982, were now *de rigueur* for competitiveness, and some of the hideously primitive refuelling devices used by the lesser teams had to be seen to be disbelieved. It was a time for keeping clear of the pits.

27 MARCH 1983 - USA WEST GP (LONG BEACH) The McLarens qualified 22nd and 23rd at Long Beach - and finished 1-2 in the race! Mainly, it was a problem with Michelin's qualifying tyres, which had been developed primarily for Renault, with their turbo horsepower; the McLarens simply didn't have enough power to generate the requisite heat in them, but on race tyres the cars worked just fine.

JOHN WATSON: "I can't explain it to you, I really can't - I would if I could. We still had too much understeer, but the grip was good all through - better than at any time in practice. I'm delighted, of course, but also baffled. Believe me, I'd rather start from near the front."

1 MAY 1983 - SAN MARINO GP (IMOLA) PATRICK TAMBAY: "Sometimes a Grand Prix makes you feel there is, after all, a God. This was one such. I had left the track the previous year in dismay: dismay that the FOCA teams had so wantonly broken their bond by striking, and dismay that Pironi's duplicity had stolen the Villeneuve victory that Gilles had earned, that the crowd so much wanted."

In 1983, though, the race had hallmarks of a sentimental movie script. Tambay, Villeneuve's close friend and the man who had replaced him at Ferrari, righted a wrong. Afterwards he seemed to have a problem in associating himself with the victory, as if he'd been willed to it. He was never to win another Grand Prix, but it is doubtful whether he would swap this one for a dozen others.

PATRICK TAMBAY: "The year before, Gilles had qualified third, and someone painted a Canadian Maple Leaf on the third place on the grid. By coincidence, I qualified third this time, and when I lined my car up there, I completely broke down - I was crying like a child.

"In the race, though, I was OK and it was the most emotional day of my career. To win at Imola, in Ferrari number 27... it's difficult to put it into words, but what happened was more than just winning a race. Really, it wasn't me driving the car that day - it was as if Gilles was with me all the way through. Number 27 *should* have won at Imola in '82, and I felt a great peace that now it had."

15 MAY 1983 - MONACO GP (MONTE CARLO) FRANK WILLIAMS: "Keke at Monaco? Well, it was one of the great drives, wasn't it? Quite brilliant. Slippery track, slicks... I don't think anyone improvises like he does. Made the rest look flat-footed."

NELSON PIQUET (second in the race): "I hate that circuit. It's like riding a bicycle in your bathroom."

22 MAY 1983 - BELGIAN GRAND PRIX (SPA) ALAIN PROST: "Since I've been in Formula 1, I've had great respect for Villeneuve, Pironi, Jones, Reutemann...but now they're all gone. At the moment I don't think we have one driver who is right at the top, clear of the rest. I think we are good, professional drivers, but not real stars."

14 AUGUST 1983 - AUSTRIAN GP (OSTERREICHRING) ALAIN PROST: "After I won in Austria, I had a 14-point lead, and the Renault people thought I was crazy when I said we would lose the championship to Piquet and Brabham. From somewhere, though, the BMW engine suddenly had a lot more power. 'Look,' I said, 'we can't get pole position anywhere, because our engine won't accept a lot of boost, so Piquet will always start ahead of us - and with his power he'll be impossible to pass in the race.' But Renault were simply too complacent, too *big*, to be able to respond quickly."

Personally, I think refuelling is fantastic - for TV, for the public, for everyone. And as far as safety is concerned, what worries me more is having about 2000 people wandering about the pit lane, looking the other way, when cars are coming in at 100mph. BERNIE ECCLESTONE

The dangerous race to refuel fastest ignited fears of fireworks that mercifully failed to materialise. Brabham (left) parlayed quick pitwork into victory over Williams (right) to win the 1983 team title.

15 OCTOBER 1983 - SOUTH AFRICAN GP (KYALAMI)
The World Championship decider involved three drivers, Prost (Renault), Piquet (Brabham-BMW) and Arnoux (Ferrari). In late August, the title had looked like a shoo-in for Prost, but if Renault were smugly confident, BMW had better engines. Piquet won the championship by driving conservatively to finish third.

Nelson won the championship, but gave the race away. I don't pay drivers to lose races.

BERNIE ECCLESTONE

You get paid so little by Bernie that you have to get something else out of it - and all I wanted was the championship. I'm very happy to have the title again, but it didn't change my life the first time, and it won't now. NELSON PIQUET

Right: Bernie Ecclestone gets a word in his ear from Nelson Piquet.

of my life to that point, and, yes, there was a bit of revenge involved, even if I don't like to admit it. Some of the French press gave me a very hard time when I left Renault. But the problem disappeared after Brazil."

EDDIE CHEEVER: "Sure, I finished fourth, but I wasn't racing - not at all. It was a matter of stroking round. A Grand Prix is supposed to be a sprint event, no holds barred, and it seems crazy to me that anything such as fuel consumption should come into it. What the hell kind of a race is it when the drivers have to back off from a duel because they're worried about running out of gas?"

FISA did a one-eighty for the 1984 season. Having permitted fuel stops the previous year (thereby allowing the teams to use as much as they wished for a 200-mile race), they banned them for '84 - and introduced a tankage limit of 220 litres. For all the turbo teams, in varying degrees, this brought problems, and Alfa Romeo, accustomed to working through 300 or more litres in a race, never did solve it. The whole notion of bringing 'economy' into Grand Prix racing seemed anathema to the drivers, and who could blame them? What was this thing? Racing, or not?

25 MARCH 1984 - BRAZILIAN GP (RIO DE JANEIRO)
ALAIN PROST: "You can't imagine the importance of that win, in my first race for McLaren. It was the most satisfying

3 JUNE 1984 - MONACO GP (MONTE CARLO) Ayrton Senna gave notice of intent this day. At Monaco, the sixth race of his Formula 1 career, he qualified only 13th in the Toleman-Hart, but race day was wet, and a combination of that track and those conditions was heaven-sent for a genius in the bud: ninth on lap one, seventh on lap six, he relentlessly climbed the order, until by lap 16 only the McLarens of Prost and Lauda were ahead.

They were in trouble, too, their carbon brakes snatching, thanks to uneven heat build-up in the torrential conditions. Ayrton passed Niki on lap 19, and set off after Alain, every lap taking seconds out of a sizeable lead. Even more remarkable, perhaps, was that another novice, Stefan Bellof, was up to third in his Tyrrell - and closing on both of them.

In the event, though, Senna and Bellof had to settle for second and third, for the rain worsened to the point that visibility was negligible, and Jacky Ickx, the Clerk of the Course, decided to bring proceedings to a halt after 31 laps.

In fact, the red flag was displayed at the end of the 32nd, and as they went past it Senna actually passed Prost on the road, and briefly believed he had won. Thus, when he stopped at the end of his slowing-down lap, he was not exhilarated by a brilliant drive, but livid that he was only second. Clearly, this was not a young man of ordinary expectations.

AYRTON SENNA: "I was very angry when the race was stopped, because I felt sure to win, but later, when I thought about more about it, I realised that actually I had been quite lucky - that the rain had given me a chance to show what I could do."

ALAIN PROST: "Obviously, I think it was a good decision to stop the race! And for sure it was bad for Senna and Bellof, but that's the way it is. I think it's stupid to say the race was stopped because I was leading. I don't know Jacky Ickx very well, but does anyone really imagine that a guy like that was going to stop the race because I have a Porsche engine, and he drives for Porsche?

Ayrton Senna (top left) astonished in Monaco, where Alain Prost and Nigel Mansell (opposite) started from the front but were rapidly caught by the audacious newcomer.
Below: Rising star Prost (left) and the veteran Niki Lauda (right) engaged in a season-long struggle for supremacy at McLaren.

It was my first win at Monaco, and that night I got completely drunk - for the first time in my life.

ALAIN PROST

Where are the FISA people? Not here, because it's too bloody hot for them. This sort of situation degrades Grand Prix racing, right? But we'll just have to bite the bullet. In the end, we're all whores - if the money's right, we'll do our stuff for anyone. KEKE ROSBERG

8 JULY 1984 - USA WEST GP (DALLAS) The FIA rule book stipulated that no circuit new to Formula 1 could run a Grand Prix without first holding a race of lesser consequences - a trial run, if you wish. But street tracks were exempt from this rule, and in Dallas the folly of that was clear to all. By the Friday afternoon the temperature was 107, and the surface was breaking up, badly. The following day, a 50-lap Can-Am race served to chew up what little remained of the racing surface. Dallas Fair Park looked like a dirt track.

An over-night bodge job with epoxy concrete compound proved ineffective: in the furnace heat it needed too long to cure properly. There arose rumours that the race would be postponed - maybe even cancelled altogether. And all the while the stands were filling up. By late morning on race day there were 90,000 folk on hand.

Above: Cowboy Keke got a ten-gallon hat for beating de Angelis and Arnoux in the bizarre stampede through the streets of Dallas. Even Sue Ellen (Linda Gray) was there.
Opposite: Niki Lauda capped his comeback by taking McLaren's turbo-powered TAG Porsche to his third driving title.

KEKE ROSBERG (winner) "We don't want to break bones. Everyone worries about pain. It's crazy to race, but what are you going to do? There's a huge crowd out there, and a lot of countries waiting for TV. There's no point in blaming anyone here in Dallas - this is FISA's fault for not insisting on new circuits having a try-out race before a Grand Prix."

DEREK WARWICK: "I threw that race away, spinning into the wall while trying to pass Mansell for the lead. I walked back to the Renault pit, and I really wanted someone to hurt me for being so bloody stupid - but they made me feel even worse by saying nothing. Then my wife arrived - and she had things to say, all right!"

5 AUGUST 1984 - GERMAN GP (HOCKENHEIM) ALAIN PROST: "Actually, the French are strange. They don't like winners - they prefer the guy who is second. Do you remember Raymond Poulidor, the cyclist? He was unbelievably popular - and he never won the Tour de France. Then there was Jacques Anquetil, one of the best ever, who won it five times, and he wasn't popular at all!

"I think maybe I have not been so popular in France, because in *everything* I want to win. I've always been like that, and it's not vanity. It's because life is a game, and I want to be the best. Otherwise the game is not worth playing. Even at cards I want to win, and if I begin to think otherwise, I don't play. That's me."

21 OCTOBER 1984 - PORTUGUESE GP (ESTORIL) In the championship decider, Prost did all he could, winning the race conclusively, but after a slow start his McLaren team mate Lauda duly came through for the second he needed to take the title - by half a point.

NIKI LAUDA: "Alain is *extremely* quick. Having him as a team mate has stimulated me, but it has also haunted me. There is no break in the pressure. He is always right there, always on form. I was never in this position with a team mate before. Sometimes one of them would beat me, but I always felt it would be me in front next time. With Prost it's different. I have had to drive faster and faster, better and better, all the time."

KEKE ROSBERG: "Niki has driven harder this year than I have ever seen before. He's had Prost so big in his eyes. I've been with him in a few corners, and I've been given a very clear picture: either I lift, or something's going to happen. Absolutely clean - but also absolutely uncompromising."

In my karting days, Niki was my idol. I used to model myself on him, dream of achieving success like him, and to be in a team with him, with the same equipment, same chances, was something fantastic. ALAIN PROST

7 APRIL 1985 - BRAZILIAN GP (RIO DE JANEIRO) Following the Brazilian Grand Prix, René Arnoux was 'released' from his Ferrari contract in circumstances that were mysterious, to say the least. Vague references were made to 'health problems', and Ferrari decided to run Stefan Johansson alongside Michele Alboreto for the balance of the season.

STEFAN JOHANSSON: "It was April 16, I remember, a Tuesday, and I was in a black mood. Although I had a contract with Toleman, we couldn't go racing because Pirelli wouldn't give us any tyres. I had nothing, in effect. Then the phone rang, and it was Marco Piccinini from Ferrari, telling me to get the first flight I could. I packed my bag in about ten minutes, went straight to Heathrow, and got a three o'clock flight to Milan. Eventually I got to the factory at about 8.30 that evening. It was incredible - all the mechanics and staff were standing outside, saying 'Welcome to Maranello.' Can you imagine how I felt?

   "The following morning I met Mr Ferrari. It was an incredible experience, and I was nervous as hell - I mean, it was like meeting royalty! As I shook his hand, I thought, 'Well, even if I don't get the drive, one of my dreams has been fulfilled.'"

21 APRIL 1985 - PORTUGUESE GP (ESTORIL) It was a rainy April weekend in Estoril, and the people stayed away. It was their loss. On the Saturday Senna took the first of his 65 pole positions, and on the Sunday the first of his 41 Grand Prix victories. Did it wonderfully, too; a drive for the gods.

AYRTON SENNA: "The big danger was that conditions changed all the time. Sometimes the rain was very heavy, sometimes not. I couldn't see anything behind me. It was difficult even to keep the car in a straight line sometimes, and for sure the race should have been stopped. Once I nearly spun in front of the pits, like Prost, and I was lucky to stay on the road. People think I made no mistakes, but that's not true - I've no idea how many times I went off! Once I had all four wheels on the grass, totally out of control... but the car came back on the circuit. Everyone said, 'Fantastic car control.' It was just luck. People later said that my win in the wet at Donington in '93 was my greatest performance - no way! I had traction control! OK, I didn't make any real mistakes, but the car was so much easier to drive. It was a good win, sure, but, compared with Estoril '85, it was nothing, really."

Senna... it's Villeneuve all over again, isn't it? A racing driver who's ahead of his car. DENIS JENKINSON

Ayrton Senna stormed sensationally off into the sodden distance in Portugal, winning for the first time and delighting Team Lotus.

19 MAY 1985 - MONACO GP (MONTE CARLO)

MICHELE ALBORETO: "Senna set quickest time, and then deliberately blocked my qualifying laps. I said to him, 'Now listen, you are young and everything, but that is not right,' He said he didn't see me! Lauda was also very angry with him, and to make Niki angry, you have to do something very wrong. I think Senna has to change. He is so good and so quick that he doesn't need to do things like that."

AYRTON SENNA: "After Monaco I didn't go out of my way to talk to Niki. I knew he was upset. That's his problem. I know I didn't do anything really wrong. I blocked him once when he was on a quick lap. Everyone blocks everyone. It was an accident. But then Niki started this crazy story about me holding him up for seven laps or something, so I kept away from him. Now we talk again. Not a lot, but we talk. As for Alboreto, I have no time for him. He said some very bad things about me, but I've done nothing wrong. He says I'll never be World Champion. Maybe not. But it won't be Alboreto who will stop me."

21 JULY 1985 - BRITISH GP (SILVERSTONE) Spots of rain were beginning to come down as Keke Rosberg hurtled up to Woodcote, so probably it had to be this lap or never, the last chance of a 160mph lap at Silverstone. Brake at the very latest, crank the wheel over in that familiar, darty style - and Keke is *really* on it. Through the middle part of the Woodcote chicane, he is all over the place, bouncing over the kerbs. Now he eases off, cruises through Copse - and we wait for the track announcer...

ANNOUNCER: "One-sixty! It's been done at last! Keke Rosberg! Williams-Honda!... One minute five point nine six seven!"

KEKE ROSBERG: "It was just plain silly to go and play again when I was already half a second ahead on pole. But I just couldn't resist it because I thought we could go a lot quicker - and we did.

"It was probably one of the few occasions when I felt I had lost my self control. I should have stayed in the garage and said: 'I've got pole, thank you very much.' But sheer enjoyment overtook professionalism."

KEITH DOUGLAS (Silverstone announcer): "The crowd rose as he came through the bends and he looked just like he was low-flying. The car looked like an airplane, twitching as it cornered. Quite incredible! It was almost as if the car was off the ground. It lives in my memory as one of the most outstanding sights I've seen yet."

IAN PHILIPS (Silverstone announcer): "Keke came through on the damp track. The line was dry but he was so fast his outside wheels were in the wet, kicking up spray. With only Woodcote corner to go I thought he was on for it. I knew what the man was capable of. In 40 years of watching Grand Prix racing, it is still the most exciting thing I've ever seen."

I got carried away, and that shouldn't be the case if you want to survive. But it only happened that one time.

KEKE ROSBERG

Rosberg's sensational lap at Silverstone was set in stone. At the time the fastest track, it was subsequently reconfigured to reduce speeds - as were most circuits - in the interests of improving safety.

Oh, Bellof was unbelievable - the nearest thing to Villeneuve we had seen. MARTIN BRUNDLE

Nelson Piquet, irked by his Brabham boss's parsimoniousness, had a move for more money on his mind.

NELSON PIQUET: "Sometimes I think about Pele and Garrincha, and how they finished their football days. Everywhere in the world they were superstars, but they finished their playing days with nothing! Pele had to go to the New York Cosmos when he was an old man, to make some money, so now he's OK, but otherwise... I tell you one thing, that's not going to happen to me.

"I've been World Champion twice, stayed loyal to Brabham - and Prost is earning three times as much as I am. I don't know how you rate us, but for sure Alain isn't three times better! If I stay with Brabham another year, people will think I'll never leave, and I know Bernie thinks that. I spoke to Ron Dennis about going to McLaren, and he mentioned so many days a year working for Marlboro, five for this, six for that... Forget it, I lost interest. I won't waste my life talking to people who don't understand racing.

"It's true I could make much more money if I found some personal sponsors, like Keke, but I don't want to do that kind of work. When I'm not at a track, racing or testing, I like to get back to my boat and disappear. That's the way I am, and when I turn up at a race I feel fresh.

"Anyway, now I've had this offer from Williams. I'm getting $1m from Bernie, and I asked him for double for next year - which is still a lot less than Prost is getting. He's offered me $1.6m, plus a thousand dollars a championship point, and I'm sure he's thinking it will be just enough to keep me.

"I'm not going to get into an argument over it, and I've told Williams I'm ready to sign: Frank has offered me $3.3m, plus *ten* thousand dollars a point! I don't want to leave Brabham; I like the team, the way things are done here. But I don't want to finish up like Garrincha."

25 AUGUST 1985 - DUTCH GP (ZANDVOORT) ALAIN PROST (second): "I knew where I stood. Niki had told me before the race he would win if he could, and that was fine. I would have been mad if, like Arnoux at Ricard in '82, he had promised to help me, then not done it. He wanted to win a race in his final year, and I understood that. Are we still friends? Of course! Maybe it was a little bit crazy in the last few laps, but it was fun."

NIKI LAUDA: "I promised that at the end of the season I would do everything to help Alain to the championship - but it's not the end of the season yet!"

1 SEPTEMBER 1985 Stefan Bellof was killed at the wheel of a Porsche 962 sportscar in the Spa 1000 Kms. In typical style, he was trying to do the impossible, overtaking Jacky Ickx into - of all places - Eau Rouge. The cars touched, and Bellof's Porsche, after spinning once, hit a barrier head on.

GERHARD BERGER: "Bellof was one of the best - I mean, one of the *very* best. I don't say that lightly. He was a future World Champion, for sure, maybe many times. He was going to be the big rival of Senna, I think. They don't come along very often like him. He was very special."

MARTIN BRUNDLE: "Stefan Bellof had fantastic talent. He'd always be the last to brake, and he'd get into extraordinary situations and somehow get away with it. He was totally fearless - way too brave, really."

KEN TYRRELL: "Stefan - he was the great lost talent, wasn't he? Incredibly fast and brave, and a lovely lad, too. He was going to Ferrari for 1986, and although I hated the idea of him leaving my team, it was inevitable one of the big guns would get him. Who knows what he might have achieved?"

8 SEPTEMBER 1985 - ITALIAN GP (MONZA)

ALAIN PROST: "I don't particularly enjoy celebrations at the track when I've won. I prefer to go somewhere with some friends and have a nice dinner, or, ideally, get home on the Sunday night. Niki and Keke have this Learjet race back to Ibiza afterwards, but they have a good advantage over me because usually they finish the race earlier."

6 OCTOBER 1985 - EUROPEAN GP (BRANDS HATCH)

ALAIN PROST: "Now I've won the championship with an English car, with a German engine, with American tyres and sponsorship - and all the French journalists could talk about was how fantastic it was for France! I said, 'Look, today I celebrate for *me*! Next week we can talk about France.'"

PATRICK TAMBAY: "Prost is World Champion now, and, you know, he is *still* underrated! People talk about 'natural talent', a gift for driving racing cars, and I suppose we must all have it in different degrees. But during my time racing I would say there have been three with something extra: Villeneuve, Senna, Prost. I don't know what this extra quality is, only that it exists."

NIGEL MANSELL: "Keke helped me win my first race, in that he helped me get past Senna, and I have to thank him for that. At first he didn't want me at Williams - at all - but I think now we actually like each other.

"Keke is completely honest. If he thinks you're a rat, he'll call you a rat. The great thing about him is that you know where you are - there's no bullshit at all about him. That's not true of certain other people."

19 OCTOBER 1985 - SOUTH AFRICAN GP (KYALAMI)
When he started to win, there was no stopping Nigel Mansell.

JAMES HUNT (BBC TV): "Mansell had tooled around for a long time, and what changed him was winning. There was a certain amount of luck in his first couple of wins, and it just changed the way he drove - he just drove better and better. Perhaps he was lucky to get those first results, but - my God! - he didn't half make the most of it. Once they were under his belt, he was a new man."

Opposite: Stefan Bellof, another talent lost too early.
Below: Nigel Mansell's first victory (here at Brands Hatch, where Prost clinched his first driving title) gave him a winning mindset.

The 1986 season got away to a very bad start, when Frank Williams, *en route* from Paul Ricard to Nice, had a road accident, suffering injuries which would put him in a wheelchair for the rest of his life. For many weeks his life hung in the balance, but before the year was out he was back at his desk.

FRANK WILLIAMS: "When I broke my neck, it obviously changed the way I had to live. Prior to that, I'd been a lot more... up front, let's say, and there might well have been one clash of wills too many. As it was, my life changed, and in many, many ways perhaps it worked for the better."

PATRICK HEAD: "Before his accident Frank was a very sort of bouncy character, with a very strong ego that would sometimes cause him to make poor judgements. In fact, we both believe that, had it not been for his accident, it's unlikely we would still be working together.

"Frank is a very pragmatic character. In the old days, when he didn't have any money for engines, or whatever, his attitude was always, 'How am I going to get out of this?' He's never been one to say, 'It's not fair.' He's always coped with whatever he's been presented with, and it was exactly the same with his accident.

"I'm sure at the time he had massive regrets: driving a not very good road car too quickly, and rolling it over at a remarkably low speed, and having the roof cave in. But once it had happened, he's the sort of person who says, 'OK, this is the position I'm in, this is what I have left to me - how am I going to make best of it?' He's a man of astonishing self-discipline."

NELSON PIQUET: "When I signed for Williams, Frank told me I was number one, no problem. It would have been different if he'd said then that it would be equal terms with Mansell, but no, I was to be number one. Then, of course, Frank had his accident, and suddenly he was in hospital with problems a million times worse than mine. When things were not working for me, I had to be a bigger man, and shut up."

NIGEL MANSELL: "Piquet had a big ego and would not want to be shown up by his number two driver. I knew him a bit and did not like what I saw. He had sloppy values and his sense of humour was the irritating kind, but as long as we were both professional I didn't think there would be a problem. How wrong I was."

23 MARCH 1986 - BRAZILIAN GP (RIO DE JANEIRO)

NIGEL MANSELL (after an incident with Senna): "I accept blame in that I was in charge of my car, and I let the team down because I should have remembered that the person in the other car thinks he's God.

"I had a talk with Senna before the season began. I said we were both going to be quick this year, and it would be better if we were both professional - if one of us won a corner, it was better for the other to let him go, and vice versa. We talked, and he said 'Yes, fine, we start again.'

"In the race at Rio I thought, rightly or wrongly, that I had done enough down the straight. I was alongside, on the inside, going into a very fast left-hander. I started to brake, still alongside, but Senna came across and hit me. I couldn't believe he would do that, so I braked to avoid a shunt. Then he came across and hit me again, very hard, with his left rear

wheel against my right front wheel. That made the front of my car jump sideways, and because of that I had my accident - trying to avoid a very big accident because of what he'd done.

"That was my mistake. Next time he does that, I won't move. If he wants a very big accident... all I will say is that I'm a professional, I'm paid by my team to do my job, and if he wants to carry on being crazy, that's up to him.

"At the moment I'm trying to avoid everything; I don't want to get near him, I don't really want to race with him. With Alain, with Keke, guys like that, there's never been a problem, but Senna has demonstrated that anybody who tries to overtake him he has complete disregard for, and he'll knock them off the road if he has to.

"The other day I heard someone comparing him with Villeneuve, and it's an insult to Gilles's name to say that Senna is anything like the man he was. Gilles was a brilliant driver, but also a totally fair one."

15 MAY 1986 A few days after the Monaco Grand Prix, Elio de Angelis crashed during a test at Paul Ricard. Help came first from his fellow drivers, who stopped to see what, if anything, could be done. They found the car upside down and on fire. Nearly ten minutes passed before it was righted, and before de Angelis was released from the cockpit. Although a doctor was in attendance at this time, no helicopter was present, and half an hour passed before one arrived. The injuries that de Angelis had suffered as a result of the crash were not themselves life-threatening. He died of asphyxiation.

ALAN JONES (making a comeback with the new Lola Haas team): "I'd just come out of the pits, and I was the first on the scene. There was no fire when I first got to the car, just some black smoke. The problem was that we just couldn't right the car because it was too heavy. There were a couple of guys there - marshals - who were in normal clothes. Shorts, in fact. They had these piddling little fire extinguishers which did nothing at all.

"Finally a truck arrived, with a big extinguisher. They parked it too far away, and then at first they couldn't get it to work. Then they stood about eight feet away, and blew all the extinguisher powder in towards the cockpit and not the engine. Apart from anything else, that powder will have done him no good.

"It's the same old story. We're all idiots, we should have checked this, that and the other - and we didn't. Ultimately, I guess it has to be down to the teams themselves. If they're not happy with facilities they shouldn't run. But of course we just front up, and assume everything's under control.

"At a race it's different. There you have people like Professor Watkins making sure nothing starts until the helicopter's arrived, and so on. On this occasion the helicopter had to come from the hospital in Marseilles, and about half an hour after that the local fire brigade arrived. Hopeless.

"I never felt so frustrated in my life - just stood there with my hands in the air. It was a carbon copy of Roger Williamson's accident at Zandvoort all those years ago. Bloody dreadful."

EDDIE CHEEVER: "I'm a fatalist, absolutely. When it's time, it's time. I've been around long enough that I've lost lots of people I've known and respected: Peterson, Villeneuve, Depailler, and so on.

Above: The loss of the popular Elio de Angelis in a needless accident was particularly hard to take.
Opposite: Frank Williams (here with his drivers Mansell and Piquet) came back from his crippling road accident to run his team better than ever.

"Look at Elio. If you were to take a whole colour range, where danger is red and safety is green, Elio had found a place somewhere in there, where there was hardly any risk factor at all. And he goes testing on Tuesday morning at Ricard, and loses the rear wing... There are people who live 24 hours a day in that red zone, like Gilles did, and sooner or later you have to pay the bills. It's like overdrawing your bank account - you can only do it so long before someone taps you on the shoulder. The problem, of course, is that the most enjoyment you get is when you're in that red zone."

JO RAMIREZ: "I really liked Elio a lot. He came from an extremely rich family in Italy, but he was a very down-to-earth person. He used to come to my house, and play the piano - like François Cevert, he was a classically trained pianist, and he played beautifully. We had a great relationship, and I think he was a very good driver, very stylish, very quick.

"Elio was a wealthy man, but he wouldn't go and buy what he wanted just because he could. I remember there was a particular Rolex he wanted, but it was a very expensive one, and it took him weeks of deliberating before he said, 'Yes, I'm going to buy it.' Then he took off the watch he had, and gave it to me. It was a gold Baume-Mercier, and I still have it. I wear it very rarely, but I happened to be wearing it the day he actually died. That was such a waste of a life. It upsets me to think of it even now, the way he suffered - he was not hurt in any way, but he just couldn't breathe. Shameful."

AYRTON SENNA: "Elio was a very special sort of driver, because he did what he did out of love for the sport, not for any commercial reason. He was well-educated, a gentleman, someone who was good to know as a person. I'm sure he wasn't responsible for the accident, because he was someone who never went over the limit, never pushed his luck."

15 JUNE 1986 - CANADIAN GP (MONTREAL) NIGEL MANSELL: "As far as my relationship with Piquet is concerned, I talk to my engineer, and he talks to his, and that's about it. Make no mistake, Nelson is bloody quick, and he's no fool. But basically I've found that we talk when he wants to talk. Since Montreal, for example, he's probably said two words to me. Zilch, really. And I don't understand that. If he'd won, I wouldn't have hesitated to congratulate him afterwards."

NELSON PIQUET: "The difficult part of competing with a driver in the same team - particularly an English driver in an English team - is that all the time you're trying to withold information, and that's not nice."

6 JULY 1986 - FRENCH GP (PAUL RICARD) JACKIE STEWART: "Mansell's a changed man, isn't he? Look at him - he's come here *expecting* to win. He's had to wait a long time for success, but it's transformed him like it does everyone. The trick now is not to become overconfident."

No problem, Formula 1 in a Communist country. We are only Communists when someone is listening. BUDAPEST CAB DRIVER ON THE HUNGARIAN GP, AUGUST 1986

Above: The Hungarian Grand Prix 1986 - the most rampantly capitalistic of sports shrieked through a crack in the iron curtain, spewing vast amounts of money from exhaust pipes in front of 250,000 spellbound East Europeans.

Hmmm...Three people ahead of me on the grid - Mansell, Piquet, Senna - and they all hate each other! ALAIN PROST

13 JULY 1986 - BRITISH GP (BRANDS HATCH) For Mansell, the momentum just built and built. He broke a CV joint within yards of the start at Brands Hatch, but a multiple shunt brought the red flag - and another chance for Nigel. It meant using the spare Williams, set up for Piquet, but 22 laps in he passed Nelson for the lead - and that was it. The pair of them put a lap on the whole field.

If the best of the day was Mansell, the worst was Jacques Laffite, who suffered severe leg injuries, and faced a long spell in hospital. He would never race a Grand Prix car again. However, 'Happy Jacques' never lost his enthusiasm for the sport and stayed in it as an adviser to several teams and as a commentator for French television.

7 SEPTEMBER 1986 - ITALIAN GP (MONZA) DEREK WARWICK: "One of my great racing memories was experiencing the power of the BMW turbo engine in the Brabham. I will remember qualifying at Monza for the rest of my life. Because at Monza I had five and a half bar boost, from a 1500 cc engine, and we had 1300 horsepower! A seven speed gearbox and I was still on the rev limiter in top gear! It was like being in a bloody rocket!

"I've never been in a rocket but it's how I imagine it must be. It was a lay down car so your head was tilted way back. I remember when I started the qualifying lap, - with a seven speed box, remember - and I could not change gear quick enough before I was on the limiter.

"And going through the chicane I'd already gone 500 meters on the limiter and thought I was on a perfect lap. It was wonderful. But we'll never know because going into the Parabolica the thing just self-destructed. I mean the engine just blew to pieces. Threw the crank, pistons and everything right out the sides. It was one of the BMW hand grenades. But what a ride that was."

Above: Between them Senna, Prost, Mansell and Piquet would win 146 races and 11 world championships, though winning was about all they had in common.

26 OCTOBER 1986 - AUSTRALIAN GP (ADELAIDE) The build-up was highly-charged and this proved to be one of the great races. Only Williams and McLaren mattered at Adelaide: Mansell, Piquet and Prost were down in Oz to settle the matter of the World Championship, and for Rosberg this would be the last time around, the end of a great career.

There were three different leaders on the opening lap; there was Rosberg's towering aggression in leading most of the way; there was Prost's puncture, then his superb comeback drive; there was Mansell's tyre explosion; there was Piquet's late tyre stop. And there was the little fellow who shook his head in disbelief as he saluted the crowd as the World Champion - at the last Alain Prost took it all.

KEKE ROSBERG: "Do I think Prost is the best I've ever seen? No - I *know* he is. As an all-round race driver, he's head and shoulders above everyone else, because he's strong in every department. For me, it would be a joke for anyone else to be World Champion, and I'm going to do everything possible to help him."

ALAIN PROST: "Keke and I talked before the start, and he told me that if he was leading, and I was second, then he would let me through. I knew how much he must have wanted to win his last Grand Prix, and I was very touched by that. As it was, he did a fantastic job for me, leading the way he did, forcing Piquet and Mansell to keep going hard."

KEKE ROSBERG: "I was enjoying myself so much I began to wish I hadn't decided to retire, but it's just as well my tyre punctured when it did, because I certainly wouldn't have finished the race, and might have had a huge accident. I found out afterwards that my brake discs were literally breaking up! So I don't have any bad memories of my last race at all: I think I drove well, and I walked away."

PATRICK HEAD: "I always think it's nice to see drivers' characters come through in their driving. Alan Jones was very much that way - when he got his head down, you knew it was Alan, from the way he was going. Rosberg was the same. As for Prost, often we'd be way ahead of him at first, and think, 'Where the hell's Alain?' He'd qualify third or fourth, make a slow start, and you'd think, 'Great, he's ninth or whatever, that's him out of the way.' Then you'd see that he was sixth, fifth, fourth, third, and you'd think, 'Ooooh, shit!' That was very much him, wasn't it? This inexorable quality. It was just like that in Adelaide."

ALAIN PROST: "When I got the puncture, I lost a lot of time on the slow lap back to the pits, so then all I could do was push as hard as possible. There was nothing to lose. Even second place was no use to me. From the halfway point, my fuel read-out had been telling me I was five litres the wrong side - that I wouldn't make the finish unless I backed off. But of course I couldn't do that because I was so far behind, so I just had to hope that, for once, the computer was wrong. Fortunately, it was..."

PATRICK HEAD: "Towards the end, Piquet and Prost were running 1-2, with Mansell in the third place he needed, and at that stage he could have stopped for tyres and still gone on to get the championship, because there was no one close behind him."

NIGEL MANSELL: "On lap 64, as I pulled sixth gear approaching 200mph, the left rear tyre exploded. It took nearly a quarter of a minute to bring the car under control, the thing was pitching about all over the place. When it stopped, I slumped. It was so hard to take. It suddenly struck me like a thunderbolt that the World Championship had gone. I had been a mere 44 miles away from clinching the title. Everything had been going fine. The car felt good, I was in a comfortable third place. Now it was all over. I was destroyed. I felt a deep sense of despair in the pit of my stomach. It was without doubt the biggest disappointment of my entire life."

Above: Mansell returns to the pits in Adelaide after his tyre and his World Championship aspirations had blown, leaving the way open for Alain Prost (opposite) to take the spoils.

PATRICK HEAD: "After Nigel's tyre had failed, we were between a rock and a hard place, with regard to Nelson. If we'd left him out there, and he'd made it, we'd have looked like heroes, but if he'd had an accident, and hurt himself, we'd have looked idiots. There was no choice to be made, in fact: we called him in, and changed his tyres."

NELSON PIQUET: "It was the right decision, to stop. I knew I might be losing the championship, but I didn't care. I was alive."

ALAIN PROST: "I must find Nigel to say how sorry I am for him today. Twice I lost the title at the last race, so I know how he must be feeling - it's terrible when that happens. But luck changed for me, and I hope he realises it can for him, also."

As for Alain... well, I used to think he and Piquet were on a par, but not any longer. Nelson's had a quicker car this year, without a doubt, but he's made a lot of mistakes, and that's the difference. Prost makes incredibly few errors. For me, he's undoubtedly the best driver in the world.

JACKIE STEWART

The animosity between Williams team mates Nelson Piquet and Nigel Mansell took the form of constant verbal sniping off the track and some torrid duels on it. Williams and McLaren had the best cars in 1987, but Berger succumbed to the enduring lure of Ferrari.

12 APRIL 1987 - BRAZILIAN GP (RIO DE JANEIRO) GERHARD BERGER: "I had the choice of signing for Mr Ferrari or Ron Dennis for 1987. My head said go to Dennis, and my heart said go to Ferrari. I had days when my head was in control, and days when my heart spoke a little bit louder - and it was on one of those days that I signed.

3 MAY 1987 - SAN MARINO GP (IMOLA) NELSON PIQUET: "After my practice accident at Imola, I really had a big problem. I was not so well - and I was slower than Mansell. I had to finish races, keep my car in one piece, because I couldn't catch him. For a long time I couldn't sleep well - two or three hours a night, and then not deeply. I couldn't relax. Only towards the end of the season I started to feel better, and then my confidence came back, and I was quick again."

PROFESSOR SID WATKINS: "Piquet tried everything to get me to say it was all right for him to race - crying, begging, threatening, the lot! But it was obviously out of the question after the bang on the head he'd had. 'Nelson,' I said to him, 'just remember that, two hours after the shunt, you didn't even know you were a racing driver. Forget it!'"

17 MAY 1987 - BELGIAN GP (SPA) In addition to the friction with Nelson Piquet, Nigel Mansell also found himself sparring with Ayrton Senna.

AYRTON SENNA: "When Mansell and I had our accident, I really didn't expect him to go for it. I expected him to try, so I kept to the middle of the circuit - and suddenly I realised he was going for it! I was committed. Being in the middle of the circuit, I didn't have much room, and I was in a critical situation already. At that moment, I realised we were in the shit.

"I was out immediately, and really pissed off. He was able to carry on for a bit, and on the next lap he made some signs at me - and I gave him one back. Then I went back to the pits, and cooled down.

"Eventually Mansell retired, and came down to the Lotus pit. I knew he hadn't come to apologise, because his face wasn't right for that - and you know someone isn't apologising when they get hold of you by the throat! He went completely mad! Well,

> You wouldn't think Nelson had a care in the world. He sleeps before a race, relaxes and tells silly jokes all the time, in shocking English. FRANK WILLIAMS

where does that take you? Nowhere. It's bad for him, bad for me. If it carries on like this between us, one of us - or both of us - is going to get hurt."

NIGEL MANSELL: "There's no question that Senna either missed a gear or backed off or did something strange, because I flew past him. And it's very clear from the video - leaving personalities out of this completely - that he was totally on the wrong line. He was right on the inside, and at the speed he was going he had no chance of getting round that corner - even if I hadn't been there! He was on the marbles, and he just came into me, used me as a brake, and punted us both off."

JOHN WATSON: "At Spa Mansell showed he is still not fully mature, and at ease with himself, as a driver. He needed desperately to win the World Championship to gain the full self-belief he lacks, and, more important, he needed *other* people to recognise it, to reassure himself that he's good. If he'd won the championship, I believe he would have developed into an even greater driver than he is, but now I don't know if we'll ever see the completely developed Mansell."

12 JULY 1987 - BRITISH GP (SILVERSTONE) This was a Honda race, nothing else. The Japanese engines powered Williams and Lotus, and Mansell, Piquet, Senna and Nakajima finished 1-2-3-4. On horsepower, nothing else was close; qualifying suggested it, the race confirmed it.

Even within the ranks of Honda, though, it was a two-class race, for Williams were way superior to Lotus, and if either Nelson or Nigel had retired, the British GP would have been a stone drag. As it was, a lost wheel balance weight sent Mansell to the pits at mid-race; on fresh tyres he began pursuit of his team mate. The closing minutes were mesmeric.

NIGEL MANSELL: "On lap 63 I had chased Piquet down and sat on his gearbox as we went out onto Hangar straight. I lined up right behind him, in his slipstream, disappearing momentarily from view in his mirrors. I was going to sell him a dummy. I watched his hands and his head from behind, knowing they would tell me when to make my move...

"I went right to pass him, just to make him act. He had his head inclined to the right and was watching me in the mirror. Immediately he moved right to cover the line. Straight away I went left, this time bolder, more aggressive to make him think I was trying to pass. His head swung frantically over to the left to check his other mirror. He bought my fake move and decided to block it, his hands turning the wheel well over to the left and his head decked over. This was it. I shot out from his slipstream and made for the inside line into the right-hander at Stowe. Too late he realised his mistake and tried to cover it.

"He came over on me but I had the momentum. We were both doing about 190mph into the braking zone for Stowe, but I knew I had the corner. He tried to chop me but nothing was going to stop me now and I never even lifted off the throttle. I was too pumped up after 25 flat-out laps to be intimidated by that sort of thing and when I crossed the finish line the cheers from the grandstand drowned out the screaming Honda engine. The fans went berserk. It was an unashamedly emotional moment. There will never be another race in my whole career which will mean as much to me as this one."

20 SEPTEMBER 1987 - PORTUGUESE GP (ESTORIL) GERHARD BERGER: "Money pushes you a lot, you know. I led most of the way in Portugal, and I was tired, and they showed me a board, saying how many laps were left, how much Prost was closing. And I knew I had to fight for my contract for next year - how could I get good money if I gave in? So I kept pushing, pushing, and eventually I spun, and lost the race! Stupid, isn't it, that money should figure in thinking like that? But it does."

18 OCTOBER 1987 - MEXICAN GP (MEXICO CITY) NELSON PIQUET: "Some people wrote some things about my relationship with Mansell which were not fair. In Mexico they said I tried to put Nigel out. I said that if I want to put someone out of a race, I do it. Very professionally. I don't try. I do it."

1 NOVEMBER 1987 - JAPANESE GP (SUZUKA) Everybody went to see Piquet and Mansell settle the championship, and expected them to dominate at Suzuka, but such was not the case. In practice Mansell spun into a tyre barrier, injuring his back in the process, so that was the end of him for 1987, and Piquet, now confirmed as World Champion, qualified a poor fifth, and blew up late in the race.

MICHELE ALBORETO: "We needed to win - especially for Mr Ferrari, who is not so well these days. He needs it like a blood transfusion."

15 NOVEMBER 1987 - AUSTRALIAN GP (ADELAIDE) GERHARD BERGER: "Over my career, the best driver was Ayrton Senna, for sure, then Alain Prost, then Nelson Piquet. And the best car? The 1987 Ferrari turbo, because it suited my style more than any other."

PATRICK HEAD: "Oh, that season of '87... We'd finish 1-2, and I'd go back to the motorhome afterwards, knowing that the loudest noise would be the moaning of the guy who'd finished second! Mind you, we're in this to win, so I suppose I'd rather have a quick guy who's a pain than a nice guy who's losing a second a lap."

Top right: A stalking Mansell brilliantly outfoxed Piquet at Silverstone, but the Brazilian won their private battle for the championship.

I DON'T GIVE A SHIT FOR FAME, I DON'T GIVE A SHIT FOR SOCIETY. I DON'T WANT TO

MAKE FRIENDS WITH ANYBODY WHO'S IMPORTANT. I JUST WANT TO WIN. NELSON PIQUET

There never was much doubt that McLaren would clean up in 1988, given their driving strength and their Honda turbos. Some, though, still questioned that a turbo would be the thing to have in this final year of its eligibility; boost was down from 4 bar to 2.5 (horsepower from, say, 1000 to 670), and fuel from 195 to 150 litres. The non-turbo brigade, by contrast, were not restricted on fuel, and, with a minimum weight of 500, were allowed to run 40 kilos lighter than the turbos. This 'transition' year, FISA had intended, would favour the atmospherics. It didn't work out that way and McLaren won all but one of the races.

JOHN WATSON: "I'm curious to see how Senna will fit into the McLaren machine this year, as he represents their long-term driver future. This season could make him into an old man."

3 APRIL 1988 - BRAZILIAN GP (RIO DE JANEIRO) After Piquet left Williams at the end of 1987, it seemed that perhaps the feud with Mansell would end. It had been a matter of a man who took life too seriously against one who didn't take it seriously enough, and Nelson's interview with the Brazilian edition of *Playboy* guaranteed him further ill-will.

The story came out as a kind of all-purpose attack on sundry racing folk, including not only Mansell, but also his wife Rosanne. Most thought that beyond the pale. For good measure Piquet came up with some kindergarten remarks about Senna while talking to a Rio newspaperman. At the Brazilian Grand Prix he was emphatically not flavour-of-the-month.

NIGEL MANSELL: "I found it very offensive - especially what he said about Rosanne, of course. But I think what Piquet did, more than anything else, was hurt himself. Perhaps for the first time, the world could see through the veneer of this 'great World Champion'.

"I know he dislikes me intensely, because I blew his bubble apart in our two seasons together at Williams. This vindictive attack on me and my family - and, while he was about it, Senna, Prost, Enzo Ferrari, and who knows who else - just shows the true character of the man.

"He has to be very careful, to watch me far more closely than I watch him, doesn't he? With his horsepower, it's not easy to get near him this year, but I managed it a couple of times, and he was shitting himself, believe me."

Alain and Ayrton will fight like hell, and they will have a difficult year, just as I did with Mansell at Williams in '86 and '87.

NELSON PIQUET

Though their boss Ron Dennis had his hands full managing the egos of Senna and Prost, McLaren only lost once during a one-sided season.

14 MAY 1988 QUALIFYING FOR MONACO GP The spine-tingling spectacle of the late Ayrton Senna on a qualifying lap provided some of the most thrilling moments in the history of the sport. There has never been a faster driver over a single lap - his record of 65 pole positions is unlikely to ever be broken - nor has anyone thought so deeply about it. When he talked about his most memorable lap, the one that left the most indelible impression on his exceptional mind, Senna's eyes shone with a faraway look and his voice quavered with intensity...

Suddenly I realised that I was no longer driving the car consciously. I was kind of driving by instinct, only I was in a different dimension. I was way over the limit, but still I was able to find even more. It frightened me because I realised I was well beyond my conscious understanding. AYRTON SENNA

Senna is a genius. I define genius as just the right side of imbalance. He is highly developed to the point where he is almost over the edge. It's a close call.

MARTIN BRUNDLE

Ayrton has a small problem. He thinks he can't kill himself because he believes in God and I think that's very dangerous for the other drivers.

ALAIN PROST

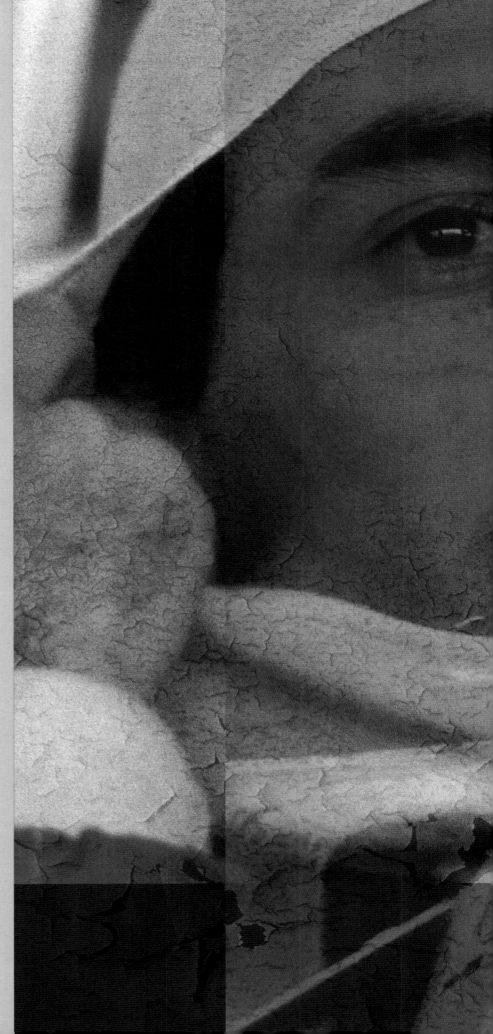

I think the guy is a nutter.
He is completely out of control.
EDDIE IRVINE

If anybody ever sold their soul to win a championship, Senna did; the commitment was just frightening. Every time he was in the car he was out to prove to everyone he was the next World Champion. Now he has done it, and has the chance to turn down the wick that he's been burning so intensely all year, he may be able to go on to this thing called greatness and become the best driver of his era.

JOHN WATSON

14 AUGUST 1988 Enzo Ferrari died at the age of 90. Ferrari's love of his cars was an abstract thing. For the actual machinery there was no sentiment whatever. Millionaires across the world may devote themselves to collecting Ferraris, but the Old Man did not have a sliver of interest in what he saw as museum pieces. The future was the thing, and the cars were routinely broken up once their useful purpose had been served.

At any given time, however, his passion for the current cars was the major force in his life. Maybe he had long ago given up going to races, but for hours he would sit in the farmhouse at Fiorano, watching and listening as Regazzoni or Villeneuve or Alboreto pounded round. There were Ferrari drivers, indeed, who suggested that this, rather than its efficacy as a test track, was Fiorano's true function.

Still, the lure of Ferrari was always very real. He had a powerful effect on people, this immaculately dressed old man with the ever-present sunglasses. At Ferrari press conferences, the journalists always felt like schoolboys again, waiting for Morning Assembly. When Ferrari died, much of the racing world felt the last of their gods had gone.

FRANK WILLIAMS: "I can't say I ever admired Ferrari as such, because he - the man - has had such a disruptive influence on motor racing. But I admired him tremendously for his success. He was the yardstick, wasn't he?"

BERNIE ECCLESTONE: "Enzo was the sort of guy I like. You could shake hands with him. You could rely on him. And he did great things. A great man. And you can go anywhere in the world and mention Ferrari and people know what you mean."

28 AUGUST 1988 - BELGIAN GP (SPA) AYRTON SENNA (on pole, again): "Before a qualifying lap, everything within me - my personality, my education, my strong points, my weaknesses - makes it fundamental to me that I concentrate as deeply as I can. I isolate all outside interference, whether it's photographers, fans, people around me. And in that state I am somehow able to get to a level where I am ahead of myself - maybe a fifth of a second, who knows? When my car goes into a corner, I am already at the apex, and so on. It's the same whether I'm braking, changing gear, putting on the power, or whatever. In effect, I'm predicting what I'm going to face, so that I can correct it before it actually happens.

"You need a lot of concentration for that, as well as instant reactions, so a lot of tension goes through the body - like electricity. Every single movement is instant, and has to be 100% precise, on the throttle, the brakes, the steering, the judging of your speed, and so on. It's not easy to explain. I use everything I have, and I'm still finding things out. In race conditions, though, you can't

keep to that level - there's too much stress, both mental and physical. You try to perform in the same way, but you have to be content to come down a little bit."

JOHN WATSON: "It's difficult to know if Senna is absolutely the best, because with him you always know you're seeing 100% of him and his ability. He gives himself totally to what he's doing - there's nothing else in his life. He's quite literally dedicated to being the fastest racing driver there is, and that doesn't stop when he leaves the race track. I don't believe we ever see 100% of other drivers' ability - certainly not all the time, anyway. That's where I think Ayrton's unique."

ALAIN PROST: "Realistically, the championship is over now. I congratulate Ayrton - he's been the best driver this year, and he deserves it."

11 SEPTEMBER 1966 - ITALIAN GP (MONZA) The only race of the year not won by a McLaren, when Senna made a rare mistake and collided with a backmarker, went to Ferrari. The *tifosi* went mad and the race winner was ecstatic.

GERHARD BERGER: "Mr Ferrari is gone now, and I miss him. To drive for *him* was different from driving for 'Ferrari, part of the Fiat company'. He was a big personality, a great man, and I'm so happy to have driven for him. But I would love to have been able to go to Maranello the day after Monza, and to have seen his face."

25 SEPTEMBER 1988 - PORTUGUESE GP (MONZA) After his 33rd Grand Prix win, Prost was back in the lead of the World Championship, and that delighted him. What did not was the drama in passing Senna for the lead at the beginning of lap two. As he drew alongside, down the pit straight, Ayrton did not so much edge him towards the pit wall as swerve at him, obliging Alain to squeeze through a dangerously narrow gap - and people on the pit wall ducked.

ALAIN PROST: "I was very close to the wall, and I could do nothing at that point - if I'd backed off, I might have hit Senna's rear wheel, or something like that. If we'd touched at that speed, it would have been like a plane crash - and we had the whole pack close behind us. If Ayrton wants the championship that badly, he can have it."

30 OCTOBER 1988 - JAPANESE GP (SUZUKA) AYRTON SENNA: "At the moment I can't take in that I'm World Champion, but I feel as if I've lost a great weight from my shoulders. Because of my terrible start, the race was amazingly hard, through the traffic, through the slippery conditions. Until today, you know, I always said my best drive was at Estoril in '85 - my first win. But not any more: this was my best."

I believe that today's work conditions the future, that men pass and their work remains. And each example of their work, created for the present, is a stairway of the future.

ENZO FERRARI

Turbocharged engines were now banned, but as in the previous year the 1989 season revolved around McLaren. Ferrari and Williams ensured it was less one-sided than before, but Ron Dennis's was always the team at which to aim. By their performance standards of the previous year, in fact, McLaren had a positively mediocre season, contriving to lose six of the 16 Grands Prix.

In human terms, their season was far worse than mediocre: it was catastrophic. Through the last few races, McLaren's previously Masonic togetherness was nowhere in sight, Prost and Senna no more than two individuals who happened to operate out of the same pit. You thought Mansell and Piquet didn't get along? Bosom buddies they were, compared with the McLaren pair.

RON DENNIS: "The relationship between any two human beings is a very complicated thing, like in a marriage, and our drivers' relationship is very, very complicated. But the negative aspects of having two such drivers can be a motivating force. However, as in any finely tuned situation, you are walking a tightrope between falling off into failure and successfully getting to the other side. The challenge is to try to understand their negative differences, try to isolate them, then turn them into positives.

"I'm not a marriage counsellor, but I think guidance and support are the words to use when it comes to handling drivers, both in racing problems and in human problems. In the current situation you might say it's a form of ego management."

FRANK WILLIAMS: "We've lost Mansell to Ferrari, and we've now got Boutsen alongside Patrese. Thierry I think is very underrated, actually, and Riccardo is still extremely quick on his day. What we like about him is that he's absolutely loyal, and never slags off the team. After the experiences we've had with people like Mansell and Piquet, that counts for a lot.

"All the top drivers are difficult people with complex personalities. I wouldn't go so far as to say nice guys finish last, but the best Formula 1 drivers are driven, motivated, pushy, won't-accept-second-best, immensely competitive people. That's what makes them good - because they're bastards!"

23 APRIL 1989 - SAN MARINO GP (IMOLA) Senna beat his team mate, though his method of doing so left Prost seriously peeved.

ALAIN PROST: "Senna and I started out quite well this season, but it changed at Imola. Something was broken there. We had such an advantage at that time, and he suggested that whoever got the lead at the start should keep it until we were clear of the rest. I agreed. OK, at the start he beat me away, and I stayed behind. Then the race was stopped, after Gerhard's accident.

"On the restart, I got ahead of him, didn't bother to protect the line because of our agreement - and when we got to Tosa he passed me! Later on he denied having suggested an agreement, but fortunately John Hogan [of Marlboro] had been there, and heard him. Then he argued that it wasn't the start - it was the restart, so it didn't apply! What do you do in this kind of situation? I mean, you can hit him - that would be one solution. I'm not joking! That could be the best way of resolving it, because then maybe you can be friends afterwards."

JAMES HUNT: "To some extent I criticise Prost for Imola, because he got the jump on Senna, so why did he leave

Their antipathy turned to hatred as Prost and Senna (above at the Monaco Grand Prix) sped angrily through a season that was bound to end in a crash of wills.

the door open? I blame him for having faith in Senna, I'm afraid. If I'd been Prost, with that arrangement, there's no way I'd have left the door wide open.

"I think a lot of Alain's anger was at himself - for being taken in. I flew back with him that night, so I knew about the 'arrangement' which Senna proposed. I told him he was stupid to agree to something like that with anyone - let alone Senna. And he agreed."

GERHARD BERGER: "After my crash at Tamburello, I said to the Imola circuit people, "Could we not move the wall back at that point, and put in a proper run-off area?" 'Not possible,' they said, 'because there's a river behind it.' And I just said, 'Oh, OK.' When Senna died there, five years later, I thought about that. Many times."

MARIO ANDRETTI: "After Gerhard's accident, I got a call from Maranello, just like in '82, when Pironi was hurt. Here I was, 49 years old, and they wanted me to do Monaco! I was tempted, no question, but there was no opportunity to test beforehand, and by now Ferrari were running the semi-automatic gearbox. I figured Monte Carlo wasn't a great place to learn a new way of shifting, so in the end I said no. But it wasn't easy."

7 MAY 1989 - MONACO GP (MONTE CARLO)
JAMES HUNT: "Senna seems even more intense this year. I thought winning the World Championship might lighten him up a bit, but not so. He has a very strange personality, hasn't he? In Monte Carlo, during the opening laps, he tooled around, just in front of Prost, obviously holding him up, and then suddenly - as they were getting towards traffic - he went two or even three seconds a lap quicker.

"After the race I saw Ron Dennis, and said, 'What the hell was going on? I got the impression that Senna was playing silly buggers with Prost.' And Ron said, 'There's no other explanation - he never said a word on the radio about any problems with anything.' So I think Senna was trying to taunt Prost, to wind him up, and if that was the case, it's a big flaw in Senna's personality - Grands Prix are too important for you to start winding up your own team mate in the middle of a race."

28 MAY 1988 - MEXICAN GP (MEXICO CITY)
BERNIE ECCLESTONE: "I'm happy for Senna to win all the races. I just wish he'd do it on the last bleedin' lap."

AYRTON SENNA: "Now some people are starting to say I should be handicapped in the races in some way. Unbelievable... something from ET people, not human beings."

RON DENNIS: "A couple of years ago Prost and I had a £1000 bet on some technicality in the rules. He was right, but I never got around to paying him, and it's been mentioned a time or two. Well, last night we were all out for dinner, and there were rows of things on the table, some hot, some very hot. There was this bowl of *particularly* hot stuff, and Senna bet me $5000 I couldn't eat all of it, straight off.

"Well, it was a weak moment by him, wasn't it? I couldn't let it go by, so I shut my eyes, and went for it. Finished the lot, and probably removed a layer of skin from inside my mouth. But I won the bet. Ayrton gave me the money - and I immediately handed over $1750 to Alain in settlement of our previous bet. A good night's work, I thought."

18 JUNE 1989 - CANADIAN GP (MONTREAL)
JAMES HUNT: "Prost is very wound up at the moment - and I think, to some extent, he's wound himself up. It's the first time I've ever seen him lose his cool. Unfortunately, it seems that Senna has got the psychological war completely won. At the moment I think Alain's motivation is suspect, although his ability is certainly not. But I think being bonked on the head by Senna has, if anything, pushed it downhill rather than uphill."

9 JULY 1989 - FRENCH GP (PAUL RICARD)
HARVEY POSTLETHWAITE (Tyrrell Technical Director): "Fourth in his first Grand Prix! I'm reluctant to say too many nice things about Jean Alesi, because I'm frightened someone's going to come along and nick him! The first thing is, he has all those nice attributes of a young driver. He isn't sitting on a pile of gold, and he hasn't got 15 kids, and all the rest of it - which means he's got the killer instinct you want in a racing driver.

"He's aggressive without being silly, and he's one of those guys who'll get in a car, and be at the limit by the third lap. And he's also unbelievably consistent in a race, reeling off good laps indefinitely. Oh, and there's one other thing - he's *quick*! If he isn't World Champion in the coming years... well, there's something wrong with motor racing."

16 JULY 1989 - BRITISH GP (SILVERSTONE)
AYRTON SENNA: "Four races without a finish, yes, but you have to put it out of your mind. The past is just data, information to consider. I only see the future."

13 AUGUST 1989 - HUNGARIAN GP (BUDAPEST) This was the finest victory of Mansell's career, for on this occasion he emphatically did not have the best car. Indeed, he started the race only 12th, having failed to get his Ferrari to work on qualifying tyres, but he made a superb start, and after 50 laps had only Senna's McLaren in front of him. When the pair of them came up to lap Johansson's Onyx, Ayrton hesitated fractionally, and that was all Nigel needed to sneak through.

NIGEL MANSELL: "Of all the races I have won and all the moves I pulled, that one is most talked about. The move to pass Piquet at Silverstone in 1987 was sweet, but also inevitable. He was never going to resist me that day.

"After I passed him Ayrton fell back and the fight seemed to go out of him. No one can deny that he was one of the greatest drivers of all time, but he wasn't always good at being put under intense pressure. I was one of the few drivers who put him under this kind of pressure and he didn't like it. I won this race by almost half a minute and it was one of the most incredibly satisfying wins of my career."

27 AUGUST 1989 - BELGIAN GP (SPA) DENIS JENKINSON: "This is the circuit that matters, and when I was watching Senna and Prost today, it struck me that in my lifetime I'll never see two drivers of that class competing against each other again. Artists, aren't they?"

NIGEL MANSELL: "The more I think about it, the more I think Prost's coming to Ferrari next year will be good for the team, and therefore for me. I respect him more than any other driver - he's the only one I can learn from. He came to me at Spa, and asked if I had any objections to his joining Ferrari. I said no, and I meant it. He told me about some of the problems he's had with Senna, and of course I knew all about things like that from my two years with Piquet. So neither of us wants any more of that."

10 SEPTEMBER 1989 - ITALIAN GP (MONZA) ALAIN PROST: "By Monza things had got really bad between me and McLaren. I had about four mechanics on my car, that's all, with everyone else working with Senna. In the race he retired, and I won.

"Afterwards, on the podium, I handed the trophy down to the crowds, and I did it quite spontaneously. Can you understand how hard it is, after so much tension, when you win - especially at Monza? I'd already signed for Ferrari, the fans were there... it was a special moment, you know.

"I'd never thought for a second about giving away Ron's trophy - it would have been a ridiculous thing. I could have given them my watch or something. I was sorry afterwards, of course, but still I didn't understand Ron's reaction. He was furious!

"I spoke to Jo Ramirez and asked him to make another trophy for Ron. I told Jo I was sorry, and gave him my word that I hadn't done it on purpose. Jo got an identical one made, and years later, at the McLaren Christmas party, I gave it to Ron. He was quite pleased, I think."

24 SEPTEMBER 1989 - PORTUGUESE GP (ESTORIL) GERHARD BERGER: "I'm going to McLaren next year, so Senna will be my team mate, and I'm pleased about that. For sure he is now the best driver in F1, and I like him - I liked him already in F3. Away from the track, he is a very charming and interesting guy. You cannot see it at the track, and that's a shame."

22 OCTOBER 1989 JAPANESE GP (SUZUKA) Senna and Prost once more fought out not only the race, but also the outcome of the World Championship. With a few laps remaining, Ayrton lunged to the inside before the chicane, whereupon Alain slammed the door, and the two cars touched, then came to a halt, engines dead. Prost at once climbed out, but Senna frantically waved for a push - to which he was entitled, given that his McLaren was in the middle of the track, in 'a dangerous place'.

The problem was, when this was forthcoming, Ayrton allowed himself to be shoved into the escape road - and was therefore no longer in 'a dangerous place'. For all that, he beckoned for a push start, duly got it, and went back into the race. And he might just have got away with it, had he first turned round, and rejoined the track where he had left it. As it was, though, he drove out of the escape road, thereby by-passing the chicane.

After a stop for a new nose, Senna caught and passed Sandro Nannini, and took the chequered flag, apparently the winner. Later, though, he was disqualified, and thus Prost - subject to McLaren's unsuccessful appeal against Senna's exclusion - was the World Champion of 1989.

ALAIN PROST: "As for the accident at Suzuka, I know everybody thinks I did it on purpose: I did not open the door, and that's it. I took my corner, and that was the end of it. I couldn't believe he tried it on that lap, because I looked in my mirrors before the chicane, and he was so far back. I saw where he was, came off the throttle, braked - and turned in. At first I didn't realise he was trying to overtake me, but at the same time I thought, 'There's no way I'm going to leave him even a one-metre gap. No way!'"

KEKE ROSBERG: "You could tell Alain had never done anything like that in his life - he did it so badly!"

MARIO ANDRETTI: "If I'd been in Prost's shoes, I would have done exactly the same. And if the situation had been reversed, Senna would have done the same. That's got to be understood, and Senna should have expected it. But I can't fault him for trying."

AYRTON SENNA: "I think what happened after Suzuka '89 was unforgivable, disgraceful. After I rejoined that race, I won it, but they decided against me, and that was not justice. I was prevented from going to the podium, and I never forget that.

"We were fighting in the same team, with Prost, and we had a bad time with FISA - I had a bad time with

Above: Following their collision at Suzuka Senna raced on and won, only to be disqualified, which left Prost the champion and Senna incensed.
Opposite: Thierry Boutsen won (inset, left, with Alain Prost), but Prost refused to race in the appalling conditions at Adelaide.

Balestre. You know what took place: I won the race, and I was robbed of it. I did the right thing when we crashed at the chicane, when Prost turned the car over me, and pushed me out. From there on, the only way I could go was straight, and return to the race. And I won the race, and they took it away from me. And that was not justice."

5 NOVEMBER 1989 - AUSTRALIAN GP (ADELAIDE) The weather was truly atrocious, torrential rain, worse - from a visibility point of view - than anyone could remember. After a single lap, Prost pulled into his pit and climbed from his car.

ALAIN PROST: "On the grid Bernie Ecclestone told me it was OK to start, because they'd cleared all the puddles. Jesus, it was raining like hell while we were talking! Everyone agreed there was no way to start - apart from Ayrton, anyway, and

I understand that: he had to race because he was thinking about the championship. But the rest of us agreed it was ridiculous, and we wouldn't start. I went to the Clerk of the Course, and asked for another delayed start, and he said no. I said, 'OK, one lap, and I stop.' And I did."

GERHARD BERGER: "We agreed we wouldn't start, but then the pressure began, from team managers, officials, and so on. In conditions like these, it shouldn't be up to the drivers; the FISA stewards should have said it was too dangerous. The guy who let this race start should be put in the electric chair. A lot of us, including me, agreed that we would stop after one lap - and Prost was the only one with the balls to go through with it. Believe me, it was easier to carry on than stop, and I knew I was doing the cowardly thing. In all my career, it's the thing I am most ashamed of."

AYRTON SENNA: "I understand why Prost did what he did - in his position, I would have done the same. The conditions were absurd, and he had nothing to gain by racing. I can't understand why they didn't stop the race. Nothing could happen any more which would affect the championship, and it would have been better to stop it, rather than continue to risk everyone out there.

"In my accident with Brundle, I didn't see a thing until I hit him. At the time I was lapping Piquet, who was over on my right, doing maybe 230kph, and just about to change up."

MARTIN BRUNDLE: "I just felt a whack - and then Ayrton came by me on three wheels! He was lucky, actually. If his front wheel had hit my rear one, it could have been like Pironi's accident at Hockenheim all those years ago - it would have launched him over me."

NELSON PIQUET: "I had tyre marks on my helmet, and I guess I was lucky. A day like this is a lottery, not a race. I was very scared beforehand. We were stupid to start."

RICARDO PATRESE: "When the officials turned down our request for a second postponement to the start, I didn't think it was a very kind decision. OK, I know TV was waiting, but our lives were at stake."

In this business, you can survive or die in the blink of an eye. How could FISA send us out to drive in conditions like that? They were the worst I have ever seen. NELSON PIQUET

The Nineties

The last decade of Formula 1's first half century saw it become the richest sport in the world. While some purists argued that it was no longer a sport but a business, the ever-higher stakes created a pressure-packed environment that often made the Formula 1 circus seem like a high-speed soap opera. Heroes and villains emerged from a fascinating cast of characters. Prost and Senna feuded bitterly, but established records that seemed unlikely ever to be broken. Mansell dominated for one season, then abruptly retired. Senna and Ratzenberger were killed in a shocking weekend that led to controversial safety measures. Williams, Benetton, McLaren and Ferrari were the teams to beat. Schumacher established himself as Formula 1's resident superstar.

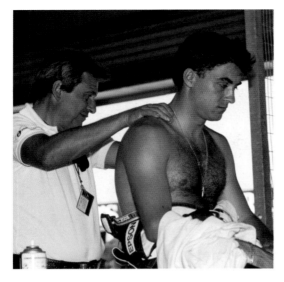

Opposite: In his ninth Grand Prix, Jean Alesi (above receiving a massage) distinguished himself by audaciously dicing with Senna in the streets of Phoenix. But Senna won - for the 21st time in 95 Grands Prix.

The 1980s having been a decade of such controversy and strife, it was perhaps inevitable that the 1990s should start the same way. The fallout from the Prost/Senna collision in the 1989 Japanese Grand Prix dragged well into the New Year. FISA president Jean-Marie Balestre hit Senna with a fine of $100,000. In Senna's mind, there was no question of paying it. At one stage, it seemed that McLaren would not be allowed to participate at all, but later it came down to Senna apologising for his criticisms of Balestre - or his licence would not be issued. Eventually the fine was paid.

AYRTON SENNA: "I practically gave up racing. If I'd pushed for what I thought was right and true, I would have created a major problem for everybody on the team. I had to give in, not for myself, but for all those who work so hard day after day."

With Prost now playing himself in at Ferrari, they no longer had to face each other except on the track. The big question for Ferrari was: would there be sparks between Prost and Mansell?

ALAIN PROST: "I find here they respond to me with terrific enthusiasm, like at McLaren until Senna arrived. I think I'm a normal guy, you know, quite natural. I like it when people recognise what I do. The ambience is good. I'm happy again now. No regrets."

NIGEL MANSELL: "It's very, very positive. Obviously a bit of persuasion was required, as I was number one and we had to renegotiate to put the deal together. But for the team to move forward as quickly as we have done reflects well on the arrangement. I've never seen Alain so motivated, in fact. He's going to make my job more difficult."

11 MARCH 1990 - US GP (PHOENIX) Ferrari endured a disastrous season opener, and the main opposition to McLaren came from an unexpected source. Helped by Pirelli tyres, Tyrrell's newcomer, Jean Alesi indulged in an audacious dice for the lead with Senna.

AYRTON SENNA: "When I caught him, we had a good moment or two at the end of the pit straight - I had a look there a couple of times, just to be sure, because it was very slippery off-line, and then I had a go. It was good - but then he went around the outside! It was a clean, exciting fight."

JEAN ALESI: "I was excited, but I was sure that I wouldn't win. I'm a realist. I decided to hold onto the lead for as long as possible. That's why I pushed so hard from the beginning. I was at 100% concentration."

25 MARCH 1990 - BRAZILIAN GP (INTERLAGOS) The tide turned in Sao Paulo, where Prost recorded his first win for Ferrari after Senna tangled with a backmarker. He still finished third, behind team mate Gerhard Berger. Afterwards it was clear that Suzuka had not been forgotten.

NIGEL ROEBUCK: "It was a sad picture of modern sport. Three of the world's greatest drivers gathered together, and not the slenderest trace of camaraderie between them. Prost, obviously, knew better than to attempt conversation with Senna; he had tried unsuccessfully to shake Ayrton's hand during practice in Phoenix, and assuredly will not try again. They stood there, on the first and third plinths, looking straight ahead, avoiding eye contact. Berger, clearly exhausted, seemed not to know where to look."

AYRTON SENNA: "Things that happened between us when we were working for the same team showed me his destructive character, for which I had to pay a very high price. I've decided to stay away from him. To be honest with oneself is the most important thing in life and, right or wrong, I felt I shouldn't offer my hand to someone who didn't mean what he was doing."

13 MAY 1990 - SAN MARINO GP (IMOLA) The Williams-Renault package was on the way up, the main competition to McLaren and Ferrari. This victory for Riccardo Patrese was only the second of his long career.

RICCARDO PATRESE: "I wouldn't say you consciously take more risks when you're younger, it's just that it may seem that way because you have less experience. Speed is something you either have or you don't. I wouldn't say there's any difference between when I started and now, except that I've probably actually gained motivation over the years."

15 JULY 1990 - BRITISH GP (SILVERSTONE) Clearly, however, there were only two genuine contenders. Prost had swiftly gained the upper hand over his Ferrari team mate and, after a series of non-finishes, Mansell began to take it personally. A failure at Silverstone was the final straw. After the race, he called a press conference, and announced his intention to retire.

NIGEL MANSELL: "I'm looking forward to putting my family first - for the first time in my life. It's not sudden. There comes a time in everyone's life when they call it a day. I'm 37 this year, and I'd rather quit while I'm at the top."

The most important thing about today is what it will do for my motivation. After this winter, quite honestly, my motivation had gone - disappeared. But here, at a race, my natural instinct took over.

AYRTON SENNA

SEPTEMBER 1990 - ITALIAN GP (MONZA) After Prost's run of success, it was Senna's turn again, with a sequence of three wins and a second on the tortuous Hungaroring, where Thierry Boutsen won a follow-my-leader race for Williams. Strangely, as Senna and Prost soared ahead of the rest in the points battle, their attitudes to each other seemed to mellow. After the post-race media conference in Italy, where Prost was second, a journalist's question prompted a public truce.

AYRTON SENNA: "Although we don't have many things in common, we share the same passion for Formula 1, and that's very important for us. When he's able to say he's sincere - in front of everyone — I'll accept it. I don't have a problem with that."

ALAIN PROST: "He has his ideas about what happened last year, and I have mine. Whatever happened, though, I'd like to forget it. As he rightly said, we have the same passion for the sport. I believe I've changed a lot since last year, and understand some things perhaps more clearly than I did. And I think it would be good for our sport if today, as we go into the last four races, we could get together somehow. So, if Ayrton agrees..."

NIGEL ROEBUCK: "Alain held out his hand, and Ayrton shook it. The press room broke into applause. As they stood up, the two men even slapped each other on the shoulder. Probably they will never be friends, but at least some of the furies are gone. They are the greatest drivers of this generation, and each acknowledges it of the other. The moment was moving."

The race was red-flagged when Derek Warwick had a huge, first-lap crash at the Parabolica. Warwick had endured a terrible season with the fading Lotus team and his resilience here and throughout the season earned him respect.

DEREK WARWICK: "I was conscious all the time. As soon as the car started to slide upside down, I started to organise mentally, because I was afraid of fire. When the car stopped, I thought of getting out, but I was scared someone might hit me. My first reaction after that was, 'I'm OK,' and my second was, 'Spare car...'"

23 SEPTEMBER 1990 - PORTUGUESE GP (ESTORIL) Mansell angered Prost by swerving at him as they left the grid, but scored his only victory of the season. Prost was annoyed that his team mate would not help his championship cause.

ALAIN PROST: "Ferrari doesn't deserve to be World Champion. It's a team without direction or strategy - against a united and well-structured team like McLaren. Berger helped Senna to the maximum in this race."

It's not only unsporting, it's disgusting. ALAIN PROST

30 SEPTEMBER 1990 - SPANISH GP (JEREZ) Martin Donnelly's career was ended by an extraordinarily violent crash that pulverised his Lotus and threw him onto the track. After many months of painful recovery, he would never race a Formula 1 car again.

DEREK WARWICK: "It's the most unbelievable escape. God must have been smiling on him."

AYRTON SENNA: "I went to the place where he was on the ground. When I saw the immediate consequences of the accident with my own eyes, on my own, it was very difficult to cope with it, and to go forward from there."

Senna's way of coping was to take pole position, but he retired from the race, leaving Prost and Mansell to a 1-2. Two races remained, and Prost had to win them. The next round was Suzuka.

RON DENNIS: "If it comes to it, Ayrton will remember what happened last year..."

21 OCTOBER 1990 - JAPANESE GP (SUZUKA) Senna took pole, with Prost second. At the start, Prost surged ahead. As they headed into the first corner, the McLaren thumped into the back of the Ferrari. Both cars spun off the road, out of the race. Senna

was the World Champion. As the two men walked back to the pits, the body language was graphic.

ALAIN PROST: "He saw I'd made a better start and had a better car and he had no chance to win - so he pushed me off. I'm not prepared to fight against irresponsible people who are not afraid to die."

AYRTON SENNA: "He tried to destroy me in the past on different occasions and he hasn't managed [it] - and he won't manage [it] because I know who I am and where I want to go. He can do what he likes. I don't really care."

RON DENNIS: "World Championships are won over a batch of races, not just one. But perhaps, after what happened here last year, there's a bit of rough justice."

4 NOVEMBER 1990 - AUSTRALIAN GP (ADELAIDE) Nelson Piquet's wins in Japan and Australia gave him third place in the championship for Benetton.

JAMES HUNT: "It is very significant that Piquet's two consecutive wins - though they were both inherited - came after he was pushed by a new team mate [Roberto Moreno], called in to replace the injured [Sandro] Nannini. Piquet shouldn't need to be pushed to pull his finger out. He should be racing because he wants to race, not because he wants the money to support his lifestyle."

Another bout of road rage at Suzuka. This time the controversial knockout blow felled both Senna's McLaren and Prost's Ferrari. They walked away, Senna as champion and Prost enraged.

NELSON PIQUET: "I'll go on racing until they throw me out."

Mansell would race too despite having previously announced his retirement. It seemed Frank Williams had made him an offer he couldn't refuse for 1991.

NIGEL MANSELL: "I'm amazed myself that my decision has been reversed, and the reasons are many and very positive. I've worked towards the World Championship for so many years and never achieved the complete backing I would have wished. To turn down at this stage what I've been working for all my life would be very sad."

The 1976 World Champion found the whole driver scene farcical. In his role as an outspoken TV commentator and newspaper columnist, he attacked - the way he used to drive.

JAMES HUNT: "Most of the people who run them know nothing whatever about racing drivers. You've only got to look at some of the old lags who are still employed - most of whom were never good enough in the first place. And of course, there are these ridiculous obsessions the entire paddock gets over one particular driver. Most of the so-called 'talent-spotters' couldn't spot a new talent if it ran them over."

In Adelaide, sparks flew when Jackie Stewart interviewed the new World Champion for Australian TV. Senna was incensed when Stewart censured him for unruly driving.

JACKIE STEWART: "A critic analysing the great champions would perhaps say that Ayrton Senna has had more coming-togethers than perhaps the last 15 or 20 other years of champions."

AYRTON SENNA: "It's not true! There was an incident at Suzuka last year, an incident at Suzuka this year. But what else? I've won more races than anybody over the past few years. I've been on pole position more than anybody in history. I've won two titles in the last three years. And I can't comprehend how you can try to turn things around to say that I've been involved in more accidents than anybody, because it's not true."

Stewart was often at a loss to understand this man who had joined him in the ranks of the sport's all-time greatest drivers.

JACKIE STEWART: "I never thought he looked like he was getting the degree of pleasure he deserved for all the hard work he put into mastering his art. He was so totally committed to racing that sadly, I thought, he didn't necessarily have a happy disposition in life. Other great drivers, Fangio, Clark, Prost and so on, lived full lives and had a quality of life outside racing which Ayrton doesn't give himself the privilege of having."

AYRTON SENNA: "I never smile much, because that's my way to be. But I'm very happy inside. I work very hard with the technicians, and we all won this championship together, step by step, race after race. But my life is not only racing. To do it time after time, year after year, and find the energy, happiness and health to do it, would be impossible for me if I didn't have a good family, friends and special people around me. I do keep that side of my life separate from my racing, for my peace and equilibrium, but it's fundamental for my life."

JAMES HUNT: "Senna really came of age in 1990, using his keen intelligence along with his exceptional driving talent. When a driver of Senna's type comes along, then adds brainpower to his natural brilliance, it's bad news for everybody else."

I can't be responsible for his actions. He's always trying to destroy people.

AYRTON SENNA

Senna is ready to take any risk to win the championship. I'm not ready to play this game.

ALAIN PROST

Most observers expected a three-way fight in 1991 between McLaren, Ferrari and Williams. Ferrari would surely continue its momentum with Prost and Alesi, and Williams, with the highly rated Adrian Newey now heading its design team and Patrese now partnered by the returning Mansell, was optimistic.

FRANK WILLIAMS: "Nigel's presence has done a tremendous amount for motivation around here. He's changed considerably from the last time around. I find him much more mature, but at the same time he's every bit as aggressive. There's no question about his will to win the title - he really doesn't want to retire without a World Championship."

JAMES HUNT: "Previously, when Mansell left Williams to go to Ferrari, he was pretty much unloved by everybody. But Williams have said 'To hell' with the problems you get when you have a superstar behaving like a superstar - at least we'll be racing again. They know only too well the penalties of working with mediocre drivers. They've had two years of soldiering along in the middle order, despite having very competitive cars."

NIGEL MANSELL: "On the circuit I think I can deliver as well if not better than any other driver. What I'm not good at is the politics off the circuit... the underhanded, back-stabbing manipulation which is done by some of the people. I simply can't compete in that arena."

24 MARCH 1991 - BRAZILIAN GP (INTERLAGOS) In front of his home crowd, yet another scintillating lap secured Senna the 54th pole of his career. The man who had now achieved such an astonishing number of pole positions thought carefully about his quest for the perfect qualifying lap, and spoke of it often.

AYRTON SENNA: "It's always my objective to concentrate on the task by taking into account everything within me: my personality, my training, my strong points, my weak points. I can then somehow get to a level where I am ahead of the car. I'm some split of a second ahead halfway through a corner, exiting a corner, just before braking, just before changing a gear, just before putting [on] the power. I can almost predict what I'm going to face, and correct it before it happens. That takes a lot of concentration as well as instant reactions.

"Sometimes I know why I do things the way I do in the car, and sometimes I don't. There are some moments that seem to be only natural instinct. Whether I've been born with it, or this has grown in me more than other people, I don't know. But it's

inside me and it takes over with great space and intensity. It takes a lot of energy. In every session in the car, I give everything I have, and this drains me completely.

"Because we [racing drivers] are in a close relationship with fear and danger, we learn how to live with it better than other people. In the process of learning to live with it, we have extraordinary emotions when we get near to an accident. There's the feeling of - 'Oh! I've just almost gone over the limit.' It's fascinating, even attractive in a way - living in a very narrow band, between being too easy, and overdoing it. The challenge to stay within that band is very much a motivation.

"When I push, I find something more. Then I go again, and I find something more. That's perhaps the most fascinating motivating factor for me. You're like an explorer finding a different world. You have this desire to go into places where you've never been before. I've experienced on many occasions the feeling of finding new things - even if I've thought, 'OK, that was my maximum.' Suddenly I find something extra. It's the challenge of always doing better. That process is almost non-stop in terms of excitement and motivation.

"There are times when your sensitivity is higher, when your ability to react to the things you feel in the car is almost infinite. You can sense the car touching the track, you can smell the brakes, hear very clearly the engine's sound, feel the vibrations from the steering wheel, or the chassis, or the turbulence from the air that touches part of your body. They are all happening at the same moment, and yet you can separate each of them in such a clear way that it makes everything fantastic and challenging.

"A lot of tension goes through the body, because you're like electricity. Every single movement is instant and has to be precise: as close to 100% precision as possible. The driving becomes automatic because your brain controls the throttle, your braking points, your gearchange points. It depends on your eyesight before a corner, on your ear for the engine revs, to make a judgement of your speed into a corner.

"So a fast lap requires a high level of sensitivity between body and mind. It's the combination of the two that gives the performance. It all happens so amazingly fast, it's a mystical feeling, focused on an inner point so far away my eyes can't see it and my mind can't project [it].

"But I've never done a perfect lap. I know, in looking back, that there was always room somewhere for perhaps a tenth [of a second], or a hundredth. It's very absorbing."

12 MAY 1991 - MONACO GP (MONTE CARLO) Senna had dominated the opening races, all from pole position. Apart from a few laps behind Patrese at Imola, he had led all four races from start to finish. His team mate had trouble keeping pace.

GERHARD BERGER: "I think that, in comparison to Ayrton, my speed is OK. He's just perfect. He's confident within himself after all the success he has had. It's rubbish to say I can beat him. He's consistently perfect."

Prost had started the season with a solid second at Phoenix, but it was soon evident that Ferrari was in trouble.

ALAIN PROST: "Internal crisis is a normal thing at Ferrari. When the team wins, it's a crisis of optimism. When that happens, everything stops. That's what happened in the off-season."

HARVEY POSTLETHWAITE (former Ferrari designer): "There are now 300 people working on the Formula 1 team. When things start to go wrong, they go wrong in a big way, with everyone blaming each other. I know. I've been there..."

2 JUNE 1991 - CANADIAN GP (MONTREAL): As expected, Williams was offering a challenge to McLaren, and Mansell seemed set to win in Canada. On the very last lap, his car crawled to a halt. His former team mate was in the right place to take advantage for Benetton.

NELSON PIQUET: "It's good to win in any circumstances, but not the same when it comes because of someone else's bad luck - not the same as leading all the way."

Opposite: From his finger tips to the depth of his soul, Senna's search for perfection took him into places where no one had been before.
Above: Newcomers Schumacher and Hakkinen quickly made an impression, but Prost and Senna were still the men to beat.

NIGEL MANSELL: "It's almost unbelievable. I went into the hairpin and I started to change down from fifth to fourth - as I had the previous 68 laps. It went to neutral and the engine cut simultaneously. It just stopped - as simple as that. Like someone had switched off the engine. The name of the game is finishing, and we didn't finish."

MAURICE HAMILTON: "Mansell was waving to the crowd; the engine revs dropped dramatically; when Nigel went to select a lower gear, the semi-automatic box baulked momentarily and found neutral instead and, at that very moment, the engine revs were so desperately low that the V10 cut out. Make of that what you will."

7 JULY 1991 - FRENCH GP (MAGNY-COURS) Williams' luck changed with Patrese's victory in Mexico, and then Mansell's in France.

JAMES HUNT: "Mansell's passing manoeuvres on Prost were quite superb, great opportunistic stuff, and he really has established himself as a master overtaker. Senna may dispose of backmarkers better because he's prepared to take more risks but, in a straight racing mode, Mansell is at least his equal."

14 JULY 1991 - BRITISH GP (SILVERSTONE) Mansell's victory from pole at Silverstone was a personal turning point. He had previously failed to outqualify his team mate but, from here on, he gained the upper hand over Patrese.

FRANK WILLIAMS: "Nigel is an immensely tough bastard and, if things are going wrong in the car, he'll give me (or usually Patrick Head) a hard time. He's not slow in coming forward. That's the unpleasant side of him. It's actually a good side too, because I bet Senna gives Ron Dennis a hard time. And Alain Prost. All these guys - the best - are not there because they're Mr Nice. They're bastards. Mean. When the lights go green, Nigel goes red…"

28 JULY 1991 - GERMAN GP (HOCKENHEIM) Senna was having a difficult summer. The thirsty Honda V12 ran out of fuel at Silverstone and again at Hockenheim, where Mansell won again. In Germany, Senna also got involved in a controversial scrap with Prost - their first confrontation since Suzuka the previous year.

ALAIN PROST: "He did everything to stop me passing him. He weaved, he braked early, he drove across me. The next time he does that to me, I'll push him out of the race, for sure, in the sense that I won't back off for him. That's the only thing that will make him understand. I'm out of the championship now. I have nothing to lose."

11 AUGUST 1991 - HUNGARIAN GP (HUNGARORING) In a FISA press release issued in Hungary, Prost's speech on French TV was quoted verbatim. Both Prost and Senna were summoned before FISA to receive admonishments for misbehaving in Germany. Senna got off with a warning about dangerous driving. Prost was given 'a suspension for one Grand Prix with suspended effect' for his remarks. Closeted in the Elf motorhome, while receiving the FISA lecture from its president, Senna and Prost declared a new peace treaty to replace the broken one they had made at Monza the previous September.

ALAIN PROST: "I think it's very different now. We talked for about two hours, and we clarified a lot of things. OK, maybe we raised our voices sometimes, but generally it was friendly."

AYRTON SENNA: "I have to think it will work. What's happened in the past between us was very unpleasant, frustrating and stressful for everyone, not just us. My honest feeling now is that, as much as I've had enough, he [Senna still refused to mention his rival by name] has had more than enough."

25 AUGUST 1991 - BELGIAN GP (SPA) Senna's wins in Hungary and Belgium put him back on track, although Mansell had dominated at Spa until retiring. However, the big story here was the arrival of Michael Schumacher. The Mercedes 'junior' sportscar driver stepped into the new Jordan team to replace Bertrand Gachot, who had been jailed in England for an assault.

WILLI WEBER (Schumacher's manager): "There was no hotel booking for us, so we went to a youth hostel. There were two small beds, and in the middle was the toilet and the basin. But I think we would have slept under the truck, you know. It was such a superb feeling for me. Michael maybe didn't realise it so much, but I knew what it meant to come to Formula 1."

JAMES HUNT: "Michael Schumacher's future would seem to be very bright indeed after a most impressive debut. Granted, he had the benefit of the excellent Jordan car, but Schumacher's immediate and confident pace signifies the arrival of a major new talent."

Tom Walkinshaw and Flavio Briatore pounced. They signed Schumacher for Benetton with immediate effect, and Roberto Moreno had to make way. Eddie Jordan was furious, but there seemed little he could do.

8 SEPTEMBER 1991 - ITALIAN GP (MONZA) Mansell struck back with a victory at Monza after a sometimes fraught battle with Senna, but the Italian weekend was dominated by intense off-track wrangling.

In Portugal, Mansell (above right with Senna) lost a wheel in the pits. In Spain (opposite, top right), he went wheel-to-wheel with Senna in a breathtaking battle of the bravest.

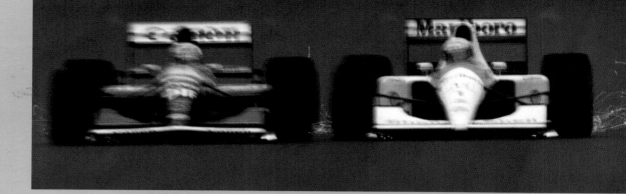

JAMES HUNT: "Schumacher's being poached by Benetton from Jordan I find quite deplorable. It has much more to do with big business, vested interests and pure greed than motor racing. Particularly distasteful to me is the horse trading, the tearing up of contracts and generally amoral behaviour which saw decisions being made with scant regard given to the welfare of the drivers involved."

JOHN WATSON: "The political situation in my day wasn't nearly as bad as now. Sure, there were broken contracts and differences of opinion, but there was also more honour. But now you've got multi-million dollar commitments and you're not playing tiddleywinks here. It's very, very serious. All this has changed the heart of Formula 1, but today's drivers adapt to the situation. And they look back at people like James Hunt and John Watson and call us silly old farts."

The 1961 World Champion was on a visit to Monza, where he had clinched his title when his Ferrari team mate, Wolfgang von Trips, was killed.

PHIL HILL: "Yes, there are a lot of memories for me here, both bad and good. But I had a lot more good times than bad and I always liked to race here. But I'm happy to have driven when I did - I don't think I would like it at all today. The worst part is the concentration camp atmosphere, especially in the paddock. It's really nasty. In my day, motor racing was treated with some kind of reverence and the sport always took care of its own people. Now, it's become such a huge business that, if you can't be of service somehow, you're out."

PATRICK TAMBAY: "The way this sport is developing in terms of technology, media coverage and public interest is exceptional. I went away from Formula 1 [in 1986] and had no contact for several years. Now I've come back with a fresh outlook and my passion has come back. But I do find the day a little long if I stand around listening to all the bullshit in the paddock…"

Welcome to the Piranha Club.

RON DENNIS TO EDDIE JORDAN

22 SEPTEMBER 1991 - PORTUGUESE GP (ESTORIL) Patrese won at Estoril after Mansell lost a wheel because his pit crew waved him out too early from a routine stop.

29 SEPTEMBER 1991 - SPANISH GP (BARCELONA): Mansell struck back with a brilliant win at the new Barcelona circuit, after a memorable, side-by-side chicken-run down the straight with Senna.

MAURICE HAMILTON (*Autocourse*): "There they sat at over 180mph for what seemed like an eternity, the two cars dancing dangerously close more than once. It was as daring a move as you could wish to see, but you had to doubt the wisdom of it."

JAMES HUNT: "It was thrilling to watch but there was an element of unnecessary macho posturing. It might have ended in disaster but this was a symptom of two charged-up World Championship protagonists unwilling to yield."

Before the next race, the FISA presidential election ushered in a new era, as long-time president Jean-Marie Balestre was defeated.

JEAN-MARIE BALESTRE: "Some people say I am a dictator. But that's not true because, although the sporting power is very strong, we're very democratic. We're an elected governing body of 32 people, each one from a different country. Our policy is that the commercial interests must come after the sport. I'm an enthusiast of Formula 1. I know all the drivers and think of them as my sons. I love them because they take risks and are very courageous."

Balestre lost the election to the former FOCA lawyer and March founder Max Mosley. The incoming president paid tribute to his controversial predecessor.

MAX MOSLEY: "It was a lot of work, but it wasn't just me. I think people decided it was the moment to change. That's not a criticism of Balestre. Everyone agreed that he'd done good work but, often in large companies or governments, there's a moment when it's necessary to change."

JEAN-MARIE BALESTRE: "My main hobby isn't Formula 1, it's my lawn. I have the most beautiful lawn in the south of France, perhaps in the country. And the best lawnmower in the world."

20 OCTOBER 1991 - JAPANESE GP (SUZUKA) The popularity of Formula 1 in Japan created a tremendous demand for the 100,000 seats at Suzuka, which was settled in a national lottery, entered by 4,400,000 hopeful fans. With two races to run, Mansell still had a title chance, but he blew it with an early spin. Berger led much of the race from the pole, but dropped back after a pitstop delay. With the title secure, Ayrton waved his team mate through to victory - on the last corner.

RON DENNIS: "It was a nice gesture, but I don't think it was particularly well executed. It [looked] condescending of Ayrton, as opposed to the gesture it should have been, which was to pay back the support that Gerhard had given him through the season, sometimes to the detriment of his own race. It could have been done more magnanimously."

Senna, World Champion again, then indulged in an extraordinary, sometimes profane outburst at the post-race press conference. He harked back to being 'robbed' of the title after winning at Suzuka in 1989, then being forced to apologise for criticising FISA. He said that, at Suzuka in 1990, FISA had then overturned a prior agreement and decreed that pole position should be on the 'dirty' side of the track. Senna implied this was an example of Balestre's personal crusade against him.

AYRTON SENNA: "To change the pole was an order from Balestre - I know from people inside the system. And this is really shit, you know. And I tell myself 'OK, you try to work clean.' You try to do your job properly, and you get fucked all the time by stupid people.

"I'm just telling the fucking truth, 100% truth. I said to myself: 'If on Sunday, because I'm on the wrong side for pole position, Prost gets the jump at the start, I'm going for it at the first corner, regardless. And he had better not turn in ahead of me, because he's not going to make it.' And it happened like this. I really wished it didn't happen, because I wanted a clean fight. He turned in, I hit him, and it was a shit end to the championship. It was a result of the politicians who made stupid and bad decisions."

Senna was condemned by his many critics in the media, although not everyone disapproved.

JAMES HUNT: "I must say I was surprised, but not dismayed, by Senna's outburst and his obvious intensity of feeling. After harbouring all that anti-Balestre vitriol for so long, he released it with considerable gusto, resorting to rather basic Anglo-Saxon expletives in the process. His vehemence served to humanise a man who sometimes seems almost robot-like in the brilliant execution of his profession."

Senna's old rival was also in trouble for speaking his mind. Throughout the season, Prost had grown increasingly critical of both his team and the media, particularly in Italy.

ALAIN PROST: "All year long, they [the media] have been writing that it's all my fault that Ferrari is not winning, and it gets on my nerves. In Japan [fourth], the car was like a horrible truck to drive. No pleasure at all. I've underlined the defects of Ferrari throughout the season, but no one has listened to a word."

Well, this time they did. A few days before the finale in Australia, Ferrari's managing director announced that test driver Gianni Morbidelli would replace Prost, who was fired with more than a year left on his contract.

CLAUDIO LOMBARDI: "We're always prepared to take constructive criticism as a team, but Prost made too many critical comments outside the team."

ALAIN PROST: "Ferrari's treatment of me has been brutal. I will say no more in case of possible litigation."

JAMES HUNT: "Prost was wrong to use the media as a method of dealing with Ferrari and certainly deserved censure for that. But such an abrupt dismissal is unseemly and amounts to the public humiliation of a great driver."

3 NOVEMBER 1991 - AUSTRALIAN GP (ADELAIDE) As in 1989, Adelaide proved to be a farcical, wet race. With Senna in front, it was stopped after just 14 laps, 32.822 miles. It was the shortest Grand Prix in history (and the surviving top six received only half points).

NIGEL MANSELL (second): "It was one of those situations where you know it's foolish to race but you're aware that the whole world has turned on their TV sets and you don't want to disappoint them. It was a crazy situation, really very dangerous."

AYRTON SENNA (first): "All I could see behind me were cars flying off and hitting the wall. One of the reasons I survived was that I was in the lead. I could see! We should have had the courage as a group - drivers, teams, organisers - not to race."

The 1981-83-87 World Champion announced that he would not continue with Benetton in 1992.

NELSON PIQUET: "I don't drive Formula 1 cars because I need a job. When I joined Benetton, there was light at the end of the tunnel. Well, the light went out."

Above: Mansell's championship chances ended in a cloud of dust in Japan.
Opposite: The 1991 season ended in a cloudburst in Australia, where the shortest race in history should never have started.

It was impossible out there. I felt as if the car was floating, with no real control. AYRTON SENNA

Through the winter, the talk was as much about who would not be racing in 1992, as who would be. Nelson Piquet declined to admit that he was retiring, but no decent seats were open to him, and he drifted off to the Indianapolis 500 – where, in May, he would shatter his legs in a dreadful crash. Dumped by Ferrari, Alain Prost was linked with Ligier and a French 'superteam'. He even tested the new JS37, but engine supplier Renault seemed wary of supporting the deal. Eventually negotiations collapsed, and Prost resigned himself to a sabbatical season as a TV pundit.

The first woman to make it to Formula 1 since Lella Lombardi in 1975-76, Giovanna Amati started the season with the ailing Brabham team. The 29-year-old Italian appeared three times but failed to qualify.

GIOVANNA AMATI: "It is difficult to keep your concentration with all the media attention. Sometimes I'm not nice about it. In South Africa, there were photographers who insulted me because I didn't smile at them. Come on, I'm not here to smile! They expected me to be a glamour girl, always available and smiling. I'm a racing driver like the others, but maybe with more problems. This is a male environment and they want to keep it that way: the drivers, the journalists, everyone."

Amati later had a romance with a former World Champion.

GIOVANNA AMATI: "When I was seeing Niki Lauda, he gave me an engagement ring and said: 'Right, now you quit racing.' I agreed to spend a year away to see how we got on. It was terrible. I realised that a man can't give the same emotional high as a racing car."

Amati was soon replaced by Williams test driver Damon Hill. He would only make it into the field twice, before the team finally ran out of money. With a record of 35 Grand Prix wins from 399 starts, the Brabham name was gone...

1 MARCH 1992 - SOUTH AFRICAN GP (KYALAMI): The season began at the rebuilt Kyalami circuit near Johannesburg, where the superiority of Patrick Head's outstanding Williams FW14B was immediately apparent.

NIGEL ROEBUCK: "Perhaps events will prove me wrong, but I felt, as I watched Mansell on one of his innumerable hot laps, that this was the beginning of a new era. The next step. It was the same when Mario Andretti began hustling the Lotus 79, a car plainly faster than anything else, yet producing this speed with nonchalance."

17 MAY 1992 - SAN MARINO GP (IMOLA) Mansell enjoyed the best start to a season in Formula 1 history: five successive victories, and on four occasions Patrese made it a Williams 1-2. Had they been equally matched, we might still have had an interesting season, but Patrese was no longer Mansell's equal. The accepted explanation was that he did not feel as comfortable with the 'active' suspension.

Some thought the Williams FW14B heralded the end of Formula 1 as we knew it, and soon there was talk of reining in the technology. At mid-season, a Safety Car regulation was introduced in an attempt to spice up the action.

ALAIN PROST: "If you have the best car, you simply put tyres on it and fuel in it, and that's it, you win. There aren't too many choices for the driver. So if you don't have the best car, there isn't as much you can do to help yourself as before."

JAMES HUNT: "Credit is due to the top teams for their technical achievements but the technology race has become so out of hand that the gap between the haves and have-nots is becoming farcical. Such innovations as automatic gearchanging and computerised traction control replace the human skills and instincts which formerly tested the drivers. Throughout Formula 1 history, the cars have had to be slowed by changing the regulations, and I believe it's time for substantially rewriting the regulations again."

NIKI LAUDA: "It's becoming more and more interesting and sophisticated, and to a degree technology is taking over. People have to learn to live with these advances. You can't turn back the wheels of time."

31 MAY 1992 - MONACO GP (MONTE CARLO) The end of Mansell's winning streak. He led comfortably until pitting with a loose wheel. Afterwards Senna fended off his persistent advances and won this famous race for the fifth time.

JAMES HUNT: "When he caught the McLaren, Mansell treated us to a tremendous display of aggressive driving that saw him do everything but climb into the cockpit with Senna. The Williams superiority has hitherto provided him with easy wins. Here, he had to fight back and it enabled him to remind us what a terrific 'racer' he is."

NIGEL MANSELL: "I thought I saw three McLarens in front of me, but no sour grapes. Ayrton was in the right place at the right time. That's racing."

JAMES HUNT: "Equally impressive was Senna's defence of his position. His tyres, in an advanced state of wear, left him with very little grip and it required all his considerable skills to keep the determined Mansell at bay. He did this firmly, but fairly."

14 JUNE 1992 - CANADIAN GP (MONTREAL) Mansell lost again in Montreal, this time after crashing out at the end of the first lap, claiming that Senna had forced him off the road.

5 JULY 1992 - FRENCH GP (MAGNY-COURS) The Williams bandwagon was back in action in France, where Patrese briefly offered resistance. Mansell was now looking forward to another success on home ground. As Silverstone approached, 'Mansellmania' among the British fans reached new heights.

You can blame progress, the amount of money in the sport. But I believe if people were just a little bit more sensitive, everyone in Formula 1 would enjoy themselves so much more. I think that some people here get out of bed in the morning, and no matter what hat they wear or whatever coat they put on, some of them think their job is to be a pain in the arse to everybody.

NIGEL MANSELL

Opposite: Mansell immediately announced his intentions and won the first five races of the 1992 season. Even Senna's McLaren (above) couldn't hold back the Williams onslaught.

261

12 JULY 1992 - BRITISH GP (SILVERSTONE) Mansell duly scored a superb win in Britain but, at the end of the race, the track was invaded by an unruly mob.

NIGEL MANSELL: "People can see that basically I am an honest person and that on the track I drive my hardest, whether for the lead or second or third. I think they respect that. But what some of the fans have said they'd like to do to the other drivers is unprintable. Woe betide anyone who does something they shouldn't on that day. They won't get out of the track alive."

THE DAILY EXPRESS: "Nigel Mansell and Silverstone: a combination so exciting it should carry a health warning."

NIGEL MANSELL: "I actually ran one person over, but I was only going a few miles an hour and he loved it."

LA GAZZETTA DELLO SPORT: "No longer can the British condemn the performances of the tifosi at Monza."

JAMES HUNT: "We saw examples of the extreme nationalism which has spread from its roots in soccer hooliganism and is an embarrassment to British sporting traditions. The abuse meted out to Ayrton Senna, who combines being supremely competitive with a high degree of dignity and sportsmanship, and who, incidentally, has achieved all his success in British cars, was totally unjustified."

Such aggressive hysteria is unique to Britain. In Italy, where a similar degree of passion prevails, it's leavened with a sense of humour and fun that makes it more acceptable.

JAMES HUNT

26 JULY 1992 - GERMAN GP (HOCKENHEIM) Rumours gathered pace to the effect that Honda might pull out at the end of the season - in which case it was unclear where McLaren would get an engine. Without a competitive power unit, would Senna stay? His logical destination seemed to be Williams, but Prost was another obvious candidate. Then there was Mansell, who wanted more money to stay with Williams. So began an extraordinary saga as the three greatest drivers of the era fought over two Williams seats.

NIGEL MANSELL: "I feel deflated to be in this position. It's the finest period of my life, and there's an air of uncertainty about what's going to happen next. I'm just trying to get the job done."

16 AUGUST 1992 - HUNGARIAN GP (BUDAPEST) Mansell finally achieved his target in Hungary. After pitting with a puncture, he finished second, securing the title in August with five races still to go.

NIGEL MANSELL: "Ayrton had won the race and, as I stood on the podium and tried to take in the enormity of it all, he was in a most benevolent mood. He put his arm around me, hugged me, and said: 'Well done, Nigel. It's such a good feeling, isn't it? Now you know why I'm such a bastard. I don't ever want to lose the feeling or let anybody else experience it.'"

Meanwhile, it soon became apparent that Prost was definitely going to Williams.

AYRTON SENNA: "Prost has a Williams contract and he has a clause in there which vetoes me driving, and there's nothing you can do about it. He simply doesn't want to compete with me in the same car."

30 AUGUST 1992 - BELGIAN GP (SPA) Just a year after his debut, Schumacher scored his maiden victory. It was a brilliant tactical success for the young Benetton ace, who had been growing in stature with a string of impressive podiums.

MICHAEL SCHUMACHER: "I had water in my eyes for the first time when I was third at Hockenheim, and here even more so. I feel this is a victory we really deserved, and I thank the team for giving me such a fantastic car today."

JAMES HUNT: "Next year's driver line-up at Williams was the subject of much conjecture in Belgium. Slowly the picture, if not the resolution, is becoming clearer, and it's not a pretty one. It seems Alain Prost has done a very good deal for himself, but a bad one for the Williams team, and for the sport of motor racing.

"Prost's agreement with the team, signed some time ago, precluded either Mansell or Senna from being his team mate. Subsequently, in the light of the excellent performances of their cars, and Mansell, Williams have tried to persuade Prost to forego his 'exclusion clauses'. So far they have only succeeded in the case of Mansell, only because Prost thinks he can beat him, and the current stalemate is over the 'No Senna' clause. While Senna waits in the wings, Mansell is understandably miffed at appearing to be third choice."

13 SEPTEMBER 1992 - ITALIAN GP (MONZA) It was revealed that, for 1993, Gerhard Berger had signed for Ferrari, and that American IndyCar star Michael Andretti would join McLaren, which would not have Honda engines. The long anticipated announcement of Honda's withdrawal came on Friday. In its farewell statement, the company said it had achieved all its objectives over the last 10 years.

On Sunday morning, Mansell was to make a statement to the media. Just before he started to speak, a Williams employee tried to intervene, telling him that his demands had been met, but it was too late. Mansell began reading his prepared statement.

NIGEL MANSELL: "Due to circumstances beyond my control, I've decided to retire from Formula 1 at the end of the season. Those who know me well understand the importance of the human side and the mutual trust, good will, integrity and fair play that are the basis of all human relationships. All these issues have suffered in recent weeks..."

He said his decision was partly based on money: Williams, having previously agreed to Mansell's figure, had asked him to take a reduced salary for 1993 after Senna had volunteered to drive for nothing. Mansell said he would look elsewhere for 1993, perhaps IndyCar racing. (He would replace Andretti in the Newman/Haas team, and win the US-based series.)

JAMES HUNT: "Like Mansell's previous decision to leave the sport, this one was made impulsively. The final stressful hours prior to a race are not the time for a driver to be deliberating such momentous matters."

AYRTON SENNA: "As far as Formula 1 is concerned, Mansell has always been a character: very aggressive, very competitive - winning, losing, crashing, overtaking. He's been a source of news, of motivation, of thrills, of emotions good and bad. Formula 1 needs those things."

27 SEPTEMBER 1992 - PORTUGUESE GP (ESTORIL) Mansell was true to his word before taking to the track at Estoril.

NIGEL MANSELL: "My motivation is to get away from Formula 1 as quickly as I can. If that means getting pole and winning the race as early as I can - that's what I'll do."

I hope that the sober thought of being World Champion will give him a more mature approach off the track. JOHN SURTEES

A spectacular accident occurred when Patrese ran into the back of Berger as the McLaren slowed to enter the pits. The Williams was launched high into the air and everyone was amazed when its driver emerged unscathed.

MAURICE HAMILTON: "Riccardo was livid. He understood what had happened and accepted that there was no malicious intent in what Berger had done. 'But no warning, no signal!' he fumed. Berger would say later that signalling was impossible at the exit of such a long, high G-force corner, claiming that he had moved to the right to allow Patrese through. Neither Patrese nor his team accepted this and a protest was lodged. The Stewards rejected it. The main thing was that Riccardo was unharmed."

Berger finished second in the race, Senna third. The Brazilian then made unwelcome headlines by complaining about Prost preventing him from taking the second Williams seat.

AYRTON SENNA: "If Prost wants to come back and maybe win another title, he should be sporting. He must be prepared to race anybody, under any conditions, under equal terms. It is like going for a 100-metre sprint in running shoes while everyone else has lead shoes. That's the way he wants to race. That's not racing."

Mansell noted that IndyCar racing was refreshingly free of politics and that former Formula 1 stars Emerson Fittipaldi and Mario Andretti had offered to help him come to grip with the unfamiliar oval tracks.

NIGEL MANSELL: "That's very refreshing. It shows you the difference between Formula 1 and IndyCars. I can honestly say that, in my whole Formula 1 career, in 12 years, other than the late great Gilles Villeneuve and Colin Chapman, I've had no assistance at all."

8 NOVEMBER 1992 - AUSTRALIAN GP (ADELAIDE) After handing the Japanese victory to his team mate as a gesture of thanks for his support, Mansell came to Adelaide for what was supposed to be his final Formula 1 appearance. If he wanted to go out with a bang, he succeeded - in a collision with Senna that spun them both off the road.

AYRTON SENNA: "People have said I was crazy to try and overtake there - but I wasn't even thinking of it. I never expected him to brake at that point."

NIGEL MANSELL: "Senna has no business on the track. He has a screw loose in his head. All I know is that someone hit me at about 40-50mph up the back as I was turning into the corner. I thought I'd do it honourably and go and see the Stewards. They're totally gutless. They said it was a sporting incident."

With the two stars out of the way, Berger went on to score his second victory of the year, and the fifth for McLaren. Joining him on the podium were the Benetton pair, Schumacher and Martin Brundle. The Englishman had rebuilt his reputation, but he had been overshadowed by his mercurial German team mate. Schumacher had enjoyed a brilliant first full season, scoring enough points to pip Senna for third place in the title battle.

JAMES HUNT: "The 1992 season featured more bickering, backbiting, name-calling, mud-slinging and public washing of dirty linen than we've ever seen before. One's view of the negative media reaction depends on whether one subscribes to the theory that any publicity is good publicity. Certainly, the processional racing was detracting from the sport's image and, regrettable though it might have been, all the petty wrangling helped keep the interest level up. Quite frankly, 1992 would have been unbearably boring had everyone's behaviour been beyond reproach."

FRANK WILLIAMS: "It's been wonderfully satisfying for us all and this season must rank among our very best. Winning the constructors' championship is a greater source of pride to me, because it means we got it right as a team. More importantly, Renault has invested in Formula 1 for 15 years and this makes it all worthwhile for them.

"In 1980, we had about 60 people in the team. In the late 1980s, we had about 120. Now we've got 200. Formula 1 never stands still and you have to keep up with the times. Still, I don't have the attitude that the good old days are over. They were fun at the time, but I've always been more interested in today and tomorrow. My energy is limited, being stuck in this bloody wheelchair, but as long as I've got the drive, I'll continue."

Williams still needed a team mate for Prost. Though Hill had earned a solid reputation as a test driver, promotion to the race team was by no guaranteed. Having been kept on tenterhooks for months, Hill was finally summoned to the Williams factory.

DAMON HILL: "When I got there, Frank said, 'You'll be astonished to learn that I've made up my mind.' Then it was down to business. I didn't celebrate until I got home. I videotaped the contract coming through the fax machine!"

Opposite: Shortly after becoming World Champion Mansell surprised everyone, including Williams, by saying he was finished with Formula 1.
Above: Sparks flew on the track - from the likes of Hakkinen, Schumacher and Alesi (here at Spa) - and off it, in a season full of dirty linen being laundered in public.

Williams was unable to enjoy the winter of 1992/93 due to its own administrative error. The team submitted its 1993 entry one day late, which meant that, technically, Prost and Hill could not compete unless all the other teams agreed. Inevitably, the situation was used to gain concessions from Frank Williams, who had steadfastly refused to support any effort to ban the 'driver aids' that his team had perfected.

BERNIE ECCLESTONE: "It's hard to get Frank Williams to give up his technical advantage. All the teams want to beat Williams on equal terms. We need to change the regulations to bring Formula 1 into the 1990s. When they were written, there was no TV to speak of. Now we have huge TV audiences and therefore we must take the sport to the TV companies. In the old days, it was pure racing, the drivers made the difference. Now teams must be involved in the spectacle. They are more important than individuals."

FRANK WILLIAMS: "I'm not happy. I've not been blocking everything alone and I won't submit to threats. I'm not going to back down, but I am very embarrassed that my actions have brought Formula 1 such bad publicity. Perhaps Williams could be guilty of some sloppy office work, but the penalty is out of all proportion to the crime."

Riccardo Patrese had gone to Benetton and Gerhard Berger back to Ferrari, but there was uncertainty elsewhere. In December, Ayrton Senna, disillusioned with McLaren's relative uncompetitiveness in 1992 and Honda's withdrawal, tested a Penske IndyCar. He was reluctant to commit to McLaren, which signed Mika Hakkinen from Lotus as insurance. McLaren finally solved its engine problem by paying for the 'customer' Ford HB, an older-specification engine than that used by the works team, Benetton. Eventually (though it was several months before he would sign a contract) Senna tested the new car, and agreed to race at Kyalami alongside McLaren's new recruit, the son of the 1978 World Champion, Mario Andretti.

RON DENNIS: "Michael Andretti has the ability to overtake cars and the aggression that goes behind that manoeuvre. Only four, maybe six drivers in Formula 1 have that quality.

He should have no trouble with the unfamiliar circuits. A true racer will dial into a circuit within an hour."

JAMES HUNT: "Michael Andretti, like his father, has a reputation for being a real charger, but it remains to be seen if his undoubted speed in IndyCars is up to Formula 1 standards."

14 MARCH 1993 - SOUTH AFRICAN GP (KYALAMI) It was no surprise when Prost won first-time-out in Johannesburg.

ALAIN PROST: "Williams is a wonderful team. I feel everyone is 100% behind me, and I haven't felt that in a long time - not since McLaren back in 1987. And that feeling is so important, you know, because you have more confidence, more motivation. It's like having another 20 horsepower."

11 APRIL 1993 - EUROPEAN GP (DONINGTON) Having scored a memorable home win, after Prost had spun off, Senna underlined his brilliance in a one-off fixture at Donington Park, in England. Rain made the track treacherous, and the first lap went down in Formula 1 legend.

NIGEL ROEBUCK: "After Schumacher's clumsy attempt to usher him off the road in the opening seconds, Senna was instantly back at the Benetton driver, taking him through the first corner, then passing Wendlinger through the Craner Curves in a move to make you gasp. By the end of that opening lap, he had also dealt with both Williams drivers, and was in the lead. People use the word 'awesome' with fatuous ease these days, but that's what it was."

JAMES HUNT: "His command of the race was absolute. While the changing weather caught out many drivers, it provided Senna with the opportunity to use his superior skills to overcome the handicap of having the second-best car. The win was set up by the most sensational first lap I can remember in a Grand Prix. Displaying pure genius in mastering the constantly changing track conditions, his brilliant driving was matched by superb

tactics. One wonders how Prost was ever regarded as the master tactician. Senna saved the final, crushing humiliation for the post-race press conference. There, a rather sheepish Prost cited a variety of technical trivia (incorrect tyre pressures, faulty gearbox, difficult clutch) by way of excuse. Senna, with incisive timing, quietly suggested that perhaps Prost would like to swap cars..."

25 APRIL 1993 - SAN MARINO GP (IMOLA) After both its cars faltered in front of the partisan Italian crowd, Ferrari announced that Jean Todt would run the team after his Peugeot commitments had finished at Le Mans in June.

GERHARD BERGER: "We have only two problems at Ferrari. One is performance. The other is reliability."

9 MAY 1993 - SPANISH GP (BARCELONA): Prost was closely followed to the chequered flag by Senna, whose new team mate finally scored his first points by finishing fifth, a lap down.

JAMES HUNT: "Andretti's performance to date puts him further down the field than a front-running team can afford, especially when McLaren has a driver of the calibre of Hakkinen waiting in the wings. There's really no excuse for number two drivers to sit back and collect points. They're not going to win prizes for simply soldiering around at half-cock. If they want to further their careers, they have to go racing. That's the name of the game."

23 MAY 1993 - MONACO GP (MONTE CARLO) Senna struck again at Monaco, where a sixth win here broke Graham Hill's record. His afternoon was made easier by a controversial jump-start penalty for Prost, after which he could finish only fourth.

JAMES HUNT: "Despite his car disadvantage, Senna has again overtaken Prost in the championship, a remarkable accomplishment and further testimony to the abilities of the best driver in the world."

13 JUNE 1993 - CANADIAN GP (MONTREAL) A few hours after writing his newspaper column about this race, James Hunt died of a heart attack, aged only 45.

JAMES HUNT: "Though it tended to be processional, I found the Canadian Grand Prix thoroughly entertaining. While the intensity of action in the early laps made them quite obviously thrilling, the last half of the race was equally engrossing. Less becoming to the sport is the awkward way the powers-that-be announced that fully 24 of the 25 cars on the grid in Canada were illegal, although it was decreed they would be allowed to race.

"What worries me is that, instead of wasting enormous amounts of energy in fighting each other over procedures and detail, FISA and the McLaren/Williams alliance should be combining all their considerable knowledge and experience on the real issue. The goal should be to create an environment similar to the halcyon days of the mid-1970s, when the sport was at its most competitive and affordable."

Senna's opening lap at Donington was one of the greatest I've ever seen. Simple as that. KEKE ROSBERG

4 JULY 1993 - FRENCH GP (MAGNY-COURS) Senna was finally confirmed as a McLaren driver for the rest of the season, although there was more to it than met the eye.

ALAN HENRY: "Senna's commitment to McLaren was initially presented to the world as a race-by-race deal. Only later did Ron Dennis concede that this was a necessary strategy, agreed between the two men, to provide time to find the funds to meet Senna's financial aspirations - reputedly in the region of $16 million."

AYRTON SENNA: "I want to have the maximum in all areas. I give my maximum, I want the maximum. That means the best car, the best people to work [with], a pleasant atmosphere, a competitive situation, and the material benefits from that. Maybe it seems too simple, but that's the way I see it."

After declaring in Canada that almost all the cars did not comply with the rules, the FISA technical delegate decided in France that all the cars were actually ineligible. The rules in question concerned 'active' suspension systems - "which influence the car's aerodynamic performance but do not remain immobile in relation to the sprung part of the car" - and traction control - "their propulsion systems are not under the control of the driver at all times." Furthermore, it was implied that fuel samples taken from the leading cars in the previous four races showed traces of high-performance additives. As in Canada, the cars were allowed to race.

The new FISA president, Max Mosley insisted that this highly public controversy, which put the results of five of the eight races to date in doubt, did not make Formula 1 look absurd. Drastic action was necessary, Mosley said, to force the teams to stop bickering among themselves, and agree forthwith to a ban on all electronic 'driver aids', in order to give designers time to get new cars ready for the next season, and to save the teams money on wasted technology.

RON DENNIS: "The issues that are on the table are not about money. Money is the camouflage on a fundamental desire to remove from the 'haves' the technical advantages that the 'have-not' teams don't have. The 'have-nots' must get their acts together. If they aren't capable, they'll die."

11 JULY 1993 - BRITISH GP (SILVERSTONE) Having nearly beaten Prost in France, Hill led his home race until the engine blew.

NIGEL ROEBUCK: "Hill pulled off, the back of the car temporarily ablaze. Then he climbed out, took off his helmet, and sadly walked away. There were no histrionics. His old man could not have handled the situation with more dignity. On the way back to the pits, he dropped into the BRDC clubhouse for a beer."

Michael Andretti also made an early departure from the race when he spun off at the first corner - his fifth accidental retirement in nine races and the third time he had failed to complete the first lap.

MICHAEL ANDRETTI: "I don't know what the hell has gone wrong. I can't seem to get it right. I'd bet that even Nigel Mansell [now winning races with Andretti's former IndyCar team] would have struggled in my situation."

25 JULY 1993 - GERMAN GP (HOCKENHEIM) Prost again suffered a dubious penalty, this time after he went down an escape road to avoid a spinning car. But he still managed to recover to win. Andretti ran into Berger on the fifth lap and retired.

RON DENNIS: "I don't think anybody is more disappointed with Michael's performance than Michael. I don't need to increase the agony that he puts on himself. If it served a function for me to be tough, I'd be tough - I'm not recognised as a pussycat. But it serves no purpose. If anything, he's too hard on himself."

At a meeting in a restaurant, the teams, under the direction of Bernie Ecclestone, unanimously agreed to accept a ban on 'active' suspension and traction control in 1994, providing FISA allowed their continued use for the rest of 1993. Why the sudden accord?

BERNIE ECCLESTONE: "Terrorism! Seriously, everybody agreed it was a farce to continue arguing and they decided to look at the long term of the sport instead of self-interest. I'm very proud of all my teams - for the first time in a long while."

15 AUGUST 1993 - HUNGARIAN GP (BUDAPEST) On a track ideally suited to his driving style, the Williams number two secured his maiden victory.

DAMON HILL: "There's enormous pressure in a race when you know it could be make-or-break, that you have the opportunity of winning and you haven't won before. It's more important than anything else you've ever done."

PATRICK HEAD: "When choosing a driver, after you've assessed a guy's skill and commitment and all those rubbish words, then you take a look at his character. And we decided Damon was one of those odd bastards who can do it."

29 AUGUST 1993 - BELGIAN GP (SPA) On the Friday morning, Alessandro Zanardi escaped from an enormous accident at Eau Rouge. The Lotus flew out of control and smashed itself to smithereens against the barriers on both sides of the circuit, coming to rest with little more than the cockpit in one piece.

PROFESSOR SID WATKINS: "We were in the Safety Car at the exit of the pit-lane and saw from the TV there had been a big shunt. It's not that far down to Eau Rouge, but there were tyres and bits and pieces still coming down the hill at us when we got there. It looked like a war."

Above: Michael Schumacher admired the winning ways of Prost, who would retire after the Australian Grand Prix in Adelaide (opposite) with a record 51 victories.

under the guidance of Professor Sid Watkins, the chief medical officer of Formula 1 and an internationally renowned neurosurgeon, Zanardi was carefully extracted from the wreckage and whisked away to hospital in Liège for a checkup and a precautionary brain scan.

SID WATKINS: "We're going to take the opportunity to look inside his head to see if there's anything there."

DAMON HILL: "I saw Zanardi's accident, and it was the worst I have ever seen in Formula 1."

ANDREA DE CESARIS: "They've been trying to take out the most difficult corners on various circuits, and this is one where you can see the difference in ability between drivers. I wouldn't change the corner. I'd just increase the run-off area."

2 SEPTEMBER 1993 - ITALIAN GP (MONZA) After finishing a respectable third at Monza, a dispirited Andretti announced that he was returning to America. Hakkinen would henceforth partner Senna. Michael Andretti's father, former world champion Mario, gave the family's side of the story.

MARIO ANDRETTI: "The facts are simply these: With Senna not signed at the start of the season, Dennis has to cover his bases, so he signs Hakkinen. Now Dennis has three drivers and only two cars. He's promised seat time to Hakkinen, so who gets the testing? Mika. Michael, after every race, is begging to go testing. They don't even look at him. They don't

even respond to his question. What the hell is he going to do? Sit in the garage?

The luckiest man in Italy was Minardi's Christian Fittipaldi (nephew of the 1972-74 World Champion), who survived a bizarre flip after hitting his team mate, Pierluigi Martini, as they crossed the finish line.

CHRISTIAN FITTIPALDI: "I kept my eyes open all the time, and it seemed like I was in the air for an hour. People will say I'm crazy but, when I was upside down, I was thinking about a rollercoaster ride I once had in America. I just kept praying that the car would land on its wheels. I didn't want to close my eyes because I was afraid I would never open them again."

26 SEPTEMBER 1993 - PORTUGUESE GP (ESTORIL) Hakkinen stunned everyone by qualifying third, behind the Williams cars but ahead of Senna – the master of the pole position. Schumacher's victory was overshadowed when Prost, having clinched his fourth title by finishing second, announced that this would be his last season. It became clear that Senna would replace him at Williams in 1994. Senna had gone without a win since Monaco, but he struck back with a double success in the final two races of the season.

24 OCTOBER 1993 - JAPANESE GP (SUZUKA) Senna dominated, but was not in a peaceful mood after the race, in which he had been repassed by the lapped Eddie Irvine, making his debut for

Jordan. After the podium ceremony, Senna and three McLaren team members paid Irvine a visit in the crowded Jordan garage. Senna told Irvine that, as a backmarker, he should stay out of the way of the front-runners.

EDDIE IRVINE: "Hey, I'm out there to do the best I can for me."

AYRTON SENNA: "You want to do well. I understand because I've been there, I understand. But it's very unprofessional. If you're about to be lapped, you should let the leader go by."

EDDIE IRVINE: "But I'm racing! I'm racing! You just happened to..."

AYRTON SENNA: "You're not racing! You're driving like a fucking idiot! You're not a racing driver, you're a fucking idiot!"

Irvine refused to concede he had done anything wrong and Senna became more incensed. He lashed out at Irvine and, still shouting, was dragged away by his McLaren colleagues.

EDDIE IRVINE: "Senna is a nutter."

7 NOVEMBER 1993 - AUSTRALIAN GP (ADELAIDE) At the conclusion of their final racing confrontation, Prost extended a hand of friendship to Senna. On the podium, a misty-eyed Senna hauled Prost up onto the top plinth to share the limelight and embraced him warmly.

It's the last time you will put on your helmet, the last time you put on your gloves, get in the car, think about the start. ALAIN PROST

Mentally, it was not easy today, knowing it was the last race. I am very tired now and have a strange feeling that I can't explain. ALAIN PROST

I come from a different time, so I didn't have a chance to see Fangio. But looking at his career, for me he is the undisputed number one. Lauda was another outstanding driver, and Prost is the next one. The four championships he has achieved are reality. No one can dispute that. AYRTON SENNA

After four titles without a serious accident, I don't believe I'm prepared to take the risks any longer. There will be no comeback. ALAIN PROST

It has been a delight to have Alain driving for us. He has been an absolute gentleman. As a driver, the faster he seemed to go, the smoother he seemed to look. FRANK WILLIAMS

Above: Hakkinen's McLaren flew in Adelaide, and his team mate Senna beat Prost to win.
It was Prost's last race and Senna's last victory.

When you're in Formula 1, it is very important to have a friend. They don't have to have anything to do with racing, they just have to be a good friend. My friend is Alain Prost. It is not because he is a four-time World Champion. He is my friend because he is my friend. I like him, he likes me. It's difficult to explain, but we're very close. JEAN ALESI

After Prost's retirement there had been great anticipation at the end of the 1993 season about the potential rivalry between Schumacher and Senna (with McLaren in '93, near right and driving for Williams, opposite, in '94). Such speculation was sadly destined to be short-lived.

The teams had to adjust to some significant rule changes, in particular the ban on electronic, computer-controlled 'driver aids' that had increasingly given the men in the cockpits less to do. Forbidden now were such devices as active suspension, anti-skid control, ABS braking, fully automatic gearboxes and 'fly by wire' throttle systems. With fewer high-tech gizmos and more of a premium placed on driving skill, it was hoped that Formula 1 would be more popular than ever, though the FIA's VP of promotional affairs disagreed.

BERNIE ECCLESTONE: "That's rubbish. People go to Formula 1 because it's a spectacle, like a big boxing match. People go because it's happening. The fight may be no good, but it's a bit like sex: it's what you think is going to happen rather than what happens."

However, the powers-that-be were convinced that the spectacle would be improved, and overtaking opportunities enhanced, by the re-introduction of mid-race pit stops for refuelling - which had been banned in 1984 for safety reasons. Critics felt that the re-introduction of mid-race refuelling was an unnecessarily artificial and dangerous means of spicing up the TV action.

DAMON HILL: "If fuel stops make the racing more exciting, then fine. If it flambées ten mechanics, it's a bad decision."

The prospect most relished by insiders and onlookers alike was that of Ayrton Senna, back in a competitive car, racing against the new young lion, Michael Schumacher.

FRANK WILLIAMS: "Seeing Ayrton in other cars, he always appears to give 100%, like Nigel did. Alain was a gentleman - laid back, didn't seem to push, did his thing. Ayrton is a mixture of Nigel and Alain. He's certainly very aggressive, but he's also very polite. He knows exactly what he wants, and won't stop at getting it."

FLAVIO BRIATORE (Benetton): "Ayrton and Michael are the two top drivers, and if you go running, you prefer to go with the younger guy. Ayrton is a mature driver and Michael will take more risks. Last year he made fewer mistakes than the season before, and I hope this year he makes none."

MARTIN BRUNDLE: "Schuey's just like Senna. He has a natural gift and the incredible self-belief that goes with it. These guys are winners who will push the limits beyond everyone else. They have the most intense, almost dangerous desire, and need to win at all costs and somehow they convince themselves that they are not wrong."

At a pre-season test in Portugal, the new Williams driver spoke about the dangers of his profession.

AYRTON SENNA: "If I'm going to live, I want to live fully and very intensely, because I'm an intense person. It would ruin my life if I had to live partially. So my fear is that I might get badly hurt. I wouldn't want to be in a wheelchair. I wouldn't like to be in a hospital suffering from whatever injury it was. If I ever happen to have an accident that costs my life, I hope it happens in one instant."

27 MARCH 1994 - BRAZILIAN GP (INTERLAGOS) Senna laid down a marker by taking pole at Interlagos, ahead of Schumacher, and he led the first part of the race. But in this new era of refuelling, Schumacher got ahead at the first stops. Senna spun off near the end as he tried to keep up.

TONY DODGINS: "There was widespread feeling that we'd just witnessed the most significant Grand Prix for a very long time. People were talking about the dawn of a Schumacher era. A little premature perhaps, but there appeared to be a case. Here we were in Senna's backyard, with Schumacher blowing away the man everyone thought was God."

This race was also notable for an accident in which Benetton debutant Jos Verstappen rolled. Eddie Irvine was given a one-race ban for causing the crash. His Jordan team appealed the decision - and the ban was extended to three races.

17 APRIL 1994 - PACIFIC GP (AIDA) At Aida – an ersatz circuit built by a multi-millionaire businessman on a remote Japanese mountainside - Senna was again on pole, but Schumacher beat him away. At the first corner, Senna was tagged by Hakkinen's McLaren, and spun into the path of the Ferrari of Nicola Larini (deputising for Jean Alesi, injured in a testing crash). Senna was out on the spot, and Schumacher went on to win.

With no points on the board, Senna knew he would have to turn the situation around at Imola. The 1994 San Marino Grand Prix would be the most infamous weekend in Formula 1 history.

1 MAY 1994 - SAN MARINO GP (IMOLA) It started on the Friday, when Rubens Barrichello had a violent crash in his Jordan. Only prompt intervention by Professor Sid Watkins prevented the Brazilian from swallowing his own tongue.

RUBENS BARRICHELLO: "When I came round in the medical centre after my accident, the first face I saw was Ayrton's, with tears in his eyes. I had never seen that with Ayrton before. I had the impression that he felt as if the accident was like one of his own. He said to me, 'Stay calm. It will be all right.'"

Worse was to come on Saturday. Rookie Roland Ratzenberger, trying to qualify the new Simtek, suffered a high-speed front wing breakage and lost all steering control. The car flew off the road and hit the wall at massive speed. Ratzenberger suffered critical head injuries and, despite the best medical attention, could not be revived.

NICK WIRTH (Simtek owner): "You can't really describe the emotions. I just have an extremely vivid memory of Roland having heart massage on the grass. I felt like I was going to end up in a heap on the ground - I just couldn't believe what I was seeing. I remember having real difficulty walking from the pit wall back to the garage.

"It was just awful. He wasn't conceited, he wasn't arrogant. The sad thing was that Formula 1 didn't get to know him. What level he would have reached, I wouldn't like to say, but I don't think it's important. His dream was Formula 1, and I'm just pleased that we had that Aida race, and he did it. That's about the only thing that you can cling on to."

Gerhard Berger also witnessed the fatality on TV monitors in the pits. The veteran Austrian, who had survived a fiery accident at Imola's Tamburello corner in 1989, frankly discussed the agony of his decision to get back in his Ferrari.

GERHARD BERGER: "I felt sick and my whole body was shaking. In our job, you must be prepared to see situations like this. But it was another Austrian driver, and a personal contact, so it was even worse. It gave me again the picture of how close sometimes we are between life and death. Then I knew the difficult question was coming. I had to ask myself if I was prepared to take risks like this. It was a difficult decision, very hard. But I said I was going to race."

Senna visited the scene of the Ratzenberger accident, and it was clear that the tragedy had a profound effect on him. On Sunday, he started from his third pole of the season, but JJ Lehto stalled his Benetton, which was hit hard by the Lotus of Pedro Lamy, throwing debris into the crowd and injuring several people. The Safety Car was deployed and, for several laps, Senna led Schumacher and the rest of the field slowly around. The restart was calamitous.

AYRTON SENNA: "Once I heard somebody say that the ideal would be to have two lives: one you learn with, the next one you use all the experience you gain in the first, and you don't make the same mistakes again. It was a very easy statement, you know: it's right, but it's not perfect. You need a third life, and a fourth, because you won't ever get to the bottom of it..."

Shortly after the restart, Senna's Williams hurtled off the road at Tamburello, the scene of many major accidents over the previous decade. Although it was a big accident, the TV pictures suggested that the car was not seriously damaged. But the medical team saw instantly that Senna's helmet had been penetrated by a broken suspension component.

PROFESSOR SID WATKINS: "He looked serene. I raised the eyelids and it was clear from the pupils that he had a massive brain injury. We lifted him from the cockpit and laid him on the ground. As we did so, he sighed. Although I'm agnostic, I felt his soul departed at that moment. More help arrived, and Dr Pezzi, one of the trackside medical team, got on with intubating Senna. We got several IV infusions into the inert form and, although I could feel his pulse, I knew from seeing the extent of his injury that he could not survive."

After the second restart, the drama continued when a bouncing wheel from Michele Alboreto's Minardi struck several mechanics in the pits.

Shortly after the finish, it was confirmed that Ayrton Senna was dead. Race winner Michael Schumacher and most of his peers wept openly. All were stunned.

NIGEL MANSELL: "There is not a driver in the world who will not be shocked and deeply affected by this terrible news."

DAMON HILL: "I watched Ayrton closely, and tried very hard to appreciate what it was that made him so special."

MICHAEL ANDRETTI: "He might have been the greatest driver of all time. There was no weakness in Ayrton Senna. He was also the most misunderstood person out there, because he got such a bum rap in the media. He comforted me when I was having trouble at McLaren and he called to congratulate me when I won again this year in IndyCars. I just want everybody to know that I knew Ayrton first-hand and he was a very good person."

The twin tragedies, the first since Elio de Angelis's testing crash in 1986, and the first at a race meeting since Ricardo Paletti's death in 1982, led to a debate over Formula 1 safety that would rage for a long time. In Italy, the cause of Senna's crash became a legal issue that would haunt the Williams team for several years.

Above: Barrichello's huge crash on Friday was followed by Ratzenberger's fatal accident on Saturday and Senna's on Sunday.

Roland was just a great, great guy. He'd be top of the list if you were going out for a drink with the boys. NICK WIRTH

Out of the car, Ayrton was a bit special too. He was a great man, actually. Probably a greater person than he was a racing driver.

FRANK WILLIAMS

I WAS LEFT WITH THE IMPRESSION THAT HE PUT HIS VERY SOUL INTO FORMULA 1. I CONSIDER

MYSELF ENORMOUSLY PRIVILEGED TO HAVE BEEN A TEAM MATE TO A DRIVER OF HIS GREATNESS.
DAMON HILL

15 MAY 1994 - MONACO GP (MONTE CARLO) The nightmare continued in Monaco, where Sauber's Karl Wendlinger suffered head injuries in a practice crash. In hospital, he was kept in a coma and on a respirator to relieve brain damage, from which he would eventually recover. Peter Sauber withdrew his other car because the team was "not in an emotional condition to race."

Before the start, all the drivers stood for a moment of silence at the front of the grid, on which the first two places were left empty as a mark of respect for Ayrton Senna and Roland Ratzenberger. Schumacher drove his Benetton flawlessly to win easily, Martin Brundle was an encouraging second for McLaren, and Berger - who, like the other drivers, overcame his personal fears about racing - finished a fighting third for Ferrari.

MARTIN BRUNDLE: "I had trouble keeping my head together. I cried when I saw a film tribute to Ayrton. My son asked me if he was really dead."

GERHARD BERGER: "I remember when I was young and danger didn't exist. Now it exists always more."

At Monaco, the drivers met to discuss safety issues, and they revived the Grand Prix Drivers Association. This was to be run by Berger (as an experienced driver), Schumacher (from a top team), Christian Fittipaldi (from a 'middle' team) and Niki Lauda (a leader of the old GPDA and now a Ferrari adviser).

"The gravity of the situation and the force of public opinion" were cited by the FIA in announcing radical measures to improve safety and reduce the performance of the cars. A range of new aerodynamic regulations was intended immediately to reduce downforce (and therefore cornering performance) by about 15%. Cockpit security was enhanced by increased lateral protection and other measures. To reduce horsepower, engine airboxes were to be eliminated, and genuine pump fuel was to be used. By mid-season, all the projected 1995 regulations, reducing aerodynamic performance by 50%, were to brought in early. And in 1995, the FIA ruled that measures would be taken to reduce power outputs to below 600bhp (from as much as 800bhp), and that the minimum car weight would be significantly raised.

The FIA president was asked to defend the morality of Formula 1.

MAX MOSLEY: "It's a matter of personal liberty. If people wish to participate in a dangerous sport, they should be free to do so. My first Formula 2 race was the race in which Jim Clark was killed and, of the 21 people on the grid, three were dead within four months. But I personally wanted to race. Today, all our drivers know exactly what they're doing and it's our job to make sure that they can do it in safety."

The spate of accidents continued when Pedro Lamy suffered broken legs after a rear wing failure pitched his Lotus over the barriers and into an empty spectator area at a Silverstone test.

29 MAY 1994 - SPANISH GP (BARCELONA) Hill's victory in Barcelona was a highly emotional one for the shocked Williams team, and came at the end of a weekend that had begun with a distinct possibility that there might not be a race at all.

The drivers were worried that the hastily introduced (and untested) aerodynamic restrictions would make the cars unstable. On the Thursday, they demanded several changes to the circuit defences, and these were duly made. But when the organisers said there was no time to change a particular high-speed turn, most of the drivers said they would not race unless something was done. A temporary chicane was placed at the entry to this corner, and the drivers agreed to compete. But most of their teams did not…

On the Friday morning, only nine cars went out for practice - three fewer than the minimum required for a race to qualify as a World Championship event. Arrows, Benetton, Ligier (now owned by Benetton), Lotus, McLaren, Pacific, Simtek and Williams all refused to race until they had had an audience with the FIA president. After a tense confrontation, it was agreed that the teams' engineers would have a say in any rule changes affecting the cars. Following this "full and frank exchange of views", as Mosley put it, the race went on as scheduled. Bernie Ecclestone, an FIA vice-president but also the head of FOCA (which he and Mosley had founded), was believed to have been behind the move by the teams which, in effect, held the FIA to ransom.

Before the start at Monaco their still-shocked peers stood in silent tribute to Roland Ratzenberger and Ayrton Senna.

BERNIE ECCLESTONE: "Whoever said this would undermine Max is an idiot. But sometimes you need a family squabble to sort out what's what..."

MAX MOSLEY: "Suggestions that the FIA or any of its officers have made concessions or abandoned powers are wholly false. The FIA owns and runs the Formula 1 World Championship. Teams will participate on that basis, or not at all."

12 JUNE 1994 - CANADIAN GP (MONTREAL) Schumacher won in Montreal, where an exchange of letters between the FIA and FOCA was made public, in a risible attempt to counteract media suggestions that a mutiny was looming over Mosley's dictatorial methods.

MAX MOSLEY: 'Dear Bernie: Please do something about stopping the fabrication and spread of these rather tiresome falsehoods. Yours sincerely, Max.'

BERNIE ECCLESTONE: 'Dear Max: Such stories are pure rubbish and you should simply ignore them. Very best regards, Bernie.'

Mosley was asked how his friend Ecclestone could be both the head of the teams' organization (FOCA) and a vice-president of the governing body.

MAX MOSLEY: "As Lyndon Johnson, the political scientist, said - if you'll excuse the vulgarity - 'Better to have him inside the tent pissing out, than outside the tent pissing in.'"

3 JULY 1994 - FRENCH GP (MAGNY-COURS) There was an unlikely turn of events when David Coulthard stood down from the second Williams to make way for IndyCar champion Nigel Mansell - brought back by Ecclestone, Renault and Williams in an effort to generate some positive media attention. Mansell initially signed up for a one-off appearance. In a test at Silverstone, over 5000 fans (and 300 journalists) turned up to watch him prepare himself for a comeback that heralded the revival of 'Mansellmania'.

KATE BATTERSBY: "It is one of the great conundrums of British sporting life that this man, not over-endowed with natural charisma, should hold such enormous public appeal."

RON DENNIS: "The big question is how used has he become to the comfort of IndyCar racing [Mansell had gained 5kg in body weight], and how much of a shock will it be when he gets back to the bed of nails?"

The motivated Hill just beat Mansell to pole position. Mansell retired from the race, in which Hill finished second to Schumacher. The Benetton star now led Hill by 66 points to 29 but, in the coming weeks, he would stumble from controversy to controversy, as his title challenge imploded.

10 JULY 1994 - BRITISH GP (SILVERSTONE) DAMON HILL: "I'm going to win my home race, believe me. I know how disappointed my dad was not winning the British Grand Prix. I intend to put our name on the trophy. If I can do that, I don't care if I never win another race."

Hill was on pole at Silverstone, and Schumacher was black-flagged after overtaking him on the formation lap. Schumacher was told by his team that he would have to serve a time penalty in the pits, but continued racing while an argument raged between Benetton personnel and the stewards. He eventually did stop, and finished second on the road to Hill, but was subsequently excluded from the results and banned for two races for ignoring the black flag. Benetton was fined $500,000 for failing to obey the officials. The FIA decreed that Schumacher could continue to compete until an appeal was heard, at the end of August. This ruling enabled Schumacher to race in Germany, Hungary and Belgium.

MICHAEL SCHUMACHER: "It's all a lot of hot air and I don't think it is right to interfere with the championship like this. All this theatre is rather stupid."

31 JULY 1994 - GERMAN GP (HOCKENHEIM) Schumacher retired early in Germany, where a first-lap crash wiped out half the field and allowed Berger to score the first Ferrari victory of the Jean Todt era, ahead of the Ligiers of Olivier Panis and Eric Bernard. Meanwhile, Jos Verstappen was engulfed in a horrific fire in the pits that graphically proved the dangers of mid-race refuelling. Mercifully, the blaze was extinguished in seconds, and the burns suffered by five Benetton mechanics and their driver were minor. There were accusations that Benetton had illegally tampered with the refuelling equipment to speed up its pitstops.

STEVE MATCHETT (Benetton mechanic, on the rear jack): "I saw the fuel spraying into the air [from] between the nozzle and the filler valve. My initial reaction was disbelief. For a moment or two, the fuel didn't catch fire. About two seconds after the fuel spray, it finally ignited. My vision of the car was suddenly replaced by a bright light as a sea of white flame erupted. It washed over and engulfed the car in an enormous fireball, with a loud rushing noise, similar to the air movement in an underground station just before the train arrives. A fraction later, I felt the heat of the burning fuel through my gloves, but there was no shock or panic at this stage. I just thought the whole situation seemed very odd. I remember thinking, 'OK, you're alive – you're on fire, but at least you're alive. Try rolling on the floor.' Rolling over and over on the ground, I saw flames coming from me every time I was facing skyward. I was heading for the McLaren pit, and the mechanics came to meet me half way. Then I felt people jumping on me and hitting the flames out."

The race winner admitted that he was a changed man since the deaths at Imola.

GERHARD BERGER: "While sitting in the car, it's no problem at all. But outside the car, if I start thinking about everything, I'm still suffering and it hurts. The only thing that's really clear is that I try to enjoy life even more, to appreciate even the little things, to live more intensely - because I've seen how quickly everything can be ended."

Like Schumacher, Hill failed to finish at Hockenheim, where partisan feelings for the local hero took on a sinister note in the form of a death threat to Hill.

I was not sure I could continue racing like normal. I think Ayrton would wish us all to continue in his sport. MICHAEL SCHUMACHER

DAMON HILL: "The message was that, if I was ahead of Michael in the race, I'd be shot. As things turned out, I wasn't in a position to challenge him. But the thought of having someone take a shot at me made the weekend a nerve-wracking experience, to say the least."

14 AUGUST 1994 - HUNGARIAN GP (BUDAPEST) Benetton's troubles with the FIA continued when Schumacher's seventh win of the season was overshadowed by more suggestions of irregularities in his team's equipment. Before the race, the FIA had fined Benetton $100,000 for a delay in revealing their computer access codes, and made public the results of an FIA investigation which implied that the team might have been using illegal traction control. Immediately after the race, the FIA removed the computer 'black-box' from Schumacher's car for inspection.

FLAVIO BRIATORE: "No team should suffer like we have done. I must protect the Benetton name and will consider legal action if necessary."

28 AUGUST 1994 - BELGIAN GP (SPA) Schumacher won on the road but, hours after the finish, it was deemed that his Benetton's wooden skidplate -

intended to stop cars running too close to the ground - was worn past the margin of error. He was excluded, and the victory was awarded to Hill.

NIKI LAUDA: "When you build a car on the threshold of legality, which Benetton has apparently done all year long, and you get caught again and again, then that's simply not right. Benetton always want to know how far they can go."

11 SEPTEMBER 1994 - ITALIAN GP (MONZA) Hill won at the historic Autodromo, as his championship rival began serving his two-race ban. The FIA Court of Appeal had also denied Benetton's protest against Schumacher's exclusion from the results in Belgium. However, regarding the charge of tampering with the fuel rig, which might have caused the pit-lane fireball in Germany, the FIA decided not to exclude Benetton from the championship, as the rules stated.

The FIA's reason for such leniency was Benetton's defence (presented by a hotshot British criminal lawyer who charged up to $200,000 an hour). It included evidence that "a junior member of the team" had removed a filter. The FIA decided it would be inappropriate to impose a penalty because "Benetton undertook to make substantial

management changes so as to ensure that a similar event could never happen again".

In response to accusations that the FIA had been spineless for not throwing out Benetton, its president had to defend his position for nearly two hours in a Monza press conference.

MAX MOSLEY: "Previously I was accused of having a personal vendetta against Benetton. Now I'm being accused of excessive leniency. Make up your minds."

Schumacher chose not to come to Italy (where he was replaced by JJ Lehto), even to offer Benetton moral support. Although the team believed it had an ironclad contract, it was rumoured that a bidding war between Williams and McLaren put a price on Schumacher's head of over $20 million for 1995.

16 OCTOBER 1994 - EUROPEAN GP (JEREZ) Schumacher returned from his banishment and promptly won at Jerez, but Hill was second, and his once huge points lead had all but evaporated. With three races remaining, Williams had hired Mansell again. Collecting a reported $1.5 million for each of his guest appearances, the 1992 World Champion claimed he was confident.

Above: Mercifully, there were no serious injuries in the inferno in Benetton's pit at Hockenheim.
Opposite: A controversial collision with Hill in Adelaide made Schumacher the world champion.

NIGEL MANSELL: "Given the motivation and the encouragement, I can go and win another World Championship without batting an eye. I can beat Schumacher. I can beat anyone."

Mansell spun out late in the race.

6 NOVEMBER 1994 - JAPANESE GP (SUZUKA) In Japan, Ayrton Senna had been revered to the point of sainthood, and many thousands of mourning fans wept during a memorial service before the start. Then a helicopter, painted in the yellow and green colours of his helmet and the Brazilian flag, descended through the mist. It landed on pole position on the grid, and Senna's sister, Viviane emerged. She gave a short, emotional speech.

VIVIANE SENNA: "During his life, Ayrton won hundreds of trophies. But from the Japanese people, he received a very special trophy: a trophy made of honour, admiration, respect and love. The other trophies, made of gold and silver, he could not take with him from our world. This trophy he took with him. This is a trophy made of eternal values, and eternal values, like our spirit, never die."

In the race, Hill's brilliant win over Schumacher meant that the points scores were 92-91 in the latter's favour. The showdown would go all the way to the season finale in Australia – but now Hill was dissatisfied with his team.

DAMON HILL: "I don't feel like driving my nuts off for the sort of money you pay someone with no experience. I'm continually under pressure to prove my worth. I've won nine Grands Prix in two seasons. I'm one point off the World Championship with one race to go, and I think I'm a better driver than my contract says I am."

FRANK WILLIAMS: "Damon is a top-flight driver but he's still very young in Grand Prix terms. He has a fair way to go before he reaches the level of Prost and Mansell."

NIGEL MANSELL: "I managed to hold off Berger to win the race, my first since 1992. Gerhard made me laugh on the podium by calling me 'an old bastard'. In some ways, it was a lucky victory, but it was a fairytale finish to the season for me."

But it was not the main post-race talking point. Hill had pressured Schumacher until the 36th lap, when the Benetton, leading by a few seconds, ran wide and struck a barrier. Schumacher scarcely managed to steer back onto the track. Hill did not realise that his rival was in terminal difficulty, and tried to pass. The Benetton seemed to steer straight into the Williams, there was a collision - and suddenly both men were out of action. Schumacher was the World Champion.

NIGEL MANSELL: "What people don't realise is that, in those split-second moments, which can be the defining moments of your life, instincts take control. Sometimes those instincts are right, sometimes they're wrong..."

WILLI WEBER (Schumacher's manager): "When I saw that Damon was unable to rejoin the race, then it came back to me that we were one point ahead, so Michael had won the championship. It was like High Noon. If you look back, he's the one who could say he had the most wins this year. They [the FIA] took a lot of points away from him."

Schumacher's eight Grand Prix victories certainly went some way to defending his reputation, but this was a messy, unsatisfactory way to decide the outcome of a difficult season.

BERNIE ECCLESTONE: "The FIA is at liberty to deduct existing points - even take someone out of the World Championship. My feeling overall is that the right guy won the championship, but that doesn't help in a case like this."

MICHAEL SCHUMACHER: "For me, it was always clear that I was not going to win the World Championship - that Ayrton was. Even when I won the first two races, I thought it was just going to delay him. At the time it was difficult for me to show my feelings. But now is the right time to take something which I have achieved, and give it to him. This is for Ayrton Senna."

You can't have drivers deliberately running into each other, can you? It's quite naughty, that sort of thing, and shouldn't be allowed. BERNIE ECCLESTONE

The great name of Team Lotus disappeared at the end of the 1994 season, when not a single point was scored, and the money finally ran out. This was not all that put Formula 1 in an uneasy mood over the winter break. After the previous traumatic season, it was a busy time for the aerodynamicists and engine designers. As part of the FIA's safety package, downforce was reduced, and the maximum engine swept volume lowered from 3.5 to 3.0 litres.

There were big changes among the engine suppliers. Benetton switched from Ford to Renault, Jordan from Hart to Peugeot, Sauber from Mercedes to Ford, Ligier from Renault to Mugen, Footwork from Cosworth to Hart. McLaren switched from Peugeot to Mercedes, and once again there was intrigue about its drivers. Ultimately, the new recruit was none other than Nigel Mansell.

RON DENNIS: "Nigel has an explosive nature and probably he'll lose control a couple of times, which will be counter-productive from an emotional standpoint. I expect it. It will be understandable because I think we're going to be in for the odd disappointment."

If McLaren was not confident, Benetton's new partnership with Renault - the package used by the man beginning his first title defence - would clearly take time to gel.

MICHAEL SCHUMACHER: "In 1994, we thought Williams would be invincible, and it worked out completely differently, so it's hard to tell how it will be. People tell me I'm favourite, but it doesn't add pressure. I feel relieved after my first title - nobody can take it away. On the other hand, I've gone from being the hunter to the hunted."

FLAVIO BRIATORE: "Running a team is more difficult than any other business, because emotion is such a big part of Formula 1. Apart from that, it is like any other company. The main difference is that you have to present your balance sheet every Sunday."

26 MARCH 1995 - BRAZILIAN GP (INTERLAGOS) It turned out that the new rules made the cars slower by about three seconds a lap. The engineers, of course, had reacted to the 500cc reduction in swept volume by stepping up their quest for more RPM. The greater the number of cylinders, the higher the pitch, but even the V8s now made thrilling sounds.

At the pre-season weigh-in (to establish the official minimum car weights), Schumacher had gained about 7kg over his normal body weight. The new rules required that the cars should weigh 595kg (an 80kg increase), with the driver on board in all his gear. If its driver was heavy, a car could race lighter. When he actually raced in Brazil, Schumacher had slimmed down again.

MAX MOSLEY: "Whether he had drunk a huge amount of water before, or hadn't gone to the loo, whatever it was,

it was extraordinary that he should have lost so much weight so quickly."

Mansell, visibly overweight, had struggled to fit into the cockpit of the new McLaren. He was replaced for the first two races by Mark Blundell while a wider chassis was built. Hill was impressive at the season opener, but a gearbox malfunction caused him to spin off. That left Schumacher to head home Coulthard. Initially, irregularities with their fuel caused their disqualification, but both were later reinstated.

LUCA DI MONTEZEMOLO: "I feel uncomfortable with some of the situations I encounter today in Formula 1. It is almost as if some people regard the sporting ethic as something that is optional."

9 APRIL 1995 - ARGENTINE GP (BUENOS AIRES) David Coulthard took his first pole, but Hill won ahead of a struggling Schumacher.

DAMON HILL: "It's easy to crack under pressure, but the team gave me three perfect stops and the car didn't miss a beat. I haven't enjoyed driving a car throughout a Grand Prix as much as that before."

30 APRIL 1995 - SAN MARINO GP (IMOLA) The return to Imola a year after the twin tragedies brought back painful memories. At the Curva Tamburello, where

David Coulthard cringed when he crashed in Monaco (above), Jean Alesi wept when he won in Montreal (opposite, top right) and Gerhard Berger (opposite, bottom) was third six times in a season dominated by Schumacher and Hill.

Ayrton Senna had died, fans erected an improvised shrine. People wept openly when they saw the large photograph of their hero, the bouquets of flowers, the Brazilian flags and the tributes to him scrawled on the concrete wall. Hill scored an appropriate win for Williams, after Schumacher had crashed heavily.

DAMON HILL: "I was very emotional in the car at the end of the race. I felt elation from winning, but then looked across at the picture of Ayrton on the wall at the spot where he crashed. I really felt his loss at that moment. I was told that some drivers [Salo and Herbert] laid flowers where Roland Ratzenberger had crashed. And remembered all the things that had happened last year."

4 MAY 1995 - SPANISH GP (BARCELONA) When Schumacher struck back, suddenly Benetton seemed to be on top. Hill's day was spoiled by a hydraulics malfunction that dropped him from second to fourth.
     After a terrible time at Imola, Mansell stopped his car in Barcelona, complaining about its handling. Before the next race in Monaco, he had split with McLaren - never to race in Formula 1 again.

BERNIE ECCLESTONE: "Unless it's a personal problem with Ron, I'm surprised he's given up so quickly and easily. Nigel is good value and a good guy to have in Formula 1, but there was nothing good in the last two races."

NIGEL MANSELL: "Inevitably some people said I just gave up. I'm fascinated by the critics. These people give the public the benefit of their enormous wisdom, but they have never actually driven a Formula 1 car, and have no idea what it's like to drive flat-out for almost two hours in a Grand Prix. Do they know what it's like to race wheel-to-wheel with Ayrton Senna at 190mph? Or have a suspension breakage going fully committed into a 160mph corner? Would they make the supreme sacrifices, take the enormous risks and push themselves beyond all reasonable human limits?
     "Here I was, driving for McLaren, and it wasn't working out. I'd tried to put my heart and soul into it, but the car wasn't up to it. I had a meeting with Ron Dennis and we talked it through. We were both disappointed about the car, and it was agreed - amicably, at my request - that I should stand down. It was one of the toughest decisions I ever made."

11 JUNE 1995 - CANADIAN GP (MONTREAL) After Schumacher's defeat of Hill in Monaco, there was a new winner in Canada. Amidst tumultuous scenes of congratulation, Jean Alesi won his maiden Grand Prix victory after 91 attempts, on his 31st birthday, on the circuit named after his boyhood hero Gilles Villeneuve, in a Ferrari bearing the number 27 which Villeneuve had made famous.

When I knew it was possible to win, I started to cry. I wasn't able to see the road because, when I braked, all the teardrops went on the visor inside my helmet.

JEAN ALESI

JEAN ALESI: "After the finish line, I was so happy I got out of the car to say hello to the fans. And when I got back in, the engine stopped!"

The ecstatic Alesi took the remainder of his victory lap riding on Schumacher's Benetton, which had seemed set for a runaway win until its gearbox jammed in third.
The Simtek team had run out of money and was unable to make the trip to Montreal. McLaren's boss had little sympathy for impoverished backmarkers.

RON DENNIS: "The race is at the front. That's what Formula 1 is all about. And that's life. This is a sport and a business. The sport begins when the flag waves at either end of the race. The rest is all business."

These comments drew an indignant response from Roberto Moreno, struggling to survive with the tiny Forti team.

ROBERTO MORENO: "Does Ron Dennis forget he was once a small team? Does he forget that if you don't have small teams then there might not be enough to hold Grand Prix races? Does he forget that you must have losers to have winners?"

16 JULY 1995 - BRITISH GP (SILVERSTONE) Again beaten into second place in France, Hill tried to force his way past Schumacher at Silverstone, but the move was never on, and the two cars bounced into the gravel. Once the crowd got over that shock, they realised they would still have a British winner. Leading now was Schumacher's team mate, Johnny Herbert, ahead of David Coulthard. When the McLaren driver was given a 10s penalty for speeding in the pit-lane, Herbert cruised to his maiden Formula 1 victory.

JOHNNY HERBERT: "The last lap was the thing. I'd overcome the problems I'd had at Benetton. I'd

overcome the accident that injured my legs in 1988 [in Formula 3000]. I was thinking about those things on the last lap, knowing I was going to win my first Grand Prix. It was very, very vivid. And it felt really good doing it at Silverstone."

MICHAEL SCHUMACHER: "There was no room and Damon came from nowhere. It was completely unnecessary, what he did - in fact, it was really stupid."

DAMON HILL: "I thought I saw an opportunity, but Michael is a harder man to pass than that, and we had an accident - what I would describe as a 'racing accident'. Michael is the greatest talent of the last ten years. I don't want to have a personal quarrel with him. I don't even know him."

30 JULY 1995 - GERMAN GP (HOCKENHEIM) Hill spun off at the start of the second lap. The crowd went wild. Schumacher won. The crowd went wild again. By now, there were rumours that Germany's young ace would be in a Ferrari in 1996. Meanwhile Jacques Villeneuve, the son of the late Formula 1 hero Gilles and the Indianapolis 500 winner on his way to the CART IndyCar title, tested a Williams at Silverstone.

JACKIE STEWART: "Formula 1 is more sophisticated than IndyCar racing. It is more structured and its drivers are well educated and better developed. Jacques is not well enough prepared. The top Formula 1 teams need experienced drivers who have gone through the preparatory work and know the circuits. They need winners. They can't afford to waste time teaching someone for four or five years."

13 AUGUST 1995 - HUNGARIAN GP (BUDAPEST) Schumacher had a troubled weekend but, by then, it had been confirmed that he was heading to Maranello and a huge salary.

MICHAEL SCHUMACHER: "For a long time, I've felt that I don't want to be in the best car. I want to have the

situation where I can develop a team up to a standard. I wouldn't have joined Ferrari if I didn't think I could win races or the title. Certainly money is important as well - I want to feel I'm being paid what I'm worth."

BERNIE ECCLESTONE: "People are tending to write off Michael and Ferrari. I'm not saying they'll win the World Championship next year, but I think that, within the next two years, they will. I think he'll bring to the team what it has been lacking, in the same way that Senna, Prost and Lauda brought it to McLaren in the 1980s."

27 AUGUST 1995 - BELGIAN GP (SPA) This was a memorable encounter. Rain at the start of qualifying put the Ferraris on the front row, with Schumacher apparently stranded in 17th position. The race brought everything - more rain, Safety Cars, and a bitter fight between Hill and Schumacher.

DAMON HILL: "Michael drove a stupendous race to come from so far back, and we had some hairy moments. He drove very defensively, to the point of actually touching wheels. That's all well and good if it's accidental, but if it's meant on purpose, I'd be very upset."

MICHAEL SCHUMACHER: "I was defending my position and it got very tight. But we didn't do it in high-speed corners. And if you're driving that close in slower corners, nothing can happen."

DAMON HILL: "I don't mind racing against someone and they are entitled to make it difficult to overtake, but my understanding is that physical contact is to be avoided. If he's honestly suggesting it's OK because it's a slow corner, then we know where he stands."

Williams lodged a post-race protest that Schumacher had unfairly blocked their man.

10 SEPTEMBER 1995 - ITALIAN GP (MONZA) For his *contretemps* with Hill in Belgium, Schumacher was given a suspended ban by the FIA. After Monza, Hill got one too. As the pair lapped backmarker Taki Inoue, Damon thumped into the back of Schumacher, in a repeat of the Silverstone incident.

DAMON HILL: "Obviously Michael is very upset, but I am too, because I wanted to race him to the end. It was just ridiculous - Inoue let Schumacher past and then blocked me. I would never, ever want to tangle deliberately."

MICHAEL SCHUMACHER: "I would expect a driver who wants to become World Champion to be able to handle a situation like that. It wasn't a slight touch - he really crashed into me. Hill just seems to lose control once he's in a situation he doesn't like - behind me."

BERNIE ECCLESTONE: "If these guys want to carry on like this, it's OK by me. But they must be prepared to accept the consequences, which are that they might get hurt, killed, or find themselves in trouble. Maybe the cars are too safe and they think they won't get hurt, or maybe the FIA will have to look harder at punishments."

Once again, the Schumacher/Hill clash allowed Herbert to come through to win in the second Benetton – and perhaps to rue comments he had made beforehand.

JOHNNY HERBERT: "Michael Schumacher is the most selfish driver I ever worked with. He saw me as a threat and didn't like it. He has this thing about being 'Mr Mega' and he tries to block people out. I'm frustrated and disillusioned at being made to look second-rate compared with my team mate. The focus on the one driver leaves me feeling like an outcast."

MICHAEL SCHUMACHER: "In reality, there is never a number one driver. A team can't slow down a quick driver, and I've never known a team to try it."

24 SEPTEMBER 1995 - PORTUGUESE GP (ESTORIL) Coulthard had thrown away pole position at Monza by spinning off on the formation lap but, at Estoril, he got his act together to score his maiden win.

DAVID COULTHARD: "I arrived in Brazil and had tonsillitis and was pretty much wiped out, and that took away confidence and a bit of an edge. It meant that I was on the back foot and, instead of being on top of it all, I was playing catch-up. Once I had that rectified, I still wasn't quite as fit as I should have been, so I made some mistakes. All this was at the front end of the grid, and that's a very public place."

1 OCTOBER 1995 - EUROPEAN GP (NÜRBURGRING) A return to the 'new' Nürburgring, after a decade away from the Eifel mountains, brought all too familiar weather. Hill and Schumacher battled on a dramatic, wet afternoon. Michael won after a memorable fight with Alesi. Hill's crash effectively ended his title challenge.

DAMON HILL: "I just felt I wasn't driving well, and I had to understand why. It boiled down to the fact that I was unhappy. It's a vicious circle: if you don't enjoy it, you don't perform well, you get kicked when you're down, so you don't perform well. I had to work out how to create the atmosphere that I needed to get it right. When I lost the championship, it was easy

Mika regained consciousness on Saturday morning. When I told him that he had a big accident, his first words were, 'Was it my fault?' PROF. SID WATKINS

to chuck it in the bin, to tell myself to forget it. It was like having something cut out. I felt better again…"

12 NOVEMBER 1995 - AUSTRALIAN GP (ADELAIDE) Schumacher's double in Japan secured the Constructors' title for Benetton, so the Australian Grand Prix should have been a holiday for everyone, with both the titles won, and the last trip to Adelaide before the race moved to Melbourne. However, a frightening practice crash befell Mika Hakkinen. The Finn's McLaren caught a kerb, flew out of control and smashed with great force into a cement wall. It was the worst accident of the season.

PROFESSOR SID WATKINS: "When I arrived at the accident, two minutes after the crash, Mika was unconscious and having serious difficulty breathing. We removed him from the car and had to perform a tracheotomy at the trackside. Fortunately, although he had a fractured skull, his brain injury was not severe.

"Reassuring him that it was due to a puncture, I gave him further good news that Mr Dennis was giving him a few days off and that he didn't have to drive in the race the next day. He grinned crookedly in response to this and, knowing his sense of humour was returning, I felt very optimistic about his recovery."

Come the race, Schumacher and Alesi were eliminated in a collision, Coulthard crashed in the pit entry while leading, and Hill was able to finish the season on a high.

MICHAEL SCHUMACHER: "Considering Damon started racing late in life, he has really surprised me. Despite his lack of experience, he has done a bloody good job this year."

"I would say I'm going to stay another five years in Formula 1, but I'm not going to get old here. I always said I would stay as long as I have fun. I will always drive. I might get old in karting."

Opposite: The British crowd was silenced at Silverstone when Hill hit Schumacher and both retired. The German crowd at Hockenheim (background) went wild when Hill crashed and Schumacher won.
Above: Hakkinen's serious accident in Adelaide brought out the red flag. It took him several months to recover from his head injuries.

There was no room and Damon came from nowhere. It was completely

unnecessary what he did - in fact, it was really stupid. MICHAEL SCHUMACHER

The winter of 1995/96 produced one of the biggest driver shake-ups in years. Most of the interest surrounded Ferrari, where Michael Schumacher and Eddie Irvine provided a fascinating combination. Their predecessors, Jean Alesi and Gerhard Berger, had gone together to Benetton, while David Coulthard's move to McLaren to join Mika Hakkinen allowed Jacques Villeneuve to slot in at Williams with Damon Hill.

JACQUES VILLENEUVE: "I've a lot to learn but I'm not coming to Formula 1 as some rookie from Formula 3000. I'm coming as the IndyCar champion and the winner of the Indy 500. In some ways I feel an obligation to prove an IndyCar driver can successfully move to Formula 1."

MICHAEL ANDRETTI: "He's a Canadian, but he grew up in Europe, and that's a big plus. The feeling for Americans in Europe is different. Americans welcome people with open arms and make you feel at home. Europeans make it as difficult as possible for you. Villeneuve is a European at heart, but his first year won't be the greatest. The Formula 1 teams purposely put pressure on you. They expected me to win after the first or second race. And the press can be ruthless, especially the British press. One or two bad races, and they'll crucify him."

Villeneuve had spent much of the winter in the cockpit of Williams test cars, and arrived as the best prepared rookie in Formula 1 history. Yet the son of the legendary Gilles had a lot to live up to.

JACQUES VILLENEUVE: "Racing is not like a gene that you can inherit. But when you come from a family where racing was always there, you get used to speed at an early age. I'm really proud of my father. No matter how much success I have, it will never diminish his accomplishments, nor what his memory means to the fans."

FRANK WILLIAMS: "We're taking a risk with Jacques, like we did with Damon, and with David. It's the same with every driver you switch to. The only people you don't take a risk with are people like Prost, Schumacher, Mansell and Senna - the guys you know are winners whatever equipment they're in. Anyone else is a risk."

10 MARCH 1996 - AUSTRALIAN GP (MELBOURNE)
Villeneuve made a sensational debut, pipping Hill to the pole at the new Albert Park venue. Everyone was relieved to see Jordan's Martin Brundle emerge unscathed from a first-lap rollover, after which Hill pressured his new team mate, who went over the kerbing but aggressively regained the lead. An oil leak gradually worsened, so the team told him to slow and let Hill past.

JACKIE STEWART: "What we've just seen is the birth of a new superstar. I never thought it would happen so fast, but we're going to see Villeneuve in the winners' circle many times."

ALAN JONES: "I used to race against his old man, and he has the pedigree to go a long way. I don't think anybody expected him to make such a sudden impact."

STIRLING MOSS: "Villeneuve looks like a kid, but he's very mature, bloody impressive. I certainly wouldn't like being his team mate and having him come in and piss on me like that."

BERNIE ECCLESTONE: "It was exactly what I thought Villeneuve would do when I got Williams to sign him. I think he'll win the championship this year."

31 MARCH 1996 - BRAZILIAN GP (INTERLAGOS)
While Hill led all the way from the pole, Villeneuve showed his wet-weather inexperience by spinning off when challenged by Alesi.

28 APRIL 1996 - EUROPEAN GP (NÜRBURGRING)
After winning from pole again in Buenos Aires, Hill a made a bad start at the Nürburgring and was swamped by the pack. Villeneuve withstood intense pressure from Schumacher to score his maiden victory.

JACQUES VILLENEUVE: "Even when you win, you're strongest desire is to leave the circuit and go home. You've done your job, the climax is over, you've shut down mentally. But you have to go up on the podium and then the press conferences.

"To this point, you haven't seen anybody from the team, and you're left feeling that something is missing from the human side of racing. It may seem strange to feel isolated from humanity when you're surrounded by so much of it, but that's often the way it is."

5 MAY 1996 - SAN MARINO GP (IMOLA) Schumacher stole the pole for Ferrari, and Coulthard led early on for a resurgent McLaren. But Hill won. Villeneuve tangled with Alesi on the first lap, pitted for a new tyre, and retired near the end with suspension damage. By now Hill was looking like a champion, and the ghosts of the past seemed exorcised.

DAMON HILL: "I feel more accomplished now. I really feel good about what I've done in the sport, about what I've achieved for myself. I feel more confident, and I'm able to contribute better to the team as well, I think. Much has been said about a new Damon, but the way I'd put it is, I'm actually more myself now. I've just settled in."

19 MAY 1996 - MONACO GP (MONTE CARLO) Schumacher took pole again in Monaco, but crashed on a damp first lap. Hill built up an apparently unassailable lead, only to be halted by a rare Renault engine failure. Out of nowhere came a surprise winner in the form of Ligier's Olivier Panis, the beneficiary of an inspired tyre change in changing track conditions.

2 JUNE 1996 - SPANISH GP (BARCELONA) The start of a new chapter in Ferrari history: Schumacher's first win for his new employers was achieved in sensational style.

He qualified third, behind the Williams drivers, but then it rained on race day, setting the stage for Schumacher to shine. He almost stalled at the start and dropped to ninth place. Within five laps, he had splashed his way up to third. On lap 12, he swept past Villeneuve and into the lead. In torrential rain and almost zero visibility, he made his rivals look as though they were racing on slicks.

Opposite: Martin Brundle's airborne Jordan got the season off to a flying start in Australia, where Williams rookie Jacques Villeneuve nearly won. By the time they got to Hungary (below) Villeneuve was challenging team mate Damon Hill for the title.

My girlfriend Sandrine is not really a race fan. But having her here provides a feeling of normality and helps take away some of the stress. JACQUES VILLENEUVE

16 JUNE 1996 - CANADIAN GP (MONTREAL) Much was expected of Villeneuve in his first appearance at the Circuit Gilles Villeneuve. But Hill beat him to pole and they finished 1-2 in the race.

JACQUES VILLENEUVE: "It gets really hectic, and you're not a person any more. You become owned by the fans, basically. You can't just do something stupid, or get drunk. You have to be careful with all that little stuff that's purely human, and that gets annoying. But I'm not complaining, because it brings me everything I want."

DAMON HILL: "I went to New York on the way to Montreal, and nobody recognised me. It was a shock! But it was nice being able to go about my business without being hassled. Secretly, I loved it. The great thing about being famous is [that] it's a little easier to go up and introduce yourself to someone you're a fan of!"

28 JULY 1996 - GERMAN GP (HOCKENHEIM) On the Thursday before Hill's German victory, the British *Autosport* magazine broke a story that, despite his good form, he was to be dropped by Williams at the end of the season. The story was denied by all parties.

DAMON HILL: "When I turned up at Hockenheim, there was great deal of speculation that the deal had been struck. I didn't believe it. I didn't know what the truth was."

25 AUGUST 1996 - BELGIAN GP (SPA) JACQUES VILLENEUVE: "I had never seen Spa before, so I watched a video of Ayrton Senna on one of his great qualifying

laps from a few years ago, and I also played a new video game which gives a quite realistic impression of the track. It may sound like a childish way to get ready, but it helped me learn the basics of the layout. In the video game, my best time was only good enough for 18th on the grid, but in real life I managed to get pole."

Villeneuve took the lead at first, but the Safety Car slowed the field for an accident, and, when it rained, an inspired Schumacher got ahead with better pit strategy.

Before the next race, at Monza, Williams confirmed the *Autosport* story: Hill was out, Frentzen in for 1997.

DAMON HILL: "Frank was obviously uncomfortable about breaking the news to me, but he had made his decision. It was a shock, and I'm disappointed. I'd turned myself around over the winter as a driver, and I'd been leading the championship all season. My view is that the reward for winning races [should be] the opportunity to continue to drive the best equipment. You could say I was being naïve. But I've had worse shocks in my life and in Formula 1, so I'll certainly get over this one. It makes me more determined to win. My only goal is to win the championship before I leave. I expect it to be a professional situation."

8 SEPTEMBER 1996 - ITALIAN GP (MONZA) Hill had the chance to clinch the title at Monza, and things looked good after he took pole position and got ahead at the start. But a slip in concentration caused him to spin out with broken suspension after only six laps. Schumacher stepped forward to score his third win of the year, to the delight of the local fans.

MICHAEL SCHUMACHER: "Below me was a sea of red - and it was so incredible to see all those people going completely crazy. Never in my life have I seen so many people have so much emotion. It gave me goosebumps all over my body!"

22 SEPTEMBER 1996 - PORTUGUESE GP (ESTORIL) Villeneuve was still mathematically in contention, but Hill just beat him to pole, made an aggressive start and pulled away. Late in the race, Villeneuve pulled off a stunning move on Schumacher to claim third, and then passed Alesi during the pitstops. Thereafter he outpaced Hill, and got in front during the final stops.

JACQUES VILLENEUVE: "That race was fun. When I came to Formula 1, everyone told me that you couldn't overtake. Before the race, the guys in the team said that, if I tried passing anybody at the last corner, they would have to scrape me off the wall. But it worked."

MICHAEL SCHUMACHER: "I was surprised when he overtook me. I looked in my mirror and couldn't find him - then suddenly he was beside me. It was a scary moment, but we got away with it."

JACQUES VILLENEUVE: "With some other drivers, I probably would have ended up in the wall. But Michael is always in complete control. It's good to know that you can be inches away from another driver and still not bang wheels, and really go for it."

JOHN WATSON: "Jacques is an out-and-out racer, more ruthless than Damon, who races more on percentage terms, like Alain Prost. Jacques is unlikely to allow anyone or anything stand in his way. He can risk making a win-at-all-costs manoeuvre."

JACQUES VILLENEUVE: "I race for myself, then the team. I understand that what matters to the team is winning, whoever the driver is, and the constructors' championship is what counts most. However, a driver has got to think of himself. In some teams there's a number one and a number two. That's not the case at Williams."

PATRICK HEAD: "It would be a great pity if Damon finished his career with Williams without taking the championship. I think he deserves it, but of course it's not for us to bias things in any way - and we won't."

13 OCTOBER 1996 - JAPANESE GP (SUZUKA) Villeneuve won a Williams battle for pole, but made a poor start, and then flew off the track when a rear wheel came adrift. Knowing he was the World Champion, Hill kept his concentration and withstood pressure from Schumacher to the chequered flag. The title was his.

FRANK WILLIAMS: "Damon is a rare breed, a true gentlemen. He spent the last 30 seconds of his final lap on the radio, telling the team what a great job they'd done, how grateful he was, how it was all down to them. It was fantastic. Genuine stuff. What he's done is truly admirable. He's been climbing the mountain for four years, and now he's got to the top and fully deserves to be there."

MICHAEL SCHUMACHER: "I really feel he deserves the championship. He's waited a long time for it and worked hard for it this year. Eight victories is not just luck."

Hill was in good form at a raucous, post-race party where Villeneuve, Salo and Coulthard turned up with their heads shaved. It turned out the Canadian had persuaded the other two to celebrate the end of the season this way.

JACQUES VILLENEUVE: "Before I came here, I heard about all the back-stabbing and how everybody in Formula 1 hated each other's guts. But it's not true. There are a few guys that you can party with. It's important that you can do that once in a while, that you can be competitors on the race track, and then share a laugh."

It was a time of mixed emotions for the new champion, whose triumph was offset by the fact that his team had forsaken him.

DAMON HILL: "It was a tremendous relief finally to end all the waiting, the training, the preparation, the sleepless nights. Jacques was a match for me by the end of the season but my motivation was to keep ahead and win the championship. I'm the first to appreciate that fate could have stepped in and he could have been champion. He won four races and has been a revelation. I've no doubt that he'll be a World Champion. It's an experience I can strongly recommend."

Below: Although the championship was won in Japan, Damon Hill's euphoria was undermined by the fact that Williams had chosen not to keep him.

I don't think because you were a World Champion driver necessarily means you're going to be a champion team principal. JACKIE STEWART

Two former champions became entrants in 1997. Alain Prost acquired control of the Ligier team and renamed it for himself, while Jackie Stewart and his son, Paul, graduated from Formula 3000 with their Stewart Grand Prix team - landing the works Ford engine deal. Both planned to use the new Bridgestone tyres, which heralded the start of a tyre war with Goodyear.

Although Ferrari hoped that its new F310B would allow it at least to challenge Williams, the new combination of Villeneuve and Heinz-Harald Frentzen was clearly the one to beat.

FRANK WILLIAMS: "We take nothing for granted, [but] Jacques has the momentum. He knows the team and the car and the technology. The cars and the teams themselves are very complex, so it takes a long while

for a driver to learn how to get everything out of his equipment. He knows what to do now."

JACQUES VILLENEUVE: "The difference now is that, set-upwise, people know what I need and what I enjoy. It took a while for Jock Clear [his engineer] and myself to push our situation and make people believe what we thought. And I'll know the tracks as well, so I can be more aggressive from the beginning. It's going to make the big difference."

9 MARCH 1997 - AUSTRALIAN GP (MELBOURNE)
Villeneuve's campaign got off to a terrible start. After taking pole, he was eliminated in a first-lap altercation with Herbert and Irvine. Coulthard beat Schumacher to score a first win for McLaren in its new silver colours - and the first for the team since Senna had won in Adelaide in 1993.

JACQUES VILLENEUVE: "It was a stupid, kamikaze move. Irvine braked later than anybody else and his mistake cost him, Johnny and myself the race after only 300 metres. When we met the Stewards after the race to explain what had happened, he wouldn't take the blame, which really irritated me."

EDDIE IRVINE: "I can understand Villeneuve being angry. When you have the sort of car superiority he enjoys at Williams, and you're on pole position, all you have to do is make a good start and the race is yours. And he didn't do that."

13 APRIL 1997 - ARGENTINE GP (BUENOS AIRES)
Villeneuve made up for the setback in Melbourne by scoring a South American double. The Argentine Grand Prix was the 600th race since the Formula 1 World Championship began in 1950. To mark the

Former champions Stewart and Prost put their racing reputations at stake by returning to the Formula 1 circus as team entrants.

occasion, several drivers who had established previous milestones were special guests for the weekend - Stirling Moss, Jackie Stewart, Niki Lauda and Nelson Piquet, winners of the 100th, 200th, 400th and 500th races respectively. Ronnie Peterson, the winner of the 300th race, was honoured posthumously.

27 APRIL 1997 - SAN MARINO GP (IMOLA) Things finally started to go right for Schumacher in front of Ferrari's *tifosi*. He mixed it with the Williams pair and, after Villeneuve retired, chased home Frentzen, who secured his maiden victory. It would prove to be his only victory for Williams.

Proposed rule changes for 1998 were the main topic of discussion at Imola. Especially controversial was a move to grooved tyres, instigated by FIA president Max Mosley and intended to slow the cars and promote more overtaking. After testing the grooved tyres, Villeneuve was dismayed.

JACQUES VILLENEUVE: "They're a joke. It takes all the precision out of driving. It's ridiculous to have to drive like that at what is supposed to be the pinnacle of motor racing."

MAX MOSLEY: "In the 1960s, one in every ten accidents resulted in the driver getting badly injured or killed. Now you have more than 300 accidents before you would expect an injury or death. Obviously we want to improve that figure still further."

11 MAY 1997 - MONACO GP (MONTE CARLO) Schumacher's title challenge now switched into top gear. On a soaking wet track, he produced a majestic performance. Among the mere mortals left in his wake were the Williams drivers, who started on slicks and flopped miserably. Instead, Rubens Barrichello finished second for Stewart, scoring the first points for the new team.

JACKIE STEWART: "I have never been happier in my whole career! Not from a victory, not from a championship. Never! I've never been emotional about my racing, either. Paul and I sat together throughout the race and, when Rubens crossed the line, we both burst out crying."

15 JUNE 1997 - CANADIAN GP (MONTREAL) Schumacher won in Canada, but the race was stopped prematurely after Panis, who had finished second to Villeneuve in Spain, crashed heavily and suffered broken legs. Villeneuve spun out early, perhaps distracted by an enforced detour to Paris a few days before his home race.

Although fluent in English, French and Italian, Villeneuve's linguistic expertise did not extend to understanding the finer points of cursing in German. When he was interviewed, in French, for the German magazine *Der Spiegel,* he used a common slang expression for excrement to describe his distaste for the new rules that would come into effect in 1998. Villeneuve's statement was deemed by the FIA to be offensive and he was summoned to Paris for a disciplinary hearing at the World Motor Sport Council. After apologising, he was given a reprimand.

29 JUNE 1997 - FRENCH GP (MAGNY-COURS) EDDIE IRVINE: "They might as well give Michael the crown now. The season is only half over but Jacques has no chance. The truth is, Jacques is not good enough to beat Michael in a straight fight - no one is."

JACQUES VILLENEUVE: "In Formula 1, there's a game within a game which goes on - a game of words - and it's dangerous. There are psychological battles and Irvine is better at them than driving. I'm not there to beat a guy off the track, I'm there to beat him on it."

FRANK WILLIAMS: "Michael is very much in control now, but Jacques is still the best challenger there is. He's an intelligent individual who's just a brilliant racer. His attitude is - 'Let's go for it.' That's what I like about his character. Jacques is very strong mentally."

In the paddock, everyone was startled to see the non-conforming Villeneuve's latest flight of fancy: a bleached blond, punk rocker-style hairdo. Then he provoked more controversy by criticising the emphasis on improving safety, which had escalated when Panis broke his legs in Montreal.

JACQUES VILLENEUVE: "As a driver, you know that you take risks every time you go out there. If you're not ready to accept that, then maybe you should stop racing. The risks are ten times less than they were a few years back and we make ten times more money. So we have nothing to complain about. I'm not against safety – it's very important. I'm not saying that racing should be more dangerous. But I don't want safety measures to destroy the racing.

"Death is something totally natural. My father died on the track so I know what I'm talking about. Death touched me. We are not immortal. But that doesn't mean that we should do suicidal things on the track and make death nearer to us than it is in reality. If you like to live with risk, you have to accept that, one day, you'll risk making a bigger accident than normal - that's all."

27 JULY 1997 - GERMAN GP (HOCKENHEIM) After inheriting a fortunate win at Silverstone, Villeneuve crashed out at Hockenheim, where Schumacher was

second in his home race. But Berger dominated the weekend and took a superb victory. The 37-year-old Austrian had missed three races with a sinus ailment, then lost his father in a plane crash three weeks prior to this race.

GERHARD BERGER: "For sure I had big emotions today and the last lap is one I will always remember. Although I am not at peak fitness I felt strong throughout the race. I really felt I was getting some special power out there and I think I know where it was coming from."

10 AUGUST 1997 - HUNGARIAN GP (BUDAPEST) The tortuous Hungaroring seemed tailor-made for another Schumacher success, and he duly took pole, and led. But, as in Spain, he damaged his tyres, and slipped back. To everyone's astonishment, he was overtaken by Damon Hill, who looked set to score a first win for Arrows (after 299 races), Yamaha and Bridgestone. However, Hill was smitten by a hydraulics leak on the last lap - and Villeneuve passed him.

DAMON HILL: "The car nearly stopped three times, so I'm really pleased to get second. Have I lost a win, or won a second place? I would say second is a good result. Still, when you're running at the front, leading by half a minute and feeling fantastic, really in a groove, you're a little disappointed."

TOM WALKINSHAW (Arrows): "As far as I'm concerned, we should have won, but we lost. I don't see why we should be happy about that."

24 AUGUST 1997 - BELGIAN GP (SPA) Schumacher was head and shoulders above the rest in the sodden Ardennes hills. A downpour came before the start, and he disappeared from the view of the vain pursuers. Fisichella was an impressive second, Villeneuve a dejected fifth.

At this stage, it seemed as if Schumacher could do no wrong. No sane person would have suggested that he would score only two points in the next three races.

7 SEPTEMBER 1997 - ITALIAN GP (MONZA) A bad day for Ferrari, as Schumacher trailed home sixth. His only comfort was that Villeneuve was just a place ahead.

21 SEPTEMBER 1997 - AUSTRIAN GP (A1-RING) The new A1-Ring in Austria was built on the site of the Osterreichring, last used for Formula 1 in 1987. Jarno Trulli, deputising at Prost for the injured Panis, was a sensation here. He qualified third and led for 37 laps before halted by an engine failure, gifting it to Villeneuve. Schumacher was sixth after being penalised for passing Frentzen under yellow.

28 SEPTEMBER 1997 - LUXEMBOURG GP (NÜRBURGRING) The Nürburgring was Schumacher's 100th GP, and it seemed time for a change of luck. Instead he was bundled out at the first corner - by his younger brother Ralf, in his rookie season with Jordan. After both McLarens suffered engine failures, Villeneuve won his second race in a row, and Ferrari's title dream seemed to be over.

12 OCTOBER 1997 - JAPANESE GP (SUZUKA) Schumacher was thrown a lifeline when Villeneuve passed a car under yellow during practice. Having committed a similar infraction at Monza, he was excluded from further participation at Suzuka, although this was suspended when Williams lodged an appeal, and he was allowed to start from pole position.

JACQUES VILLENEUVE: "I find it difficult to accept giving up a first championship because of this penalty, but if they're ready to do that, they're the ones making the rules. Sportwise, it's a bit difficult to accept. I would have driven differently if I didn't have the disqualification in my mind. I would have battled more. Anyway, Irvine decided to reject his first Formula 1 victory and block me. It was a Ferrari team game and it was in front of all the people."

When Williams withdrew its appeal, Schumacher was handed a one-point lead going into the last race of the season.

26 OCTOBER 1997 - EUROPEAN GP (JEREZ) The championship showdown in Spain was a sensational affair. The tension escalated throughout the weekend.

EDDIE IRVINE: "For someone who has consistently had the fastest car, Villeneuve doesn't deserve to win the title. He makes too many mistakes."

JACQUES VILLENEUVE: "Eddie is definitely the wrong man to make statements like that. Everybody makes mistakes, we're human beings. It would be sad if we were machines. Whenever I hear what he says, it makes me laugh."

PATRICK HEAD: "The man who goes into the last race in the lead is in a position where, as we've seen before, he can be very aggressive with the person behind. I view what happened to Damon in 1994 as the deliberate removal of a competitor. Only Schumacher knows the truth about what happened. Jacques has no record of causing accidents. I just hope this championship is settled on the track and not in a gravel trap."

MICHAEL SCHUMACHER: "I've no reason to feel guilt about the past, so I'm not upset by this kind of talk. I hope this will be a good, clean race between us. Whoever is in front at the finish will be the World Champion. The situation is ideal. But if Villeneuve tries to shut the door on me, he had better be prepared for me to push against it. This is not a sport where players give flowers to each other."

Astonishingly, the top three qualifiers - Villeneuve, Schumacher and Frentzen - were credited with exactly the same lap-time, to the thousandth of a second. Villeneuve, awarded the pole because he set his time first, complained that Irvine had again deliberately blocked him.

JACQUES VILLENEUVE: "He's a fucking idiot. He just waited for me and then slowed me down. We all know he's a clown but there's no point in playing games like that. It just goes to show what Irvine is prepared to do to help Michael."

MICHAEL SCHUMACHER: "On these occasions, it is wise to listen to both sides. Irvine says he drove normally. Villeneuve is always complaining about Irvine. Maybe the pressure is getting to him..."

JACQUES VILLENEUVE: "Yes, there's pressure. I'm the underdog here because Michael is one point ahead. There's no choice of strategy for us, we just have to be in front. That makes it easier in a way."

EDDIE IRVINE: "I'll do everything I can to help Michael claim the title, within the rules. I won't be aiming to take Villeneuve out, but I'll certainly put my car in his way whenever possible."

JACQUES VILLENEUVE: "If team mates come into this race, it could be a good thing for us, because Heinz-Harald is a much better driver than Irvine."

HEINZ-HARALD FRENTZEN: "I will help Jacques all I can, but I won't be more unfair than Irvine. One thing is for sure - I am in the right spot to see the action in front of me."

When Schumacher seized the lead, the title seemed within his grasp. But Villeneuve caught him napping after a pitstop, and dived down the inside going into a corner. Schumacher jinked to the right in a clumsy attempt to block him. They touched - and it was the Ferrari that speared into the gravel trap, out of the race.

JACQUES VILLENEUVE: "I was hoping to get him in the pits, but I came out just behind him. In two laps, I ate the difference up. I knew I had to make my move. I was set on it. Going into the corner, I braked as late as I could, and I got him. It was, 'Wow, I'm in, he didn't see me!' I wasn't surprised when he turned in on me. I knew I was taking a risk. When he came over on me, I couldn't move any further, because I was already on the grass."

MICHAEL SCHUMACHER: "Jacques had nothing to lose, and he obviously went for it. Being behind me, he would have lost the championship, so he had to do that. I would have done the same. I braked as late as possible but he braked even later, so I don't feel I made a mistake.

Above and opposite: His failed attempt to ram his rival off the road left a rueful Schumacher watching Villeneuve win the championship.

"I was called in to see the Stewards and no action was taken against me. They called it a racing accident, which it was."

JACQUES VILLENEUVE: "He hit me really, really hard and I was sure the crash had broken something. It was lucky he went off the road, because afterwards my car felt really weird. I'm surprised I was able to finish the race. When I saw Mika coming up in my mirrors, it was a question of pushing like a maniac and risking going off, or letting him through. So I let him through. When David got very close, I didn't fight him either."

Coulthard then got ahead of his team mate, but controversial McLaren orders forced the Scot to move over and give the win to Hakkinen.

MIKA HAKKINEN: "It was fantastic to win my first Formula 1 race. I would like to thank David, the perfect team mate. The more I realise what happened, the happier I feel."

DAVID COULTHARD: "Mika deserves his victory, Jacques deserves the championship, and I'm very happy to be on the podium for the last race of the season. The good guys won!"

FRANK WILLIAMS: "It was a great title fight. Jacques was cool, never gave up, attacked, attacked, attacked, took the opportunity with both hands and won the championship today. He showed great morale to fight through from behind and attack Michael. It was hand-to-hand fighting between those two."

Many felt that Schumacher had attempted to knock out his rival with a low blow. Replays of the incident (captured on the Ferrari's in-car camera) revealed an unsubtle turn of the steering wheel into the Williams. Even a celebrity singer thought this was a soap opera...

PLACIDO DOMINGO: "It was a great pity, because there has been so much emotion building into this last race. Both are great drivers, and perhaps Schumacher is one of the greatest drivers ever. He didn't need to do that. It can't be possible among champions. It was quite clear it was done deliberately."

BERNIE ECCLESTONE: "Good for Villeneuve, and good for Formula 1. He's a real racer and he put on a great show. In the end, Michael was a little stupid and made things easier for him."

GERHARD BERGER: "You've got to consider the stress and strain drivers are under. Yes, Michael was stupid, but only for a tenth of a second. To create a murder over this is wrong."

LUCA DI MONTEZEMOLO: "Schumacher is a man who made a mistake, just like all men can make a mistake. Let's not forget that, above all, he damaged himself, losing what should have been his third title."

Overleaf: A TV camera perched over Schumacher's shoulder captured him swerving his Ferrari into Villeneuve's Williams.

JACQUES VILLENEUVE: "The whole season has been hectic - testing between every race, PR, media. It's been heavy going. I'm tired. And I know Michael is tired, too, because he told me. It's hard to realise that I'm the World Champion. Since the moment I stepped out of the car at Jerez, I've been shaking hands with hundreds of people. The most amazing thing for me has been seeing all the good feelings coming from so many people. It makes me feel proud and at the same time very humble."

Meanwhile Schumacher was being swamped by a swelling tide of condemnation. Even notoriously pro-Ferrari Italian newspapers demanded that Schumacher either apologise to Villeneuve, and to Ferrari fans around the world, or be fired by the team.

CORRIERE DELLO SPORT: "It was a dirty trick, an unworthy blow which in everyday life would have criminal consequences."

LA GAZZETTA DELLO SPORT: "Let's disown the stain left by Schumacher's naïve and twisted attempt to force Villeneuve out."

LA STAMPA: "Schumacher's image as a champion is shattered."

And even in his native country:

BILD: "Michael, why on earth did you do it?"

The pressure for some sort of punishment became so great that the FIA decided to summon Schumacher to appear before an extraordinary meeting of the World Motor Sport Council.

FIA STATEMENT: "It was found that Michael Schumacher's manoeuvre was an instinctive reaction and, although deliberate, not made with malice or premeditation. It was a serious error."

For this 'error', Schumacher was excluded from the final results of the entire 1997 season. The judgement erased his 78 points from the record books - although he was allowed to 'keep' his five race wins. The FIA president said that it was intended to be a deterrent, to show that, in future, no driver could ever win a championship by deliberately crashing into an opponent. He said that banning Schumacher from competing the following season would have been futile.

MAX MOSLEY: "There's no driver competing who wouldn't be ready to accept a ban next year if he could win the championship this year."

Wild West manners! The way he sought a collision with his opponent's car throws

a bad light on him. Gone is his image as the nice boy next door. *FRANKFURTER ZEITUNG*

RALF SCHUMACHER: "Hopefully this year there are five teams at the top, not only four. It could help the smaller teams that there's been a regulation change and everybody has to build a new car. But again, Ferrari or McLaren have resources like hell. It should be easier for them because they don't need to think about money."

8 MARCH 1998 - AUSTRALIAN GP (MELBOURNE) The McLarens were in a class of their own in Australia. On the podium, the race winner wept with emotion.

MIKA HAKKINEN: "This victory in the same country where I almost died has helped me forget what happened to me in 1995. When you've been through so much, and tried so hard for so long, and you're standing on the podium and hear your national anthem being played, it's such a strong emotion. Hopefully, I'll get used to this and not cry again."

In preparing their 1998 cars, the designers had much to think about. The controversial grooved tyre regulation was introduced, while a narrower track gave the cars a curiously 'squeezed' appearance. This was the biggest package of changes for some time, and it remained to be seen who got it right. The defending World Champion was aware of the challenges that lay ahead.

JACQUES VILLENEUVE: "The best thing about having the number one on your car is that it proves you were the best last year. But I won't take it for granted that it will stay on the car. When you're on top, you become the target for everybody. I have to make sure it's a moving target."

But Williams no longer had a works Renault engine supply. While basically the same engine was to be used (badged for Mecachrome), it was expected that Williams would lose its edge, partly due to the defection of its star designer, Adrian Newey, to McLaren. The McLaren team opted for Bridgestone tyres, leaving Ferrari to fly the Goodyear flag. Among other changes, Damon Hill moved from Arrows to join Ralf Schumacher at Jordan, while Giancarlo Fisichella went to Benetton, where he was partnered by former test driver Alex Wurz. Jean Alesi moved across to Sauber, alongside fellow veteran Johnny Herbert.

Yet there was outrage when it was revealed that Hakkinen's win over Coulthard had been staged by the drivers. A pre-race agreement not to race each other meant that whoever led at the start would get the victory. Hakkinen had started from pole but then misheard a radio signal and pitted unnecessarily – so Coulthard moved over later to let him past once more.

DAVID COULTHARD: "A deal is a deal. The smart thing in the first race of the season is not to think about the entertainment value, but on the results for the team. I don't see the problem."

MIKA HAKKINEN: "What David did today was remarkable, a very gentlemanly way to go racing. If I'm in a similar situation in the future, I will do the same for him, no question."

RON DENNIS: "I'm particularly delighted at the sportsmanship of our two drivers. McLaren is contesting a championship over 16 races, not one, and we would look very silly if our cars crashed at the first race because the drivers were pushing each other."

BERNIE ECCLESTONE: "It was disgusting - unnecessary. An insult to people's intelligence. They were so superior, they could have done things in a much nicer way and still achieved the same result. The guys are here to race each other."

Top left: In Australia, Hakkinen's 'staged' win over his team mate Coulthard provoked outrage.
Main picture: Their collision in Argentina sparked a feud between Coulthard and Schumacher.

A media backlash over 'race fixing' led to the FIA strongly implying that such tactics would not be welcome in the future.

29 MARCH 1998 - BRAZILIAN GP (INTERLAGOS) McLaren dominated again in Brazil, but the second successive Hakkinen-Coulthard 1-2 was overshadowed by a bizarre episode of wrangling over the Technical Regulations.

Early in the weekend, Ferrari protested McLaren's 'auxiliary' rear braking system, claiming that it functioned like illegal four-wheel steering. Since Williams and Jordan had similar systems, they were also protested by other teams. Until decisions could be made, the teams in question were forced to disable the devices. The whole exercise seemed futile. McLaren completely dominated the weekend.

12 APRIL 1998 - ARGENTINE GP (BUENOS AIRES) The McLaren train was derailed in Argentina, where Schumacher collided with poleman Coulthard, then beat Hakkinen fair and square.

EDDIE IRVINE: "Some people still suggest the McLaren guys are faster than Michael, but that's plain rubbish! Give me a break. Hakkinen and Coulthard are good drivers, but Schumacher they ain't."

24 MAY 1998 - MONACO GP (MONTE CARLO) RON DENNIS: "I can understand people looking at our current dominance as boring, but we're here as a team to do the best we can. It's taken us years and a lot of hard work to get back into this position of apparent dominance - years when other teams have dominated. So we intend to enjoy it."

Hakkinen's win in Monaco, achieved in superb style, impressed his manager and fellow-Finn.

KEKE ROSBERG: "Mika is very good on all issues. He makes fewer mistakes than any other top guy. He hasn't crashed with other drivers, he hasn't gone off, his qualifying performance has been there. If there's anything to improve, maybe he could be a bit more cheerful in press conferences…"

7 JUNE 1998 - CANADIAN GP (MONTREAL) After a spectacular, multi-car pile-up at the first corner, Schumacher was given a 10-second stop-go penalty for running Frentzen's Williams off the road in the restarted race. But Schumacher won, although incensed after it appeared that Hill had swerved deliberately in front of him.

MICHAEL SCHUMACHER: "Damon was in a position to see me, and you can't get away with weaving like that at 300kph. Cars touching at those speeds can easily go into the crowd or something. I don't know why Damon and I have so many incidents. I have ideas, but it would be wrong to say them in public."

12 JULY 1998 - BRITISH GP (SILVERSTONE) The British Grand Prix took place in soaking conditions, and Schumacher scored a third straight victory, helped by Coulthard crashing out soon after taking the lead, and Hakkinen twice going off the road. The Finn recovered to finish second, ahead of Irvine, who goaded McLaren.

26 JULY 1998 - AUSTRIAN GP (A1-RING) Schumacher's *blitzkrieg* was halted when he damaged his car's nose in a gravel trap. He finished third, and Hakkinen won. The championship pendulum swung to and fro.

Jacques Villeneuve, disenchanted with not being able to defend his title, announced that he would leave Williams at the end of the season and move to a new team being set up by his personal manager.

CRAIG POLLOCK: "Some people think Jacques is too weird and grungy, but a lot of people like the fact that he's independently minded. We don't want him doing anything stupid in our new team, but at the same time we won't discourage him from doing his own thing, which includes being the real racer that we need."

JACQUES VILLENEUVE: "Nobody knows what to expect. There's a lot of work to be done, a lot of things to build up, so that side of it is very interesting. But you don't want to take that challenge if you don't believe that it can be competitive. You have to believe. You have to dream a little."

DAVID COULTHARD: "Jacques will probably have to buy a bigger piggy bank."

Asking me whether I was trying to kill him is totally unacceptable. I can't find words to describe how disappointed I am in Michael as a man.

DAVID COULTHARD

16 AUGUST 1998 - HUNGARIAN GP (BUDAPEST) In Hungary, a simmering feud between Ferrari and McLaren was made public. McLaren's suggestion that Ferrari might have a secret braking/traction control system provoked an outburst from Ferrari's technical director.

ROSS BRAWN: "There's a very nasty, malicious process going on. Somebody has said that our car has traction control, but it's done so cleverly that nobody can find it. When Ron Dennis came along and said he was going to protest our car, we welcomed that, because it would have cleared the air. But then he didn't protest it."

RON DENNIS: "In Austria, we informed [Ferrari sporting director Jean] Todt that we thought his braking system did not comply with the rules. He immediately leaked this to the press. It should have been discussed quietly behind closed doors."

At the Hungaroring, Schumacher, masterminded by Brawn's brilliant tactics that required him to make an extra pitstop, won superbly.

MICHAEL SCHUMACHER: "Absolutely outstanding! There was an amazing amount of emotion, standing on the podium and facing so many German and Ferrari fans. This is one of the best wins of all."

30 AUGUST 1998 - BELGIAN GP (SPA) Two nasty accidents heralded a shambolic weekend at Spa. In Friday practice, Villeneuve's car flew out of control in the awesome Eau Rouge corner. The Williams slewed sideways, skipped over a gravel trap, and slammed backwards into a tyre wall. The violent impact ripped off both rear wheels, and tore the tyre wall to shreds. All the other drivers were relieved to see him clamber unhurt from the wreckage.

DAMON HILL: "Jacques is fortunate because that was a big hit. It's very difficult to take Eau Rouge flat and you saw what happened when he tried it. I know he's pleased with the spectacular outcome, because he's that sort of bloke."

JACQUES VILLENEUVE: "It was my best accident in Formula 1! I was doing over 290[kph] going into the apex of the corner. It was too fast, I got sideways and just lost it. I saw the wall coming up and thought: 'This could hurt.' I'm OK. I just bruised my knee a bit. Nothing major."

On Saturday, Mika Salo suffered an equally heavy accident in the same place, losing control of his Arrows, which destroyed itself against a wall. After being taken to hospital for a brain scan, Salo hopped in the spare car and qualified 18th in the 22-car field.

And the race itself may have set a record for accidents, partly due to a wet track and poor visibility. It began with a massive pile-up in the first corner. Thirteen of the 22 starters were involved in the mêlée, which sent wheels and debris flying in all directions. The red flag was shown and the restart delayed for nearly an hour while the track was cleared. Several of those who restarted the race in their spare cars were later involved in yet more collisions, and the final tally was 23 damaged cars. Only eight made it across the finish line. All this carnage allowed Damon Hill to head home team mate Ralf Schumacher (under team orders) to score Jordan's maiden Grand Prix victory.

DAMON HILL: "I'm speechless!"
EDDIE JORDAN: "This is a great result for Formula 1. It's another winner. I know Damon is happy for us, but he was smiling from ear-to-ear because people had said he couldn't win in anything other than a Williams."

But Michael Schumacher admonished the team for not letting his younger brother win.

DAMON HILL: "The gall of the man. Frankly, he should shut up and mind his own business."

Indeed, the elder Schumacher had had other business to attend to. He had held a commanding lead in the race until the 24th lap. While attempting to lap Coulthard (who was several laps down after an earlier crash), Schumacher's Ferrari rammed the rear of the McLaren. The impact tore off the Ferrari's left front wheel, but Schumacher managed to manhandle it to the pits, where Coulthard also went for repairs. The enraged German leaped out of his car and strutted into the McLaren garage, where he had to be restrained.

MICHAEL SCHUMACHER: "Were you trying to kill me?"
DAVID COULTHARD: "This is completely unacceptable! I did nothing deliberate, and you crashed into me from behind."
MICHAEL SCHUMACHER: "It was clear that we would have taken the lead in the championship, because I was by far the fastest car on the track. Obviously, lifting on the straight, like he did when I hit him, was very dangerous. He has the experience to know you shouldn't do that. So one could think he did it deliberately."

13 SEPTEMBER 1998 - ITALIAN GP (MONZA) Although most observers saw Coulthard as the innocent victim in Belgium, the incident had inflamed the passions of the Italian fans. In a test session at Monza the week before the race, the *tifosi* jeered Coulthard and brandished offensive banners.

Above: In Belgium, their collision ended in a war of words between Schumacher and Coulthard.
Opposite: The spectacular spate of smashes at Spa left Hill an ecstatic winner for Jordan.

Bernie Ecclestone tried to defuse the volatile situation by brokering a peace treaty in a meeting with the two drivers. Also discussed was Schumacher's shoving Coulthard off the road to win in Argentina in March. After the meeting, the two men shook hands publicly.

DAVID COULTHARD: "It was useful for both of us to clear the air. I feel comfortable with the situation now. It's all behind us and I look forward to racing wheel-to-wheel with Michael again."

MICHAEL SCHUMACHER: "I'm now confident David did not purposely put me out of the race. He's not the type of person to do this. I hope what I have said calms down the *tifosi*. This is a sport. We have a lot of emotion for Ferrari here. But the *tifosi* should not go beyond their emotions."

Ferrari held a banquet to celebrate its 600th Grand Prix. Among those honoured were the 32 drivers who had won 118 races for the team.

LUCA DI MONTEZEMOLO: "Ferrari is a unique combination of passion, technology and competition. It was founded on the passion of Enzo Ferrari and it still runs on his emotion today."

MICHAEL SCHUMACHER: "Ferrari is at least 50% of Formula 1 racing, and the rest of the teams make up the other 50%."

NIKI LAUDA: "Ferrari. Among the many thoughts this word conjures up is a plunge into a sea of emotions, there either to drown or to take flight and soar into the incomparable."

When Schumacher won the Italian Grand Prix, the Monza multitude went mad with delight.

27 SEPTEMBER 1998 - LUXEMBOURG GP (NÜRBURGRING) Schumacher and Hakkinen were now tied on 80 points. In the Luxembourg Grand Prix in Germany, McLaren turned the tactical tables on Ferrari. The red cars were quicker in qualifying, but Hakkinen went longer to his first pitstop and managed to emerge ahead. Schumacher finished a frustrated second, in front of Coulthard, whose points meant that McLaren was now within shouting distance of clinching the titles it had not won since 1991.

DAVID COULTHARD: "Mika deserves the championship. All his wins have been very clean, very sporting. Meanwhile, Michael has been banging into other drivers."

JACQUES VILLENEUVE: "You don't change someone's personality. I was brought up believing you should behave in the right way, so you can sleep at night. Michael doesn't seem to care about such things. Mika should win it in Japan. All he has to do is stay cool. He just needs to keep putting the pressure on Michael, because that's when he makes mistakes."

1 NOVEMBER 1998 - JAPANESE GP (SUZUKA) In a perfect build-up to the showdown at Suzuka, Schumacher and Hakkinen qualified on the front row. But the titles were effectively decided even before the lights went out: the Ferrari stalled on the line.

Schumacher's futile recovery drive was ended by a puncture after he had climbed back to third. Hakkinen won as he pleased, and McLaren clinched the double.

MIKA HAKKINEN: "When I saw Michael's Ferrari parked beside the track, I knew it was over. I started whistling to myself in the car, and slowed down a bit. The team came on the radio and told me to speed up, go for the win. But there was no rush. I'm very happy. We're all very happy. And I guess everybody in Finland is upside-down."

DAVID COULTHARD: "Mika is an unusual character, very reserved and, because of that, hard to get to know. But he's a good person, even-tempered with no nasty traits. I don't believe he has an argumentative bone in his body."

ERJA HAKKINEN (Mika's wife): "Mika has a very good way of seeing things. He believes you have to have your private life, not spread out everything about yourself in public. The results talk for you, but not what is inside of you. That's a sort of protection, and that's why he's so strong mentally."

MIKA HAKKINEN: "It takes a really long time to sink in. It's not a thing where you wake up in the morning, look in the mirror and say, 'Hey, I'm World Champion, I feel great!' The process takes a long time. Every day, you realise more how important it is to have won the championship, to get the confidence in yourself, to know you've done it."

A historical footnote: Suzuka marked the final Grand Prix for the famous team founded by Ken Tyrrell, who had been bought out by British American Tobacco to form the basis of the new BAR team in 1999.

There is so much to think about that sometimes smoke comes out your ears. No question, Formula 1 is a mind game. If you don't keep your head in gear your car will overtake it. MIKA HAKKINEN

Above: In Japan, Hakkinen won both the race and the championships, for himself and McLaren.

Any time someone new comes up against the establishment, it pisses some people off. Having people against you makes it more fun when you win. JACQUES VILLENEUVE

Goodyear's withdrawal left Bridgestone with a tyre monopoly in 1999, so now it would be much easier to judge Ferrari's performance against that of McLaren. There were no driver changes in the two top teams but, at Williams, Ralf Schumacher joined from Jordan and Alex Zanardi returned to Formula 1 from a successful American foray in ChampCar racing. Heinz-Harald Frentzen went to Jordan alongside Damon Hill, but the biggest development was the appearance of a brand new team. After a year as the low-key owner of Tyrrell, British American Racing hit the scene with a huge media splash.

JACQUES VILLENEUVE: "We're aiming very high with our goals, considering the team was only organised a few months ago. You've got to aim high if you want to win, and that's what we plan to do. The only reason you go racing is to win."

7 MARCH 1999 - AUSTRALIAN GP (MELBOURNE) Mika Hakkinen began his title defence with the pole, and McLaren's prospects looked even better when Michael Schumacher had a problem on the grid and had to start from the back. However, the tables were soon turned. Both Hakkinen and David Coulthard were forced out with mechanical problems, and Ferrari's Eddie Irvine secured his maiden win.

EDDIE IRVINE: "In the second part of the race, I just cruised. Michael did a lot of pre-season testing for me, which made the car reliable. Hats off to him, he did a good job! Last year I did all the tyre testing which helped close the gap to McLaren, and he got all the victories, so this year the roles are reversed."

JOHN WATSON: "It's very difficult being in Eddie's position at Ferrari. He's got to put up with tremendous pressures. Today he gave his answer in the most emphatic way he can. He won a Grand Prix with one of the finest drives I've ever seen. He never put a wheel wrong."

2 MAY 1999 - SAN MARINO GP (IMOLA) Before Imola, the Formula 1 circus was rocked by the sudden death of Harvey Postlethwaite, one of its most accomplished engineers, who had been busy trying to put together a Honda project that would subsequently be aborted.

As in Brazil, McLaren was on top in qualifying but, to the delight of the *tifosi*, Hakkinen lost concentration and crashed out, and then Schumacher beat Coulthard with an aggressive drive and a two-stop strategy.

27 JUNE 1999 - FRENCH GP (MAGNY-COURS) If Formula 1 needed a break from the domination by Ferrari and McLaren, Magny-Cours certainly brought something quite different. After a wet qualifying session, Rubens Barrichello's Stewart found itself on pole ahead of Jean Alesi's Sauber and the Prost of Olivier Panis. More rain during the race led to a brilliant strategic victory for Frentzen.

But his Jordan team mate, having been underperforming all season, announced that 1999 would be his last year in Formula 1.

DAMON HILL: "There has to be a time when we all stop. There's a finite limit. There's only so much toothpaste in a tube and, when you get to the very bottom, it gets very difficult to get the last bit out. That's a good analogy. I've said before that if I wasn't enjoying it and I didn't think I could be competitive, then it would be time to stop. Those two criteria were met this year. Maybe making this announcement now will give me a breathing space to enjoy what's left of the season."

JACKIE STEWART: "I don't know when Damon is retiring, and I don't think Damon knows. It's a difficult decision for a driver, but you can't be a bit pregnant. You're either retiring, or you're not. I think it's time for Damon to retire now. He should do his home race and then call it a day."

Hill *was* retiring but Irvine was coming on strong. The colourful Irishman's newfound status as a winner confounded his image as a Blarney Stone-kissing braggart. 'Motormouth' Irvine lived most of the time on board his 30-metre yacht, the *Anaconda*, cruising the Mediterranean with a crew that featured a retinue of bikini-clad beauties. But the fun-loving 33-year-old bachelor could hold his own in a Ferrari, as the team's shrewd technical director pointed out.

ROSS BRAWN: "People get the impression that Eddie is a playboy driver, but he is actually very serious and it is no surprise to see how far he has come along. When he joined us he wasn't as fast as Michael, but he has learned Michael's sense of commitment and how to get the best out of his car. He has a marvellous way of divorcing himself from everything and getting on with the job."

Irvine now found himself an internationally popular figure with the fans.

EDDIE IRVINE: "Even though I'm hardly ever there I get loads of mail sent to my house in Dublin. It comes from every country you can think of. Lots from Italy, naturally, and even more from Germany, which is surprising when you consider Michael is their hero. Most of the mail is just addressed to 'Eddie Irvine, Ireland'. It still arrives on my doorstep."

> When I started racing, there were guys mouthing off that I would never make it as long as I had a hole in my arse. Well, they got that bit wrong. The hole's still there and here I am at the top.
>
> EDDIE IRVINE

11 JULY 1999 - BRITISH GP (SILVERSTONE) Hakkinen now led Schumacher by 40 points to 32, and they qualified first and second in that order at Silverstone. But the Ferrari made a poor start. As Schumacher tried to make up ground on the first lap, he speared off the road at Stowe corner, and hit the tyre wall with a sickening thud. It was immediately obvious that this was serious, and the race was red-flagged.

After the restart, Coulthard won from Irvine, while a lost wheel proved expensive for Hakkinen. After an operation for a broken tibia and fibula in his right leg, Schumacher was expected to be out of action for at least six weeks. His surprise replacement had earlier subbed for an injured Ricardo Zonta at BAR, but was still without a permanent drive.

MIKA SALO: "On Sunday I was at London Heathrow, just leaving for Helsinki. I saw the start of the race on TV in the departure lounge, and then I had to go to the plane. On Monday morning my manager called me and said, 'Pack up your stuff, go to the airport. You have a flight to Bologna in one hour.' I didn't have time to pack anything! I just took a pair of jeans and T-shirt and left. I didn't really believe it. When I landed, somebody from Ferrari was there to meet me, and it was only then I was sure it wasn't a joke."

The points table now read Hakkinen 40, Schumacher and Irvine 32. Irvine had the chance of a lifetime.

EDDIE IRVINE: "All of a sudden, I wasn't just there just to bring back a few points. Normally my job was to beat Coulthard, and suddenly my job was to beat Hakkinen. Trying to beat such a good driver in a quicker car is not what most people would want as a job! It was a big challenge."

25 JULY 1999 - AUSTRIAN GP (A1-RING) Against all the odds, Irvine scored a brilliant win in Austria, albeit with involuntary assistance from Coulthard, who punted Hakkinen into a spin at the second corner.

BERNIE ECCLESTONE: "The beautiful thing about Formula 1 is its unpredictability. Who would have foreseen Eddie Irvine winning in Austria? I would certainly never have put my money on him. Now we'll have to see if Eddie is as good as he thinks he is."

1 AUGUST 1999 - GERMAN GP (HOCKENHEIM) Hakkinen non-finished at Hockenheim, and Irvine won again, thanks to his stand-in team mate. After an exceptional drive, Salo was ordered to move over by Ferrari.

MIKA SALO: "I'm so happy with the best result of my Formula 1 career. When I saw 'P1' on my pit board, I couldn't believe it. I was happy to let Eddie past, because this is a team effort. When I asked Michael Schumacher how to approach this job, he told me: 'Just drive the car and Ferrari will do the rest.' He was right."

Irvine now found himself leading Hakkinen 52-44.

EDDIE IRVINE: "Now I have to start thinking like a title contender!"

15 AUGUST 1999 - HUNGARIAN GP (BUDAPEST) But McLaren quickly struck back. Both Hakkinen and Coulthard headed Irvine home in Hungary.

29 AUGUST 1999 - BELGIAN GP (SPA) While the tense race for the titles occupied most of the attention, the well-funded BAR team was battling with the tiny Minardi outfit at the back of the pack.

CRAIG POLLOCK: "We had huge expectations at the start of the season, and we've under-achieved hugely since then. With zero points and almost zero finishes [four], it's been a huge disappointment. It's been a season of hard lessons learned."

At Spa, however, Villeneuve's pride got the better of him again, and he had another massive accident at Eau Rouge - and so did his BAR team mate, Ricardo Zonta. Neither was injured but the cars were destroyed.

JACQUES VILLENEUVE: "Pretty much the same as last year - I tried to take Eau Rouge flat, and it didn't work. I think the impact was smaller this time. But I rolled, so that was a bonus. But maybe Ricardo's accident was more impressive to look at…"

The race was won by Coulthard, who forced his way past Hakkinen at the start, causing some to wonder about McLaren's wisdom in not issuing team orders. However, Ferrari's team orders incensed the Williams technical director.

PATRICK HEAD: "Unfortunately, Ralf fell foul of Ferrari's cynical approach of running a one-car team, with a blocking tactic to protect Irvine's position. I'm very surprised that Mika Salo was prepared to accept such orders from the pits. Ferrari has been doing this for the last number of years, and I have to say that I very much appreciate the more sporting approach of McLaren in running a two-car team. They'll thoroughly deserve the drivers' and constructors' championships which I fervently hope they'll achieve this year."

> I was with Michael within 85 seconds of the accident. When I arrived, he said, 'Hello Sid, it's just my leg, not a big problem.' So we got him out of the car and laid him down. I checked his neck, and it was OK. I splinted his right leg, because it was obviously broken - you could see the angle of deformation in the shin. PROFESSOR SID WATKINS

Opposite: Michael Schumacher's chances of becoming Ferrari's first champion since 1979 ended with rear brake failure at Silverstone's Stowe corner.

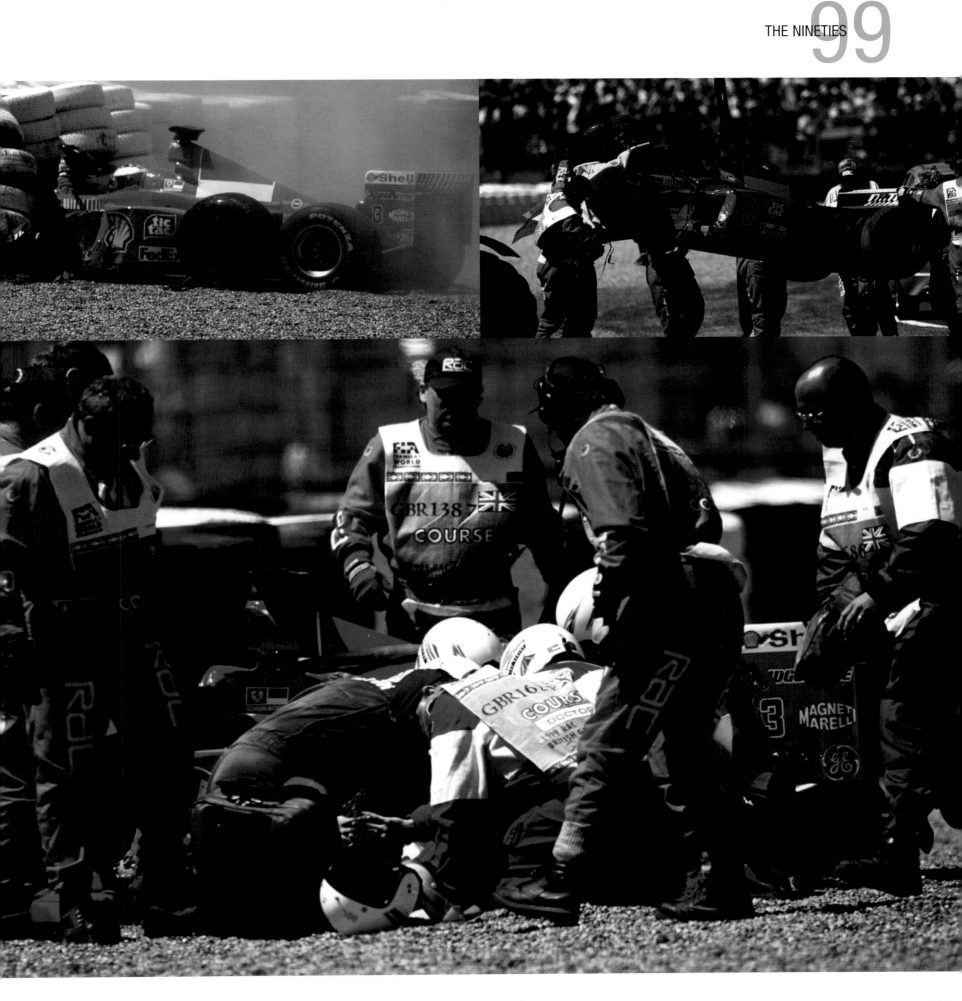

12 SEPTEMBER 1999 - ITALIAN GP (MONZA) It was now Irvine 56, Hakkinen 54. McLaren's contender established a lead at Monza, but crashed out of the race. He jumped out of his car and wept at the trackside, in view of the TV cameras.

ERJA HAKKINEN: "It was a terrible moment for Mika, but in a way I also felt relieved, because I don't like this picture which is sometimes given about Formula 1 drivers that they are cold people, like robots. I think Mika did the right thing. For once he shared his feelings with the fans, and I think that brought him closer to them. Mika's mental power is coming from mistakes, but he told me that he had never made such a mistake as this, even when he was a child in karts. He will react, and make himself better for the next race."

Hakkinen was fortunate that, as Frentzen came through to win, Irvine could finish only sixth.

26 SEPTEMBER 1999 - EUROPEAN GP (NÜRBURGRING) The most spectacular race of the season was a matter of surviving the hazards caused by two separate rain showers. These left only nine of the 22 starters still on the Nürburgring when the chequered flag flew.

Of the contenders, only Hakkinen scored. He staged a stirring comeback to fifth place after a wrong tyre choice by McLaren had sent him down the order. Those two hard-earned points gave him the lead in the championship. Among those he overtook was Irvine, whose seventh place was the result of badly timed tyre changes by Ferrari.

The star in the sodden circumstances was Johnny Herbert, who scored the first victory for Stewart Grand Prix after getting the tyre choice just right. His team mate, Rubens Barrichello was third (behind Jarno Trulli's Prost). On the podium, their team leader fervently embraced and kissed them both.

JACKIE STEWART: "This is undoubtedly the most important moment in my racing career. I've won 27 Grands Prix and three World Championships, but to win as a constructor is the highest emotion imaginable."

JOHNNY HERBERT: "I must be honest - it was a surprise. People have asked which was better, this win or the first one, and I must say this one was much better. Lots of things are happening around it that have been very, very positive. It's much more emotional."

Hakkinen now led Irvine 62-60. Two races remained. And to make things interesting, Michael Schumacher was back for the first ever Malaysian Grand Prix at the new Sepang track.

17 OCTOBER 1999 - MALAYSIAN GP (SEPANG) Schumacher took pole and then allowed Irvine past, leaving Hakkinen a frustrated third. After the race, however, came news of the disqualification of both Ferraris for a minor infringement on the dimensions of their aerodynamic 'bargeboards'. That would have made Hakkinen champion on the spot, but inevitably Ferrari filed an appeal.

Amid much controversy, the FIA subsequently overturned the original decision of the Stewards. The Ferraris were reinstated, ensuring a showdown in Suzuka.

31 OCTOBER 1999 - JAPANESE GP (SUZUKA) Hakkinen's superlative reaction to the FIA's decision was to drive like a champion in Japan. He won the race from the front, putting the matter beyond doubt. Schumacher and Irvine followed him to the chequered flag to clinch the constructors' title for Ferrari.

MIKA HAKKINEN: "Brilliant! What a great English word to express how I feel. This was one of my best races, after my hardest season, and I shall never forget it. To have won the championship in the last race is nerve-wracking. It's an experience that I can't recommend to anyone!"

EDDIE IRVINE: "I have to say Mika did a fantastic job. He deserved the title and he won it in style. At least Ferrari has a consolation prize - the constructors' championship. It is my leaving present for the team."

Above: Jackie Stewart, Johnny Herbert and Paul Stewart celebrate Stewart Grand Prix's first win.
Opposite: Ron Dennis hugs Hakkinen following the Finn's second successive title triumph.

After coming so close to the title, Irvine was transferring to Stewart, which had been purchased outright by Ford and would be rebadged for Jaguar in 2000.

EDDIE IRVINE: "Never winning the championship must be a massive cross for any driver to bear, especially when you have been so close. But you've got to forget about it, and just recharge the batteries, and then get stuck in next season."

Suzuka 1999 was the last Grand Prix for the 1996 World Champion, who had been totally overshadowed by his Jordan team mate.

DAMON HILL: "I'm disappointed I couldn't have done better, but I must say that I've succeeded in everything I've wanted to achieve in Formula 1. There's absolutely no doubt in my mind - I never want to do a Grand Prix again."

So many people misunderstand so many aspects of Mika. His very occasional mental fatigue can't detract from the discipline that he brings to his racing. Suzuka was a complete demonstration of this discipline. He is the iceman. RON DENNIS

The New Millennium

Formula 1 gathered momentum, racing faster than ever around the world in front of an increasing international audience. In a throwback to earlier times, more automobile manufacturers formed alliances with teams. Ford bought Stewart and renamed it Jaguar. Mercedes continued to supply engines to McLaren, Renault returned with Benetton, BMW with Williams and Honda supplied powerplants to BAR and Jordan. Michelin's comeback meant a tyre war with Bridgestone, while the return of previously banned computer-managed launch and traction control devices made it easier for the drivers, but harder for the purists. And, led by a masterful Michael Schumacher, Ferrari dominated as never before in its long history.

With Michael Schumacher rested and fully fit, it was arguable that Ferrari had the momentum going into the new millennium. The Italian team had recruited Rubens Barrichello, who swapped places with Irvine. Meanwhile Williams, preparing for its first season with BMW power, replaced the disappointing Alex Zanardi with Jenson Button, who had only just turned 20 and was extremely inexperienced. His extremely experienced boss still loved the sport.

FRANK WILLIAMS: "I just love Formula 1. I love the noise. I love watching the cars, even the slower ones. When a car is on the limit, it's pure pleasure. When drivers go out on the track, especially a wet track, with 800bhp behind them, I simply shake my head, because I still don't understand how they do it. They might be pains in the backside out of the car but, behind the wheel, they're heroes."

12 MARCH 2000 - AUSTRALIAN GP (MELBOURNE) The McLarens started their campaign from the front row, but both were stopped early by engine failures. That left Michael Schumacher free to lead his new team mate to the flag. While Ralf Schumacher brought Williams a surprise third place on BMW's debut, Jacques Villeneuve finally gave BAR its first points with fourth place.

MICHAEL SCHUMACHER: "When I got in my new car, I immediately felt this is the car I'm going to win with. Now I've proved that it's reliable as well as being bloody fast. It's so good, I almost feel sorry for our opposition."

RON DENNIS: "We outqualified them! And we were leading the race comfortably before our problems. There's no question they have a good car, but to have the arrogance to tell the world how wonderful you are is just a waste of time."

Dennis also implied that Ferrari had forced Barrichello to make an extra pitstop to ensure that Schumacher would win.

ROSS BRAWN: "Ron is talking a load of nonsense. Our record shows we have a better grasp of what goes on in races than he does. I can only assume he's upset about the performance of his cars and he's become a bit irrational."

26 MARCH 2000 - BRAZILIAN GP (INTERLAGOS) A familiar story in Brazil: the McLarens quickest in qualifying, Ferrari turning it around on race day. Schumacher's two-stop strategy did not appear to be working, but Hakkinen's retirement left him ahead. And then he made it three in a row.

23 APRIL 2000 - BRITISH GP (SILVERSTONE) Because of calendar congestion, the British race was moved to the Easter weekend in April. Rain and waterlogged car parks caused traffic chaos and a scandal in the national media. Barrichello took his first pole for Ferrari in a rain-affected qualifying session, but the race victor was David Coulthard. Perceived as having a bland personality, he drove brilliantly to win his home race, after which he partied late into the night.

DAVID COULTHARD: "My salary is paid by McLaren and Mercedes, two very big companies. I'm paid to develop a racing car that will improve their products, and help their image by winning races. I'm not paid to juggle four balls while singing some weird song backwards."

Top right: Soon after David Coulthard and his girlfriend Heidi celebrated his home win at Silverstone they miraculously survived a tragic plane crash in France.
Opposite: In a see-saw season Hakkinen found himself having to defend his title against Coulthard and Schumacher.

Coulthard's post-race joy was short-lived. The following week, he was in a horrific private plane crash in France, in which the two pilots were killed. Along with his girlfriend, Heidi Wichlinski, and his trainer, Andy Mathews, he had a miraculous escape.

DAVID COULTHARD: "We had time to prepare ourselves in the brace position prior to landing. On impact, the wing tanks ruptured and there was a fire on the right-hand side of the aircraft. When it finally came to rest, the front of the cockpit had broken free from the main fuselage. The only way out was through the front of the aircraft. Andy led the way through the debris and, as part of the plane was now three feet off the ground, I followed Andy so we could help Heidi out. Once we were all clear, I returned to the wreckage to see if there was anything I could do for the pilots. But there was nothing to be done."

7 MAY 2000 - SPANISH GP (BARCELONA) In Barcelona, Hakkinen won and Coulthard, remarkably, was second, despite the trauma of the plane crash and the pain from cracked ribs.

The race featured a close fight for fourth place between Ralf and Michael Schumacher. The latter's Ferrari, crippled by a punctured tyre at the time, seemed to push his younger brother's Williams out of the way, enabling Barrichello's Ferrari to finish third.

RALF SCHUMACHER: "What Michael did was completely senseless."

MICHAEL SCHUMACHER: "I can't help it if he's angry with me. Racing is racing. I'm not giving anyone any favours, including my brother. If he doesn't understand that, then hard luck."

Driving is the most important thing for me. I'll be a stronger person now. It's like when I had my first proper shunt in a racing car, at a Silverstone test, years ago. Until that happened, I was nervous of the unknown. DAVID COULTHARD

FRANK WILLIAMS: "We decided to take Ralf on the basis that he'd had several years of learning, crashing and banging and going over the limit. When he stayed on the track, he was very quick, and we felt he might just have turned the corner. That's how it's worked out. But he's a hard-headed bugger. Self-willed. He could be as good as his brother some day."

In Barcelona, those of a literary bent recalled that Ernest Hemingway, a noted *aficionado* of all things Spanish, had written that there were only three real sports - bullfighting, mountaineering and motor racing – and that all the rest were merely games. The author's romantic view was not shared by everyone.

EDDIE IRVINE: "I'm not really into the romance of it all. A car is a steering wheel, four wheels, two wings and an engine. Formula 1 is about physics. It's about the amount of load on the car, the amount of grip from the tyres, the amount of fuel in it. Driver ability comes into the equation as well, but it's an exercise in physics which takes the mystery and spontaneity out of the sport."

In the paddock in Barcelona, Irvine's Jaguar Racing lost its mascot. An enormous, chrome-plated, carbonfibre replica of a jungle cat, which had adorned the top of Jaguar's monstrous motorhome, suddenly disappeared. The person who was responsible for its banishment explained why it had to go.

BERNIE ECCLESTONE: "Jaguar would have started a silly trend. First thing you'd know, Peugeot would be wanting a lion. Then you'd get Ferrari wanting a donkey, or whatever that thing is on the side of their cars. Before long, the paddock would be looking like a bloody zoo."

21 MAY 2000 - EUROPEAN GP (NÜRBURGRING) When Coulthard took pole, less than three weeks after the air crash, he was given a standing ovation at the press conference. He finished third in the wet race, behind Hakkinen and the home-grown winner.

MICHAEL SCHUMACHER: "This victory ranks very high. It's one of the best days of my life, because it is the first time I've won in Germany with Ferrari. I've seen my fans standing here for three days in this bad weather and I hope this has warmed their hearts."

4 JUNE 2000 - MONACO GP (MONTE CARLO) The pendulum swung again in Monte Carlo. What looked like an easy win for Schumacher came to nothing when a broken exhaust overheated the rear suspension and caused it to fail.

DAVID COULTHARD: "I've always said there was a handful of races I wanted to win, and this completes a personal grand slam. Spa, because it's my favourite track. Silverstone, because it's my home race. Monza, because there's nothing quite like an Italian crowd. And here, because it's technically one of the most difficult tracks."

Above: When Hakkinen wasn't fighting Schumacher, his McLaren team mate took up the cudgels.

Below: Having had the door slammed in his face by Schumacher's Ferrari, Coulthard again tried to prise it open with his McLaren. His overtaking manouevre (overleaf) was accomplished one-handed, the other being employed making a rude gesture.

2 JULY 2000 - FRENCH GP (MAGNY-COURS) After a nightmare experience in Canada, where it rained, Coulthard emerged triumphant in France in a torrid struggle with Michael Schumacher in exceptionally high temperatures. Controversial starting tactics, which were now increasingly being used from pole position by Schumacher, raised extra heat in the McLaren cockpit.

Thus fired-up, Coulthard channelled his ire into impressive aggression. First he decisively overtook Barrichello, who had slipped into second place when Coulthard backed off. Then he disposed of the race-leading Ferrari with a pass in which the wheels of their cars were briefly intertwined. As he completed the move, he aimed an impolite, one-finger salute in his adversary's direction.

DAVID COULTHARD: "I have to apologize for the gesture, which was not at all in keeping with the sport. But my emotions were running high. I was very angry."

16 AUGUST 2000 - AUSTRIAN GP (A-1 RING) The milestone of Coulthard's 100th Grand Prix was marked by McLaren with the release of some statistics. Since his debut in 1994, 'DC' had raced 29,608km in 5971 race laps, using about 790 tyres, which, if stacked, would measure as high as the Eiffel Tower (321m). He had gone through 300 race suits, 90 pairs of boots, 250 pairs of gloves and 45 helmets. But he had used only one pair of 'lucky' underpants, given to him by his grandmother,

perhaps to protect him whenever involved in the infamous road-hogging tactics of his 'villainous' championship rival.

JACQUES VILLENEUVE: "It's always the same person doing it. But he always gets away with it, so why should he stop? The drivers don't have any power to stop him, so it doesn't really matter what we say or think."

MAX MOSLEY: "It's what the lawyers would call a question of fact and degree. The real question is to decide at which point you say, 'You can do this, but you can't do that.' I understand the problem up to a point, but in this case you would have to say that, ultimately, it didn't do much harm to the French Grand Prix. Against all conventional wisdom, Coulthard caught and passed Schumacher to win that race."

In Austria, Schumacher was punted out in a mêlée at the start. Hakkinen and Coulthard were able to score an unchallenged 1-2. With more and more examples of wild driving, some critics noted how things differed from the old days.

HEINZ-HARALD FRENTZEN: "Compared with the old heroes, today's racing drivers are real cissies. On the one hand, we're driving more on the limit. On the other, the drivers in the past drove without the levels of safety we have today. If they had driven as close to the extreme as we do now, deaths would not only have been one or two a year, but a couple every race."

30 JULY 2000 - GERMAN GP (HOCKENHEIM) MICHAEL SCHUMACHER: "Is this Formula 1, or is it drinking coffee in a happy family situation? In my view, we're racing in a very hard and fair way. Nothing else. If the rules allow us to fight like this, then that's how we'll fight."

Incredibly, at the start of his home race, Schumacher again lost out at the first corner. From pole, Coulthard's McLaren appeared to zig-zag in front of the Ferrari, which was promptly rammed out of the race by Fisichella's Benetton. Many onlookers thought the swerve was deliberate.

JACQUES VILLENEUVE: "David's start was not acceptable. He only did it to repay Michael. If this is acceptable, we're all going to start doing it."

MICHAEL SCHUMACHER: "I'm a tough racing driver, but I'm no Rambo. This is two races in a row that I was pushed off the track."

More drama ensued. First, a spectator invaded the track, wielding a protest banner and triggering a Safety Car. Then it rained.

HOCKENHEIM STATEMENT: "The person who invaded and crossed the track is a 47-year-old Frenchman. The police reported the person had cut his way through the fence near the Jim Clark chicane. According to his own words, he wanted to protest against his dismissal by Mercedes-Benz. The man is in custody."

Barrichello made an inspired decision to stay out in drizzle on dry-weather tyres. He scored a popular and emotional maiden victory, after eight years and 123 races.

RUBENS BARRICHELLO: "This win has been a long time coming. I dedicate it to Ayrton Senna, my fellow Brazilian who helped me so much and inspired me until his death. I'm racing in a really competitive team, which is focused on Michael to win, but is not forgetting me. I say Michael is the present, and I'm the future."

13 AUGUST 2000 - HUNGARIAN GP (BUDAPEST) The Hungarian weekend began with an escalation of the controversy over swerving at the starts.

JEAN ALESI: "These disagreements belong in kindergarten. I remember when Ayrton Senna went to see Eddie Irvine [Japan 1993]. Irvine cut him off in the race. They argued. Ayrton punched him in the nose. That was more like real motor racing."

In the Grand Prix, Hakkinen won memorably from Schumacher and Coulthard.

MIKA HAKKINEN: "This circuit is all about the start. I went side-by-side with Michael into the first corner and we didn't touch. So it was very pleasant racing."

Hakkinen now led Schumacher 64-62, marking a remarkable turnaround, while the see-saw constructors' battle was 112-111 in McLaren's favour.

27 AUGUST 2000 - BELGIAN GP (SPA) A superb battle between Hakkinen and Schumacher, who was beaten by a brilliant overtaking manoeuvre. Hakkinen's first passing attempt was rudely chopped but, on the next lap, he cleverly used Ricardo Zonta's lapped BAR to outwit his rival: the most exciting moment of the year.

Michael was within the rules. But once again I had to lift. It should be done in a sporting way - not in a 'You lift, otherwise you crash' way. DAVID COULTHARD

I've had good fights with Hakkinen, and he had no complaints. But Coulthard,

like Hill, always seems to find something to moan about. MICHAEL SCHUMACHER

MIKA HAKKINEN: "Three laps from the end, I knew I had to go for it. There was no point in trying again to overtake Michael at the end of the straight, because he obviously wouldn't have given me room."

RICARDO ZONTA: "I saw them coming up fast in my mirrors, so I stayed in the middle of the track to give them room. It was an amazing view."

MIKA HAKKINEN: "So I switched to Plan B, and went completely to the inside, overtaking the backmarker."

10 SEPTEMBER 2000 - ITALIAN GP (MONZA) The race at Monza in 2000 will be remembered for a tragic, multi-car accident on the first lap at the second chicane, which killed a track marshal, Paolo Ghislimberti. Much of what happened was obscured by smoke and dust, but everyone involved had a harrowing tale to tell.

RUBENS BARRICHELLO: "Frentzen braked too late and hit me, provoking an incident which involved a large number of cars."

HEINZ-HARALD FRENTZEN: "I was trying to overtake Barrichello and he braked early, so we collided. I also hit Jarno [Trulli, his Jordan team mate]. I'm lucky to have got away with a bruised knee."

JOHNNY HERBERT: "As we went into the second chicane, it was obvious something had happened. I could see wheels flying high up in the air and then de la Rosa went straight into the back of me."

PEDRO DE LA ROSA: "I saw the yellow flags, braked, then saw pieces of car flying, lots of tyre smoke and dust, cars spinning in front of me. I hit Zonta's rear wheel and was launched into the air and barrel-rolled until the car stopped upside down. I wouldn't say I was unlucky – I'm lucky still to be here."

JACQUES VILLENEUVE: "The death was very sad. It's bad when someone who's working to protect the lives of the drivers loses his own. But the accident was part of racing. What do people want? If they want us to be racers, then we're sometimes going to bang wheels. And things like this will happen. It's either a fighting with some risks, or a procession. Most people prefer to see hard racing."

The race ran for many laps under a Safety Car and, after the restart, Schumacher won easily. At the finish, tens of thousands of Ferrari fans flooded onto the circuit, ecstatic at his crucial victory for the home team. In the post-race press conference, he began sobbing uncontrollably.

MICHAEL SCHUMACHER: "Delighted is the wrong word... I've no vocabulary for anything to describe it. I'm just happy. I'm just exhausted..."

The second-place finisher, Hakkinen began patting his rival on the back before he also was momentarily overcome. Ralf Schumacher, third for Williams and also trying to console his distraught elder brother, had to do the talking until the top two regained their composure.

RON DENNIS: "I don't really understand where this emotion came from. But it was obviously genuine and the other two felt Michael's discomfort. I'm not surprised with anybody showing such emotion. When you have success in difficult circumstances, sometimes the adrenaline which has controlled your emotions suddenly isn't there any more, and everything floods over you."

MICHAEL SCHUMACHER: "We're here in Italy. We obviously were in some difficulty in the last few races and now we're back on the road. The reaction of the *tifosi* was just amazing. It's... I don't know why, but it's simply a lot more... It came a lot more close to me... And it's different... It's difficult to put into words."

After the Monza tragedy, the FIA mandated stronger tethers in a bid to prevent wheels flying off the cars during impact accidents.

Above: A track marshal was killed in a frightening accident at Monza, where race-winner Schumacher was overcome with emotion.
Opposite: Ferrari's Ross Brawn (technical director), Michael Schumacher, Jean Todt (team manager) and Rubens Barrichello celebrate.

24 SEPTEMBER 2000 - US GP (INDIANAPOLIS) The first US Grand Prix since 1991 was staged on a new, purpose-built road course within the Indianapolis Motor Speedway. By bringing its act to America's hallowed shrine of speed, the Formula 1 circus invited comparisons with the American racing heroes who strutted their stuff on the big oval. One of the heroes of NASCAR happened to be a Formula 1 fan.

JEFF BURTON: "What American race fans like to see is competitive spirit. They like to see emotion, they enjoy it when drivers don't like each other, they love it when the teams have rivalries. To capture the American fans, the drivers just have to be themselves. But the really cool thing about Formula 1 is how technical it is compared to what we do. The American fans need to look at that aspect of it."

RON DENNIS: "The big difference between us running here and other categories of racing is the engine note. That's the bit that still gives me a tingle.

When you hear an engine at 18,000 revs in a relatively confined space, such as we have here in front of the pits, that's what it's all about. Fabulous!"

The weekend was a huge success, and rain on race day helped to create an intriguing race in which the timing of tyre stops was crucial. As usual, Schumacher got it right, although a late spin - when under no pressure - gave him a fright. There was a blown engine for Hakkinen and a jump-start penalty for Coulthard. The victor received a tumultuous reception from 250,000 spectators.

MICHAEL SCHUMACHER: "This is truly amazing. We saw it already on Friday when it was an unusually big crowd, and the crowd got bigger every day. I was wondering whether people would be satisfied with what they saw. But it seems we've put on a good show for them."

8 OCTOBER 2000 - JAPANESE GP (SUZUKA) Ferrari had twice lost the title in Suzuka, but this time there was no mistake. Schumacher beat Hakkinen in a furious, closely fought race as they both left their team mates far behind.

MICHAEL SCHUMACHER: "It's difficult to find the words to describe how it feels. It's similar to Monza, but don't expect me to cry! I did feel an outbreak of emotion as I crossed the finish line. This championship is more special than the others because it's with Ferrari, 21 years after it last happened for the team. We've been working so hard for this for my five years here. Imagine what's happening in Italy right now!"

MIKA HAKKINEN: "We've had a great battle this year and it's been very exciting. To be a good winner, you have to be a good loser. Now this is Michael's moment."

22 OCTOBER 2000 - MALAYSIAN GP (SEPANG) The constructors' title was not settled until Malaysia, where a fourth straight Schumacher victory gave it to Ferrari for the second year in a row. To mark the occasion, he joined many of the team members in wearing a bizarre, red wig.

MICHAEL SCHUMACHER: "We wanted to win the constructors' championship for Ferrari, and we've done it, not just by getting three points, but by finishing first and third. We're the best team in the world! After we've packed up, we'll have a big, big party, and then we can have a holiday, which everybody deserves."

CORINNA SCHUMACHER: "Michael is on top of the world. Michael is my man."

I think nature is the most beautiful thing we have and the colour I like most is green, which is related to nature. I love animals and might even like to have a farm some day.

MICHAEL SCHUMACHER

Age for age, experience for experience, Michael Schumacher is the best Grand Prix driver I have ever seen. I have watched Michael walk out to his car on qualifying days and it is one of the most thrilling sights in Formula 1. There is an air of certainty about him, and he is like a fighting cock who has won countless bouts. At Monza one afternoon, when he slipped into the cockpit, it looked as if he was entering his natural habitat and he made an entirely convincing picture. I thought to myself, 'He's really got it on' and, sure enough, Michael went out and seized pole position as if it was the easiest thing in the world. JACKIE STEWART

MICHAEL SCHUMACHER: "This is the worst thing, that people tell stories about me which are not true. A good example is that they say I am a cold person without any feelings. Ayrton Senna had to go through the same thing. It seems this is part of the procedure.

"Journalists use a few minutes of my time, ask me about my car's set up or something, then go away and try to make a complete picture of me and they often get it wrong. The story they get depends on which mood I am in, which time they get me. I can be free and relaxed but sometimes I am thinking about my car and I am not as free to concentrate on other questions. There is a big difference between the Michael Schumacher on a racing weekend and the private Michael Schumacher. You just wish the journalists had a little more understanding. These people don't really know the personal side of Michael Schumacher, they only see the business side and while I might be labelled as introverted, or arrogant, or both, it is merely a form of protection to stop people taking advantage of me.

"The first time I met Corinna I knew immediately she was the girl I would marry. The greatest pleasure I have is when I wake up in the morning and she smiles at me, and then we look at the kids and come together as a family. These are the times when I am happiest, and for those folk who write nasty things about me, well, what can I do?

"I didn't come from a rich family, and when I hear that I am supposed to be some kind of Superman I just laugh. Honestly, if you believe you know it all you will never get any better, and that means you will always go backwards, so I can't afford to take the hype seriously.

"As for being famous, it's difficult for me to think of myself in that manner and it doesn't mean a great deal to me. I'm not happy about it because it means the loss of the privacy I cherish. But I also appreciate that I have an added responsibility to those Ferrari fans who watch me race.

"Every human being makes mistakes and I am no exception to the rule. I've had many doubts at various times in my career - moments when I have wondered if I was doing something right, or whether I could have handled it better.

"There is one particular country, which is England, which struggles with me, but I think it is part of history. They have always struggled with Germans, to be honest. And me fighting against British drivers makes it even more complicated, so there's always this extra intrigue which doesn't bring over the real Michael Schumacher.

"There are 22 drivers and you get along better with some than with others. If you are a German and not getting on well with a person like Damon Hill, who is obviously favoured by the English press, then you always take the short stick.

"Formula 1 is so intense that you go through as much in one year as a normal person does in ten years. At first, so much was happening to me so soon that it was difficult for me to know who I was. You are always under such pressure and tension. This is especially true in the beginning. Later on, things change less. Personally, I'm not sure if Formula 1 has changed me much. It was difficult at first because I didn't have the chance to be relaxed. I always tried to hide myself and didn't want to cause any trouble because I didn't really understand everything that was happening. Now I can be more open because I am getting a clearer picture about Formula 1.

"When you are younger you think a nice car might fulfil your dream. When you have the car you find out very early it doesn't fulfil anything, really. It may be nice to drive, but that's it. What's around us fulfils my dreams. I am very interested in space, the moon and stars and everything around us. I can be happy just sitting watching the moonlight."

The greatest pleasure I have is when I wake up in the morning and Corinna smiles at me, and then we look at the kids and come together as a family.

MICHAEL SCHUMACHER

When Michael crashed at Silverstone in 1999 he asked me to phone his wife Corinna and tell her not to worry. A couple of days later he called me from his hospital bed and thanked me for all I'd done. **He gets so much adverse press, but I find him to be a thoroughly decent guy.** PROFESSOR SID WATKINS

If Ferrari was still the team to beat going into the 2001 season, most expected McLaren to hit back hard.

MIKA HAKKINEN: "There's no pressure. Now I don't have to defend my title - I can go hunting again and try to get it back."

Part of the latest effort by Williams to get on terms with Ferrari and McLaren was to sign ChampCar star Juan Pablo Montoya. It remained to be seen how he would work with Ralf Schumacher.

PATRICK HEAD: "There may be friction, fireworks even, but a team works best when two drivers work together. I don't mean by one being totally subjugated to the other. Mansell and Piquet didn't get on at all - they were like oil and water. The same with Jones and Reutemann. But they each had a respect for the other, and if one tested something and found it was better, then the other said, 'OK, I'll try it.' I hope Ralf and Juan have that."

FRANK WILLIAMS: "Juan is very exciting. Superb car control. Good to watch, a bit like a marching army coming down the pass. But he's short of Formula 1 experience, and that matters, because the cars are very complex. When he acquires the experience, Juan will be very, very good."

Williams would be using Michelin tyres, as the French company returned for the first time since 1984, also adding to its roster Benetton, Jaguar, Prost and Minardi. The little Italian team was taken over by Australian-born businessman Paul Stoddart shortly before the start of the season.

GIANCARLO MINARDI: "Our financial problem is like an atomic bomb - it mushrooms. Pizza, wine, ham - no money. That's the perception of Minardi."

PAUL STODDART: "Teams with budgets of hundreds of millions of dollars will beat us. But we'll be one of the most motivated teams in Formula 1. We'll also be the most friendly."

Among other changes, Prost split with Peugeot and joined Sauber in paying for Ferrari 'customer' engines, while Peugeot sold off its race engine operation to Asiatech, which joined forces with Arrows. Jordan would share works Honda engines with BAR, whose star driver had not won a race since 1997, yet was as motivated as ever.

JACQUES VILLENEUVE: "It's the romance behind the driving, behind the racing. To go back home and know that you were the only one who went through a corner without lifting or without braking - or you had a huge sideways moment that you probably shouldn't have caught, and you caught it. That's the kind of pride that drives me in racing."

4 MARCH 2001 - AUSTRALIAN GP (MELBOURNE) Schumacher started his title defence by winning pole-to-flag in Albert Park, but the weekend was marred by another marshal fatality caused by a detached wheel, just a few months after Monza 2000 and despite the strengthened tethers. Standing by an access gap in the debris fencing, Graham Beveridge was struck by a wheel from Villeneuve's BAR after its violent collision with Ralf Schumacher's Williams.

JACQUES VILLENEUVE: "I had a fast car, very easy to drive, so I was expecting to overtake Ralf in that corner. He was in the middle of the track and I didn't know whether to go left or right. When I decided to go on the outside, he jumped on the brakes and I couldn't get out of the way. It hit very hard - a big, big one. I wasn't frightened at the time. Normally when you crash, you're spinning but you're looking in your mirrors, and you know where and how you're going to hit, so you prepare yourself. This time, once I was in the air, I couldn't see where I was going, I was just thinking that I might get very hurt. I was shaken up a bit and felt some nausea, maybe some shock. When I heard the marshal had been involved, it felt even worse."

1 APRIL 2001 - BRAZILIAN GP (INTERLAGOS) After a chaotic, wet race in Kuala Lumpur, Williams returned as a contender in Sao Paulo. Montoya pulled a memorable pass on Schumacher and led impressively until he was punted off the track by the lapped Arrows of Jos Verstappen. Later in the race, rainfall seemed tailor-made for another Schumacher success, but for once Ferrari got the setup wrong, and Coulthard could pass him to the win.

15 APRIL 2001 - SAN MARINO GP (IMOLA) After three 'flyaway' races the Formula 1 circus came back to Europe, where the Williams-BMW-Michelin package came good on the Autodromo Enzo e Dino Ferrari. On a bad day for Ferrari, Ralf Schumacher qualified third but jumped into the lead and stayed there for the duration to achieve his maiden victory.

RALF SCHUMACHER: "It's a great experience and I hope it will be the first of many. After I got away from David at the start, it was a pretty long race. It took ages, to be honest..."

DAVID COULTHARD: "In the first few laps, I thought Ralf must be on a five-stop strategy - he couldn't be that quick. Then reality started to sink in and I realised there was no way I was going to catch him."

RON DENNIS: "We hate to lose but, if we have to, we prefer that it's our good friends and competitors at Williams."

29 APRIL 2001 - SPANISH GP (BARCELONA) On the Circuit de Catalunya, Hakkinen was set for his first win of 2001 when his McLaren was stranded by a clutch malfunction on the very last lap. Michael Schumacher swept past him to win, followed by Montoya and Villeneuve, who scored BAR's first podium.

MICHAEL SCHUMACHER: "I told Mika I felt very sorry for him. He did a great job, it was a great race, a good battle, and it was a shame to see him losing like that."

Above: Michael Schumacher won in Melbourne, where an accident involving his brother Ralf and Jacques Villeneuve killed a track marshal.
Opposite: Brothers in arms. At Imola Michael welcomed Ralf to the family of winners.

This race was notable for the return of traction and launch control systems – 'driving aids' that had been banned in 1993 because it was felt that drivers, not computers, should be in control of the cars. It had been widely suspected that some teams had continued to use these illegal electronic devices, and the FIA admitted that it was powerless to stop them. The new Technical Regulations became necessary because the sophistication of modern computer technology made it almost impossible for the software scrutineers to detect illegalities.

JACQUES VILLENEUVE: "It's a shame, but it had to be done. Unfortunately, it's normal human behaviour to cheat. All the money in Formula 1 makes it difficult for some people to resist. It's not something I would ever do, even alone playing a computer game, because it would take the pleasure away from doing it."

NIKI LAUDA: "A monkey could drive these cars now. Maybe not quickly, but it would be possible."

13 MAY 2001 - AUSTRIAN GP (A1-RING) Hakkinen's nightmare continued when he failed to get off the line at Zeltweg, along with three other cars whose launch controls also malfunctioned. But Coulthard won, bringing McLaren some joy on the weekend when Paul Morgan - a partner in Ilmor, the company building the team's Mercedes-branded engines - was tragically killed in a vintage plane crash. Schumacher finished second, but only after Barrichello had been told to move over - delaying until the final corner before following team orders. This provoked a storm of outrage. Even in Italy, Ferrari was accused of making a mockery of fair play, cheating the public. Concerned about the image of Formula 1, big business became involved in the debate, as, for example, the chairman of DaimlerChrysler, the 40% owner of McLaren and its engine supplier.

JURGEN HUBBERT: "If you castrate the sport, one day it is not going to be interesting any more. It's a shame that someone who runs a fantastic race doesn't get what they deserve. We see things differently from Ferrari."

JACQUES VILLENEUVE: "The team has always been built around Michael. It is in Barrichello's contract to let him win. Everybody knows that. Barrichello knows, Michael knows, the fans know, the media know. Why is anybody surprised?"

MICHAEL SCHUMACHER: "As long as we're not breaking the rules, then it's fair. A lot of things are involved in this sport - a lot of money, a lot of pressure - and all that counts in the end is the championship, to be honest."

Ralf did it in style. This is the first time that two brothers have won Formula 1 races. Our parents will be very proud.

MICHAEL SCHUMACHER

27 MAY 2001 - MONACO GP (MONTE CARLO) On the narrow streets of Monte Carlo, Coulthard took pole position with a brilliant lap on a circuit that had hardly changed since the very first race there, 72 years earlier.

It was all for nothing. On the formation lap, another launch control glitch stranded the poleman on the grid. That left Schumacher free to win for the fifth time in Monaco after an early pursuit by Hakkinen, whose season was still falling apart.

ADRIAN NEWEY: "Mika is very good at keeping himself motivated. He's very disappointed with his current position, but I think the hallmark of any great sportsman is to be able to put that behind them and just look forward."

10 JUNE 2001 - CANADIAN GP (MONTREAL) McLaren was never really in the hunt on the Ile Notre Dame. The Schumacher brothers dominated. Michael led most of the way but an ultra-late pitstop put Ralf ahead. Its 105th win proved that Williams was firmly a front-runner again. The team's 59-year-old leader had been knighted for his services to British industry.

SIR FRANK WILLIAMS: "When we've gone through bad patches, we've always bounced back. It's quite straightforward why we can do this. Without exception, everyone who works for us loves Formula 1. Most of them are nuts about it - they really adore what they do. They're highly paid, but the primary motivation is to win. And once you've got that under your belt - once it is burning away in your belly - the rest follows. You just push yourself and you arrive at your destination. Our people are extremely motivated."

1 JULY 2001 - FRENCH GP (MAGNY-COURS) But - temporarily, at least - Scuderia Ferrari put Williams and BMW in their place by winning two on the trot.

I'm very delighted about this. And I'll be much more delighted when I am retired, sitting one day on the sofa, with a cigar and a beer in my hands, thinking about it.

MICHAEL SCHUMACHER

15 JULY 2001 - BRITISH GP (SILVERSTONE)
EDDIE IRVINE: "Coulthard must kneel by his bedside, put his hands together and pray. Unless Michael Schumacher breaks another leg in the British Grand Prix, he can kiss goodbye to his World Championship dream. When I was Michael's team mate, it was like being hit over the head with a cricket bat every day. The guy is something else. He turns the steering wheel better, brakes better, accelerates better than anyone else. He simply has an innate ability to drive a car better than any of us."

Schumacher was second to Hakkinen, who finally won after a ten-month absence from the top step of the podium. Coulthard crashed on the first lap.

29 JULY 2001 - GERMAN GP (HOCKENHEIM) The race began with a heart-stopping accident at the start. Michael Schumacher's Ferrari slowed with a transmission malfunction and was struck by Luciano Burti's Prost, which cartwheeled to the first corner.

LUCIANO BURTI: "The car in front of me avoided Michael and, when I saw him, it was too late. The first impact, and then even when the car landed again, the whole thing was smooth, which really surprised me. Maybe because the car was destroying itself, it was absorbing the impacts. That shows us how safe the cars are now."

The race was red-flagged, and Michael got another chance - only to suffer a fuel pump failure. Montoya, from the pole, was well set for victory when an engine failure let in his team mate.

RALF SCHUMACHER: "It's been an unbelievable day and I'm very, very happy. It's just great for a German driver with a German engine to win the German Grand Prix."

Coulthard gained nothing from Michael's non-finish. He was stopped by an engine failure.

19 AUGUST 2001 - HUNGARIAN GP (BUDAPEST) Michael Schumacher won comfortably on the Hungaroring, with Barrichello and Coulthard chasing in vain. Apart from clinching the drivers' title and taking Ferrari to its third successive constructors' championship, the victory equalled Alain Prost's record of 51 Grand Prix successes.

ALAIN PROST: "I'm very happy for Michael, for winning his fourth championship and equalling my record. It's hard to say how far he can go, or how long. It's up to him. He could win 60 or 70 races and become five or six times the champion."

After jumping higher than ever on the podium, Schumacher sat down on the top step and led the ecstatic Ferrari team, and thousands of fans who had swarmed over the fences, in a rousing rendition of a Queen rock classic, 'We Are The Champions'.

DAVID COULTHARD: "Today is all about Michael. I congratulate him on his achievement and recommend he takes a holiday for the last four Grands Prix."

MICHAEL SCHUMACHER: "What makes it so fantastic is the team around Rubens and myself. You can't believe how wonderful these guys are, how much we stick together, in good times and especially in bad times."

2 SEPTEMBER 2001 - BELGIAN GP (SPA) In the Ardennes hills, the race was again stopped after an accident involving Burti, this time after his Prost had speared off the road following contact with Irvine's Jaguar. The blue car disappeared under the tyre wall, but amazingly the driver was not seriously hurt, although out for the season.

The restarted race was won by Michael Schumacher, whose fifth win here came on the 10th anniversary of his Formula 1 debut. Having won 52 times in his 158 Grands Prix, he was now the most successful Formula 1 driver in history.

DAVID COULTHARD: "I can't concern myself with whether Michael is making history, only whether I can beat him in a straight fight, which I've shown I can do. I have beaten him on level terms. Some day I may look back and consider myself unfortunate to have raced in the same era as Michael. For now I have to think he's beatable."

16 SEPTEMBER 2001 - ITALIAN GP (MONZA) Practice for the Italian Grand Prix came three days after the horrific terrorist attacks in America on September 11. The most eloquent summation of the sombre mood at Monza was given by Jordan driver Jarno Trulli, who received a standing ovation at a press conference.

JARNO TRULLI: "It's for sure a difficult weekend because we can all see what's happening in the USA. But it's not just a US tragedy. It is the whole world's tragedy. Normally, Formula 1 is a celebration, but there's nothing to celebrate here when we see what's happening elsewhere. We have to show to everybody that we are together with the USA, that we're all together in the whole world. Formula 1 is a sport and all sport is a way to show somehow that the whole world doesn't have to stop. We have to take care of what's happening but we can't stop. Otherwise the people who attacked the USA will have won their battle and we can't let this happen."

Ferrari ran its cars with black noses and no commercial logos, and several other cars carried American flags as a mark of respect.

The 1998-99 World Champion announced that he was going to take a sabbatical in 2002, having been feeling negatively about his profession for some time.

MIKA HAKKINEN: "It was a long and complicated process, and hard to understand why I was feeling the way I was. I've been involved in racing since I was six years old and in Formula 1 since 1991. This is a really tough business, and I've decided to take a break and recharge my batteries."

On Saturday, in qualifying, Hakkinen emerged unhurt from a frightening accident, so violent that the session was red-flagged while debris from his wrecked McLaren was removed. That same afternoon, former Grand Prix driver Alex Zanardi suffered a terrible accident and lost both legs in a ChampCar race in Germany. By Sunday, emotions were running high. Michael Schumacher attempted to get the drivers to agree to a 'no overtaking' policy for the first few corners, which led to a lot of confusion in the build-up to the race.

MICHAEL SCHUMACHER: "It's a weekend when everything is not right in the world, and we question whether we should even race. And also after what happened here last year, when a marshal was killed, we tried to have an agreement not to overtake in the first two chicanes on the first lap. One person didn't agree."

JACQUES VILLENEUVE: "I'm a professional racing driver and I get paid to race. We have to go flat out from the start and give 100% to the chequered flag. If Michael feels that strongly about it, then he shouldn't start at all."

In the event, the race passed without major drama, and Montoya scored his first Formula 1 win, ahead of Barrichello, Ralf Schumacher and a lacklustre Michael Schumacher. Then the Formula 1 circus decamped for America. Although there were fears about safety at the US Grand Prix, everyone felt a duty to go.

MAX MOSLEY: "Anyone who can help the victims of the American disaster should do so. Likewise, anyone who can help apprehend the perpetrators. The duty of the rest of us is to carry on as normal and to make no concessions to terrorism."

30 SEPTEMBER 2001 - US GP (INDIANAPOLIS)
EMERSON FITTIPALDI: "It's perfect for the race to be here at this time. It's a very special place in the history of motor sport and Indy is known around the world. America has to make a statement to the world, and this race will do that."

The race itself was a classic. After a penalty for an infringement in the warm-up had dropped him from second to fourth on the grid, Hakkinen drove beautifully to win from Michael Schumacher.

Veteran driver Jean Alesi scored a point for Jordan in his landmark 200th Grand Prix - and would announce his retirement shortly before starting his 201st.

14 OCTOBER 2001 - JAPANESE GP (SUZUKA) Michael Schumacher, the newly crowned World Champion, took pole by a massive margin with the qualifying performance of the season. He then made more history by dominating the race from lights to flag, thus extending the record for the total career points to 801, and his own record for points scored in a single season to 123.

Opposite: By the end of the season Schumacher had made 53 victory leaps on the podium, making him the most successful driver in history.
Above: Juan Pablo Montoya won at Monza, from where the Formula 1 circus travelled to Indianapolis, determined to help America defy international terrorism.

Our sport is a pure emotional sport, and we give joy to people.

It's not for nothing so many people follow Formula 1. MICHAEL SCHUMACHER

Cast of Characters

This section provides further information about some, though by no means all, of those who have performed in the Formula 1 circus over the years, ranging from legendary figures who have featured prominently in the history of the sport to some of the more influential or entertaining behind-the-scenes personalities. Further biographical information about many of those listed can be found in the main text of the book. The statistical data provided for each entry includes nationality, dates of birth (and, when relevant, death) where available - and for the drivers, their Formula 1 careers, including the years in which they drove for specific teams, the number of Grands Prix in which they competed and the number of GP wins. All information is complete to the end of the 2001 season.

MICHELE ALBORETO (I)

b. 23 December 1956 - d. 25 April 2001
F1 career: 81-83 - Tyrrell; 84-88 - Ferrari. 89 - Tyrrell, Larrousse; 90-92 - Footwork. 93 - BMS Scuderia Italia; 94 - Minardi, Scuderia Italia
GP starts: 194. **GP wins**: 5

The urbane and courteous son of a middle-class businessman, Alboreto (above) watched the 1969 Italian Grand Prix at the age of 12 and was hooked: "I was completely entranced by all I saw." On arriving in Formula 1, three productive seasons with Tyrrell earned him five with Ferrari. He won his third race in a red car, and instantly became an Italian hero. Skilful and stylish, he was unflappable as a driver, but tired of Ferrari polemics in 1989 and, after gracing lesser teams, ultimately left Formula 1 at the end of 1994, aged 38. But life to Alboreto was nothing without the race. He was testing a works Audi sports-prototype in Germany when a component failure cost him his life.

JEAN ALESI (F)

b. 11 June 1964
F1 career: 89-90 - Tyrrell; 91-95 - Ferrari; 96-97 - Benetton; 98-99 - Sauber; 00-01 - Prost, Jordan.
GP starts: 201. **GP wins**: 1

The French-Sicilian Alesi grew up with a lifesize poster of his hero Gilles Villeneuve in his bedroom. Like him, Alesi was energetic and explosive on track (though sometimes volatile off it) and his personal warmth and sheer enthusiasm for the sport made him a popular presence in the paddock for 13 years. Despite many flashes of brilliance and never-say-die commitment, his emotional win for Ferrari in the 1995 Canadian Grand Prix was his only victory, before he retired at the end of 2001 to tend his vineyard and play with his vintage car collection in Provence.

TYLER ALEXANDER (USA)

While studying aircraft engineering in America Alexander (below) helped a friend prepare a racing car and chose that as his profession. He came to Europe with Teddy Mayer (later McLaren team manager), joined Bruce

McLaren's new team in 1964 and has been there more or less ever since. Gruff and abrupt with those he considers to be time-wasters (who in turn, label him the paddock's resident curmudgeon), Alexander is in private one of the funniest and most entertaining people in the sport.

GIOVANNA AMATI (I)

b. 20 July 1962
F1 career: 92 - Brabham. **GP starts**: 0

The daughter of a wealthy Italian industrialist, Amati (above) competed in national racing before moving to F3000 in 1987, achieving limited success in 14 races. With ambitions of becoming the first female Formula 1 driver since Lella Lombardi (who raced 12 times in the 1970s) In 1992, Amati bought a ride with the cash-strapped Brabham team and failed to qualify in South Africa, Mexico and Brazil, whereupon she was replaced by Damon Hill, who did little better in the uncompetitive car. Amati was once abducted and held for ransom by kidnappers, and also had a romance with Niki Lauda.

CHRIS AMON (NZ)

b. 20 July 1943
F1 career: 63 - Lola, Lotus; 64 - Lotus; 65 - Lotus, Brabham; 66 - Cooper, Brabham; 67-69 - Ferrari; 70 - March; 71-72 - Matra; 73 - Tecno, Tyrrell; 74 - Amon, BRM; 75-76 - Ensign. **GP starts**: 95

Perhaps the best driver never to win a Grand Prix, Amon had both bullish determination and appalling luck. The Kiwi farmer's son, who learned to "slide a truck around" at the age of eight, embarked on what he called his "war" with Formula 1 at the tender age of 19. He and fellow Kiwi Bruce McLaren secured the historic first Ford GT40 victory at Le Mans in 1966, inflicting Ferrari's first defeat there of the decade, and Ferrari snapped him up to race both Sportscars and Formula 1. He became the team leader when Lorenzo Bandini was killed, and was a consistent points-scorer, which made the next two seasons all the more disappointing. He was a match for Stewart in equal March cars in 1970, but his career declined after two very competitive seasons with Matra, and his efforts to revive it by becoming a car constructor ended in failure. Back home, he now runs the family farm.

MARIO ANDRETTI (USA)

b. 28 February 1940
F1 career: 68-69 - Lotus; 70 - March; 71-72 - Ferrari; 74-75 - Parnelli; 76 - Parnelli, Lotus; 77-80 - Lotus; 81 - Alfa Romeo; 82 - Williams, Ferrari. **GP starts**: 128. **GP wins**: 12. **World Champion**: 1978

As a teenage member of a poor immigrant family from Montona in Italy, Mario Andretti bought his first car (a Hudson) at 18 and modified it for stock car racing, sharing it with his twin brother Aldo. Mario won his first 16 races in a row, and had similar success in US Sprint car racing before making it to IndyCars, where he won his first title in 1965. He went on to become a household name, an embodiment of the American Dream. He was still dominating the US series when he competed in a handful of Formula 1 races for Colin Chapman, whose Lotus 49 he put on pole on his Formula 1 debut in his home race. In 1971, he accomplished a childhood dream by racing for Ferrari. His only Grand Prix victory in a red car came on his debut in South Africa, but he co-drove 312P Sportscars to several big wins with Ickx. After a spell with Parnelli Jones, in both Indy and Formula 1 cars, he returned to Team Lotus and capitalised when Chapman introduced the ground-effect Type 78, with which he became World Champion almost without challenge. There was less success in the seasons that followed, and he returned home to win the IndyCar title again in 1984.

MICHAEL ANDRETTI (USA)

b. 5 October 1962

F1 career: 93 - McLaren. **GP starts**: 13.

It was no surprise when Mario Andretti's son swiftly made an impact in US racing - the shock was his failure in Formula 1. Having finished in the top three in the IndyCar series every year between 1986 and 1992 (bar 1988), he was signed to partner Ayrton Senna at McLaren, but rarely featured. The adventure ended prematurely, but with a degree of credibility, when he finished third at Monza, before going home to continue in IndyCars.

RENE ARNOUX (F)

b. 4 July 1948

F1 career: 78 - Martini, Surtees; 79-82 - Renault; 83-85 - Ferrari; 86-89 - Ligier. **GP starts**: 148. **GP wins**: 7

A qualified mechanic, whose hobbies are woodworking and restoring old cars, the earthy little Frenchman stepped up to Formula 1, where success came with the turbo V6 Renault. Shy and with a perpetually astonished facial expression, Arnoux (above, right) had more cultured team mates in Jabouille and Prost, and at times these were uneasy partnerships. A brave, if untidy, charger in the car, he won three times in his first season at Ferrari and was third

in the championship, but the results and the motivation tailed off, and he was released amidst some acrimony. He endured three seasons with unreliable Ligiers before retiring and returning to his hobbies.

ALBERTO ASCARI (I)

b. 13 July 1918 - d. 26 May 1955

F1 career: 50-53 - Ferrari; 54 - Maserati, Ferrari, Lancia; 55 - Lancia. **GP starts**: 31. **GP wins**: 13. **World Champion**: 1952, 1953

The son of one of Italy's greatest racing drivers, Ascari was developing his skills on motorcycles and in sportscar events when WW2 intervened. He was 29 when motor racing resumed, and won several races before participating in the inaugural World Championship in 1950. Farina, Fangio and Alfa Romeo were tough adversaries, but he earned a win at the Nürburgring in 1951. The Ferrari 500 was tailor-made for the 2-litre formula of 1952 and he was unbeaten in all six Grands Prix, then became the first back-to-back World Champion by winning five of eight races in 1953. At Monaco in 1955, he escaped both drowning and serious injury when he crashed a Lancia D50 into the harbour - but only four days later he was killed testing a Ferrari sportscar at Monza.

ANTONIO ASCARI (I)

b. 1888 - d. 1925

As an Alfa Romeo dealer in the early 1920s, Antonio Ascari was successful in local events and was recruited as a works driver. Once promoted to the Grand Prix squad, he proved scintillatingly fast, and scored 13 wins from 32 starts. After winning the 1924 Italian and 1925 Belgian Grands Prix, he crashed to his death

while dominating the 1925 French Grand Prix at Montlhéry. His son Alberto - a future double World Champion - was then six years old.

GIANCARLO BAGHETTI (I)

b. 25 December 1934 - d. 27 November 1995

F1 career: 61-62 - Ferrari; 63 - ATS; 64 - BRM; 65 - Brabham; 66 - Ferrari. 67 - Lotus. **GP starts**: 21. **GP wins**: 1

The son of a Milan industrialist, Baghetti was the first (and currently only) driver to win on his Formula 1 debut. That historic victory in the 1961 French Grand Prix at Reims was followed by occasional appearances spanning the next seven seasons. In the finest Italian tradition, he made more headlines by dating famous women than with his endeavours on the track. He turned to photo-journalism and continued living life to the full until succumbing to cancer, aged 61.

> "I assessed him as a cool, calm and collected young man. Put him in a car, however, and he revealed another side of his nature. His career began brilliantly - but he failed to live up to his new-found fame, and his star soon set." ENZO FERRARI

JEAN-MARIE BALESTRE (F)

During WW2, Balestre served in the French regiment of the Reich's Waffen SS, and was imprisoned in France after VE Day - only to be released and awarded a *Croix de Guerre* when it was established that he had been a double agent for the Resistance. He formed a successful publishing company and set himself up as a motorsport administrator, eventually becoming the president of FISA (then the sporting arm of the FIA). Much given to spectacular table-thumping and shouting, he absolutely loved polemics. The first Concorde Agreement resolved his tortuous 'FISA-FOCA war' in 1980-81 with Bernie Ecclestone and Max Mosley over control of Formula 1, and he became relatively quiet. Ultimately he was deposed as the man in charge by Mosley's superior political skills, and retired to his fine house in the south of France.

LORENZO BANDINI (I)

b. 21 December 1935 - d. 10 May 1967

F1 career: 61 - Cooper; 62 - Ferrari; 63 - BRM, Ferrari; 64-67 - Ferrari. **GP starts**: 42. **GP wins**: 1

A qualified engineer pursuing a dream, Bandini gained experience in self-prepared racecars. He finished third at Monaco in his first race for Ferrari, but did not become a full team member until 1964, when he thrived alongside Surtees and won in Austria. In 1967, battling through the streets of his favourite Monaco, he clipped the chicane at the harbour and was trapped when fire engulfed his upturned Ferrari, and remained in the inferno for some time. He succumbed to appalling injuries three days later.

> "A young man of great integrity, he has a sound automobile grounding because he started as a mechanic. He drives any kind of car with equal ease." ENZO FERRARI

RUBENS BARRICHELLO (BR)

b. 23 May 1972

F1 career: 93-96 - Jordan; 97-99 - Stewart; 00-01 - Ferrari. **GP starts**: 147. **GP wins**: 1

Born virtually next to the Interlagos circuit, Barrichello's earliest recollection of Formula 1 was watching Gilles Villeneuve in a Ferrari. Not yet six years old, the boy knew there and then what he wanted to do with his life, and was later inspired by his countryman, Ayrton Senna. His maiden Grand Prix win, at Hockenheim in 2000, came at the wheel of a Ferrari and prompted copious tears on the podium from this highly emotional man. He proved to be the perfect team mate for Michael Schumacher, although his contracted role as Schumacher's understudy at Ferrari made future winning difficult.

JEAN BEHRA (F)

b. 16 February 1921 - d. 1 August 1959

F1 career: 52-54 - Gordini; 55-58 - Maserati; 59 - Ferrari. **GP starts**: 52. **GP wins**: 0

Somehow, a Grand Prix victory eluded this very popular Frenchman, who switched to cars after a successful motorcycle racing career. Driving for the perennial underdog, Amedee Gordini, Behra was a menace to the mighty factory teams and regularly came close to causing real upsets. He did win non-championship Formula 1 races and Sportscar events, and showed no ill-effect from losing an ear in a 1955 crash in a Maserati, but his hopes were often dashed by mechanical failures. He was killed in his own Porsche on the dangerous Avus circuit in Germany when he crashed on the rain-soaked banking and was hurled out of the cockpit during a race supporting the 1959 German Grand Prix.

> "Only those who do not move do not die. But are they not already dead?" JEAN BEHRA

STEFAN BELLOF (D)

b. 20 November 1957 - d. 1 September 1985
F1 career: 84-85 - Tyrrell. **GP starts**: 20

In 1982, Bellof startled the establishment by winning his first two Formula 2 races, and some amazing 1983 performances for the works Porsche Group C team further marked him as a future Formula 1 champion. His break came in 1984, and no one present at a sodden Monaco has any doubt that he would have won that race, but for its premature stoppage. Sadly his aggressive style caused his death, at Spa. A daring but foolhardy attempt to pass Jacky Ickx through Eau Rouge resulted in an inevitable collision, and his Porsche struck the barrier head-on. Many felt he was one of the greatest natural talents of all time.

JEAN-PIERRE BELTOISE (F)

b. 26 April 1937
F1 career: 66-71 - Matra; 72-74 - BRM. **GP starts**: 86. **GP wins:** 1

A mechanic and multiple French motorcycle champion, Beltoise's four-wheel career began at Le Mans in 1963 - and almost ended at Reims in 1964. A fiery crash left him with scars and a permanently damaged arm, but he recovered to race for Matra. The man to beat in Formula 2, he won the European title in 1968. But his finest hour came in 1972 with BRM, when rain levelled the playing field at Monaco, and he manhandled a normally uncompetitive car to his only Grand Prix victory.

GERHARD BERGER (A)

b. 27 August 1959
F1 career: 84 - ATS; 85 - Arrows; 86 - Benetton; 87-89 - Ferrari; 90-92 - McLaren; 93-95 - Ferrari; 96-97 - Benetton. **GP starts**: 180. **GP wins**: 10

A joyful *bon viveur* and avid prankster (he once tossed his friend Ayrton Senna's briefcase out of a helicopter), Berger (above) was able to instil a sense of fun into his profession. He broke into Formula 1 with ATS, thanks to strong connections with BMW, its engine supplier. Those ties took him on to Arrows, and then Benetton, where he scored its first Grand Prix victory with the most powerful Formula 1 engine of all time. Eight more wins resulted from two spells at Ferrari, either side of a stint at McLaren, before he saw out his career back at Benetton, winning perhaps his greatest race, the 1997 German Grand Prix, in his final season. He returned to Formula 1 as the good-humoured director of motorsport for BMW.

GEORGES BOILLOT (F)

b. 1885 - d. 1916

Arguably racing's first superstar, Boillot (right) was a spectacular driver who became a household name in pre-WW1 France with a meteoric career in Peugeots. After coming to prominence in *voiturette* racing, he won on his Grand Prix debut in France in 1912. He repeated the victory the following year. In 1914 - as well as setting pole and a lap record on his Indy 500 debut - he fought a magnificent but doomed race against superior Mercedes in the French Grand Prix, his final race. A pilot in the French Air Force, he was killed in action in 1916 - attempting to take on seven enemy planes single-handed.

JOAKIM BONNIER (S)

b. 31 January 1930 - d. 11 June 1972
F1 career: 57-58 - Maserati; 59-60 - BRM; 61-62 - Porsche; 63 - Cooper; 64-65 - Brabham; 66-67 - Cooper; 68 - McLaren, Honda; 69 - Lotus; 70-71 - McLaren. **GP starts**: 103. **GP wins**: 1

The scion of a Swedish publishing family, he owned his own art gallery in Lausanne and a private collection of over 60 paintings, including works by Picasso, Fernand Léger and other modern masters. Although he was a Formula 1 regular from 1958 to 1968, including two seasons driving for his own team, a BRM P25 brought him his only F1 victory, at Zandvoort in 1959. He said it was "the most beautiful racing car of all time", and hung it on the wall of his living room like a sculpture. Bonnier named a son Wolfgang, after his friend von Trips. Goateed and inscrutable (his face rarely conveyed any emotion) 'JoBo' was more successful in sportscars - only to be killed in one during the 1972 Le Mans when his Lola collided with another car and was hurled over the barriers.

THIERRY BOUTSEN (B)

b. 13 July 1957
F1 career: 83-86 - Arrows; 87-88 - Benetton; 89-90 - Williams; 91-92 - Ligier; 93 - Jordan. **GP starts**: 163. **GP wins**: 3

Having cut his teeth with Arrows, Boutsen moved to Benetton in 1987 and became a regular on the podium the following season. His big break came in 1989, when he replaced Ferrari-bound Nigel Mansell at Williams, where he won three races. Mansell's return signalled his departure, and a poor stint with Ligier and a

disastrous half-season at Jordan brought the curtain down on Boutsen's Formula 1 career.

SIR JACK BRABHAM (AUS)

b. 2 April 1926
F1 career: 55 - Cooper; 56 - Maserati; 57-61 - Cooper; 62-63 - Lotus; 64-70 - Brabham. **GP starts**: 126. **GP wins**: 14. **World Champion**: 1959, 1960, 1966

The only son of a greengrocer in Sydney, Brabham became the only driver to win the championship with a car of his own make. 'Black Jack' was a doer not a talker - he hated being interviewed - and a straight-thinking engineer as well as a crack driver, who honed his skills in a variety of racing categories on a myriad of track surfaces. He was closely involved in the development of the rear-mid-engined Cooper which transformed Formula 1 and secured his first two titles in 1959-60. He formed the Brabham Racing Organisation in late 1962 and took on Ron Tauranac as his designer, producing very successful brand-name racecars for several categories of racing. In 1966, the first year of the new 3-litre formula, Brabham quietly arranged for an Australian company, Repco, to modify an old Oldsmobile pushrod motor and, thus powered, his cars romped to the 1966 and 1967 titles. He bowed out in 1970 at the age of 44 and sold his team to Bernie Ecclestone.

> "A man who says nothing, just looks and listens, sits there calmly taking in everything, and if someone is very far wrong, he won't even give him the benefit of his resentment. He'll just pack it away in his filing cabinet and write the man off. The central fact about Jack is that very few people know anything about him." JACKIE STEWART

VITTORIO BRAMBILLA (I)

b. 11 November 1937- d. 26 May 2001
F1 career: 74-76 - March; 77-78 - Surtees; 79-80 - Alfa Romeo. **GP starts**: 74. **GP wins**: 1

The 'Monza Gorilla' was a Formula 1 debutant at 37, and lived up to his nickname by crashing a lot during 1974. Transformed into a regular top-ten qualifier during his second season, he was even credited with a pole position - although his team management

admitted years later that they had cheated the timing system. His career highlight came with victory in that year's Austrian Grand Prix, when he famously spun into the barriers after jubilantly greeting the chequered flag with his hands in the air.

ROSS BRAWN (GB)
b. 23 November 1954

An astute and inventive engineer, he successfully designed racing sportscars before coming into Formula 1 with Benetton. He and Rory Byrne then produced a car specifically to suit Michael Schumacher's driving style, which won the 1994 and 1995 titles. Schumacher took them both with him to Ferrari and these three, with Jean Todt, engineered the Scuderia's impressive resurgence. Owlishly bespectacled, studious and very clever, technical director Brawn's superior strategy, devised from his perch on the pit wall, has helped Michael Schumacher win many races.

CHRIS BRISTOW (GB)
b. 2 December 1937 - d. 19 June 1960
F1 career: 59-60 - Cooper. **GP starts**: 4

A regular winner in sportscar racing with the British Racing Partnership team, he defeated the likes of Brabham, Salvadori and McLaren and became BRP's Formula 1 team leader in 1960 after his team mate Harry Schell was killed early in the season. Only months later, Bristow lost his life in a fearful accident at Spa while challenging for the lead of the Belgian Grand Prix.

TONY BROOKS (GB)
b. 25 February 1932
F1 career: 56 - BRM; 57-58 - Vanwall; 59 - Ferrari, Vanwall; 60 - Cooper, Vanwall; 61 - BRM. **GP starts**: 38. **GP wins**: 6

The son of a dentist, Brooks was studying for that profession and playing good rugby when he became a works racing driver. He was second to Fangio at Monaco in only his second Grand Prix start and then shared a victory at Aintree when, suffering from the effects of a crash at Le Mans, he handed over his Vanwall to Moss when the latter's car had broken. His three 1958 victories, at Spa, the Nürburgring and Monza, underlined his brilliance on fast tracks, and helped Vanwall to win the first constructors' title. He raced the

front-engined Ferrari 246 to success at Reims and on the Avus in 1959, but finished runner-up in the championship. Deeply affected by the loss of several close racing colleagues, he retired and turned his attentions to his family and his garage business.

DAVID BRUCE-BROWN (USA)
b. 1890 - d. 1913

An all-American hero from the immediate pre-WW1 period, he was a winning machine. He made his international reputation with a victorious run in the 1910 Savannah Grand Prize, a race in which the top Europeans and Americans competed together. When FIAT entered in 1911, it made sure he was one of their drivers - and he won again. This led to a place on the Grand Prix team in 1912, and he was narrowly leading when forced to retire. He was killed a year later, while practising for an American race.

MARTIN BRUNDLE (GB)
b. 1 June 1959
F1 career: 84-86 - Tyrrell; 87 - Zakspeed; 88 - Williams; 89-91 - Brabham; 92 - Benetton; 93 - Ligier; 94 - McLaren; 95 - Ligier; 96 - Jordan. **GP starts**: 158

Brundle's season-long battle with Senna for the 1983 British Formula 3 title marked him out as a future star, though breaking both his ankles in Dallas in 1985 delayed his early progress, and while he went on to make five trips to the podium, none were to the top step. Winning the 1988 World Sportscar title for Jaguar interrupted stints with five Formula 1 teams. Brundle's business acumen is now put to good use in his UK car dealerships, and his wit and intimate knowledge of the sport serves Formula 1 well in the TV commentary box.

RONNIE BUCKNUM (USA)
b. 5 March 1936 - d. 14 April 1992
F1 career: 64-66 - Honda. **GP starts**: 11

An established Sportscar racer, Bucknum joined Honda's fledgling Formula 1 team to drive its new 1.5-litre V12-powered car, which on its debut suffered steering failure and crashed at the Nürburgring. Lesser mechanical failures accounted for two further retirements in that first season, but another steering failure, during winter testing at Suzuka, left him with a broken

leg. Well into the 1965 season, it was Richie Ginther who registered Honda's first Grand Prix victory, in Mexico, while Bucknum picked up his first and only World Championship points in fifth place. He returned to the USA and continued racing in CanAm, USAC and TransAm.

ETTORE BUGATTI (I,D,F)
b. 15 September 1881 - d. 21 August 1947

The talented young Italian engineer designed and personally built every component of a dual-engined racing tricycle in his native Milan at the age of 18, and raced it in the 1899 Paris-Bordeaux. Bugatti first moved to Alsace to design cars for the De Dietrich company, then switched to Deutz as its chief engineer, moving to Cologne and taking German nationality. He still built his own jewel-like cars in his spare time and in 1910 set up his own business back in Strasbourg, where he set about developing his reputation as a technical genius. His company produced aircraft engines during WW1, after which the Alsace region became part of France. He turned to producing luxury cars in Molsheim to finance his trend-setting racing models, which were raced by the factory team and many satisfied customers. His son, Jean, began to assume control of the company during the 1930s but was killed testing a Le Mans racer in 1939. This, and the effects of WW2, broke his father's heart. The Bugatti works was transferred to Bordeaux, but its founder lost interest after the German invasion. Post-war, he took French nationality, but his former Molsheim factory was confiscated by France as enemy property, and he died a sad man two years later. A vintage Bugatti is worth millions of pounds today.

GIUSEPPE CAMPARI (I)
b. 1892 - d. 1933

A contemporary of the young Enzo Ferrari, Campari was briefly his team mate at Alfa Romeo in 1920, but was much the better driver. He developed into a consistent Grand Prix winner with the Alfa Romeo P2 from 1924-28, latterly for Scuderia Ferrari, and also won many big sportscar races for the company in a long and successful career. Known as '*Il Negher*' on account of his dark complexion, he had a passion for opera - he was married to singer Lina Cavalleri - and fine food. He weighed 16 stone and would unexpectedly break into song in a fine baritone while driving. Ironically, his last

victory came in a Maserati in the 1933 French Grand Prix. He jubilantly announced that he would retire after his next race, and devote himself to opera. He never made it: he and Umberto Borzacchini, battling for the lead of the Monza Grand Prix, both crashed on oil from another car's blown engine and were killed.

RUDOLF CARACCIOLA (D)
b. 30 January 1901 - d. 28 September 1959

Undeniably one of the greatest drivers of all time, Caracciola made his reputation with an unsuitable, stripped-down sports Mercedes SSK in the late 1920s. He was recruited by Alfa Romeo in 1932, when he won twice and earned instant acclaim by going wheel-to-wheel with Nuvolari, racing's incumbent superstar. In practice for the 1933 Monaco Grand Prix, he badly injured a leg, and did not return until late the following season - as a member of the new Mercedes Grand Prix team. He was the European champion in 1935, 1937 and 1938, displaying astounding 'feel' on wet circuits. He did not re-enter Grand Prix racing after WW2, and died in 1959.

EUGENIO CASTELLOTTI (I)
b. 10 October 1930 - d. 14 March 1957
F1 career: 55 - Lancia, Ferrari; 56-57 - Ferrari. **GP starts**: 14

A dashing young man who made his mark with Ferrari sportscars, he was signed by the factory Lancia team. Affected by heatstroke in Buenos Aires, he crashed his Lancia on his Grand Prix debut but then finished second at Monaco, in the race in which his team mate, Ascari, crashed into the harbour. When Ascari was killed four days later, Castellotti briefly became number one, but the team was soon to regroup under the wing of Ferrari. He excelled in Sportscar events, winning the Mille Miglia and at Sebring, when he partnered Fangio. Recalled from a holiday to test the latest Ferrari at Modena, he crashed on a wet track, struck a concrete barrier and was killed, aged 28.

FRANÇOIS CEVERT (F)
25 February 1944 - d. 6 October 1973
F1 career: 70 - March; 72-73 - Tyrrell. **GP starts**: 47. **GP wins**: 1

Cevert was born François Goldstein, to a family of Paris jewellers who decided their son might have an easier life if he used his mother's maiden name: Cevert. Hired by Tyrrell midway through 1970, he developed rapidly under Jackie Stewart's tutelage and concluded the 1971 season with a superb win at Watkins Glen. Tyrrell lost momentum in 1972, but was back on form a year later and he dutifully rode shotgun to Stewart as the Scot eased to his third title. In his spare time, the outrageously handsome Frenchman dated the likes of Brigitte Bardot. It was ironic that his fatal accident should occur at the scene of his only victory, but the tragedy was compounded when it became known that Stewart was to retire and Cevert promoted to team leader. He died never knowing his apprenticeship had been served.

COLIN CHAPMAN (GB)

b. 9 May 1928 - d. 16 December 1982

Chapman was the archetypal British 'wheeler-dealer', but a remarkable original thinker, who began to build spindly, Austin 7-based 'specials' as an engineering student in 1948. This led him to found Lotus Cars in 1995, and to own one of the most accomplished and famous of all Formula 1 teams, which he operated with prodigious energy. His reputation as motorsport's foremost technical innovator was justified - with the proviso that he could be slow in denying credit for work initiated by his talented Team Lotus engineering team. Lotus Formula 1 innovations included the monocoque type 25, the almost unbeatable DFV-engined 49, the wedge-shaped 72, and the 'ground-effect' 79 - not to mention cigarette sponsorship, in 1968. He died of a heart attack in 1982 when embroiled in the DeLorean scandal. He had started Lotus with £25 borrowed from his wife, Hazel, and left her £1.3 million in his will. Lesser men could not keep his once-great team alive for long. Team Lotus was never a force again, and folded at the end of 1994.

> "He was the hub of Lotus. The rest of our people were spokes. It was too difficult to rebuild the wheel." PETER WARR

FERNAND CHARRON (F)

A former cycle racer, Charron was the most successful of the pioneer city-to-city racers, driving for Panhard. He won most of the big events between 1898 and 1900, but then his career faded.

EDDIE CHEEVER (USA)

b. 10 January 1958

F1 career: 78 - Theodore, Hesketh; 80 - Osella; 81 - Tyrrell; 82 - Ligier; 83 - Renault; 84-85 - Benetton; 86 - FORCE; 87-89 - Arrows.
GP starts: 132

As a baby-faced youth, born in the USA but raised in Italy, Cheever rose through the Formula 3 ranks, made his name in Formula 2, and seemed destined for the top after a Ferrari test. But the deal never materialised. Instead he endured torrid times in uncompetitive cars, although he secured several good results with Tyrrell and Ligier. His best Formula 1 season came with Renault as Prost's team mate, when he was sixth in the championship. The following seasons were disappointing, and he was not consoled by winning performances in Jaguar Group C cars. Whatever his results Cheever could be relied upon to have something interesting, usually funny, to say. Eventually he returned to the USA to race IndyCars, and is now a successful owner/driver in the Indy Racing League.

JIM CLARK (GB)

b. 4 March 1936 - d. 7 April 1968

F1 career: 60-68 - Lotus; **GP starts** - 72. **GP wins**: 25. **World Champion**: 1963, 1965

Clark learned to drive as a child - on a tractor on his father's farm in Scotland - and showed extraordinary talent in racing cars as a youth. After winning 12 sportscar races with a Lister Jaguar in 1959, he was to have joined the Aston Martin Grand Prix team for 1960, but the project was delayed. Colin Chapman snapped up the introspective, unassuming 24-year-old after receiving a sound thrashing by him in identical racing Lotus Elans. The long partnership between the brilliant engineer and the genius driver set new standards that often demoralised the opposition. Twice the undisputed World Champion, he drove 28 fastest laps and 33 pole positions up to the 1968 season-opener at Kyalami - his last Formula 1 appearance. His unexplained fatal accident, in a relatively unimportant Formula 2 race at Hockenheim, shook the motor racing world. He never drove a bad Formula 1 car, but his reputation as one of the all-time greats is secure.

> "I think his most profound influence, certainly on me and his close associates, was not his ability as a driver but his success

as a man. He was so thoroughly adjusted to life and its problems, and had such personal integrity it is very difficult for others to compare themselves in the same street. He was a man who set an example for others." COLIN CHAPMAN

PETER COLLINS (GB)

6 November 1931 - d. 3 August 1958
F1 career: 52-53 - HWM; 54 - Vanwall; 55 - Maserati; 56-58 - Ferrari.
GP starts: 32. **GP wins**: 3.

A gifted driver who never fulfilled his potential, Collins graduated from post-WW2 500cc racing, progressing through Formula 2 and Sportscar racing, at which he excelled. His reputation spiralled at Ferrari in 1956 when he partnered Fangio and - although himself contending for the title - handed him his fourth championship by generously giving up his car when his team leader's had broken. Handsome, gregarious, and a lover of laughter, Collins lived with his wife Louise King, a glamourous American actress, on their yacht *Mipooka*, moored in the harbour at Monaco. The best friend of his team mate Mike Hawthorn, Collins was also a personal favourite of Enzo Ferrari. Charging in third place and closing on the leaders, he perished at the Nürburgring in the 1958 German Grand Prix, after being thrown from his Ferrari 246 when it struck an earth bank and rolled into a field.

JOHN COOPER (GB)

With his father, Charles, Cooper (above) emerged as the foremost manufacturer of the spindly little single-seaters that revived British motorsport after WW2. Built to race on the smooth perimeter roads of de-commissioned airfields, they had 500cc motorcycle engines (the only power sources still in plentiful supply) mounted in the back. Later, with a little development and more power, these simple but highly adjustable cars defined the ultimate format of the Formula 1 chassis. They could outperform the bigger, front-engined Italian cars, developed for European races on bumpy street circuits, and the Coopers saw the future when they put a twin-cylinder JAP car on the grid for the 1950 Monaco GP, the second race in the inaugural World Championship. They were unable to field a pukka works team until 1957. It was their first customer,

Rob Walker, who landed the marque's first Formula 1 wins in 1958, but the works team secured the 1959-60 titles with Jack Brabham, and ultimately every constructor had to follow Cooper's lead. But Cooper himself (above) was not cut out for the developing business aspects of Formula 1 and built his last Formula 1 car in 1968.

DAVID COULTHARD (GB)

b. 27 March 1971
F1 career: 94-95 - Williams; 96-01 McLaren.
GP starts: 123. **GP wins**: 11

A tenacious, square-jawed Scot, Coulthard landed a Williams test driver deal for 1994 after solid performances in Britain's junior single-seater divisions. Only weeks later, Ayrton Senna's death saw him promoted to the Formula 1 grid alongside Damon Hill. Disappointed at being replaced (by Mansell) for the last three races of 1994, Coulthard bounced back the next season, but his career did not gain real impetus until 1996, when he formed his long and fruitful partnership with Mika Hakkinen at McLaren. Also noted for a succession of glamourous girlfriends, 'DC' developed a reputation as an unselfish team player, and a hard but fair racer, though he remained a reluctant tabloid-style celebrity.

> "I know a lot of people would love me to kick the wing mirror of my car in frustration when things go wrong, but I think to show your emotions to a competitor is a great weakness." DAVID COULTHARD

PIERS COURAGE (GB)

b. 27 May 1942 - d. 21 June 1970

F1 career: 66 - Lotus (F2); 67-68 - BRM; 69 - Brabham; 70 - De Tomaso. **GP starts**: 28

Born into the British brewing company, Courage (below) was educated at Eton and articled as an accountant, but took up racing as a sport and found he excelled at it. He and Frank Williams were hired for Charles Lucas's 1965 Brabham Formula 3 team and formed a lasting friendship before going their separate

ways, Courage to start a Formula 1 career with Reg Parnell and BRM, Williams to start his own team. Williams chose his friend to drive his new Formula 1 Brabham in 1969, and Courage stayed on the following season to race the embryonic team's new car, which was branded for De Tomaso. It overturned and caught fire, trapping its driver, in a dreadful crash at Zandvoort.

"After Piers and Jochen [Rindt] and Jimmy [Clark] died, both Jackie and I were afraid to make friends with other drivers and their wives. It was deliberate. We didn't want to go through it all again."
HELEN STEWART

GEOFFREY CROSSLEY (GB)

b. 11 May 1921 - d. 31 December 2001

F1 career: 50 - Alta. **GP starts**: 2

Crossley was an enthusiastic amateur who bought one of Geoffrey Taylor's little Alta single-seaters in 1949 and raced it in two events in the inaugural Formula 1 World Championship, at Silverstone and Spa.

ELIO DE ANGELIS (I)

b. 26 March 1958 - d. 15 May 1986

F1 career: 79 - Shadow; 80-85 - Lotus; 86 - Brabham. **GP starts**: 108. **GP wins**: 2

The son of a prosperous Roman builder, de Angelis was initially regarded as just another rich kid, but silenced his critics with solid performances. Cultured and well-educated, and a gifted pianist, he was able to mix easily even with those who lacked his social graces, and came to be well-liked by everyone in the sport. A fourth place for Shadow at Watkins Glen in 1979 resulted in offers from Tyrrell and Lotus. Naïvely, he signed for both. Lotus duly won its man and he secured two victories over six mostly competitive seasons. He switched to Brabham for 1986 but, four races into the season, de Angelis lost his life while testing at Paul Ricard.

COUNT CAREL GODIN DE BEAUFORT (NL)

b. 10 April 1934 - d. 3 August 1964

F1 career: 57-64. **GP starts**: 28

A perennially cheerful, if oversized, aristocratic Dutch amateur, who always raced in his socks, he became a serious competitor when he bought Rob Walker's Porsche 718 in 1961. He was into his fourth season with this car when he crashed in practice for the 1964 German Grand Prix, and succumbed to his injuries three days later.

ALBERT, COMTE DE DION

A wealthy Parisian aristocrat who had a reputation for gambling and duelling, but also had engineering interests, de Dion pioneered the early steam cars in partnership with Georges Bouton and competed in them in the first city-to-city events. He initiated the committee that later became the Automobile Club de France (ACF), which gave motor racing almost all of its early impetus. He subsequently confined his car interests to production models.

ALFONSO DE PORTAGO (E)

b. 11 October 1928 - d. 12 May 1957

F1 career: 56-57 - Ferrari. **GP starts**: 5

A Spanish nobleman, his full name was Don Alfonso Cabeza de Vac y Leighton, 17th Marquis de Portago - nicknamed 'Fon'. He was the best gentleman steeplechase jockey in the world, a competitive swimmer, an accomplished

bobsledder, highly literate (he tried to read a book a day) and very attractive to women. His pit stop to kiss his then girlfriend, the actress Linda Christian, just before taking off to crash fatally (killing 11 others) in the 1956 Mille Miglia, is part of racing's tragic folklore.

"I think the Marquis de Portago had a more traditional Latin approach to the thing. He was an extremely brave guy. I think he may have lacked the engineering know-how that many of us had, and that might have upped the odds of his having a serious accident. I think he kind of said his prayers before the event, relying on the Good Lord to protect him, and then sort of let it all hang out." DAN GURNEY

LUCA DI MONTEZEMOLO (I)

b. 31 August 1947

A nobleman by birth, a brilliant administrator by intellect, di Montezemolo studied commercial law at La Sapienza University in Rome, then gained a Masters at Columbia in New York, before joining Fiat. He was placed at Ferrari in 1973 and began running the Formula 1 team a year later, aged 27, overseeing Lauda's title seasons in 1975 and 1977. He then became the youngest senior manager in the history of the FIAT empire, and successively ran the *La Stampa* newspaper, the Cinzano drinks company and Juventus football club. He took time out when he was asked to organise Italia 90, the soccer World Cup. After a spell running RCS Video, he returned to Ferrari in 1991 to become its CEO, and to take some of the credit for its resurgence in its Michael Schumacher era.

RON DENNIS (GB)

b. 1 June 1947

A racing mechanic (notably in Formula 1 with Cooper in 1966), his fierce ambition and acute intelligence led him to start his own team - which became Project Four, bought into McLaren and ultimately took it over. Since then all the McLaren Formula 1 cars have reflected the alliance in the designation 'MP4', but Dennis has taken the company into a business empire reaching far beyond Formula 1, thanks to a fruitful partnership with his Franco-Arabian

partner Mansour Ojjeh. Their TAG McLaren Group is now a major company, supplying a range of technology to customers worldwide, and the racing division has been solidly established as one of the Formula 1 front runners for two decades. Dennis, who says he experiences physical pain the morning after not winning a race, has also become very wealthy, though money is not what drives him.

"The driving force has got to be a desire to be the best, not just to make money. Fortunately, if you are winning Grands Prix you can have both. I've often said I would prefer to be recognised as a successful businessman before a successful motorsport director. But if it came to a choice, I would most certainly choose winning a Grand Prix over making a million dollars."
RON DENNIS

PATRICK DEPAILLER (F)

b. 9 August 1944 - d. 1 August 1980

F1 career: 72-78 - Tyrrell; 79 - Ligier; 80 - Alfa Romeo. **GP starts**: 95. **GP wins**: 2

The racer's racer, Depailler missed Tyrrell's final two Grands Prix of 1973 because he broke a leg in a motorcycle accident. It could have cost him his Formula 1 career, but Tyrrell forgave him and he was hired full-time in 1974. His move to Ligier in 1979 proved successful, only for a hang-gliding accident to curtail his season midway. Despite badly damaged legs, he fought through the pain and was back on the grid with Alfa Romeo at the beginning of 1980, but died in a testing accident at Hockenheim.

MARK DONOHUE (USA)

b. 18 March 1937 - d. 19 August 1975

F1 career: 71 - McLaren; 74-75 - Penske. **GP starts**: 14

A qualified engineer, 'Captain Nice' was an unusually versatile racing driver in American TransAm, sportscar and IndyCar racing. Donohue's long partnership with the fabulously successful entrepreneur Roger Penske first took him into Formula 1 in 1971, when a McLaren M19 was hired for the end-of-season North American races. Donohue was lured out of retirement when Penske built his own car,

but the project was spiked in mid-1975. Driving Penske's new March, he had a massive accident at the Osterreichring. Initially it seemed not to have seriously harmed him, but complications arose, and Donohue (above) died in hospital the following Tuesday.

RENE DREYFUS (F)

b. 1905 - d. 1993

As a Bugatti salesman, Dreyfus harangued his way into minor league competitions with the cars and met with much success. A wealthy benefactor bought a Grand Prix Bugatti for him to drive for 1930 and he beat Chiron's works car to win the Monaco Grand Prix. Thereafter he drove for Bugatti and Scuderia Ferrari, scoring regular successes. After retiring from the cockpit, he opened a successful restaurant in New York.

BERNIE ECCLESTONE (GB)

b. 28 October 1930

The ambitious, hard-working son of a Suffolk trawlerman, Bernard Charles Ecclestone became a motorcycle dealer and then a property owner in south-east London, and began to race 500cc Formula 3 cars as a hobby in the 1950s. An astute businessman, he became involved in Formula 1 as the manager of Stuart Lewis-Evans and an owner of the Connaught team. Later he managed Jochen Rindt and then purchased Jack Brabham's team. After founding the Formula One Constructors Association (FOCA), he found his niche in life by utterly transforming Formula 1 - almost single-handed - into a multi-billion dollar global business. In 1980-81, he fought a long and acrimonious war for control of the sport with FIA mandarin Jean-

Marie Balestre. Ultimately he gained effective control of the entire world governing body when his friend and colleague, Max Mosley, became its president. This dynamic duo - and Formula 1 - has never looked back. Ecclestone's dealings are merciless but famously fair, and his single-minded determination is balanced by a genuine sense of humour. For all his tycoon image, Bernie is a very funny man - and one of Britain's wealthiest, with a fortune of over £2 billion. Above all, he is a real racer.

> "I'm just a bloke doing a job. Fire-fighting, mostly. That's the thing that really excites me - the fact that I get up in the morning and have no idea what's going to happen next. The fires can be big or small, and they all need to be put out, one way or another. Sometimes we have to light a few." BERNIE ECCLESTONE

LUIGI FAGIOLI (I)

b. 8 June 1898 - d. 20 June 1952

The 'Abruzzi robber' was one of the most pugnacious characters of Grand Prix racing in the 1930s. He established his reputation in the emergent Maseratis before switching first to Scuderia Ferrari, then Mercedes. At the German team, he was in constant conflict with team manager Alfred Neubauer, whom he felt favoured Caracciola. He once retired a healthy car rather than accept team orders, pulled a knife on a team mate and threw tools with malicious intent in the pit-lane. On his day, though, he was formidably fast and won major races for all three teams, although a later move to Auto Union was not a success.

JUAN MANUEL FANGIO (RA)

b. 24 June 1911 - d. 17 July 1995
F1 career: 50-51 - Alfa Romeo; 53-55 - Mercedes; 56 - Ferrari; 57-58 - Maserati.
GP starts: 51. **GP wins**: 24. **World Champion**: 1951, 1954, 1955, 1956, 1957

Fangio (below) has the best Formula 1 record of all time. The son of an Italian emigrant builder, he started work in a garage aged 11, and played soccer before driving his first race in a converted Ford taxi. He was long established as Argentina's top road race driver when he finally settled in

Europe in 1949, aged 38, stocky, slope-shouldered, balding and nicknamed 'El Chueco' (bow-legged). When he retired nine years later, he had contested 51 Grands Prix, with 29 pole positions, 48 front-row starts, 23 fastest laps, 35 podiums, 24 wins and five World Championships. Out of the car, he was calm and courteous, even humble. In it, Fangio (below) was impeccable, earning the admiration and respect of all his rivals without exception. He died at home in Argentina at the age of 84.

> "I always drove with prudence and serenity, not like an ill-tempered person going to the cemetery. I always wanted to finish first in everything, but in death I preferred to finish last."
> JUAN MANUEL FANGIO

GIUSEPPE FARINA (I)

b. 30 October 1906 - d. 30 June 1966
F1 career: 50-51 - Alfa Romeo; 52-55 - Ferrari.
GP starts: 33. **GP wins**: 5. **World Champion**: 1950

A doctor of engineering, Farina was the son of a founder of the famous Italian family coachbuilding firm. He started racing in 1932 with an Alfa Romeo, but switched to a Maserati, then to Scuderia Ferrari's Alfas in 1938-39. After the war, he again drove a Maserati, winning the 1948 Monaco Grand Prix before rejoining Alfa as its team leader in 1950. He was 44 years old when he won the inaugural World Championship that year, though the 1951 season was the start of his decline. He retired in 1955, but lost his life in a road accident en route to watch the 1966 French Grand Prix.

> "I copied Farina's straight-arm posture at the wheel, not because it was more efficient, but because I thought one looked better driving that way. I didn't like it all at first, but kept going until it felt comfortable." STIRLING MOSS

ENZO FERRARI (I)

b. 1898 - d. 1988

The future founder of the team bearing his name shod mules for the Italian army in WW1. Ferrari (below) wanted to be an opera singer or a sports journalist, but went racing instead, starting as a moderately successful driver - winning 13 of his 47 races - and a 'fixer' for a small Italian team, CMN, before performing a similar role for the emergent Alfa Romeo team in the 1920s. After playing a prominent part in poaching key FIAT staff for Alfa, thereby establishing the latter as a potent Grand Prix force, he formed Scuderia Ferrari to campaign Alfas for a variety of drivers. After WW2 he began to manufacture his own road and racing cars and had three 125 models on the grid for the 1950 Monaco Grand Prix, the second round of the inaugural World Championship. Scuderia Ferrari dominated the 2-litre formula of 1952-53 and never looked back, establishing a large factory at Maranello to produce both chassis and engines. It became the most charismatic team and has remained so ever since, establishing such a worldwide following that it is impossible to imagine Formula 1 racing without its red cars. Until near the end of his long life Enzo Ferrari still came into his office

at 7:30 every morning and greeted most of his staff by their first names. He was one of the most powerful figures in Formula 1 history and left a permanent legacy: the most famous racing team in the world.

> "I am the living expression of the fantasy of journalists. So much has been said about me that when I die, I would rather be quickly forgotten." ENZO FERRARI

> "I want to end my career there, even if Ferrari's car is as slow as a Volkswagen Beetle, I still want to be driving it in my last race, on my last lap. Ferrari is the myth of Formula 1, the tradition, the soul, the passion." AYRTON SENNA

EMERSON FITTIPALDI (BR)

b. 12 December 1946

F1 career: 70-73 - Lotus; 74-75 - McLaren; 76-79 - Copersucar; 80 - Fittipaldi. **GP starts**: 144. **GP wins**: 14. **World Champion**: 1972, 1974

Sporting the biggest sideburns ever seen, 'Emmo' was a Team Lotus new boy when he was thrown into the deep end by Jochen Rindt's fatality in 1970. He proved himself equal to the challenge by winning the penultimate race, which guaranteed that the title would go to his deceased team leader. Two years later, aged 25, he became the youngest ever World Champion, and won his second title with McLaren in 1974. He stunned McLaren by announcing he was leaving at the end of 1975 to join elder brother Wilson to run his new Fittipaldi Automotive team. Five seasons behind the wheel of cars bearing the family name resulted in just two podiums, and the team folded in 1982. He moved to the USA to win the CART championship, and twice won the Indy 500 before retiring and becoming a born-again Christian.

MAURO FORGHIERI (I)

b. 13 January 1935

Described as a madman, but also a genius, by Niki Lauda, Forghieri got an engineering degree from the University of Bologna, took over the Ferrari racing department in 1961 and stayed there for three decades, running

the engineering side and the racing teams with a furious application that sometimes extended to flaming rows with the drivers, all of whom respected his expertise. On retirement he turned his artistic talents to designing jewellery for his wife, and furniture for the 17th-century villa he restored in Modena. He studied and collected paintings, noting that his favourite, Michelangelo, was an engineer as well as an artist.

> "I put 28 years of my life in Ferrari, you know. I like to think there is a little bit of myself still there. I was involved in 55 of the victories they had. It is a nice memory. Me with Ferrari. Sometimes bitter, sometimes sweet." MAURO FORGHIERI

HEINZ-HARALD FRENTZEN (D)

b. 18 May 1967

F1 career: 94-96 - Sauber; 97-98 - Williams; 99-01 - Jordan, Prost. **GP starts**: 127. **GP wins**: 3

Frentzen (below) learned to drive in his undertaker father's hearse, and later used artistic talents inherited from his Spanish mother to design rugs. Personable and laid-back, his engaging sense of humour served him well in times of an occasionally stressful career which never fulfilled a promise that once had him labelled as a superior talent to his countryman Michael Schumacher. In 1996 Williams fired newly crowned World Champion Damon Hill to accommodate Frentzen. The relationship failed to match expectations and,

with only one win from two seasons, he moved to Jordan. More comfortable in these new surroundings, he won two races in 1999 and another in 2000 but, by the mid-point of the following season, it had all turned sour, and he was sacked on the eve of his home race. He finished off 2001 with the doomed Prost team. After his former girlfriend, Corinna, became Mrs Michael Schumacher, Frentzen (above) married Tanya, and said the birth of their child made him drive better because he had another mouth to feed.

OLIVIER GENDEBIEN (B)

b. 12 January 1924 - d. 2 October 1998

F1 career: 56-59 - Ferrari; 60 - Cooper; 61 -Ferrari, Lotus. **GP starts**: 14

A fine-mannered Belgian aristocrat and an accomplished athlete who could run 100 metres in 10.9s and was wooed by a professional soccer club, Gendebien served as a WW2 paratrooper, then worked for four years as a forester in the Belgian Congo jungle, where he hunted buffalo. He entered motorsport in rallying and was hired by Ferrari in 1955, mainly to race its sportscars, with which he was very successful. Over seven seasons, he won many of the sportscar 'classics', including Le Mans four times, although he scored only 18 points in Formula 1.

> "He is a gentleman who never forgets that noblesse oblige and, when he is at the wheel, he translates this code of behaviour into an elegant and discerning forcefulness." ENZO FERRARI

PETER GETHIN (GB)

b. 21 February 1940

F1 career: 70-71 - McLaren; 72-73 - BRM; 74 -Lola. **GP starts**: 30. **GP wins**: 1.

A jockey-sized son of a jockey, Gethin was almost unbeatable in Formula 5000 through the late 1960s and early 1970s, and was also a winner in CanAm sportscars, yet his Formula 1 career was limited to sporadic races over five seasons. But his name is in the record books as the winner of the fastest, and most closely finished, Grand Prix ever run - at Monza in 1971, when his BRM P160 averaged 150.75mph.

RICHIE GINTHER (USA)

b. 5 August 1930 - d. 20 September 1989

F1 career: 60-61 - Ferrari; 62-64 - BRM; 65 - Honda; 66 - Cooper, Honda. **GP starts**: 51. **GP wins**: 1

Small, freckle-faced and always sporting a crewcut, Ginther (below) honed his skills in California and came to Europe aged 29 in 1960 to become Ferrari test driver for about $160 a month. He was given a Formula 1 debut in the 1960 Italian Grand Prix and

impressed Ferrari with a solid drive into second place behind his friend Phil Hill. After a full season in the red cars in 1961, he embarked on a three-year stint as Graham Hill's number two at BRM. His technical knowledge earned him a drive with Honda's new Formula 1 team in 1965, when he won in Mexico. This final race of the 1.5-litre formula was the first win for Honda, Goodyear and the driver. Ginther retired in 1967 and went home to America where he became something of recluse. On holiday in France he died from a heart attack in 1989.

JOSE FROILAN GONZALEZ (RA)

b. 5 October 1922

F1 career: 50 - Maserati; 51 - Talbot, Ferrari; 52-53 - Maserati; 54-55 - Ferrari; 56 - Maserati, Vanwall; 57 - Ferrari; 60 - Ferrari. **GP starts**: 26. **GP wins**: 2

Fearsome in appearance, soft-hearted by nature, Gonzalez had an ample physique which made him an unlikely racing driver, but his quick car control and tenacity were 'discovered' by his compatriot Fangio, who brought him to Europe. Gonzalez famously defeated the works Alfa Romeos at Silverstone in 1951 to score Ferrari's first Formula 1 victory and, although his car control seemed persistently precarious, he remained invariably competitive in both Ferraris and Maseratis.

"Gonzalez, the 'Cabezo' as he was called, was just the opposite of Fangio. Whereas the latter could keep going as regularly as clockwork, Gonzalez instead alternated bursts of furious speed with spells in which he seemed to be taking his time. I was never able to understand why he was so extraordinarily inconsistent - indeed, seeing the fatigued, worried and perspiring state he got into, I wondered why he ever raced at all." ENZO FERRARI

MASTEN GREGORY (USA)

b. 29 February 1932 - d. 8 November 1985

F1 career: 57-58 - Maserati; 59 - Cooper; 60 - Porsche, Cooper; 61 - Cooper, Lotus; 62 - Lotus; 63 - Lotus, Lola; 65 - BRM. **GP starts**: 38

From a wealthy mid-western American family, and wearing impressively thick spectacles and speaking with an equally impressive deep voice, Gregory chose motorsport as a means of spending a massive inheritance. He bought the 1954 Buenos Aires 1000-winning Ferrari sportscar to race in Europe - and stayed. He mixed a varied Formula 1 career with forays into sportscar racing, where his exploits included a win at the Nürburgring in a Camoradi team 'birdcage' Maserati, and a Le Mans victory in a Ferrari 250LM, co-driving with Jochen Rindt. A charming and modest man, he had three bad habits: crashing racing cars, bailing out of racing cars just before they crashed (which he did twice), and smoking strong cigarettes. It was the tobacco that killed him, in Rome, where he had set up a leather goods importing business and where he died of a heart attack in his sleep.

"He has survived more crashes than any living driver of racing cars. To break down in a Grand Prix is, for Gregory, a most prosaic ending to a race." ROBERT DALEY

DAN GURNEY (USA)

b. 13 March 1931

F1 career: 59 - Ferrari; 60 - BRM; 61-62 - Porsche; 63-65 - Brabham; 66-67 - Eagle; 68 - Eagle, Brabham, McLaren; 70 - McLaren. **GP starts**: 86. **GP wins**: 4

The handsome, all-American son of opera singers, Gurney (above) raised hell 'street racing' in souped-up hotrods in the 1950s, served as an anti-aircraft gunner in the Korean War, moved from New York to California, then started 'legal' racing with a Triumph TR2. American Ferrari importer Luigi Chinetti took him to Europe to race in the 1958 Le Mans, where he impressed Enzo Ferrari. He was signed up for $160 a month, and then given four Formula 1 outings in 1958. Full seasons with BRM and Porsche produced his maiden win with the latter, and he became a real contender when he moved to Brabham in 1963. Although disarmingly laid-back out of the car, he showed both skill and bravery: only he and Clark did not need to 'lift' through the awesome, multiple downhill esses at Rouen in 1964. He decided to become a constructor and won in 1967 at Spa with one of his beautiful, UK-built Eagles, before returning to the USA to build and operate IndyCars and IMSA GTP sportscars.

"At Jim Clark's funeral Jim's father told the friendly tall American Dan Gurney that he had been the only driver Jim truly feared. Gurney never forgot it, but typically kept it to himself." ERIC DYMOCK

MIKE HAILWOOD (GB)

b. 2 March 1940 - d. 23 March 1981

F1 career: 63 - Lotus, Lola; 64-65 - Lotus; 71-73 - Surtees; 74 - McLaren. **GP starts**: 50

Unaffected by being the son of a prosperous businessman, Hailwood chose unfashionable motorbike racing as his sport, mastered the discipline and was nine times a World Champion on two wheels when he first tried racing on four in Formula 1. But Reg Parnell's

team could not give him a winning car and, after a dozen Grands Prix, he returned to motorcycles. Six years later he came back to Formula 1 with John Surtees - the only man ever to win world titles on two wheels and four - but the cars were unreliable. In 1973, 'Mike the Bike' earned himself a George Medal for bravery when he rescued Clay Regazzoni from his burning BRM at Kyalami. His final season, with a third works McLaren, was more fruitful, but his Formula 1 career ended prematurely when he broke a leg on the Nürburgring. After another successful bike racing comeback, he was killed in a road accident caused by a reckless truck driver.

"Switching from bikes to cars I had to learn a completely different set of techniques, with vastly varying mechanical hazards to master. I was almost dizzy trying to unravel the mysteries." MIKE HAILWOOD

MIKA HAKKINEN (FIN)

b. 28 September 1968

F1 career: 91-92 - Lotus; 93-01 - McLaren. **GP starts**: 161. **GP wins**: 20. **World Champion**: 1998, 1999

After training as a unicyclist at a circus school, he added the skilful handling of three more wheels to his repertoire, raced to prominence by winning the British Formula 3 championship, and was promoted to Formula 1 by Lotus in 1991, where promising potential took him to McLaren in 1993. He famously outqualified team mate Ayrton Senna on his McLaren debut, and took over as team leader in 1994. The following year, he very nearly died after crashing heavily in Adelaide, and was only saved by an emergency tracheotomy performed at trackside by Professor Sid Watkins and the medical team. Returning to his flat in Monaco, where he kept a pet tortoise named Caroline, Hakkinen was nursed back to health by his girlfriend Erja, whom he subsequently married. As the McLaren-Mercedes partnership gelled, Hakkinen (ably assisted by his team mate Coulthard) quickly emerged as a race winner, taking his first title in 1998 with eight victories, and another the following season after more of a struggle. His partnership with David Coulthard at McLaren became the longest in Formula 1 history.

"Mika is an unusual character, very reserved and because of that hard to get to know. But I like him. He's essentially a good person, even-tempered and with no nasty traits. I don't think he would ever deliberately do anyone any harm. I don't believe he has an argumentative bone in his body. He is just a driver who wants to go racing. And that is something he does extremely well." DAVID COULTHARD

MIKE HAWTHORN (GB)

b. 10 March 1929 - d. 22 January 1959

F1 career: 52 - Cooper; 53-54 - Ferrari; 55 - Vanwall, Ferrari; 56 - Maserati, BRM, Vanwall; 57-58 - Ferrari. **GP starts**: 45. **GP wins**: 3. **World Champion**: 1958

Hawthorn raced wearing a trademark bow-tie and a full-faced plexiglas helmet that more often than not revealed a wide grin. Driving his father's Formula 2 Coopers, he impressed in five Grands Prix in 1952, and the following season became a Ferrari driver and a Grand Prix winner - just two years after his first circuit race. In 1957 and 1958, he was partnered at Ferrari by his close friend, Peter Collins, and was devastated by the death of his 'ami mate' in the 1958 German Grand Prix. He finished the season as the World Champion, but immediately announced his retirement, then crashed his Jaguar in a road accident and was killed early in 1959.

"I think he might have been driving too fast. I drove with him once, on the road. Frightened me to death. Too fast for me." STIRLING MOSS

PATRICK HEAD (GB)

b. 5 June 1946

Blessed with an acute engineering brain, Head (opposite, bottom right) established Williams Grand Prix Engineering with its eponymous co-owner, and his reputation as an innovator ultimately matched Colin Chapman's. An admirable straight-talker, with a powerful voice capable of carrying a considerable distance when making a strong point, he remains motivated by the technology of Formula 1 and dislikes reading magazines if they have pictures. He lives in London with his young family (his wife Betise was PA to the late Ayrton Senna) and commutes daily to the Williams factory in Oxfordshire by helicopter.

JOHNNY HERBERT (GB)

b. 25 June 1964

F1 career: 89 - Benetton, Tyrrell; 90-93 - Lotus; 94 - Lotus, Ligier, Benetton; 95 - Benetton; 96-98 - Sauber; 99-00 - Stewart/Jaguar. **GP starts**: 161. **GP wins**: 3

A cheerful disposition helped Herbert (above) recover from a devastating F3000 accident in 1988, but that same trait probably hindered him in Formula 1. Undoubtedly a natural talent, Herbert's fun-loving demeanour counted against him when the top drives became available, because team owners were unable to convince themselves that he was serious about his career. His only real break was rejoining Benetton when it was on top form, but his team mate was Michael Schumacher, whose complete command of the team left no room for Herbert to manoeuvre. Yet he persevered and remained popular with his peers, none of whom, with the possible exception of Schumacher, resented his three victories.

"I've been criticised for being too cheerful and not appearing to take things seriously, but that's a mask I adopted after the accident. Before then, I wasn't a bubbly sort of guy." JOHNNY HERBERT

ALEXANDER HESKETH (GB)

b. 28 October 1950

Lord Thomas Alexander Fermor-Hesketh inherited his father's title when he was five - but the family's wealth was withheld until he was 21, at which point he began spending large quantities of it as a race team proprietor. Described then as a 'Falstaffian figure' and an 'eccentric British peer', the portly 'Good Lord' and his friend 'Bubbles' Horsley hired James 'Hunt the Shunt' to drive a Formula 2 Surtees, an old Formula 1 Surtees and later a March. He enlisted the services of several glamorous young women to serve as pit crew and used a pin-striped Rolls Royce and a Jet Ranger helicopter as team transporters. At their headquarters, the vast Hesketh family estate near Silverstone, Harvey Postlethwaite PhD designed the first Hesketh car in 1974 and, in 1975, it won the Dutch Grand Prix with Hunt aboard. But even Hesketh was unable to continue funding the sponsorless team and he sold it to Walter Wolf. A member of the House of Lords, Hesketh turned to politics, and has since been a Tory government whip, a junior minister at the DTI, and a Privy Counsellor. From 1994-99, he was the president of the British Racing Drivers Club.

DAMON HILL (GB)

b. 17 September 1960

F1 career: 92 - Brabham; 93-96 - Williams; 97 - Arrows; 98-99 - Jordan. **GP starts**: 115. **GP wins**: 22. **World Champion**: 1996

Despite having a famous Formula 1 name, Damon Hill had to make it on his own, and he did, with the same gritty determination as his father Graham. Having begun by successfully racing motorcycles, he swapped to cars in his mid-twenties and by the early 1990s was considered an F3000 driver of quality. This was recognised by Frank Williams, who signed him as a test driver in 1992 and allowed him the chance to get Formula 1 race experience for half a season with Brabham. When Mansell deserted to the USA, Hill hung on to fend off rival bids to line up alongside Prost for 1993. He went on to win his first Grand Prix later that year and pushed Michael Schumacher hard for the title in the next two seasons, before finally making it his own in 1996, whereupon Williams dumped him. Thereafter, though he bounced back to win the first Grand Prix for Jordan, Hill's career petered out and he left Formula 1 with little fanfare.

GRAHAM HILL (GB)

b. 15 February 1929 - d. 29 November 1975

F1 career: 58-59 - Lotus; 60-66 - BRM; 67-70 -Lotus; 71-72 - Brabham; 73 - Shadow; 74-75 -Lola. **GP starts**: 176. **GP wins**: 14. **World Champion**: 1962, 1968

A well-known oarsman for the London Rowing Club, Graham Hill was an unashamed opportunist, and talked his way into a job as a mechanic with the emerging Team Lotus. He picked up the odd drive in Lotus and Cooper sportscars, and was on hand when Lotus entered Formula 1 in 1958. In 1960, he left to join BRM, which took him to his first title two seasons later. He was loyal to BRM until returning to Lotus in 1967 and, on Clark's death, steered the team through its darkest days by winning the 1968 championship. A year later, he famously fought to return to the cockpit after badly breaking his legs at Watkins Glen. The only man to win the Formula 1 World Championship, the Indy 500 and the Le Mans 24 Hours, he formed his own team in 1973 and, unpredictably irascible as he grew older, could put the fear of God into his employees. He had just become a constructor when he died in an awful aircraft accident. With his Errol Flynn moustache, he was the life and soul of any party - another outstanding virtue was his stubborn determination. These are what killed him: his refusal to accept air traffic control advice to abort a landing in thick fog because he was late for a party. The immensely talented driver Tony Brise and other team members died with him.

"Very intense and dedicated, or perhaps the word is determined, Graham never gives up, whether it be with his golf game, his jokes, daily exercises, or racing. His competitiveness has always been closely linked to his pride and probably is responsible for his staying on so long, which hasn't been an altogether good thing." JACKIE STEWART

PHIL HILL (USA)

b. 20 March 1927

F1 career: 58 - Maserati, Ferrari; 59 - Ferrari; 60 - Ferrari, Cooper; 61-62 - Ferrari; 63 - ATS, Lotus; 64 - Cooper. **GP starts**: 48. **GP wins**: 3. **World Champion**: 1961

Small, dapper and highly focused, Phil Hill (above) worked hard as a youth to finance his racing and was spotted by US sportscar entrant Alan Guiberson, for whom he raced a Ferrari in International events. Soon his talent came to the attention of Luigi Chinetti, and then the Scuderia itself. He was signed up in 1956 and developed into an outstanding sportscar driver, eventually winning Le Mans three times (all with Gendebien). Frustrated by being excluded from the Formula 1 team, he hired a Maserati 250F to make his debut in the 1958 French Grand Prix and finished seventh. Enzo Ferrari relented and Hill went on to become America's first World Champion, clinched at Monza in 1961, in the race marred by the fatal accident to his team mate von Trips and many spectators. He threw away his Formula 1 career two years later with an ill-advised commitment to Carlo Chiti's doomed ATS project. An operagoer between races, he would listen to symphonies in his hotel room and in his retirement continued to build up a collection of classical records and piano rolls, as well as rebuilding classic cars.

"A reliable, intelligent driver who started on sports cars and had some useful experience as a mechanic in California. He likes sweeping bends and long straights, being less fond of winding courses that require continuous driving precision. This precision he prefers to show where speed is the factor that counts." ENZO FERRARI

ANTHONY 'BUBBLES' HORSLEY (GB)

b. 1943

He spent part of the 1960s wandering around Europe as a nomad with the Formula 3 circus, ending his driving career at the Nürburgring when he crashed his car into the already crashed car of Frank Williams. Horsley then tried the hippy life, driving to Bhutan in a Land Rover before returning to London as proprietor of Horsley's Horseless Carriages, a car trading venture, and supplementing his income by working as an actor in TV commercials promoting sausages and beer. With his friend Alexander Hesketh, "partly out of boredom, as a sort of weekend hobby, we decided to go racing." From 1973 until its demise in 1978 Horsley ran Hesketh's team with considerable acumen, transforming it from a joke into a serious contender.

DENIS 'DENNY' HULME (NZ)

b. 18 June 1936 - d. 4 October 1992

F1 career: 65-67 - Brabham; 68-74 - McLaren; **GP starts**: 112. **GP wins**: 8. **World Champion**: 1967.

With his father in the trucking business, Hulme learned to drive and service vehicles at an early age. In 1961 he came to England under New Zealand's 'Driver to Europe' scheme and financed his racing by working as a mechanic for Jack Brabham. In 1962, a first-ever victory for a Brabham car, in a Formula Junior race at Brands Hatch, earned him a Formula 1 trial. He became Brabham's full-time team mate in 1966, and secured his first two victories the following season en route to the title. An offer from fellow Kiwi Bruce McLaren tempted him away and the balance of his Grand Prix career was spent mainly as team leader, following the death of his friend. As retirement drew closer, 'The Bear' - big and gruff on the outside, inwardly a sweetie - grew less enamoured with his environment, but he won the 1974 Argentine race during his final season. He still loved to compete, and raced on for another 18 years - until he died of a heart attack behind the wheel of a BMW during the 1992 Bathurst 1000 race in Australia.

> "I don't like fame. Deep down inside it's nice to know I've done it, but the speeches and social functions are agony." DENIS HULME

JAMES HUNT (GB)

b. 29 August 1947 - d. 15 June 1993

F1 career: 73 - March; 74 - March, Hesketh; 75 - Hesketh; 76-78 - McLaren; 79 - Wolf. **GP starts**: 92. **GP wins**: 10. **World Champion**: 1976

The son of a London stockbroker, Hunt was educated at Wellington, one of Britain's leading schools. His early career as an amateur in Formula 3 was notable only for spectacular accidents, but his background and cultivated accent seemed to be sufficient to gain promotion with Lord Hesketh's new Formula 1 team in 1973. Once in Formula 1, his development as a driver was astonishing. The team's one victory at Zandvoort in 1975 propelled him to McLaren the following year, where his championship battle with his friend Niki Lauda, who nearly died in his flaming Ferrari, was one of the most dramatic ever. Hunt won the title, delighting his young fans and offending the establishment with his often wild behaviour. He remained competitive over the next two seasons but was disheartened by poor reliability, and with increasing fears about the dangers of his profession, he walked away from the sport in 1979. His achievements should be judged against his terror of racing, which often caused him to vomit just before the start. He showed no such fear when he became an outspoken and perceptive TV commentator, to the great benefit of viewers. All were shocked when he died suddenly from a heart attack.

> "James was a total non-conformist, a curious mixture of wit, intelligence, stubbornness and sometimes appalling behaviour. Whatever else he might have been, he was never boring." STIRLING MOSS

JACKY ICKX (B)

b. 1 January 1945

F1 career: 67 - Cooper; 68 - Ferrari; 69 - Brabham; 70- 72 - Ferrari; 73 - Ferrari, McLaren, ISO; 74-75 - Lotus; 76 - Williams, Ensign; 77-78 - Ensign; 79 - Ligier. **GP starts**: 116. **GP wins**: 8.

The son of a motorsport journalist, Ickx might have been a multiple World Champion, but instead his name will forever be linked to Le Mans, where he won the great 24 Hours race on six occasions. In Formula 1 he burst onto the scene with impressive performances in a Formula 2 Matra for Tyrrell. At Ferrari in 1968, he gained the distinction of scoring the first Grand Prix win with a winged racecar (at Rouen). Noted for extreme bravery, bordering on the foolhardy, he nonetheless seemed to have what it took to take the title, but it never came. Some thought his extreme self-

confidence ventured into outright conceit, though it served him well on wet tracks where his skill was simply astonishing. Ickx (below) won five times for Ferrari, in spite of the situation he found there.

> "At Ferrari confusion is permanent. Changing of mind is continuous. Whatever happens, the Ferrari car is never at fault, not the Ingegnere Forghieri. The driver is always guilty. It is not pleasant or easy to work for Ferrari. When you must, it is probably better that you do not understand Italian." JACKY ICKX

INNES IRELAND (GB)

12 June 1930 - 22 October 1993

F1 career: 59-62 - Lotus; 63-64 - BRM; 65 - Lotus; 66: BRM. **GP starts**: 50. **GP wins**: 1

Ireland, the son of a veterinary surgeon, did his British National Service as a paratrooper - and would often swear like one. Yet he was highly literate, with a personal library of books by Chekhov, Sophocles, Hugo, Conrad, Huxley and Kipling. Refusing to wear seat belts, he survived a violent accident in the tunnel at Monaco that threw him out the car with such force he left his shoes behind in the cockpit. Ireland was a fiercely determined competitor who never forgave Lotus for dropping him in favour of Jim Clark, just after he had won the US Grand Prix with a faultless drive. His career declined over subsequent seasons and he applied his refreshing, hell-raiser attitude to racing journalism until succumbing to cancer at the age of 63.

> "In my day we didn't strap ourselves in with those 'hysterical' safety belts. Stewart was the one that started all that crap, going about with his blood group tattooed on his underpants, that kind of thing." INNES IRELAND

EDDIE IRVINE (GB)

b. 10 November 1965

F1 career: 93-95 - Jordan; 96-99 - Ferrari; 00-01 - Jaguar. **GP starts**: 117. **GP wins**: 4

Having forged a financially sound niche in Japanese F3000, and made money speculating on the stock market, he took a risk and a salary cut to join fellow-Irishman Eddie Jordan in Formula 1. His baptism at the 1993 Japanese Grand Prix ended in a punch-up with Senna, and was followed immediately by an accident in Brazil that caused him to be banned for several races. Within a few years he would be enjoying millionaire status as a Ferrari driver, coming close to winning the title when his team mate Michael Schumacher broke his leg in 1999. Moving to Jaguar, his earning power remained high, unlike his lifestyle.

> "Boozing, clubbing, women - you name it. I really lived it up. I went bananas. Then I realised that the only thing you get out of doing that are headaches." EDDIE IRVINE

JEAN-PIERRE JABOUILLE (F)

b. 1 September 1942

F1 career: 75 - Tyrrell; 76-80 - Renault; 81 - Ligier. **GP starts**: 49. **GP wins**: 2

Almost boring to watch behind the wheel, Jabouille's real talent was as a development driver, but he led Renault's first foray into Formula 1 in 1977, taking the turbo V6 engine programme to the winner's circle in just two years. He suffered broken legs in an accident during the penultimate race of 1980, and quit Formula 1 following an unsuccessful comeback attempt with Ligier in 1981. Peugeot plucked him from its World Sportscar driver line-up to front its new Formula 1 engine project, but he became a high-profile casualty when it foundered.

CHARLES JARROTT (GB)

b. 1877 - d. 1944

Britain's leading racing driver of the pioneering era of motorsport, Jarrott raced motorised tricycles at Crystal Palace before graduating to cars in 1901, and was the winner of the world's first major circuit race, the 1902 Circuit des Ardennes. His last major race was in 1904, after which he devoted his time to his various car-related businesses. He was a co-founder of the AA.

ALAN JONES (AUS)

b. 2 November 1946

F1 career: 75 - Hesketh, Lola; 76 - Surtees; 77-81 - Williams; 83 - Arrows; 85-86 - Lola-Haas. **GP starts**: 116. **GP wins**: 12. **World Champion**: 1980

A straight-talking, iron-willed, hard-driving tough guy, Jones fought his way to the forefront, where he defended his territory with ruthless determination and large doses of intimidation. The rugged Australian, who once tackled three large adversaries with his fists in a bout of civilian road rage, could also be very funny and delighted in being politically incorrect.

> "Alan was a man's man. And he was great fun to be with. He never needed propping up mentally, because he was a very determined and bullish character. He didn't need any babysitting or hand-holding, and that's the way it should be. It's shouldn't be necessary for me to ask a driver if he is happy, or if he needs his underwear changed."
> FRANK WILLIAMS

EDDIE JORDAN (GB)

b. 30 March 1948

A former Dublin bank clerk and would-be rock star drummer, Jordan wheeled and dealed his way from journeyman Formula 3 driver to fun-loving Formula 1 team owner.

> "The way I run the team is on a fairly casual basis. Anyone can have a chat and a laugh. The Irish play the role of the underdog beautifully. But behind this façade is a man so desperately serious I'm just glad I haven't blown my cover."
> EDDIE JORDAN

JACQUES LAFFITE (F)

b. 21 November, 1943

F1 career: 74 - Iso; 75 - Williams; 76-82 - Ligier; 83-84 - Williams; 85-86 - Ligier. **GP starts**: 176. **GP wins**: 6.

Laffite was a popular member of the Formula 1 fraternity for over a decade. When practice for the 1984 Dallas Grand Prix started very early to avoid the intense heat, he appeared in the pits wearing his pyjamas. His lengthy career was terminated prematurely following leg injuries sustained in an accident at the start of the 1986 European Grand Prix, though he continued to travel with the Formula 1 circus as a team adviser and TV pundit.

HERMANN LANG (D)

b. 6 June 1909 - d. 19 October 1987

A Mercedes mechanic, Lang graduated from working on Luigi Fagioli's car to become a full-time driver from 1937, soon establishing himself as the team's fastest driver with some formidable performances.

NIKI LAUDA (AUS)

b. 22 February 1949

F1 career: 71-72 - March; 73 - BRM; 74-77 - Ferrari; 78-79 - Brabham; 82-85 - McLaren. **GP starts**: 171. **GP wins**: 25. **World Champion**: 1975, 1977, 1984

The son of a prosperous Viennese businessman, Nikolas Andreas Lauda traded on the family name to borrow money from banks to rent his first Formula 1 rides. Deeply in debt, he drove his way out of it by transforming himself into a winner, though he very nearly paid the ultimate price in an appalling accident at the Nürburgring in 1976. Terribly burned and given up for dead, he recovered by what doctors described as sheer force of will and raced on - carving himself a permanent niche as one of the sport's greatest heroes. As a driver, besides being incredibly brave and tenacious, he had one of the best racing brains in the business and was known variously as 'The Computer', 'The Technician' and 'The Calculator'. Gruff and notoriously unsentimental - he gave away his "useless" trophies - his often brutal frankness was leavened by an acerbic wit used to express an ironic sense of humour. "Tired of driving around in circles", he abruptly hung up his helmet in 1979 and turned his talents to aviation, another of his enthusiasms, and founded Lauda Air. Returning to the racing life, Lauda won a third driving title in 1984. The battle-scarred veteran then served as an adviser to Ferrari for several years, before taking over as boss of the Jaguar team in 2001.

> "A tremendous character and personality. A living legend."
> JOHN WATSON

EMILE LEVASSOR

b. 21 January 1843 - d. 14 April 1897

An engineer by profession, Levassor won the first proper motor race, the 1895 Paris-Bordeaux-Paris. He was a partner in the company Panhard et Levassor that manufactured cars powered by Daimler engines. He was leading the 1896 Paris-Marseilles race when his car overturned after hitting a dog. Though he subsequently finished the race, internal injuries led to his death the following year.

STUART LEWIS-EVANS

b. 20 April 1930 - d. 25 October 1958

F1 career: 57 - Connaught, Vanwall; 58 - Vanwall. **GP starts**: 14

A friend of Bernie Ecclestone, Lewis-Evans made rapid progress in his first few races and was marked for future stardom. But his career was cut short when his Vanwall's transmission seized and he crashed in Casablanca. Badly burned, he died in hospital a few days later.

WILLY MAIRESSE (B)

b. 1 October 1928 - d. 4 September 1969

F1 career: 60 - Ferrari; 61 - Lotus, Ferrari; 62-63 - Ferrari. **GP starts**: 12

Mairesse was the prototypical 'accident waiting to happen'. Brave beyond his skill, the passionate little Belgian miraculously survived several massive crashes, until serious head injuries ended the racing for which he lived. He became despondent and died by his own hand in a shabby hotel room in a dreary seaside town in Belgium.

> "Mairesse is a man who takes many risks, a strange kind of fellow, of undaunted will and unfathomable courage, who is fired by a sort of sacred zeal in whatever he puts his hand to."
> ENZO FERRARI

NIGEL MANSELL (GB)

b. 8 August 1953

F1 career: 80-84 - Lotus; 85-88 - Williams; 89-90 - Ferrari; 91-94 - Williams; 95 - McLaren. **GP starts**: 187. **GP wins**: 31. **World Champion**: 1992.

Mansell came up the hard way, literally breaking his neck and his back *en route* to Formula 1, where it took him 72 Grands Prix to win for the first time. From then on he was often unstoppable, in the process becoming one of the most exciting drivers of all time. Every time he took to the track, Mansell attacked. He was guaranteed to do something sensational, occasionally making silly mistakes but more frequently staging scintillating performances that smacked of pure aggression. He seemed to thrive on adversarial situations, using them to fuel his motivational fires, and if they didn't exist he would invent them. His 'me against the world mentality' upset many. At Williams Patrick Head said "he thinks everybody is trying to shaft him at all times, and that can be extremely wearing", and Frank Williams called Mansell "a pain in the arse". Mansell was ridiculed in the media, particularly in Britain, where he was rubbished as a chronic complainer and made fun of for affecting a bristling moustache and whingeing in a 'Brummie' accent. But the fans weren't fooled. In Britain, 'Our

Nige' provoked feverish 'Mansellmania' amongst millions. In Italy, for Ferrari, '*Il Leone*' was a huge hero to the *tifosi*. Universally, his 'British Bulldog' determination was admired.

> "Nigel was a difficult man. But he would never give up. On race day he was somebody you really had to look out for."
> GERHARD BERGER

ONOFRE MARIMON (ARG)

b. 19 December 1923 - d. 31 July 1954

F1 career: 51-54 - Maserati. **GP starts**: 11

A protégé of Fangio, and also a friend of their fellow-Argentinian Gonzalez, Marimon showed great promise until the fatal accident at the Nürburgring which left Fangio and Gonzalez distraught.

JOCHEN MASS (D)

b. 30 September 1946

F1 career: 73 - Surtees; 74 - Surtees, McLaren; 75-77 - McLaren; 78 - ATS; 79-80 - Arrows; 82 - March. **GP starts**: 105. **GP wins**: 1

A burly former merchant seaman, who still owns a fine sailing barge, Mass (below) became interested in racing at 21 and progressed

steadily from amateur hillclimbs and touring car racing into F1, where his only win came with McLaren in the 1975 Spanish GP. He excelled as a sportscar driver with the factory Porsche and Sauber Mercedes teams, winning the 1989 Le Mans - a race he detested. Popular and easy-going (he was nicknamed 'Herman the German' by James Hunt), his career was unfortunately blighted by his involvement in Gilles Villeneuve's fatal accident in 1982. Mass was haunted by the incident for many years, until a chance meeting on a street in Monaco in 1996.

> "I was walking around one day and suddenly was stopped by this young woman saying hello to me. I did not recognise her and she said, 'Do you remember me? I am Melanie, daughter of Gilles Villeneuve.' I was shocked and did not know what to say. But she took away all my uneasiness in a couple of seconds. She was very friendly and told me nobody in the family was angry about me, or is blaming me because of what happened in 1982. Later, I often met Jacques Villeneuve at the races, and he was always very kind."
> JOCHEN MASS

BRUCE McLAREN (NZ)

b. 30 August 1937 - d. 2 June 1970

F1 career: 58-65 - Cooper; 66-70 - McLaren. **GP starts**: 101. **GP wins**: 4

The son of an Auckland garage owner, McLaren contracted a rare disease at the age of nine, and was unable to walk for two years. It left him with a permanent limp, but he started in motorsport soon after his 16th birthday while studying engineering. His national sporting authority sponsored him as its first 'Driver to Europe' in 1958, and he raced an F2 Cooper to such good effect that he was offered a full-time F1 drive in 1959 alongside Brabham - and ended his debut season by winning the inaugural US GP at Sebring. He also won in Argentina in 1960 and in Monaco in 1962 during his eight seasons with Cooper, and then established Bruce McLaren Motor Racing, initially to run Coopers. It began tragically when his partner and team mate, Tim Mayer, was killed at Longford during the Tasman Series, but the team survived the setback and, in 1966 (the year when McLaren himself won Le Mans for Ford), it was ready to build its own chassis. Its F1 project was slow to make a mark, as were subsequent IndyCar and F2 programmes, but its sports-racers became almost unbeatable in the CanAm series, which they would dominate for five seasons. F1 success arrived in 1968 with the Cosworth DFV engine. McLaren won in Belgium and team mate Hulme in Italy and Canada and, by 1969, the team was an established front-runner. Sadly its owner was killed testing a new CanAm model at Goodwood a year later, and never knew that his name would eventually signify so much F1 glory.

> "I thought Bruce might have become World Champion because he had the ability to think about it. He wasn't going to be the world's quickest driver, but then the world's quickest driver isn't always World Champion." KEN TYRRELL

JUAN PABLO MONTOYA (COL)

b. 20 September 1975

F1 career: 01 - Williams. **GP starts**: 17. **GP wins**: 1

Montoya's first racing experience came at the age of five months, on his architect father's knee in a go-kart in Bogota, from where he sped through the ranks of racing, winning all the way. Having conquered all comers in American CART racing, where he gained a reputation for bravery bordering on madness, the former Williams test driver moved up to the main team, where his unharnessed aggression saw him deliver both 'bull-in-a-china-shop' and 'diamond-in-the-rough' performances, Gradually, Montoya (below) settled down and became a steadier, though still spectacular, performer.

> "He's a charger, like an army coming through the pass."
> FRANK WILLIAMS

MAX MOSLEY (GB)

b. 13 April 1940

Son of controversial politician Sir Oswald Mosley and Lady Diana Mitford (of the literary family), Mosley was educated in France and Germany and at Christ Church, Oxford, where he studied

physics, and honed his wily debating skills as the secretary of the Oxford Union. He then read law in London, qualifying in 1964 while dabbling in racing as an amateur. He and Chris Lambert formed a team together to graduate to Formula 2, but his partner was killed at Zandvoort and he joined Piers Courage in Frank Williams's team. Mosley quit racing in 1969 to co-found March Engineering. As a brand-name racecar maker, the company was very successful, less so as an Formula 1 team, winning only two GPs (in 1975 and 1976). But Mosley (above) became increasingly involved with Bernie Ecclestone and his emerging FOCA organisation and, in 1977, was appointed as its legal adviser. In this role he was centrally involved in the FISA-FOCA war of 1980-81, and co-wrote the Concorde Agreement that resolved it. Later he became the president of the FISA Manufacturers Commission, and subsequently stood in the 1991 FISA presidential election, defeating the incumbent, Jean-Marie Balestre. Having merged FISA with the FIA, he was elected in 1993 as the FIA president, and has since been increasingly engaged in representing the motor industry in European government circles.

SIR STIRLING MOSS (GB)

b 17 September 1929

F1 career: 51 - HWM; 52 - HWM, ERA, Connaught; 53 - Connaught, Cooper; 54 - Maserati; 55 - Mercedes-Benz; 56 - Maserati; 57 - Vanwall, Maserati; 58 - Vanwall, Cooper; 59 - Cooper, Porsche, BRM; 60 - Cooper, Lotus; 61 - Lotus, Cooper, Ferguson. **GP starts**: 66. **GP wins**: 16.

Undoubtedly the best driver never to win the World Championship, Moss was a brilliant all-rounder, and probably also the greatest sportscar racing driver of all time. The dentist's son forsook showjumping to take up a 500cc single-seater racing in 1947, and rose to international prominence three years later when he won the Tourist Trophy with a privately owned Jaguar XK120. His Formula 1 debut quickly followed, but not in competitive cars. In 1954, Moss (below) and his father bought a Maserati 250F to accelerate his career, and his immediate third place at Spa led to a works drive, then on to Mercedes-Benz. He very ably backed up Fangio, and was first across the line in the 1955 British Grand Prix to score the first of his 16 career victories - although this paled into insignificance next to his fabulous winning drive in the Mille Miglia in the company's 300SLR sportscar. Back at Maserati, he won two more races in 1956 before taking up an offer from

Vanwall, which made him a title contender in both the next two seasons. However, three wins in 1957 were insufficient to defeat Fangio who, ironically, had replaced him at Maserati. Then his strong sense of fair play famously cost him the 1958 championship. He stepped forward to offer a successful defence of Hawthorn when his rival faced a penalty in Portugal, where Moss had won. He went on to lose the title to the Ferrari driver by a single point, despite having four victories to Hawthorn's one. Thereafter, spurning offers from Ferrari and works teams, he did most of his Formula 1 racing for privateer Rob Walker, with whose Cooper he had won in Argentina at the start of that 1958 campaign. He secured six more victories, including an outstanding success with a Lotus 18 at Monaco in 1960. This was followed by a serious accident at Spa when a wheel fell off the car, but he heroically fought to recover from his back injuries, and came back to win the US race at season's end. His career ended abruptly and mysteriously, when his Lotus left the road at Goodwood during the Easter meeting in 1962, and he received critical head injuries. Moss eventually came round from a coma and recovered fully. He is still occasionally to be seen racing Historic cars.

"I only once saw Stirling nervous, and that was at Oporto following his very bad accident at Spa in 1960. After that race he had such a violent reaction that he was physically sick all night. I'm sure it was nerves, and never saw any further signs of it." ROB WALKER

LUIGI MUSSO (I)

b. 28 July 1924 - d. 6 July 1958
F1 career: 53-55 - Maserati; 56-58 - Ferrari.
GP starts: 24. **GP wins**: 1

The athletic son of a wealthy diplomat, Musso was adept at shooting, fencing and riding, but envied his elder brothers, whose sport was motor racing. He had to wait until 1952 before one of them loaned him a little Stanguellini single-seater, and he was immediately the fastest racing driver in the family. He was chosen for a Maserati 'junior' team in 1953 and won his national sportscar title, also getting a run in the Italian Grand Prix. He was retained in the works team to race sportscars and occasionally F1 machines in 1954-55, and was head-hunted by Scuderia Ferrari in 1956. His only Formula 1 victory came with its Lancia D50 that season, when he handed over his car to team leader Fangio. Later in the year, at Monza, he refused to do so again, and was heading for victory when a broken steering arm caused a crash only three laps from the finish. In 1958 he crashed fatally at 150mph into a ditch at Reims during the French Grand Prix.

ALFRED NEUBAUER (D)

b. 29 March 1891

Born in what is now the Czech Republic, Neubauer was a motor pool manager in WW1 with the Austrian army and was hired by Austro-Daimler in 1922 to drive the Sascha car, designed by Ferdinand Porsche. In 1924 he raced in the Italian GP, but was withdrawn when his team mate, Count Louis Zborowski, was killed. He became Daimler's motorsport manager in 1925, the year before the merger of Daimler and Benz, which created the Mercedes-Benz brand. He developed Porsche's Mercedes-Benz SSK for sportscar racing and occasional GPs in 1928-29, and went on to set new standards of team direction during the second half of the 1930s, when the awesome 'Silver Arrows' had their heyday in Grand Prix racing. Always an eccentric, larger-than-life character, he said that a driver on the race track

was "the world's loneliest human being," and set out to keep his men fully supported and informed during races, though he was also a stern taskmaster given to loud rages. After WW2, he masterminded the company's run of F1 successes in 1954-55 before the Le Mans disaster led it to withdraw from motorsport, whereupon he helped look after the Mercedes museum in Stuttgart.

ADRIAN NEWEY (GB)

b. 28 December 1958

The first 'superstar' designer, the son of a vet, Newey began by assembling scale model Formula 1 cars as a hobby, before building his own go-kart; at 15 he designed an electronic ignition system. After getting an aeronautical engineering degree, he applied his energies to designing Formula 1 cars that won many races and several championships - first with Williams, then from 1997 with McLaren, where he became technical director.

GUNNAR NILSSON (S)

b. 20 November 1948 - d. 20 October 1978
F1 career: 76-77 - Lotus. **GP starts**: 31.
GP wins: 1

Nilsson (below), the fun-loving and carefree 'Viking Driver' once said every lap at the Nürburgring was "like a blue movie". His promising career was cut short by cancer. Before

succumbing to the disease he helped found the Gunnar Nilsson Cancer Treatment Campaign.

TAZIO NUVOLARI (I)

b. 18 November 1982 - d. 11 August 1953

Believed by many to be the greatest driver who ever lived, Nuvolari was a motorcycle champion and already in his late 30s before his sporadic successes led to him being given a works drive by Alfa-Romeo in 1930. His awesome talent and breathtaking daring made him a legend. The

image was merely accentuated later in the decade when his cars were rendered obsolete by German machinery, but he continued to confound belief by taking them on and occasionally beating them, never more spectacularly than in his victory in the 1935 German Grand Prix. He later joined Auto-Union and continued his winning form. He was an ill man post-war, with a lung disease believed to have been brought on by prolonged breathing of the fumes from the exotic fuels of the times, but nonetheless he continued to produce heroic performances. He died in 1953 at the age of 60 and was buried in his leather helmet, Italian flag tricolour scarf, yellow shirt and blue trousers.

"I will do anything to win. Anything, anything, anything. Win first and let them lodge their objections afterwards has always been my code." TAZIO NUVOLARI

JACKIE OLIVER (GB)

b. 14 August 1942
F1 career: 67-68 - Lotus; 69-70 - BRM; 71 -McLaren; 72 - BRM; 73: Shadow. **GP starts**: 50

A victim of mechanical failures and a brave survivor of several large accidents, Oliver never won a Grand Prix but made a lasting mark on the sport by becoming a founding member of the Arrows team.

CARLOS PACE (BR)

b. 6 October 1944 - d. 18 March 1977
F1 career: 72 - March; 73-74 - Surtees; 74-77 - Brabham. **GP starts**: 72. **GP wins**: 1

Nicknamed 'Moco,' Pace (above) was intelligent, handsome and superstitious. His wife and two children all shared the same birthday. In 1974 he changed his helmet design when a spiritualist advised him that it was unlucky to wear an arrow on his forehead. His Brabham boss Bernie Ecclestone claimed Pace would have been a champion had he not been killed in a private plane crash before the 1977 season began.

RICCARDO PALETTI (I)

b. 15 June 1958 - d. 13 June 1982

F1 career: 82 - Osella. **GP starts**: 1

Paletti died just seconds after starting his first Grand Prix, from the back of the grid in Montreal. His Osella rammed Pironi's stalled Ferrari and the young Italian succumbed to the massive internal injuries he incurred.

OLIVIER PANIS (F)

b. 2 September 1966

F1 career: 94-96 - Ligier; 97-99 - Prost; 01 - BAR. **GP starts**: 108. **GP wins**: 1

An optimistic and hard-working team player, Panis needed these attributes during his tenures with not particularly competitive teams. An opportunistic but deserved win in Monaco in 1996 was followed the next year by a serious accident that left him with badly broken legs. Manager Keke Rosberg masterminded a career-resurrecting move to the new BAR team in 1999, though equipment deficiencies continued to impede much forward progess.

REG PARNELL (GB)

b. 2 July 1911 - d. 7 January 1964

F1 career: 50 - Alfa Romeo, Maserati; 51 - Ferrari, BRM; 52 - Cooper; 54 - Ferrari. **GP starts**: 6.

Best remembered as a team manager, firstly during the 1950s with Aston Martin, then Yeoman Credit and his own team in the 1960s, Parnell was also quite capable behind the wheel and scored points in three of his six Championship starts.

TIM PARNELL (GB)

b. 25 June 1932

F1 career: 61 - Lotus. **GP starts**: 2.

Following the untimely death of his father, Reg, Tim Parnell took on managerial roles at Reg Parnell Racing and at BRM in the late 1960s, then retired to run the family pig farm in Derbyshire.

RICARDO PATRESE (I)

b. 17 March 1954

F1 career: 77 - Shadow; 78-81 - Arrows; 82-83 - Brabham; 84-85 - Alfa Romeo; 86-87 - Brabham, Williams; 88-92 - Williams; 93 - Benetton. **GP starts**: 256. **GP wins**: 6

After an uneasy start as a rambunctious rookie, Patrese matured into a steady performer - in fact the steadiest of all, competing in a record 256 Grands Prix. On his debut in 1978, he was wrongly condemned by his peers for being responsible for Ronnie Peterson's fatal accident. Self-confessed as both arrogant and shy as a newcomer, Patrese (below) was a highly-respected and well-liked veteran when he retired

in 1993, after 17 seasons, thereafter devoting himself to his favourite pursuits of golf, skiing and collecting watches and model trains. A real team player, Patrese is remembered fondly by those he drove for.

> "He's not a selfish man, which is quite rare in a racing driver. His ego is under control too. Which is also quite rare."
> FRANK WILLIAMS

RONNIE PETERSON (S)

b. 14 February 1944 - d. 11 September 1978

F1 career: 70-72 - March; 73-76 - Lotus; 77 - Tyrrell; 78 - Lotus. **GP starts**: 123. **GP wins**: 10.

An abundance of natural talent, coupled with an all-out driving style, guaranteed Peterson cult status in the 1970s, although his spectacular, full-opposite lock powerslides were in direct contrast to his demeanour out of the cockpit, as

he was a reserved man whose hobby was tropical fish. Without doubt World Champion material, he simply never found himself in quite the right place at the right time. At Monza in 1978 he was in the wrong place at the wrong time and was fatally injured.

> "In natural car control and ability, Ronnie got a very high ranking, but in my opinion he wasn't a complete driver. I admired his driving very much - the seat of the pants thing - but beyond that there was a lack of mental application that prevented him from winning more Grands Prix." JACKIE STEWART

NELSON PIQUET (BR)

b. 17 August 1952

F1 career: 78 - Ensign, McLaren, Brabham; 79-85 - Brabham; 86-87 - Williams; 88-89 - Lotus; 90-91 - Benetton. **GP starts**: 204. **GP wins**: 24. **World Champion**: 1981, 1983, 1987

His real name was Nelson Piquet Sauto Maior, though he never used his father's surname because he hid his early racing from his disapproving parents and later found that the press had an easier time pronouncing his mother's maiden name. His family wanted him to be a tennis pro - and sent him to the US for a year to perfect his game - but their son preferred racing, turning up in the Brabham garage in 1974, where he made tea, swept the floors and slept beside the cars as a watchman. Seven years later he won his first World Championship. He also fancied himself as a champion practical joker, though on one occasion a ruse backfired spectacularly. When a female photographer left her camera in the Brabham garage Piquet had a mechanic take a full frontal shot of his manhood, not realising his name - embroidered on the belt of his dropped trousers - was also captured by the lens. A short time later an intimate portrait of Nelson Piquet appeared in an adult magazine.

DIDIER PIRONI (F)

b. 26 March 1952 - d. 23 August 1987

F1 career: 78-79 - Tyrrell; 80 - Ligier; 81-82 - Ferrari. **GP starts**: 70. **GP wins**: 3

In 1981, with his team mate Gilles Villeneuve as passenger in a Ferrari 308GTB1, Pironi averaged 136mph over 95 miles of the *autostrada* in

heavy traffic between Milan and Modena on the way to a test session at Ferrari's Fiorano track. The next year, after the team mates fell out at Imola, Villeneuve was killed at Zolder and Pironi suffered a career-ending accident at Hockenheim. He took up powerboat racing and had some success before being drowned when his boat flipped during a race off the coast of southern England.

> "I remember thinking while I was flying through the air at Hockenheim that it was a shame because I was going really well and now I'm going to crash. Then I saw the line of pine trees and saw I was flying very high. Then came the fall and I thought it was all over. But then - voila! - I was still conscious."
> DIDIER PIRONI

ALAIN PROST (F)

b. 24 February 1955

F1 career: 80 - McLaren; 81-83 - Renault; 84-89 - McLaren; 90-91 - Ferrari; 93 - Williams. **GP starts**: 199. **GP wins**: 51 wins. **World Champion**: 1985, 1986, 1989, 1993

Once he had decided not to play soccer for a living, Prost tried karting instead, which ultimately led to a prize drive in Formula Renault in 1976. He so dominated his national series that Renault took him to Formula 3, in which he won the European and French titles in 1979. His immaculate win at Monaco led to a McLaren test. He was signed for 1980, as a stopgap until Renault could run him in 1981, when he secured the first three Grand Prix victories that put him on the road to becoming a multiple champion. After narrowly losing the 1983 championship, Prost was fired by Renault, so he returned to McLaren and vied for the 1984 title with team mate Lauda. Becoming known as 'The Professor', because of his thinking approach to the sport, he won his first titles in 1985 and 1986. His famous rivalry with Senna began when they became McLaren team mates in 1988, when Prost won seven of 16 Grands Prix, Senna eight. The McLaren-Honda domination continued in 1989, but the team mates had become enemies, and the season ended with a collision at Suzuka which handed Prost the championship. He moved to Ferrari and won five times in 1990, but Senna beat him to the title by

returning the compliment and driving into him at Suzuka. Prost (above) was fired by Ferrari before the end of 1991 for his public criticism of the team, and he had to sit out the 1992 season as a TV commentator. But he returned in 1993 with Williams and Renault to lift his fourth title, with seven more wins. He retired when Williams signed the hated Senna. Three years later, he bought Guy Ligier's team and renamed it Prost Grand Prix, and continued his often stormy Formula 1 adventure as a constructor.

> "He is one of the greatest in history, born with a steering wheel in his hands. He achieves a perfect communion with his car."
> CARLOS REUTEMANN

TOM PRYCE (GB)

b. 11 June 1949 - d. 5 March 1977
F1 career: 74 - Token, Shadow; 75-77 - Shadow.
GP starts: 42. **GP wins**: 0.

Often compared to Ronnie Peterson as a quite spectacular controller of cars, the Welshman was, also like the Swede, a quiet and private individual. Pryce made an immediate impression and in only his second season scored both a pole and a podium finish, and was touted by many as sure championship material. Sadly, his life was snuffed out in an accident that was as bizarre as it was appalling. During the South African Grand Prix a misguided track marshal ran across the track in front of Pryce's speeding Shadow. Both were instantly killed, the marshal by the car and Pryce by a fatal blow on the head from a fire extinguisher.

DAVID PURLEY (GB)

b. 26 January 1945 - d. 2 July 1985
F1 career: 73 - March; 77 - LEC. **GP starts**: 7

A dedicated daredevil, Purley was an officer in the British Army's crack Parachute Regiment before taking up motorised thrills at the end of the 1960s. In Formula 1 he became a reluctant hero for his valiant efforts to save Roger Williamson in the 1973 Dutch Grand Prix and was awarded the George Medal for his bravery. Four years later Purley suffered an enormous accident at Silverstone, slamming into barriers with such terrific force that the impact was officially registered as the highest degree of g-force ever inflicted on a man without killing him - though every bone in Purley's body was broken. Although he did race again on an amateur level, his legs still troubled him and he took up piloting stunt aircraft. Purley lost his life when he failed to pull his Pitts Special out of a dive off the coast of his hometown of Bognor Regis.

JO RAMIREZ (MEX)

b. 20 August 1941

Born in Mexico City, Ramirez (below) followed his friend Ricardo Rodriguez to Ferrari, where he served as a 'gofer' ("go fer this, go fer that"). Though devastated when Rodriguez was killed in their home race in 1962, Ramirez stayed in the sport because "I was hooked on the look of the cars, the sound of engines, the smell of the fuel and the tyres". After working as a mechanic, then manager with several

teams, he joined McLaren in 1984 as team co-ordinator, and stayed there, inspiring everyone with his infectious good humour and an all-consuming passion for the sport.

ROLAND RATZENBERGER (A)

b. 4 July 1962 - d. 30 April 1994
F1 career: 94 - Simtek. **GP starts**: 1.

Ratzenberger was attempting to qualify his Simtek for only the third time when he crashed fatally at Imola's Villeneuve corner. An extremely popular, talented and highly active member of the band of European drivers who raced in Japan, he was late in arriving in Formula 1 by modern standards, which made his breakthrough all the sweeter, then all the more tragic with his death.

CLAY REGAZZONI (CH)

b. 5 September 1939
F1 career: 70-72 - Ferrari; 73 - BRM; 74-76 - Ferrari; 77 - Ensign; 78 - Shadow; 79 - Williams; 80 - Ensign. **GP starts**: 132. **GP wins**: 5

Amongst his wins 'Regga' is best known for scoring the first victory for Williams, at the 1979 British Grand Prix. A year later his Ensign suffered brake failure at Long Beach, leaving him with spinal injuries that have confined him to a wheelchair ever since. Always popular, always good-humoured, always a racer, he remains all three - still showing up at occasional Formula 1 races and still competing in saloon cars fitted with hand controls that he has helped to develop for other handicapped drivers.

LOUIS RENAULT (F)

b. 12 February 1877 - d. 24 October 1944

Renault was the son of a prosperous button manufacturer. In his early twenties he devised a gearbox for his de Dion car that was a big improvement on the original and he soon had orders from friends for replicas. Backed by his brothers Marcel and Fernand, he set up a factory to build cars of a fully Renault design. Both Louis and Marcel competed in these machines in the city-to-city races at the turn of the 20th century and performed brilliantly. Using engines much smaller than was fashionable in racing at the time, they frequently beat the monster Panhards and Mors. In the 1903 Paris-

Madrid, Louis finished a superb second but as the race was halted he learned that Marcel had been fatally injured in one of the many crashes of that race. Louis retired from race driving and over the years built up his company into one of the world's great industrial empires. The company withdrew from racing after 1908 and did not return for almost 70 years.

CARLOS REUTEMANN (RA)

b. 12 March 1942
F1 career: 72-76 - Brabham; 77-78 - Ferrari; 79 - Lotus; 80-82 - Williams. **GP starts**: 146.
GP wins: 12

He arrived in Europe in 1970 as a member of his 'national' Formula 2 team and was immediately competitive, pressing Peterson closely for the 1971 title. This earned a Formula 1 drive in 1972 with Bernie Ecclestone's newly acquired Brabham team. He thrilled his compatriots by qualifying on the pole on his debut in Buenos Aires, but victory on his home soil always eluded him. Utterly brilliant on good days, 'Lole' had too many bad days to mount a consistent championship challenge. His five-year term at Brabham yielded only four victories, but he was much more competitive at Ferrari, for which he scored four wins in two seasons, among 11 podiums. He remained a regular points-scorer with both Lotus and Williams and should have won the title in 1981, but, despite starting from pole, he lost out to Piquet by a single point in the series finale in Las Vegas. An introspective character, he was an enigma until the abrupt end of his career: without explanation, he stepped from the cockpit forever, two races into the 1982 season. He later turned to politics, campaigning on an anti-corruption ticket. He became a provincial governor in Santa Fe, where his father had been a cattle farmer, and a senator for whom his backers formed presidential aspirations.

> "Carlos was too much on and off. If he felt like it, he was superb, but often you would forget he was in a race. His temperament was far too emotional and that stopped him from being great."
> JACKIE STEWART

PETER REVSON (USA)

b. 27 February 1939 - d. 22 March 1974

F1 career: 64 - Lotus; 71 - Tyrrell; 72-73 - McLaren; 74 - Shadow. **GP starts**: 30. **GP wins**: 2.

The suave and debonair heir to the Revlon cosmetics empire was a dedicated racing driver, despite the trauma of his brother Doug's death in a Danish Formula 2 race. Often accompanied by his girlfriend Marjorie Wallace, an American beauty queen who became Miss World, he won in most of the major US categories, including becoming the CanAm champion and claiming pole for the Indy 500 in works McLarens. These efforts led to his promotion to the McLaren Formula 1 team, where he won his two Grands Prix. Signing with Shadow in 1974, he was at a pre-season test at Kyalami in South Africa when news filtered through from England that Marjorie Wallace was keeping company with Welsh crooner Tom Jones. When Revson was killed at Kyalami, it was at first suggested that the newspaper stories had caused him to lose concentration, but subsequent investigations revealed that his Shadow had suffered suspension failure.

> "Everything is sweetened by risk." PETER REVSON

JOCHEN RINDT (A)

b. 18 April 1942 - d. 5 Sept 1970

F1 career: 64 - Brabham; 65-67 - Cooper; 68 - Brabham; 69-70 - Lotus. **GP starts**: 60. **GP wins**: 6. **World Champion**: 1970

Shortly after Rindt's birth, his parents were killed in an air raid in Mainz, Germany. His grandmother took him to Graz in Austria, raised him and also bought him his first cars, with money from a family fortune made in the spice business, to which Rindt was heir. He suddenly shot to international prominence in 1964 when he convincingly won a Formula 2 race at Crystal Palace with his own Brabham, displaying incredible car control to defeat such as Clark, Hill and Hulme. He was snapped up by Cooper in 1965, moved to Brabham in 1968, then the next year to Lotus, where he fulfilled his potential. His good friend Bernie Ecclestone became his manager, and Rindt married Nina, a glamorous Finnish fashion model (their daughter, Natasha, would one day work for Ecclestone's Formula 1 digital TV enterprise). His win at Monaco in 1970 was one of the most spectacular drives of all

time, but later that season he became the first posthumous World Champion. Unwilling to buckle the crotch strap of his safety harness, he was killed in an innocuous accident in practice at Monza.

> "I am impatient. It is one of my mistakes. You push a bit more and people don't like it. It makes life more difficult."
> JOCHEN RINDT

PEDRO RODRIGUEZ (MEX)

b. 18 January 1940 - d. 11 July 1971

F1 career: 63 - Lotus; 64-65 - Ferrari; 66 - Lotus; 67 - Cooper; 68-71 - BRM. **GP starts**: 55. **GP wins**: 2

Their wealthy father bought fast sportscars for Pedro and his younger brother Ricardo to race when they were in their mid-teens. Before a race the Rodriguez boys would kneel on the tarmac to be blessed by their mother, who then went away and read a book. Though devastated by Ricardo's death, Pedro continued in the sport, always charging hard and gradually earning respect as he went from frighteningly fast to just plain fast. He died at the Norisring in Germany when his Ferrari sportscar crashed and burned.

> "Racing is something that comes out of you. You have something in your blood. It unwinds itself."
> PEDRO RODRIGUEZ

RICARDO RODRIGUEZ (MEX)

b. 14 February 1942 - d. 1 November 1962

F1 career: 61-62 - Ferrari. **GP starts**: 5

More flamboyant than his older brother (he owned 100 suits and 60 pairs of shoes), and even more of a risk-taker, Ricardo Rodriguez told his worried wife, Sarita, that he would stop racing after he won his first Grand Prix. He was killed in front of Sarita in his home Grand Prix.

> "I recall thinking to myself that Ricardo Rodriguez is a holy terror, who drives with a frightful lack of any restraint and a waste of physical energy that is without comparison. If this young fellow will only learn to curb his eagerness and improve

his style, he will be a big success. A short time afterwards, his luck ran out. He was a really good lad - always happy, with that innocent face of a mischievous schoolboy."
> ENZO FERRARI

KEKE ROSBERG (FIN)

b. 6 December 1948

F1 career: 78 - Theodore, ATS, Wolf; 79 - Wolf; 80-81 - Fittipaldi; 82-85 - Williams; 86 - McLaren. **GP starts**: 114. **GP wins**: 5. **World Champion**: 1982

The original 'Flying Finn,' Keijo 'Keke' Rosberg was a chain-smoking swashbuckler whose dash and flair and daring, darting style of driving enlivened every race he was in. Colourful, irreverent, outspoken and commercially shrewd, he wore a gold Rolex, carried a Gucci briefcase and later managed the careers of Mika Hakkinen and Olivier Panis.

> "An aggressive driver, highly talented and a modern-style businessman who wheels and deals tremendously hard and competitively." JOHN WATSON

BERND ROSEMEYER (D)

b. 14 October 1909 - d. 28 January 1938

As a racer for the DKW motorcycle team that was part of the Auto-Union group, Rosemeyer made his car racing debut in 1935 in the monstrous V16 Auto-Union. Remarkably, given his lack of experience, he was immediately successful. He dominated 1936 and picked up the European Drivers Championship along the way. Apparently fearless, his talent enabled him to tame the notoriously demanding machines in a way none of his team mates could quite manage. He was killed early in 1938 when attempting a straightline speed record for the team on a German *autobahn*.

MIKA SALO (FIN)

b. 25 September 1966

F1 career: 94 - Lotus; 95-97 - Tyrrell; 98 - Arrows; 99 - BAR, Ferrari; 00 - Sauber. **GP starts**: 93

This fun-loving, fresh-faced Finn lost a season-long duel with Mika Hakkinen for the 1990 British Formula 3 title and has raced in the

shadow of his compatriot ever since. Yet Salo startled everyone with strong performances when he briefly stood in for the injured Michael Schumacher at Ferrari in 1999, and would have won easily at Hockenheim had the Scuderia not required him to lift off so that Irvine could catch him up. Though he once claimed James Hunt was his hero, because he drank, smoked and chased women, Salo gave up all three, marrying his Japanese girlfriend, Noriko Endo, and leading the new Toyota entry in 2001, prior to its entry into Formula 1.

ROY SALVADORI (GB)

b. 12 May 1922

F1 career: 52 - Ferrari; 53 - Connaught; 54-56 - Maserati; 57 - Vanwall; 57- 59 - Cooper; 59 - Aston Martin; 60 - Aston Martin, Cooper; 61 - Cooper; 62 - Lola. **GP starts**: 47. **GP wins**: 0

The English-born son of Italian parents, slick-haired Roy Francesco Salvadori started a business in London as a motor trader in 1946 and began racing the following year, eventually graduating to Formula 1 after establishing an 'all-rounder' reputation in a huge variety of cars. His Grand Prix debut came in 1952 but, apart from his 1958 season with Cooper, he was an irregular Formula 1 competitor, and was much more successful in sportscars, notably for Aston Martin. He drove his last Formula 1 race in 1962, and quit sportscar racing in 1964. He briefly returned to Formula 1 as Cooper's team manager in 1966-67, before retiring to his apartment overlooking the Grand Prix startline in Monaco.

JODY SCHECKTER (ZA)

b. 29 January 1950

F1 career: 72-73 - Mclaren; 74-76 - Tyrrell; 77-78 - Wolf; 79-80 - Ferrari. **GP starts**: 112. **GP wins**: 9. **World Champion**: 1979

Erratic and crash-prone as a talented but rash rookie, Scheckter (opposite, top) straightened himself out by relaxing his heavy right foot and relying more on a head that proved to contain a fine racing brain. With single-minded determination he applied himself to the goal of becoming champion. Achieving the ultimate success in the sport, he abruptly abandoned it and went off to found a highly lucrative high-tech security business in America, which he later sold and retired from the workaday world to shepherd the racing careers of his two sons.

> "Temperamental, argumentative, sulky at times, he was outspoken but at the same time had a charming touch of innocence and a shy sense of humour."
> PROFESSOR SID WATKINS

HARRY SCHELL (USA)

b. 26 June 1921 - d. 13 May 1960

F1 career: 50 - Cooper, Talbot; 51-52 - Maserati; 53 - Gordini; 54 - Maserati; 55 - Maserati, Ferrari, Vanwall; 56 - Vanwall, Maserati; 57 - Maserati; 58 - Maserati, BRM; 59 - Maserati, Cooper; 60 - Cooper. **GP starts**: 55

Born in Paris to well-off parents (a French father and an expatriate American mother, whose citizenship he took), Henry O'Reilly 'Harry' Schell (above) was an adventurer whose exploits included serving as a tail gunner in the Russo-Finnish war. He loved women, raising hell, living high and, especially, racing. He was killed on a Friday the 13th at Silverstone, when his Cooper spun off the wet track and flipped, breaking his neck.

> "Racing is a drug. I am addicted to it." HARRY SCHELL

JO SCHLESSER (F)

b. 18 May 1928 - d. 7 July 1968
F1 career: 68 - Honda. **GP starts**: 3

At the age of 40, Schlesser fulfilled a life's ambition by taking part in a Grand Prix at the wheel of a proper Formula 1 car (his previous appearances were in Formula 2 cars). He died horribly, on the second lap of his home Grand Prix at Rouen in heavy rain, when his Honda crashed and burst into flames. Team owner Guy Ligier subsequently added the 'JS' prefix to all his cars as a mark of respect to his fun-loving and enthusiastic friend and business partner.

MICHAEL SCHUMACHER (D)

b. 3 January 1969

F1 career: 91 - Jordan, Benetton; 92-95 - Benetton; 96-01 - Ferrari. **GP starts**: 161. **GP wins**: 53. **World Champion**: 1994, 1995, 2000, 2001

Outstanding all-round ability is the hallmark of all great sporting champions but, as the most complete racing driver of his era, Schumacher has set new standards. Overly aggressive tactics have courted controversy on many occasions, but these have also served to underline his exceptional commitment to winning. After displaying his early potential in karts, he rose through the ranks of Formula Ford and Formula 3, but it was his rapid development in Group C, as a member of Sauber's Mercedes-Benz 'junior' squad, that propelled him into Formula 1. He qualified seventh on his debut with Jordan at Spa in 1991 and was immediately poached by Benetton. At Monza, only a fortnight later, he opened his Formula 1 points tally with fifth place. A string of podiums in 1992 preceded his maiden Grand Prix win on his return to Spa. Benetton evolved into a consistent front-running team and he opened 1994 with two wins, but his car was excluded from second place at Silverstone and then first place at Spa due to technical infringements, and then he had to serve a two-race suspension. Against expectation, the championship was still open at the Australian finale in Adelaide. There was uproar after what appeared to be a deliberate mid-race collision with title rival Damon Hill, but no action was taken, and he became Germany's first Formula 1 World Champion. Equipped with Renault engines in 1995, he achieved back-to-back titles in his final term with Benetton, and departed for Ferrari when the Scuderia offered to restructure its entire operation around him. Success was not immediate against the superior Williams-Renault cars, although he contrived victories at Spa and Monza. There was another controversial end to the 1997 season, when he tangled with championship rival Jacques Villeneuve at Jerez, for which the FIA subsequently excluded him from second place in the standings. Ferrari continued to improve and he took his share of race wins in 1998, but now Hakkinen and McLaren-Mercedes were the class of the field. Then his 1999 season was ruined when he broke a leg at Silverstone. But the two seasons of dominance that followed brought Ferrari its first drivers' championship since 1979, and made Schumacher a four-time World Champion and the 'winningest' F1 driver of all time.

> "Michael would remain a formidable challenge if he was driving a pram." FRANK WILLIAMS

RALF SCHUMACHER (D)

b. 30 June 1975

F1 career: 97-98 - Jordan; 99-01 - Williams. **GP starts**: 83. **GP wins**: 3

Successful in karting and then establishing himself as a winner in Formula 3, Ralf Schumacher was always on course to follow his brother into Formula 1, where he also started his career at Jordan - although he stayed a while longer. With a double World Champion in the family, there was a lot to live up to, and he knew that any mistakes would be magnified. But his strong performances in his first season at Williams showed maturity, even though it was not until 2001 that he became a Grand Prix winner.

> "I thought the world could only bear one Schumacher. Now we have two." MIKA HAKKINEN

RICHARD SEAMAN (GB)

b. 4 February 1913 - d. 25 June 1939

An exceptionally promising young driver, Seaman crashed fatally whilst leading the 1939 Belgian Grand Prix for Mercedes. As a Briton, his place in the team had required the permission of Hitler. His presence there caused some embarrassment when he won the 1938 German Grand Prix in front of watching Nazi party officials.

HENRY SEGRAVE (GB)

b. 1896 - d. 1930

Segrave became the first 'British' driver (his ancestry was British, but he was born in the USA) to win a Grand Prix when he took his Sunbeam to victory in France 1923. His frontline racing career was with Sunbeam throughout and he then set about taking the Land Speed Record, becoming the first man to exceed 200mph, in a special Sunbeam V12 in 1927. He upped this to 231mph in 1929 with the Golden Arrow. The following year he died from injuries received during an attempt on the water speed record at Lake Windermere when his boat hit a log.

AYRTON SENNA (BR)

b. 21 March 1960 - d. 1 May 1994
F1 career: 84 - Toleman; 85-87 - Lotus; 88-93 - McLaren; 94 - Williams. **GP starts**: 161. **GP wins**: 41. **World Champion**: 1988, 1990, 1991

One of the greatest drivers of all time, Ayrton Senna da Silva was also one of the sport's most charismatic personalities and probably the most cerebral. Here was a genius of a driver with a formidable intellect. If his bitter rival Prost was 'The Professor' then Senna (below) was 'The Philosopher' - a man for whom racing was a metaphor for a life - a life about which he thought deeply and spoke eloquently. In his mesmerising press conferences you could hear a pin drop as Senna's musings about everything under the sun held even the most cynical members of the media contingent absolutely spellbound. His sensitive soul and gently

questioning spirit were replaced by a frightening intensity of attack on the track. There, Senna (above) pushed himself harder and harder, seeking new personal revelations through his driving, daring his rivals to come near him, hating it - sometimes them - if they beat him. Inevitably, his relentless aggression and uncompromising attitude earned him enemies. Some critics crucified him, yet millions deified him, and after his shocking death Senna was elevated to sporting sainthood.

> "He was the only driver I respected. With his death half my career has gone." ALAIN PROST

JO SIFFERT (CH)

b. 7 July 1936 - d. 24 October 1971

F1 career: 62-63 - Lotus; 64 - Lotus, Brabham; 65 - Brabham; 66 - Brabham, Cooper; 67 - Cooper; 68 - Cooper, Lotus; 69 - Lotus; 70 - March; 71 - BRM. **GP starts**: 96. **GP wins**: 2

Jo 'Seppi' Siffert spent much of his career driving for private entrant Rob Walker, though he was with the BRM team when he was killed. Over 50,000 people attended his funeral in his home town of Fribourg, Switzerland, where the procession to the cemetery included a faithful mechanic walking behind the hearse, carrying Siffert's famous red helmet with the white cross.

> "In the fullness of time Seppi and I developed what I suppose you could almost call a father and son relationship. He was a superb driver who was just so brave it scared me witless, and I admired him enormously." ROB WALKER

ALAN STACEY (GB)

b. 29 August 1933 - d. 19 June 1960

F1 career: 58-60 - Lotus. **GP starts**: 7

Stacey suffered from unusual circumstances in life and also in the manner of his death. Handicapped by an artificial right leg, he drove with special hand-operated throttles on his cars. Having won in Lotus sports cars he was given rides in the Lotus Formula 1 team on several occasions, including the 1960 Belgian Grand Prix where he was hit full in the face by a bird, lost control of his car and was killed.

LOUIS STANLEY (GB)

Stanley was the chairman of BRM for many years, then relaunched it as Stanley BRM in 1974, but closed it down four years later. The portly, opinionated and rather pompous Stanley was dismayed by the "slovenly dress sense" and "uncivilised buffoonery" of the spectators at races in the New World, particularly America. Yet he made important contributions to motor racing safety when he established and arranged funding for the mobile Grand Prix Medical Unit, and to motorsport history with several superbly researched, and entertainingly written, books.

> "Louis is a big man, a daunting character in many ways with an imperious manner and I always deferentially called him Mr. Stanley when he was there and, like everybody else, 'Big Lou' when he was not." JACKIE STEWART

SIR JACKIE STEWART (GB)

b. 11 June 1939

F1 career: 65-67 - BRM; 68-69 - Matra; 70 - March, Tyrrell; 71-73 - Tyrrell. **GP starts**: 99. **GP wins**: 27. **World Champion**: 1969, 1971, 1973

Although his brother Jimmy had raced for several seasons, John Young Stewart's initial sporting interest was clay pigeon shooting, in which he competed to Olympic standards. His famous racing partnership with Ken Tyrrell began after he had outpaced Bruce McLaren in a test at Goodwood but, after a dominant 1964 Formula 3 season with Tyrrell's Cooper-BMC, he elected to embark on his Formula 1 career at BRM. His arrival came soon after Clark's, and he soon established himself as another emerging Scottish talent. His maiden Grand Prix victory came at Monza in 1965, and he followed up that with a victory at Monaco in 1966. Renewing his relationship with Tyrrell, he won five Formula 2 races in an Formula 2 Matra, then broke his wrist. He returned to dominate the 1969 Formula 1 season. Born on 11 June, he became the 11th different World Champion on the day he won his 11th Grand Prix, 11 years after the inception of Formula 1. He won the title again in 1971, but his hyperactivity led to a debilitating stomach ulcer in 1972. His final World Championship success was marred by the death of his team mate, François Cevert, in practice for the 1973 US

Grand Prix, which was to have been Stewart's 100th and final race. As a mark of respect, however, he and the team withdrew. This unhappy episode led him to redouble his efforts to transform safety in motorsport. Renowned for his precision-smooth style in the cockpit, he was the ultimate professional and maintained his diligent approach as a safety campaigner. Stewart was knighted in 2001 in recognition of his services to motorsport.

> "Sometimes a racing car is very much like a woman. Sometimes you have to be extremely sympathetic. You have to caress it. You have to coax it into doing the things you want it to do. You have to tempt it, be very gentle. With others, on some occasions, you have to give them a really good thrashing." JACKIE STEWART

JOHN SURTEES (GB)

b. 11 February 1934

F1 career: 60 - Lotus; 61 - Cooper; 62 - Lola; 63-65 - Ferrari; 66 - Ferrari, Cooper. 67-68 - Honda; 69 - BRM; 70 - McLaren, Surtees; 70-72 - Surtees. **GP starts**: 111. **GP wins**: 6. **World Champion**: 1964

Seven times a motorcycle champion before he moved to four wheels, Surtees (right) recovered from being nearly killed in a sportscar accident in Canada. He then joined Ferrari and won the drivers' championship, abruptly left the team after a violent argument, won for Cooper and then for Honda. Surtees (below) suffered through several season with uncompetitive cars, including his own, before retiring to a quiet life in a splendid home in the English countryside.

> "I was a bit nuts, really." JOHN SURTEES

> "That stark, take-it-or-leave-it glare has not mellowed. It is an instinct, not a pose." LOUIS STANLEY

FERENC SZISZ (H)

b. 20 September 1873 - d. 21 February 1944

Formerly the riding mechanic for Louis Renault, Szisz drove a Renault car to victory in the first Grand Prix, at Le Mans in 1906. The massive machine, scarcely more than a bare chassis with

a bench, had a 13-litre engine developing 96bhp, weighed around 1000kg and was mounted on Michelin tyres. Szisz, 33 years old at the time, and driving for 12 hours over two gruelling days, averaged 62.88mph. His triumph generated excellent publicity for Renault, who sold 1000 cars in 1907. Szisz was still racing in 1923 when he tried but failed to track down the car that brought him fame and fortune.

PATRICK TAMBAY (F)

b. 25 June 1949

F1 career: 77 - Ensign; 78-79 - McLaren; 81 - Theodore, Ligier; 82-83 - Ferrari; 84-85 - Renault; 86 - FORCE. **GP starts**: 113. **GP wins**: 2

Debonair, cosmopolitan, educated in both France and America, Tambay was the 1977 CanAm champion, but was going nowhere in Formula 1 when he was suddenly offered a chance with Ferrari in 1982, as a replacement for his friend, the

late Gilles Villeneuve. Tambay won that year's German Grand Prix after team mate Pironi had been critically injured in practice, and won again at Imola in 1983. Well-liked and easy-going, he remained a front-runner with Renault, but never did add to these two victories. When he quit Formula 1, he started an event management company.

> "I don't see why you should have to be a bastard to succeed." PATRICK TAMBAY

PIERO TARUFFI (I)

b. 12 October 1906 - d. 12 January 1988

F1 career: 50 - Alfa Romeo; 51-52-54 - Ferrari; 55 - Ferrari, Mercedes; 56 - Mercedes, Vanwall. **GP starts**: 18. **GP wins**: 1

A Roman doctor of engineering, Taruffi's prematurely grey hair led to his nickname 'The Silver Fox'. Taruffi was a successful motorcycle racer in the 1920s and, either side of WW2, ran the Gilera team alongside his own car racing ventures. Before the war, he raced for Scuderia Ferrari in Alfa Romeos, then for Maserati and Bugatti, and set off on a long quest to win the Mille Miglia which became his claim to motor racing fame. He had one Grand Prix outing in 1950 for Alfa Romeo and was then engaged by Ferrari for two full seasons as Ascari's team mate, winning the 1952 Swiss race at Bremgarten. Thereafter his only wins came in Lancia, Ferrari and Maserati sportscars. In 1957 - 27 years after making his debut in the event and at his 13th attempt - he finally won the Mille Miglia (the last such road race), then retired to establish a race driving school.

JEAN TODT (F)
b. 25 February 1946

The Parisian doctor's son started his career as a rally co-driver in 1969 with the works Ford France team, and rose in his profession to win big events alongside many of the top drivers of his day, such as Piot, Nicolas, Aaltonen, Ove Andersson, Warmbold, Mikkola and Frequelin, in Fiats, Peugeots and Sunbeams. He retired to become the competitions director of Peugeot Talbot, and to develop the prodigiously effective Group B 205 Turbo 16, which dominated the World Rally Championship in 1985-86. When Group B was banned, Todt took Peugeot to rally-raids, winning four Paris-Dakars, and then to FIA Sportscar racing, in which its 905 prototypes won two Le Mans races and the World titles in 1992-93. He was awarded a *Légion d'Honneur*, France's equivalent of a knighthood. Formula 1 was next on his agenda, but Peugeot was not ready, and instead he went to Ferrari in 1993. Short, stocky and single-minded, he has been central to the Scuderia's impressive resurgence.

MAURICE TRINTIGNANT (F)
b. 30 October 1917
F1 career: 50-53 - Gordini; 54-55 - Ferrari; 56 - Vanwall, Bugatti; 57 - Ferrari; 58 - Cooper, Maserati, BRM; 59 - Cooper; 60 - Cooper, Aston Martin; 61 - Cooper; 62 - Lotus; 63 - Lola, BRM; 64 - BRM. **GP starts**: 82. **GP wins**: 2

Trintingnant was competing in his Bugatti in the very first race in Europe after WW2, the Coupe de la Libération in Paris in September 1945, when he was halted by a blocked fuel feed. This turned out to have been caused by rats making their home in the car's fuel tank during its wartime storage in a French barn. Thereafter Trintingnant had to live with the unkind nickname '*Le Petoulet*' ('rat shit'). The dapper, moustachioed son of a vineyard owner recovered from serious injuries at Berne in 1948 to become a reliable professional whose Formula 1 career spanned 15 seasons. His consistency brought him two wins at Monaco, in 1955 with Ferrari and three years later with Rob Walker, this being the maiden success for Cooper. He closed his long career with his own BRM in 1964, before retiring to become mayor of his home town Ste-Cécile-Les-Vignes.

KEN TYRRELL (GB)
b. 3 May 1924 - d. 25 August 2001

When he died of cancer, at the age of 77, Tyrrell was described by Jackie Stewart as "the single most important man in my life". Aged 16, Tyrrell joined the RAF in 1939 as a fitter, and later served in WW2 as a flight engineer on Halifax and Lancaster bombers. After the war, 'Chopper' Tyrrell established a timber business and took up 500cc racing as a hobby. He was good enough to win an international race at Karlskoga in Sweden in 1955, and to be given a test by John Wyer's Aston Martin sportscar team. But he decided to give up driving to become an entrant, initially in partnership with Alan Brown and Cecil Libovitz. In 1960, he quietly established his own front-running professional team, first in Formula Junior (running Surtees in his first car races), then in Formula 3, and finally in Formula 2 to run Matra's works team. The French aerospace and automobile manufacturer then helped to launch him into Formula 1 in 1968, when Ford made the Cosworth DFV engine readily available. He built up Tyrrell Racing Organisation to become one of the most successful Formula 1 teams in history, with 33 victories to its name (including 23 with its own cars). It undertook 29 F1 seasons between 1970 and 1998 and, such was the astonishing growth of the sport during this period, each year would ultimately be worth a million dollars when Tyrrell sold out to BAR. He was universally respected in Formula

1, and 'Uncle Ken' - along with his wife Norah, who made tea and sandwiches for the team in the old days - inspired extraordinary loyalty among all who worked for him. He loved Grand Prix racing even more than cricket, which he followed avidly.

> "When we started, Ken and I were racing at the same time together. Then he developed the Tyrrell team and I bought Brabham. We went back a long way, and we remembered what it was all about when we started. With Ken's death, I suppose, one of those last bridges with the old days is gone." BERNIE ECCLESTONE

TONY VANDERVELL (GB)
b. 1898 - d. 1967

The man behind the winner of the inaugural Formula 1 constructors' title in 1958, Vandervell (below) was the son of a prosperous businessman and competed in motorcycle and car events at pre-WW2 Brooklands. He was one of the financiers of BRM before embarking on his own projects, the Thinwall Special and the original Vanwall, built by Cooper in 1954, which were funded by his successful bearings company. Later designs benefited from the technical expertise of Frank Costin and Colin Chapman. Ultimately he achieved his aim to take on and defeat the incumbent Italian teams, and his British Racing Green cars won nine Grands

Prix in 1957-58. In both years, Moss fought valiantly against Ferrari, only to finish runner-up in the drivers' championship, first to Fangio, then Hawthorn. However, the 1958 success was overshadowed by the loss of Stuart Lewis-Evans, who crashed in the final race at Casablanca and later succumbed to terrible injuries. Vandervell, himself suffering ill health, withdrew the factory team.

ACHILLE VARZI (I)
b. 1904 - d. 1948

Initially defined by his intense rivalry with Tazio Nuvolari, Varzi's ruthless ambition and velvety talent made him the most successful driver of the early 1930s, driving Alfas, Bugattis and Maseratis. A switch to Auto-Union in 1935 brought some early success but in early 1936 he became hooked on the drug morphine and his mental and physical health suffered badly. After being dismissed by the team he did not reappear until the early post-war years when, back in full health once more, he was successful with Alfa-Romeo. He was killed in practice for the 1948 Swiss Grand Prix, trying to beat the pole time of team-mate Jean-Pierre Wimille.

GILLES VILLENEUVE (CDN)
b. 18 January 1952 - d. 8 May 1982
F1 career: 77 - McLaren, Ferrari; 78-82 - Ferrari. **GP starts**: 67. **GP wins**: 6

During his brief career Villeneuve made an indelible impression on the sport out of all proportion to the results he achieved. His legend owes much to its classic elements of tragedy, for he was a charming young man of humble origins (his father was an itinerant piano tuner) who achieved undreamed-of fame and fortune by giving his all to the sport which ultimately took his life. It was a life lived at the limit, behind the wheel of a Ferrari, where his exceptional skill and daring, his brilliant car control, tremendous fighting spirit and pure passion for driving produced so much high drama and deeply felt emotion that Villeneuve became one of the greatest Formula 1 heroes. Some critics thought the little French-Canadian daredevil was simply a crazed speedfreak, but the vast majority felt his seemingly superhuman efforts to control runaway speed captured the very essence of racing. His boss Enzo Ferrari compared him to the great Nuvolari. Villeneuve's death, during qualifying for the 1982 Belgian Grand Prix and following a controversial feud with his Ferrari team mate Didier Pironi, was one of the saddest days in the sport.

"I will miss Gilles for two reasons. First, he was the fastest driver in the history of motor racing. Second, he was the most genuine man I have ever known. But he has not gone. The memory of what he has done, what he has achieved, will always be there." JODY SCHECKTER

"Gilles was loved above all others because he was so clearly working without a net."
NIGEL ROEBUCK

JACQUES VILLENEUVE (CDN)

b. 9 March 1971

F1 career: 96-98 - Williams; 99-01 - BAR. **GP starts**: 98. **GP wins**: 11. **World Champion**: 1997

Though his father's illustrious name opened doors for him early in his career, Gilles Villeneuve's son went on to make an impressive name for himself. After winning the 1995 CART championship and the Indy 500, he entered Formula 1 with Williams, very nearly won his first Grand Prix and was narrowly beaten to the 1996 driving title by his team mate Damon Hill. Villeneuve won it the next year, fending off the worst efforts of Michael Schumacher in their infamous coming together at Jerez. Following a downturn in Williams competitive fortunes, Villeneuve was paid a fortune to follow his manager Craig Pollock to the new BAR team, which started slowly in its 1999 debut, then tapered off. Very much his own man, he also appreciates the company of women, and was once engaged to Australian songstress Dannii Minogue. His current fiancée is Elly Green, an American ballerina. Though he has not won a race since 1997, Villeneuve remains a colourful, outspoken character and, car permitting, is still quite capable of putting on the impressively aggressive shows that are a family trait.

"I love the feeling when you're right on the edge and pushing it. The greatest pleasure is when you're going through a corner and the car starts sliding, and you hold it there. You're really on the limit, you can feel it, you're controlling it, you wonder how much further you can push it before you lose control - and then you push it further to find out. Your heart pumps a bit, you get an adrenaline rush, you've got a big grin on your face and you say to yourself, 'Wow! That was cool.'"
JACQUES VILLENEUVE

MANFRED VON BRAUCHITSCH (D)

b. 15 August 1905

Born into a Prussian military family - his father was an army major and his uncle would ultimately become Hitler's WW2 commander-in-chief - von Brauchitsch was unfit for military service after fracturing his skull in a motorcycle accident. So he took up motorsport and his career took off when he sensationally won the Avus Grand Prix. His rivals laughed when they saw the streamlined bodywork he had fitted to his Mercedes SSKL, but, on race day, he passed Caracciola's works Alfa Romeo and won by a length. Now he was invited to join the Mercedes team for its 1934 Grand Prix season. A ragged but very effective driver, he won on his professional debut in the Eifel Grand Prix but crashed in the German Grand Prix and suffered many broken bones - including another skull fracture. He resumed in 1935 with tremendous drives at Spa and the Nürburgring, where he was holding Nuvolari's Alfa at bay when a tyre burst. Von Brauchitsch was inconsolable, even after Nuvolari had given him a bouquet of flowers. His 1936 season was also plagued by bad luck and he earned the nickname the 'Pechvogel' ('unlucky bird'). But he achieved his finest hour by winning the 1937 Monaco Grand Prix after repeatedly (and bravely) ignoring Neubauer's team orders, racing wheel-to-wheel with his team leader, Caracciola, and setting a lap record that would stand for 18 years. Later in the season, Neubauer pulled his rebellious driver from his burning car in a Nürburgring pitlane fire. In

Belgrade for the 1939 Yugoslavia Grand Prix, von Brauchitsch heard the news that Britain had declared war on Germany, and bought a ticket on a flight to Geneva in neutral Switzerland. Neubauer reached the aircraft before it took off and hauled him back to the circuit, and he spent WW2 in Germany. After the war, unable to progress due to his military connections, he tried but failed to make a new life in Argentina, and returned to West Germany a bitter man. In 1951, he was arrested under suspicion of being a Communist spy, and jumped bail to defect to East Germany. His wife committed suicide, but he stayed in the GDR to become the president of the 'national society for the Olympic ideal' for over 30 years. Mercedes-Benz honoured him in Stuttgart on his 95th birthday in August 2000.

WOLFGANG VON TRIPS (D)

b. 4 May 1928 - d. 10 September 1961

F1 career: 57-58 - Ferrari; 59 - Porsche, Ferrari; 60 - Ferrari, Cooper; 61 - Ferrari. **GP starts**: 27. **GP wins**: 2

Enzo Ferrari wrote this pen portrait of von Trips: "A foreign driver who was especially dear to me was the great-hearted Wolfgang von Trips. The sole descendant of a baronial family, one of those families of *junkers* who still today represent the feudal land-owning class in Germany, he was fond of all sports, but especially motorsport. A very fast driver who was always as much a gentleman at the wheel as in everyday life, he was capable of the utmost daring without ever losing his slightly melancholy smile. Just when the World Championship was within his grasp, he was killed in the 1961 Monza Grand Prix that should have been the scene of his triumph. He was involved, during the second lap, in a collision with another car that was hanging closely on to him, and the irreparable happened in a flash. A year that had been a glorious one for us thus closed tragically. That day at Monza should have been a triumphant one for us after all the efforts we had made; instead it only brought us bitter sorrow."

ROB WALKER (GB)

b. 1917 - d. 2002

Walker was the most famous of all Formula 1 private entrants, and a scion of the Johnnie Walker whisky family. He came to prominence

at the end of the 1950s when he ran Moss from his little Dorking raceshop, and beat the works teams in landing maiden Formula 1 victories for both Cooper and Lotus. Moss's historic defeat of the Ferraris and Maseratis in Argentina in 1958 was the first post-war victory by a mid-engined car, and the first by a Coventry Climax engine, although his

triumph in Walker's Lotus 18 at Monaco in 1960 is just as famous. In all, Walker's team secured nine Grand Prix victories (seven with Moss), the last in the 1968 British race with Jo Siffert and a Lotus 49. Invariably accompanied by his charming wife Betty, who baked delicious brownies for their drivers, Walker (above) continued as an entrant until 1973, when the costs became too prohibitive even for him, and he became an immensely popular Formula 1 columnist. Despite his wealth, he was known for his self-deprecation and a very attractive, upper-class sense of humour. Reporting how much he had enjoyed staying on the *Queen Mary* floating hotel while covering the inaugural Long Beach Grand Prix, he remarked in his languid style, "They were so sweet to me, you know. Put me in my old cabin..."

DEREK WARWICK (GB)

b. 27 August 1954

F1 career: 81-83 - Toleman; 84-85 - Renault; 86 - Brabham; 87-89 - Arrows; 90 - Lotus; 93 - Footwork. **GP starts**: 147

Although he drove for some of the biggest teams in Formula 1, each spell invariably coincided with their downturn in fortunes and

Warwick (below) never won a Grand Prix. However, his driving career did include such successes as becoming World Hot Rod Champion in his teens, British Formula 3 Champion in 1978 and winner of the Le Mans 24 Hours in 1992.

"You know, I think there are two sides to motor racing. First of all, about 95% of the time, you have the lows. And the remaining 5% of the time you have the highs. But that 5% of highs outweighs the lows 100%." DEREK WARWICK

PROFESSOR SID WATKINS (GB)

The universally respected FIA-appointed Formula 1 medical delegate qualified as a doctor at Liverpool University in 1952 and, after National Service with the Royal Army Medical Corps, specialised in neurosurgery in

Oxford. During his spare time, he became a volunteer trackside doctor at UK race meetings, a service he continued to provide at Watkins Glen after being appointed as the professor of neurosurgery at Syracuse University in New York state. Formula 1 impresario Bernie Ecclestone offered him a permanent role as the resident Formula 1 doctor, which he took up when he became the head of neurosurgery at the London Hospital. Watkins (bottom left) continues to press constantly for motorsport safety improvements and has become an international authority on the subject.

"I make a lot of jokes about the fact that as a neurosurgeon I shouldn't really be required at a Formula 1 race because the drivers don't have any brains - otherwise they wouldn't race." PROFESSOR SID WATKINS

JOHN WATSON (GB)

b. 4 May 1946

F1 career: 73-74 - Brabham; 75 - Surtees, Lotus, Penske; 76 - Penske; 77-78 - Brabham; 79-85 - McLaren. **GP starts**: 152. **GP wins**: 5

Watson (above) arrived in England in 1970 from Belfast as a wild, bearded young man in a silly hat, and shocked the establishment with a competitive performance in his debut Formula 2 race at Thruxton. His abundant natural talent was clear and took him into a professional career spanning two decades. After his 1976 Austrian Grand Prix victory Watson shaved off his beard to pay off a bet

with team owner Roger Penske. His most sensational performances came at Detroit in 1982 and Long Beach a year later, when he drove his McLaren from the back of the grid to victory. After quitting Formula 1, he had a second career as a successful sportscar driver in Porsches and Jaguars. He fell in love with Ronnie Peterson's widow, Barbro, but was devastated by her early death. With his soft Irish accent and his readiness to speak his mind, Watson is now a popular TV commentator and in his private time an avid angler and wine connoisseur.

"The thing you must remember about a driver who is killed is that the man was doing something he enjoyed - maybe more than anything else in the world. He probably had it easier than the rest of us because it was over with very quickly. The rest of us have to live with it." JOHN WATSON

SIR FRANK WILLIAMS (GB)

b. 6 April 1942

This fiercely patriotic son of an RAF officer is an entirely self-made man and still the driving force behind an immensely successful Formula 1 team, despite his confinement to a wheelchair since a road accident in 1986. He has been involved in motorsport since he was a 19-year-old grocery salesman racing an Austin A30, when he met fellow racers Piers Courage, Jonathan Williams and Charlie Crichton-Stuart, and shared a famously decadent flat with them in Pinner, near London. He acted as a Formula Junior mechanic for Williams and scraped together enough money to do some Formula 3 racing himself by selling old racing cars and spares. He established Frank Williams Racing Cars for this purpose and became a team entrant, running Courage, whose death at Zandvoort in 1970 was a devastating setback that left Williams in the wilderness for several years. In 1977, he teamed up with new designer Patrick Head to form Williams Grand Prix Engineering, headquartered in a former carpet warehouse in Didcot, and the second chapter of the Williams story began. His old friend Crichton-Stuart arranged sponsorship from Saudia

Airlines and, in 1979, Head's ground-effect FW07 achieved the team's first victory. It was followed by World Championships for Alan Jones in 1980 and Keke Rosberg in 1982. A Honda engine deal in 1983 led to another drivers' title in 1987, with Nelson Piquet. The team went on to more championships with Renault in 1992 and 1993, with Nigel Mansell and Alain Prost, and - after recovering from the dreadful setback of Senna's fatal accident - there were championships for Damon Hill in 1996 and Jacques Villeneuve the following year. Also the winner of nine constructors' championships, Frank Williams was knighted in 1999. The present Formula 1 partnership with BMW began in 2000 after Williams had built the BMW sportscar that won the 1999 Le Mans.

"A Grand Prix weekend for me is 72 hours of pumping adrenaline." FRANK WILLIAMS

'WILLIAMS' (GB)

William Grover-Williams (an Englishman with a French mother), who raced under the pseudonym 'Williams', won the first Monaco Grand Prix in 1929. He enjoyed further successes as a works Bugatti driver until the mid-1930s. As a British secret services operative during WW2, he co-ordinated the efforts of Resistance fighters, including fellow racers Robert Benoist and Jean-Pierre Wimille. Intelligence security policies mean that his subsequent history is unclear. Recent doubt has been cast on the official line that he was executed by the Gestapo in 1945, and that the mysterious Williams may have lived a long, though still secret, life.

ROGER WILLIAMSON (GB)

b. 2 February 1948 - d. 29 July 1973

F1 career: 73 - March. **GP starts**: 2

The dreadful circumstances in which Williamson lost his life at Zandvoort in 1973 remain one of the most shameful episodes in Formula 1 history. The sadly short life of this charming and most promising young driver is commemorated among the exhibits in the Donington Museum, which is the world's largest collection of Formula 1 cars, owned and operated by Williamson's mentor and entrant, Tom Wheatcroft.

The Winners

The following list covers the 680 Formula 1 World Championship Grands Prix held from 1950 to 2001, at 60 separate venues in 23 different countries and featuring 52 World Champions. Information given includes each race date, the name of the Grand Prix, the venue, the winner, his car and, each year, the World Champion.

1950

13 MAY 1950 - BRITISH GP (SILVERSTONE): GIUSEPPE FARINA (ALFA ROMEO)
21 MAY 1950 - MONACO GP (MONTE CARLO): JUAN MANUEL FANGIO (ALFA ROMEO)
4 JUNE 1950 - SWISS GP (BREMGARTEN): GIUSEPPE FARINA (ALFA ROMEO)
18 JUNE 1950 - BELGIAN GP (SPA): JUAN MANUEL FANGIO (ALFA ROMEO)
2 JULY 1950 - FRENCH GP (REIMS): JUAN MANUEL FANGIO (ALFA ROMEO)
3 SEPTEMBER 1950 - ITALIAN GP (MONZA): GIUSEPPE FARINA (ALFA ROMEO)

1950 WORLD CHAMPION: GIUSEPPE FARINA (ALFA ROMEO)

1951

27 MAY 1951 - SWISS GP (BREMGARTEN): JUAN MANUEL FANGIO (ALFA ROMEO)
17 JUNE 1951 - BELGIAN GP (SPA): GIUSEPPE FARINA (ALFA ROMEO)
1 JULY 1951 - FRENCH GP (REIMS): JUAN MANUAL FANGIO (ALFA ROMEO)
14 JULY 1951 - BRITISH GP (SILVERSTONE): FROILAN GONZALEZ (FERRARI)
29 JULY 1951 - GERMAN GP (NÜRBURGRING): ALBERTO ASCARI (FERRARI)
16 SEPTEMBER 1951 - ITALIAN GP (MONZA): ALBERTO ASCARI (FERRARI)
28 OCTOBER 1951 - SPANISH GP (PEDRALBES): JUAN MANUEL FANGIO (ALFA ROMEO)

1951 WORLD CHAMPION: JUAN MANUEL FANGIO (ALFA ROMEO)

1952

18 MAY 1952 - SWISS GP (BREMGARTEN): PIERO TARUFFI (FERRARI)
22 JUNE 1952 -BELGIAN GP (SPA): ALBERTO ASCARI (FERRARI)
6 JULY 1952 - FRENCH GP (ROUEN): ALBERTO ASCARI (FERRARI)
19 JULY 1952 - BRITISH GP (SILVERSTONE): ALBERTO ASCARI (FERRARI)
3 AUGUST 1952 - GERMAN GP (NÜRBURGRING): ALBERTO ASCARI (FERRARI)
17 AUGUST 1952 - DUTCH GP (ZANDVOORT): ALBERTO ASCARI (FERRARI)
7 SEPTEMBER 1952 - ITALIAN GP (MONZA): ALBERTO ASCARI (FERRARI)

1952 WORLD CHAMPION: ALBERTO ASCARI (FERRARI)

1953

18 JANUARY 1953 - ARGENTINE GP (BUENOS AIRES): ALBERTO ASCARI (FERRARI)
7 JUNE 1953 - DUTCH GP (ZANDVOORT): ALBERTO ASCARI (FERRARI)
21 JUNE 1953 - BELGIAN GP (SPA): ALBERTO ASCARI (FERRARI)
5 JULY 1953 - FRENCH GP (REIMS): MIKE HAWTHORN (FERRARI)
18 JULY 1953 - BRITISH GP (SILVERSTONE): ALBERTO ASCARI (FERRARI)
2 AUGUST 1953 - GERMAN GP (NÜRBURGRING): GIUSEPPE FARINA (FERRARI)
23 AUGUST 1953 - SWISS GP (BREMGARTEN): ALBERTO ASCARI (FERRARI)
13 SEPTEMBER 1953 - ITALIAN GP (MONZA): JUAN MANUEL FANGIO (MASERATI)

1953 WORLD CHAMPION: ALBERTO ASCARI (FERRARI)

1954

17 JANUARY 1954 - ARGENTINE GP (BUENOS AIRES): JUAN MANUEL FANGIO (MASERATI)
20 JUNE 1954 - BELGIAN GP (SPA): JUAN MANUEL FANGIO (MASERATI)
4 JULY 1954 - FRENCH GP (REIMS): JUAN MANUEL FANGIO (MERCEDES)
17 JULY 1954 - BRITISH GP (SILVERSTONE): FROILAN GONZALEZ (FERRARI)
1 AUGUST 1954 - GERMAN GP (NÜRBURGRING): JUAN MANUEL FANGIO (MERCEDES)
22 AUGUST 1954 - SWISS GP (BREMGARTEN): JUAN MANUEL FANGIO (MERCEDES)
5 SEPTEMBER 1954 - ITALIAN GP (MONZA): JUAN MANUEL FANGIO (MERCEDES)
29 OCTOBER 1954 - SPANISH GP (PEDRALBES): MIKE HAWTHORN (FERRARI)

1954 WORLD CHAMPION: JUAN MANUEL FANGIO (MASERATI & MERCEDES-BENZ)

1955

16 JANUARY 1955 - ARGENTINE GP (BUENOS AIRES): JUAN MANUEL FANGIO (MERCEDES)
3 MAY 1955 - MONACO GP (MONTE CARLO): MAURICE TRINTIGNANT (FERRARI)
5 JUNE 1955 - BELGIAN GP (SPA): JUAN MANUEL FANGIO (MERCEDES)
19 JUNE 1955 - DUTCH GP (ZANDVOORT): JUAN MANUEL FANGIO (MERCEDES)
16 JULY 1955 - BRITISH GP (SILVERSTONE): STIRLING MOSS (MERCEDES)
11 SEPTEMBER 1955 - ITALIAN GP (MONZA): JUAN MANUEL FANGIO (MERCEDES)

1955 WORLD CHAMPION: JUAN MANUEL FANGIO (MERCEDES)

1956

22 JANUARY 1956 - ARGENTINE GP (BUENOS AIRES): JUAN MANUEL FANGIO (FERRARI)
13 MAY 1956 - MONACO GP (MONTE CARLO): STIRLING MOSS (MASERATI)
3 JUNE 1956 - BELGIAN GP (SPA): PETER COLLINS (FERRARI)
1 JULY 1956 - FRENCH GP (REIMS): PETER COLLINS (FERRARI)
14 JULY 1956 - BRITISH GP (SILVERSTONE): JUAN MANUEL FANGIO (FERRARI)
5 AUGUST 1956 - GERMAN GP (NÜRBURGRING): JUAN MANUEL FANGIO (FERRARI)
2 SEPTEMBER 1956 - ITALIAN GP (MONZA): STIRLING MOSS (MASERATI)

1956 WORLD CHAMPION: JUAN MANUEL FANGIO (FERRARI)

1957

13 JANUARY 1957 - ARGENTINE GP (BUENOS AIRES): JUAN MANUEL FANGIO (MASERATI)
19 MAY 1957 - MONACO GP (MONTE CARLO): JUAN MANUEL FANGIO (MASERATI)
7 JULY 1957 - FRENCH GP (ROUEN): JUAN MANUEL FANGIO (MASERATI)
20 JULY 1957 - BRITISH GP (AINTREE): STIRLING MOSS (VANWALL)
4 AUGUST 1957 - GERMAN GP (NÜRBURGRING): JUAN MANUEL FANGIO (MASERATI)
18 AUGUST 1957 - PESCARA GP (PESCARA): STIRLING MOSS (VANWALL)
8 SEPTEMBER 1957 - ITALIAN GP (MONZA): STIRLING MOSS (VANWALL)

1957 WORLD CHAMPION: JUAN MANUEL FANGIO (MASERATI)

1958

19 JANUARY 1958 - ARGENTINE GP (BUENOS AIRES): STIRLING MOSS (COOPER)
18 MAY 1958 - MONACO GP (MONTE CARLO): MAURICE TRINTIGNANT (COOPER)
26 MAY 1958 - DUTCH GP (ZANDVOORT): STIRLING MOSS (VANWALL)
15 JUNE 1958 - BELGIAN GP (SPA): TONY BROOKS (VANWALL)
6 JULY 1958 - FRENCH GP (REIMS): MIKE HAWTHORN (FERRARI)
19 JULY 1958 - BRITISH GP (SILVERSTONE): PETER COLLINS (FERRARI)
3 AUGUST 1958 - GERMAN GP (NÜRBURGRING): TONY BROOKS (VANWALL)
25 AUGUST 1958 - PORTUGESE GP (OPORTO): STIRLING MOSS (VANWALL)

1986

23 MARCH 1986 -BRAZILIAN GP (RIO DE JANEIRO): NELSON PIQUET (WILLIAMS)
13 APRIL 1986 - SPANISH GP (JEREZ): AYRTON SENNA (LOTUS)
27 APRIL 1986 -SAN MARINO GP (IMOLA): ALAIN PROST (McLAREN)
11 MAY 1986 - MONACO GP (MONTE CARLO): ALAIN PROST (McLAREN)
25 MAY 1986 - BELGIAN GP (SPA): NIGEL MANSELL (WILLIAMS)
15 JUNE 1986 - CANADIAN GP (MONTREAL): NIGEL MANSELL (WILLIAMS)
22 JUNE 1986 - USA EAST GP (DETROIT): AYRTON SENNA (LOTUS)
6 JULY 1986 - FRENCH GP (PAUL RICARD): NIGEL MANSELL (WILLIAMS)
13 JULY 1986 - BRITISH GP (BRANDS HATCH): NIGEL MANSELL (WILLIAMS)
27 JULY 1986 - GERMAN GP (HOCKENHEIM): NELSON PIQUET (WILLIAMS)
10 AUGUST 1986 - HUNGARIAN GP (BUDAPEST): NELSON PIQUET (WILLIAMS)
17 AUGUST 1986 - AUSTRIAN GP (OSTERREICHRING): ALAIN PROST (McLAREN)
7 SEPTEMBER 1986 - ITALIAN GP (MONZA): NELSON PIQUET (WILLIAMS)
21 SEPTEMBER 1986 - PORTUGUESE GP (ESTORIL): NIGEL MANSELL (WILLIAMS)
12 OCTOBER 1986 - MEXICAN GP (MEXICO CITY): GERHARD BERGER (BENETTON)
26 OCTOBER 1986 - AUSTRALIAN GP (ADELAIDE): ALAIN PROST (McLAREN)

1986 WORLD CHAMPION: ALAIN PROST (McLAREN)

1987

12 APRIL 1987 - BRAZILIAN GP (RIO DE JANEIRO): ALAIN PROST (McLAREN)
3 MAY 1987 - SAN MARINO GP (IMOLA): NIGEL MANSELL (WILLIAMS)
17 MAY 1987 - BELGIAN GP (SPA): ALAIN PROST (McLAREN)
31 MAY 1987 - MONACO GP (MONTE CARLO): AYRTON SENNA (LOTUS)
2 JUNE 1987 - USA GP (DETROIT): AYRTON SENNA (LOTUS)
5 JULY 1987 - FRENCH GP (PAUL RICARD): NIGEL MANSELL (WILLIAMS)
12 JULY 1987 - BRITISH GP (SILVERSTONE): NIGEL MANSELL (WILLIAMS)
26 JULY 1987 - GERMAN GP (HOCKENHEIM): NELSON PIQUET (WILLIAMS)
9 AUGUST 1987 - HUNGARIAN GP (BUDAPEST): NELSON PIQUET (WILLIAMS)
16 AUGUST 1987 - AUSTRIAN GP (OSTERREICHRING): NIGEL MANSELL (WILLIAMS)
6 SEPTEMBER 1987 - ITALIAN GP (MONZA): NELSON PIQUET (WILLIAMS)
20 SEPTEMBER 1987 - PORTUGUESE GP (ESTORIL): ALAIN PROST (McLAREN)
27 SEPTEMBER 1987 - SPANISH GP (JEREZ): NIGEL MANSELL (WILLIAMS)
18 OCTOBER 1987 - MEXICAN GP (MEXICO CITY): NIGEL MANSELL (WILLIAMS)
1 NOVEMBER 1987 - JAPANESE GP (SUZUKA): GERHARD BERGER (FERRARI)
15 NOVEMBER 1987 - AUSTRALIAN GP (ADELAIDE): GERHARD BERGER (FERRARI)

1987 WORLD CHAMPION: NELSON PIQUET (WILLIAMS)

1988

3 APRIL 1988 - BRAZILIAN GP (RIO DE JANEIRO): ALAIN PROST (McLAREN)
1 MAY 1988 - SAN MARINO GP (IMOLA): AYRTON SENNA (McLAREN)
15 MAY 1988 - MONACO GP (MONTE CARLO): ALAIN PROST (McLAREN)
29 MAY 1988 - MEXICAN GP (MEXICO CITY): ALAIN PROST (McLAREN)
12 JUNE 1988 - CANADIAN GP (MONTREAL): AYRTON SENNA (McLAREN)
19 JUNE 1988 - US GP (DETROIT): AYRTON SENNA (McLAREN)
3 JULY 1988 - FRENCH GP (PAUL RICARD): ALAIN PROST (McLAREN)
10 JULY 1988 - BRITISH GP (SILVERSTONE): AYRTON SENNA (McLAREN)
24 JULY 1988 - GERMAN GP (HOCKENHEIM): AYRTON SENNA (McLAREN)
7 AUGUST 1988 - HUNGARIAN GP (BUDAPEST): AYRTON SENNA (McLAREN)
28 AUGUST 1988 - BELGIAN GP (SPA): AYRTON SENNA (McLAREN)
11 SEPTEMBER 1988 - ITALIAN GP (MONZA): GERHARD BERGER (FERRARI)
25 SEPTEMBER 1988 - PORTUGUESE GP (MONZA): ALAIN PROST (McLAREN)
2 OCTOBER 1988 - SPANISH GP (JEREZ): ALAIN PROST (McLAREN)
30 OCTOBER 1988 - JAPANESE GP (SUZUKA): AYRTON SENNA (McLAREN)
13 NOVEMBER 1988 - AUSTRALIAN GP (ADELAIDE): ALAIN PROST (McLAREN)

1988 WORLD CHAMPION: AYRTON SENNA (McLAREN)

1989

26 MARCH 1989 - BRAZILIAN GP (RIO DE JANEIRO): NIGEL MANSELL (FERRARI)
23 APRIL 1989 - SAN MARINO GP (IMOLA): AYRTON SENNA (McLAREN)
7 MAY 1989 - MONACO GP (MONTE CARLO): AYRTON SENNA (McLAREN)
28 MAY 1989 - MEXICAN GP (MEXICO CITY): AYRTON SENNA (McLAREN)
4 JUNE 1989 - US GP (PHOENIX): ALAIN PROST (McLAREN)
18 JUNE 1989 - CANADIAN GP (MONTREAL): THIERRY BOUTSEN (WILLIAMS)
9 JULY 1989 - FRENCH GP (PAUL RICARD): ALAIN PROST (McLAREN)
16 JULY 1989 - BRITISH GP (SILVERSTONE): ALAIN PROST (McLAREN)
30 JULY 1989 - GERMAN GP (HOCHENHEIM): AYRTON SENNA (McLAREN)
13 AUGUST 1989 - HUNGARIAN GP (BUDAPEST): NIGEL MANSELL (FERRARI)
27 AUGUST 1989 - BELGIAN GP (SPA): AYRTON SENNA (McLAREN)
10 SEPTEMBER 1989 - ITALIAN GP (MONZA): ALAIN PROST (McLAREN)
24 SEPTEMBER 1989 - PORTUGUESE GP (ESTORIL): GERHARD BERGER (FERRARI)
1 OCTOBER 1989 - SPANISH GP (JEREZ): AYRTON SENNA (McLAREN)
22 OCTOBER 1989 - JAPANESE GP (SUZUKA): ALESSANDRO NANNINI (BENETTON)
5 NOVEMBER 1989 - AUSTRALIAN GP (ADELAIDE): THIERRY BOUTSEN (WILLIAMS)

1989 WORLD CHAMPION: ALAIN PROST (McLAREN)

1990

11 MARCH 1990 - US GP (PHOENIX): AYRTON SENNA (McLAREN)
25 MARCH 1990 - BRAZILIAN GP (INTERLAGOS): ALAIN PROST (FERRARI)
13 MAY 1990 - SAN MARINO GP (IMOLA): RICCARDO PATRESE (WILLIAMS)
27 MAY 1990 - MONACO GP (MONTE CARLO): AYRTON SENNA (McLAREN)
10 JUNE 1990 - CANADIAN GP (MONTREAL): AYRTON SENNA (McLAREN)
24 JUNE 1990 - MEXICAN GP (MEXICO CITY): ALAIN PROST (FERRARI)
8 JULY 1990 - FRENCH GP (PAUL RICARD): ALAIN PROST (FERRARI)
15 JULY 1990 - BRITISH GP (SILVERSTONE): ALAIN PROST (FERRARI)
29 JULY 1990 - GERMAN GP (HOCKENHEIM): AYRTON SENNA (McLAREN)
12 AUGUST 1990 - HUNGARIAN GP (BUDAPEST): THIERRY BOUTSEN (WILLIAMS)
26 AUGUST 1990 - BELGIAN GP (SPA): AYRTON SENNA (McLAREN)
9 SEPTEMBER 1990 - ITALIAN GP (MONZA): AYRTON SENNA (McLAREN)
23 SEPTEMBER 1990 - PORTUGUESE GP (ESTORIL): NIGEL MANSELL (FERRARI)
30 SEPTEMBER 1990 - SPANISH GP (JEREZ): ALAIN PROST (FERRARI)
21 OCTOBER 1990 - JAPANESE GP (SUZUKA): NELSON PIQUET (BENETTON)
4 NOVEMBER 1990 - AUSTRALIAN GP (ADELAIDE): NELSON PIQUET (BENETTON)

1990 WORLD CHAMPION: AYRTON SENNA (McLAREN)

1991

10 MARCH 1991 - US GP (PHOENIX): AYRTON SENNA (McLAREN)
24 MARCH 1991 - BRAZILIAN GP (INTERLAGOS): AYRTON SENNA (McLAREN)
28 APRIL 1991 - SAN MARINO GP (IMOLA): AYRTON SENNA (McLAREN)
12 MAY 1991 - MONACO GP (MONTE CARLO): AYRTON SENNA (McLAREN)
2 JUNE 1991 - CANADIAN GP (MONTREAL): NELSON PIQUET (BENETTON)
16 JUNE 1991 - MEXICAN GP (MEXICO CITY): RICCARDO PATRESE (WILLIAMS)
7 JULY 1991 - FRENCH GP (MAGNY-COURS): NIGEL MANSELL (WILLIAMS)
14 JULY 1991 - BRITISH GP (SILVERSTONE): NIGEL MANSELL (WILLIAMS)
28 JULY 1991 - GERMAN GP (HOCKENHEIM): NIGEL MANSELL (WILLIAMS)
11 AUGUST 1991 - HUNGARIAN GP (HUNGARORING): AYRTON SENNA (McLAREN)
25 AUGUST 1991 - BELGIAN GP (SPA): AYRTON SENNA (McLAREN)
8 SEPTEMBER 1991 - ITALIAN GP (MONZA): NIGEL MANSELL (WILLIAMS)
22 SEPTEMBER 1991 - PORTUGUESE GP (ESTORIL): RICCARDO PATRESE (WILLIAMS)
29 SEPTEMBER 1991 - SPANISH GP (BARCELONA): NIGEL MANSELL (WILLIAMS)
20 OCTOBER 1991 - JAPANESE GP (SUZUKA): GERHARD BERGER (McLAREN)
3 NOVEMBER 1991 - AUSTRALIAN GP (ADELAIDE): AYRTON SENNA (McLAREN)

1991 WORLD CHAMPION: AYRTON SENNA (McLAREN)

1992

1 MARCH 1992 - SOUTH AFRICAN GP (KYALAMI): NIGEL MANSELL (WILLIAMS)
22 MARCH 1992 - MEXICAN GP (MEXICO CITY): NIGEL MANSELL (WILLIAMS)
5 APRIL 1992 - BRAZILIAN GP (INTERLAGOS): NIGEL MANSELL (WILLIAMS)
3 MAY 1992 - SPANISH GP (BARCELONA): NIGEL MANSELL (WILLIAMS)
17 MAY 1992 - SAN MARINO GP (IMOLA): NIGEL MANSELL (WILLIAMS)
31 MAY 1992 - MONACO GP (MONTE CARLO): AYRTON SENNA (McLAREN)
14 JUNE 1992 - CANADIAN GP (MONTREAL): GERHARD BERGER (McLAREN)
5 JULY 1992 - FRENCH GP (MAGNY-COURS): NIGEL MANSELL (WILLIAMS)
12 JULY 1992 - BRITISH GP (SILVERSTONE): NIGEL MANSELL (WILLIAMS)
26 JULY 1992- GERMAN GP (HOCKENHEIM): NIGEL MANSELL (WILLIAMS)
16 AUGUST 1992 - HUNGARIAN GP (BUDAPEST): AYRTON SENNA (McLAREN)
30 AUGUST 1992 - BELGIAN GP (SPA): MICHAEL SCHUMACHER (BENETTON)
13 SEPTEMBER 1992 - ITALIAN GP (MONZA): AYRTON SENNA (McLAREN)
27 SEPTEMBER 1992 - PORTUGUESE GP (ESTORIL): NIGEL MANSELL (WILLIAMS)
25 OCTOBER 1992 - JAPANESE GP (SUZUKA): RICCARDO PATRESE (WILLIAMS)
8 NOVEMBER 1992 - AUSTRALIAN GP (ADELAIDE): GERHARD BERGER (McLAREN)

1992 WORLD CHAMPION: NIGEL MANSELL (WILLIAMS)

1993

14 MARCH 1993 - SOUTH AFRICAN GP (KYALAMI): ALAIN PROST (WILLIAMS)
28 MARCH 1993 - BRAZILIAN GP (INTERLAGOS): AYRTON SENNA (McLAREN)
11 APRIL 1993 - EUROPEAN GP (DONINGTON): AYRTON SENNA (McLAREN)
25 APRIL 1993 - SAN MARINO GP (IMOLA): ALAIN PROST (WILLIAMS)
9 MAY 1993 - SPANISH GP (BARCELONA): ALAIN PROST (WILLIAMS)
23 MAY 1993 - MONACO GP (MONTE CARLO): AYRTON SENNA (McLAREN)
13 JUNE 1993 - CANADIAN GP (MONTREAL): ALAIN PROST (WILLIAMS)
4 JULY 1993 - FRENCH GP (MAGNY-COURS): ALAIN PROST (WILLIAMS)
11 JULY 1993 - BRITISH GP (SILVERSTONE): ALAIN PROST (WILLIAMS)
25 JULY 1993 - GERMAN GP (HOCKENHEIM): ALAIN PROST (WILLIAMS)
15 AUGUST 1993 - HUNGARIAN GP (BUDAPEST): DAMON HILL (WILLIAMS)
29 AUGUST 1993 - BELGIAN GP (SPA): DAMON HILL (WILLIAMS)
12 SEPTEMBER 1993 - ITALIAN GP (MONZA): DAMON HILL (WILLIAMS)
26 SEPTEMBER 1993 - PORTUGUESE GP (ESTORIL): MICHAEL SCHUMACHER (BENETTON)
24 OCTOBER 1993 - JAPANESE GP (SUZUKA): AYRTON SENNA (McLAREN)
7 NOVEMBER 1993 - AUSTRALIAN GP (ADELAIDE): AYRTON SENNA (McLAREN)

1993 WORLD CHAMPION: ALAIN PROST (WILLIAMS)

1994

27 MARCH 1994 - BRAZILIAN GP (INTERLAGOS): MICHAEL SCHUMACHER (BENETTON)
17 APRIL 1994 - PACIFIC GP (AIDA): MICHAEL SCHUMACHER (BENETTON)
1 MAY 1994 - SAN MARINO GP (IMOLA): MICHAEL SCHUMACHER (BENETTON)
15 MAY 1994 - MONACO GP (MONTE CARLO): MICHAEL SCHUMACHER (BENETTON)
29 MAY 1994 - SPANISH GP (BARCELONA): DAMON HILL (WILLIAMS)
12 JUNE 1994 - CANADIAN GP (MONTREAL): MICHAEL SCHUMACHER (BENETTON)
3 JULY 1994 - FRENCH GP (MAGNY-COURS): MICHAEL SCHUMACHER (BENETTON)
10 JULY 1994 - BRITISH GP (SILVERSTONE): DAMON HILL (WILLIAMS)
31 JULY 1994 - GERMAN GP (HOCKENHEIM): GERHARD BERGER (FERRARI)
14 AUGUST 1994 - HUNGARIAN GP (BUDAPEST): MICHAEL SCHUMACHER (BENETTON)
28 AUGUST 1994 - BELGIAN GP (SPA): DAMON HILL (WILLIAMS)
11 SEPTEMBER 1994 - ITALIAN GP (MONZA): DAMON HILL (WILLIAMS)
25 SEPTEMBER 1994 - PORTUGUESE GP (ESTORIL): DAMON HILL (WILLIAMS)
16 OCTOBER 1994 - EUROPEAN GP (JEREZ): MICHAEL SCHUMACHER (BENETTON)
6 NOVEMBER 1994 - JAPANESE GP (SUZUKA): DAMON HILL (WILLIAMS)
14 NOVEMBER 1994 - AUSTRALIAN GP (ADELAIDE): NIGEL MANSELL (WILLIAMS)

1994 WORLD CHAMPION: MICHAEL SCHUMACHER (BENETTON)

1995

26 MARCH 1995 - BRAZILIAN GP (INTERLAGOS): MICHAEL SCHUMACHER (BENETTON)
9 APRIL 1995 - ARGENTINE GP (BUENOS AIRES): DAMON HILL (WILLIAMS)
30 APRIL 1995 - SAN MARINO GP (IMOLA): DAMON HILL (WILLIAMS)
14 MAY 1995 - SPANISH GP (BARCELONA): MICHAEL SCHUMACHER (BENETTON)
28 MAY 1995 - MONACO GP (MONTE CARLO): MICHAEL SCHUMACHER (BENETTON)
11 JUNE 1995 - CANADIAN GP (MONTREAL): JEAN ALESI (FERRARI)
2 JULY 1995 - FRENCH GP (MAGNY-COURS): MICHAEL SCHUMACHER (BENETTON)
16 JULY 1995 - BRITISH GP (SILVERSTONE): JOHNNY HERBERT (BENETTON)
30 JULY 1995 - GERMAN GP (HOCKENHEIM): MICHAEL SCHUMACHER (BENETTON)
13 AUGUST 1995 - HUNGARIAN GP (BUDAPEST): DAMON HILL (WILLIAMS)
27 AUGUST 1995 - BELGIAN GP (SPA): MICHAEL SCHUMACHER (BENETTON)
10 SEPTEMBER 1995 - ITALIAN GP (MONZA): JOHNNY HERBERT (BENETTON)
24 SEPTEMBER 1995 - PORTUGUESE GP (ESTORIL): DAVID COULTHARD (WILLIAMS)
1 OCTOBER 1995 - EUROPEAN GP (NÜRBURGRING): MICHAEL SCHUMACHER (BENETTON)
22 OCTOBER 1995 - PACIFIC GP (AIDA): MICHAEL SCHUMACHER (BENETTON)
29 OCTOBER 1995 - JAPANESE GP (SUZUKA): MICHAEL SCHUMACHER (BENETTON)
12 NOVEMBER 1995 - AUSTRALIAN GP (ADELAIDE): DAMON HILL (WILLIAMS)

1995 WORLD CHAMPION: MICHAEL SCHUMACHER (BENETTON)

1996

10 MARCH 1996 - AUSTRALIAN GP (MELBOURNE): DAMON HILL (WILLIAMS)
31 MARCH 1996 - BRAZILIAN GP (INTERLAGOS): DAMON HILL (WILLIAMS)
7 APRIL 1996 - ARGENTINE GP (BUENOS AIRES): DAMON HILL (WILLIAMS)
28 APRIL 1996 - EUROPEAN GP (NÜRBURGRING): JACQUES VILLENEUVE (WILLIAMS)
5 MAY 1996 - SAN MARINO GP (IMOLA): DAMON HILL (WILLIAMS)
19 MAY 1996 - MONACO GP (MONTE CARLO): OLIVIER PANIS (LIGIER)
2 JUNE 1996 - SPANISH GP (BARCELONA): MICHAEL SCHUMACHER (FERRARI)
16 JUNE 1996 - CANADIAN GP (MONTREAL): DAMON HILL (WILLIAMS)
30 JUNE 1996 - FRENCH GP (MAGNY-COURS): DAMON HILL (WILLIAMS)
14 JULY 1996 - BRITISH GP (SILVERSTONE): JACQUES VILLENEUVE (WILLIAMS)
28 JULY 1996 - GERMAN GP (HOCKENHEIM): DAMON HILL (WILLIAMS)
11 AUGUST 1996 - HUNGARIAN GP (BUDAPEST): JACQUES VILLENEUVE (WILLIAMS)
25 AUGUST 1996 - BELGIAN GP (SPA): MICHAEL SCHUMACHER (FERRARI)
8 SEPTEMBER 1996 - ITALIAN GP (MONZA): MICHAEL SCHUMACHER (FERRARI)
22 SEPTEMBER 1996 - PORTUGUESE GP (ESTORIL): JACQUES VILLENEUVE (WILLIAMS)
13 OCTOBER 1996 - JAPANESE GP (SUZUKA): DAMON HILL (WILLIAMS)

1996 WORLD CHAMPION: DAMON HILL (WILLIAMS)

1997

9 MARCH 1997 - AUSTRALIAN GP (MELBOURNE): DAVID COULTHARD (McLAREN)
30 MARCH 1997 - BRAZILIAN GP (INTERLAGOS): JACQUES VILLENEUVE (WILLIAMS)
13 APRIL 1997 - ARGENTINE GP (BUENOS AIRES): JACQUES VILLENEUVE (WILLIAMS)
27 APRIL 1997 - SAN MARINO GP (IMOLA): HEINZ-HARALD FRENTZEN (WILLIAMS)
11 MAY 1997 - MONACO GP (MONTE CARLO): MICHAEL SCHUMACHER (FERRARI)
25 MAY 1997 - SPANISH GP (BARCELONA): JACQUES VILLENEUVE (WILLIAMS)
15 JUNE 1997 - CANADIAN GP (MONTREAL): MICHAEL SCHUMACHER (FERRARI)
29 JUNE 1997 - FRENCH GP (MAGNY-COURS): MICHAEL SCHUMACHER (FERRARI)
13 JULY 1997 - BRITISH GP (SILVERSTONE): JACQUES VILLENEUVE (WILLIAMS)
27 JULY 1997 - GERMAN GP (HOCKENHEIM): GERHARD BERGER (BENETTON)
10 AUGUST 1997 - HUNGARIAN GP (BUDAPEST): JACQUES VILLENEUVE (WILLIAMS)
24 AUGUST 1997 - BELGIAN GP (SPA): MICHAEL SCHUMACHER (FERRARI)
7 SEPTEMBER 1997 - ITALIAN GP (MONZA): DAVID COULTHARD (McLAREN)
21 SEPTEMBER 1997 - AUSTRIAN GP (A1-RING): JACQUES VILLENEUVE (WILLIAMS)
28 SEPTEMBER 1997 - LUXEMBOURG GP (NÜRBURGRING): JACQUES VILLENEUVE (WILLIAMS)

12 OCTOBER 1997 - JAPANESE GP (SUZUKA): MICHAEL SCHUMACHER (FERRARI)

26 OCTOBER 1997 - EUROPEAN GP (JEREZ): MIKA HAKKINEN (McLAREN)

1997 WORLD CHAMPION: JACQUES VILLENEUVE (WILLIAMS)

1998

8 MARCH 1998 - AUSTRALIAN GP (MELBOURNE): MIKA HAKKINEN (McLAREN)

29 MARCH 1998 - BRAZILIAN GP (INTERLAGOS): MIKA HAKKINEN (McLAREN)

12 APRIL 1998 - ARGENTINE GP (BUENOS AIRES): MICHAEL SCHUMACHER (FERRARI)

26 APRIL 1998 - SAN MARINO GP (IMOLA): DAVID COULTHARD (McLAREN)

10 MAY 1998 - SPANISH GP (BARCELONA): MIKA HAKKINEN (McLAREN)

24 MAY 1998 - MONACO GP (MONTE CARLO): MIKA HAKKINEN (McLAREN)

7 JUNE 1998 - CANADIAN GP (MONTREAL): MICHAEL SCHUMACHER (FERRARI)

28 JUNE 1998 - FRENCH GP (MAGNY-COURS): MICHAEL SCHUMACHER (FERRARI)

12 JULY 1998 - BRITISH GP (SILVERSTONE): MICHAEL SCHUMACHER (FERRARI)

26 JULY 1998 - AUSTRIAN GP (A1-RING): MIKA HAKKINEN (McLAREN)

2 AUGUST 1998 - GERMAN GP (HOCKENHEIM): MIKA HAKKINEN (McLAREN)

16 AUGUST 1998 - HUNGARIAN GP (BUDAPEST): MICHAEL SCHUMACHER (FERRARI)

30 AUGUST 1998 - BELGIAN GP (SPA): DAMON HILL (JORDAN)

13 SEPTEMBER 1998 - ITALIAN GP (MONZA): MICHAEL SCHUMACHER (FERRARI)

27 SEPTEMBER 1998 - LUXEMBOURG GP (NÜRBURGRING): MIKA HAKKINEN (McLAREN)

1 NOVEMBER 1998 - JAPANESE GP (SUZUKA): MIKA HAKKINEN (MCLAREN)

1998 WORLD CHAMPION: MIKA HAKKINEN (McLAREN)

1999

7 MARCH 1999 - AUSTRALIAN GP (MELBOURNE): EDDIE IRVINE (FERRARI)

11 APRIL 1999 - BRAZILIAN GP (INTERLAGOS): MIKA HAKKINEN (McLAREN)

2 MAY 1999 - SAN MARINO GP (IMOLA): MICHAEL SCHUMACHER (FERRARI)

16 MAY 1999 - MONACO GP (MONTE CARLO): MICHAEL SCHUMACHER (FERRARI)

30 MAY 1999 - SPANISH GP (BARCELONA): MIKA HAKKINEN (McLAREN)

13 JUNE 1999 - CANADIAN GP (MONTREAL): MIKA HAKKINEN (McLAREN)

27 JUNE 1999 - FRENCH GP (MAGNY-COURS): HEINZ-HARALD FRENTZEN (JORDAN)

11 JULY 1999 - BRITISH GP (SILVERSTONE): DAVID COULTHARD (McLAREN)

25 JULY 1999 - AUSTRIAN GP (A1-RING): EDDIE IRVINE (FERRARI)

1 AUGUST 1999 - GERMAN GP (HOCKENHEIM): EDDIE IRVINE (FERRARI)

15 AUGUST 1999 - HUNGARIAN GP (BUDAPEST): MIKA HAKKINEN (McLAREN)

29 AUGUST 1999 - BELGIAN GP (SPA): DAVID COULTHARD (McLAREN)

12 SEPTEMBER 1999 - ITALIAN GP (MONZA): HEINZ-HARALD FRENTZEN (JORDAN)

26 SEPTEMBER 1999 - EUROPEAN GP (NÜRBURGRING): JOHNNY HERBERT (STEWART)

17 OCTOBER 1999 - MALAYSIAN GP (SEPANG): EDDIE IRVINE (FERRARI)

31 OCTOBER 1999 - JAPANESE GP (SUZUKA): MIKA HAKKINEN (McLAREN)

1999 WORLD CHAMPION: MIKA HAKKINEN (McLAREN)

2000

12 MARCH 2000 - AUSTRALIAN GP (MELBOURNE): MICHAEL SCHUMACHER (FERRARI)

26 MARCH 2000 - BRAZILIAN GP (INTERLAGOS): MICHAEL SCHUMACHER (FERRARI)

9 APRIL 2000 - SAN MARINO GP (IMOLA): MICHAEL SCHUMACHER (FERRARI)

23 APRIL 2000 - BRITISH GP (SILVERSTONE): DAVID COULTHARD (McLAREN)

7 MAY 2000 - SPANISH GP (BARCELONA): MIKA HAKKINEN (McLAREN)

21 MAY 2000 - EUROPEAN GP (NÜRBURGRING): MICHAEL SCHUMACHER (FERRARI)

4 JUNE 2000 - MONACO GP (MONTE CARLO): DAVID COULTHARD (McLAREN)

18 JUNE 2000 - CANADIAN GP (MONTREAL): MICHAEL SCHUMACHER (FERRARI)

2 JULY 2000 - FRENCH GP (MAGNY-COURS): DAVID COULTHARD (McLAREN)

16 AUGUST 2000 - AUSTRIAN GP (A-1 RING): MIKA HAKKINEN (McLAREN)

30 JULY 2000 - GERMAN GP (HOCKENHEIM): RUBENS BARRICHELLO (FERRARI)

13 AUGUST 2000 - HUNGARIAN GP (BUDAPEST): MIKA HAKKINEN (McLAREN)

27 AUGUST 2000 - BELGIAN GP (SPA): MIKA HAKKINEN (McLAREN)

10 SEPTEMBER 2000 - ITALIAN GP (MONZA): MICHAEL SCHUMACHER (FERRARI)

24 SEPTEMBER 2000 - US GP (INDIANAPOLIS): MICHAEL SCHUMACHER (FERRARI)

8 OCTOBER 2000 - JAPANESE GP (SUZUKA): MICHAEL SCHUMACHER (FERRARI)

22 OCTOBER 2000 - MALAYSIAN GP (SEPANG): MICHAEL SCHUMACHER (FERRARI)

2000 WORLD CHAMPION: MICHAEL SCHUMACHER (FERRARI)

2001

4 MARCH 2001 - AUSTRALIAN GP (MELBOURNE): MICHAEL SCHUMACHER (FERRARI)

18 MARCH 2001 - MALAYSIAN GP (SEPANG): MICHAEL SCHUMACHER (FERRARI)

1 APRIL 2001 - BRAZILIAN GP (INTERLAGOS): DAVID COULTHARD (McLAREN)

15 APRIL 2001 - SAN MARINO GP (IMOLA): RALF SCHUMACHER (WILLIAMS)

29 APRIL 2001 - SPANISH GP (BARCELONA): MICHAEL SCHUMACHER (FERRARI)

13 MAY 2001 - AUSTRIAN GP (A1-RING): DAVID COULTHARD (McLAREN)

27 MAY 2001 - MONACO GP (MONTE CARLO): MICHAEL SCHUMACHER (FERRARI)

10 JUNE 2001 - CANADIAN GP (MONTREAL): RALF SCHUMACHER (WILLIAMS)

24 JUNE 2001 - EUROPEAN GP (NÜRBURGRING): MICHAEL SCHUMACHER (FERRARI)

1 JULY 2001 - FRENCH GP (MAGNY-COURS): MICHAEL SCHUMACHER (FERRARI)

15 JULY 2001 - BRITISH GP (SILVERSTONE): MIKA HAKKINEN (McLAREN)

29 JULY 2001 - GERMAN GP (HOCKENHEIM): RALF SCHUMACHER (WILLIAMS)

19 AUGUST 2001 - HUNGARIAN GP (BUDAPEST): MICHAEL SCHUMACHER (FERRARI)

2 SEPTEMBER 2001 - BELGIAN GP (SPA): MICHAEL SCHUMACHER (FERRARI)

16 SEPTEMBER 2001 - ITALIAN GP (MONZA): JUAN PABLO MONTOYA (WILLIAMS)

30 SEPTEMBER 2001 - US GP (INDIANAPOLIS): MIKA HAKKINEN (McLAREN)

14 OCTOBER 2001 - JAPANESE GP (SUZUKA): MICHAEL SCHUMACHER (FERRARI)

2001 WORLD CHAMPION: MICHAEL SCHUMACHER (FERRARI)

BIBLIOGRAPHY

The following publications were used as reference (and quoted from as indicated by page numbers) in the preparation of this book.

ALL ARMS AND ELBOWS Innes Ireland (Pelham Books 1967) 86, 87, 88, 93, 118
ALL BUT MY LIFE Stirling Moss (William Kimber 1963) 89, 91, 112
A RACING DRIVERS' WORLD Rudolf Caracciola (Cassell, 1961) 30, 35, 37
A RACING MOTORIST S.C.H Davis (Iliffe & Sons 1949) 19, 20, 21, 23
AUTOCOURSE ANNUALS (Hazleton Publishing, various)
CHALLENGE ME THE RACE Mike Hawthorn (William Kimber 1958) 51, 52, 74
COOPER CARS Doug Nye (Osprey 1983) 70
DAVID'S DIARY David Coulthard with Gerald Donaldson (Simon & Schuster 1998)
DRIVING AMBITION Alan Jones and Keith Botsford (Stanley Paul 1981) 197, 202
ENZO FERRARI Brock Yates (Doubleday 1998) 100, 103, 114
FANGIO: MY RACING LIFE Juan Manuel Fangio with Roberto Carozzon (Patrick Stephens 1987) 40, 44, 60, 64, 66, 67, 72
FASTER Jackie Stewart and Peter Manso (William Kimber 1972) 137, 138, 139, 140, 147, 148, 153
FERRARI - THE GRAND PRIX CARS Alan Henry (Hazleton 1984) 114
FERRARI'S DRIVERS Michel Fenu (William Kimber 1980)
FIFTY YEARS OF THE FORMULA ONE WORLD CHAMPIONSHIP Bruce Jones (Carlton Books 1999)
FOR THE RECORD Niki Lauda with Herbert Volker (William Kimber 1977) 156, 178, 179, 189
FORMULA ONE DRIVER BY DRIVER Alan Henry (The Crowood Press 1992)
FROM THE COCKPIT Bruce McLaren (Frederick Muller Ltd. 1964) 84, 96
GILLES VILLENEUVE Gerald Donaldson (Motor Racing Publications 1989) 208
GRAND PRIX DATA BOOK David Hayhoe & David Holland (Duke Marketing 1996)
GRAND PRIX GREATS Nigel Roebuck (Patrick Stephens Ltd 1986) 112
GRAND PRIX PEOPLE Gerald Donaldson (Motor Racing Publications 1990) 238, 240, 242, 255
GRAND PRIX RACING George Monkhouse (GT Foulis 1950) 30
GRAND PRIX WHO'S WHO Steve Small (Travel Publishing Ltd. 2000)
GRAND PRIX WINNERS Jenkinson, Roebuck, Henry, Hamilton, Small (Hazleton Publishing 1995)
INSIDE FORMULA 1 Nigel Roebuck (Patrick Stephens Limited 1989)
IT WAS FUN Tony Rudd (Patrick Stephens Ltd 1993)
JACKIE STEWART - WORLD CHAMPION Jackie Stewart and Eric Dymock (Pelham Books 1970) 109, 145
JAMES HUNT Gerald Donaldson (CollinsWillow 1994) 158, 172, 173, 181, 182, 187
JIM CLARK AT THE WHEEL Jim Clark (Arthur Barker Ltd. 1964) 86, 92
JIM REDMAN Jim Redman (Veloce Publishing 1998)
JOCHEN RINDT Heinz Pruller (William Kimber 1970) 111, 103, 126, 140, 141
JUAN MANUEL FANGIO Gunther Molter (Foulis 1958)
KEKE Keke Rosberg and Keith Botsford (Stanley Paul 1985) 111, 194, 202, 211
LIFE AT THE LIMIT Graham Hill (William Kimber 1969) 96, 98, 107, 118, 123
LIFE AT THE LIMIT Professor Sid Watkins (Macmillan 1996) 285
MARLBORO GRAND PRIX GUIDES Jacques Deschenaux (Marlboro, annual)
MICHAEL SCHUMACHER James Allen (Transworld Publishers 1999) 231
MIKE HAILWOOD Ted Macauley (Buchan & Enright 1984) 150
MON AMI MATE Chris Nixon (Transport Bookman 1991) 75
MY CARS, MY CAREER Stirling Moss with Doug Nye (Patrick Stephens 1987) 48, 55, 58, 59, 61, 62, 70, 72, 75
MY FIRST SEASON IN FORMULA 1 Jacques Villeneuve with Gerald Donaldson (CollinsWillow 1996) 288, 290, 291
MY GREATEST RACE (Jackie Stewart) Adrian Ball (Hart-Davis MacGibbon Ltd 1974) 107, 122, 123
MY TERRIBLE JOYS Enzo Ferrari (Hamish Hamilton 1963) 22, 25, 26, 30, 45, 53, 56, 58, 62, 64, 72, 76, 77, 101, 114, 149, 178
MY TWO LIVES Rene Dreyfus (Aztec Corporation 1983) 26, 30. 32, 37
NIGEL MANSELL Nigel Mansell with James Allen (CollinsWillow 1995) 230, 233
NUVOLARI Giovanni Lurani (Cassell 1959)
RACERS APART David Tremayne (Motor Racing Publications 1991) 147
RACING THE SILVER ARROWS Chris Nixon (Osprey 1986)
ROB WALKER Michael Cooper-Evans (Hazleton Publishing 1993) 71, 98, 121, 142
ROSEMEYER! Eilly Beinhorn & Chris Nixon (Transport Bookman Publications 1986)
SPEED WITH STYLE Peter Revson and Leon Mandel (Doubleday & Co. 1974) 151, 152, 156
STIRLING MOSS Robert Edwards (Cassell & Co 2001)
STIRLING MOSS'S MOTOR RACING MASTERPIECES Stirling Moss with Christopher Hilton (Sidgwick & Jackson 1995)
TEAMWORK: WEST McLAREN MERCEDES Gerald Donaldson (CollinsWillow 1998)
TEN YEARS OF MOTORS AND MOTOR RACING, Charles Jarrott (Grant Richards Ltd, 1906) 14, 15, 16, 17, 18, 19
THE CHEQUERED FLAG Ivan Rendell (Weidenfeld & Nicolson 1993)
THE CRUEL SPORT Robert Daley (Prentice-Hall 1963) 92, 93, 96
THE COMPLETE HISTORY OF GRAND PRIX RACING Adriano Cimarosti (Aurum Press Ltd 1997)
THE COOPER GOLDEN YEARS Cooper Car Company 84, 87
THE DESIGNERS Leonard Setright (Follett Publishing 1976)
THE EXCITING WORLD OF JACKIE STEWART (Collins 1974) 156
THE GRAND PRIX CAR Laurence Pomeroy (Motor Racing Publications 1949)
THE GRAND PRIX CHAMPIONS Mary Heglar (Bond Parkhurst Publishing 1973)
THE GREAT ENCYCLOPEDIA OF FORMULA 1 Pierre Menard (Constable & Robinson Ltd 2000)
THE JIM CLARK STORY Bill Gavin (Leslie Frewin Publishers 1967)
THE LURE OF SPEED, Henry Segrave (Hutchinson & Co. 1928) 13
THE RACING DRIVER Denis Jenkinson (Robert Bentley Inc 1969)
THE THREE POINTED STAR David Scott-Moncrieff (Cassell) 20
THE ULTIMATE ENCYCLOPEDIA OF FORMULA ONE Bruce Jones (Hodder & Stoughton 1995)
TO HELL AND BACK Niki Lauda with Herbert Volker (Stanley Paul 1986) 162, 163, 169, 172, 173
VROOOM! Peter Manso (Funk & Wagnalls 1969)
WHEN THE FLAG DROPS Jack Brabham (William Kimber 1971) 86, 90, 109, 112
WORKS DRIVER Piero Taruffi (Temple Press Books 1964) 34

Other sources of reference and shorter quotes include the following publications: *Autocar, Autosport, F1 Racing, Grand Prix International, Motoring News, Motor Racing, Motor Sport, The Autocar, The Engineer*

The majority of material in this book is original, obtained by the contributors from private interviews and press conferences. In the case of copyrighted material, every effort has been made to contact and receive permission to reproduce the passages used in this book. Any errors, oversights or omissions will be corrected in subsequent editions.

PICTURE CREDITS

LAT 6, 12 (2x inset), 16, 17, 19, 27, 30, 31 2 x inset, 38, 40, 42, 43, 45, 47/47, 48 top, 48 bottom, 49, 50, 51, 52, 53, 54, 55, 56/57, 58/59, 60, 61, 62, 63, 66/67, 68, 69, 71, 72, 72 inset, 73,74, 76, 77, 78, 79, 80, 81, 82 2x inset, 83 inset, 86, 87, 90, 90/91, 144, 152 bottom, 156, 160, 164/165, 172, 172 inset, 173 top, 199 bottom, 209 top, 217, 218, 220, 221 top, 224, 225, 228, 241, 242, 244, 246 inset, 294, 295, 298 inset, 305, 307 all, 308, 309, 310 1x inset, 314/315, 316/317, 319, 322, 323, 331 right, 343 left, 347 bottom left, 349
Geoffrey Goddard Collection 13 inset, 15, 36, 75, 76, 332 right
Mercedes Archive 12/13, 12 2x inset, 18, 328/329
Offside/LflEquipe back cover, 20/21, 21 inset, 22/23, 25, 38, 44, 334, 336 centre
Spitzley/Zagari 23 inset, 24, 32/33, 34
Hewitt/Sporting Pictures 28/29, 31, 35, 37, 41
Sporting Pictures 246 inset, 250 top, 256/257, 280, 281 left
FOA 296/297
GPL 1, 38/39, 38 2 x inset, 39 inset, 64, 65 top right/bottom right/bottom left, 79 3x inset, 80 inset, 219 top, 222/223
Olympia Publifoto 61 3x inset, 93 3 sequence
Phipps/Sutton 82/83, 82 2 x inset, 84, 85, 88/89, 92, 93, 94/95, 96, 96/97, 98, 99, 100, 101, 102, 103, 103 inset, 104/105, 106, 107 inset, 107, 108, 109, 113, 114, 114 inset, 115, 117/116, 119, 119 2x inset, 119 top, 120, 121, 122, 123, 124/125, 126, 127 inset, 127, 128/129, 130/131, 131 4 x inset, 132 inset, 132, 133, 134, 134/135, 136, 137, 138, 140, 141, 142, 143, 145, 146, 147, 148, 149 top, 150, 151 left, 153, 154/155, 157, 158, 159 bottom, 161, 162, 170/171, 173 bottom, 174, 175, 176, 177, 180, 182, 182 inset, 183, 184/185, 186 top, 186 bottom, 187, 188 left, 189, 190/191, 192 4x inset, 192/193, 193 inset, 194, 195, 195 top, 196, 198, 199 top, 200, 201 top, 201 bottom, 202, 203, 204, 206, 207, 210, 330 centre, 335, 336 left/right, 337 right, 338 left, 339 right, 340 top/bottom, 342 left, 343 centre/right, 347 top left, 348 right, 350, 351 top left/centre
Sutton Motorsport Images cover, 211, 213, 214/215, 216 top, 219 bottom, 221 bottom, 226, 227, 229, 230, 231, 232, 233, 236/237, 240, 243, 245, 245 inset, 246/247, 246 inset, 248, 249, 250 bottom, 251, 254 top, 254 bottom, 255, 256 inset, 257 inset, 258, 259, 260, 261, 262/263, 264, 265, 268, 269, 270, 271, 272, 273, 274 sequence, 275 top, 275 bottom, 276/277, 278, 281 right, 282, 283 bottom, 284 inset, 285, 286/287, 288, 291 right, 298/299, 310 3x inset, 311 inset, 310/311, 312, 313, 314, 318, 324, 325, 326/327, 330 left/right, 331 left, 332 left, 337 left, 338 right, 342 centre/right, 345 left/centre, 347 right, 351 bottom left
Rainer Schlegelmilch 2/3, 110, 111, 149 bottom, 151 top right, 159 top, 163, 167, 168, 178, 179, 181, 190/191, 197, 238/239, 284 (flags), 289, 291 (left), 292, 300
Michael Cooper 139 top and bottom
Cor Mooy/Omnipress 152 sequence
DPA 168/169, 169 top,
Grand Prix Photo 188 right
DPPI 205
IPA 208/209
AFP 208 inset
Paul Henri Cahier 216 bottom, 234/235, 246 inset, 247 inset, 252, 253, 266/267, 283 inset, 301, 302, 303, 304, 344 centre
Rothmans 290
Michel Comte 321
Grantour 320
Hochzwei/West 9
Juan Carlos Ferrigno 239

ACKNOWLEDGEMENTS

Gerald Donaldson would like to thank Michael Dover, Publisher, for commissioning the book, editorial consultant Philip Dodd for managing the project and David Costa and Emil Dacanay of Wherefore Art? for designing the book.

As well as all the contributors, thanks also to Stuart Dent, Peter Dick and Paul Harmer for their assistance, and special thanks to editorial consultant Quentin Spurring.